Conte

G000146629

CHAPTER 7: Performing Basic Image Tasks

53 About Image Information

54 Arrange the View of Multiple Images in the Editor

55 Zoom In and Out with the Zoom Tool

56 Zoom In and Out with the Navigator Palette

57 Scroll a Large Image

58 Magnify Your Work

59 About Size and Resolution

60 Change Image Size or Resolution

61 Rename, Resize, Reformat, and Retouch a Group of Images

62 Increase the Area Around an Image

63 Change Color Mode

CHAPTER 8: Printing Images

64 About Printing Images

65 Set Print Options

66 Print an Image

67 Print a Contact Sheet

68 Print a Picture Package

69 Print an Image Using an Online Service

CHAPTER 9: Selecting a Portion of an Image

70 About Making Selections

71 Make Areas of an Image Easier to Select

72 Select a Rectangular or Circular Area

73 Draw a Selection Freehand

74 Select a Straight-Edged Area

75 Select an Object by Tracing Its Edge

76 Select Areas of Similar Color

77 Paint a Selection

CHAPTER 10: Modifying a Selection

78 Expand or Shrink a Selection

79 Add Areas Similar to the Current Selection

80 Smooth a Jagged Selection Edge

81 Move the Selection Marquee

82 Soften the Edge of a Selection

83 Select Everything but the Current Selection

CHAPTER 11: Using Selections to Edit Images

84 Save a Selection for Reuse

85 Reload a Previously Saved Selection

86 About Copying, Cutting, and Pasting Data Within a Selection

87 Create a New Image from a Selection

88 Create a New Layer from a Selection

89 Rotate the Data in a Selection or Layer

90 Copy Data into a Selected Area

CHAPTER 12: Using Multiple Layers to Edit Images

91 About Layers and the Layers Palette

92 Create a New Image Layer

93 Create a Layer Filled with Color, Gradient, or Pattern

94 Create an Adjustment Layer

95 Convert a Background Layer to a Regular Layer or Vice-Versa

99 Move, Resize, Skew, or Distort a Layer

100 Mask an Adjustment or Fill Layer

101 Group and Organize Layers

102 Merge or Flatten Layers into One

PART 3: EDITING IMAGES

CHAPTER 13: Making Quick Corrections to a Photograph

103 About Color Management

104 About Adobe Gamma

105 Ensure That What You See Is What You Get

106 Rotate an Image or Layer

107 Crop a Portion of an Image

108 Straighten an Image

109 Apply a Quick Fix

Chapter 14: Retouching Photos with the Tools

110 About the Toolbox

111 About Tool Options

112 About Preset Manager

113 Select a Color to Work With

114 Select a Color Already in Your Image

115 Draw on a Photo with a Pencil

116 Paint an Area of a Photo with a Brush

117 Paint an Area of a Photo with the Airbrush

118 Fill an Area with a Pattern

119 Fill an Area with a Gradient

120 About Drawing Shapes

121 Add Thought Bubbles to a Photo

Continued on next page

Contents at a Glance

Continued from previous page

CHAPTER 15: Repairing Photographs

122 About Removing Scratches, Specks, and Holes
123 Remove Scratches
124 Remove Specks and Spots
125 Repair Minor Tears, Scratches, Spots, and Stains
126 Repair Large Holes, Tears, and Missing Portions of a Photo
127 Restore Color and Tone to an Old Photograph
128 Restore Quality to a Scanned Photograph

CHAPTER 16: Improving Portraits

129 Create a Soft Focus Effect
130 Correct Red Eye
131 Remove Wrinkles, Freckles, and Minor Blemishes
132 Whiten Teeth
133 Awaken Tired Eyes
134 Remove Glare from Eyeglasses
135 Brighten a Face with Digital Makeup

CHAPTER 17: Correcting the Brightness and Contrast in a Photograph

136 About an Image's Histogram
137 Improve Brightness and Contrast
138 Improve a Dull, Flat Photo
139 Lighten a Subject on a Snowy Background
140 Lighten or Darken Part of an Image
141 Improve a Nighttime Photo
142 Fix a Flash That's Too Close
143 Fix a Flash That's Too Far Away

CHAPTER 18: Correcting Color and Saturation

144 Correct Color Manually
145 Correct Color, Contrast, and Saturation in One Step
146 Adjust Hue, Saturation, and Lightness Manually
147 Adjust Saturation for a Specific Area

CHAPTER 19: Controlling Sharpness and Clarity

148 About Sharpness
149 Sharpen an Image
150 Blur an Image to Remove Noise
151 Blur a Background to Create Depth of Field
152 Create a Spin Effect
153 Soften Selected Details
154 Add Motion to an Image

PART 4: SHARING, CREATING, AND HAVING FUN

CHAPTER 20: Sharing Images

155 About Emailing
156 Set Up Photoshop Elements for Emailing
157 Manage Contacts
158 Share Images Using Email
159 Select an Online Service
160 Share Images Using an Online Service
161 Send Images to a Mobile Phone

CHAPTER 21: Improving a Photograph's Visual Impact

162 Remove Unwanted Objects from an Image
163 Mask an Image Layer
164 Replace a Background with Something Else
165 Fix a Bland-Looking Sky

166 Frame a Photograph
167 Blend Two Images into One
168 Create a Scrapbook Page
169 Create a Composite Image
170 Create a Panorama

CHAPTER 22: Applying Visual Effects

171 "Melt" an Image
172 Wrap an Image Around an Object
173 Create the Illusion of Snow or Rain
174 Simulate a Water Reflection

CHAPTER 23: Creating Artistic Photographs

175 Make a Photograph Look Old
176 Change a Color Photograph to Black and White
177 Create a Negative Image
178 Colorize a Photograph
179 Make a Photograph Look Like an Oil Painting
180 Turn a Photograph into a Watercolor
181 Make a Photograph Look Like It Was Drawn
182 Make a Photograph Look Like Andy Warhol Painted It

CHAPTER 24: Adding and Embellishing Text

183 Add a Text Caption or Label
184 Bend Text
185 Create a Sales Sign
186 Add a Backscreen Behind Text
187 Create Metallic Text
188 Create Text That Glows
189 Emboss Text
190 Fill Text with an Image
191 Add Copyright Information

Adobe®
Photoshop®
Elements 3

Jennifer Fulton
Scott M. Fulton III

SAMS
Teach
Yourself

Sams Publishing, 800 East 96th Street, Indianapolis, Indiana 46240 USA

Adobe® Photoshop® Elements 3 in a Snap

Copyright © 2005 by Sams Publishing

International Standard Book Number: 0672-32668-X

Library of Congress Catalog Card Number: 2003099240

Printed in the United States of America

First Printing: December 2004

07   06   05   04   4   3   2   1

Trademarks

All terms mentioned in this book that are known to be trademarks or service marks have been appropriately capitalized. Sams Publishing cannot attest to the accuracy of this information. Use of a term in this book should not be regarded as affecting the validity of any trademark or service mark.

Warning and Disclaimer

Every effort has been made to make this book as complete and as accurate as possible, but no warranty or fitness is implied. The information provided is on an "as is" basis. The author and the publisher shall have neither liability nor responsibility to any person or entity with respect to any loss or damages arising from the information contained in this book.

Bulk Sales

Sams Publishing offers excellent discounts on this book when ordered in quantity for bulk purchases or special sales. For more information, please contact

U.S. Corporate and Government Sales

1-800-382-3419

corpsales@pearsontechgroup.com

For sales outside of the United States, please contact

International Sales

1-317-428-3341

international@pearsontechgroup.com

Acquisitions Editor
Betsy Brown

Development Editor
Alice Martina Smith

Managing Editor
Charlotte Clapp

Project Editor
George Nedeff

Production Editor
Michael Henry

Indexer
Julie Bess

Proofreader
Carla Lewis

Technical Editors
Dallas Releford
Doug Nelson

Team Coordinator
Vanessa Evans

Designer
Gary Adair

About the Authors

Jennifer Fulton is an experienced trainer, consultant, and author who has used nearly every graphics editor and organizer ever produced, for both work and home. She is partnered in business with her husband, Scott. They work and live in the midwest United States with their daughter, Katerina—the subject of many illustrations in this book.

Scott M. Fulton, III is a veteran author, editor, programmer, and artist with 27 years' experience in the field of computing. As one of *Computer Shopper* magazine's original editorial team, he introduced North America to CorelDraw, and has since written many books and articles on the subject of graphic art and design.

Dedication

Jennifer and I dedicate this book to the memory of Maria DeLaJuen (1931–2004), who taught thousands through the process of art to draw what they see and to see beyond themselves, and who, as my mother and my mentor, moved me to seek beyond myself, to seek God, and to apply myself to all that is right and beautiful in the world.

Acknowledgments

Scott and I would like to acknowledge several people, without whom this book would not be as good, and may very well have not made it to press. First of all, we thank Betsy Brown, who stood by us when it seemed that the world itself was coming down, giving us not only understanding but the time we needed to produce our best effort. Next, we would like to thank Alice Martina Smith, who is not only a good friend but also a great editor, and whose heart and soul are in this book with ours. We'd also like to thank Doug Nelson, who provided a thorough technical edit, with comments that were both insightful and accurate. Our thanks go also to the staff of Adobe, with whom we worked during the formation of this book and of Photoshop Elements 3.0, so that both our teams could build a better product.

Tell Us What You Think!

As the reader of this book, *you* are our most important critic and commentator. We value your opinion and want to know what we're doing right, what we could do better, what areas you'd like to see us publish in, and any other words of wisdom you're willing to pass our way.

You can email or write me directly to let me know what you did or didn't like about this book—as well as what we can do to make our books stronger.

Please note that I cannot help you with technical problems related to the topic of this book, and that due to the high volume of mail I receive, I might not be able to reply to every message.

When you write, please be sure to include this book's title and author as well as your name and phone or email address. I will carefully review your comments and share them with the authors and editors who worked on the book.

Email: graphics@samspublishing.com

Mail: Mark Taber
            Associate Publisher
            Sams Publishing
            800 East 96th Street
            Indianapolis, IN 46240 USA

Reader Services

For more information about this book or others from Sams Publishing, visit our website at **www.samspublishing.com**. Type the ISBN of the book (excluding hyphens) or the title of the book you're looking for in the Search box.

PART I

Organizing Items in the Catalog

IN THIS PART:

CHAPTER 1   Start Here   3

CHAPTER 2   Importing Items into the Organizer
             Catalog   33

CHAPTER 3   Viewing and Sorting Items   81

CHAPTER 4   Organizing Items in the Catalog   105

CHAPTER 5   Finding Images, Movies, and Audio Files   137

1

✔ Start Here

You might not have discovered it yet, but Photoshop Elements is actually two programs designed to work seamlessly together: the *Editor* and the *Organizer*. You use the Editor to make changes to digital images, such as brightening and sharpening them. Use the Organizer to catalog your images so that you can quickly locate and edit, print, or email them when needed.

Given the recent advancements in the field of digital photography, you might be surprised how relatively easy it is to take a bad picture. Even when your digital camera is taking pictures in Automatic mode, it might not properly compensate for less-than-favorable lighting conditions, unexpected movement of your subject matter, and poor composition. Luckily, in the digital world of photography, you can correct most mistakes with the help of a *graphics editor* such as the Photoshop Elements Editor.

Perhaps you don't use a digital camera; the quality of film photography is often far superior to that of digital images. Unfortunately, when you scan a photo print into a digital file, you often lose the qualities that made the original print superior in the first place—its sharpness, depth of tone, and color. Again, with the aid of graphic editors such as the Photoshop Elements Editor, you can restore the beauty your prints might have lost in translation. In this chapter, you'll learn everything you need to know about working with digital images, including how to use the Organizer and the Editor to categorize and manipulate them.

The Nature of Digital Photography

If you use a digital camera, you are more likely to print your photos at home rather than have a photo shop print them. Your computer essentially becomes the "film lab," making you responsible for the touch-ups and corrections you'd otherwise trust to a lab technician. Don't let this new responsibility overwhelm you. As you'll learn in this book, the *Editor* provides many simple-to-use tools for fixing just about any problem caused by a digital camera, scanner, or simple human error. In addition, with the Editor, you'll be able to create special effects your neighborhood film lab couldn't create.

Before Editing, This Image Is Dark and Rotated Incorrectly

After Brightening and Cropping, the Image Is Ready for Printing

With the Editor, you become your own photo lab technician.

With digital photography and Photoshop Elements, you become the photo processor, so you'll have to learn these principles of the digital trade:

- **Film can record more detail than digital media.** It's simply the nature of the beast. To compensate, always take photos at your digital camera's highest *resolution*. Yes, this means you won't be able to store as many photos on the camera's memory card, but the photos you do save will be worth printing.

- **Digital photos require digital storage media.** Early on in your digital photography career, you should develop a plan for managing your images. The simplest method is to copy photos from your camera to the hard disk and then back them up immediately onto a CD-R, DVD-R, or other high-volume, permanent storage medium. Next, print *thumbnails* of each image, select the best ones to keep, and delete the rest of the image files to reclaim storage space. You'll find that the *Organizer* is uniquely designed to help you with all stages in this process.

- **After making changes to your images, save copies of them.** Save your images in a universal format that's recognized by other applications—perhaps the same format your digital camera used to begin with—so that they're easier to share. Compressed TIFF and JPEG are the two most common universal formats for digital photographs. Using the Organizer, back up these edited images onto a separate CD-R or other storage medium.

- **Printing good-quality photos requires a printer designed and tested not only for color, but for use with photo paper.** Not all color printers are photo printers, capable of dealing with thicker, photo-quality paper. In addition, photo printers typically use six or seven tones of ink, including black, as opposed to the standard four inks you find with common color printers. So, a photo printer is well worth the extra money when you want prints that are worth archiving in albums and scrapbooks, not just thumb-tacking to your wall. If less than half of your everyday printing tasks are devoted to photos, and you want to save money, you can find a four-tone printer model that *does* print nice photos, if you use photographic paper specifically designed for that particular model or its brand. When comparing printer prices, compare not only the photo quality but also the price of the exclusive inks they use because that's where your greatest expense will be.

As an alternative to buying your own color photo printer, consider those do-it-yourself printing kiosks that let you insert a CD-R or PhotoCD and print photos on high-quality photo paper. Find a kiosk in your neighborhood (many discount department stores and drug stores have one) and study the instructions so that you'll save

If you're given a choice of formats to use with your digital camera, choose RAW or TIFF format over JPEG, because RAW and TIFF record and save more photographic detail than JPEG. Save these original digital images onto CD or DVD as your "digital negatives," and make copies to work on, preferably in PSD format. See the upcoming section that discusses PSD format in more detail.

You'll find yourself overrun with digital images not long after you've purchased your digital camera. One tool for keeping them all organized and easy to locate is the Organizer portion of Photoshop Elements. See the upcoming section, Use Photoshop Elements to Organize Photos, for more information.

NOTE

For optimum results, use only the photo paper that's compatible with your particular printer. Another consideration when printing photos at home is longevity. Archival inks and papers, although expensive, produce the best results.

your photos in a compatible format on a compatible medium. For occasional photo printing needs, **online services** such as Adobe Photoshop Services (provided by Ofoto, a Kodak company) enable you to upload your photos over the Internet, have them printed on quality stock, and delivered to you for reasonable fees.

- **If you intend to use the Editor to repair images scanned from old prints, invest in a good quality scanner with high resolution.** Some premium scanner models include special features such as a film reader for scanning film strips and/or slides.

What You Should Know About Resolution

A digital image is comprised of a series of small dots of color and brightness called *pixels*. Digital TV images and the images on your computer monitor are also comprised of pixels. The higher a digital photo's *resolution*, the more pixels it has per inch, and thus the more detail and clarity the image can contain.

KEY TERM

Resolution—In digital images, the number of pixels per inch/centimeter. The more pixels (dots) of color, the more detail an image holds. To compute resolution, multiply the number of pixels in width by the number of pixels in height for an image.

DPI (dots per inch)— Because a printer uses dots of ink to produce an image, DPI is used to describe printer output. The higher the DPI, the more pixels are used to print an image, and the more detail you get in your printed image.

PPI (pixels per inch)—A monitor uses pixels to display an image, so PPI (pixels per inch) is used to describe the quality of onscreen images. The higher the PPI, the larger the image file and the higher its resolution.

When editing digital images, you must always consider that the resolution you are using directly affects the quality of the final result. Onscreen, images are rendered at somewhere between 72 and 106 pixels per inch (**PPI**), which is quite a bit less than the 4,800 dots per inch (**DPI**) of most ink jet photo printers sold today. (Dye sublimation printers use a different printing technology and need only an average of 300 DPI to produce high-quality photo prints.) Because an onscreen pixel is larger than a printed dot, an onscreen image needs fewer pixels to produce the highest quality result. In other words, an onscreen image doesn't need very high resolution for you to think it looks good. So, if you are editing an image for use on the Web, in a PowerPoint presentation, or as a Windows desktop background image, a low-resolution photograph (larger pixels and fewer of them) will do just fine.

But because a printer reproduces photos by printing a greater number of dots per inch, to produce a high-quality, detailed, printout, you'll need to start with an image that has a lot of pixels (a high resolution). In other words, an image with low resolution that looks great onscreen will not look very good when printed.

Adding Text and Objects

If you view a digital photo at high magnification, it's easy to see that the image is comprised of many pixels arranged in perfect, horizontal rows. A row of pixels is called a *raster*. On your computer monitor, at 800×600 *resolution*, the display is comprised of 600 rasters. To display a black circle onscreen using raster technology, the Editor simply arranges a series of black dots in a circle pattern, and fills in the remaining spaces in each raster row with dots of the *background color*. The process of rendering raster objects onscreen is similar to using a Lite-Brite toy to draw a picture using rows and rows of small lights.

A vector is a mathematical formula that describes a line or a curve. A *vector* shape (such as a flower or a house) is comprised of one or more vectors; a circle or rectangle is made up of just one. A vector circle, for example, is computed by the Editor *geometrically,* as a series of dots set the same distance from a chosen point.

Rasters and vectors are not important in image editing until you decide to add text or drawn objects to a photo. It's at that point you'll need to choose between *raster data* and *vector data*.

In the *Editor*, geometric elements such as shapes, curves, lines, and text are rendered on a vector layer. Image content (such as a digital photograph or a scanned image) and objects you paint with the **Brush** tool or draw with the **Pencil** tool on a *layer* are rendered on a raster layer. On the vector layer, the boundaries of objects and text are plotted mathematically and filled in with color. Normally, the edges of vector objects are smooth and clean because they are rendered mathematically. But because the Editor renders the contents of its vector layer on a grid with the same *resolution* as all the other raster layers in an image, curved or diagonal content might appear jagged or stair-stepped when viewed at a high magnification. This fact makes that same data look jagged when printed.

Not to worry though; the Editor automatically compensates for the "jaggies" through a process called *anti-aliasing*. Anti-aliasing smoothes curves by adding semi-transparent pixels that "fuzz" the edges and fool the eye. Your eye, as it turns out, will more readily forgive the watery borders caused by anti-aliasing than it will ignore the stair-step look of a non-anti-aliased curve. When creating text, you can turn on anti-aliasing to smooth curved letters and numbers.

NOTE

The size of an onscreen image will vary depending on the screen resolution of the monitor it is being viewed on. In other words, if you're viewing an image with your monitor resolution set at 1280 by 1024, that same image will appear bigger (but with the same quality or level of detail) on a monitor set to a resolution of only 1024 by 768.

KEY TERM

Raster data—Data comprised of individual pixels, each with its own hue, saturation, and brightness value.

Vector data—Data stored as a series of mathematical formulas that plot the coordinates of points along the edges of a shape, such as a star or a bit of vector text.

Anti-aliasing—The addition of semi-transparent pixels along the curved edge of a shape or selection. Anti-aliasing helps curves look smooth and not jagged.

Anti-aliased Text

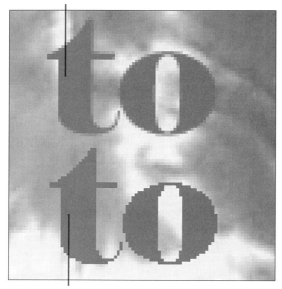

Non-anti-aliased Text

Anti-aliasing of this text blends otherwise jagged edges with their background by adding shades of the object color along its edges.

So, why does the Editor use vector technology on drawn objects and text, and then typically reduce images to raster data? One advantage in using vector data is that it can be easily changed. After drawing a vector object, you can reselect it with one click and change its size, position, color, and so on. And the edges of the vector object will be just as smooth even if you enlarge the object by a great deal. Because text is created using vector data, you can also easily edit it without damaging the image beneath it. On the other hand, raster data (which you create with the painting tools) is really only a series of dots. So, the only way to "edit" a diagonal line comprised solely of pixels painted onto an image is to systematically repaint each dot.

About Color Models and Optics

Digital images (such as photographs) are comprised of a series of pixels; each pixel has various characteristics that describe its color. For example, a pixel might be pale yellow-green. How the computer decides to make that pixel pale yellow-green depends on a specific color model. The *Editor* uses two color models interchangeably: RGB and HSB. This means that for any given pixel, there are two different ways to describe its color: as a mixture of the optical primaries red, green, and blue (RGB); or as given hue with a specific *saturation* and brightness (HSB).

Color models become important whenever you're asked to make a color choice in the Editor. For example, if you want to add some text or paint with one of the painting tools, you must choose the color you want to apply. You can use the RGB color model or the HSB color model by using the **Color Picker** to do just that—neither color model is necessarily better than the other; you simply use the one you prefer.

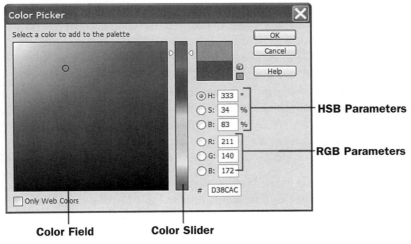

Color Field   **Color Slider**

The Color Picker represents pixel colors using two models simultaneously.

In the RGB model, the three optical primaries red, green, and blue are expressed in terms of their relative intensities, from 0 to 255. As you choose a color from the **Color Picker**, the relative amount of red, green, and blue contained in that color is displayed in the corresponding R, G, and B boxes. The purest, brightest red would be defined as an RGB value {255, 0, 0} or red with no green or blue. Cyan is created by mixing equal parts of green and blue with no red {0, 255, 255}. Medium gray is produced by mixing red, green, and blue equally, at roughly half strength {129, 129, 129}. White is produced by mixing the three colors evenly at full strength {255, 255, 255}. Black is produced on your monitor by adding no light at all {0, 0, 0}.

NOTE

When you look at colors displayed in the **Color Picker**, you'll discover the absence of certain colors you would swear were real—khaki colors, "earth tones," sandy shades. They're blends that can't be described by an optical color model—one based on light. A digital photograph (whether captured by a digital camera or scanned in using a scanner) simulates these natural colors by placing two or more pixels with often wildly different hues next to each other and letting the mind create the color by blending the pixels.

The second color model, named for the three attributes hue, saturation, and brightness (HSB), also describes every color that Windows and your monitor can display. In the HSB model, the hue (H) value is represented by a color's location on the optical color wheel. There are 360 degrees in a circle, and thus each hue is represented by its angle or degree on this circle. The color wheel begins at red, transitioning through magenta, blue, cyan, green, and yellow, then back to red again. When the **H** for **Hue** is enabled, all possible hues are represented on the **Color Picker** by the **color slider**, located to the right of the **color field**.

NOTE

Okay, there's a third way to specify color in the **Color Picker**: by entering a specific HTML color code in the # box. The code uses six hexadecimal (base-16) digits, where the first pair stands for the red value, the second pair for green, and the third pair for blue. Whereas we commonly use digits 0 through 9 with everyday numbers (base-10), hexadecimal proceeds from 0 to 9 and up to A through F (to represent 10 through 15). So, A0 represents 160, and FF represents 255.

The saturation level (S) refers to how *much* of that hue appears in the blended color. To "remove" the hue from the final color, the color opposite that hue on the color wheel is *added*. To you, adjusting the saturation of a color will look like you're adding white, because optically, when you equally blend two colors that are opposite on the color wheel, you get white. When the S option is enabled in the **Color Picker**, the color slider shows colors from the pure hue to white. A value of **0%** S for Saturation means that none of the hue is present in the final color, so it will therefore look completely white. A value of **100%** for Saturation means that the final color is completely saturated with the chosen hue, without a hint of its opposite added (such as a pure yellow).

Brightness (B) represents the blended color's degree of light. Here, a value of **0%** represents total darkness (black), and **100%** is a color with no black added at all. When the B option is enabled in the **Color Picker**, the colors on the color slider range from the blended color to pure black. You'll learn the specifics behind selecting a color using both the RGB and HSB color models in **113** **Select a Color to Work With**.

Why Printing a Photograph Isn't So Easy

Until now, you're probably used to printing mostly cards, letters, spreadsheets, and other everyday work documents, and you've come to expect that your printed results will match your onscreen view pretty closely. When you first enter the realm of digital photography, however, there may come a moment after printing your first image when you think, "That isn't how it looked onscreen." It's then that you start to realize that no two devices ever worked so differently from one another as your monitor and your printer.

A computer monitor uses varying intensities of the three optical primary colors to create each pixel—even the white ones. These optical primaries

See Also

→ **64** About Printing Images

→ **105** Ensure That What You See Is What You Get

are red, green, and blue. The science of light (optics) is an *additive process*. You start with the absence of light (black), and then add light to make color. Theoretically, every hue in the rainbow can be created with any combination of the three primaries. Imagine shining a red flashlight and a green flashlight at the same spot, and watching their combined output become a yellow light, and you'll get the idea.

Your color inkjet printer mixes colors following the rules of *pigment*, in which cyan, magenta, and yellow are the primary colors of ink or dye. A color inkjet has as few as four inks (with black being the fourth), or as many as seven different inks to work with. Rather than employing the optical process of *adding* light to attain the desired color, printing employs what's called a *subtractive* process. This theory works in precisely the opposite direction of optics. The subtractive process presumes that the purest light an object can reflect is white, so an object's color can be simulated by applying colored pigment or dye to mask out, or subtract, just those hues that an object absorbs and does *not* reflect. During printing, magenta is applied to the color of an object because the object appears to reflect red and blue light (megenta's two optical components) and absorb—or not reflect—green light.

Theoretically, if your inkjet printer were to mix equal amounts of cyan, magenta, and yellow ink in a given area, the inks would cancel out all reflected light, and the product would be black. In practice, however, because inks tend to introduce certain impurities, the product is actually a muddy brown. So, printers add a fourth pass, with black ink, to make darker portions bolder. Thus the name commonly given to the four-pigment process, CMYK (where the "K" stands for black). Recall from our earlier discussion of optics that cyan, magenta, and yellow just happen to be the three secondary hues in optics. This is the critical connection between optics and pigment, and this is why cyan, magenta, and yellow are the three basic inks used in process printing. Still, because the monitor and the printer use two different color models to create color, it's up to your program (in this case, Photoshop Elements) to do the best job it can in translating between the two. Photoshop Elements uses certain files called *ICC color profiles* to help it do just that. ICC color profiles help translate color information from your monitor's RGB color model to your printer's CMYK color model.

Windows typically installs a color profile for translating optical shades to printed shades so that what you see onscreen looks the same when

NOTE

Because your monitor mixes light to make colors, in its system, red and green make *yellow*, green and blue make *cyan*, and red and blue make *magenta*. This might be a foreign concept for you, especially because it's so different from what you may have done as a child, when mixing yellow and blue made blue, red and blue made purple, and so on. A color printer uses a color mixing system known as CMYK, where the three primary colors are cyan (the closest thing to blue in a transparent ink), magenta (a kind of red), and yellow.

NOTE

You'll learn more about color profiles and how to install them in **105** **Ensure That What You See Is What You Get**

TIPS

Do not put batteries in your pocket unless they are enclosed in a plastic case; if the batteries come in contact with metal (keys, change, and the like) they will discharge and burn you.

If you use a card reader to transfer images to the computer, don't ask your computer to format a memory card for you because it might cause errors. Instead, format your memory card in the camera by selecting that option off the camera's menu.

NOTES

Low-resolution digital images are always much grainier than their higher-resolution cousins—a problem you cannot really fix, even with the help of a graphics editor. So, don't skimp on image resolution when taking photographs—you will always regret it.

Photoshop Elements supports some digital cameras' RAW formats. If yours is supported, you can save your images using the camera's RAW format, which basically preserves all the image information without loss, as a kind of "digital negative." A list of supported cameras appears on Adobe's Web site at **http://www.adobe.com/products/photoshop/cameraraw.html**.

printed. When you installed your printer, the software it uses might have overridden this default color profile with one that's better suited to your printer. But it might not have done so. In any case, this book will show you not only how to install the best color profiles for your system, but also how to make subtle color corrections to your images onscreen so that you'll get the best printed result.

How to Take Better Photographs

Even with the help of a good *graphics editor* such as the Photoshop Elements *Editor*, learning a few things about what makes a more optically appealing photograph will save you time editing your images later on. Here are some simple things you should know:

- **Be prepared**. You can't take a picture if your camera's batteries are low or if you're out of memory. Invest in some extra batteries and plenty of memory cards or sticks and always keep them handy and ready to use. With ample backup power and storage media on hand, you'll be more relaxed, so when you take a shot you know isn't perfect, you can easily try again.

- **Don't skimp on quality**. Unless you're capturing an image for email or Web use *only*, always shoot at the highest *resolution* your camera allows. If you decide after the fact that a particular photo will make a nice 8"×10" print, you won't be able to get a quality result if you skimped on the resolution when taking the picture. In addition, if image compression is a variable on your camera, select low or even none.

- **Take lots of pictures**. The reason professional photographers can get that one really great shot is because they take far more than just one. This is especially true of candid moments, group photos, subjects in motion, or with less-than-perfect lighting conditions. Taking more than one photo also enables you to easily experiment with exposure and shutter speed settings, and maybe even a different lens (such as a wide-angle, telephoto, or fisheye lens). Later, you can choose the best image and discard the rest.

- **Study the light**. Locate the brightest and darkest areas of the scene you're capturing and determine how one affects the other. Is the sun shining right in your subject's face, causing her to squint and frown? Does the sunlight falling from behind put her face in shadow? Is your subject much brighter or darker than the background?

If so, you might want to change your position, or adjust the exposure value (plus or minus) to compensate for low light/bright light conditions. For example, you might be trying to take a nice picture of your child playing in the snow, but the camera sets the exposure automatically for the brightest object (the snow); as a result, your child's face is underexposed. The same situation happens when the sun is behind your subject and his face is in shadow, or the sun is in the picture when you're trying to capture the sunset. To compensate for over-bright elements in a scene, set the exposure value to plus 1 or 2 and reshoot. To compensate for deep shadows, dark foliage, or a dark subject against a light background, adjust the exposure value to minus 1 or 2.

- **Get white right**. Whenever the lighting conditions change, *white balance* your camera. Typically, white balancing involves making a lighting choice from a menu or the mode button (such as indoors, outdoors, snow, cloudy day, nighttime, stage lighting, and so on). More sophisticated digital camera models enable you to select the white balance option, point it toward something white or near white, and white balance automatically, so that the temperature and quality of the light you capture is adjusted for the light in the scene you're shooting. Unless you white balance the camera to match the current lighting conditions, flesh tones can look too blue or too orange.

- **Don't "auto" everything**. Get involved in the picture-taking process. Use the flash to provide fill light even in the daytime, softening shadows on a subject's face. Some cameras enable you to adjust the flash output so that the flash won't overwhelm a subject and drain its color.

   Control light by manually selecting the f-stop (aperture). A large aperture such as F2 helps you capture images under low-light conditions; a smaller aperture such as F16 is more appropriate for daylight conditions. When needed, you might choose to manually set the shutter speed instead.

- **Throw the background out of focus**. A great way to bring out your subject (and improve a photo's composition) is to blur the background behind it. This is easily accomplished by manually

---

KEY TERM

White balance—To adjust the color balance of the camera to the current lighting conditions so that the colors in the resulting photo are "true."

NOTE

White balancing allows the camera to compensate for color shifts caused by the source of light. For example, under a florescent light, things can look a bit blue because the light source is cool; outdoors, things tend toward orange because the light source is warmer. If conditions change after you white balance the camera (you move indoors or it starts to cloud up for example) be sure to white balance the camera again.

KEY TERMS

Depth of field—The distance between the closest and farthest in-focus objects.

NOTE

Two other factors affect depth of field: zoom and camera-to-subject distance. As you zoom in on a subject, the depth of field gets smaller. To increase the depth of field, zoom out. In addition, as you move closer to a subject and refocus, the depth of field becomes more shallow. To increase the depth of field, move back from your subject and refocus.

TIP

The world is your tripod if you only look—a park bench, car roof, tree branch, stone railing, or countertop all make perfectly legitimate tripod substitutes. If you can't find a reasonable "tripod," bring your elbows in, take a breath, and release it slowly as you gently press the shutter. Never stab at the shutter because doing so can move the camera.

selecting a large aperture (such as F2 or F4) to create a small *depth of field*. To capture a subject and the detail in the background around it, create a large depth of field by selecting a small aperture such as F12 or F16.

By blurring the background, this little girl, and not the festival crowd, becomes the most important element in this photograph.

- **Get rid of the shakes.** Whenever you can, use a tripod. For most digital cameras, there's an interminable wait between the time you press the shutter release and the time the camera records the image. Holding a camera perfectly still during this waiting period can be almost impossible. Invest in a small pocket tripod to steady your camera and remove unnecessary blur, especially when you've zoomed in on a far-away subject or are shooting in low-light conditions. Alternatively, use your surroundings as a surrogate tripod.

- **Be careful of zoom.** Most digital cameras offer a digital zoom, where the camera artificially increases its maximum optical zoom factor by essentially cropping a region from the optical image and magnifying that same region. Digitally zoomed images are grainy, even blocky, as a result. If you want a quality photograph, don't zoom in past the natural optical zoom level of your digital camera's lens. Some digital cameras even give you the option of turning off the digital zoom so that you can't accidentally engage it.

- **Frame it right.** Some digital cameras come with a viewfinder and a larger liquid crystal display (LCD) screen for displaying pictures. To properly frame subjects that are close to the lens, you must use the camera's LCD and not the viewfinder, because the viewfinder renders the scene a bit to one side.

- **Take better landscapes.** One mistake new photographers often make when taking pictures of a far-off vista is to simply press the shutter button, making the camera focus on that far away mountaintop. The result is a blurring of most of the foreground. To keep more of the foreground in focus, focus on something about 1/3 of the distance from you to that mountaintop and then press the shutter button partway. Then, while still holding the shutter button partway down, reframe the picture and press the button the rest of the way to take the photograph.

Use Photoshop Elements to Organize Photos

After beginning your foray into digital photography, it won't take long before you'll realize that your collection is getting almost too big to manage. This is where the Photoshop Elements *Organizer* comes in: Its purpose is to provide the tools you need to catalog images so that you can locate them quickly, regardless of where they are stored—on the hard disk, CD-R, DVD, or a digital camera's memory card. Basically, you import images into the Organizer's *catalog*, and then tag them with special markers that indicate what those images contain (for example, Fourth of July, Oklahoma City, Granddad and Nana), or their purpose (for example, Family Reunion Invitation). Next, you'll use these markers to locate specific images for editing, printing, or using in *creations*. If you choose to edit an image, the *Editor* portion of Photoshop Elements appears, displaying its unique set of tools designed for making changes to images. To learn how to start the Editor and the Organizer, refer to **Use the Welcome Window**, later in this chapter. You'll learn how to use the Organizer and its tools in **About the Organizer**.

TIP

If you want a great photograph of a friend or relative, become an observer. At get-togethers, blend into the background and discretely take photos only when the moment is right. Your patience will be rewarded with a candid photo that captures people as they really are—beautiful and human. This trick also works well with nature photographs of birds, butterflies, and squirrels at play. As a diver once put it, take only pictures and leave only bubbles.

NOTE

The Organizer (essentially Photoshop Album 3.0) sports many new or improved features, including *collections*, grouped versions of the same image, *photo review*, and **Photo Compare** mode.

KEY TERM

Creations—Greeting cards, calendars, Web galleries, slideshows, and other things you can make with Organizer's help, using the images in the catalog.

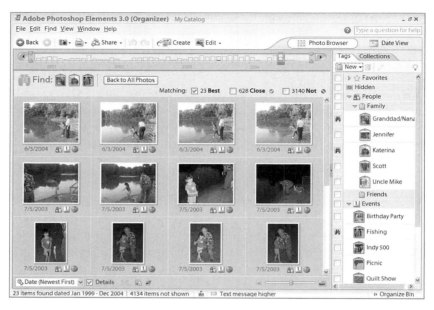

The Organizer enables you to quickly categorize your collection of digital images.

Use Photoshop Elements to Edit Photos

NOTE

The Editor sports many new or improved features, including the **Healing Brush**, **Spot Healing Brush**, **Cookie Cutter** tool, *Histogram palette*, dedicated **Quick Fix** mode, *Multi-window Mode*, *Maximize Mode*, Photo Bin, and *Palette Bin*.

As you learned earlier, the portion of Photoshop Elements that enables you to edit and create graphic images is called the *Editor*. Although you can use the Editor to create buttons, banners, and other graphical gadgets for your Web pages, its main purpose is to edit photographs. You can use the Editor's tools to retouch photographs, add text and other objects, and apply special *effects*. You'll learn how to start the Editor in **Use the Welcome Window**, later in this chapter, and to use the Editor's tools in **43 About the Editor**. Right now I want to show you how a *graphics editor* such as the Editor can make your images look better.

What You Can Do with a Graphics Editor

With the help of a *graphics editor* such as the Photoshop Elements *Editor*, you can fix errors in your photographs such as bad lighting and *red-eye*. You can also perform some special effects wizardry. Here are just a few of the tasks you can accomplish with the Editor and a little help from this book:

- If a photo is slightly out of focus, you can make it sharper. However, you can't "fix" a blurry photo (although you can improve it somewhat).

- If you've taken a picture of a person standing in front of the sun, her face is probably in shadow and the background is probably too light. Using the Editor, you can lighten her face and darken the background.

- You can remove unwanted elements from a photograph—such as an electric cord draped along the floor, a price tag or a logo on a shirt, or a hunk of lettuce stuck in your subject's teeth—by selectively copying elements from elsewhere in the photo and using those elements to mask the unwanted ones.

- You can perform digital cosmetic surgery on your subject, removing gray hairs, wrinkles, blemishes, uneven skin tone, tired eyes, and eyeglass glare. You can even whiten teeth and add makeup if you want.

TIP

To a certain degree, you can remove the effects of a flash that was either too close or too far away.

 Before

 After

Removing the mailbox from this snowy scene improves the composition by placing the focus on the subject.

- You can improve the composition of a photograph and bring out your subject by blurring the background.

- You can improve a photo's composition by straightening a slanting horizon and cropping out areas to the left, right, top, or bottom of your subject that aren't needed.

TIP

You can draw a frame around a photograph, or add text, cartoon bubbles, or other objects.

—Before   —After

Selectively cropping, lightening, sharpening, and color balancing makes a world of difference in this photograph.

- You can apply a variety of special **filters**, **effects**, and **layer styles** to make your photograph look as though it were drawn by Picasso, Titian, Toulouse-Lautrec, or Andy Warhol.

- You can restore the appearance of a very old and damaged photograph by scanning it into the **Organizer catalog** or the Editor, and then using the Editor to repair rips, scratches, and other mutilations. You can even fill in missing areas of a photo by copying material from other places on the same photograph or another photograph.

- You can add color to black-and-white photos by painting in faces and clothing, just like they used to do long ago. If your old photo is already in color, you can remove the color and give it a more old-fashioned sepia tone.

- You can remove a friend from an office setting and place her on the beach, in a parade, or at the signing of the Declaration. You can also place her on an artistic background you create yourself.

Before

After

Restoring this old photograph involved lightening it, filling in a missing area, and removing several scratches.

There are a few things you can't do with the Editor, at least not easily. For example, as I noted earlier, although you can sharpen a slightly blurry photograph, you can't restore focus to one that's completely out of focus. To sharpen a photo, the Editor simply increases the contrast between pixels along the edges of objects, making those edges more distinct. However, extreme digital sharpening can reveal details that weren't obvious before, such as the texture of hair or skin, small spots, and background objects.

You cannot easily create animated images in the Editor, although it does enable you to preview and save simple animations such as a ball bouncing up and down.

✍ **NOTE**

The Editor is not a publishing program. By that, I mean it wasn't designed to produce multi-page birthday cards, invitations, newsletters, and the like. Although it includes tools that enable you to add text to a picture, the Editor wasn't designed for typesetting long passages of text. So, use the Editor to improve the appearance of your graphics, and then use the *Organizer* or some other application—such as Microsoft Publisher or Word—to produce the newsletters, greeting cards, and other documents you need.

You cannot restore extremely damaged photographs; for such wizardry, you should use a high-end graphics editor such as Photoshop CS.

When to Use Layers

While editing or building an image, the *Editor* enables you to place data on multiple *layers*. The key purpose of layering is to give you a way to isolate multiple, individual parts of what will eventually comprise a complete image. For example, you might place a subject on a separate layer so that you can apply brightness and contrast changes just to it and not the entire photograph. Also, placing an element such as a photo caption on its own layer enables you to resize, recolor, or reposition it without overwriting portions of the photo beneath that element. In addition, data on upper layers can be used to obscure data on the layers below. For example, if you copied a person onto a lower layer, you could place him behind other people or objects in a photograph. After using layers to manipulate different elements of an image individually, you merge them together to create a flattened, single-layer image.

You can build a complex image by isolating each element on its own layer.

You can blend two layers together in a multitude of ways, achieving effects you couldn't create otherwise. For example, you might blend two copies of the same image using the **Exclusion, Hard Mix,** or **Vivid Light** blend mode to create instant pop-art as the colors from each layer are blended. When needed, you can add a special *adjustment layer* to test an adjustment on the layers below (such as a brightness change) without making that adjustment permanent, to control the amount of an adjustment or to apply the same adjustment to several layers at once.

The **Layers** *palette* shows you which layers are on top of others and which are beneath. Like a series of animation cels, layers of an image are laid one on top of the other, with each layer obscuring the layers beneath it. You can control the capability of a layer to block the data in the layers below it by changing the layer's opacity. A layer that's 100% opaque is like new paint on a wall—it completely blocks the wall color beneath. Set the opacity to 50% however, and the layer will cover lower layers only partially—like a sheer veil. You can also control which areas of an image layer are seen by applying a *clipping mask*, which you'll learn how to do in **Mask an Image Layer**. In a similar manner, a *mask* on a fill layer can block the fill from covering up portions of the layers below. On an adjustment layer, a mask can act as a blanket, protecting selected parts of a layer from changes such as a color adjustment. You'll learn how to create fill and adjustment layer masks in **100** **Mask an Adjustment or Fill Layer**.

A digital photograph starts out with a single layer; the Editor treats that layer as the *background layer*, and lists it as such in the **Layers** palette. The background layer is locked and cannot be moved within the layer stack; its opacity and blend mode also cannot be changed. The name of the current layer is highlighted in the **Layers** palette; with a few exceptions, any changes you make apply only to the data on the current layer. To select a layer for editing, click its name in the **Layers** palette. To move, transform, copy, paste, or merge multiple layers, link them together as explained in **91** **About Layers and the Layers Palette**.

 TIP

If you're not careful with layers, you might get into a situation where you start painting but nothing seems to be happening—for some reason, your paintbrush is dry. The reason is probably that you've accidentally chosen another layer and are painting in an area obscured by pixels in a higher-order layer—the changes you're making on that layer are not visible to you. So, be sure to watch your layers!

NOTE

When you select a region of an image to restrict editing to that region, you're also restricting your edits to that region *on the currently selected layer*—unless you specify otherwise when making the selection. In addition, you can have the Editor copy data from the region you select in the current layer plus every other layer if you choose the **Copy Merged** command. See **86** **About Copying, Cutting, and Pasting Data Within a Selection** for details.

NOTE

A selection doesn't have to be comprised of just one region of adjacent pixels; it can be several nonadjacent regions. In addition, as mentioned earlier, a selection can include pixels from all layers and not just the current layer.

Since the Text Is Fully Opaque, It Obscures the Layers Below

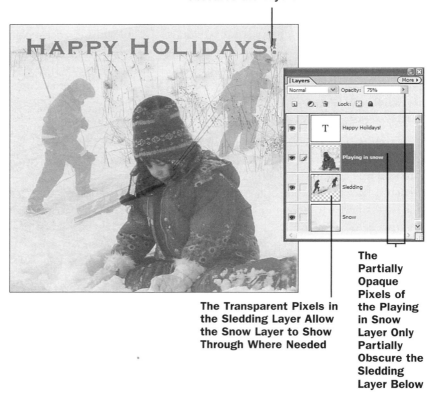

The Transparent Pixels in the Sledding Layer Allow the Snow Layer to Show Through Where Needed

The Partially Opaque Pixels of the Playing in Snow Layer Only Partially Obscure the Sledding Layer Below

Upper layers can obscure lower layers, depending on their opacity.

Why Select a Portion of a Photo?

The *Editor* enables you to select a portion of a *layer* or layers when needed. For example, if you select a portion of a layer and then begin painting, the paint affects only the selected area on that layer and none of the pixels outside it. Here, the selection acts as a kind of painter's tape, preventing the paint from spilling outside its borders and affecting the pixels you don't want to change. This same protection applies to any effect you might apply; for example, if you adjust the brightness after making a selection, only the pixels within the selected area are affected. You might also select an area when you want to copy or move its pixels to another image or layer. Here, the selection helps to mark the data you want to copy or move.

The Editor gives you a variety of tools and methods you can use to select the area you want to affect. The selected area is marked with a *selection marquee*. The marquee is always in motion (like marching ants) so you can easily see the area you selected and distinguish that area from the rest of the image (the unselected area).

—— Selection Marquee

With a selection tool, you define where changes are to take place— here, the head of a mallard duck has been selected.

Filters, Effects, and Layer Styles

Professional photographers often attach a filter to the front of the camera lens to bend the light coming into the camera and create visual effects. In the *Editor*, a *filter* can also be used to create a visual effect, but far beyond the capability of a mere lens attachment. For example, you can use a filter to change any or all of your image as though it were rendered by a watercolor brush, sketched with a charcoal pencil on coarse-bond art paper, or burned into a plate of steel with a blowtorch. You choose a filter from the **Filter** menu and configure its options using the dialog box that appears. You can also select a filter from the **Styles and Effects** *palette* by first choosing **Filter** from the first drop-down list. You'll learn how to apply various filters in upcoming tasks.

If your image doesn't appear crisp or clear, a sharpen filter can detect the narrowest areas where colors appear to contrast and draw out those contrasts to create a sharper image. By blending some color values with

KEY TERM

Selection marquee— Flashing dashes that mark the boundary of a selection.

NOTE

When a selection is *feathered*, data from the pixels along the outside edge of the selection are selected only partway. This way, the edge of the area that's affected by whatever change you make is soft and fuzzy instead of hard and chunky; however, the marquee of a feathered selection surrounds only the non-soft part of the selection—in other words, only those pixels that are entirely opaque. So in a feathered selection, the selection boundary is actually a bit larger, by the amount of the feathering.

The Editor provides several tools for selecting the area you want to affect: the **Marquee** tools (which help you select a regularly shaped region such as a rectangle or circle), the **Selection Brush** and **Lasso** tools (which enable you to select any region you can draw freehand or by tracing the edge of an object), and the **Magic Wand** (which selects pixels of a similar color with a single click). You'll learn how to use each of these tools later in this book.

🔍 **KEY TERM**

Filter—A series of computer instructions that modify the pixels in an image.

🖌 **NOTE**

Filters typically work on only **RGB Color** images, although most work on **Grayscale** images as well. See **63** **Change Color Mode** for help in changing color modes. In addition, you can't apply a filter to text unless you convert that text to *raster data* first. If you want to apply the filter to only a portion of an image, select that area first and then apply the filter.

others in their immediate proximity, a blur filter can generate the illusion of motion. Other filters can remove scratches, blemishes, and *moiré* patterns from a photo, especially a photo imported from a scanner where dust specks often abound.

Filters can apply many special effects to your images.

💡 **TIP**

Most of the tasks in this book use filters of a more practical nature to clean up photographs and such, but you should take time to experiment with the artistic filters to create special effects and add some fun to an otherwise ordinary picture.

Although some filters exist for the purpose of correcting images, most are, quite frankly, created purely to exploit a new form of artistic expression. Using a filter, you can take all or part of an image and wrap it around a sphere or a three-dimensional box. You can create circular ripples in an image as though it were rendered on the surface of a pond or a lake of mercury. You can give an image the texture of stained glass, mosaic tiles, or a patchwork quilt.

Effects are timesavers—typically, an effect is a collection of several filters and other image adjustments, applied automatically in a particular sequence, to create a special effect. Effects can be applied to an entire layer, to a selection, to text, or to a flattened image with no layers. You can't make adjustments to an effect as you can with a filter; effects are a take-it-or-leave-it kind of thing. To apply an effect, choose **Effects** from the first drop-down list on the **Styles and Effects** palette. Then double-click the effect thumbnail to apply that effect. You can narrow the list of effects by choosing an effects group from the second drop-down list. If an effect's name includes the notation (**selection**), the Editor will flatten all layers first, copy the data in the selected area to another layer, and apply the effect. If an effect's name includes the notation (**type**), that effect can be applied only to a text layer. If an effect's name includes the notation (**layer**), that effect will be applied to a new *layer* above the current one.

A *layer style* is often applied to the edges of objects or text on a shape or text layer. These "edge styles" are listed in the first grouping in the **Layer Style** list box on the **Styles and Effects** palette. For example, you can add a bevel layer style to create a chiseled look for your text. You can also apply a layer style to the object itself, filling that object with a special texture or pattern. For example, using the **Orange Glass** layer style, you can make an object or some text look as if it were made from orange glass. These "filler styles" are listed in a second grouping in the **Layer Style** list on the **Styles and Effects** palette.

If you apply a layer style to a regular layer instead of a shape or text layer, the layer style may replace all the data on that layer, depending on what that data is. If the layer is filled with an image, for example, the "filler styles" typically replace the image and fill the layer. If the layer contains pixels you've painted or drawn with the **Brush** or **Pencil** tool, or if it contains objects you've simplified to bitmap data, the "filler styles" will fill only the interior of those drawings and not the entire layer. With filters, effects, and layer styles, it's typically best to apply the filter, effect, or style you're thinking about, and then use the **Undo** button to remove it if it doesn't work out as you thought.

KEY TERMS

Effect—A unique combination of filters and other image manipulations, applied together automatically, to achieve a particular look such as bricks, asphalt, or a wooden frame.

Layer style—A design that's applied to all the objects on a layer, such as text or drawn objects, or to the layer as a whole. As new data is added to the layer, the style is applied to that data as well.

TIPS

You can adjust the scale of a layer style after applying it if you don't like the result. For example, if you apply the **Puzzle** layer style and want the puzzle pieces to look smaller, choose **Layer, Layer Style, Scale Effects**. Then choose a percentage (less than 100% makes the pattern smaller; more than 100% makes it bigger).

When a layer style is added to a layer, a small cursive *f* appears next to the layer's name on the **Layers** palette. Click this **f** to display the **Style Settings** dialog box, which enables you to make small changes to the layer style. Right-click the **f** and select **Clear Layer Style** to remove the layer style altogether.

The **Blizzard** effect adds a chilly air to this scene, whereas the **Angled Spectrum** layer style applied to the border adds whimsy.

When to Use the Photoshop File Format

Your digital camera stores its photos in one of the universal image formats: perhaps JPEG (named for the Joint Photographic Experts Group, which devised the format), Tagged Image File Format (TIFF), or a version of RAW format customized by your specific camera manufacturer. Your digital scanner probably uses one of these formats as well. RAW format is uncompressed and can be considered a "digital negative" of your image, provided you have a program that can read the format. (Photoshop Elements can read most RAW formats, but you should check first before recording images in RAW format that you might want to edit later.) Both JPEG and TIFF images can be mathematically compressed so that they consume less storage space than a format that represents the entire image as a *bitmap*—as colored dots in multiple rows, left-to-right, top-to-bottom. (For TIFF files, compression is optional.) But even compressed, a JPEG file is made up of one single image component—that is, one picture and not several *layers* of an image laid on top of each other. And although a TIFF file can support layers, a layered TIFF file might not be readable by some programs and might be considerably larger than the format I'm about to suggest—Photoshop format. If you compress your layered TIFF file to make it smaller, you might introduce *artifacts* if you resave your work often. RAW format is great for bringing all your data into Photoshop Elements, but not good for saving your changes.

The *Editor* has a special format you use to store works in progress: the Photoshop format. (Files in Photoshop format can have either a **.PSD** or **.PDD** extension; the **.PDD** extension is older but is still recognized by Photoshop Elements. The **.PSD** extension is assigned to your files when you save them with Photoshop Elements.). When you save an image in Photoshop format, all image data is saved, such as *layers*, *masks*, saved selections, areas of transparency, and hidden data. And as long as you turn off the **Maximize Compatibility** option when saving a PSD image (in other words, you have no need to save the PSD file so that it can be read by earlier versions of Photoshop or Photoshop Elements), the file will remain relatively small even as it preserves all your work. When you complete your work on an image, you can merge all the layers and data into a single layer, and then save the single-layer image in a smaller, universal format such as JPEG or TIFF. If you want the file to be useable on another computer, and you want the layers preserved, you can choose not to merge the layers and save them in a TIFF file that should be readable by most image viewers. Even so, quite a lot of image viewers these days can read PSD files quite easily, so converting your file to a layered TIFF might not be necessary for you.

How to Use a Pen Tablet with the Editor

The prices of digital cameras and digital scanners have plummeted sharply in the last half-decade, making true digital photo processing feasible and affordable not only to professionals but also to hobbyists. Add to this list of more affordable tools the *pen tablet*. In the *Editor*, you can use a tablet instead of a mouse to make the same kind of drawing or painting motions on a computer that you'd make with a real pencil or paintbrush. (Although you can use a pen tablet to make selections in the *Organizer*, its usefulness is more apparent within the Editor.)

Today's tablets, such as the Wacom Graphire, are touch-sensitive; the tablet can record the difference between a light touch and a firm press. Specifically, it senses 255 different degrees of pressure. If you're using the airbrush function of the **Brush** tool, for example, the degree of "air pressure" in the brush, and/or the radius of the spray, is determined by how firmly you press the pen against the tablet. (You can't make this same kind of variation or adjustment using the mouse to paint.) If you're not accustomed to making precise movements with your mouse device—and

NOTE

You won't want to share photos in Photoshop format, even if your friend also uses Photoshop or Photoshop Elements, because the files are simply too large. Converting finished images to JPEG or TIFF format is smart because the resulting files are typically smaller. Back up your original Photoshop Elements files onto CD for retrieval later on should you need to make additional changes.

KEY TERM

Pen tablet—Input device that enables you to draw and paint on a computer using a natural hand motion and a special pen.

many people aren't—you might find a wireless pen much easier to learn and control. And that will make it much easier for you to make minute changes to your photographs or drawn artwork. You can even switch back and forth between a pen and a mouse (the Graphire comes with a wireless mouse), so that you can still select menu commands and control Windows with the mouse while you're drawing with the pen.

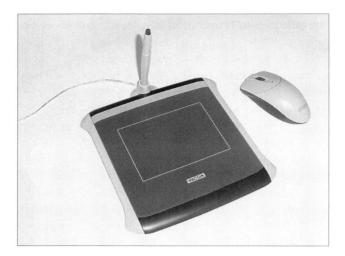

The Wacom Graphire pen tablet (ruby edition).

 NOTE

Most modern tablets, including Wacom models, have a special button on the pen that assumes the function of *double*-clicking the left mouse button. Press this button once, not twice, to double-click.

With a pen tablet, operations can be a little different than using a mouse. To make an adjustment to a tool setting, for example, lift the pen completely off the tablet—the pointer will stay where it is. Then *hover* your pen over the spot on the tablet that corresponds with the tool setting location onscreen; the pointer will snap to that spot like a magnet. To move the pointer without actually drawing with it, hover the pen just over the tablet without touching it. To select something with the pen, *tap*, just once. To draw, touch the pen to the tablet and draw normally, remembering that the degree of pressure you use is registered by the tool you're using.

The process of picking up and moving something—such as a flower petal you've selected—is different with a pen tablet than it is with a standard mouse. You'll see how to do this in proper detail later in this book; in brief, after you've selected the portion you want to move, plunk the pen down right in the middle of it, move the pen in the same direction you want to move the selection, and then lift the pen when the selection is in place. From the point of view of your hand, you might as well have used a real pen to scoot a piece of paper along the top of your desk; it feels pretty much the same.

Believe it or not, many tablets (including the Wacom Graphire) have *erasers* on the back end of the pen. To erase something in a photograph, you can literally turn the pen around and use the blunt eraser end to wipe away unwanted content in an image. The Editor associates the eraser end of the pen with its own **Eraser** tool.

When the pen procedure for a task differs significantly from the mouse procedure for the same task, I'll tell you how to do it both ways. But when the procedures are pretty much the same, I'll defer to explaining the task as though you're using the mouse (drag, click, drag-and-drop, double-click). When there's something you can do with a pen that you cannot do with a mouse (for example, vary the radius of an airbrush stroke *while* you're painting or using the eraser tip), I'll show you how to do that using pen tablet language.

Use the Welcome Window

Every time you start Photoshop Elements, you're greeted by the **Welcome** window. You can use its controls to start either the *Editor* or the *Organizer*, so that you can quickly locate an image for editing, review a tutorial on an unfamiliar feature, watch the product overview, or start a new image or *creation*. To dismiss the **Welcome** window, click its **Close** button; to redisplay the **Welcome** window at any time, choose **Window, Welcome** from the menu bar.

The buttons at the top of the **Welcome** window provide quick access to the most common tasks you'll want to perform at the start of a work session, such as importing images into the Organizer *catalog*, editing an image using **Quick Fix** or **Standard Edit** modes, beginning a new image, or starting a creation. You'll learn the specific steps for performing each of these actions in upcoming tasks.

To view the product overview, click the **Product Overview** button. To start a tutorial, click the **Tutorials** button at the top of the window. To open your Web browser and display Adobe's Home page, click the **Adobe** button at the bottom of the window.

TIP

If you don't want to display the **Welcome** window every time you start Photoshop Elements, then before closing its window, open the **Start Up In** drop-down list at the bottom of the window and select either **Editor** or **Organizer**. If you choose **Editor**, for example, the **Welcome** window does not display when you start Photoshop Elements, but the Editor will. Regardless of which component you choose to start up in, it's an easy matter to start the other component (such as the Organizer, for example) whenever you need it.

Start a New Image or Creation

Start a
Tutorial

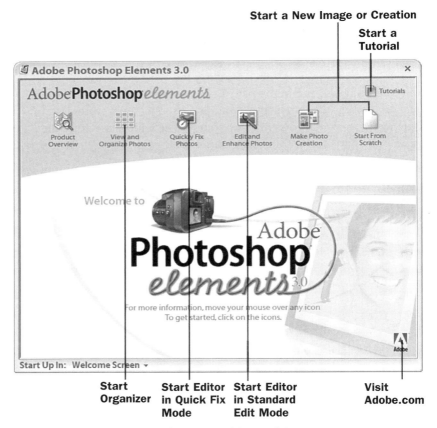

Start
Organizer

Start Editor
in Quick Fix
Mode

Start Editor
in Standard
Edit Mode

Visit
Adobe.com

*The **Welcome** window provides you with a quick way to start your image editing session.*

Change Preferences

Like most other programs, Photoshop Elements enables you to tweak its default settings to suit your needs. To change preferences in the *Editor* or the *Organizer*, choose **Edit, Preferences** and then select the type of preferences you want to change from the submenu that appears. For example, in the *Editor*, choose **Edit, Preferences, Saving Files** to change the way in which images are saved; in the *Organizer*, choose **Edit, Preferences, Scanner** to change the default file type and *resolution* for images scanned into the Organizer *catalog*. The **Preferences** dialog box is then displayed with the appropriate page open.

PART I: Organizing Items in the Catalog

After making changes to a set of preferences, you can save those changes by clicking **OK**. To change from one set of preferences to another in the Editor **Preferences** dialog box, choose the set of options you want to view from the drop-down list at the top of the dialog box or click the **Next** button to view the next set of preferences in the list. Return to a previous set of preferences by clicking **Prev** instead. To change to a different preference set in the Organizer **Preferences** dialog box, select that set from the list on the left.

 TIP

If you want to reset the currently displayed set of preferences back to default settings, click **Reset** or **Restore Default Settings**.

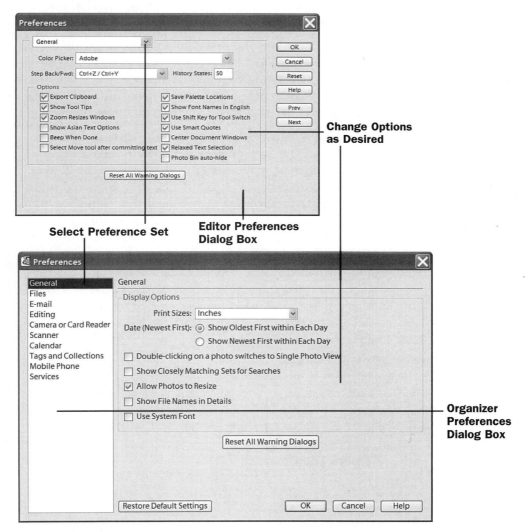

Select Preference Set

Editor Preferences Dialog Box

Change Options as Desired

Organizer Preferences Dialog Box

*Use the **Preferences** dialog box to change the way in which the Editor or the Organizer performs basic tasks.*

🔦 **TIP**

If you save an image while you're working on it, you can undo changes you've made. Once you close the image, you can't undo saved changes.

📝 **NOTES**

To change the limit for the number of changes to an image the Editor can undo, choose **Edit, Preferences, General**. Then adjust the **History States** value (the maximum value is 100) and click **OK**.

So, what's a "change"? Any complete action is a change. If you paint a blob on an image using the **Brush** tool, lift the brush and paint another blob, that's two actions. If you paint a large squiggle and a blob without releasing the mouse button, that's one action. If you select a filter, set its options, and click **Apply**, that's one action. If you select a region, copy its data to a different layer, and then move that data around, that's three actions. Changes made to the program (such as moving a *palette* or changing a preference) cannot be undone by clicking **Undo**.

If you have several images open, the Editor remembers separate sequences of changes or "diaries," for each image. So, when you display the **Undo History** palette, it only lists changes for the current image.

How to Undo Mistakes

Like a lot of programs, both the *Editor* and the *Organizer* remember the changes you make to an image or the *catalog* and enable you to undo those changes as needed. When you click the **Undo** button on the **Shortcuts** bar or select **Edit, Undo XXX** from the menu (where *XXX* is the name of the action you want to undo), Photoshop Elements resets the image or the catalog to the state it was before you made the most recent change. To undo the next most previous change, click **Undo** or choose **Edit, Undo** again.

Whatever can be undone can also be redone. Every time you undo an operation—thereby going back one step—that operation is remembered in a separate redo sequence for the image or catalog. If, after you click **Undo**, you click the **Redo** button or select **Edit, Redo**, the active image or catalog is re-reset to the stage it was in before the **Undo** command.

If you want to undo multiple changes, rather than clicking the **Undo** button repeatedly, use the **Undo History** palette in the Editor. Select **Window, Undo History** from the menu to display a listing of all the image changes you can undo. Changes are listed in the order in which they occurred, with the most current change appearing at the bottom. Drag the slider up from the bottom to undo changes, or simply select any change from the list. All the changes made up to that point will be undone in one step (changes that have been undone appear faded to indicate that they no longer apply to the current image). You can still redo the changes by dragging the slider back down or clicking a change that's lower in the list than the last retained change. To clear the history list of all changes for the current image, click the **More** button and select **Clear Undo History** from the **More** menu.

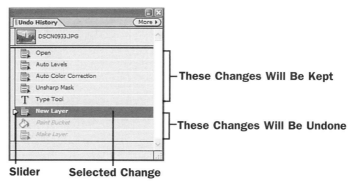

*The **Undo History** palette makes it possible for you to undo multiple changes in one step.*

2

Importing Items into the Organizer Catalog

IN THIS CHAPTER:

1 About the Organizer

2 Perform an Initial Scan for Media

3 Import Media from a Folder

4 Import Media from a CD-ROM or DVD

5 Import Images from a Digital Camera

6 Import a Scanned Image

7 Import and Separate Multiple Scanned Images

8 About Importing Images from a Cell Phone

9 Capture Images from a Video File

10 Import Images from a PDF Document

11 Import New Media Automatically

12 Remove an Item from the Catalog

13 Locate Moved Files

14 Back Up the Organizer Catalog

15 Copy Items onto CD-ROM or DVD

By now you have probably accumulated quite a collection of digital images and are more than ready to start organizing them using the Photoshop Elements' *Organizer*. With the Organizer, you can quickly categorize your images and easily locate them later. At the heart of the Organizer is its *catalog*—in the catalog, you can organize all your images, regardless of their location, into whatever categories you choose. For example, if you want to organize all the photos of your son into a single grouping, you can do so even if those photos are stored in various locations on the hard disk and on several CDs or DVDs. To keep the Organizer running smoothly, you must keep its catalog in order, so in this chapter you'll learn not only how to add images to the catalog, but also to remove them when needed, to update the catalog when an image's location has changed, and to back up the catalog periodically (a process that backs up the catalog information and the media files it contains). Finally, you'll learn how to back up the images themselves onto CD-ROM or DVD—something you might do to easily share images or take them to a kiosk (such as Kodak Picture Maker) for printing.

1 About the Organizer

See Also

→ **2** Perform an Initial Scan for Media

→ **14** Back Up the Organizer Catalog

→ **15** Copy Items onto CD-ROM or DVD

KEY TERMS

Catalog—A collection of organized media files. Each member of your family can create his or her own unique collection (catalog) of files.

Captions—A text or audio description of a media file.

The *Organizer* helps you categorize your digital images, video, and audio files by creating a list of those media files and their locations. In addition, the catalog keeps track of any *creations* you make using these media files. To create this initial listing of media files, you simply indicate the general location you want the Organizer to search. You'll learn the details of this procedure in **2** **Perform an Initial Scan for Media**. After compiling this initial listing (which is called the *catalog*), you'll want to repeat this process from time to time to add new media files, such as those located on a CD-ROM, DVD, digital camera, or scanner.

After your media files (images, video, and audio) are listed in the Organizer, you begin organizing them by adding *tags* and *collection* markers. After adding these special markers, you can use them to quickly display a group of similar files, regardless of where they are stored— even if they are stored *offline* on a CD or DVD. For example, you might want to display all the photos of your dog so that you can pick out the best one to include in a family photo album. After displaying a set of similar images, you can browse through them full screen, or select a single image for editing within the *Editor*. If you've located a favorite video or audio file, you can play it without leaving the Organizer. You can perform other image tasks as well, including printing, sharing, and creating cards and calendars.

You can add *captions* to your media files, making it easier to locate and identify them. Captions can be added as text to images, sound, video files, and creations, and also as sound attachments (*audio captions*), bringing a new dimension to your media collection. For example, you might select a photo and add an audio description of the party or event at which it was taken. You can then include this audio in a slideshow of photos or in a video CD of images. Text captions appear under images included in Web Photo Galleries, photo albums, and calendars, so it's well worth the extra time and effort to add them.

Because the catalog contains a list of each media file and its location, date, size, caption, markers, and other *properties*, it's important to create a backup copy of the catalog from time to time. The backup copy aids in data recovery, should something happen to the original catalog file. See **14** **Back Up the Organizer Catalog**. Backing up the catalog also copies your image, audio, and video files onto the backup disc, so performing a backup from time to time is critical. If you're ready to offload your images, video, and audio files to a permanent location such as a CD-ROM or DVD, you can copy just those files to disc. See **15** **Copy Items onto CD-ROM or DVD**. As another protection against the loss of your original images, any changes you initiate from within the Organizer (whether you use the Editor or another *graphics editor* such as Photoshop to complete them) can be easily saved to a new image file.

A Look at the Organizer Work Area

You can start the *Organizer* from the **Welcome** window (by clicking the **View and Organize Photos** button) or from within the *Editor* (by clicking the **Photo Browser** or **Date View** button on the **Shortcuts** bar). The Organizer work area is then displayed. If this is your first time using the Organizer, you should perform an initial search for media files, as described in **2** **Perform an Initial Scan for Media**. After importing some media files into the *catalog*, you're ready to familiarize yourself with the Organizer work area. The work area can appear in one of two ways: as a browser or as a calendar. For now, I'll assume that you're using **Photo Browser** view because that's the default view. If you're using **Date View** (where images are displayed within a large calendar), see **38** **Find Items with the Same Date** for more information.

NOTE

The Organizer recognizes only particular image file types (PSD, JPEG/JPG, TIFF/TIF, BMP, PNG, and GIF to name a few), so it can import images in only these file types. The Organizer also recognizes MP3 and WAV audio files, AVI, MPEG, and MOV video files, and *PDF documents* (Adobe portable document format files, which often contain images).

NOTE

The **Status bar** appears below the **Options bar**, and lists the total number of items currently being displayed. Occasionally, a **Notification** icon may appear in the middle of the Status bar; click it to display messages from Adobe, such as a new update or a sale on photo services

In the Organizer work area, you'll find the tools you need to organize and use your media files. At the top of the work area is the menu bar. Just like any other program, you click a menu to open it, and then click the menu command you want. Below the menu bar are the **Shortcuts** bar, **Timeline**, **Organize Bin**, **Find** bar, photo well, and **Options** bar. Let's take a closer look at each of these features.

The Organizer work area.

Shortcuts Bar

See Also

→ **38** Find Items with the Same Date

→ **64** About Printing Images

→ **109** Apply a Quick Fix

→ **155** About Emailing

Below the menu bar, you'll find the **Shortcuts** bar—a toolbar of buttons for common commands such as importing media files into the *catalog*, sharing and printing images, and making *creations*. Some buttons on the **Shortcuts** bar require a bit more explanation than others. After you've searched for and displayed a group of similar media files, you can redisplay a previously selected group of items by clicking the **Back** button. To return to the most recent search results, click the **Forward** button. If you select an image in the photo well and click the **Edit** button, you'll see a menu of choices. Select either **Go to Quick Fix** or **Go to Standard Edit**, and the *Editor* automatically appears with the image displayed so that you can make changes to it. Choose **Auto Fix Window**, and you'll display the **Auto Fix** dialog box—a simple Organizer tool you can use to apply a series of automated changes to an image. At the far right end of the **Shortcuts** bar, you'll see two buttons: click **Photo Browser** to display items in the photo well as shown here; click **Date View** to display items within a calendar. By clicking any date in the calendar that appears when you switch to **Date View**, you can review images taken and other media files created on that date, one by one. See **38** **Find Items with the Same Date**.

 TIP

If you're unsure of the purpose of any button on the **Shortcuts** bar, simply move the mouse pointer over the button; a tooltip appears, displaying a description for that button.

NOTE

Some buttons on the **Shortcuts** bar (such as the **Get Photos** button) have down-pointing arrows; click the arrow to reveal a menu of commands related to the button. Click a command on this menu to select it.

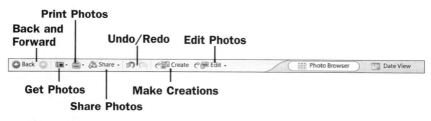

The Organizer Shortcuts bar.

Timeline

Under the **Shortcuts** bar, you'll find the **Timeline**. With it, you can quickly display items created on a particular date or within a range of dates. You'll learn to use the **Timeline** in **39** **Find Items Within a Date Range**.

You can also get some quick information from the **Timeline**: Dates on which items were created are represented by a bar on the **Timeline** graph; the more items associated with a particular date, the taller the bar.

See Also

→ **39** Find Items Within a Date Range

Find Bar

By dragging *tags* or *collection* markers onto the **Find** bar, you can display items that have the same content or purpose. You can also remove these restrictions quickly, redisplaying all media files in the *catalog*, by clicking the **Back to All Photos** button. The **Find** bar also displays how many items match or closely match your criteria, and how many do not. See **34** **Find Items with the Same Marker**.

See Also

→ **34** Find Items with the Same Marker

See Also

→ **27** Attach a Marker to an Item

NOTE

To quickly view the *properties* of any item in the catalog, display the **Properties Pane** in the **Organize Bin**. See **53** **About Image Information.**

See Also

→ **18** Sort Items
→ **19** Stack Items
→ **21** Play an Audio File
→ **22** View a Video
→ **23** Change Image Date and Time

NOTE

Actually, audio files are not initially displayed in the photo well at all, even if they are added to the catalog. To control which file types are displayed, select **View, Media Types**, select the types to display (such as **Photos** or **Audio**), and click **OK**.

KEY TERM

Thumbnail—A small version of an image generally appearing in a group of other small images, but just large enough so that you can easily distinguish it from the others.

Organize Bin

The **Organize Bin** displays the current list of *tags* and *collection* markers that you can attach to items in the *catalog* to identify their content or purpose. When you see a binocular icon in front of a particular tag or collection in the **Organize Bin**, it indicates that only items with that tag or collection marker are currently being displayed. To display all images again, click the **Back to All Photos** button on the **Find** bar. You'll learn how to attach tags and collection markers to images and other media files in **27** **Attach a Marker to an Item.**

Photo Well

Images, video, audio files, and *creations* matching the current search criteria are displayed in the photo well, typically in date order with the more recent files displayed first. You can change the order of display, arranging files in reverse date order, by folder location, by the batch in which they were imported into the *catalog*, by color similarity, by *collection* or *tag*, photo *stack*, or *version set*. You can also change the size of the *thumbnails* in the photo well.

Each item in the photo well is displayed with the date and time the file was originally created or scanned. Typically, items appear in reverse date order, with newly created or scanned images appearing at the top of the photo well. If you edit an image, the date it was modified is saved, but the image's creation date is not changed. This enables you to always display images grouped with other images taken that same day, whether or not you edit one of them. The date on which an item was imported into the catalog is also noted, so you can group items by import batch. You can modify these dates if you find they don't reflect what you expect; see **23** **Change Image Date and Time.**

The thumbnails for selected files are surrounded by a blue outline. You might select several images, for example, to include them in a slideshow you want to create. To select one item, click it. To select multiple contiguous items, click the first item, press and hold the **Shift** key, and then click the last item in the group. To select items that are not contiguous, press and hold the **Ctrl** key as you click each item.

Icons appear with each item as well, indicating various things:

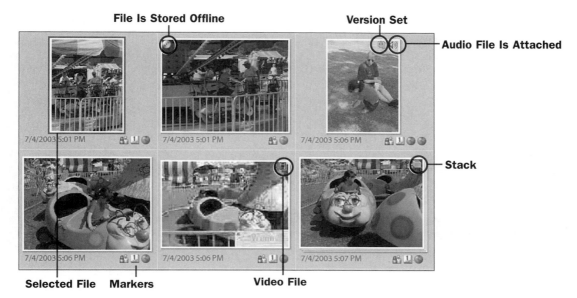

File Is Stored Offline   **Version Set**

Audio File Is Attached

Stack

Selected File   Markers   **Video File**

Icons in the photo well indicate various things.

- Whether the file is stored locally or offline (on a CD, for example)

- Whether an *audio caption* is attached to the file

- Whether the file is a video file

- Whether the file has been edited and stacked with the original in a *version set*

- Whether the image has been manually placed together with similar images in a *stack*

- Any associated *tags* or *collection* markers, such as a particular family member or event

Options Bar

The **Options** bar helps you control the sort order and size of the *thumbnails* in the photo well. (See **17** **Change Thumbnail Size** and **18** **Sort Items**.) You can also use the **Options** bar to quickly rotate an image, display the **Properties** pane (with which you can change an item's *properties*, such as its text *caption*), and display each item's date, time, markers, and other properties. You can also start a *photo review*, in

See Also

→ **16** Review Images
→ **17** Change Thumbnail Size
→ **18** Sort Images
→ **19** Stack Items

which the currently displayed items appear full-screen, one at a time, automatically.

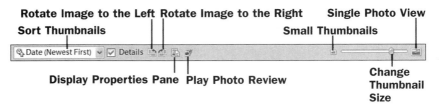

*The **Options** bar.*

2 Perform an Initial Scan for Media

See Also

→ **3** Import Media from a Folder

→ **4** Import Media from a CD-ROM or DVD

→ **5** Import Images from a Digital Camera

→ **6** Import a Scanned Image

→ **7** Import and Separate Multiple Scanned Images

→ **8** About Importing Images from a Cell Phone

→ **11** Import New Media Automatically

Before you can use *Organizer*, you must import some media files into its *catalog*. You begin by telling Organizer to search the hard disk for media files—images, music, and movies. Organizer provides two methods you can use to perform this initial scan. This first method is presented to you when you start Organizer for the first time. Here, you select a single folder and import all the media files in that folder (and its subfolders too, if you like). This method, although simple and straightforward, does not allow you to import media in several different folders at the same time or to place limits on the files that are imported.

Whether or not you import media when you first start Organizer, you can perform a different type of scan to import the bulk of your media files. This method is useful for locating all the applicable files on your computer, regardless of where they are located. It enables you to exercise more control over the files that are imported. You usually begin this method by performing a scan of all hard disks or just drive C. As it scans, the Organizer makes a note of each media file's name, file type, and location. After this initial scan, you select the folders containing the media files you want to add to the catalog, ignoring any folders with media files you don't often use. For example, Microsoft Office comes with lots of clip art files; although these are media files, you probably don't want to add them to the Organizer catalog because you typically will not use these clip art files outside of Microsoft Office. The media files contained in the folders you select are then added to the catalog listing.

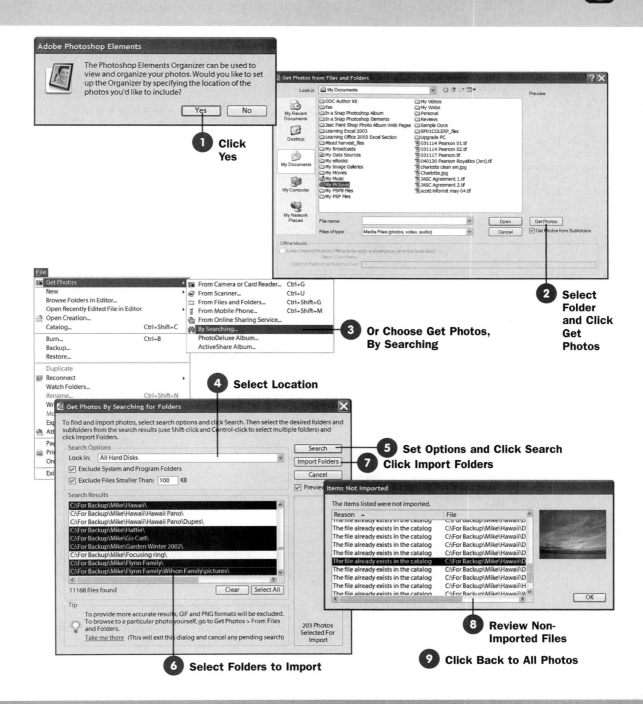

Adobe Photoshop Elements

The Photoshop Elements Organizer can be used to view and organize your photos. Would you like to set up the Organizer by specifying the location of the photos you'd like to include?

Yes   No

1 Click Yes

2 Select Folder and Click Get Photos

3 Or Choose Get Photos, By Searching

4 Select Location

5 Set Options and Click Search

7 Click Import Folders

6 Select Folders to Import

8 Review Non-Imported Files

9 Click Back to All Photos

TIP

You can tell Organizer to scan particular locations for new media files periodically, and add any new files it finds to the catalog automatically. The Organizer can even import images automatically from your camera phone's folder. See **11** Import New Media Automatically.

TIP

You can start the Organizer from the **Welcome Window** by clicking the **View and Organize Photos** button. From the Editor, you can start the Organizer by clicking **Photo Browser**.

Regardless of how you import this initial set of media files, you use *tags* and *collection* markers to organize the imported media files into whatever categories you choose. If you create more images, sound files, or movies after this initial scan, you can perform similar steps to add these new media files to the catalog. See **3** Import Media from a Folder, **4** Import Media from a CD-ROM or DVD, **5** Import Images from a Digital Camera, **6** Import a Scanned Image, **7** Import and Separate Multiple Scanned Images, **8** About Importing Images from a Cell Phone, **9** Capture Images from a Video File, and **10** Import Images from a PDF Document for help in adding any new images you acquire after performing an initial scan as described in this task.

This task assumes that you have media files on your computer ready to import. If you haven't copied images from your digital camera to your computer yet, you can import them into the Organizer directly from the camera or card reader. See **5** Import Images from a Digital Camera.

1 Click Yes

When you start Organizer for the first time, you'll see a dialog box asking you if you want to add images to the catalog. If you're not sure where your media files are located, or if they are simply scattered over several hard disks and folders, skip to step 3 for a different method you can use to import your initial files. Otherwise, click **Yes** to continue.

2 Select Folder and Click Get Photos

By default, Organizer wants to search the **My Pictures** folder for images, videos, and audio files to add to the catalog. If you'd rather search a different folder, click that folder to select it.

To search subfolders of the main folder you've selected, enable the **Get Photos from Subfolders** option. When you're ready, click **Get Photos** to begin. Skip to step 6.

3 Or Choose Get Photos, By Searching

Whether or not you imported files into the catalog the first time you started Organizer, you can still perform a massive search for images, videos, and audio files, and then import all the ones you find, or just selected folders.

In the Organizer, choose **File, Get Photos, By Searching** from the menu bar. The **Get Photos by Searching for Folders** dialog box appears.

4 Select Location

From the **Look In** drop-down list, select the location you want to search. To search your entire computer, select **All Hard Disks**. To search only the main drive, select **Drive C**.

5 Set Options and Click Search

By default, the Organizer does not search the computer's system folders or any folders for programs you've installed, but you can disable the **Exclude System and Program Folders** check box and search there anyway if you like.

Also, by default, the Organizer does not look for files smaller than 100KB, under the assumption that smaller files are unlikely to be of high quality. You can disable the **Exclude Files Smaller Than 100k** check box, or modify the value as desired to include smaller files in the search. You might want to do this, for example, if you take a lot of low-quality photos that you want to store in the catalog.

After changing any options, click the **Search** button to begin the initial scan. Depending on the location you selected to search, the scan might take a while.

6 Select Folders to Import

After the scan is complete, a list of folders that contain media files is displayed in the **Search Results** pane. Select the folders whose contents you want to list in the catalog by either pressing the **Ctrl** key and clicking each folder or pressing **Shift** and clicking the first and last folder in a group. Selected folders are highlighted in blue. If you want to import all the media files from the folders listed, click **Select All**.

7 Click Import Folders

After selecting the folders you want to import, click the **Import Folders** button.

 NOTE

It's recommended that you select either **All Hard Disks** or **Drive C** from the **Look In** list so that you can locate all your media files. You can still limit what's imported by selecting folders in step 6. However, if you know that your media files are stored in a particular folder, you can choose **My Documents** or **Browse** from the **Look In** list (so that you then can choose a specific folder).

NOTE

The Organizer does not include GIF or PNG files in its **Search Results** list because you'll probably not want to import and organize Web graphics unless you've created them yourself. To import GIF and PNG files manually, see **3** Import Media from a Folder.

TIP

If you're not sure why a specific folder was included in the list, you can click it to display its contents in the column to the right of the **Search Results** frame. You can't select specific files within a folder, but you can at least preview what you're importing by choosing a particular folder from the **Search Results** list.

 NOTE

If the imported images contain metadata keywords (tags), the **Import Attached Tags** dialog box appears. You can add new tags to the **Organize Bin** to match the attached photo tags, or associate the attached tags with existing tags in the **Organize Bin**.

8 Review Non-Imported Files

The **Getting Photos** dialog box appears, displaying each photo as it's added to the catalog. You can click **Stop** if you want to interrupt the importing process for some reason; only photos already imported at that point will appear in the catalog.

After the import process is complete, the **Items Not Imported** dialog box appears; it lists any files that were not imported. For example, a file might be smaller than the limit specified, be in an unsupported format, or already exist in the catalog. (This dialog box does not appear if all the files were imported correctly.) After reviewing the list, click **OK**.

The Organizer might display a reminder telling you that the only images being displayed right now are those you have just imported; click **OK** to dismiss this warning box.

9 Click Back to All Photos

After the importing process is complete, the Organizer displays only the "just imported" media files in the photo well. To redisplay all the images in the catalog, click the **Back to All Photos** button on the **Find** bar.

3 Import Media from a Folder

Before You Begin

✔ **2** Perform an Initial Scan for Media

See Also

→ **4** Import Media from a CD-ROM or DVD

→ **5** Import Images from a Digital Camera

→ **6** Import a Scanned Image

→ **7** Import and Separate Multiple Scanned Images

→ **8** About Importing Images from a Cell Phone

After you import an initial set of media files into the *catalog* by following the steps outlined in **2** **Perform an Initial Scan for Media**, you can import additional media files whenever you like. Suppose that you recently received some photos by email and saved those photos to the hard disk. Because *Organizer* can categorize your images, you don't have to organize images on the hard disk into particular folders. So, you could have simply saved all the email images with your other photos in the **My Pictures** folder, or you could have created a special folder just for those photos. Anyway, to view and organize those photos within the Organizer, you must import the files into the catalog.

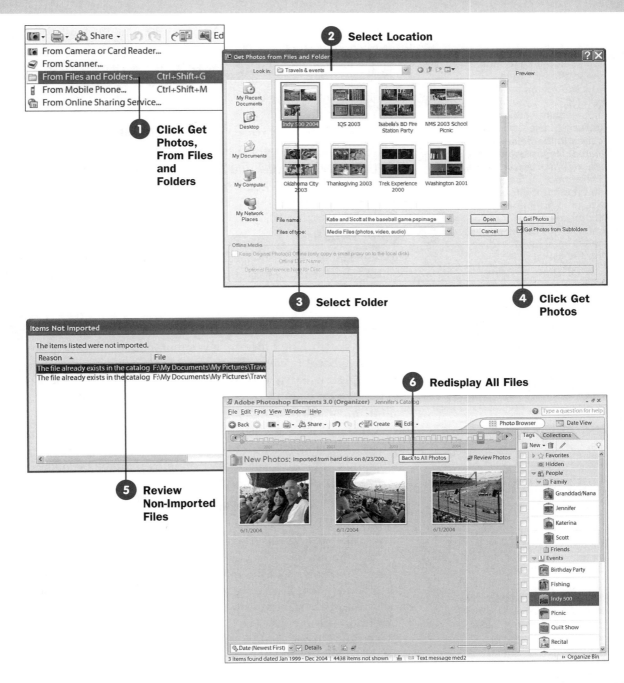

2 Select Location

1 Click Get Photos, From Files and Folders

3 Select Folder

4 Click Get Photos

6 Redisplay All Files

5 Review Non-Imported Files

If you open a noncataloged image in the Editor and make changes to it, you can add the image to the catalog when you save your changes. Just enable the **Include in the Organizer** option in the **Save As** dialog box. If you use a different *graphics editor* such as Photoshop, you can drag an image from its window and drop it right in the photo well to add it to the catalog. You can also drag and drop image files from the file listing in **My Computer** into the photo well.

You can start the Organizer from the **Welcome Window** by clicking the **View and Organize Photos** button. From the Editor, you can start the Organizer by clicking **Photo Browser**.

TIPS

If you want to import media files from a network drive, select **My Network Places** from the **Look in** drop-down list. Then select the network folder that contains the media files you want to import.

You don't have to import all the images in a folder; if you double-click the folder and display its contents, you can select just the images you want to import by pressing **Ctrl** and clicking each image file.

This task shows you exactly how to import new files from the hard disk into the catalog. Importing does nothing to the files themselves; the process simply adds the files' names, file types, and locations to the catalog. You can then organize the photos within the catalog however you like, and edit or print them as desired.

1 Click Get Photos, From Files and Folders

In the Organizer, click the **Get Photos** button on the **Shortcuts** bar and then select **From Files and Folders** from the list that appears. You can also choose **File, Get Photos, From Files and Folders** from the menu bar.

2 Select Location

From the **Look in** drop-down list, select the location of the folder that contains the images you want to import. For example, if the files are located on the main drive, select **Local Disk (C)**.

3 Select Folder

Select the folder whose contents you want to import. For example, if you chose **Local Drive (C)** from the **Look in** drop-down list, you can double-click the **My Documents** folder to display its contents, and then click the **My Pictures** folder to select only that one. If you want to import the contents of any subfolders of the selected folder (for example, if you have several subfolders within the **My Pictures** folder and you want to scan all of them), enable the **Get Photos from Subfolders** check box. You can select multiple folders by pressing **Ctrl** and clicking each one.

For my scan, I navigated to the **My Documents** folder, and then double-clicked the **My Pictures** folder to display its contents. I then double-clicked the **Travels & Events** folder in which I keep images collected from my travels or other special events. In this folder, I have a subfolder for each destination or special event. (Obviously, with Organizer, you don't have to keep your images in such a well-structured folder tree, but this was the organization I had adapted before using Organizer, so I've just stuck with it.) I then clicked the **Indy 500 2004** folder icon (located in my **Travels & Events** folder) to select just that folder for scanning. I enabled the **Get Photos from Subfolders** check box to include any subfolders within the **Indy 500 2004** folder in the scan.

4 Click Get Photos

Click the **Get Photos** button to begin the importing process. The **Getting Photos** dialog box appears, displaying each photo as it's added to the catalog. You can click **Stop** if you want to interrupt the importing process for some reason; only photos already imported at that point will appear in the catalog.

5 Review Non-Imported Files

After the import process is complete, the **Items Not Imported** dialog box might appear; it lists any files that were not imported. For example, a file might be in an unsupported format (such as Paint Shop Pro's native **.pspimage** format), or might already exist in the catalog. After reviewing the list, click **OK**. The Organizer might display a reminder telling you that the only images being displayed right now are those you have just imported; click **OK** to dismiss this warning box.

6 Redisplay All Files

The files you've just imported are the only ones displayed in the photo well; to display all files in the catalog, click the **Back to All Photos** button on the **Find** bar.

NOTE

If the imported images contain metadata keywords (tags), the **Import Attached Tags** dialog box appears. You can add new tags to the **Organize Bin** to match the attached photo tags, or associate the attached tags with existing tags in the **Organize Bin**.

TIP

If you don't want to see the warning box that reminds you that only recently imported images are displayed after an import process, select the **Don't Show Again** option before clicking **OK** to dismiss the box.

---

4 Import Media from a CD-ROM or DVD

After importing images into the *Organizer* for the first time and creating a *catalog* as described in **2** **Perform an Initial Scan for Media**, you might want to import additional images as you create them. If the images are stored on CD-ROM or DVD, you can copy them to the hard disk at the same time you add them to the catalog, or you can continue to store them *offline* on the CD-ROM or DVD. With the offline approach, the catalog still knows that the images exist, but you won't use up hard disk space to store images you might not use that often. Perhaps you took several photos using your film camera and had them processed, printed, and copied to a CD, or perhaps a friend has given you a DVD of images she created. You can use this task to import those photos into the Organizer.

Before You Begin

✔ **2** Perform an Initial Scan for Media

See Also

→ **3** Import Media from a Folder

→ **5** Import Images from a Digital Camera

→ **6** Import a Scanned Image

→ **7** Import and Separate Multiple Scanned Images

→ **8** About Importing Images from a Cell Phone

KEY TERM

Offline—Images in the Organizer catalog that are stored on a CD-ROM or DVD, and not copied to the hard disk.

TIPS

You can copy images from a CD or DVD onto the hard disk and then rename, resize, retouch, and reformat them at the same time. See **61** Rename, Resize, Reformat, and Retouch a Group of Images. After processing the images, you can import them into the catalog by following the steps in **3** Import Media from a Folder.

You can start the Organizer from the **Welcome Window** by clicking the **View and Organize Photos** button. From the Editor, you can start the Organizer by clicking **Photo Browser**.

If you choose to store images offline (and not copy them to the hard disk), a low-*resolution* copy of the image is kept in the catalog so that you can still view offline images and organize them as you like. However, if you attempt to perform some task that requires the actual image (such as adjusting the image's contrast or creating a greeting card using that image), you'll be asked whether you want to use the low-resolution copy or the offline file, which is typically of much higher quality. If you choose to use the offline file, you'll be prompted to insert the CD-ROM or DVD on which the image file is stored.

When you add images to the catalog that are stored offline, you'll be prompted to create a reference name. This name is used later on whenever you're prompted to insert the CD-ROM or DVD on which the image is stored. This name helps you insert the correct CD-ROM or DVD. So, it's a good idea to create easily identifiable reference names that you also write on the disc itself or its jewel case.

1 **Click Get Photos, From Files and Folders**

In the Organizer, click the **Get Photos** button on the **Shortcuts** bar and then select **From Files and Folders** from the list that appears. You can also choose **File, Get Photos, From Files and Folders** from the menu bar.

If you've already inserted the CD or DVD, do not attempt to start Organizer from the dialog box that Windows automatically displays (by selecting **Organize and Edit pictures using Adobe Photoshop Elements** from the **What do you want to do?** list). Instead, you'll end up starting the Editor and displaying the contents of the disc within its **File Browser**, which will not help you import the files into the Organizer catalog.

2 **Select Drive**

From the **Look in** drop-down list, select the CD-ROM or DVD drive that contains the images you want to add to the catalog.

3 **Select Folder**

Select the folder whose contents you want to import. If the CD or DVD doesn't contain any folders, you can skip this step.

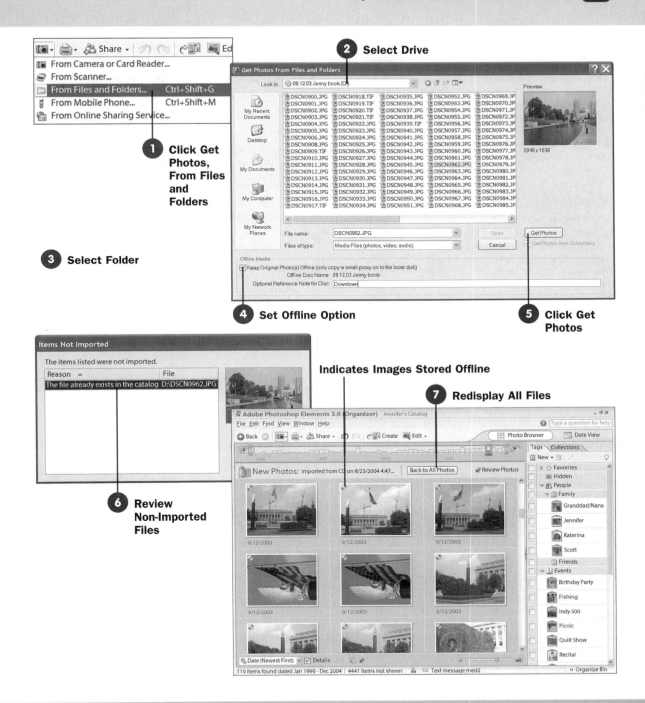

2 Select Drive

1 Click Get Photos, From Files and Folders

3 Select Folder

4 Set Offline Option

5 Click Get Photos

Indicates Images Stored Offline

7 Redisplay All Files

6 Review Non-Imported Files

If you want to import the contents of any subfolders of the selected folder, enable the **Get Photos from Subfolders** check box. You can select multiple folders by pressing **Ctrl** and clicking each one.

4 Set Offline Option

If you want to keep the images offline (that is, you want to keep only low-resolution images in the catalog and leave the larger original images on the CD or DVD), enable the **Keep Original Photo(s) Offline** check box and type a name for the disc in the **Optional Reference Note for Disc** text box. If you do not enable the **Keep Original Photo(s) Offline** check box, the Organizer copies the files from the CD or DVD to the hard disk.

5 Click Get Photos

Click **Get Photos** to begin the importing process. The **Getting Photos** dialog box appears, displaying each photo as it's added to the catalog. You can click **Stop** if you want to interrupt the importing process for some reason; only photos already imported at that point will appear in the catalog.

6 Review Non-Imported Files

After the import process is complete, the **Items Not Imported** dialog box might appear; it lists any files that were not imported. For example, a file might be in an unsupported format (such as Paint Shop Pro's native **.pspimage** format) or already exist in the catalog. After reviewing the list, click **OK**. The Organizer might display a reminder telling you that the only images being displayed right now are those you have just imported; click **OK** to dismiss this warning box.

7 Redisplay All Files

The files you've just imported are displayed in the photo well. If you kept the images offline, a small CD icon appears in the upper-left corner of each small *thumbnail*. To display all files in the catalog rather than just the images you've imported, click the **Back to All Photos** button on the **Find** bar.

5 Import Images from a Digital Camera

You can import images directly from a digital camera and add them to the *Organizer catalog*. The method you use to do that, however, varies as much as digital cameras vary from one another. For a great many cameras, when you connect them to your computer using a USB, SCSI or FireWire cable, Windows automatically detects the camera, reads its memory card, and displays the contents in a new drive window (a virtual drive) within **My Computer**. For example, your computer might have only one hard disk—drive C—but when you connect your digital camera, Windows presents you with a window that displays all the files on drive D, which is really the memory card inside your camera. At the same time, Photoshop Elements detects the virtual drive and launches its **Photo Downloader** to help you import the images into the catalog.

This same process occurs if you use a memory card reader. When you take the memory card out of the camera, insert it into the reader, and connect the reader to your computer using a cable, Windows treats the contents of the memory card as a virtual (pretend) drive D or other drive letter. Once again, Photoshop Elements detects the virtual drive and launches the **Photo Downloader**.

① Connect Camera or Card Reader

Connect the camera to the computer, or insert the camera's memory card into the card reader and connect the card reader to the computer. Adobe's **Photo Downloader** should automatically start and display the **Adobe Photo Downloader** dialog box.

If the **Photo Downloader** does not start automatically, you can start it manually. In the Organizer, click the **Get Photos** button on the **Shortcuts** bar and select **From Camera or Card Reader** from the list that appears. You can also choose **File**, **Get Photos**, **From Camera or Card Reader** from the menu bar. The **Get Photos from Camera or Card Reader** dialog box (which looks similar to the **Adobe Photo Downloader** dialog box shown here) appears.

Before You Begin

✔ **2** Perform an Initial Scan for Media

See Also

→ **3** Import Media from a Folder

→ **4** Import Media from a CD-ROM or DVD

→ **6** Import a Scanned Image

→ **7** Import and Separate Multiple Scanned Images

NOTE

If the **Photo Downloader** does not launch when you connect your camera or memory card reader to the computer, you might have to use the driver that came with the camera to read its memory card. After copying the images to the hard disk using the camera's software, follow the steps in **3** Import Media from a Folder to import those images into the catalog.

② Select Device

The card reader or camera should already be listed in the **Get Photos from** drop-down list. If not, open the list and select your camera or card reader (or its virtual drive letter) from the devices listed. After the memory card has been read, its images appear on the left side of the dialog box.

③ Select Folder

Your digital images will be copied to the **My Documents\My Pictures\Adobe\Digital Camera Photos** folder. To change to a different folder, click the **Browse** button, select the folder into which you want to copy the new image files, and click **OK**.

④ Set Options

You can place the images you are importing into a subfolder of the folder you selected in step 3: first enable the **Create Subfolder Using** check box. Then select either the **Date/Time of Import** option (if you want the subfolder to use the current date and time as its name) or **New Name** (if you want to name the subfolder yourself). If you chose the **New Name** option, type a name for the subfolder in the text box provided.

Because digital camera image files are typically given nondescript names such as **DSC00035.JPG**, you might want to tell the Organizer to rename the files as it imports them into the catalog. Just enable the **Rename Files to** check box and type a descriptive name in the text box provided. The Organizer automatically adds a two-digit number to this description to create the filename. For example, if you type "**Aunt Jane's Bday 2004** " as the filename (notice the space I added at the end to separate the name from the number Organizer adds), files will be named **Aunt Jane's Bday 2004 001**, **Aunt Jane's Bday 2004 002**, and so on.

⑤ Click Get Photos

Click the **Get Photos** button to begin the importing process. The files are copied to the hard disk; if Organizer is not already started, it is started for you automatically. The **Getting Photos** dialog box appears, displaying each photo as it's added to the catalog. You can click **Stop** if you want to interrupt the importing process for

TIPS

You can change the camera preferences, such as the default folder in which images are stored, using the **Preferences** dialog box. Select **Edit, Preferences** from the Organizer main menu and then click **Camera or Card Reader**. You can also select your camera from a list and prevent the **Photo Downloader** from automatically starting when you connect your camera or card reader by using the **Preferences** dialog box. You might want to do this if the **Photo Downloader** is not detecting the camera or card reader properly or is reading its data incorrectly.

To select a catalog to upload the images to (that is, if you use more than one catalog), click the **Advanced Options** button, click **Browse**, select the catalog to use, and click **Open**. To create a new catalog, click the **New** button instead of **Browse**, type a name for the catalog, and click **Save**. Click **OK** to return to the **Adobe Photo Downloader** dialog box.

TIP

You can copy images from your camera onto the hard disk and rename, resize, retouch, and reformat them at the same time. Although you can rename digital images as you import them, this alternative process might be useful because digital images typically need retouching and possibly reformatting as well. See **61** Rename, Resize, Reformat, and Retouch a Group of Images. After processing the images, you can import the images into the catalog by following the steps in **3** Import Media from a Folder.

 NOTE

If the imported images contain metadata keywords (tags), the **Import Attached Tags** dialog box appears. You can add new tags to the **Organize Bin** to match the attached photo tags, or associate the attached tags with existing tags in the **Organize Bin**.

some reason; only photos already imported at that point will appear in the catalog.

6 Delete Files from Memory Card

After the files are imported into the Organizer, you'll see a dialog box asking whether you want to remove the images from the camera's memory card. Click **Yes** or **No** as desired.

7 Redisplay All Files

You might see a dialog box listing images that were not imported; typically this is because the images are already in the catalog. Anyway, if you see the **Items Not Imported** dialog box, make a note of the images that were not imported and click **OK** to continue.

Next, the Organizer might display a reminder telling you that the only images being displayed right now are those you have just imported; click **OK** to dismiss this warning box.

Even if the warning box does not appear, the files you've just imported are the only ones displayed in the photo well; to display all files in the catalog, click the **Back to All Photos** button on the **Find** bar.

You can review the photos you've just imported and perform various tasks such as marking them with tags or collections markers, marking them for printing, and performing minor retouching by clicking the **Review Photos** button that appears on the **Find bar**. See **16** Review Images.

---

6 Import a Scanned Image

Before You Begin

✔ **2** Perform an Initial Scan for Media

See Also

→ **7** Import and Separate Multiple Scanned Images

→ **128** Restore Quality to a Scanned Photograph

You can import images into the *catalog* directly from your digital scanner. The *Organizer* talks directly to your scanner through its driver, enabling you to begin the scanning and importing process with one click. In rare cases, the Organizer cannot work with the scanner driver; you must then scan in the photo manually, save it to the hard disk, and import the image into the catalog by following the steps outlined in **3** Import Media from a Folder.

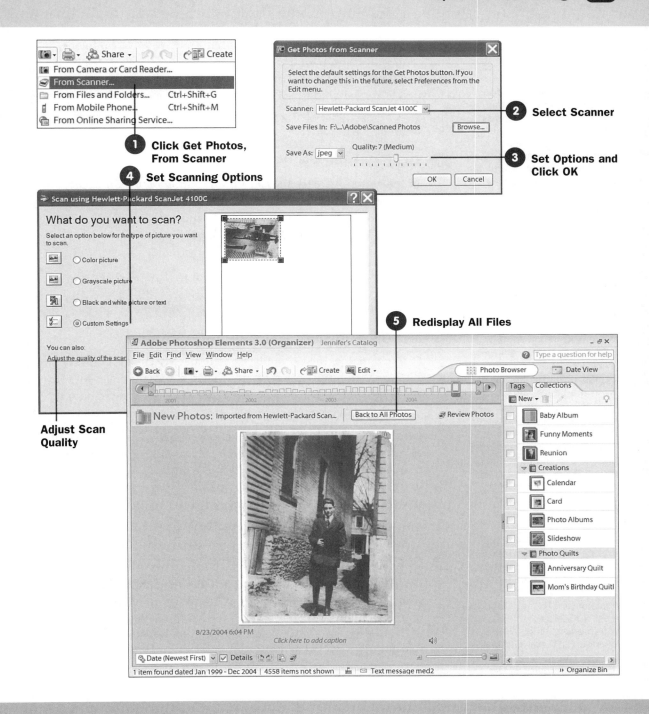

1 Click Get Photos, From Scanner

4 Set Scanning Options

2 Select Scanner

3 Set Options and Click OK

5 Redisplay All Files

Adjust Scan Quality

💡 TIPS

To change the default scanning options normally displayed in the **Get Photos from Scanner** dialog box, choose **Edit, Preferences, Scanner** from the menu bar, select the default options you want to use (such as the default image format and quality of the resulting scan), and click **OK**.

You can scan multiple images at one time and let the Editor automatically save them in separate image files. See **7** **Import and Separate Multiple Scanned Images.**

You can start the Organizer from the **Welcome Window** by clicking the **View and Organize Photos** button. From the Editor, you can start the Organizer by clicking **Photo Browser**.

To import a scanned image directly into the Editor and save it to the catalog after editing, see **7** **Import and Separate Multiple Scanned Images.**

In the scanning dialog box that appears, remember to adjust the scanning *resolution* to fit your intended output: use 150 PPI for onscreen images and at least 300 PPI for images you intend to print. In the Windows XP scanning dialog box shown here, click the **Adjust quality of the scanned picture** to display another dialog box in which you can adjust the resolution of the scan.

Scanning a printed photo into digital format may result in an image that's darker, less sharp, and with a lower range of tone than the original photograph. Thus, after scanning an image and importing it into the catalog, you will most likely want to edit the image using the *Editor*, to restore its original quality. See **128** **Restore Quality to a Scanned Photograph** for help.

❶ Click Get Photos, From Scanner

In the Organizer, click the **Get Photos** button on the **Shortcuts** bar and then select **From Scanner** from the list that appears. You can also choose **File, Get Photos, From Scanner** from the menu bar. The **Get Photos from Scanner** dialog box appears.

❷ Select Scanner

From the **Scanner** drop-down list, select your scanner from the devices listed.

❸ Set Options and Click OK

Scanned images are normally saved to the **My Documents\My Pictures\Adobe\Scanned Photos** folder, but if you prefer to store the scanned image in some other folder, click the **Browse** button and select that location.

From the **Save As** drop-down list, choose the file format you want to use for the scanned image. If you choose **TIFF** or **PNG**, you'll get a higher-quality image and a much larger file. If you select **JPEG**, you can adjust the **Quality** slider and affect the resulting file size (lower-quality images result in smaller files).

After setting the options for the scan, click **OK**.

❹ Set Scanning Options

The scanning program starts and displays the options available to your scanner. Adjust the options as desired (for more information on these options, see your scanner manual). The dialog box shown here is for the default Windows XP scanning program; the dialog box you see might look different.

Click **Scan** to begin the scanning process. After the image has been scanned, the **Getting Photos** dialog box appears, and the image is automatically imported into the Organizer catalog.

5 Redisplay All Files

The scanned image is the only one displayed in the photo well; to display all the files in the catalog, click the **Back to All Photos** button on the **Find** bar.

Scanned images are marked with a date that matches the date on which they were imported into the Organizer, and thus, appear with other images scanned or taken on that same day. To change the date associated with the scanned image to the date on which the photo was taken, see **23** **Change Image Date and Time**.

7 Import and Separate Multiple Scanned Images

Although you can scan a photograph directly into the *Organizer*, as explained in **6** **Import a Scanned Image**, you might not want to. For example, if you think you'll need to edit the scan to remove spots and other imperfections or to improve the photograph's color and contrast, why not import the scan directly into the *Editor*? After making changes, you can still add the image to the Organizer when you save your edits.

Another reason why you might want to scan directly into the Editor is to exploit its capability to deal with multiple-image scans. If you've got multiple photographs to scan, you can lay them all on the scanner bed and perform a single scan. The Editor can then break up these images for you, creating the separate image files you need.

1 Choose File, Import

Lay the photographs you want to scan on the scanner bed, leaving a small amount of space between them. This space enables the Editor to separate the images later on.

Before You Begin

✔ **2** Perform an Initial Scan for Media

✔ **47** About Saving Images

See Also

→ **6** Import a Scanned Image

→ **128** Restore Quality to a Scanned Photograph

NOTE

In this task, I'll show you how to scan several images at one time and use the Editor to create the various image files to save in the Organizer catalog. However, as noted earlier, you can follow these same basic steps to scan a single image directly into the Editor and later save it in the Organizer catalog.

TIP

If your scanner is not listed, select **WIA Support** from the menu. This option enables you to access the WIA support built into Windows, which might be able to clear up the problem by scanning for WIA- and TWAIN-compliant devices.

KEY TERM

WIA and TWAIN—WIA stands for *Windows Image Acquisition*. TWAIN comes from the phrase, "and never the twain shall meet," although some prefer to think that it stands for Technology Without an Interesting Name. WIA and TWAIN are technologies that allow graphical software programs to communicate directly with digital cameras and scanners. TWAIN was replaced by WIA in Windows Me and Windows XP.

NOTE

Sometimes the Editor crops the scan incorrectly, resulting in a poor separation of the individual images. If that happens, you can rescan the photos, adding a bit more space between them, or you can undo the crop on an individual image file, and recrop it yourself.

Choose **File, Import** from the menu bar and select your scanner from the list that appears. The program for your scanner automatically appears. My scanner happens to appear twice in the list—because it is *WIA* compliant, I'll choose that option.

② Perform Scan

The dialog box that appears displays the options available to your particular scanner. Adjust the options as desired (for more information on these options, see your scanner manual). The dialog box shown here is for the default Windows XP scanning program; the dialog box you see might look different.

Click **Scan** to begin the scanning process.

③ Choose Image, Divide Scanned Photos

The images appear in the Editor in a single, unsaved file. To use the Editor to separate the images for you (rather than manually selecting and copying each image to a file yourself), choose **Image, Divide Scanned Photos** from the menu. The Editor creates separate image files for you.

④ Click Save

None of the image files are saved at this point. Click its **Close** button (the **X**) to close the original scan window (the one with the multiple scanned images). Click **No** because you do not want to save this file.

Click each of the other image windows, make changes as desired, and then click the **Save** button on the **Shortcuts bar** to save the image. The **Save As** dialog box appears.

1 Choose File, Import

2 Perform Scan

3 Choose Image, Divide Scanned Photos

4 Click Save

5 Save Image in Catalog

About Importing Images from a Cell Phone

TIP

Scanned photographs often suffer from low brightness, poor contrast, and low saturation. They often lack sharpness and may even contain moiré patterns. See **128** **Restore Quality to a Scanned Photograph** for help in improving your photographs after you scan them.

⑤ Save Image in Catalog

Select the folder in which you want to save the image from the **Save in** drop-down list at the top of the dialog box. Type a name for the image in the **File name** box. Select an image type from the **Format** list. Select other options as desired (see **47** **About Saving Images**), but be sure to enable the **Include in the Organizer** option so that the image is placed in the Organizer catalog. Click **Save** to save the image.

You Should Know

✔ **2** Perform an Initial Scan for Media

NOTE

Typically, digital images captured with a cell phone have a resolution somewhere between 1 and 3 MP, but even so, given the lower quality lens and digital sensor incorporated into most cell phone cameras, the resulting images are most likely going to be fairly low quality. So you might not want to import a lot of these cell photos into the Organizer, or attempt to print them in a large size because they will probably look fairly grainy.

Many modern cell phones come equipped with a built-in digital camera. Granted, the resulting photos are usually small and of poor quality, but these cell phones are useful in capturing those unexpected moments that happen from time to time. For example, you might use your cell phone to record an accident scene before the arrival of the police, to capture the sudden appearance of a celebrity, or to preserve a funny moment. If you've captured important photos using your cell phone, you'll want to import them into the catalog where they can be organized, retouched, and printed as needed.

The folks at Adobe recognize the popularity of cell phones with digital cameras and have anticipated your need to occasionally preserve and organize these images, even if they are of low-resolution and small size. Unfortunately, although cell phones are fairly similar in nature, the way in which they implement their digital camera technology isn't. Therefore, Photoshop Elements provides several different methods for importing cell phone images into the Organizer catalog. You'll have to use the method that works with your particular cell phone:

- If your cell phone stores its digital photo images on a removable memory card, you can import the images directly from the card reader. See **5** **Import Images from a Digital Camera**.

- If you can connect your cell phone directly to the computer using a cable, or through some type of wireless connection (such as infrared or Bluetooth), you can manually copy the images to the computer. First, set up a folder you want to use exclusively for cell phone photos and then tell Organizer which folder you're using: choose **Edit, Preferences, Mobile Phone** from the Organizer menu. The **Preferences** dialog box appears. Click **Browse**, select the cell phone image folder, and click **OK**. You return to the **Preferences** dialog box. Click **OK** again to finalize your changes. Whenever you transfer photos from your cell phone into the designated folder, import them into the catalog by clicking the **Get Photos** button on the **Shortcuts** bar and choosing **From Mobile Phone** from the menu. You can also choose **File, Get Photos, From Mobile Phone**.

- If your cell phone carrier is an Adobe service partner, you'll be able to import your images after uploading them to a special Web site on the Internet. First, upload the images as described in your cell phone manual. Then start Organizer, click the **Get Photos** button on the **Shortcuts** bar, and select **From Online Sharing Service** from the list that appears. You can also choose **File, Get Photos, From Online Sharing Service** from the menu bar. The **Get Photos from Online Sharing Service** dialog box appears. Select your service and click **OK**. Then follow the onscreen instructions to import the images into the Organizer catalog.

Select your carrier from those listed on the right and click **OK**. The Organizer connects to the Web and downloads your images onto the hard disk—and into the catalog.

TIPS

If your cell phone is compatible with Nokia Suites 6.2, and you have installed that software, you'll be able to use the program to import images directly into the catalog. See **5** **Import Images from a Digital Camera**.

You can start the Organizer from the **Welcome Window** by clicking the **View and Organize Photos** button. From the Editor, you can start the Organizer by clicking **Photo Browser**.

If you set up a cell phone image folder, you can tell Organizer to watch that folder and automatically import new images into the catalog whenever it detects any. See **11** **Import New Media Automatically**.

9 Capture Images from a Video File

With the plethora of digital recording equipment available to the consumer today, it's often difficult to choose what to bring to an event such as a graduation or wedding. If you tote along your digital camera, you can of course record the action in a series of stills; depending on your camera, you might also have the option of recording a short video (although not with the highest quality). If you bring along your digital video camera to an event, you can record high-quality video, and when needed, capture a single digital image (although again, not with the same quality as your digital camera can provide).

You Should Know

✔ **2** Perform an Initial Scan for Media

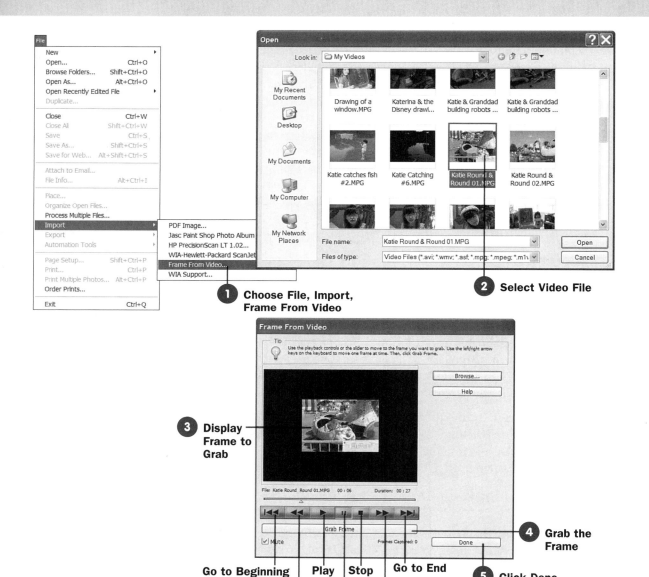

① Choose File, Import,
Frame From Video

② Select Video File

③ Display
Frame to
Grab

④ Grab the
Frame

⑤ Click Done

Go to Beginning   Play   Stop   Go to End

Rewind   Pause   Fast Forward

Sometimes, even after making the decision of which equipment to take, you might find yourself making the impossible choice between stills and video when an important moment arrives. No need to worry: If you've recorded some digital video using either your digital camera or your digital video camera, you can capture a single frame of that video and save it as a digital image (although not with as high a quality as you might have had if you had captured the image with your high resolution digital camera to begin with).

1 **Choose File, Import, Frame From Video**

In the *Editor*, choose **File, Import, Frame From Video** from the menu bar. The **Frame From Video** dialog box appears.

2 **Select Video File**

Click the **Browse** button to display the **Open** dialog box, then change to the folder that contains the video file from which you want to grab a still image, select the video file, and click **Open**. (Supported video formats include AVI, MPG/MPEG, WMV, ASF, and M1V.) The first frame of the video appears in the preview window of the **Frame From Video** dialog box.

3 **Display Frame to Grab**

Click the **Play** button. Watch the video until the frame you want to capture is displayed in the preview window and click **Pause** to stop the playback. You can use the other video control buttons (if they are enabled in the particular video format you're using) to locate and display the correct frame. For example, to jump to the last frame in the video, click the **Go to End** button. You can also drag the video slider (located just above the video control buttons) left or right to jump to a particular place in the video.

If you don't want to hear the video sound as you're reviewing the video, enable the **Mute** check box.

4 **Grab the Frame**

When the frame of video you want to convert into a single image is displayed in the preview window, click the large **Grab Frame** button. The image is captured and displayed in the Editor window.

TIPS

To improve the quality of your captured image somewhat, you might want to apply one of the sharpening *filters*, such as the **Unsharp Mask** filter. See **149** **Sharpen an Image**.

You can start the Editor from the **Welcome Window** by clicking the **Quick Fix Photos** or **Edit and Enhance Photos** button. From the Organizer, you can start the Editor by clicking **Edit** button and selecting either **Go to Standard Edit** or **Go to Quick Fix**.

NOTES

The frames you've captured are not yet permanently saved; if you're satisfied with the quality of a capture, be sure to click the **Save** button on the **Shortcuts** bar to save it. If you don't like the captured image, simply close its window without saving the file. To add an image to the *catalog* when you save it, enable the **Include in the Organizer** button.

If you're using **Quick Fix** mode, only the last frame you grab is displayed; however, the other frames are safe and sound in their windows. To change to a different image window, select it from the **Window** menu.

5 **Click Done**

Repeat steps 3 and 4 to advance the video and capture additional frames as desired. When you're through grabbing frames as still images, click the **Done** button.

10 Import Images from a PDF Document

You Should Know

✔ **2** Perform an Initial Scan for Media

EY TERM

PDF document—A document format by Adobe that allows text and graphics to be displayed using the same layout, regardless of the user's particular computer model and operating system. Adobe Reader (formerly Acrobat Reader) is required for viewing PDF documents.

NOTE

If a PDF image is selectable within Adobe Reader, you can import it into the Editor by following the steps in this task. Based on how they were laid out within the PDF document, some images cannot be selected, and therefore cannot be imported into the Editor.

PDF documents are used quite often to display text and graphics, especially on the Internet. The beauty of PDF format is its consistency—if you use it, you can be assured that your document will appear the same on everyone's computer, regardless of the type of computer they use or its operating system. For example, if you create a user manual for a product you've designed, you can save the manual in PDF format and know that an image won't accidentally overlay some important text if the reader happens to use a lower monitor *resolution* than the one you used when you created the document.

Another key feature of PDF documents is the variety of ways in which a user can work with them within Adobe Reader. A user might print the document, search through it for particular keywords while reading it onscreen, or display *thumbnails* of each page and then jump to a particular page with a single click. By following the steps in this task, you can import an image in a PDF document directly into the *Editor* window, and then adjust, print, or view it at higher magnification as desired. This task is also useful in importing a single image from a PDF slideshow created using the *Organizer*. So, if a friend or relative also uses Organizer (or an older version of Photoshop Album) to create and share PDF slideshows with you, you can import a particularly good image into the Editor and print it if you like.

1 **Choose File, Import, PDF Image**

In the Editor, choose **File**, **Import**, **PDF Image** from the menu. The **Select PDF for Image Import** dialog box appears.

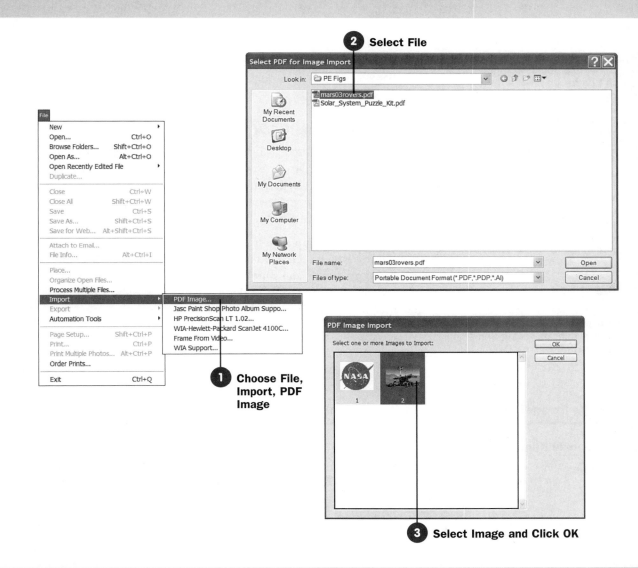

② Select File

Select PDF for Image Import

Look in: 📁 PE Figs

📄 mars03rovers.pdf
📄 Solar_System_Puzzle_Kit.pdf

My Recent Documents

Desktop

My Documents

My Computer

My Network Places

File name: mars03rovers.pdf   Open

Files of type: Portable Document Format (*.PDF,*.PDP,*.AI)   Cancel

File

New	▶
Open...	Ctrl+O
Browse Folders...	Shift+Ctrl+O
Open As...	Alt+Ctrl+O
Open Recently Edited File	▶
Duplicate...	
Close	Ctrl+W
Close All	Shift+Ctrl+W
Save	Ctrl+S
Save As...	Shift+Ctrl+S
Save for Web...	Alt+Shift+Ctrl+S
Attach to Email...	
File Info...	Alt+Ctrl+I
Place...	
Organize Open Files...	
Process Multiple Files...	
Import	▶
Export	▶
Automation Tools	▶
Page Setup...	Shift+Ctrl+P
Print...	Ctrl+P
Print Multiple Photos...	Alt+Ctrl+P
Order Prints...	
Exit	Ctrl+Q

PDF Image...
Jasc Paint Shop Photo Album Suppo...
HP PrecisionScan LT 1.02...
WIA-Hewlett-Packard ScanJet 4100C...
Frame From Video...
WIA Support...

① Choose File, Import, PDF Image

PDF Image Import

Select one or more Images to Import: OK

Cancel

NASA
1   2

③ Select Image and Click OK

TIP

To import all the images in a PDF file and save them in Photoshop .PSD format automatically, choose **File, Automation Tools, Multi-Page PDF to PSD**. Select the PDF file, set the range of pages to import images from (or leave the option set to **All**), choose a color mode, type a base file-name to use (the Editor adds a three-digit number to the end of this name for each image), select a desti-nation folder, and click **OK**.

NOTE

Be careful of images you import; some images might be copyright protected and have restrictions on their legal use.

2 Select File

In the **Look in** drop-down list, change to the folder that contains the PDF document you want to scan for images, select the file, and click **Open**.

3 Select Image and Click OK

The document is scanned, and thumbnails for all the importable images within the PDF document are displayed in the **PDF Image Import** dialog box. Click an image's thumbnail to select it and then click **OK** to import the image. The image appears in the Editor window.

The image you've imported is not yet permanently saved; if you want to save the image to your system, click the **Save** button on the **Shortcuts** bar. If you simply imported the image so that you could view it better or print it, close its window without saving the file after you're through.

 Import New Media Automatically

You Should Know

✔ Perform an Initial Scan for Media

After importing images, audio, and video files currently on the hard disk into the *catalog*, you can import new media files manually by following the steps outlined in **Import Media from a Folder**. You can also set up the *Organizer* so that it periodically scans the hard disk for new media and imports that media automatically for you. If you'd like to exercise discretion over the images that Organizer finds and wants to import, you can tell Organizer to simply notify you when it finds new media.

1 Choose File, Watch Folders

In the Organizer, choose **File, Watch Folders** from the menu bar. The **Watch Folder** dialog box appears.

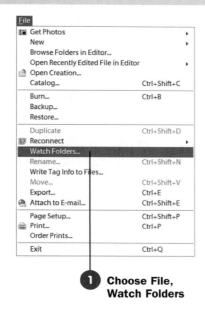

1 Choose File,
Watch Folders

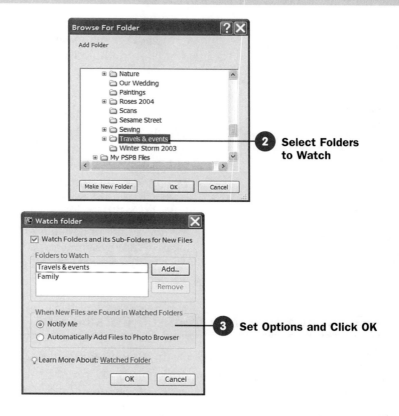

2 Select Folders
to Watch

3 Set Options and Click OK

---

2 **Select Folders to Watch**

Click **Add**. In the **Browse for Folder** dialog box that opens, select the folder you want the Organizer to watch and then click **OK**. You return to the **Watch Folder** dialog box; repeat this step to add as many folders to the watch list as you want.

3 **Set Options and Click OK**

To have Organizer watch sub-folders of the folders you've selected, enable the **Watch Folders and its Sub-Folders for New Files** check box.

TIP

If you take digital photos with your cell phone, you can have the Organizer watch the folder into which you normally import cell photos and then either automatically import them or notify you when you need to import new images into the catalog. After designating a folder for your cell phone photos (as described in **8** About Importing Images from a Cell Phone), follow the steps in this task to watch the folder for new images.

You can start the Organizer from the **Welcome Window** by clicking the **View and Organize Photos** button. From the Editor, you can start the Organizer by clicking **Photo Browser**.

You can remove folders from the watch list later on: just choose **File, Watch Folders** to redisplay the **Watch Folder** dialog box, select a folder name from those listed, and click **Remove**.

Next, select what you want the Organizer to do when it discovers new media in the specified folders: **Notify Me** or **Automatically Add Files to Photo Browser**. After selecting the options you want, click **OK**.

When new images are saved, moved, or copied to a watched folder, one of two things happens. If you chose to have the Organizer notify you, you'll see a message asking whether you want to add the new files. If you click **Yes**, you'll see a dialog box with thumbnails for each image. Enable the check box in front of each image you want to import and click **OK**. The images are imported into the catalog. If you chose to have new files automatically added to the catalog, you won't see any notification. Instead, the images are imported into the catalog, and the listing changes to show just those images. Click the **Back to All Photos** button on the **Find** bar to redisplay all items in the catalog.

Remove an Item from the Catalog

Before You Begin

✔ **2** Perform an Initial Scan for Media

If you want to delete a group of related items such as all the images of your recent house renovation, use the **Find** bar to display them first. (See **33** **About Finding Items in the Catalog**.) Then press **Ctrl+A** or choose **Edit, Select All** to quickly select the displayed images. If the catalog is sorted by batch or folder, you can click the gray bar above a group to select all the items in that group.

To make the *Organizer* useful, its *catalog* must list all the images and other media files you want to work with. In earlier tasks in this chapter, you learned how to import the items you want to track. After an image is displayed in the catalog, you can make changes to it or incorporate it into a *creation* such as a calendar or slideshow. If the catalog lists an image you no longer want to work with, you can remove that image just as easily as you imported it. You can also remove unwanted audio and movie files from the catalog.

Remember that the catalog is simply a *listing* of files, not the files themselves. Removing an item from the catalog does not actually remove the file from the hard disk, unless you specifically tell the Organizer you want to do that.

① Select Item(s) to Remove

In the Organizer, click the first item and then press **Ctrl** and click each additional item in the photo well that you want to remove. Selected items appear with a blue outline.

1 Select Item(s) to Remove

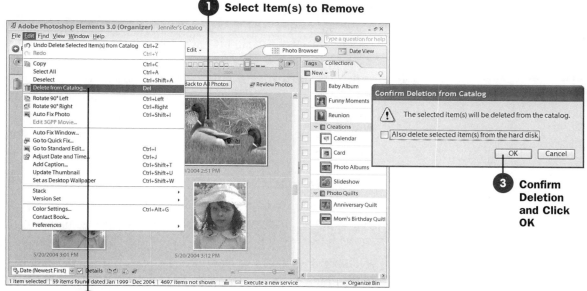

2 Choose Edit, Delete from Catalog

3 Confirm Deletion and Click OK

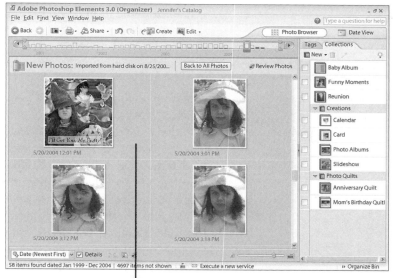

4 View the Result

② Choose Edit, Delete from Catalog

Choose **Edit, Delete from Catalog**. If you selected multiple items, choose **Edit, Delete Selected Items from Catalog** instead.

③ Confirm Deletion and Click OK

The **Confirm Deletion from Catalog** dialog box appears. If you want to remove the actual item(s) from the hard disk as well as from the catalog, enable the **Also delete selected item(s) from the hard disk** check box. Click **OK**.

④ View the Result

The selected item(s) are removed from the catalog and are no longer displayed in the photo well. The item(s) are also removed from the hard disk, if you chose that option in step 3.

If you deleted an item you didn't want to remove from the catalog, you can immediately choose **Edit, Undo Delete Selected Items from Catalog** to return that item to the catalog. If you deleted the item from the hard disk it's restored to the hard disk as well.

⑬ Locate Moved Files

Before You Begin

✔ Perform an Initial Scan for Media

As you are probably well aware by now, the *Organizer catalog* is not a collection of media files, but rather a listing of those files and their various locations on your hard disks, CDs, and DVDs. The Organizer is designed to keep track of any changes you initiate within its program (such as renaming, deleting, or editing images), but it is unaware of any file maintenance activities you perform on its media files outside of the program. If, for example, you use **My Computer** to move a file from one folder into another, the Organizer assumes that the file has simply disappeared. Similar problems arise if you rename or delete a file outside of the Organizer. To properly rename a file, make the change within the Organizer using the **File, Rename** command. Move a file using the **File, Move** command. To delete a file from the Organizer catalog and from the hard disk, see ⑫ **Remove an Item from the Catalog**.

2 Choose File, Reconnect, Missing File

3 Click Browse

1 Select Moved Item

Missing File Icon

4 Locate Actual File

7 View the Result

5 Click Reconnect

6 Click Close

💡 TIPS

To tell Organizer to check for missing files periodically and to automatically reconnect them, choose **Edit, Preferences, Files** from the Organizer menu. Enable the **Automatically Search for and Reconnect Missing Files** option and click **OK**. If, however, the Organizer has not yet realized that an image has been renamed or moved, follow the steps in this task to manually reconnect the file yourself.

If you've moved a lot of files, you can reconnect them all in one step by selecting **File, Reconnect, All Missing Files**. A listing of missing files appears on the right side of the **Reconnect Missing Files** dialog box. Select as many files as you like, choose the folder in which they are located, and click **Reconnect**.

If you find that you have accidentally moved or renamed a file using **My Computer** and not the Organizer, you must update the catalog by following the steps in this task. If you have deleted an item from the hard disk, you can remove it from the catalog as described in ⓬ **Remove an Item from the Catalog**.

① Select Moved Item

When an item in the catalog is no longer connected to the actual file, a missing file icon appears at the bottom of the image in the photo well. In the Organizer, click the item to select it.

② Choose File, Reconnect, Missing File

Choose **File, Reconnect, Missing File** from the menu bar. You can also double-click the item in the photo well to display the image in **Single Photo View**, which might also trigger the reconnect process, depending on your preferences (see the first Tip). A message box appears, telling you that the Organizer is searching the hard disk for the missing file.

③ Click Browse

You can wait for Organizer to locate the moved file for you, but if it takes more than a few seconds, it's often faster to look for the file yourself. Click the **Browse** button in the message box. The **Reconnect Missing Files** dialog box appears.

④ Locate Actual File

In the **Reconnect Missing Files** dialog box, the original location and *thumbnail* of the missing image appear on the left. On the right side of the dialog box, from the drop-down list on the **Browse** tab, navigate to the folder in which the file is now located.

Organizer should locate the file immediately and display its thumbnail in the lower-right corner of the dialog box. If not, select the file from those listed on the right.

⑤ Click Reconnect

After you've verified that the image shown in the lower-right area of the dialog box is indeed the missing file, click the **Reconnect** button to update the file's location in the catalog.

If you can't relocate the missing file and you no longer want the item in the catalog, click **Delete from Catalog** instead of **Reconnect**.

6 **Click Close**

You can reconnect additional files while the **Reconnect Missing Files** dialog box is open; just repeat steps 4 and 5. When you're through reconnecting files, click **Close**.

7 **View the Result**

After the file's new location is updated in the catalog, its thumbnail appears as normal in the photo well and the missing file icon is removed.

14 Back Up the Organizer Catalog

After you've imported lots of images into the *Organizer catalog* and have used its features to organize your images, you won't want to risk losing your hard work. True, the catalog does not contain the images themselves (only a listing of their locations and names), so if something were to happen to the catalog, you wouldn't lose any photographs. What you would lose, however, are the *properties* of each image, such as the various *tags* and *collections* to which an image is associated, plus any *audio captions* or text notes you've appended to the images. You would also lose your *creations* and organizational information, such as an item's location, file size, file type, and *thumbnail*. If something happened to the catalog (but your media files were still okay), you could always reimport all your media files and then retag, annotate, and caption them, but that would be a lot of work. Therefore, periodically, you should back up *both* the Organizer catalog *and* your media files onto CD, DVD, or another drive in case something happens to your media files or the catalog. Lucky for you, the Organizer provides an easy method for you to do both in one simple process.

See Also

→ **15** Copy Items onto CD-ROM or DVD

🔍KEY TERM

Properties—Information associated with each media file, such as its creation date, modification date, tags, collections, audio or text captions, or notes.

1 **Choose File, Backup**

In the Organizer, choose **File**, **Backup** from the menu bar. The first page of the **Burn/Backup** wizard appears.

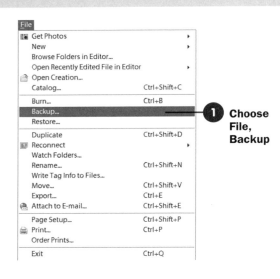

1 Choose File, Backup

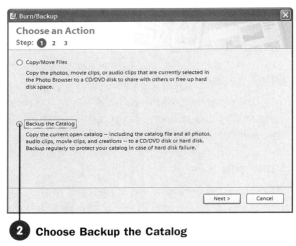

2 Choose Backup the Catalog

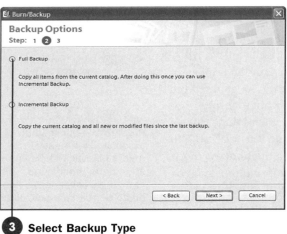

3 Select Backup Type

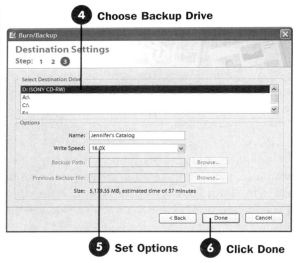

4 Choose Backup Drive

5 Set Options

6 Click Done

2 Choose Backup the Catalog

In Step 1 of the **Burn/Backup** wizard, select the **Backup the Catalog** option and click **Next** to continue.

The **Missing Files Check Before Backup** dialog box might appear; if it does, use it to reconnect any moved files before continuing with the backup (see the Note for more information).

③ Select Backup Type

In Step 2 of the **Burn/Backup** wizard, select the type of backup you want to perform: To back up the entire catalog and all your media files, select **Full Backup**. To make an incremental backup that contains a copy of the entire catalog plus any new media files added to the catalog since the last backup, select **Incremental Backup**. Click **Next**.

④ Choose Backup Drive

In Step 3 of the **Burn/Backup** wizard, select the drive to which you want to copy the catalog and media files from the **Select Destination Drive** list. If you select a CD or DVD drive, you'll be prompted to insert the disc. Do so and click **OK** to return to the **Burn/Backup** wizard.

⑤ Set Options

If you are backing up the data onto a CD or DVD, you can adjust the write speed by selecting a different speed from the **Write Speed** list. You might do this if you have been having trouble with your CD-R drive and want to compensate for that by having the computer write the data more slowly.

If you are backing up to another hard drive and not a CD-ROM or DVD, you must select a folder into which you want the data copied. If you are performing an incremental backup, the folder you select must be different from the one you originally selected when you did the full backup. Click the **Browse** button next to the **Backup Path** text box, select a folder, and click **OK**.

If you're performing an incremental backup, you must tell the Organizer where the original backup file is located. Click the **Browse** button next to the **Previous Backup File** text box, select the file that contains the original backup, and click **OK**. If you backed up previously onto a CD or DVD, you'll be prompted to insert that disc so that the Organizer can determine the backup set to which you want to add. You'll remove the disc later so that you can insert a new disc on which to copy the incremental backup.

NOTE

You should make sure that all your media files are properly linked to the catalog before you back it up. If needed, click **Reconnect** in the **Missing Files Check Before Backup** dialog box to relink lost files; see ⑬ **Locate Moved Files** for help. If you don't want to be reminded of this step, select the **Don't Show Again** option and click **Continue**.

NOTE

If something occurs to the catalog later on (such as a power surge that damages the file), you'll be prompted to recover the file—a process that fixes the damage. Simply choose **File, Catalog** from the menu to display the **Catalog** dialog box. Click the **Recover** button, and then click **OK** to proceed. If the catalog file is so badly damaged that it can't be repaired using this method, or if you want to return to an earlier version of the catalog at some later date, you can restore that version. First create an empty catalog by choosing **File, Catalog** and clicking **New**. Then choose **File, Restore** from the menu, locate the incremental backup file (if any, because it must be restored first), and click **Restore.** If you selected an incremental backup file, after it's restored, you'll be prompted to select the full backup file so its data can be restored as well.

▲NOTE

This process backs up the currently displayed catalog only. If you are using more than one catalog (for example, if each family member has his or her own catalog file), you must first open the catalog you want to back up (by choosing **File, Catalog**), and then repeat steps 1 through 6 to back up that catalog.

⑥ Click Done

Click **Done** to begin the backup process. If you are backing up the data onto a CD or DVD, you'll see a dialog box telling you how many discs you'll need to complete the backup. Click **Yes** to continue, and then follow the onscreen instructions.

If you are performing an incremental backup, the original backup disc is probably still in the drive (if you backed up to CD or DVD). If so, you'll be prompted at the proper time to remove the first disc and insert an additional disc on which to store the incremental backup.

When the backup is complete, be sure to label any removable discs with the date and time of the backup.

Copy Items onto CD-ROM or DVD

See Also

→ ⑭ **Back Up the Organizer Catalog**

→ ⑮⑧ **Share Images Using Email**

→ ⑯⓪ **Share Images Using an Online Service**

→ ⑯① **Send Images to a Mobile Phone**

In ⑭ **Back Up the Organizer Catalog**, you learned how to protect both your media files and the information in the *catalog* by backing it up onto disc. That way, if something goes wrong and the *Organizer* cannot open the catalog file or if one of the image, audio, or movie files is damaged, you can restore the needed file from the backup disc.

But what if you want to protect only certain media files, and not all the files in the catalog? Or what if you want to share particular media files with friends or family—do you have to back up the entire catalog to disc? Well, the answer is no. In this task, you'll learn how to copy just the items you want onto CD-ROM or DVD discs.

During the process of creating the CD or DVD, you can instruct the Organizer to change the status of the items to *offline*. If you choose this option, the Organizer copies the files from your hard disk to the CD or DVD, creates low-*resolution* copies of any image files for display purposes within the photo well, and then removes the files from the hard disk. Archiving files in this manner frees up hard disk space and yet still enables you to continue to view and work with those images, audio files, and movie files within the catalog. Offline images are marked with a small CD icon; if you attempt to edit one of these images or to use any offline media file in a *creation*, you'll be prompted to insert the disc onto which the original copies were transferred.

2 Choose File, Burn

3 Choose Copy/Move Files

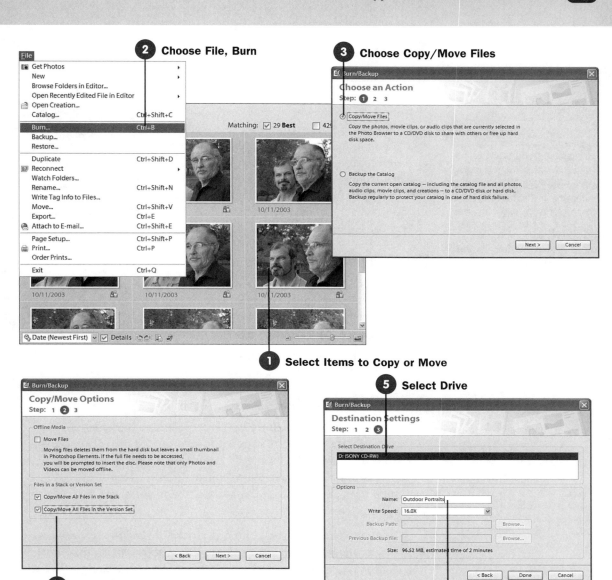

1 Select Items to Copy or Move

5 Select Drive

4 Set Offline Options

6 Type Name and Click Done

7 Burn the Discs

8 Verify the Process

TIP

If no items are selected, the Organizer copies/moves only those items currently displayed in the photo well. Rather than selecting individual items to copy/move, you can use the **Find** bar to display just the items you want. See **33** **About Finding Items in the Catalog** for more help.

 NOTE

Creations are not copied to the disc even if they are selected.

1 Select Items to Copy or Move

Only the currently displayed items are archived, so if the items you want to archive are the only ones displayed, skip this step.

If you want to copy or move only particular media files to the disc, select them in the Organizer first. You can select a contiguous group of items by pressing **Shift**, clicking the first item in the group, and then clicking the last item. To select noncontiguous items, press **Ctrl** and click each *thumbnail*. If the catalog is sorted by batch or folder, you can click the gray bar above a group to select all the items in that group. (See **18** **Sort Items** for more information.)

2 Choose File, Burn

Choose **File, Burn** from the menu bar. The first page of the **Burn/Backup** wizard appears.

3 Choose Copy/Move Files

In Step 1 of the **Burn/Backup** wizard, choose the **Copy/Move Files** option (if needed) and click **Next** to continue.

4 Set Offline Options

In Step 2 of the **Burn/Backup** wizard, set the offline options. For example, if you want to copy images to the CD or DVD and then erase them from the hard disk, enable the **Move Files** option. The images are then considered "offline," and if you want to access them from within the Organizer, you'll have to insert this disc when prompted.

If the selected images contain any *stacks* or *version sets*, you can copy or move all the images in the stack or version set (and not just the one used as a thumbnail), by enabling the **Copy/Move All Files in the Stack** and/or **Copy/Move All Files in the Version Set** options.

After selecting the offline options, insert a disc if you haven't already and click **Next** to continue.

5 Select Drive

In Step 3 of the **Burn/Backup** wizard, select the CD-ROM or DVD drive to which you want to copy the media files from the **Select Destination Drive** list.

NOTE

You can copy items only to a CD-ROM or a DVD, and not to the hard disk.

6 Type Name and Click Done

In the **Name** text box, type a name (up to 70 characters) for the collection of items you want to copy. Use a name that will remind you later on which items are contained on the discs. I wanted to copy some portraits I recently had taken, so I typed **Outdoor Portraits** as the name of my collection.

You can adjust the write speed by selecting a different speed from the **Write Speed** list. You might do this if you have an old CD drive and want to select a speed that matches it, or if you've been having trouble with your CD-R drive and want to compensate for that by having the computer write the data more slowly.

Click **Done**. If the selection includes any creations, you'll see a warning box telling you that they will not be copied to the disc. Click **OK** to continue.

7 Burn the Discs

The Organizer takes a moment to calculate how many discs you'll need and displays that information in the next dialog box. Click **Burn** to initiate the copy/move process. After a disc is completed, you'll see a reminder to label the disc properly. Click **OK** to continue. If an additional disc is needed to copy or move the files, you'll be prompted to insert additional discs until the procedure is complete.

8 Verify the Process

A message appears asking whether you want to verify the new disc. This process takes a while, but it also guarantees that the discs were created properly and can be read (which is time well spent if you later have to recover items from the discs). Click **Verify** to continue. At the end of the verification process, you'll be told whether everything is okay. If the verification detects any errors, repeat these steps to create a new series of discs. Otherwise, click **Don't Verify** to return to the Organizer window.

3

Viewing and Sorting Items

IN THIS CHAPTER:

16 Review Images

17 Change Thumbnail Size

18 Sort Items

19 Stack Images

20 Update an Image in the Catalog

21 Play an Audio File

22 View a Video

23 Change Image Date and Time

⚒ NOTE

The tasks in this chapter assume that you are using the Organizer in **Photo Browser** view. If you're currently displaying items in **Date View** (on a calendar), you can change to **Photo Browser** view by clicking the **Photo Browser** button at the right end of the **Shortcuts** bar.

After importing images into a *catalog*, you can begin to work with them in the *Organizer*. Several tasks you perform have nothing to do with editing an image or creating anything, but simply reviewing what you've got. In this chapter, you'll learn how to review images one at a time in an automated slideshow, adjust the size of the *thumbnails*, compare images side by side, sort items, organize different versions of the same image, play audio and video files you've imported, sort images, and update an image's thumbnail if it ever gets out of sync with the actual contents of the image file.

16 Review Images

Before You Begin

✔ **33** About Finding Items in the Catalog

See Also

➔ **17** Change Thumbnail Size

➔ **31** Add a Text Caption or Note

➔ **32** Add an Audio Caption

➔ **68** Print a Picture Package

➔ **69** Print Images Using an Online Service

After importing all your media files, you might find that the *catalog* contains too many images to easily review when needed. One way to deal with this problem is to reduce the size of the *thumbnails* so that you can review more images at one time (see **17** Change Thumbnail Size). The problem with this method is that the reduced size of the image thumbnails can make it difficult for you to distinguish one image from another, so if you wanted to review images to mark them with *tags* and *collection* markers, reducing the thumbnail size might not be the best method to use. Another way you can review particular images is to use the tag and collection markers to group similar items together and then display just those items when you want to review them. (See **34** Find Items with the Same Marker.) Although this approach requires some upfront work, it at least enables you to limit the display to just those images you're interested in. You could then display them one at a time in **Single Photo** view (see **17** Change Thumbnail Size). But even so, you might find yourself wondering, "Is there an easier way to review some images?"

🔍 KEY TERM

Photo review—A controllable slideshow in which each image is displayed onscreen, one at a time, in whatever order and at whatever speed you want.

The answer is to use a full-screen *photo review*. In a photo review, you can automatically review a set of images one at a time, stop the review when needed, and edit, rotate, or delete an image, mark an image for printing, or add a tag or collection marker. You can also control the replay as you like, jumping out of order to a particular image when desired. In addition, you can split the screen and compare two images when needed. In this task, you'll learn the ins and outs of conducting your own private photo review.

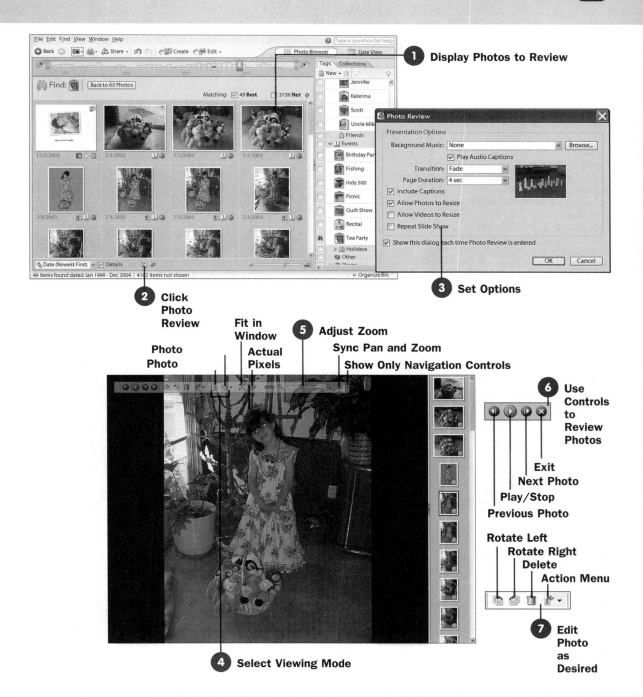

1 Display Photos to Review

2 Click Photo Review

3 Set Options

Fit in Window

Photo Photo

Actual Pixels

5 Adjust Zoom

Sync Pan and Zoom

Show Only Navigation Controls

6 Use Controls to Review Photos

Exit

Next Photo

Play/Stop

Previous Photo

Rotate Left

Rotate Right

Delete

Action Menu

7 Edit Photo as Desired

4 Select Viewing Mode

1 Display Photos to Review

In the Organizer, display the photos to review by using the **Find** bar to limit the display. (See **33** **About Finding Items in the Catalog**.) For example, you might drag several markers from the **Organize** bin to the **Find** bar to display only items with those markers.

You can also limit the items used in the photo review by selecting them first. Click the first photo you want to review, hold down the **Ctrl** key, and click the other items. To select a contiguous series of photos from the well, click the first photo in the series, hold the **Shift** key, and click the final photo in the series.

2 Click Photo Review

Click the **Photo Review** button on the **Options** bar at the bottom of the photo well. The **Photo Review** dialog box appears.

3 Set Options

To play music while you're reviewing your photos, select a music file from the **Background Music** list. If the music you'd like to play does not appear in the list, click **Browse**, select the file, and click **OK**.

To have *audio captions* you've recorded for an image automatically play when that image appears, enable the **Play Audio Captions** option. To display text *captions* you've added to images, enable the **Include Captions** option.

Select the number of seconds you want each image to appear onscreen from the **Page Duration** list. From the **Transition** list, select the tansition you want to use to segue from one image to the next. A sample of the transition you select appears in the preview window on the right.

To allow photos to resize to fill the window, enable the **Allow Photos to Resize** option. To allow video files to resize to fill the window, enable the **Allow Videos to Resize** option. This option, however, can make low-*resolution* videos very grainy and hard to see. If you want the slideshow to automatically repeat itself over and over until you stop it manually, enable the **Repeat Slide Show** option. Click **OK**.

4 Select Viewing Mode

The first photo is displayed in the review area on the left; other photos are listed as thumbnails on the right. The **Photo Review** toolbar also appears. By default, the **Photo Review** button on the **Photo Review** toolbar is enabled, which causes one image to appear at a time, automatically.

If you'd rather compare two images by dividing the review area into two separate panes, click the arrow on the **Photo Compare** button and select either **Side by Side** or **Above and Below**. Be sure to see this image in the Color Gallery to see all the details.

5 Adjust Zoom

Adjust the zoom so that you can display the portion of the photo you want to review. Click the **Actual Pixels** button to display the photo in its original size (for a high-resolution photo, you'll have to scroll to see it all); click **Fit in Window** to shrink the photo so that all of it is displayed. You can also drag the **Zoom** slider to the left or right to adjust the zoom level. Click the **Sync Pan and Zoom** button to synchronize scrolling and zooming when using **Photo Compare** mode to display two images at a time.

6 Use Controls to Review Photos

If you're using **Photo Review** mode, click **Play** to begin the slideshow. Click **Stop** to pause the slideshow temporarily when you want to perform some action such as adjusting the zoom or editing an image, and then click **Play** to resume. If you do nothing but watch, each image appears for the number of seconds you chose, then fades into the next image until the whole sequence is played (unless you selected the **Repeat Slide Show** option in step 3, in which case the slideshow will continue to repeat until you exit the photo review or stop it by clicking **Stop** on the review toolbar. You can skip to an image at any time by clicking its thumbnail on the right. The slideshow will simply resume from that point.

If you're using **Photo Compare** mode, you must switch from image to image manually. Click a pane to make that pane active (the active pane appears with a blue border), and then click a thumbnail to display that image in the active pane.

TIP

Click the **Show Only Navigation Controls** button at the end of the toolbar to remove the edit buttons from view, making it easier to see more of your photo. To redisplay the edit buttons, click the **Show All Controls** button.

In either mode, you can also use the controls to skip from image to image. Click the **Next Photo** button to display the next photo in the set. Click the **Previous Photo** button to return to the previous photo in the set.

7 Edit Photo as Desired

If you're using **Photo Review** mode, click **Stop** to pause the slideshow so that you can edit the displayed image. If you're using **Photo Compare** mode, click the pane that contains the image you want to edit.

Click the **Rotate Left** or **Rotate Right** button in the **Photo Review** toolbar to rotate the image sideways. Click **Delete** to remove the image from the catalog. (From the dialog box that appears, you can also choose to remove the image from the hard disk.) Click the arrow on the **Action Menu** button to display a list of actions you can take, such as adding a tag or collection marker to the current image, or marking an image for printing later on.

When you're through, click the **Exit** button to stop the review and return to the main Organizer window. If you've marked photos for printing, a dialog box appears. Click **Print** to print those photos locally; click **Order Prints** to send the images to an *online service* for printing.

17 Change Thumbnail Size

Before You Begin

✔ Perform an Initial Scan for Media

By default, the *Organizer* displays the items in its active *catalog* (photos, movies, audio files, and *creations*) in reduced sizes. Each of these miniature media files is called a *thumbnail*, which is a name borrowed from the realm of professional photography. There, *contact sheets* are often printed separately for each developed roll of film, containing miniatures of each print on the roll. These contact sheets were often used by the photographer for cataloging purposes. The size of each miniature on the contact sheet was usually just larger than an actual thumbnail, hence the name.

You can adjust the size of the Organizer's thumbnails to suit the task at hand. By default, the photo well displays thumbnails in a medium size.

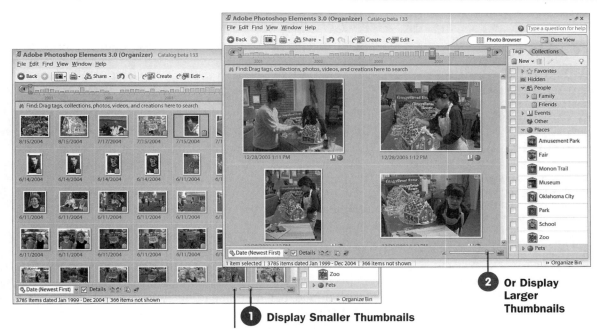

1 **Display Smaller Thumbnails**

Small Thumbnail Size Button

2 **Or Display Larger Thumbnails**

3 **Or Display a Single Photo**

1 **Display Smaller Thumbnails**

To display images in a smaller thumbnail size than normal—so that there are more of them displayed onscreen at one time—in the Organizer, drag the **Thumbnail size** slider (located on the **Options** bar at the bottom of the screen) to the left.

2 **Or Display Larger Thumbnails**

To display images in a larger thumbnail size than normal—so that image details are easier to see—drag the **Thumbnail size** slider to the right.

As thumbnails grow in size, their file date and time and the individual markers associated with a specific image are easier to see. To display the name of a marker, hold the mouse pointer over it.

3 **Or Display a Single Photo**

To display images one at a time in the largest size possible, click the **Single Photo View** button (located just to the right of the **Thumbnail size** slider on the **Options** bar). In **Single Photo** view, you can then scroll from one image to another by using the scrollbar, pressing the **Up** or **Down** arrow key, or pressing the **Page Up** or **Page Down** key. To reduce the size of the thumbnail and display multiple images again, drag the **Thumbnail size** slider to the left.

To display an image in **Single Photo** view quickly, just double-click its thumbnail. If you double-click the image again while in **Single Photo** view, you'll be returned to the view you used previously.

18 Sort Items

The *thumbnails* that appear in the photo well are laid out in some kind of order, from left to right, and then top to bottom. By default, the newest photo in the well appears in the upper-left corner. You can change this sort order very easily, and you might find yourself re-sorting the *catalog* quite often—especially when you're working to organize and make better sense of several hundred or more digital images, movies, and audio files freshly imported from your camera or hard disk.

The *Organizer* does not sort its thumbnails in the photo well by file-name because the filenames of digital images tend to be rather generic (for instance, **DSC00425.JPG**). Instead, the Organizer sorts its thumb-nails generally by *file date*.

1 Sort by Date (Newest First)

In the Organizer, select **Date (Newest First)** from the **Photo Browser Arrangement** list on the **Options** bar. This option arranges items by file date, with newer images and other media appearing at the top. This is how items are normally arranged in the photo well.

2 Or Sort by Date (Oldest First)

Select **Date (Oldest First)** from the **Photo Browser Arrangement** list on the **Options** bar. This option arranges items within the photo well in reverse date order, with older items appearing near the top.

Before You Begin

✔ **2** Perform an Initial Scan for Media

See Also

→ **19** Stack Images

→ **27** Attach a Marker to an Item

→ **41** Find Items with Similar Color

TIPS

If you scan a photo, the file date shows the date the image was scanned and not when the photo was actually taken. For this rea-son, you'll want to adjust the file date of all your scans so that the scans appear with other images taken around that same time. See **23** Change Image Date and Time.

You can also sort items by selecting the appropriate command from the **View, Arrangement** submenu.

1 Sort by Date (Newest First)

2 Or Sort by Date (Oldest First)

Click a Folder to Display Its Contents

Click to Select All Items in This Batch

Click to Select All Items in This Folder

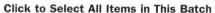

3 Or Sort by Import Batch

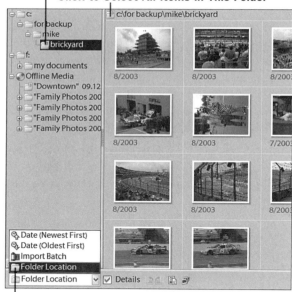

4 Or Sort by Location

3 Or Sort by Import Batch

Select **Import Batch** from the **Photo Browser Arrangement** list on the **Options** bar. This option arranges items into groups based on their *import date*. A gray bar appears at the top of each import batch, containing the date the batch was imported, and the general location (CD or hard disk for example) of the items in that batch. To select all the items in a batch, click the gray bar above that batch.

The most recently imported batch of items appears at the top of the photo well. Within each batch, items are arranged so that the oldest items appear first (the items with the oldest file date).

4 Or Sort by Location

Select **Folder Location** from the **Photo Browser Arrangement** list on the **Options** bar. This option arranges items into subgroups, each of which contains items located within the same folder on a hard disk, CD-ROM, or DVD. Items within each folder are arranged in date order (oldest first). A gray bar appears at the top of each folder group, containing the path to that folder. To select all the items in a folder group, click the gray bar above that group.

Along the left side of the window, you'll see a directory tree. Click the plus sign in front of a drive to display the folders on that drive. *Offline* media are listed by the description you used when you imported those items from the CD or DVD. (See **4** **Import Media from a CD-ROM or DVD**.) Click a folder name to instantly scroll to that folder in the photo well.

TIP

While displaying items by **Folder Location**, you can automatically create a tag with a folder's name and assign that tag to all the items in that folder. For example, if you have items in a folder called **Vacation 2005**, you can create a tag called **Vacation 2005** and add that tag to all the items in the folder. Just click the **Instant Tag** button, located at the right end of the gray bar above a folder group. In the **Create and Apply New Tag** dialog box that appears, select the **Category** in which you want to place the tag. Edit the tag **Name** and add a **Note** if desired, then click **OK**.

NOTE

Some sort options (**Color Similarity, Collection Order, Stack Order,** and **Version Set Order**) are only available from the **View, Arrangement** menu. See **41** Find Images with Similar Color, **34** Find Items with the Same Marker, **19** Stack Images, and **47** About Saving Images.

19 Stack Images

When editing a photo, you might create several copies, each with a different set of changes. This method of editing images enables you to compare various approaches to fixing the problems in a photograph and to select the best result. The only problem with creating several versions of one image is that these extra copies can clutter the *catalog*

See Also

→ **42** Hide Items You Don't Generally Use

→ **45** About Editing Images

KEY TERM

Stack—A group of related images, typically displayed in the catalog with a single thumbnail. A stack can be expanded to display all the images in the group.

NOTE

If you use the Editor to edit an image and create a different version of it, you can create a *version set* (which includes the original image and the edited version) when you save your changes. A version set is similar to the image stack discussed here, except that an image stack is created manually and can include any images you want to stack together. (See **47** About Saving Images to learn more about version sets.)

TIP

If you want to select a group of related images (such as all the images of your sister walking across the stage and receiving her diploma), use the **Find** bar to display them, and then select the ones you want to stack. See **33** About Finding Items in the Catalog. If you want to stack all the images in the same folder or batch, sort them that way first (see **18** Sort Items), and then click the gray bar above a group to select all the images in that batch or folder.

fairly quickly. Even if you're not an editing fool like I am, you might be a picture-taking one, recording a lot of similar photos at an event, in the hopes that one of them will come out okay. And all these similar photos can clutter up your catalog as well.

In any case, if you find that you have a lot of copies of the same image—or lots of similar images taken at roughly the same time—you can still keep them all in the catalog. Simply *stack* the images as explained in this task; the *thumbnail* of the latest image is all that shows up in the photo well. When needed, you can expand the stack and display all the related images in the stack.

1 Select Images to Stack

In the *Organizer*, click the first image you want to stack, then press **Ctrl** and click additional images to stack. Selected images appear with a blue border. The images do not have to look alike for you to be able to stack them.

2 Choose Edit, Stack, Stack Selected Photos

Select **Edit, Stack, Stack Selected Photos** from the menu bar. The images you selected in step 1 are now stacked.

3 View the Result

A single thumbnail of the newest image now represents the stack of images. To remind you that the thumbnail represents a stack, the stack icon appears in the upper-right corner of the thumbnail.

4 Redisplay Images in the Stack

To redisplay the images in a stack later on, select the stack image (the one with the stack icon). Then choose **Edit, Stack, Reveal Photos in Stack**.

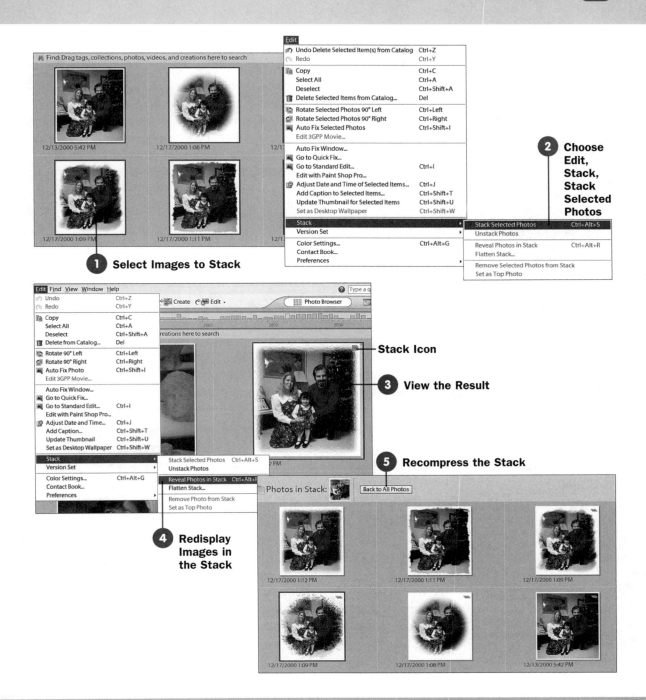

① Select Images to Stack

② Choose Edit, Stack, Stack Selected Photos

Stack Icon

③ View the Result

⑤ Recompress the Stack

④ Redisplay Images in the Stack

NOTE

To unstack a stack of images so that each image is represented in the catalog by its own thumbnail once again, select the stack thumbnail and choose **Edit, Stack, Unstack Photos**.

If you don't want to keep the extra images in the stack, and you want to retain only the top photo in the catalog (the one displayed on the thumbnail), select the stack and click **Edit, Stack, Flatten Stack**. The extra images are removed from the catalog; you'll be asked whether you want to remove the extra photos from the hard disk as well.

⑤ Recompress the Stack

The stack is expanded and all its photos are displayed in a **Find** window. At this point, you can select a new photo to represent the stack by simply selecting an image and choosing **Edit, Stack, Set as Top Photo**. To remove a photo from the stack, select it and then click **Edit, Stack, Remove Photo from Stack** (this action does not remove the photo from the catalog or the hard disk). To hide the images in the stack again (to recompress the stack so that only one thumbnail represents the stack of images), simply click **Back to All Photos**. Be sure to look in the Color Gallery to see the details of the stack.

---

⑳ Update an Image in the Catalog

Before You Begin

 ✔ **45** About Editing Images

See Also

 → **13** Locate Moved Files

 NOTE

This same problem occurs when you edit an image in the catalog using any other *graphics editor*, such as Photoshop or Paint Shop Pro, *without initiating that edit from within the Organizer*.

It's relatively easy to locate an image in the *Organizer* and then send it to the *Editor* for improvements when needed. (See **45** **About Editing Images**.) When you do this, the Organizer makes a note that you are editing the image; when you are done, it automatically updates the image's *thumbnail* in the *catalog* to reflect the changes you made.

If you open an image in the Editor the old-fashioned way (through the **File, Open** command), and make (and save) changes to an image that's currently in the catalog, the Organizer won't know you've edited the image and it won't automatically update the thumbnail to reflect your recent changes. To correct this situation, you have to tell the Organizer that you've changed the image so that it can update the thumbnail to accurately reflect the current version of the image.

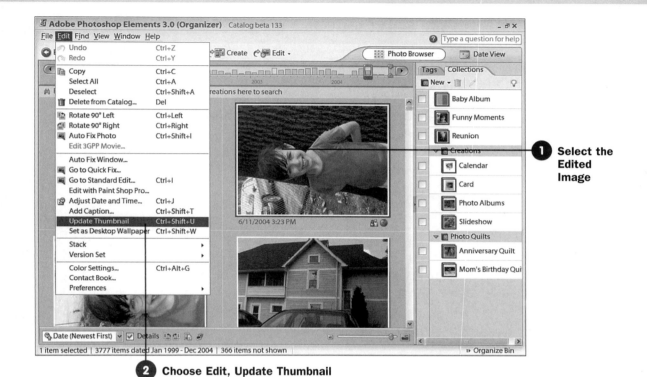

1 Select the Edited Image

2 Choose Edit, Update Thumbnail

3 View the Result

NOTE

To use another graphics editor with the Organizer, choose **Edit, Preferences, Editing**, and locate the graphics program you want to use to edit images, such as Photoshop. Then select an image in the catalog and choose **Edit, Edit with XXX**, where *XXX* is the name of your graphics editor.

TIP

If you have made changes to several images since you last used the Organizer, you can update all their catalog thumbnails in one fell swoop. Select all the edited images by **Shift**+clicking or **Ctrl**+clicking them and then choose **Edit, Update Thumbnails for Selected Items**.

① Select the Edited Image

In the Organizer, click the old thumbnail for the image you've just completed editing. The Organizer will highlight the selected thumbnail with a blue border.

② Choose Edit, Update Thumbnail

Choose **Edit, Update Thumbnail** from the menu bar. In a moment, the Organizer will update the thumbnail image to reflect your most recent changes to the photo file.

③ View the Result

As you can see here, the image thumbnail has changed to display the most recent version of the image. I liked this image of my daughter, taken on her last day of first grade, but I thought it needed work. I opened the image in the Editor, rotated and cropped the image, and adjusted the contrast a bit. Because I forgot when I opened the image in the Editor that it was also in the catalog, I had to manually update the thumbnail after I was done making changes. After following the steps given here, the newly edited image appears in the photo well.

Play an Audio File

Before You Begin

✔ **③** Import Media from a Folder

See Also

→ **22** View a Video

→ **32** Add an Audio Caption

→ **35** Find Items of the Same Media Type

Although it was primarily designed to help you organize your vast collection of digital images, the *Organizer* can also keep track of your other multimedia files, such as audio and video files. If you didn't import your audio or video files into the *catalog* when you performed the initial scan for media, see **③** Import Media from a Folder for help in adding them now. The Organizer recognizes audio files in **.WAV** format (produced by Windows's Sound Recorder and other applications that use your microphone) and **.MP3** format (used in recording high-fidelity stereo tracks).

So, you can use the Organizer to manage audio clips of your son reading his favorite book and musical clips of your favorite band.

My catalog, for example, includes not just pictures of my daughter at various ages but also recordings of her singing or talking. If your collection is similar, there's no reason you can't organize both types of files together on the hard disk. In other words, you can keep your toddler photos in the same folder with your toddler audio tracks if you want to, and look and listen to these files within the Organizer whenever you like. You can keep your musical files in a completely different folder—or several folders, organized by artist, for example—and after importing them into the Organizer, play the music files the same way you do any other audio clip.

 Display Audio Files

By default, the Organizer does not display audio files in the photo well. This is probably what you want because you cannot edit audio files in the Organizer, only play them. To display your audio files temporarily so that you can play one or two, in the Organizer, select **Find, By Media Type, Audio** from the menu. You'll see a warning telling you that audio files are not normally displayed in the catalog. Click **OK**. The photo well displays only the audio files you have imported into the catalog.

❷ Double-click Audio File

The Organizer represents audio files in the catalog with a blue horn icon, which serves as the file's *thumbnail*. In the photo well, double-click the icon for the audio file you want to play. The **Media Player** appears.

❸ Click Play

Click the **Play** button at the bottom of the **Media Player** window to begin playback. The audio plays to the end; you can replay the audio by clicking **Play** again.

 NOTE

Although the Organizer recognizes particular audio files and can play them, you can't use the program to create audio files—with the exception of brief audio annotations which are then associated with particular images, as described in **32** Add an Audio Caption.

 TIP

To display audio files all the time, choose **View, Media Types**. In the **Items Shown** dialog box, select the **Audio** option and click **OK**.

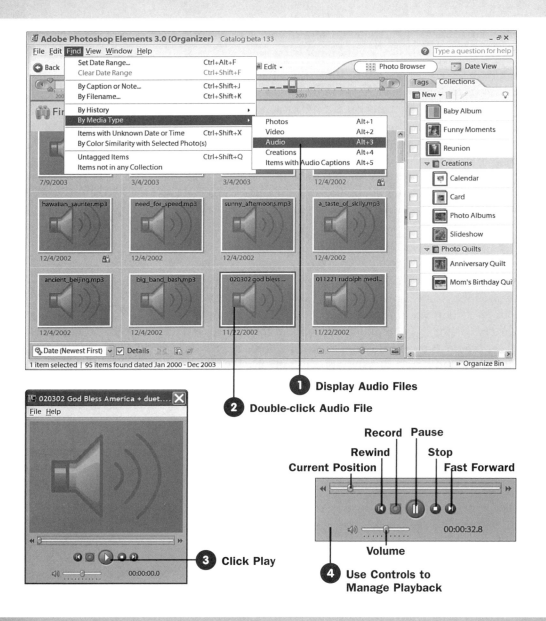

1 Display Audio Files

2 Double-click Audio File

3 Click Play

4 Use Controls to Manage Playback

Record Pause
Rewind Stop
Current Position Fast Forward

Volume

4 Use Controls to Manage Playback

You can manage the playback of the audio file using the controls in the **Media Player**. The **Current Position** slider indicates the current location of the playback relative to the entire file. Drag the slider left or right to jump forward or backward in the audio file. For example, you might drag this bar to the right to play something at the end of the audio file.

Click **Rewind** to set the slider to the beginning of the file. Click **Play** to hear the file from the point at which the **Current Position** slider is set; click **Pause** to stop playback temporarily. Click **Stop** to end playback and reset the slider to the beginning of the file. Click **Fast Forward** to set the slider to the very end of the file.

At the bottom of the **Media Player** window is a volume slider that you can use to adjust the playback volume. Setting this volume to maximum plays back the sound at the volume you've currently set for the rest of your Windows environment. In other words, the playback volume does not adjust Windows's master volume, but rather, your listening volume in relation to the Windows current maximum.

When you're through listening to your audio file, click the **Close** button on the **Media Player** window (the **X** in the upper-right corner). In the **Find** bar in the Organizer window, click **Back to All Photos** to redisplay images in the photo well and hide audio files once again.

TIP

If you've already set the Media Player volume control to maximum and you want the sound louder, adjust the volume control in Windows. If the **Volume** icon is displayed on the taskbar, click it to display the Windows volume control. If the icon does not appear, open the Windows **Control Panel**, double-click the **Sounds and Audio Devices** icon, click the **Volume** tab, and adjust the Windows volume as desired.

---

22 View a Video

Digital video cameras are becoming less expensive and thus more popular than their video tape counterparts. In addition, many digital cameras are capable of recording short bits of digital video. With the popularity of digital video recordings these days, it makes sense that the *Organizer* enables you to organize digital video files alongside your photos and audio tracks in the *catalog*. The supported video formats include .**AVI** (a common Windows format), .**MPG** (a common format for movies used by most digital cameras), and .**MOV** (QuickTime format). Thus, you can use the Organizer to organize your home videos and any short movie files you download from the Web. If you haven't imported your video files into the catalog yet, see **3** **Import Media from a Folder** for help.

Before You Begin

✔ **3** Import Media from a Folder

See Also

→ **9** Capture Images from a Video File

→ **21** Play an Audio File

→ **35** Find Items of the Same Media Type

Display Video Files

Movie Icon

2 Double-click Video File

3 Click Play

You aren't limited to simply viewing the videos you import into the Organizer. You can also incorporate those video clips into various *creations* such as slideshows and video CDs. However, playback quality in these creations might not be as smooth as when you use a dedicated video playback program such as Windows **Media Player** or **ZoomPlayer**.

 WEB RESOURCE

ZoomPlayer is a video and audio player; you can download the standard version for free for use on your Windows machine.

www.inmatrix.com/files/zoomplayer_download.shtml

① Display Video Files

The Organizer displays video files side by side with images and creations in the photo well. The first frame of a video is used as its *thumbnail*, and a movie icon appears in the upper-right corner of the thumbnail to distinguish it from photos and other types of files.

One way to locate a specific video file for playback is to temporarily display only video files in the photo well. In the Organizer, select **File, By Media Type, Video** from the menu. When you use this command, only your video files appear in the photo well.

② Double-click Video File

In the photo well, double-click the thumbnail for the video file you want to play. The **Media Player** opens.

③ Click Play

Click the **Play** button to begin playback. The movie plays to the end and then stops. Click the **Close** button (the **X** in the upper-right corner) to close the **Media Player** and return to the main Organizer window. In the **Find** bar in the Organizer window, click **Back to All Photos** to redisplay images in the photo well and hide video files once again.

> **TIP**
>
> You can create an image from a video file by clipping out a single frame. See ⑨ **Capture Images from a Video File**.

> **TIP**
>
> You can drag the border of the player to make the video window bigger, but the playback might seem grainier as a result.

> **NOTE**
>
> The same **Media Player** controls used to control the playback of audio files are used to play video files. See ㉑ **Play an Audio File** for information about those controls.

㉓ Change Image Date and Time

Several dates are associated with each image: the *import date*, the *file date*, and the *modified date*. The import date tells you the date and time the item was imported (added) into the *catalog*. The file date tells you when an image was created or scanned. The modified date indicates the last time an image was changed—rotated, brightened, saturated, and so on. The modified date is the same as the file date until you change the image by adjusting its characteristics using either the *Organizer*'s simple Auto Fix feature, the *Editor*'s more sophisticated editing tools, or another *graphics editor* such as Photoshop or Paint Shop Pro (as long as you launch that graphics editor from within the Organizer). When you make changes to an image in the catalog, the modified date changes, but the file date remains the same.

> **See Also**
>
> → ⑱ Sort Items
> → ㊳ Find Items with the Same Date
> → ㊴ Find Items Within a Date Range

KEY TERMS

Import Date—The date on which an item was imported into the catalog.

File Date—The date on which an image was taken or scanned into the system.

Modified Date—The date on which an image was modified by using either the Organizer or the Editor, or by launching another graphics editor from within the Organizer.

NOTE

The file date can be used to locate an image, which is one reason why you might want to make sure that it always reflects the date *you* associate with an image. See **38** **Find Items with the Same Date** and **39** **Find Items Within a Date Range**.

TIP

To display the **Properties** pane so that you can view the dates associated with an image, click the **Show or Hide Properties** button on the **Options** bar, or choose **Window, Properties.** To park the **Properties** pane in the **Organize Bin,** choose **Window, Dock Properties in Organize Bin.**

This date business is important because it is the file date that appears in the catalog below the image in the photo well (assuming that the **Details** button on the **Options** bar is enabled). So, it's the file date the Organizer uses to sort items in the photo well. And because the file date is not changed when you modify an image, you must have some way to manually change that date when needed. For example, you might have taken a picture with your digital camera while on vacation in another time zone, and the file date and time recorded were based on your home time, and not the local vacation time. Not that a difference of a few hours should matter much, but *it might matter to you*—especially if the difference between the two time zones (the vacation spot and your home) results in a different date, and thus, a different placement in the catalog when items are sorted.

Most often, you'll want to manually change the file dates for all your scanned images, because the date and time assigned to the resulting file is based on *when the image was scanned*, not *when the photograph itself was taken*. This means that unless you manually change the file date for all your scans, they will appear in the catalog along with photos taken the same day the scan was made, rather than appearing alongside other photos taken on the same day. For example, unless you change the file date, that picture you scanned of Great-Grandma Kaster when she was 16 might appear in the catalog next to an image of your 6-year-old daughter imported from your digital camera.

The file date, by the way, is also displayed on the **General** tab of the **Properties** pane. You can see the import date and the modified date on the **History** tab of the **Properties** pane. The modified date is for your own purposes; you can't sort by that date. You can, however, search and sort using the import date. See **18** **Sort Items** and **40** **Find Items with the Same History**.

① Select Image

In the Organizer, in the photo well, click the image whose date you want to change. The selected image appears with a blue border around it (unless you're working in **Single Photo** view).

② Choose Edit, Adjust Date and Time

Select **Edit, Adjust Date and Time** from the menu, or click the file date shown below the image *thumbnail*. The **Adjust Date and Time** dialog box appears.

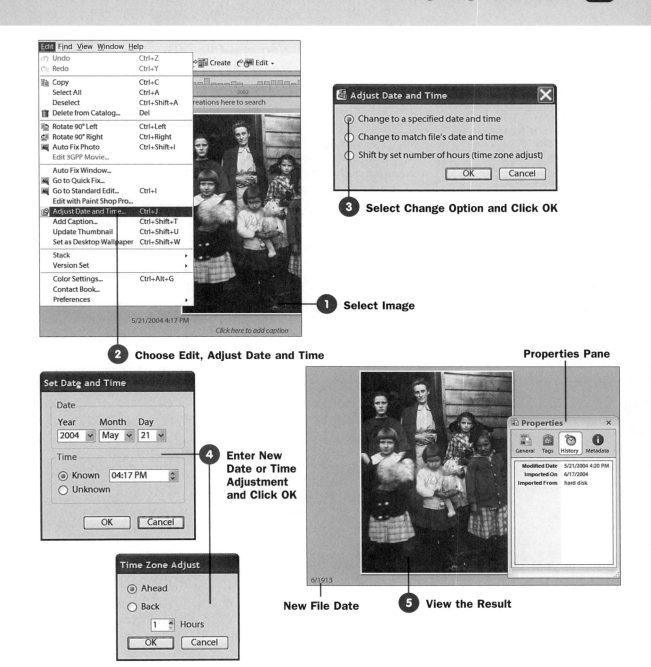

1 Select Image

2 Choose Edit, Adjust Date and Time

3 Select Change Option and Click OK

4 Enter New Date or Time Adjustment and Click OK

Properties Pane

New File Date

5 View the Result

TIP

You can change several images to the same date and time by selecting them before continuing to step 2. To make it easy to select several similar images, you might want to use the **Find** bar to display just those images. See **33** About Finding Items in the Catalog.

NOTE

If you select multiple images, you can adjust their file date by shifting it. Choose **Shift to new starting date and time** in Step 3, then enter the date and time for the earliest photo in the group. The file date and time for the selected images are shifted accordingly, using this ealiest date/time as a starting point.

③ Select Change Option and Click OK

To change the file date and time to anything you like, select the **Change to a specified date and time** option. To change the file date so that it matches the current modified date, select the **Change to match file's date and time** option. To adjust the time portion only by a few hours or so, select the **Shift by set number of hours (time zone adjust)** option. After selecting the option you want to use to change the file date, click **OK**.

④ Enter New Date or Time Adjustment and Click OK

If you selected the **Change to match file's date and time** option in step 3, the file date is changed immediately to match the modified date, and you're returned to the main Organizer window.

If you selected the **Change to a specified date and time** option in step 3, the **Set Date and Time** dialog box appears. Enter a **Year**, **Month**, and **Day**. If you don't know the actual date on which the photo was taken, and you'd rather list it as unknown, select **????** from the **Year** list. You can also select **??** from the **Month** or **Day** list if either is unknown. If you've entered a specific date, you can also specify the time the photo was taken. Click **Known** and enter the time; if you don't know the actual time the photo was taken or you don't want to bother with it, select **Unknown**. Click **OK** to save the date change.

If you selected the **Shift by set number of hours (time zone adjust)** option in step 3, the **Time Zone Adjust** dialog box appears. Select either **Ahead** or **Back** to indicate the direction in which you want the time adjusted, and then enter the number of **Hours** to adjust the time of the photograph. Click **OK**.

⑤ View the Result

The Organizer immediately adjusts the file date and time based on your choices and displays that new date/time in the photo well, just below the image. Here, the file date for this photo of my great-grandmother and her children originally displayed the date on which I scanned the photo into my computer. I changed the file date to June 1913, to correspond with when the photo was actually taken. I didn't know the exact day or time, so I chose **??** and **Unknown** for those options.

4

Organizing Items in the Catalog

IN THIS CHAPTER:

24 About Organizing Items

25 Create a Category or Group

26 Create a Tag or Collection Marker

27 Attach a Marker to an Item

28 Delete a Marker, Category, or Group

29 Change a Marker's Icon

30 Change a Marker's Category, Group, Name, or Note

31 Add a Text Caption or Note

32 Add an Audio Caption

The main reason for importing images, audio files, and movies into the *catalog* is to organize them, and that's what this chapter is all about. You group similar media files together by adding the same *tag* or *collection* marker. For example, you might add a **John** tag to several audio files, movie files, and images that feature your son, John. Similarly, you might add a **Calendar** collection marker to the images you've used in creating a family calendar for an earlier year so that you don't select the same images when creating this year's calendar. After you've created tags and collection markers, you can change anything about them that doesn't work for you—you can change a marker's name, icon, category, and even its position within the tag or collections listing. You'll learn how to perform these maintenance tasks in this chapter. Finally, you'll learn how to annotate your images with a written or audio commentary.

24 About Organizing Items

See Also

→ **18** Sort Items

→ **27** Attach a Marker to an Item

→ **34** Find Items with the Same Marker

→ **38** Find Items with the Same Date

→ **39** Find Items Within a Date Range

 TIP

If you're displaying items by folder location as shown in the figure, you can click the **Instant Tag** button above a folder group to automatically create a new tag with that folder name, and assign the tag to all the images in that folder.

The *Organizer* provides many different ways to sort, display, and categorize the items in your *catalog*. For example, in **18** **Sort Items**, you learned how to change the view in the photo well so that items are sorted in the order in which you want them to appear, such as grouped by import batch. You can also use this method to sort and group items by *file date* or their location on a hard disk, CD-ROM, or DVD. The advantage of this method of organization is that you don't have to do anything to an item (other than import it) to have that item appear in the proper sort order within the catalog.

Although you can also use the technique explained in **18** **Sort Items** to arrange items by file date, you might prefer a method that actually limits the display so that only those items created on a particular day or within a particular range of dates appear in the photo well. One way to do this is to use **Date View**, as described in **38** **Find Items with the Same Date**. With **Date View**, you use a calendar format to quickly view all the images and other items created on a particular day (all items with the same file date). If you were looking for a photo taken at the state fair last year, you could display the month the fair was held, use the daily *thumbnails* to quickly locate the exact day you want, and then browse through the state fair images taken that day until you locate the one you want to use.

**Click to Create a Tag for This Group
with the Same Name as the Folder**

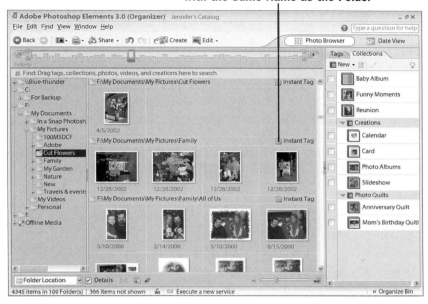

Items located in the same folder can be grouped together in the photo well.

Scroll Through Images Taken
on the Selected Day

Select a Day

*The **Date View** limits the number of items displayed to a particular date.*

NOTES

You can also use text *captions* and notes to organize images and other items. For example, if you add a text caption to an image that says, **Samantha takes a dive**, you can search for the word *dive* and locate the image. You can search the notes attached to images and other items as well. See **37** **Find Items with the Same Caption or Note.**

The tasks in this chapter assume that you are using the Organizer in **Photo Browser** view. If you're currently displaying items in **Date View** (on a calendar), you can change to **Photo Browser** view by clicking the **Photo Browser** button at the right end of the **Shortcuts** bar.

In **Date View**, you can review the photos taken on any one particular day. When you want to see photos shot over a *range* of days, **Photo Browser** view includes a **Timeline**, which works almost like a slide rule. You could limit the display of media files in the photo well to, for example, images taken between June and October 2003 simply by dragging the end markers on the **Timeline**. You can also use the **Timeline** to quickly scroll to a particular set of media files without limiting the display of items at all. For example, you might click a bar on the **Timeline** at **April 2004** to jump directly to the images taken on your birthday, plus any items you might have created that day. (As does the **Date View**, the **Timeline** looks for items with the same file date.) You'll learn more about using the **Timeline** in **39** **Find Items Within a Date Range.**

Click a Bar to Scroll to Items Created That Month   **End Markers**

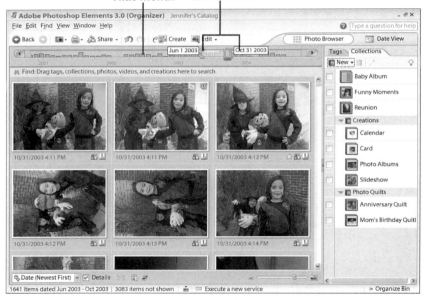

*Use the **Timeline** to scroll within the catalog or to limit the display.*

Although the **Date View** and the **Timeline** in **Photo Browser** view are useful tools, they depend on an item's file date being correct. As discussed in **23** **Change Image Date and Time,** an image's file date might be set to the date you scanned it in rather than the actual date the image was taken. So, relying on the **Date View** and **Timeline** to help you organize images and other items in the catalog is not enough. And searching for an image based on its filename (see **36** **Find Items with Similar Filenames**) might not help because digital images often use generic filenames such as **DSC00203.TIF**. The simplest and easiest method to organize your growing pile of images and other catalog items is to apply *tags* and *collection* markers, which just happen to be the subject of this chapter.

How Markers Work

With tags and collection markers, you can group similar items together quickly and easily. Tags are typically used to identify items with similar content—for instance, the same people. **Dad** and **Joan** would make great candidates for tags. Collections are used to group together photos that might contain a variety of people or different types of subjects, but are important for their collective *context* or purpose—for instance, the time in which they took place or a project you want to use them in. For example, you might create a collection called **Reunion** and use it to group the various images, movies, and audio files you're gathering for a family history CD, regardless of which particular family member is in each image, movie, or audio recording. (If you wanted to, you could use various family member tags to identify the content of each item in the **Reunion** collection.) Think of a tag as identifying the *who* or *what* of a photo, and a collection as identifying the *where* or *why*.

Another reason to create a collection is to group images you intend to use in a particular project, such as a photo quilt, scrapbook, or T-shirt with photos of each of the grandkids for Grandma and Granddad. In other words, you could create a **T-Shirt** collection marker and use it to mark all the images you intend to put on Granddad's t-shirt, regardless of who's in the photo. Another thing that sets collection markers apart from tags is your ability to display the items in a collection in any order, regardless of their file dates, folder locations, or import batch. In other words, after displaying the items in a collection, you can rearrange them in any order you choose by simply dragging and dropping them onscreen. For example, you might place the **T-Shirt** collection images in the order in which you intend to place them on the t-shirt. Similarly, you could rearrange images in the **Calendar** collection by months, making it easier for you to assemble the calendar when you're done. The freedom

KEY TERMS

Tag—A marker associated with a group of media files that contain similar content or subject matter.

Collection—A marker associated with an ordered group of media files that share the same context or purpose, whether or not they contain different subject matter.

NOTE

Although you can assign tags and collection markers to the same item, you can't search for items using both kinds of markers. For example, if you assign a **Reunion** collection marker and a **Mom and Dad** tag to an image of your mom and dad at a recent family reunion, you can search for images with the **Mom and Dad** tag *or* with the **Reunion** collection marker, but not both at the same time.

to rearrange items in a collection is especially helpful if it happens to turn out that the best image for July is one taken at a picnic in August.

**Number Icons Mark an Item's
Placement Within a Collection**

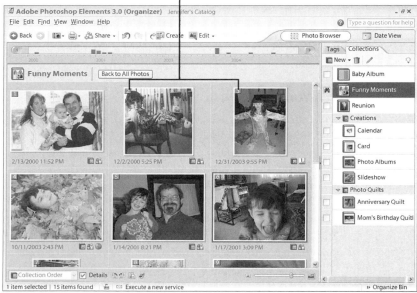

Items that share the same context or purpose can be quickly displayed on screen, in any order you choose, using collection markers.

NOTE

Markers do not appear on thumbnails in the photo well if you do not also display *file dates*. To display dates, turn on the **Details** option on the **Options** bar.

Markers assigned to an item appear as small icons beneath an item's *thumbnail* in the *catalog*. To identify the tag or collection a particular image belongs to, hover the mouse pointer over that icon and a description appears. In **Single Photo** view, you'll see not only the marker icons, but the marker description as well.

Now, if you were to create a **Joan** tag and assign it to several images, you could quickly display just the images that contain Joan (maybe alone, maybe with other people) using the steps shown in **34** **Find Items with the Same Marker**. Being able to control the catalog display is one of the powerful results of using tags and collections to organize your catalog items.

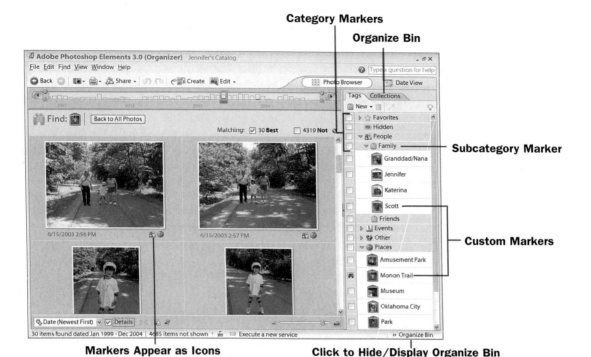

Category Markers

Organize Bin

Subcategory Marker

Custom Markers

Markers Appear as Icons

Click to Hide/Display Organize Bin

Markers help you organize your images and display just those you want to work with.

Available tags are displayed on the **Tags** tab of the **Organize Bin**, located on the left side of the Organizer window. By default, tags consist of five main categories: **Favorites**, **People**, **Events**, **Places**, and **Other**. Under the **People** category, you'll find two subcategories waiting for you—**Family** and **Friends**. You can use these existing category (**People**) and subcategory tags (**Family**) to organize your media files by content, or you can create new subcategory tags and custom tags (such as **Scott** or **Museum** within an existing category or subcategory).

Collection markers are used to group items with the same purpose or context. The Organizer does not provide any default collection markers for you, so when you want to create a collection group, you'll have to create your own. For example, a **Portfolio** collection could be used to mark your best images, regardless of their content. Because the images are grouped in a collection, you could then arrange them in order from best-of-the-best to almost-the-best. Collection markers are displayed on the **Collections** tab of the **Organize Bin**.

NOTES

The Organizer provides an additional tag category, called **Hidden**, that you can use to temporarily hide media files you don't use very often. This tag allows you to keep items in the catalog, yet keep the catalog uncluttered with images and other media files you don't use often. See **42** **Hide Items You Don't Generally Use.**

You can hide the **Organize Bin** temporarily, and then later redisplay it by choosing **Window, Organize Bin** or by clicking the **Organize Bin** button at the right-end of the **Status** bar.

TIPS

When creating a new tag or collection marker, you can place it under any category or subcategory—for example, you could create a tag marker for your son and place it in the **People, Family** subcategory. Because you start off without any collection markers, you can create categories as needed, or simply create a bunch of collection markers without categorizing them. For example, you could create a **Scrapbook** collection category and add collection markers under it for each child, such as **Shakur** and **Samone**. Then you could use the **Scrapbook, Samone** collection marker to group the best images of Samone through the years for a photo scrapbook you'll present to her on her 16th birthday.

Markers don't have to be specific (such as **Places, Chicago**); you can just as easily create a **Places** tag for **Museums** or **Parks** if you spend a lot of time in those kinds of places. Tags in the **Events** category can also be specific (**Family Reunion 2004**) or generic (**Holidays**). Just create tags and collection markers that relate *in your own mind* to a specific collection of media files. That way, you'll be able to later find any item or group of items by simply using the marker you created. As you can see, I created several tags for my catalog—one for each member of my immediate family, organized under the **Family** category. I haven't added any specific friend markers; instead, if an image contains some of my friends, I simply mark it with the **Friends** subcategory tag.

I added several places we visit often to the **Places** category, such as amusement parks and the Monon Trail (a walking and riding trail that runs through my city). In the **Event** category, I've listed a few events that reoccur often in my life, such as **Birthday Party, Picnic, Quilt Show**, and **Recital**, although I'm sure I'll add more as I expand my collection. I found that I had a lot of holiday photos, so I created a **Holiday** subcategory under **Events**, with several custom tags (**Christmas, Fourth of July**, and so on). I've created a few collection markers as well: **Calendar** (which I use to group the images I've used in my annual calendars, so I don't reuse the same ones), **Reunion** (to group my growing collection of media files for an upcoming family reunion this year), **Baby Album** (to group images I'm collecting for a special photo album I'll present to my daughter on her 16th birthday), and **Funny Moments** (to group silly photos that make me smile).

You'll learn how to create categories, subcategories, and markers in **26** **Create a Tag or Collection Marker**. As I import images, I may invent new markers to help me organize the new files. As I work with the files in the catalog, I'll reorganize the markers as needed, eliminating those that just don't seem to work after all. One thing to keep in mind when creating markers: don't create a marker for every little thing. You should instead create several general markers, and then, by associating multiple markers with specific items, narrow down broad groups. For example, you might create a tag for your friend **Juanita**. If you also have a tag called **Vacation**, you could assign both the **Juanita** and **Vacation** tags to several images, and use them together to display photos of your friend and you on vacation together. You could also use the **Vacation** tag, however, to group photos of your family on vacation. By assigning the additional tag, **Family,** to those images, you could quickly display your family on vacation in Florida without wading through the additional photos of Juanita.

Changing the Organize Bin Display

To display the **Organize Bin** at any time, choose **Window, Organize Bin** from the menu or by clicking the **Organize Bin** button at the right-end of the **Status** bar. Then click either the **Tags** or **Collections** tab at the top of the bin to display those markers. If a tag or collection marker you want to use is out of view, use the scrollbar on the right side of the **Organize Bin** to scroll through the list. You can shorten the list by temporarily hiding particular categories. Just click the down arrow to the left of a category name to hide any subcategories and markers it contains. To expand a category and display its markers, click the right arrow to the left of the category name. You can quickly expand the entire listing by selecting either **View, Expand All Tags** or **View, Expand All Collections** from the menu. To collapse the listing and show only the main categories, select **View, Collapse All Tags** or **View, Collapse All Collections**. To make the **Organize Bin** wider (so that you can read a long marker name, perhaps), drag the bin's border to the left. To make the bin narrower so that the photo well is larger, drag the bin's border to the right.

TIP

If you use a category marker to display a selected group of media files (as described in **34** **Find Items with the Same Marker**), all items associated with a subcategory or a custom marker under that category also display. For example, if you select the **People** category for display, all items tagged with the **Family** or **Friends** subcategory tag, as well as any items tagged with custom tags under that heading, also display.

NOTE

The check boxes that appear in front of each marker in the **Organize Bin** are used to control the display of items in the *catalog*. See **34** **Find Items with the Same Marker**.

TIPS

By default, the **Organize Bin** shows tags with a name and a small icon, and sorts the tag and collection lists in alphabetical order. You can change this appearance and sort order by choosing **Edit**, **Preferences**, **Tags and Collections**. Enable the **Manual** option for a particular element (such as **subcategories**) if you want to drag and drop those elements in the list to arrange them yourself rather than allow the element to appear in alphabetical order). This way, the **Mom and Dad** marker can appear above little **Isabella** if you prefer elders to precede children. By the way, on the **Tags** tab, categories appear in the order in which you add them to the list (and not in alphabetical order), unless you change to **Manual**.

In the **Tag Display** frame, you can set tags (but not collection markers) to appear without photos (as miniature folder icons) or as larger icons (big enough to see who's in them).

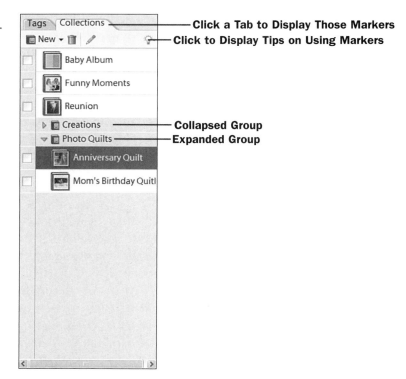

Expand or collapse categories or groups to control the listing of markers.

---

25 Create a Category or Group

See Also

→ **26** Create a Tag or Collection Marker

→ **28** Delete a Marker, Category, or Group

To make your various *tags* and *collection* markers easier to use, you'll want to keep them organized in a logical manner. The **Tags** tab of the **Organize Bin** has several pre-existing categories for you to use: **Favorites**, **Hidden**, **People**, **Events**, **Other**, and **Places**. There are some subcategories in the **People** category as well: **Family** and **Friends**. To this list you can add as many categories and subcategories as you want. You can even create sub-subcategories.

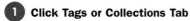

Click Tags or Collections Tab

Click New Button

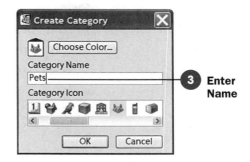

Enter Name

Enter Name

Set Options and Click OK

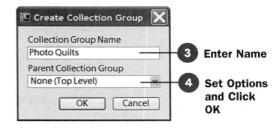

Enter Name

Set Options and Click OK

Tags are gathered together in categories; collections are gathered in groups. Collection markers do not have any pre-existing groups or subgroups, but again, you can add some whenever you want.

1 Click Tags or Collections Tab

If you want to create a new tag category or subcategory, in the *Organizer*, click the **Tags** tab on the **Organize Bin**. To create a new collections group, click the **Collections** tab instead.

NOTE

Although you'll most likely create new categories and groups to organize your tag and collection markers, the categories and groups you'll create in this task are markers in and of themselves, and can be used to organize items in the catalog.

NOTE

If the **Organize Bin** is not showing, click the **Organize Bin** button on the **Status** bar to display it, or choose **Window, Organize Bin** from the menu.

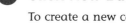 **Click New Button**

To create a new category for tags, click the **New** button at the top of the **Organize Bin** and then select **New Category** or **New Sub-Category** from the menu that appears. The **Create Category** or **Create Sub-Category** dialog box appears.

To create a new group for collections, click the **New** button at the top of the **Organize Bin** and then select **New Collection Group**. The **Create Collection Group** dialog box appears.

③ Enter Name

Type a name for the new tag category, tag subcategory, or collections group in the box provided.

TIPS

You can drag existing markers on top of a category, subcategory, group, or subgroup marker on the **Organize Bin** to add that marker to that category or group. See **30** Change a Marker's Category, Group, Name, or Note.

Subcategories, collection groups, and subgroups appear in the **Organize Bin** in alphabetical order (tag categories appear in the order in which they are added to the list). For example, on the **Tags** tab, any subcategories you add within the **Events** category appear in alphabetical order. You can rearrange things more to your liking by dragging and dropping them within the list. To enable manual rearranging, choose **Edit, Preferences, Tags and Collections**. Then enable the **Manual** option next to the item you want to manually rearrange, such as **Collection Groups**.

④ Set Options and Click OK

If you're creating a tag category, select the icon you want to represent the category from those shown in the **Category Icon** list. You can also change the color that appears at the top of the tags in this category by clicking the **Choose Color** button, selecting a color from the **Color Picker** that opens, and clicking **OK** to return to the **Create Category** dialog box.

If you're creating a tag subcategory, select the category to which you want to assign it from the **Parent Category or Sub-Category** list.

If you're creating a collections group, you can make it a subgroup by selecting the existing group to which you want to assign it from the **Parent Collection Group** list. If you leave this option set to **None**, the new group will appear on the **Organize Bin** at the top level with other top level groups.

When you're through setting options, click **OK** to create the new category, subcategory, group, or subgroup. The new category/group marker appears on the **Organize Bin**.

26 Create a Tag or Collection Marker

Although the *Organizer* provides a few category and subcategory *tags* to start you out, you'll want to create some new tags to help you organize your own catalog. Also, because the Organizer provides no *collection* markers for you, you'll definitely need to create the collections you need. You can place the markers you create into any existing category/group or subcategory/subgroup; recall that tag markers use categories and subcategories, whereas collection markers use groups and subgroups. See **25** **Create a Category or Group**.

You assign each new marker a name and add any descriptive notes in the text box provided. New markers appear in the **Organize Bin** with a generic icon that has no picture. The first time you assign the new marker to a photo, however, that photo is used as the icon for the marker. This gives your markers a visual reference that can help when you begin the process of assigning various markers to the items in the *catalog*. You can reassign the photo being used as a marker's icon whenever you like; see **29** **Change a Marker's Icon**. You can also make other changes to a marker after the fact; see **30** **Change a Marker's Category, Group, Name, or Note**.

1 Click Tags or Collections Tab

If you want to create a new tag, in the *Organizer*, click the **Tags** tab on the **Organize Bin**. To create a new collection marker, click the **Collections** tab instead.

You must create any new category, group, or subcategory *before* creating any new markers you want to assign to them (see **25** **Create a Category or Group**).

Before You Begin

✔ **24** About Organizing Items

✔ **25** Create a Category or Group

See Also

→ **27** Attach a Marker to an Item

→ **28** Delete a Marker, Category, or Group

 TIPS

You can save your tag and collection markers in a file and import them into a different catalog when needed. To save the marker list, click the **New** button at the top of the **Organize Bin**, choose **Save Tags to File** or **Save Collections to File**, select the markers you want to export, and click **OK**. Type a filename and click **Save**. To import the saved list into another catalog, click the **New** button, choose **From File**, select the file, and click **Open**.

You can enlarge the size of the icon that appears next to a tag by choosing **Edit, Preferences, Tags and Collections**, and choosing the last option from the **Tag Display** frame. Notice that you can also forgo the photo icon altogether and display a small folder icon instead. This option, by the way, does not affect the icon that appears in front of collection markers.

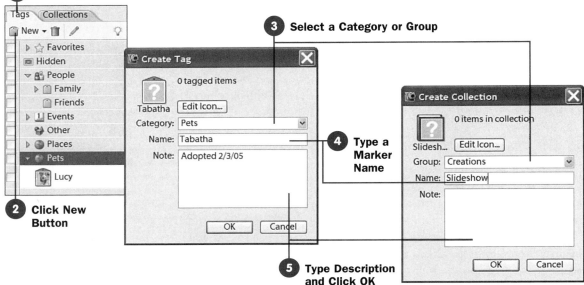

1 Click Tags or Collections Tab

3 Select a Category or Group

2 Click New Button

4 Type a Marker Name

5 Type Description and Click OK

NOTE

If the **Organize Bin** is not showing, click the **Organize Bin** button on the **Status** bar to display it, or choose **Window, Organize Bin** from the menu.

TIP

To add a marker to a specific category or group quickly, click that category or group in the **Organize Bin** just before you click the **New** button. The category/group you selected automatically appears in the **Category** or **Group** list box in the **Create Tag** or **Create Collection** dialog box.

2 Click New Button

Click the **New** button at the top of the **Organize Bin**. From the menu that appears, choose **New Tag** to create a new tag or **New Collection** to create a new collection. The **Create Tag** or **Create Collection** dialog box appears.

3 Select a Category or Group

Open the **Category** or **Group** drop-down list and select the category or group to which you want to assign this new marker.

4 Type a Marker Name

Type a name for the new marker in the **Name** text box. The name can include spaces if you like, but you are limited to 63 characters.

5 Type Description and Click OK

Click in the **Note** box and type a description of the marker if desired. This note appears only when you select a tag and display the **Edit Tag** or **Edit Collection** dialog box (see **30** **Change a Marker's Category, Group, Name, or Note**), so it's of limited use. Click **OK** to create the new marker.

The marker appears on the **Organize Bin** underneath the category or group you selected in step 3. The marker is now ready to be assigned to any item you want—although you've probably noticed that its icon is blank at the moment. When you assign a new marker to a photo for the first time, the marker will grab that photo for its icon. See **27** **Attach a Marker to an Item**.

If you decide at a later date that you want to remove a marker you've created from the Organize Bin, see **28** **Delete a Marker, Category, or Group**.

NOTES

Subcategories, collection groups, and subgroups appear in the **Organize Bin** in alphabetical order (tag categories appear in the order in which they are added to the list). For example, on the **Tags** tab, any subcategories you add within the **Events** category appear in alphabetical order. You can rearrange things more to your liking by dragging and dropping them within the list. To enable manual rearranging, choose **Edit, Preferences, Tags and Collections**. Then enable the **Manual** option next to the item you want to manually rearrange, such as **Collection Groups**.

27 Attach a Marker to an Item

To organize your media files into logical groups such as vacation photos, photos of the family dog, audio files of your daughter, movies of friends, and so on, assign *tag* and *collection* markers to them. After a marker has been associated with your media files, you can search for items with a particular marker and display just those files onscreen. For example, if you have a tag called **Hattie**, you could use it to instantly display photos of your pet Scottie dog. You can also organize audio and video clips you've imported into the *catalog* by assigning markers to them as well.

Before You Begin

✔ **24** About Organizing Items

✔ **26** Create a Tag or Collection Marker

See Also

→ **28** Delete a Marker, Category, or Group

1 Select Items

2 Click Tags or Collections Tab

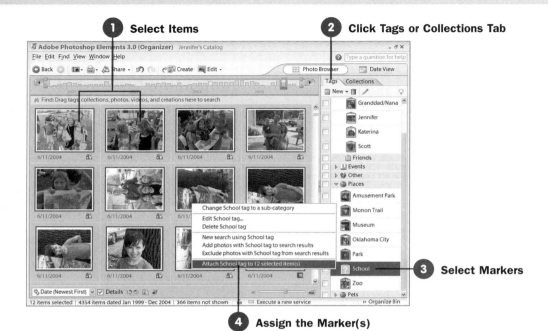

3 Select Markers

4 Assign the Marker(s)

Marker Appears on
Selected Items

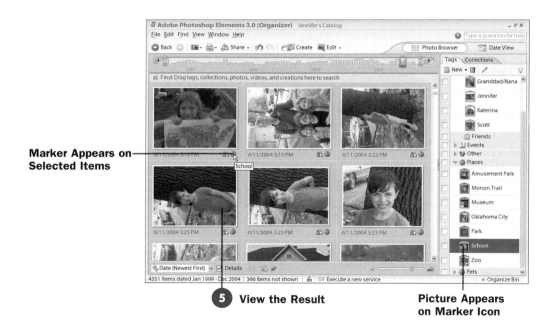

5 View the Result

Picture Appears
on Marker Icon

If you've recently created a tag or collection marker (see **26** **Create a Tag or Collection Marker**), that marker does not yet have a photo icon. The first time you assign the new marker to a photo, the marker adopts that photo as its icon. If you assign a new marker to a group of items, the marker uses the first photo in that group as its icon. So, when assigning a new marker for the first time, you'll want to be selective and choose a photo that represents that category well.

You should be aware of two special tag markers: **Favorites** and **Hidden**. Use the **Favorites** tags to mark favorite image, audio, and video files for quick retrieval. There are five different favorite tags, each with an associated number of stars as its icon. You could assign the five-star **Favorites** marker to your very best photos, the three-star **Favorites** marker to ones you like pretty well, and the one-star **Favorites** marker to ones you like "sorta kinda"—or you could use the stars to represent each family member's favorites. Most likely, you'll use the **Favorites** tag in combination with other tags; for example, if you attach the **Favorites** tag to an image that also uses the **Vacation** tag, you can locate your favorite vacation photos in a jiffy. The **Hidden** tag is used to temporarily hide items in the photo well; see **42** **Hide Items You Don't Generally Use.**

1 Select Items

In the *Organizer*, click the first item you want to mark. Then press **Shift** and click the last item in the group. Alternatively, press **Ctrl** and click each additional item you want. If items are sorted by folder or import batch (see **18** **Sort Items**), you can click the gray bar above a group to select all items in that group.

2 Click Tags or Collections Tab

If you want to assign a tag, click the **Tags** tab on the **Organize Bin**. To assign a collection marker, click the **Collections** tab instead.

TIPS

If you forget and assign a new marker to just any old photo and later decide that a different photo is more representative of the group, you can change a marker's photo icon. See **29** **Change a Marker's Icon.**

If tag and keyword metadata has already been attached to images you're importing (typically by Photoshop or similar software), you'll be asked if you want to add these image tags to the **Tags** list on the **Organize Bin**. The new tags will automatically be associated with the images you're importing. If the image tags are similar in purpose to those you already have, you can tell Organizer which existing tags you want to use instead. The imported images are then tagged with the existing tag(s) you select.

You can create new tags using the names of the folders in which images reside. Just display images by **Folder Location** and click the **Instant Tag** button (located just after the folder name at the top of a folder group). A tag is created using the name of the folder, and all the images in that folder are automatically marked with the new tag. See **24** **About Organizing Items.**

You can assign just tags or just collection markers in one step; if you want to assign both tag *and* collection markers to the same set of items, you must repeat steps 2 to 4.

You can review a group of photos and assign tags or collection markers to them during the review. See **16** Review Images.

After assigning a collection marker to a group of images, you can display that group in **Collections Order** view. Then you can rearrange the images in the group in any order you want by simply dragging them in the photo well. See **24** About Organizing Items and **34** Find Items with the Same Marker.

③ Select Markers

In the **Organize Bin**, press **Ctrl** and click each marker you want to assign to the selected items.

④ Assign the Marker(s)

Drag the selected marker(s) onto any one of the selected items and drop the markers on the item. If you don't like dragging, you can right-click a selected marker and choose **Attach selected tag(s) to XX selected items** or **Add XX selected items to selected collections** (where XX represents the number of items you selected in step 1) from the context menu.

If you've accidentally associated a marker with an item, and you feel that the marker doesn't really apply, you can remove it. Just select the items, right-click, choose **Remove Tag** or **Remove from Collection** from the context menu, and select the marker you want to remove from the list that appears.

⑤ View the Result

If you're assigning a new marker to an image for the first time, that image is used as the marker's photo icon which appears on the **Organize Bin**.

The markers you assigned appear as icons underneath the selected items. If you are using **Single Photo** view, the descriptions for the markers attached to an image also appear; to see a marker's description in other views, hover the mouse pointer over the icon to make the marker's description appear.

28 Delete a Marker, Category, or Group

Before You Begin

✔ **24** About Organizing Items

See Also

→ **25** Create a Category or Group

→ **26** Create a Tag or Collection Marker

To keep the items in the *catalog* organized, you create *tags*, *collections*, categories, and groups, and then use their markers to identify the content or purpose of individual items. Occasionally, after creating a marker, you'll realize that its purpose overlaps other markers, and that it simply isn't needed. The same thing might happen with the categories, subcategories, groups, and subgroups you create—at some point, they might no longer be needed. Luckily, it's easy to remove unwanted markers, categories, and groups from the **Organize Bin**. After a marker is deleted, its name and icon no longer appear on the **Organize Bin**. Also, the marker is automatically removed from any items that might have been using it; the items themselves are not deleted. Likewise, if you remove a category or group, any markers within that category or group are also removed from the **Organize Bin**; the category, group, tag, and collection markers are also removed from any items that use them.

1 **Click Tags or Collections Tab**

If you want to delete a tag or a tag category or subcategory you no longer use, in the *Organizer*, click the **Tags** tab on the **Organize Bin**. To delete a collectio marker or a collection group or subgroup, click the **Collections** tab instead.

2 **Select Marker, Category, or Group to Delete**

In the **Organize Bin**, click the marker, category, or group you no longer need.

3 **Click Delete**

Click the **Delete** button located at the top of the **Organize Bin** (it looks like a trash can). You'll be asked to confirm the deletion; click **OK** to continue.

You can delete multiple markers or collection groups by simply clicking the first one, then pressing **Ctrl** and clicking all the other markers or groups you want to remove. You cannot remove multiple tag categories or subcategories in one step—repeat these steps to remove additional categories or subcategories.

4 **View the Result**

The selected marker, category, or group is removed from the **Organize Bin** and from any associated items. If you removed a category or group, any subcategories, subgroups, or markers within the deleted category or group are also removed from the **Organize Bin**. These additional markers are also removed from associated items.

NOTES

You can't remove the **Favorites** or **Hidden** tag categories. You can remove other standard Organizer categories if you like, such as **Events** or **Other**.

If you want to remove a marker from a item or group of items, but not remove it from the **Organize Bin**, just select the items, right-click, choose either choose **Remove Tag** or **Remove from Collection** from the context menu, and select the marker you want to remove from the list that appears. The marker is removed from the selected items, but it remains in the **Organize Bin** where you can use it for other items.

TIP

If the purpose of a marker or markers overlaps with the purpose of another, you can merge the markers. Select the markers you want to merge into a single marker, right-click the selection, and choose **Merge Tags** or **Merge Collections** from the context menu. Select the tag or collection you want to keep from those listed in the dialog box that appears and click **OK**. Items that use the tags or collections you didn't keep are assigned the tag or collection you did keep.

3 Click Delete

1 Click Tags or Collections Tab

2 Select Marker, Category, or Group to Delete

4 View the Result

Marker Is Removed from Associated Items

Marker Is Removed from Organize Bin

29 Change a Marker's Icon

The first time you assign a new marker to an image, that image is used as the marker's icon in the **Organize Bin**. Choose carefully when making this initial assignment; by selecting a meaningful image to act as the marker's icon, you might find it easier to locate the icon on the **Organize Bin** when you decide to assign it to other images and media files later on.

Regardless of how careful you are, you might discover an image later on that better exemplifies the meaning of the marker. If that happens, follow the steps in this task to select a different image to act as a marker's icon.

1 Click Tags or Collections Tab

If you want to change the icon associated with a *tag*, in the *Organizer*, click the **Tags** tab on the **Organize Bin**. To change the icon associated with a *collection* marker, click the **Collections** tab instead.

2 Select Marker

In the **Organize Bin**, click the marker whose icon you want to change. The selected marker is highlighted.

3 Click Edit Button

Click the **Edit** button located at the top of the **Organize Bin** (it looks like a pencil). The **Edit Tag** or **Edit Collection** dialog box appears.

4 Click Edit Icon Button

Click the **Edit Icon** button in the dialog box. The **Edit Tag Icon** or **Edit Collection Icon** dialog box appears.

5 Scroll to Find Image

The number of images currently using the selected marker appears just below the image in the dialog box. Click the left and right arrows on either side of the **Find** button to scroll through each associated image and select the one you want.

Before You Begin

✔ **26** Create a Tag or Collection Marker

See Also

→ **27** Attach a Marker to an Item

→ **28** Delete a Marker, Category, or Group

→ **30** Change a Marker's Category, Group, Name, or Note

🖊 NOTE

To change the color that appears above an image on a tag icon, change the color associated with the category to which that tag belongs. Select the category, click the **Edit** button (it looks like a pencil), and then click **Choose Color** to select the tag color you want to use for that category.

💡 TIPS

The image icon is not the only thing that can help you select the right marker for a media file. You might use a marker's description (its note), for example. If a marker's note, name, group, or category is not as descriptive as it should be, you can change it. See **30** Change a Marker's Category, Group, Name, or Note.

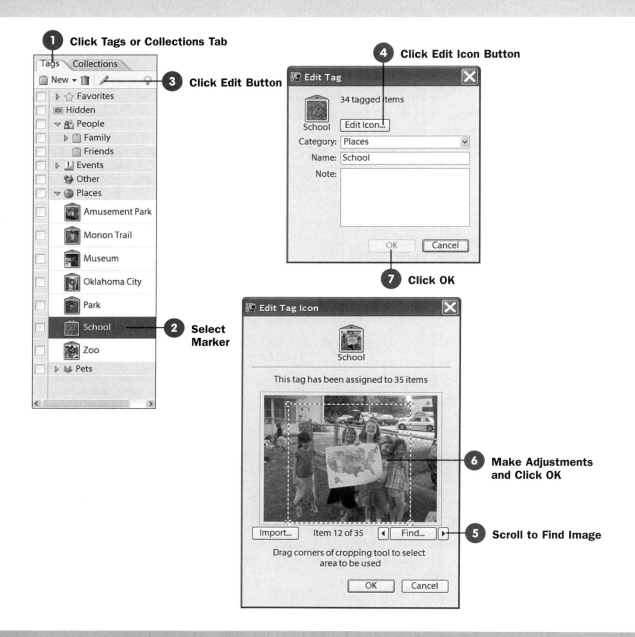

1 Click Tags or Collections Tab

3 Click Edit Button

2 Select Marker

4 Click Edit Icon Button

7 Click OK

6 Make Adjustments and Click OK

5 Scroll to Find Image

If you want to see the images together so that you can select your favorite for use as an icon, click the **Find** button instead of the arrow buttons. The **Select Icon** dialog box appears. All the items currently associated with the selected marker appear together in this dialog box. Just click the one you want to use and click **OK** to return to the **Edit Tag Icon** or **Edit Collection Icon** dialog box.

6 Make Adjustments and Click OK

You can use only a selected portion of the image as the icon if you like. Just drag the corner of the white cropping border to adjust the size of the area that will be used as the icon. Click in the middle of the cropping border and drag to adjust its position on the image. When you're through, click **OK** to close the **Edit Tag Icon** or **Edit Collection Icon** dialog box and complete the selection of the new icon.

The cropped portion of the image you've selected appears as the marker's new icon in the **Organize Bin**. (The actual image in the catalog is unaffected.)

TIP

To change the size of the icon that appears on the **Tags** tab of the **Organize Bin**, choose **Edit, Preferences, Tags and Collections**. Then select a size from the **Tag Display** pane. This selection does not affect the icons on the **Collections** tab of the **Organize Bin**, which cannot be adjusted.

NOTE

If none of the currently matching images makes a great icon, you can import an image or a piece of clip art for that purpose. Click **Import**, select an image file from your computer or network, and click **Open**. This image is not imported into the catalog, but it does replace the current icon for that marker.

---

30 Change a Marker's Category, Group, Name, or Note

As you learned in **26 Create a Tag or Collection Marker**, when you create a new marker for organizing items, you give that marker a name and select the category/group or subcategory/subgroup to which you want it assigned. You're also given a chance to add a description (a note) to help you remember the marker's purpose at a later date. In the computer world, things are rarely permanent, and markers are no exception. If they don't prove as easy to use as you might have thought, you can change a marker's name, category, group, or description at any time by following the steps in this task.

Before You Begin

✔ **26** Create a Tag or Collection Marker

See Also

→ **29** Change a Marker's Icon

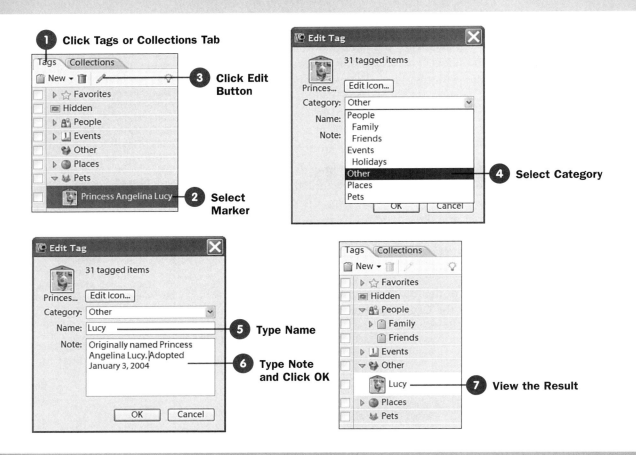

1 Click Tags or Collections Tab

3 Click Edit Button

2 Select Marker

4 Select Category

5 Type Name

6 Type Note and Click OK

7 View the Result

NOTE

You can follow these same steps to change a category or group on the **Organize Bin**. You can change the name, tag color, category icon, and parent category or group to which a subcategory or subgroup belongs. Just select the category or group, click the **Edit** button (it looks like a pencil), make your changes, and click **OK**.

1 Click Tags or Collections Tab

If you want to change a *tag*, in the *Organizer*, click the **Tags** tab on the **Organize Bin**. To change a *collection* marker, click the **Collections** tab instead.

2 Select Marker

In the **Organize Bin**, click the marker whose details you want to change. The selected marker is highlighted.

③ Click Edit Button

Click the **Edit** button located at the top of the **Organize Bin** (it looks like a pencil). The **Edit Tag** or **Edit Collection** dialog box appears.

④ Select Category

In the dialog box, you should change only the things that are wrong. If you want, open the **Category** or **Group** drop-down list and select a different category or group to which you want the marker to belong.

⑤ Type Name

If you want, select the marker's name in the **Name** text box and type a replacement name.

⑥ Type Note and Click OK

If you want, type a replacement description in the **Note** text box, or simply edit the existing description. When you're through making changes, click **OK**.

⑦ View the Result

The marker's name, category, group, and note are changed immediately. These changes, except for the note, appear in the **Organize Bin** and the **Tags** tab of the **Properties** pane (the optional note appears only in the **Edit Tag** and **Edit Collection** dialog box).

I had a tag marker called **Princess Angelina Lucy**, the name my daughter gave our new kitten. Eventually, the cat's name was shortened to just Lucy, so I changed the name on the marker. The shorter name was also easier to read on the **Organize Bin**. While changing the tag name, I decided to change the category as well. Because we have only one pet so far, it didn't make sense to have a **Pets** category. So, I moved the **Lucy** tag into the **Other** category. Next, I'll remove the unused **Pets** category as well.

◤ NOTES

To change a tag into a sub-category, right-click the tag and select **Change XX tag to a sub-category**. To change a subcategory into a tag, right-click it and select **Change XX sub-category to a tag**.

If you want to change the image that appears on a marker's icon in the **Organize Bin**, see **29** **Change a Marker's Icon**.

◤ NOTE

It's easy to delete a category or group you no longer need. See **28** **Delete a Marker, Category, or Group**.

31 Add a Text Caption or Note

See Also

→ **32** Add an Audio Caption

→ **37** Find Items with the Same Caption or Note

TIPS

When searching for a particular image, you can search for text contained in its filename, caption, or note. So, adding captions and notes also helps you locate images. See **37** Find Items with the Same Caption or Note.

To add the same caption to several images at once, select the images, and then choose **Edit, Add Caption to Selected Items** from the menu. Type your caption in the **Caption** box in the dialog box that appears, select **Replace Existing Captions** (if you don't select this option, existing captions are not replaced), and then click **OK**.

Although this task explains how to add captions while in **Photo Browser** view, you can also add captions while viewing images in **Date View**. Just use the calendar in **Date View** to locate an image, and then click the **Day View** button to display the image in a larger view where you can enter its caption.

With a text *caption*, you can provide a title for your "works of art" (your photographs). An image's caption appears in the photo well when you display the image using **Single Photo** view, and below each image in a *photo review* (see **16** Review Images). Captions also appear on the **General** tab of the **Properties** pane whenever it is displayed. Although having a caption appear beneath a photo while you're reviewing images in the *Organizer* can be fun, there is a serious purpose to all this work. After you've entered captions for your images, the captions can be made to appear in various *creations*, such as a slideshow, photo album, video CD, calendar, or Web Photo Gallery.

For longer descriptions or stories about an image, you can enter a note. Notes do not appear in the photo well, but only within the **Properties** pane. Do not confuse these notes, however, with the **Daily Notes** section displayed in **Date View** in both the **Month** and **Day** views. Daily notes are used to record a general description of the day's activities, making it easier for you to locate a specific group of images you might be looking for. See **38** Find Items with the Same Date.

1 Select Image

In the Organizer, click the image in the photo well to which you want to add a caption. The selected image appears with a blue border around it (unless you're using **Single Photo** view).

2 Display Properties Pane

If it's not already displayed, click the **Show or Hide Properties** button on the **Options** bar to display the **Properties** pane. You can also choose **Window, Properties** from the menu.

To display the **Properties** pane below the **Organize Bin**, choose **Window, Dock Properties in Organize Bin** first, and then choose **Windows, Properties**.

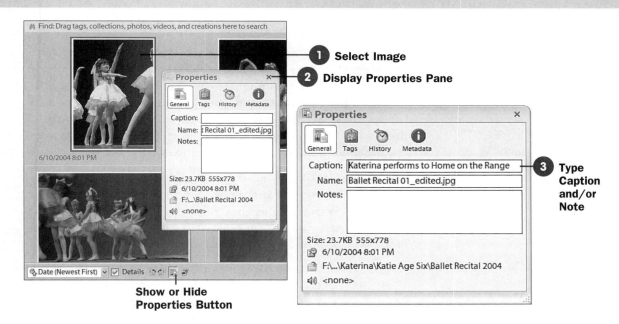

Select Image

Display Properties Pane

Type Caption and/or Note

Show or Hide Properties Button

View the Result

③ Type Caption and/or Note

If it's not already selected, click the **General** button at the top of the **Properties** pane to display the contents of the **General** tab. Then click in the **Caption** text box and type your caption, such as **Alyce on Big Bear Mountain, July 2004** or **We watched the rain under the protection of a large maple tree**. Your caption can include up to 200 characters, including spaces, but you'll want to keep it short so it displays fully onscreen and in creations.

You can make searches easier later on by using specific, easy-to-remember keywords in your notes and captions. For example, if you often search for funny shots for use in your greeting cards, you could use the keyword *funny* or *goofy* in your image notes or captions to help you locate those shots when you need them.

Longer descriptions can be typed in the **Notes** section if you like. Close the **Properties** pane by clicking the **X** button in the upper-right corner of the pane or clicking the **Show or Hide Properties** button on the **Options** bar.

You can also enter text captions when an image is displayed in **Single Photo** view. Double-click an image in the photo well to display it in **Single Photo** view. Click where it says **Click here to add caption**, type a caption, and press **Enter**.

④ View the Result

Notes can only be seen in the **Properties** pane, and they are not used in creations. To view an image's caption, change to **Single Photo** view by double-clicking the image in the photo well or by clicking the **Single Photo View** button on the **Options** bar.

Here I added a caption to my daughter's recital photo so that I would remember the name of the song she performed to. Because I was also planning on using this photo in my annual calendar, the caption served a dual purpose. To view the entire caption as I was entering it, I resized the **Properties** pane (by dragging its border) to make it wider.

TIP

You can delete a text caption from either the **Caption** text box in the **Properties** pane, or from **Single Photo** view. Click the caption and then use the mouse to highlight the entire caption. Press **Delete** to remove the caption.

32 Add an Audio Caption

Information about an image doesn't have to be stored as text, as you learned in **31** **Add a Text Caption or Note**. It can be stored instead as audio, in an *audio caption* attached to an image. After an audio caption has been recorded for an image, you can click the special audio caption icon that appears on the image's *thumbnail* to listen to its contents.

If you copy images onto a disc as described in **15** **Copy Items onto a CD-ROM or DVD**, any audio captions attached to those images are copied as well. If you give the resulting disc to a friend or relative, that person can play the audio file (it's stored in **.WAV** format) using a compatible audio program and listen to any comments you might have had about the images. In addition, if you use an image with an audio caption in a slideshow or VCD, you can include the audio caption as well.

❶ Display Image in Single Photo View

In the Organizer, in the photo well, click the image to which you want to add an audio caption, and then click the **Single Photo View** button on the **Options** bar to display it in **Single Photo** view.

❷ Click Record Audio Caption Button

Click the **Record Audio Caption** button located below the image (it looks like a speaker with sound waves coming out of it). The **Select Audio File** dialog box appears.

❸ Begin Recording

When you're ready to begin recording, click the **Record** button. Speak into the microphone.

See Also

→ **21** Play an Audio File
→ **31** Add a Text Caption or Note

⟍**K**EY TERM

Audio caption—Recorded description of an image, created in the *Organizer* and then associated with the image.

◥**NOTES**

To record an audio caption, your computer must be equipped with a microphone.

You can also create an audio recording by selecting an image, displaying the **Properties** pane, and clicking the **Add or change audio caption** button on the **General** tab.

⍭ TIP

You can attach an existing audio file in **MP3**, **WAV**, or **WMA** format to the selected image, rather than recording one now. Just choose **File**, **Browse** in the **Select Audio File** dialog box, select the audio file you want to use, and click **OK**.

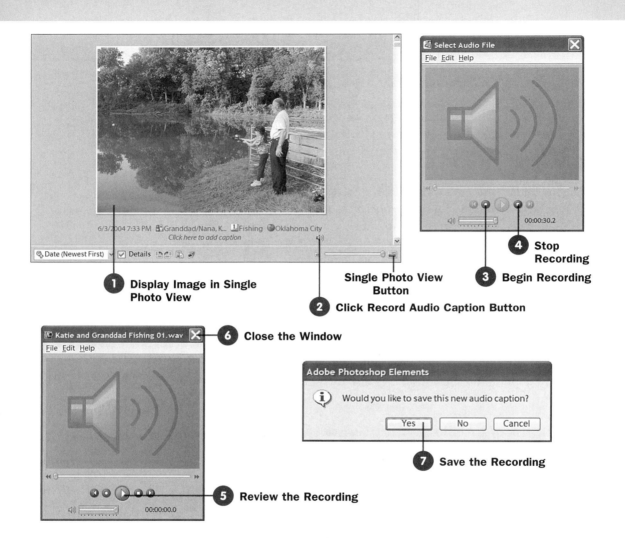

1 Display Image in Single Photo View

2 Click Record Audio Caption Button

Single Photo View Button

3 Begin Recording

4 Stop Recording

6 Close the Window

5 Review the Recording

7 Save the Recording

4 Stop Recording

When you are done recording your audio annotation, click the **Stop** button to stop the recording. The file is immediately saved in .WAV format (in the \My Pictures\Adobe\Audio Captions folder), using the image's filename as the base for the audio file's filename. At this point, the **Select Audio File** dialog box becomes the **Media Player**. The audio filename appears on the title bar of the **Media Player**, and its controls become active. For example, here, my annotation was saved to the file **Katie and Granddad Fishing 01.wav** because the image I selected for annotation was called **Katie and Granddad Fishing 01.jpg**.

This audio filename, by the way, will not change if you later change the image filename, but it will remain associated with that image so you'll still be able to play it.

⑤ Review the Recording

Click the **Play** button and listen to the recording. If you don't like what you've recorded, you can't really edit it, but you can record something else entirely by repeating steps 2, 3, and 4.

⑥ Close the Window

When you're satisfied with the recording, click the **Close** button (the **X** in the upper-right corner) to close the **Media Player** window.

⑦ Save the Recording

The Organizer displays a prompt asking whether you want to save the recording; click **Yes**. The Organizer attaches the recording to the image. (If you click **No**, the recording is not attached, and it's discarded.)

After an audio caption has been attached to an image, a special icon (a sound horn) appears on the image's thumbnail in the photo well; to listen to the audio caption, display the image in **Single Photo** view and click the **Record Audio Caption** button to redisplay the **Media Player**. If the **Properties** pane is displayed, you can play an audio caption by clicking its **General** tab and then clicking the **Add or change audio caption** button.

TIP

For help in using the other buttons in the **Media Player** window, see **21** Play an Audio File.

TIP

You can attach a text or audio caption to any item in the catalog. This includes creations, such as calendars and slide shows. These captions don't change the content of your creations, but they can help you record the purpose you had in mind for them, or any notes or reminders you want to remember about creations in progress.

5

Finding Images, Movies, and Audio Files

IN THIS CHAPTER:

33 About Finding Items in the Catalog

34 Find Items with the Same Marker

35 Find Items of the Same Media Type

36 Find Items with Similar Filenames

37 Find Items with the Same Caption or Note

38 Find Items with the Same Date

39 Find Items Within a Date Range

40 Find Items with the Same History

41 Find Images with Similar Color

42 Hide Items You Don't Generally Use

You'll know your digital photos, audio files, and movies are truly and properly organized when you're able to quickly locate any item in the *catalog* without struggling to recall its exact filename or the folder you saved it in. If you had to organize photographs, movies, and audio files with Windows alone, you'd probably create an organized system of folders, and then attempt to save each file in an appropriate folder. This limited method of organization quickly leads to all sorts of problems. Suppose that you have a photo of your two kids seated with their granddad and uncle beneath the Christmas tree. Do you file the image in the **Christmas** folder? Or in the **Kids**, **Granddad**, or **Uncle** folder? Or do you place multiple copies of the image in several folders, wasting disk space?

With the *Organizer*, you don't have to depend on a series of Windows folders to help you organize your media files. As you learned in **27** **Attach a Marker to an Item**, you can assign various *collection* or *tag* markers to an item, enabling you to locate it in multiple ways. For example, you could assign the **Christmas**, **Granddad**, **Uncle**, and **Kids** tags to the holiday snapshot, and locate it later on by searching for items with that unique combination of tags. Or you could assign a **Photo Album** collection marker to your favorite images in that group, and recall them quickly for use in a new photo album *creation*. Because you're using the Organizer to categorize images and other media files, you can store all of them in the **My Pictures** folder if you like, rather than creating separate folders for various groups. You can even store media files *offline*, on CD-ROMs or DVDs. The Organizer doesn't care where files are located; it can organize them all easily.

By the way, tag and collection markers aren't the only things you can use to locate an image or other file, as you'll discover in this chapter. You can also search for media files based on *file date*, filename, caption, note, change history, color range, and other criteria. With the Organizer and a little bit of work initially marking and captioning items, you can locate any one or any group of photos, audio files, or movies with the people you want, in the scene you want, at the time you want, without any fuss or difficulty.

33 About Finding Items in the Catalog

If you take full advantage of the power and potential of digital photography, before very long, the *Organizer catalog* will be filled with thousands of photographs. In addition, your catalog may also contain a lot of digital video, audio files, and *creations*. As you learned in **24** About Organizing Items, you don't have to store all those thousands of media files on your hard drive unless you want to. You can choose to offload your media files onto CD-R or writeable DVD media, and still include those *offline* items in the Organizer catalog. So, regardless of where items are stored, if they are in the catalog, they can be easy to find and use when needed. By the way, if you decide to edit an offline item or use it in a *creation*, the Organizer will tell you which disc to insert in your optical drive so that it can access the proper file.

Just because your catalog may have countless rows of *thumbnails* does not mean that it is less manageable, or that your media files are more difficult to find than when you had only a few dozen thumbnails to contend with. After each image file has been imported, the catalog automatically begins tracking that image's filename, location, *file date*, and file type, along with the Exchangeable Image File (*EXIF*) data that your camera/scanner stored in the file when the image was shot or scanned. If you import an audio or movie file, its filename, location, file date, and file type are tracked too. So, without doing any work other than importing a media file, you can locate an item immediately if you know any of its file data.

The true organizational magic begins, however, when you associate any number of markers to the items in the catalog. The markers enable you to keep track of what's important about a particular item—for instance, whether it's a holiday, party, or other special event, or whether the shot was taken indoors or outdoors. You can add notes and captions to your catalog items, making it even easier to locate a particular media file when needed. See **31** Add a Text Caption or Note and **27** Attach a Marker to an Item for more information.

If you make any changes to a digital image file *and* you start the editing process through the Organizer, the program will keep track of *when* these changes occurred. This is true whether you use the Organizer's Auto Fix tool, the *Editor's* tools, or some other *graphics editor* such as Photoshop

Before You Begin

✔ **24** About Organizing Items

 TIP

Because your catalog contains a listing of all your media files, markers, notes, captions, and other organizational information such as offline disc location, you wouldn't want to ever lose it. So, protect your catalog by backing it up from time to time. This process backs up your actual media files too. See **14** Back Up the Organizer Catalog.

KEY TERM

EXIF (Exchangeable Image File)—Data attached to a photo file that contains the key settings the camera used when the photo was shot. This data typically includes the resolution, color gamut (color range), image size, compression, shutter speed, and f-stop. An EXIF-aware application such as Photoshop Elements can use this data to adjust the image so that it appears, when displayed or printed, as closely to the way the image looked when shot as possible. Other programs, such as Photoshop and Adobe Acrobat, can amend the EXIF data to include tags and copyright information; these tags can be read by Photoshop Elements and imported into the Organizer with the image.

NOTES

EXIF data such as image resolution will not be saved in a scanned image if you use Microsoft Office Document Imaging to perform the scan. It's best to use the software that came with the scanner. In addition, some scanners might not be capable of recording EXIF data—see the scanner documentation.

You can add multiple tags to the **Find** bar and see just the items with all the tags, just one of them, or none of them, depending on other options you choose. You cannot, however, mix tag and collection markers on the **Find** bar to create a unique search, nor can you use more than one collection marker on the **Find** bar at a time.

or Paint Shop Pro to make the changes. This makes it possible for you to search for "the family photo I edited last month." If you include a photo in a card, photo album, or slideshow, the Organizer will keep track of that fact as well, enabling you to search for just the images or other media files used in creations. (See **35** **Find Items of the Same Media Type**.)

Because the Organizer keeps track of so much, finding the file you want is simple. For example, by dragging a marker to the **Find** bar, you can display only the photos, audio, movie files, and creations with that marker. See **34** **Find Items with the Same Marker**. Get a closer look at this photo in the Color Gallery.

Find Bar   Organize Bin

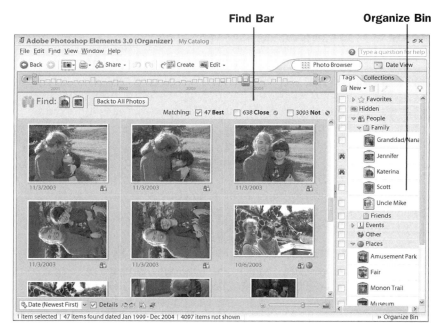

After marking the items in the catalog, you can easily locate media files with similar characteristics, such as images that include your wife and daughter.

Here are some of the other types of searches made possible by the Organizer:

- You can quickly display only audio files, home movies, or creations. See **35** **Find Items of the Same Media Type**.

- You can have the catalog show only those photos, audio, movie files, or creations that were shot or created on a particular day, or during a particular *range* of time—say, the last weekend of October. See **38** **Find Items with the Same Date** and **39** **Find Items Within a Date Range**.

- If you wrote a caption or description (note) about an image, and you remember just a single key word or phrase from that description (for instance, *Walt Disney World* or *wedding reception*), you can retrieve the photo based on that text alone. See **37** **Find Items with the Same Caption or Note**.

- Using the history stored on each item in the catalog, you can locate images you might have emailed or received, ordered prints for or shared through an *online service*, printed at home, or used in a creation. See **40** **Find Items with the Same History**.

- If you can find a photo in the catalog that looks pretty similar to the image you're actually looking for, but you know it's not the one you want, you can have the Organizer retrieve all photos in the catalog that have a similar disposition of colors. Perhaps, for instance, you've found a picture of your spouse wearing the same sweater as she is wearing in the photo you want. There's a chance that the Organizer could retrieve similarly lit photos where your spouse is wearing that sweater. See **41** **Find Images with Similar Color**.

Understand the Find Bar

Just above the photo well in the *Organizer* window is a long bar marked with a binoculars icon. It's called the **Find** bar. You don't need to worry about displaying the **Find** bar, even if you're not currently searching for particular items, because it's always there. Whenever you have a search in progress, however, the **Find** bar shows you the different criteria—the markers, notes, or *captions* you're searching for—that each item in the well currently matches. If you're searching for items with certain *collection* or *tag* markers, those markers appear in the **Find** bar. If you're looking for the photos you used in a particular slideshow, the **Find** bar reads **Used in** along with the name of that slideshow. If you're looking for only those items to which you've attached *audio captions* (see **35** **Find Items of the Same Media Type**), the **Find** bar reads **Items with Audio Captions**.

TIP

You can make searches easier by using specific, easy-to-remember keywords in your notes and captions. For example, if you often search for funny shots for use in your greeting cards, you could use the keyword *funny* or *goofy* in your image notes or captions to help you locate those shots when you need them.

NOTES

You cannot mix and match different types of searches. For example, if you're searching for items that contain one or more tags, and you begin a search for items you emailed to someone or that you included in a slideshow, the Organizer clears the current search by tags and processes your search by email or slideshow request as a new search.

Whenever the **Find** bar displays some markers or other search criteria, some type of filtering is going on. For you, this means that not all your media files are currently visible—instead, only those items matching the criteria shown on the **Find** bar are currently displayed. To redisplay all items in the *catalog*, click the **Back to All Photos** button on the **Find** bar.

*The **Find** bar shows you the criteria for the currently displayed items.*

One exception to this functionality deals with when you're searching for media files created during a particular period of time. In that case, the **Timeline** at the top of the window narrows itself to represent the range of time you've chosen, and the **Find** bar displays no search criteria at all. See **39 Find Items Within a Date Range** to learn how such a search works.

TIP

You can review the results of a previous search by clicking the **Back** button on the **Shortcuts** bar. You can return to the current search by clicking the **Forward** button.

You can add criteria to the **Find** bar to narrow a search. For example, you can start with one tag such as **Birthday** and then add another tag such as **Ramona** to display only Ramona's birthday photos, audio, movie files, and creations using those files. Instead of adding another tag to the search, you can exclude a tag from the search results. For example, you can tell the Organizer to display all the **Birthday** images that *do not include* **Ramona**. You clear that search and use the collection marker, **Funny Moments**, to help you locate the photo of Ramona throwing water on the Wicked Witch of the West at her Dorothy party, and hitting you instead. If you mean to start a new search, and there's already a search in progress, it's best to clear the **Find** bar of its current criteria first. To do that, just click the **Back to All Photos** button on the **Find** bar. This also resets the photo well so that all items in the catalog are displayed.

When there's an active search in progress, the **Find** bar displays the number of matches and non-matches. After you perform a search, the matching items are displayed in the photo well, and a check mark appears next to the **XX Best** box on the **Find** bar (where XX represents the number of exact matches to all your criteria). To show those items that *do not match* the criteria in the **Find** bar, enable the **XX Not** check box (where XX represents the number of items that do not match the criteria). With both boxes selected, the photo well will display *all the items* *in the catalog*, but on the non-matches it will show a red **Not** icon (a circle with a slash) similar to the one on the **Find** bar. Matches won't have this icon.

*You can control the display of matches, non-matches, and partial matches using the **Find** bar.*

To have the photo well show only items that do *not* match the search criteria, you must *uncheck* the **XX Best** check box and enable only the **XX Not** check box. After you do this, all the items in the photo well feature the red **Not** icon. You could use the **XX Not** option, for example, to help you search for photos that *do not include* your son.

In a situation where there's more than one marker in the **Find** bar, only items with *all* the selected markers are displayed. You can, if you want, display items that have at least one of the markers but not all of them by selecting only the **XX Close** check box. Items that meet this special condition are adorned with a blue check mark **Close** icon. You can have the photo well show items that are both partial *and* complete matches by enabling both the **XX Best** and **XX Close** check boxes in the **Find** bar and by leaving the **XX Not** check box disabled.

TIP

If you always want to display both matching and closely matching items when you conduct a new search, choose **Edit, Preferences** and select the **General** tab. Select the **Show Closely Matching Sets for Searches** option and click **OK**.

34 Find Items with the Same Marker

The payoff of using *tags* or *collection* markers to help catalog your digital photos and other media files is that they can help you can find specific items quickly and easily. There are several different methods you can use to tell the *Organizer* which tag or collection markers are attached to the items you're looking for. After the Organizer knows the markers you're interested in, it searches the *catalog* for items that have those markers attached and displays them in the photo well.

Before You Begin

✔ **27** Attach a Marker to an Item

✔ **33** About Finding Items in the Catalog

1 Drag the Marker to the Find Bar

3 Add More Search Criteria

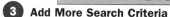

2 Or Click the Marker to Search For

When selecting a marker to use in searching for a particular set of media files, keep in mind that if you select a category, subcategory, group, or subgroup marker, you automatically include all the tag or collection markers within that category/group or subcategory/subgroup as well. Although these extra markers won't appear on the **Find** bar, they are included by implication. For example, if you place the **Events** tag on the **Find** bar, items tagged with the **Events** category tag *plus* any items tagged with a specific **Events** tag such as **Family Reunion** or **Fourth of July** will also appear in the photo well.

Another thing you need to keep in mind when making your selection for a search is that you cannot combine tags and collection markers in a single search. In addition, you can specify only *one* collection marker to use in a search at a time.

❶ Drag the Marker to the Find Bar

One method for displaying specific items is to drag the applicable tags or collection markers to the **Find** bar. In the Organizer, on the **Organize Bin**, click either the **Tags** or **Collections** tab. Then open the applicable category/group and subcategory/subgroup to locate the marker associated with the items you want to locate. Click the right-arrow beside a category/group name to open it. For example, if you want to search for photos, movies, or creations containing a certain person, or audio files of a particular person's voice, click the right arrow in front of the **People** category to display its tags.

Click and hold the marker representing the items you want to search for. Drag this marker to the **Find** bar and drop it. In a moment, the **Find** bar displays the marker next to the words **Search Criteria**.

❷ Or Click the Marker to Search For

Another method for displaying marked items is to select particular markers from the list in the **Organize Bin**. In the **Organize Bin**, first click either the **Tags** or **Collections** tab to display those markers. Then click the small box to the left of the marker you want your items to match, *or* double-click the marker itself. A binoculars icon appears in the box, and the marker appears in the **Find** bar.

NOTES

You'll have to display the **Organize Bin** to complete this task. If it's not currently showing, select **Window, Organize Bin** from the menu or click the Organize Bin button on the Status bar to display it.

After displaying the items in a single collection, you can reorder the items by dragging them within the collection. Items in a collection, when displayed as a group, appear with a number icon denoting their position within that group. By dragging an item to a different place within the collection group, you change that item's number icon and its position within the group.

You can display closely matching or non-matching items by choosing those options on the **Find** bar. For example, to display items that use any one of the tags but not all of them, select the **XX Close** check box in the **Find** bar.

TIPS

To quickly display items that do not yet have any markers associated with them, select **Find, Untagged Items.**

To exclude items with a particular a tag from an existing search, right-click that tag in the **Organize Bin** and select **Exclude photos with XX tag from search results** from the context menu.

3 Add More Search Criteria

At this point, only items with the selected marker appear in the photo well. To search for items that have multiple tags, simply click the box in front of additional tags in **the Organize Bin** to add those tags to the search criteria, or drag more tags from the **Organize Bin** to the **Find** bar. Only items that match *all the tags* are shown in the photo well.

You cannot search for items with multiple collection markers, or a combination of tag markers and a collection marker. Attempting to do either of these things resets the search criteria. To redisplay all items, click the **Back to All Photos** button on the **Find** bar.

 Find Items of the Same Media Type

Before You Begin

✔ **33** About Finding Items in the Catalog

See Also

→ **32** Add an Audio Caption

The three types of files you can import into the photo well are digital, scanned, or created images (of course), video files, and audio files. There are several file formats for each type, which Windows distinguishes from one another using a filename extension such as **.JPG** or **.JPEG** for images using the Joint Photographic Experts Group format or **.WAV** for audio files using WAVE format.

The *Organizer* is not concerned with file formats, however—only the types of media the files contain: photos, audio, or video. In this task, you learn how to display items in the *catalog* based on their media type—audio files for example. If you want to locate items by file type (such as JPG, GIF, or TIFF), search for that part of their filename (for example, search for items with **JPG** or **JPEG** as part of their filename as explained in **36 Find Items with Similar Filenames**).

The Organizer also includes in its catalog items you create using the program, such as slideshows and greeting cards. When you need to, you can have the photo well show only your *creations* (slideshows, photo albums, cards, and so on). Of course, the entire creation won't be displayed in the photo well (most of them contain multiple pages), but the first page of each one will appear as its *thumbnail*. You can also search for items (regardless of media type) that have an *audio caption* attached to them. You might do this, for example, to review the images you've annotated with audio.

NOTE

By default, the photo well does not show thumbnails representing audio files, although they can be imported into the catalog. To show audio tracks as blue speaker icons along with all your other image and movie thumbnails, select **View, Media Types**; from the dialog box that opens, enable the **Audio** check box and click **OK.**

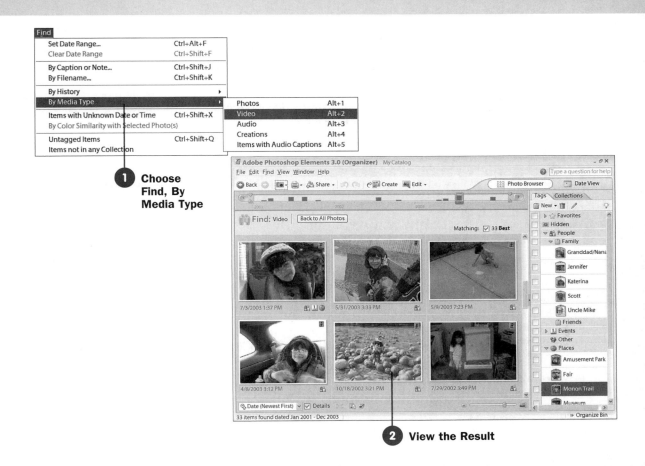

1 Choose
Find, By
Media Type

2 View the Result

---

1 Choose Find, By Media Type

In the Organizer, choose **Find, By Media Type** from the menu. From the submenu that appears, select the type of item you want to display: **Photos**, **Video**, **Audio**, **Creations**, or **Items with Audio Captions**.

2 View the Result

Here, I selected **Video** from the **By Media Type** submenu. The photo well displays only the movie files in my catalog. Notice the

NOTE

If you selected **Audio** from the **By Media Type** submenu in step 1, you might see a warning box telling you audio files (which are not normally displayed), will be displayed *now*. Click **OK** to continue. When you clear the search results, the audio files will no longer be included in the display unless you've changed your viewing options as explained in the margin note.

TIP

To redisplay all files, click the **Back to All Photos** button on the **Find** bar.

small movie icon in the upper-right corner of each thumbnail, which tells me that these are movie files. Notice also that the **Find** bar displays the words, **Find: Video**, which let you know that only video files are currently displayed.

To play a particular video, double-click the thumbnail. See ㉒ **View a Video** for help.

Find Items with Similar Filenames

Before You Begin

✔ ㉝ About Finding Items in the Catalog

NOTES

You can also search for letters in the filename extension. For example, to locate all images saved in TIFF format, enter the search text **.tif**, which will match images that use either the **.TIFF** or **.TIF** extension. Notice that, unlike searches you might conduct in other programs where you must enter an asterisk before the filename extension (for example, ***.tif**), you do not use asterisks here.

You can't search for a creation based on its filename because it doesn't have one—creations exist only within the catalog and not as separate files (at least, not until you save them manually as a PDF, if you do that). You can add a caption, note, or marker to help you search for a particular creation. See ㉗ **Attach a Marker to an Item** and ㉛ **Add a Text Caption or Note**.

If you know something about the filename of the media file(s) you're looking for, but you're not quite sure of the actual filename, you might still be able to locate the file. You simply type a bit of text, and if the filename of any item in the *catalog* contains those same characters (in uppercase or lowercase), in the order in which you entered them, the photo well will display the *thumbnail* for that item.

For example, if you know that an image has the word *spring* in its name, you can search for the text **spring** and get a list of items that contain that text, such as **Spring 2003-01**, **Jim's springer spaniel**, **Katie's spring recital**, and so on.

① Choose Find, By Filename

In the *Organizer*, select **Find, By Filename** from the menu bar. The **Find by Filename** dialog box appears.

② Enter Search Text and Click OK

Type the portion of the filename you know in the **Find items with filename containing** box. For example, type **jan** to search for files such as **January Snow**, **Jan's new car**, and **janyce 02**. The text you enter here is not case sensitive, nor does it have to be a complete word. If you typed **Erin**, for example, files whose names include **Katerina** are considered matches because the word *Katerina* contains the characters *erin*. Click **OK**.

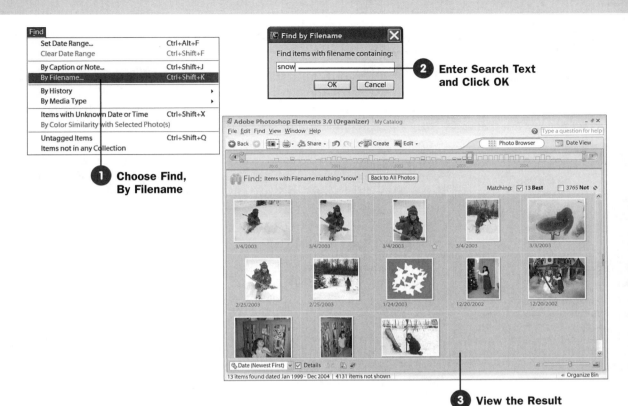

**Choose Find,
By Filename**

2 **Enter Search Text
and Click OK**

3 **View the Result**

3 **View the Result**

In a moment, the photo well displays only those items whose file-names include the text you entered *somewhere* in the filename or file extension. Here, I typed the word *snow* in the text box and the Organizer displayed several photos, videos, and audio files whose names contained those letters. I got quite a variety of items as a result of my search, including a scan of a snowflake my daughter made, several photos from a Christmas card with a snowy scene, a squirrel in the snow, and an old photo of me building a snow fort. Notice that the **Find** bar displays the search criteria. To redisplay all items in the photo well, click the **Back to All Photos** button on the **Find** bar.

TIP

To search for items that contain a particular word or words in their caption or note, see **37** **Find Items with the Same Caption or Note.**

37 Find Items with the Same Caption or Note

Before You Begin

✔ **24** About Organizing Items

✔ **31** Add a Text Caption or Note

✔ **33** About Finding Items in the Catalog

NOTE

The Organizer searches *both* captions and notes for matches to the text you supply. You cannot instruct the program to search only through one or the other.

NOTE

The search is not case sensitive, so don't worry about that when entering the search text.

Ideally, the best way to ensure that items are easily located by category is to use *tag* or *collection* markers to group items, and then to search for items using those markers. However, markers might not tell the whole story about an image, audio file, movie, or creation. Every item in the *catalog* can be annotated by way of its own note, which is a textual notation of up to 1,023 characters. Notes for an item appear in the **Properties** pane and can consist of any extra description that helps you recall the subject matter or purpose of a particular item. If your catalog contains scans of printed photos bound in albums, for instance, you could use item notes to store the identity and location of the album to which each scanned photo belongs.

Cataloged media files can also contain text *captions*. A caption appears below an item in **Single Photo View**, and captions can be made to appear in various creations under each image or movie. If using markers to locate a particular item is not working for you, you can have the *Organizer* search for any passage or bit of text you might have used in an item's caption or note.

1 **Choose Find, By Caption or Note**

In the Organizer, select **Find, By Caption or Note** from the menu bar. The **Find by Caption or Note** dialog box appears.

2 **Enter Text to Search For**

Type the known portion of the caption or note you want to search for in the **Find items with caption or note** box. The Organizer will search *both* captions and notes for this text.

3 **Choose How Matches Are Determined and Click OK**

Select the **Match only the beginning of words in Captions and Notes** option to make the Organizer search for the text you enter at the *beginning* of words only. For example, the search text **Erin** will not match the word *Katerina*. Selecting this option might speed up the search process.

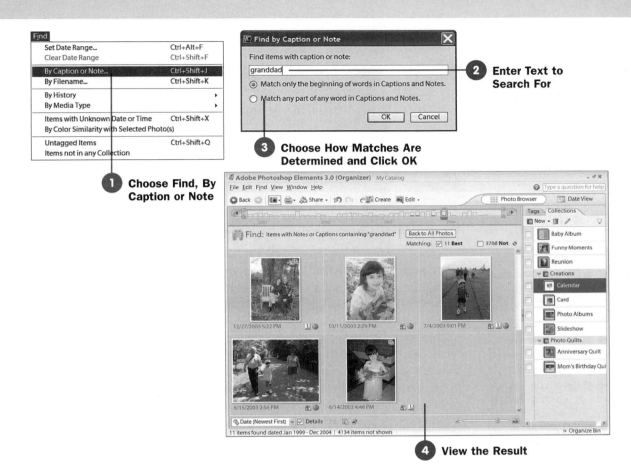

① Choose Find, By Caption or Note

② Enter Text to Search For

③ Choose How Matches Are Determined and Click OK

④ View the Result

To search for matches throughout all characters (and not just those at the beginning of words), select the **Match any part of any word in Captions and Notes** option. With this option selected, the search text **Erin** does match the word *Katerina*. Click **OK** to begin the search process.

④ View the Result

In a moment, the photo well displays only those items that match the search criteria. I needed to locate an image of my daughter

NOTE

The Organizer has no tools for searching through the contents of an audio caption. However, you can search exclusively for items that have audio captions attached to them, as explained in **35** Find Items of the Same Media Type.

skating at a park one day while we were visiting her granddad. The image had apparently been tagged only with her tag and not Granddad's, which I discovered after a search using both their tags and just his tag didn't produce the results I wanted, and a search using her tag alone resulted in too large a listing to browse through. So, I searched the notes and captions for any item that contained the word *granddad*, and came up with several matches, including the photo I was looking for.

38 Find Items with the Same Date

Before You Begin

✔ **33** About Finding Items in the Catalog

See Also

→ **18** Sort Items

→ **23** Change Image Date and Time

→ **39** Find Items Within a Date Range

NOTE

Date View is best used when you want to review a group of media created on the same day. To quickly display a larger group of media created within a specific date range, see **39** Find Items Within a Date Range.

The designers of the *Organizer* realized that a day's worth of photographs, movies, audio files, and creations represents a chronicle of an important time in your life. So, rather than make the search for media created on the same day into a dull and lifeless process, the Organizer offers you a functional calendar, called **Date View**. Here, you can leaf through the important periods of your life year by year or month by month, and review a specific day's items in a large window. Specifically, you can view each image, the first frame of each video, and the title page of each creation for the day you select from the calendar. If audio files are currently being displayed in the photo well, their *thumbnails* will appear as well.

Date View not only helps you locate the media files you created on a particular day, but also to recall the events in your life in the context in which you remember having looked forward to them: a monthly calendar. Summer vacation, family weddings, Christmas… at one time, you planned for these days by looking at a calendar, so why not use a calendar-style control to help you recall and cherish those moments? While reviewing a particular day's items, you can add an event banner to the monthly calendar for that day, such as *Aunt Rheu's 90th Birthday* or *Baby Jerlyn Takes Her First Step*. These event banners, which display in bold teal text on a particular day in the monthly calendar, help you quickly identify the day you want to review. (Holidays are shown in purple.) You can also annotate the day's events with a **Daily Note**, which might help you later identify the specific day you want to review.

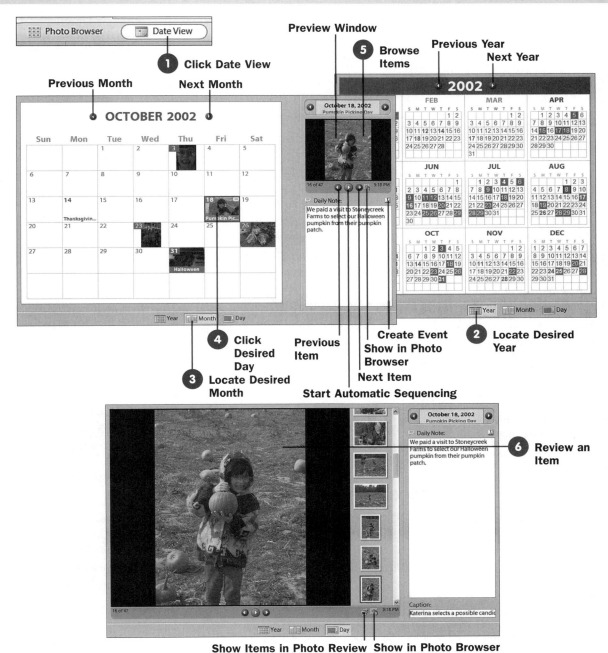

Preview Window

Previous Year

Next Year

5 Browse Items

1 Click Date View

Previous Month

Next Month

OCTOBER 2002

2002

4 Click Desired Day

3 Locate Desired Month

Previous Item

Start Automatic Sequencing

Next Item

Create Event

Show in Photo Browser

2 Locate Desired Year

6 Review an Item

Show Items in Photo Review   Show in Photo Browser

① Click Date View

In the *Editor* or the Organizer, click the **Date View** button at the right end of the **Shortcuts** bar. **Date View** appears, with items organized by month and year.

② Locate Desired Year

If the year currently being displayed is the year containing the items you want to review, skip to step 3. Otherwise, change to a different year by clicking the **Year** button below the calendar. On the left, a yearly calendar for the current year is displayed. Dates with items associated with them appear with solid squares; events and holidays appear in purple; dates with items associated with them (that are not events or holidays) appear in blue. Click the **Previous Year** or **Next Year** button at the top of the yearly calendar to page to the year you want to review.

③ Locate Desired Month

After you've changed to the year you want to review, click the **Month** button below the yearly calendar. A monthly calendar is now displayed on the left (get a closer look at this monthly calendar in the Color Gallery). For each day that has one or more items associated with it, a thumbnail for the first item appears in the block for that day. If you want to review items from a different month that year, click the **Previous Month** or **Next Month** button located on either side of the month name at the top of the window until the month you want to review is displayed.

④ Click Desired Day

Every day in the monthly calendar for which the *catalog* contains items is marked with a thumbnail of the earliest item created that day. Click the day you want to review. The selected day is highlighted in blue, and the first item for the selected day appears in the preview window, located to the right of the monthly calendar.

⑤ Browse Items

The first item created for the currently selected day appears in the preview window. Below this preview, on the left, are listed the total number of items for that day, and the number of the currently displayed item.

TIP

You can select a month or year quickly by clicking the month or year name at the top of the calendar, and then choosing a month or year from the list that appears. For example, if a monthly calendar is currently displayed, click the month name at the top of the monthly calendar, and then select a different month name from the list that appears to quickly switch to that month.

NOTE

The date that **Date View** uses to display items in groups is the date on which the item was created (its *file date*), not the *import date* or *modified date*. To arrange items by import date, see **18** Sort Items. To locate items you modified, you can try searching for the text **copy** in the filename, as explained in **36** Find Items with Similar Filenames and **45** About Editing Images.

To scroll from item to item for the currently selected day, click the **Previous Item** or **Next Item** button below the preview. To display items in sequence automatically, click the green **Start Automatic Sequencing** button. When all the items for that day have been displayed, the slideshow begins again automatically. Click this same button (now red and called **Pause Automatic Sequencing**) to temporarily stop this playback. Click the button again to restart the slideshow.

TIP

You can scroll to a different day by clicking the **Previous Day** or **Next Day** button *above* the preview window.

6 Review an Item

After you've found the item you're interested in and have displayed it in the preview window, you can perform many tasks.

You can remove selected events that display on the calendar automatically, such as Lincoln's Birthday. Choose **Edit, Preferences, Calendar**. Then disable any **Holidays** you don't want to include on your calendar and click **OK**. You can also edit events you have added manually (as explained in the following bullet points), and elect to display Monday as the first day of the week.

- To add a note that describes the events that day, click in the **Daily Notes** box and type your note.

- To add a banner to the monthly calendar that describes the events of that day more succinctly, click the **Create a new event for the selected day** button. Type a brief description or event name such as **Family Reunion**, select the **Repeating event** option if this event happens on the same day every year, and then click **OK**. The event name appears on the monthly calendar, in teal (greenish-blue), on the current day. Automatic events such as holidays, which are inserted into the calendar for you, appear in purple. The event name also appears below the date, but above the preview window, when that day is selected. In the example shown here, the event name, **Pumpkin Picking Day**, was added to **October 18, 2002**.

- To display the current item in the photo well, click the **Show this photo in the Photo Browser** button.

- To display the current item in a larger view, click the **Day** button below the monthly calendar. Other items for that day are displayed as thumbnails to the right of the large preview

NOTE

If an item's date was changed to **Unknown** (as explained in **23** Change Image Date and Time), it will not appear in **Date View**. To have the Photo Browser display items whose date was manually changed to **Unknown**, choose **Find, Items with Unknown Date and Time**. Items with an **Unknown** time *will appear* on their file date.

window. Click a thumbnail to display that item in the large preview window instead.

- To add a text caption to the current item, click the **Day** button if needed to display the item in a large preview. Then click in the **Caption** box on the right, and type your caption.

- To start a *photo review* of the items for the selected day, click the **Day** button if needed to display the item in a large preview. Then click the **View all photos of this day in Photo Review** button.

To redisplay the photo well and exit **Date View**, click the **Photo Browser** button on the **Shortcuts** bar.

39 Find Items Within a Date Range

Before You Begin

✔ **24** About Organizing Items

✔ **33** About Finding Items in the Catalog

See Also

→ **18** Sort Items

→ **23** Change Image Date and Time

→ **38** Find Items with the Same Date

 TIP

With the **Timeline**, you can narrow an existing search to display only items that fall between particular dates. For example, after searching for items in your **Scrapbook** collection, you can limit the display for only those **Scrapbook** items that fall within specific dates.

In **24** About Organizing Items, you learned about the **Timeline**, which is a graph that appears above the photo well. On the **Timeline** are bars representing how many items in the *catalog* originated in various months. Specifically, this is the number of items whose *file dates* (not *import date* or *modified date*) fall within that month. You can see which month represents the largest number of media files by looking for the tallest bar on the **Timeline**. By clicking a bar, you can instantly jump to that month of items in the catalog. Notice that the **Timeline** does not limit the display of items when you simply click a particular bar; however, the **Timeline** can be used to display only those items that fall within a particular date range if you like.

At either end of the **Timeline** are scroll arrows; use these arrows to scroll through the years. Next to the scroll arrows are *range markers*, which mark the range of file dates associated with the items currently displayed in the photo well. By dragging these range markers inward, you can limit the number of items displayed in the photo well (only items whose file dates fall between the dates represented by the range markers on the **Timeline** are displayed in the photo well). The range markers on the **Timeline** enable you to limit the display range to specific months. You can limit this range even further, to specific *days*, by using the **Set Date Range** dialog box as discussed in this task.

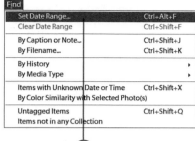

1 Choose Find,
Set Date Range

2 Set Start Date

3 Set End Date and
Click OK

Range of Dates for
Items Not Shown

Beginning of
Date Range

End of Date
Range

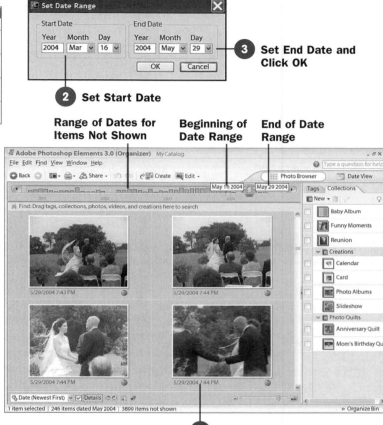

4 View the Result

1 Choose Find, Set Date Range

In the *Organizer*, select **Find, Set Date Range** from the menu bar.
The **Set Date Range** dialog box opens.

2 Set Start Date

Set the **Start Date** by typing the **Year** and selecting the **Month** and
Day from the drop-down lists.

NOTE

To use the **Set Date Range**
dialog box to limit the
items shown in the photo
well, you do not have to
display the **Timeline** first.
However, if you want to
drag the range markers on
the **Timeline** to limit the
items shown, display the
Timeline if needed by
choosing **View, Timeline**.

3 **Set End Date and Click OK**

Set the **End Date** by typing the **Year** and selecting the **Month** and **Day** from the drop-down lists. Click **OK** to display only items that have file dates between and including these two dates.

4 **View the Result**

In a moment, the photo well displays only items created during the range you selected. The range markers on the **Timeline** are also adjusted. ToolTips appear next to the range markers, displaying the start and end dates you selected. Notice also that the range of dates for items not currently being shown appears grayed out on the **Timeline** and that the valid date range is in full color.

> **NOTE**
>
> To reset the **Timeline** so that all items in the catalog are displayed, select **Find, Clear Date Range**.

40 Find Items with the Same History

You Should Know

✔ **33** About Finding Items in the Catalog

See Also

→ **3** Import Media from a Folder

→ **66** Print an Image

→ **69** Print Images Using an Online Service

→ **158** Share Images Using Email

→ **160** Share Images Using an Online Service

As soon as an item is imported into the *catalog*, a history is created. When you include an item in a *creation*, export it for use in some other application, share it via email or through an *online service*, or print it locally or through an online service, these events are noted and logged in that item's history. You can then use this history to recall a particular item for display. For example, suppose that you sent several images of a recent family outing to your brother in Colorado, and now you're ready to send some more but you can't recall which ones you've already sent! Luckily, you can simply ask the *Organizer* to display items you emailed to your brother, and then quickly review the recently sent ones.

1 **Choose Find, By History**

In the Organizer, choose **Find, By History** from the menu. A submenu of items tracked by history appears. Select an item from this list. For example, select **Find, By History, Imported On**.

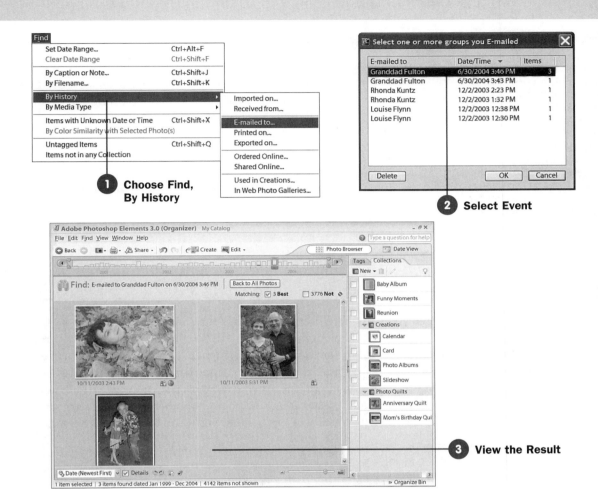

1 Choose Find, By History

2 Select Event

3 View the Result

2 Select Event

A dialog box appears, listing the dates on which you performed the action you selected in step 1. For example, if you choose **Find, By History, Printed On** in step 1, a list of dates on which you printed some images appears. If you chose an event that involves a third party—for example, you selected **Find, By History, Shared Online**, you'll see a list of online services through which you've shared some images, and a list of dates on which you did that. Select the event (the date) you're interested in, and click **OK**.

NOTE

You can remove an event from history and reduce the size of the Organizer's catalog file by a little bit. Just select an event from the dialog box in step 2 and click **Delete**. Removing events you don't want to remember anymore will also reduce the size of the list displayed in the dialog box, and make it easier for you to find the events you are interested in when needed.

The images associated with the event you selected in step 1 appear in the photo well. Here, I had recently sent some photos to my father-in-law and I wanted to send some more, but I just couldn't remember what I'd already sent! Luckily, the Organizer doesn't suffer from short-term memory loss.

After displaying the items associated with an event, you can make changes, print, share, organize, or use in a creation any of these items; when you're done, click the **Back to All Photos** button to redisplay all items in the photo well.

---

41 **Find Images with Similar Color**

Before You Begin

✔ **33** About Finding Items in the Catalog

When you take more than one photo of an event or a group of people, at or about the same time, the content of those images is generally very similar. The *Organizer* can't see the content of an image; it can't look at a photograph, determine the lines and contours of what's depicted in it, and draw any conclusions about what's there. The Organizer can, however, detect similarities in color (including brightness and intensity), and present you with a series of images that *might* contain similar content.

Suppose that you took several photos of your kids standing in front of the Eiffel Tower. The sky, background, and your children's hair, skin, clothing and so on would all look the same in every shot. Even if the photos were taken each year when you visit Paris, chances are they would still contain a similar range of colors. By selecting one of those images and then asking the Organizer to locate others of similar color, you should be able to quickly locate all your Paris memories. However, it's entirely possible that the Organizer will find other photos as well—photos that contain a similar range of colors but completely different content. Still, chances are you might be able to locate photos with similar content, even if those images were taken years apart, are stored in different places, and use dissimilar filenames, *captions*, notes, and markers.

Choose Find, By Color Similarity

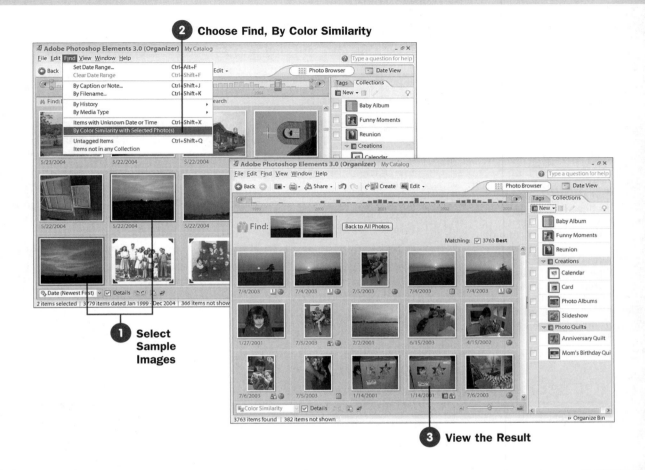

1 Select Sample Images

3 View the Result

1 Select Sample Images

In the Organizer, click the first *thumbnail* for an image whose color content is similar to that of the other image(s) you're looking for. Then press **Ctrl** and click additional, similarly colored images to use as samples (if any). By selecting multiple sample images, you can produce a more accurate color sample to search for, and increase the odds of locating other similar, related images.

NOTE

You can select only photos, not *creations*, audio files, or videos.

TIP

To locate previously marked images so that you can search for others that use similar colors, use the **Find** bar, as explained in **34** Find Items with the Same Marker.

NOTE

Unfortunately, you can't re-sort the displayed images as described in **18** Sort Items. You can, however, use the **Timeline** to limit the file dates of the displayed items. See **39** Find Items Within a Date Range. You can also use tags to limit the search results; see **34** Find Items with the Same Marker.

2 **Choose Find, By Color Similarity**

Select **Find, By Color Similarity with Selected Photo(s)** from the menu bar.

3 **View the Result**

The photo well displays images whose color and brightness resemble that of the original image(s). The **Find** bar displays thumbnails of the original photos, and those thumbnails also appear at the top of the photo well. Other images are arranged not by date, but by their color similarity to the original selected image(s).

Here, I found a few good sunset photos but wanted to see what others I might have for use in a greeting card. So, I selected two sunset images and searched for other images with similar colors. I found a few unrelated photos, but as you can see, I found several other sunsets as well. After viewing your results, to redisplay all images in the *catalog*, click the **Back to All Photos** button.

42 Hide Items You Don't Generally Use

Before You Begin

✔ **24** About Organizing Items

✔ **27** Attach a Marker to an Item

✔ **33** About Finding Items in the Catalog

Here's something you might be wondering: Why go through all the trouble of adding items to a *catalog*, along with other items that might be used later in albums or slideshows, if you're only going to hide them? Well, not every digital image or movie you might ever want to keep track of or use in a presentation is so important that you need to thumb through it every day. For example, take a shot of a closed stage curtain. It's not a terribly important image. If you lost it, you wouldn't shed any tears. But you might want to use the closed stage curtain photo as the first image in most of your slideshows as a kind of title screen, so it's certainly worth keeping in the catalog.

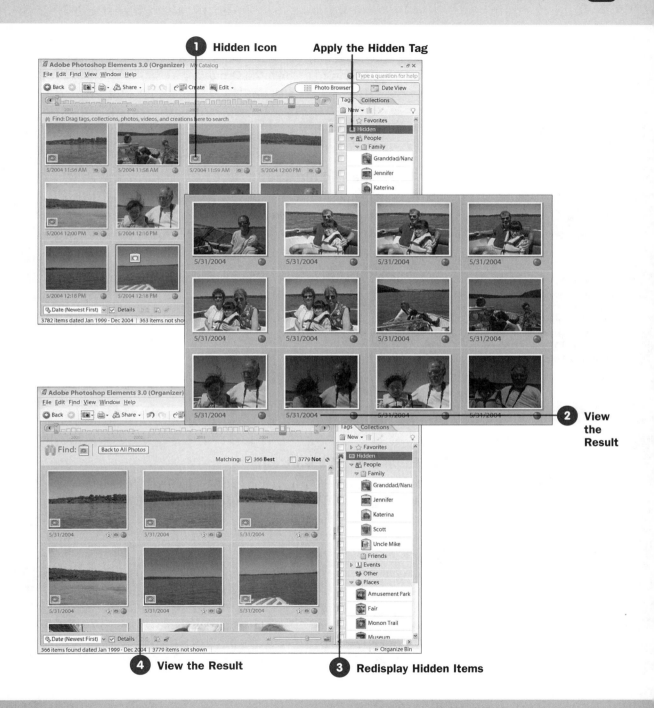

1 Hidden Icon

Apply the Hidden Tag

2 View the Result

3 Redisplay Hidden Items

4 View the Result

NOTES

Audio files are not normally displayed in the photo well anyway, so you won't need to perform this task to hide them. See **35** **Find Items of the Same Media Type**.

If you simply want to remove items from the catalog that you don't use often, move them offline. See **15** **Copy Items onto CD-ROM or DVD**.

TIP

To quickly display previously marked items so that you can apply the **Hidden** tag to them, use the **Find** bar. See **34** **Find Items with the Same Marker** for help.

NOTE

Simply scrolling through the photo well does not remove the hidden items from view.

Hiding such items from view keeps the catalog leaner and meaner, easier to load and to scroll through. You hide occasionally used items by giving them the **Hidden** *tag*. When the *Organizer* sees an item with the **Hidden** tag, it knows not to display that item in the photo well. However, the item still belongs to the catalog, so you can see it when you need to. In this task, you'll learn how to hide items and then redisplay them when needed.

❶ Apply the Hidden Tag

In the Organizer, select the items you want to hide from general view. Then drag the **Hidden** tag from the **Organize Bin** and drop it onto the selected items in the photo well to assign the tag to the selected items.

The **Hidden** icon (a closed eye) appears on the selected items; the items themselves don't actually disappear from view until you either re-sort the catalog or import new items. Here, I decided to hide some scenic shoreline photos taken during a recent boating trip because they weren't as important to me as the ones containing my family.

❷ View the Result

After I re-sorted the catalog, the items I marked with the **Hidden** tag were removed from view.

❸ Redisplay Hidden Items

You can redisplay items you've hidden when you want to view or use them. Just click the **Tags** tab on the **Organize Bin**, and then click the check box in front of the **Hidden** tag.

❹ View the Result

Only items marked with the **Hidden** tag are displayed in the photo well. Each item appears with the closed-eye icon, and the **Find** bar indicates that only items tagged with the **Hidden** tag are currently being viewed. Here, I redisplayed the shoreline photos so I could look at a house we had admired while boating. To redisplay all items in the catalog, click the **Back to All Photos** button.

PART II

Working with Images

IN THIS PART:

CHAPTER 6   Creating, Opening, and Saving Images   167

CHAPTER 7   Performing Basic Image Tasks   209

CHAPTER 8   Printing Images   243

CHAPTER 9   Selecting a Portion of an Image   267

CHAPTER 10 Modifying a Selection   295

CHAPTER 11 Using Selections to Edit Images   311

CHAPTER 12 Using Multiple Layers to Edit Images   333

6

Creating, Opening, and Saving Images

IN THIS CHAPTER:

43 About the Editor

44 Create a New Image

45 About Editing Images

46 Open an Image for Editing

47 About Saving Images

48 Save an Image in Photoshop Format (PSD)

49 Save an Image in TIFF Format

50 Compress an Image Using GIF Format

51 Compress an Image Using JPEG Format

52 Save an Image in PNG Format

The *Editor* comes with many tools for creating and manipulating graphics. With its help, you can restore old photographs, insert your missing brother into a family photo, or create a Web page background. You can also make a few simple corrections to an image from within the *Organizer*. Before you can perform any of this graphics wizardry however, you must first open the image you want to work on or tell the Editor you want to start from scratch on a new image. In the tasks presented in this chapter, you will learn not only how to start something new, but also how to locate and open image files already saved to the hard disk. In addition, you'll learn how to save new or edited images in a variety of graphic formats.

43 About the Editor

See Also

→ **1** About the Organizer

→ **45** About Editing Images

NOTE

Before you use the Editor to make changes to an existing image, be sure to read **45** About Editing Images.

TIP

You can start the Editor in **Standard Edit** mode from the **Welcome Window** by clicking the **Edit and Enhance Photos**. From the Organizer, you can start the Editor in **Standard Edit** mode by selecting an image, clicking the **Edit** button, and selecting **Go to Standard Edit**.

As you probably know by now, Photoshop Elements is made up of two components: the *Editor* and the *Organizer*. The Editor window is similar to other Windows applications, containing familiar elements such as the menu bar, work area, and **Minimize**, **Maximize**, and **Close** buttons. Still, no matter how many automobiles you've driven, there's always some new feature in the next car you buy. Windows programs are like that, too; each program comes with its own set of unique controls designed to implement the functionality unique to that program. In the case of the Editor, you'll find a set of unique controls designed to help you edit your graphics with ease. It's these controls I want to introduce you to.

At the right end of the menu bar, you'll find a **Search** box; type a word or phrase in this box and press **Enter** or click the **Help Contents** button (the question mark icon) to the left of the **Search** box to search the program's Help system. If you don't type anything in the **Search** box and press Enter or click the **Help Contents** button, you'll go directly to the home page in Help.

Open images are displayed in the work area in the middle of the window. You can have as many open images as you like; the maximum number is theoretically limited by the memory of your computer. Typically, each image is initially displayed in a manageable size within its own window. This image window contains its own **Minimize**, **Maximize**, and **Close** buttons.

Shortcuts Bar
Options Bar
Search Box
Automatically Tile Windows Button

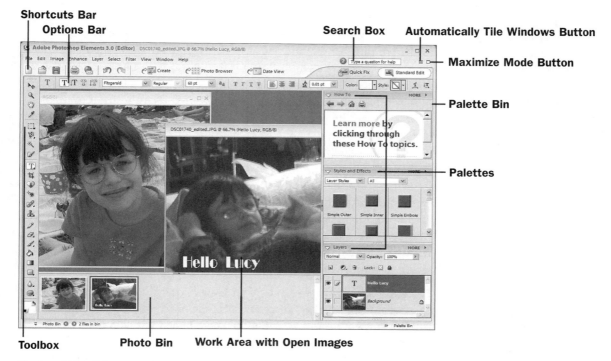

Maximize Mode Button
Palette Bin
Palettes

Toolbox   Photo Bin   Work Area with Open Images

Parts of the Editor work area.

To the right of the **Search** box, you'll find some buttons that control how images are displayed. When you see two buttons here, you're in what Adobe calls *Multi-window mode*, which enables you to display multiple image in the work area. In this mode, the first button, **Automatically Tile Windows**, causes newly opened images to be automatically arranged with already open images in a tiled formation. With this button engaged, if you open a new image, it is automatically tiled with other open images. To have Adobe stop tiling image windows, resize any window to some other size, click the **Automatically Tile Windows** button again to turn the option off, or change to *Maximize mode* by clicking the second button to the right of the **Search** box. You can cascade open windows rather than tiling them by choosing **Window, Images, Cascade**.

KEY TERMS

Multi-window mode—A setting that enables you to display more than one image in the work area at the same time.

Maximize mode—A setting that enables you to display only one image at a time, using as much of the work area as possible.

NOTE

You can also change from image to image in **Maximize Mode** by choosing the image you want to work on from those listed at the bottom of the **Window** menu.

 NOTE

Display the **Photo Bin** if needed by choosing **Window, Photo Bin** or clicking the **Photo Bin** button at the left end of the **Status** bar.

When you click the **Maximize Mode** button, four buttons appear to the right of the **Search** box: **Automatically Tile Windows, Minimize, Multi-window Mode,** and **Close.** When you open an image while in Maximize mode, the Editor displays that image as fully as possible within the limits of the work area. If an image is open when you change to Maximize mode, its size is not changed, but you can resize it to take up more space in the work area if you want. While in Maximize mode, you can display only one image in the work area at a time. Change from one open image to another by clicking its *thumbnail* in the **Photo Bin** at the bottom of the work area. You can minimize the image window (returning it to the **Photo Bin**) by clicking its **Minimize** button. This, in turn, maximizes the previously active image window, or clears the work area if no other images are open. Close the image window by clicking its **Close** button. Return to Multi-window mode by clicking the **Multi-window Mode** button; click **Automatically Tile Windows** button to return to Multi-window mode, but with automatic tiling active.

There are other ways to adjust your view of an image. For example, you can zoom in or out, and display an image onscreen in the same size it will appear when printed. See **55** **Zoom In and Out with the Zoom Tool** and **56** **Zoom In and Out with the Navigator Palette** for help. You can zoom all images to the same level as the active image (regardless of whether you're in Multi-window mode or Maximize mode) by choosing **Window, Images, Match Zoom.** To have all images match the area you're zoomed in on in the active image window, choose **Window, Images, Match Location.** These modes are helpful if you have several open photos that were taken at close to the same time—such as several portraits of the same family member—where you need to compare the same detail in each image side-by-side.

Use the Shortcuts Bar

Below the menu bar is the **Shortcuts** bar, which contains buttons for the most common commands such as opening, saving, and printing an image. Buttons with a sweeping right arrow on the left, such as the **Create, Photo Browser,** and **Date View** buttons, will launch the

Organizer so that you can complete the selected action, such as locating an image based on the date on which it was taken. To identify a particular button, hover the mouse pointer over the button and a tooltip appears, displaying the button's name. At the right end of the **Shortcuts** bar, you'll find a pair of buttons that change the Editor from a full-featured *graphics editor* into a quick touch-up program, and back again. See **109** **Apply a Quick Fix** for more information.

These Buttons Represent Common Editor Tasks

These Buttons Launch the Organizer

These Buttons Switch Between Editing Modes

*The **Shortcuts** bar provides fast access to common commands.*

Use the Toolbox and Options Bar

The **Toolbox**, located along the left side of the window, is the *Editor*'s equivalent of a caddy on your desk where you keep all your brushes, pens, erasers, and scissors. To select a tool, click its button; the currently selected tool is highlighted. Some tools with similar purposes are located in the same slot on the **Toolbox**, with one in front and the others hidden behind it. To access a hidden tool, hold the mouse down on a button to make a menu full of additional tools appear. Click one of the tools in the menu to make it active and display it in the **Toolbox**.

You can move the **Toolbox** into the work area if that makes it more convenient; just drag it by the top bar. You can't resize the floating **Toolbox**, but you can hide it quickly to get it out of the way of your work—just press **Tab** as you might do to hide all free-floating palettes (you'll learn more about palettes in the next section). Press **Tab** again to restore the **Toolbox** and your free-floating palettes. To restore the **Toolbox** to its original position on the left of the window, drag it by the blue title bar.

NOTE

To identify a specific tool, hover the mouse pointer over it. A tooltip appears with the name of the tool and its keyboard shortcut. You can press this shortcut key at anytime to activate the tool currently displayed on the **Toolbox**. To choose a hidden tool, just keep pressing the same shortcut key. For example, to cycle through the erasers until you select the eraser tool you want, keep pressing E.

Options Bar

Toolbox

Currently Selected Tool

Shortcut Key
Hidden Tools

NOTE

You can also click a tool on the **Toolbox** and then click the icon on the **Options** bar for the hidden tool you want to use.

The Toolbox contains tools you can use to edit images.

After you select a tool, its available options appear on the **Options** bar, located just under the **Shortcuts** bar. You'll learn how to use the tools in the **Toolbox** and to set options in upcoming tasks.

Use Palettes

On the right side of the *Editor* window, you'll see the *Palette Bin*, which contains a collection of *palettes*. By default, three palettes are displayed in the **Palette Bin**: the **How To** palette (which contains step-by-step instructions for completing common image modifications), the **Styles and Effects** palette (which displays *thumbnails* representing special modifications you can apply to an image), and the **Layers** palette (which provides access to the multiple *layers* an image contains). The **Palette Bin** helps you corral the palettes you currently want to use. You can add or remove palettes from the **Palette Bin** as desired, or you can display palettes in the work area. These palettes are called *floating palettes*. You can place several floating palettes together, forming a *group* (where only the tab of the active palette shows) or a *dock* (where palettes are stacked vertically).

Docked Palettes   **Floating Palette**   **More Button**   **Hidden Palette**

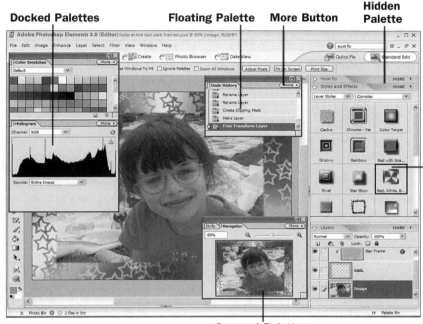

Grouped Palettes

Palettes provide valuable information and tools for modifying images.

- To display a palette, select it from the **Window** menu. If the palette is part of a group, the entire group appears; if the palette is docked with other palettes, they appear too.

- When a palette is displayed for the first time, it appears as a floating palette in the work area. You can move the palette around by dragging it by its title bar.

- To remove a floating palette from the screen, select its name again from the **Window** menu or click its **Close** button. Again, if the palette is docked with other palettes or part of a group, this affects all the related palettes, closing all of them.

KEY TERMS

Palette Bin—A gathering place for the palettes you want to keep open.

Palette—A floating dialog box that contains tools or information to help you modify images.

—Palette Bin

NOTES

If you chose a palette's name from the **Window** menu to remove it from the screen, and that palette is currently displayed in the **Palette Bin,** the entire **Palette Bin** is hidden. You can also hide and redisplay the **Palette Bin** by clicking its button on the **Status** bar.

If you drag a palette out of the **Palette Bin** and into the work area, it becomes a floating palette. But if you close it, the palette returns to its home in the **Palette Bin**. To make a palette that floats even if you close and redisplay it, click its **More** button and uncheck the **Place in Palette Bin** option.

NOTE

To place a palette in the **Palette Bin** temporarily, drag it by its tab and drop it on the bin. The temporary palette will hide and redisplay like a bin palette, but it won't cause the bin to hide if you close the palette by choosing its name from the **Window** menu.

NOTE

The **Histogram** and **Info** palettes can not be resized.

TIP

To reset all palettes to their default positions (all of them hidden but the **How To, Styles and Effects,** and **Layers** palettes, which appear in the bin), choose **Window, Reset Palette Locations** from the menu.

- To place any floating palette in the **Palette Bin**, click its **More** button and select **Place in Palette Bin** from the **More** menu, and then click its **Close** button. The palette then closes—and reappears in the bin. If you open the **More** menu again, a checkmark appears next to this command to indicate that the palette has been placed in the **Palette Bin**.

- To keep a palette in the **Palette Bin** but temporarily hide it, click the **down arrow** to the left of the palette's name on the title bar. To redisplay the hidden palette, click the **right arrow** that appears in its place, or choose the palette's name from the **Window** menu.

- To roll up a floating palette so that only its title bar shows, double-click its title bar. Double-click the title bar again to unroll it. To temporarily hide all floating palettes, press **Tab**. Press **Tab** again to redisplay them where they were.

- If a palette is located in the **Palette Bin** or docked with other palettes, you can change its size vertically by dragging its bottom border up or down. If a palette is floating, drag the **Size box** (located in the lower-right corner) to resize it.

- To relocate any palette within the **Palette Bin**, drag it by its title bar up or down to a new location, and let go.

- You can make the **Palette Bin** skinnier by dragging its left border. This makes the work area (and the **Photo Bin**, if it's displayed) wider.

The **More** button provides access to commands other than **Place in Palette Bin**. Click the **More** button and select **XXX Help** (where XXX is the name of the palette) to get help working with a particular palette. Choose **Help Contents** to display the Help Contents page instead. Other commands on the **More** menu enable you to set options related to that particular palette.

You can group palettes together in a sort of tabbed dialog box so that the palettes are easily accessible and yet take up little room. To group one palette within another, drag a palette by its tab (and not its title bar) and drop it on top of the target palette. The palettes are grouped, and a tab appears for each palette. Only one palette in the group is fully visible at any one time. To switch to a different palette, click its tab. To remove a palette from a group, drag it by its tab outside the group to return the palette to a free-floating state.

You can dock multiple palettes together, creating mini-Palette Bins. These docked palettes can be moved, hidden, redisplayed, and closed with a single click. To dock a palette with another, drag the palette by its tab to the bottom edge of another palette. A double line appears along this bottom edge; release the mouse button to dock the palette. Click the **Minimize** button to roll up this floating bin, or click the **Close** button to remove it from the screen.

You'll learn more about the individual palettes throughout this book. For now, here is a brief description of the remaining palettes: **Color Swatches** (displays various collections of colors, patterns, and textures you can use with the painting tools); **Histogram** (a graph depicting the distribution of the brightness in an image); **Info** (displays information about the pixel under the cursor, and about the size of any shape, selection, or cropping border you're currently drawing); **Navigator** (provides an alternative method for zooming and scrolling an image); and **Undo History** (displays a list of actions you can undo).

Use the Photo Bin

Under the work area you'll find the **Photo Bin**. This bin displays a *thumbnail* for every open image. You can use the bin to switch from one image to another quickly: Just click the thumbnail of the image you want to work on. You'll find this method of switching from one image to another especially useful when you are displaying images in *Maximize mode*, where the active image is automatically maximized, hiding any other open images. You can also click the left and right arrows next to the **Photo Bin** button on the left side of the status bar to change from one image to the next. Next to these arrows is a notation that tells you how many images you currently have open. When you have more images in the **Photo Bin** than it has room to show, use the vertical scrollbar to browse through the thumbnails or resize the bin by dragging its top border upwards. Of course, making the **Photo Bin** taller makes the work area smaller.

NOTE

The image thumbnails are arranged in the bin in the order in which you opened the images. You can drag thumbnails within the bin to rearrange this order to make switching between the images you're currently working on easier.

Image Thumbnails

Photo Bin Button

*The **Photo Bin** provides quick access to open images.*

To see the filename for a single thumbnail in the **Photo Bin**, hold the pointer over that thumbnail; the tooltip shows the filename. To display a filename under each thumbnail, right-click an empty space in the **Photo Bin** and select **Show Filenames** from the context menu.

If you want to maximize your work area, you can hide the **Photo Bin** when not in use by clicking the **Close Photo Bin** button, located at the left end of the status bar. Redisplay the bin by clicking this button again. To hide the bin automatically when not in use, right-click an empty space in the **Photo Bin** and select **Auto Hide** from the context menu. As soon as you activate an image window or if nothing happens in the work area for a few seconds, the bin automatically disappears; to redisplay it, simply move the mouse pointer towards the bottom of the work area.

Use the Rulers and Grid

Occasionally, you might want to turn on several tools to guide you as you make precise adjustments to an image. For example, when drawing objects of a specific size, you might want to display the ruler (choose **View, Rulers**). A vertical ruler appears along the left edge of each image window, and a horizontal ruler appears along the top edge. Using the ruler, you can make more precise selections with any of the **Selection** tools, create objects of an exact size and position, and position type more exactly. As you move the mouse pointer over the image, hash marks appear on the rulers to indicate the pointer's exact position.

Zero Origin

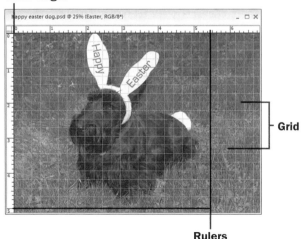

Use the rulers and the grid to help you make precise changes to an image.

If you want to measure from some point on an image, you can adjust the *zero origin*. Normally, zero is located in the upper-left corner of an image; to move the zero origin, click at the intersection of the two rulers (in the upper-left corner of the image window) and drag downwards and to the right, to the point on the image from which you want to measure. Cross-hairs appear as you drag to help you precisely position the zero origin. Release the mouse button to set the zero origin. To reset the rulers so that the zero origin is once again in the upper-left corner, double-click the intersection of the two rulers.

Another useful tool for aligning objects perfectly is the grid, a set of vertical and horizontal lines that cross all over the image forming, well, a *grid*. You can automatically align objects to the gridlines by turning on the **View, Snap to Grid** option. You can see the gridlines by choosing **View, Grid**, although the grid does tend to obstruct your image; if you chose not to display the grid, you can still snap objects to the (invisible) gridlines by choosing only the **Snap to Grid** option. When the gridlines are invisible, you still "feel" them (almost like they are magnetized) as you draw or move objects because the gridlines pull the edges of objects towards them.

Use the How To Palette

The **How To** *palette* guides you step by step through some of the more common image editing tasks, such as cropping photos and removing dust and scratches. To display the **How To** palette, choose **Window, How To**. The **How To** palette works like a small Web page, complete with hyperlinks to different sections and browser-like buttons that enable you to go back to the page you just read or to the **Home** page. Start by selecting a task from the **Home** page. The steps you must follow to complete that task appear. Sometimes, the hyperlink **Do this step for me** is included with a step to help you complete it properly.

NOTES

With gridlines invisible, don't forget to disable the **Snap to Grid** option when you no longer want objects to snap to the grid!

To change the properties of the grid—for example, to make the gridlines further apart—choose **Edit, Preferences, Grid**. Here you can choose the distance between the horizontal/vertical gridlines, and the number of subdivisions between gridlines. You can also choose the color and pattern used for the gridlines.

TIP

The **How To** palette is just like any other palette, so you can dock it, float it, or hide it temporarily. You can also resize the window.

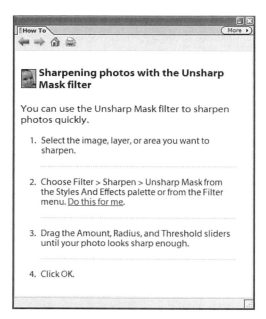

*The **How To** palette guides you through common tasks.*

44 Create a New Image

Before You Begin

✔ **59** About Size and Resolution

See Also

→ **48** Save an Image in Photoshop Format (PSD)

→ **49** Save an Image in TIFF Format

→ **60** Change Image Size or Resolution

→ **63** Change Color Mode

→ **105** Ensure That What You See Is What You Get

As with other programs, if you want to use Photoshop Elements to create new art such as a decorative Windows wallpaper or a Web page button, you must start with a new, empty image file. You might also create a new image file when you want to combine portions of several photographs into a photo collage, scrapbook page, or panorama. After creating a new image file, you should save it in Photoshop format as described in **48** **Save an Image in Photoshop Format (PSD)**.

When you create a new image file, you set several initial parameters, such as the image's width and height. You are not stuck with your initial choices; you can change your selections later on as you work. For example, it's easy to resize a photograph to make it bigger or smaller as needed. In addition to width and height, you determine how finely detailed the image will be (its *resolution*). Finally, you'll select the *background color* and the image *color mode*. As you make your selections, the resulting file size (taking into account only a single, basic *background layer*) is displayed at the bottom of the dialog box. If necessary, reduce the image size, resolution, or color mode to make the file size more manageable for your system.

1 Click New Button

In the *Editor*, change to **Standard Edit** mode and click the **New** button on the **Shortcuts** bar, or choose **File**, **New**, **Blank File** from the menu. The **New** dialog box appears.

2 Enter Name

Type a name for the new image in the **Name** box. For now, the name you type will serve as the file's temporary name until you actually save the file as described in **47 About Saving Images**. Because this is only a temporary name, you can skip this step if you like, and enter the permanent name for the file when you save it later on.

3 Select Preset

Open the **Preset** drop-down list and select one of the many common image types, such as a 5-by-7-inch photo or an 800-by-600-pixel Web background. You can modify the **Width**, **Height**, and **Resolution** settings that appear by following steps 4 and 5; otherwise, skip to step 6.

4 Adjust Width and Height

If your chosen preset doesn't match the image size you want exactly, select new **Width** and/or **Height** values.

5 Adjust Resolution

Depending on how detailed you want the image to appear, adjust the **Resolution** value to the number of pixels you want per inch/centimeter. If the image will only be viewed onscreen or on the Web, 72 pixels per inch is sufficient; for images you intend to print, consider at least 300 *DPI*.

⚲ KEY TERM

Color mode—Determines the number of colors an image can contain; the color mode (also called *color depth*) also affects an image's file size—the larger the color depth, the larger the file size.

⚙ TIPS

You can start the Editor in **Standard Edit** mode from the **Welcome Window** by clicking the **Edit and Enhance Photos**. From the Organizer, you can start the Editor in **Standard Edit** mode by selecting an image, clicking the **Edit** button, and selecting **Go to Standard Edit**.

If you want to create a new image using data currently on the Clipboard (the part of memory that holds cut or copied data before it's pasted), see **87 Create a New Image from a Selection** for help.

To create a new image that uses the same dimensions as a currently open image, select the image's name from the bottom of the **Preset** list. You might have to scroll to see the filenames of these open images.

1 Click New Button **2** Enter Name

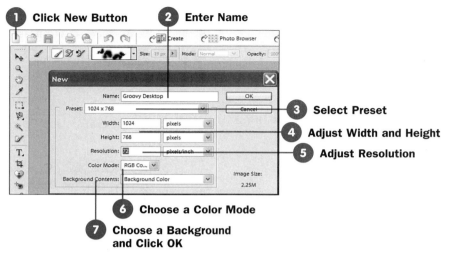

3 Select Preset

4 Adjust Width and Height

5 Adjust Resolution

6 Choose a Color Mode

7 Choose a Background
and Click OK

8 View the Result

6 Choose a Color Mode

Open the **Color Mode** drop-down list and select the color mode you want to work with: **RGB Color** (for color images), **Grayscale** (for images in black, white, and grays), or **Bitmap** (for images in black and white only).

7 Choose a Background and Click OK

Open the **Background Contents** drop-down list and select the color you want to fill the bottom *layer* of your image—the background layer. You can choose **White**, **Background Color** (which makes the background the same color as the current background color as shown on the **Toolbox**), or **Transparent**. (The **Transparent** option is not available in **Bitmap** color mode.) After selecting a background, click **OK** to create the blank *canvas* for the new image onscreen.

8 View the Result

An image window opens with the dimensions and colors you choose. Use the Editor's tools to fill the image with color or data copied from another image. Apply *filters*, *effects*, or *layer styles*. After you've worked a little in your image, you'll want to save it so you don't lose your work. The best format for works in progress is Photoshop (***.psd**), as explained in **48 Save an Image in Photoshop Format (PSD).** After you work on the image, save the result in JPEG or TIFF format as explained in **47 About Saving Images**, leaving your PSD image with its *layers* (if any) intact so that you can return at a later time and make different adjustments if you want.

Here, I created a quick image for use as a Windows background. I filled it with a purple background color, painted it with green and yellow droplets, and applied the **Glass**, **Wave**, and **Liquify** filters. Then I added some flowers using the **Custom Shape** tool, and some text.

TIPS

A typical ink jet printer uses a resolution of 600 DPI (dots per inch), so for printing purposes on a home ink jet, select at least half that, or 300 DPI (pixels per inch). Photo printers average 1200 DPI; here, you're still fine with 300 DPI resolution, although you could try 600 DPI and compare the results.

If you're not sure whether you'll be printing an image or not, use at least 300 DPI. If you're going to be working with photographs in this new image, go with 600 DPI; you can always reduce the resolution (and the file size) later if you need to.

45 About Editing Images

Before You Begin

✔ **1** About the Organizer

✔ **43** About the Editor

See Also

→ **46** Open an Image for Editing

 **TIP**

To automatically fix one or more images in the Organizer catalog, use **Auto Fix**. In the Organizer, select the images you want to adjust by clicking the first image *thumbnail*, pressing **Ctrl** and clicking as many additional thumbnails as you like. Then choose **Edit, Auto Fix Selected Photos** to automatically adjust the images for color, contrast, and sharpness or choose **Edit, Auto Fix Window** to automatically apply selected fixes to the chosen image(s).

 **NOTES**

You can switch back and forth between **Quick Fix** and **Standard Edit** modes in the Editor as often as you like. To switch between modes in the Editor, just click the **Quick Fix** or **Standard Edit** button located at the right end of the **Shortcuts** bar.

After you create a new image and save it, as explained in **44** **Create a New Image**, you can open that image later on and make further changes. You can also make changes to images you captured with a digital camera, or printed images you've scanned in. For the most part, images you like, and therefore will want to edit and improve, are probably already in the *Organizer catalog*. You can attempt to fix the image using the **Auto Fix** command in the *Organizer*, but you'll have no control over the result. For more options and therefore more control over the editing process, you'll want to send the cataloged image over to the *Editor*. This can be done in one of two ways:

- You can send the cataloged image to the Editor's **Quick Fix** window. Here you can make simple adjustments to an image's contrast, *saturation*, and sharpness, using slider controls that enable you to manipulate the amount of adjustment that occurs. See **109** **Apply a Quick Fix** for help.

- For complete control over any adjustments you apply, send the cataloged image to the Editor's **Standard Edit** window. Here you can use any of the tools in the **Toolbox**, apply variable image adjustments, add layers, or apply *filters* and *effects* to correct or enhance an image. See **46** **Open an Image for Editing**.

The Organizer knows when an image is being changed, so in the catalog, it flags the image with a marker that reads, *Edit in Progress*. The flag prevents you from attempting to share, print, or include the image in a creation while it's still being changed. The flag is automatically removed from the image thumbnail when you're done editing.

If you have a more sophisticated *graphics editor* that you prefer to use (such as Paint Shop Pro or Photoshop CS), you can send a selected image from the catalog directly to that program. First, you may have to tell the Organizer what other graphics editor you want to use—see the note for instructions. When that's done, just select an image in the catalog and choose **Edit, Edit with XXX** (where XXX is the name of the graphics editor you choose). The image automatically appears in the chosen graphics editor; there you can make your changes and save them. When you return to the Organizer, the *Edit in Progress* flag should be automatically removed, but if for some reason it's not, click the thumbnail and choose **Edit, Finish External Edit** to remove the flag.

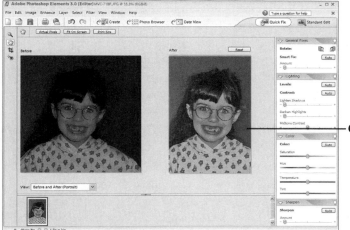

—Quick Fix Window

Standard Edit Window

*You can edit an image using either the Editor's **Quick Fix** or **Standard Edit** windows.*

You should keep a few things in mind when you decide to edit an image. First, you will probably not want to make changes to an original file. If you make changes to a *copy* instead, you can always delete the copy and go back to the original if you feel that your edits took you in the wrong direction. When you edit an image and you save your changes, you can either make a copy file, or make a copy and link the new file with the original, in a *version set*. The process of opening an

NOTES

If Photoshop is installed on your system, it is set up automatically during installation to be used as the alternative graphics editor. To set up the Organizer so that you can use a different alternative graphics editor from time to time, choose **Edit, Preferences, Editing**. The **Preferences** dialog box appears. Enable the **Use a Supplementary Editing Application** check box, click **Browse**, select the graphics editor program file (such as **paintshoppro.exe**), and click **Open**. You return to the **Preferences** dialog box; click **OK**.

If an image is not in the catalog, you can open it for editing in the Editor by clicking the **Open** button on the Editor's **Shortcuts** bar, selecting the file, and clicking **Open**. When you save your changes, you can add the image to the catalog at the same time. See **47 About Saving Images**.

image and saving it is discussed in detail in **46** **Open an Image for Editing**, but what happens basically is this: You send an image from the Organizer to the Editor. You make changes. When you save your changes, a dialog box appears that provides many options. One option creates a copy of the original file by adding **copy** to the filename. Another option adds **_edited-1** to the filename, and creates a version set. If you send an image to an alternative graphics editor such as Photoshop and then save your changes, the version set is created for you automatically, without you doing a thing.

Keeping your original images safe whenever you make changes is one important aspect of editing; another is managing the additional files you create during the editing process. If you create a copy of an image when saving your changes to it, both the original and the copy will appear as thumbnails in the catalog. This can quickly lead to a fat catalog full of similar images. Luckily, the folks at Adobe have thought about this as well and have provided you with an easy way to keep your originals and your edited copies close at hand, without cluttering the catalog. The process is simple: While saving edits to an image, you indicate that this image is a *version* of another image. The Organizer will then stack the edited image with the original automatically, leaving a single thumbnail in the catalog to represent the similar versions. The edited image is assigned the same file date as the original image, so the version set thumbnail appears where it belongs, amongst other images taken that same day. You can expand the *version set* when needed to compare the original with its edited copies. Just select the version set thumbnail and choose **Edit, Version Set, Reveal Photos in Version Set**. The Organizer displays thumbnails for the images in the set, with the newly edited version appearing first, on the far left. If you've rearranged the thumbnails in the set (as explained in the next paragraph), you can view the date on which a particular image was modified by looking on the **History** page of the **Properties** pane. See **53** **About Image Information**.

Edited Version   **Original Image**

You can display the images in a version set.

When the images in a version set are revealed, you can select a different image for use as the set thumbnail by clicking it and choosing **Edit, Version Set, Set as Top Photo**. The image you select to act as the new version set thumbnail (the top photo) will display first when you expand the stack, rather than the most recently edited version. You can remove all edited versions of an image (from the hard disk and from the catalog) and return to using the original image by selecting the original and choosing **Edit, Version Set, Revert to Original**. To close the version set and return to the catalog, click the **Back to All Photos** button on the **Find** bar. You can then remove the original image from the set (and from the hard disk if you want) by clicking the version set thumbnail choosing **Edit, Version Set, Flatten Set**.

Notice that when you edit and image and create a version set, the original file date is retained. This enabled the version stack to appear in the catalog where it did before. If you edit an image and make a copy instead of a version set, today's date is assigned to the resulting file.

NOTES

If you expand a version set that contains multiple image edits, select the original thumbnail, and delete it, the remaining images are still kept together. However, the version set is converted to a stack, because the original image is no longer a part of the set.

46 Open an Image for Editing

Before You Begin

✔ **43** About the Editor

✔ **47** About Saving Images

See Also

→ **33** About Finding Items in the Catalog

→ **109** Apply a Quick Fix

 TIPS

If you double-click a file of an associated file type in **My Computer**, the Editor starts and opens the file for you automatically. To change the file types currently associated with the Editor, choose **Edit, File Association** from the Editor menu.

You can start the Editor in **Standard Edit** mode from the **Welcome Window** by clicking the **Edit and Enhance Photos** button.

To open a recently used file, in the Editor, choose **File, Open Recently Edited File** and select the file from the submenu that appears.

Although you can perform an automated fix on an image in the *catalog* using the *Organizer's* Edit, **Auto Smart Fix** command, or make selected, automatic adjustments with the *Organizer's* Edit, **Auto Fix Photo** command, you will probably never do so because the results are often disappointing. In all likelihood, when an image needs some touchups, you'll use the *Editor* to fix it. If the image is already in the catalog, you can send it from the Organizer to the Editor with one click. Not only is this method convenient because you can use the Organizer to help you quickly locate the image you want to edit, but it also ensures that the catalog *thumbnail* reflects any changes you make. If the image is not in the catalog, you can open it from the Editor and then add it to the catalog when you're through (assuming that you want to add it to the catalog, that is).

The Editor enables you to make changes to an image using either its **Quick Fix** or **Standard Edit** windows. With the **Quick Fix** window, you can make simple changes to an image's brightness, color, and sharpness. (See **109** Apply a Quick Fix.) With the **Standard Edit** window featured in this task, you can use all the Editor's tools and commands to edit an image.

❶ Click Standard Edit

If the image you want to edit is located in the catalog, click the image thumbnail in the Organizer to select it. Click the **Edit** button on the **Shortcuts** bar and select **Go to Standard Edit** to send the image to the Editor for editing. The Editor starts and the image appears in the **Standard Edit** window.

❷ Or Click Open

If the image you want to edit is not in the catalog, click the **Open** button on the **Shortcuts** bar in the Editor. The **Open** dialog box appears; select the image file and click **Open**. The image appears in the Editor. If necessary, click the **Standard Edit** button on the **Shortcuts** bar to display the image in the **Standard Edit** window.

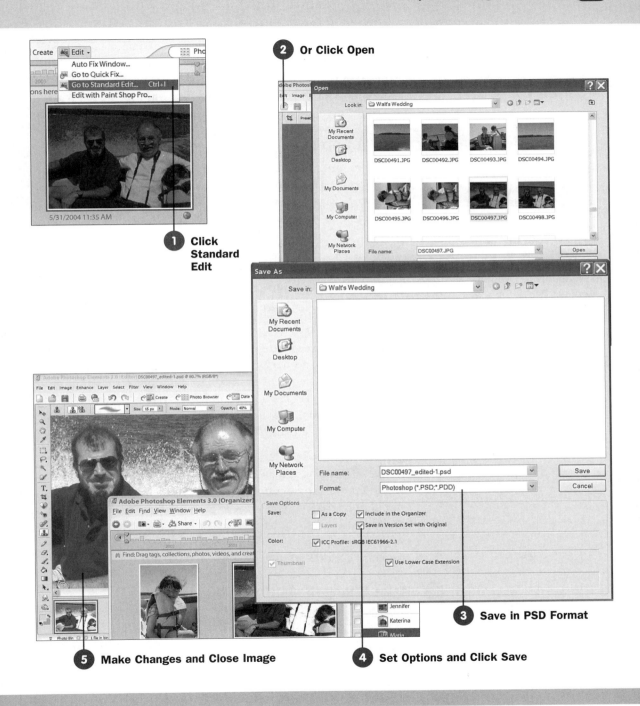

2 **Or Click Open**

1 **Click Standard Edit**

3 **Save in PSD Format**

5 **Make Changes and Close Image**

4 **Set Options and Click Save**

When you open some file types such as Kodak Photo CD and RAW, you might have to supply additional information such as width, height, *resolution*, *color mode*, and *ICC color profile*. See **44** **Create a New Image** and **105** **Ensure That What You See Is What You Get** for more information.

3 Save in PSD Format

Before you make any changes to the image, save it in Photoshop (*.psd*) format. PSD format allows you to use all the Editor's tools as you work, such as layers, filters, effects, and so on. Click the **Save** button on the **Shortcuts** bar. The **Save As** dialog box appears.

4 Set Options and Click Save

Change to the folder in which you want to save the file by selecting it from the **Save in** list. Select **Photoshop (*.PSD)** from the **Format** list.

To make sure your edited image appears in the catalog, enable the **Include in the Organizer** check box. To group this edited image with the original image in a version set that uses a single thumbnail in the Organizer catalog, enable the **Save in Version Set with Original** check box. The text **_edited-1** is added to the end of the original filename, creating a different filename for the edited copy.

For a description of the rest of the options in the **Save As** dialog box, see **47** **About Saving Images**. Click **Save** to save the image. A note might appear describing version sets; click **OK** to continue. You might be asked if you want to preserve **Maximum Compatibility** with earlier versions of Photoshop Elements; unless you go back and forth between versions, disable this option when asked and click **OK** to save your file in a smaller file size.

5 Make Changes and Close Image

Make changes to the image using the techniques you'll learn in upcoming tasks. While you're editing a cataloged image in the Editor, that same image is marked in the Organizer with a flag that reads, *Edit in Progress*. This flag prevents you from using the image in the Organizer while it's being edited.

When you're done making changes, choose **File, Save as** from the Editor menu and save the final result in an image format you can share—such as JPEG or non-layered TIFF format—leaving your PSD image with its *layers* (if any) intact so that you can return at a later time and make different adjustments if you want (see **47** **About Saving Images** for more help). Click the image window's **Close** button to close the file and remove the *Edit in Progress* flag from the image thumbnail in the Organizer catalog. The thumbnail in the catalog is updated to match your final changes; if you chose to create a *version set*, the original image is stacked beneath the thumbnail of the edited image. You can expand the version set to view both images by choosing **Edit, Version Set, Reveal Photos in Version Set**.

47 About Saving Images

In the world of computing, there is no single, universal definition of an "image file." There are any number of image formats, some of which are used by your digital camera, others within Web pages, and still others when emailing. There's even a special format used by Photoshop Elements, called the Photoshop format. To understand what you're doing when you save and copy images, you have to know more about formats, and why there are so many of them.

The More Common Formats

Digital images can be saved in any number of different formats. The format you choose for your images will depend on the purposes you have in mind for them. For example, if you want to use an image on a Web page, you'll have to save it in a Web-compatible format: GIF, JPEG, or PNG. Each of these formats uses compression—JPEG and PNG in variable amounts—to make image files smaller. Compressed images are a benefit to Web users who have lower bandwidth and, thus, longer download times. Compressed images are also great for emailing because they are smaller and easier to send. Here's a brief description of each of the more popular formats:

- **GIF.** One of the oldest compressed formats in wide use, Because a GIF file can contain only 256 colors at most, GIF is great for use with line art such as cartoons and illustrations, and artwork with large areas of similar color, rather than photographic images

See Also

→ **1** About the Organizer

→ **48** Save an Image in Photoshop Format (PSD)

→ **49** Save an Image in TIFF Format

→ **50** Compress an Image Using GIF Format

→ **51** Compress an Image Using JPEG Format

→ **52** Save an Image in PNG Format

→ **103** About Color Management

If you open an image, make changes, and then save them, certain data might be lost forever when you close that file. For example, if you add a message to an image, it's stored on its own *layer*. Unless you save the image using the Photoshop or layered TIFF format, when you open the image later on, you'll find that the text has been embedded with the image data. You won't be able to edit, move, resize, or recolor the text, nor will you be able to erase the text and see the image data that used to be below the text.

which typically require more colors to look good. GIF format supports animation—basically multiple copies of almost-the-same image stored in one file. GIFs can also include transparent pixels. When a transparent GIF is placed on a Web page, its rectangular edges disappear, and the image appears to sit right on top of the page as shown here.

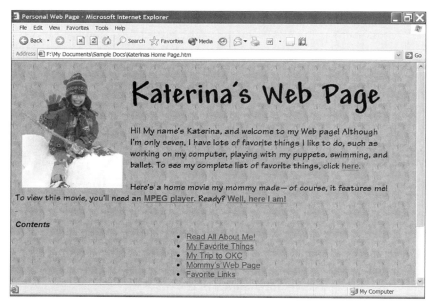

A transparent GIF blends into the Web page background.

Artifacts—Unwanted elements of a digital photo introduced by technology (by the setup of the digital camera, by the scheme used to compress an image file when saving it, or sometimes by the application used to edit the image). In a JPEG image, artifacts typically appear as rectangular blocks of slightly differing color.

- **JPEG.** JPG/JPEG images are perfect for use with photographs or other images with lots of color. JPEG uses a lossy compression technique, in which certain color values in similarly shaded regions are blended with one another in a barely noticeable way, resulting in a smaller color *palette* and a smaller image file. But if you save a JPEG file over and over again, it will develop *artifacts*. So, you should save an image in JPEG format only when you are finished editing it. When you want to retouch a JPEG image in the *Editor*, start by saving it immediately in Photoshop (*PSD) format. That way, you can save all the work you do as you work. When you're satisfied with the touchups, save a copy of the Photoshop image as JPEG. That way, you can avoid creating artifacts as you work on the image. Artifacts might also appear in a JPEG file if it is compressed too much. If that happens to you, simply go back to your Photoshop file and create a new JPEG using a smaller amount of compression. Artifacts might also appear in a JPEG file if the image contains sharp edges, such as a border, a line, or the edges of large text. If that happens, save your Photoshop file in some other format, such as TIFF or PNG.

- **JPEG 2000.** JPEG 2000 or JP2 format is similar to JPEG, but because it uses a different compression scheme, JPEG 2000 can produce smaller files, retain image quality, and produce minimal artifacts even at high compression. JPEG 2000 handles *anti-aliased* text better than JPEG, so if you have an image such as a photograph with text, JPEG 2000 might be the format to use. Be sure to see this figure, which compares JPEG and JPEG 2000 files in the Color Gallery.

  A JPEG 2000 file contains image information in its header about the color space used, which helps to ensure that the file is displayed and printed properly. JPEG 2000 supports lossless and lossy compression, *alpha transparency*, and 16-bit color. However, if you use lossy compression, then like JPEG format, a JPEG-2000 image can develop artifacts if resaved several times or if overly compressed.

- **PNG.** PNG is a fairly new format on the Web scene, so using it might mean that some users with older Web browsers won't be able to view your Web graphics correctly—and sometimes not at all, especially if the images use transparent backgrounds. PNG does offer a lossless compression method (as does GIF), so it does have that advantage over other Web-compatible formats. PNG files, when compared to GIF files, are typically smaller. They also offer other advantages, such as alpha transparency, *gamma* correction for cross-platform control, and faster *interlacing*.

NOTE

If you own a digital camera, it probably uses JPEG format. As long as you choose high quality, however, the JPEG compression should be minimal and you'll still get a good quality image. However, if your camera gives you a choice between JPEG, TIFF, or RAW format (all three are commonly used by digital cameras to save image data without loss), choose TIFF or RAW.

KEY TERM

Alpha transparency— Supported by JPEG 2000 and PNG image formats, alpha transparency is simply variable transparency, or the ability to vary the amount of transparency in an image. This enables you to gradually fade the pixels along the edge of an image against a Web page background, for example.

TIP

JPEG 2000's major drawback right now is that litigation concerning the originality of its compression scheme has compelled many manufacturers to suspend their support for it. For example, no Web browsers currently support JPEG 2000 (at least, not without third-party plugins), so you might not want to use this file type on your Web pages.

Interlacing—Also known as *interleaving*. A method of displaying a Web graphic on a user's screen in which the image is displayed progressively—typically, the image appears on the Web page quickly but without much detail, and as the download progresses, the image gains detail and sharpness.

JPEG 2000 Format

JPEG Format

This JP2 image is smaller than its JPEG counterpart, yet it retains a higher quality.

- **TIFF.** TIFF/TIF format is great to use when saving photographs or other color-intensive images because as long as you choose LZW or ZIP compression, there is no loss of image data. Unlike JPEG, which uses a lossy compression scheme, TIFF offers two lossless compression schemes (LZW or ZIP). TIFF can also save image layers which makes it a good format for saving your work in progress, if you need to use the unfinished work file on a system that does not have Photoshop Elements or Photoshop. Otherwise, use the PSD format for working images and reserve TIFF for saving copies after you've completed your work.

- **RAW.** A format used by many of the newer digital cameras today. You can think of an image in RAW format as a digital negative—uncompressed, unprocessed raw image data that's been saved in a file. The only problem with the RAW format is that there's no standard—each camera manufacturer has its own particular version of it. Thus, the file extension varies from manufacturer to manufacturer, but look for extensions such as **.dcr**, **.orf**, **.nef**, and **.crw**. Lucky for you, Photoshop Elements can read the RAW files of the most popular digital cameras, making it the perfect format for taking pictures. However, before you use RAW format on your digital camera, be sure to check Adobe's Web site for its list of compatible camera RAW formats.

 **WEB RESOURCE**

http://www.adobe.com/products/photoshop/cameraraw.html

Check Adobe's Web site for a list of compatible digital camera RAW formats.

- **Photoshop.** Before retouching a digital photo or creating an original graphic, save your file in Photoshop format (PSD), which is also supported by the *graphics editor*, Photoshop CS. Saving an image in the program's native format enables you to preserve critical image data such as *layers*, text, and *vector* objects. When you're done making changes to an image, you can always save it in a format that's more easily shareable, such as JPEG or TIFF.

If you're not going to use your image on a Web page, but simply send it over the Web using email, the image can be saved in just about any format (as long as the recipient has a program capable of reading that format). You might prefer, however, to use a compressed format such as JPEG to make the image smaller and easier to send. If file size isn't an issue, you might prefer TIFF because if you choose a lossless compression scheme such as LZW or ZIP, all your image data is preserved and the result is a high-quality image. If your purpose is to simply print the image, you can use any format compatible with the program you're using to print—in this case, any format supported by Photoshop Elements.

NOTE

If you want to be able to make changes to vector text, vector objects, or elements on layers, you *must* save the image in Photoshop format or TIFF layered format. When you save an image in any other format, vector data is converted to raster (bitmapped) data, and the image is flattened. This makes individual elements such as text and objects impossible to edit. And because Photoshop format files are typically much smaller than layered TIFF files, PSD is the format of choice for working files.

Options for Saving Images in the Editor

Saving an image in the *Editor* is roughly the same as saving a document with any other program: just click the **Save** button on the **Shortcuts** bar or choose **File, Save** and a dialog box appears with the following options:

- **As a Copy.** Select this option to save a copy of the image so that you don't overwrite the existing file. *The current image is kept open so that you can continue working*, but the image as it looks right now is saved in a new file with **copy** added to the original filename. Use this option to save copies of your working image at various stages in the editing process. Doing so allows you to go back to an earlier version if some of your edits don't work out.

- **Include in the Organizer.** Select this option to add the image to the *Organizer catalog* (if it isn't there already). By default, this option is already checked, but you can disable it if you like.

> **NOTE**
>
> If you turn off the **Layers** option when saving a layered image, the **As a Copy** option is turned on for you. This prevents you from saving a merged version of your image over top of the copy that contains the separate layers. So when you disable the **Layers** option, your layered, working image is kept open, and a merged, flattened copy is saved to the disk with a different filename.

- **Layers.** Select this option when the format you've chosen supports *layers* (Photoshop PSD or TIFF format), *and* you want to make certain that the full content and identity of all layers are saved in your file. (This option is disabled if the format you select does not support layers.) Layering is especially important when you're creating an image made up of parts of other images. With the **Layers** option disabled, the Editor merges all content in the file into a single layer before saving. See **91** **About Layers and the Layers Palette** for an explanation of layers and how they work.

- **Save in Version Set with Original.** Select this option to group the edited version of an image in the catalog, along with the original version, in a single *version set*. When this is done, both items share the same *thumbnail* in the catalog. In addition, when you chose this option, **_edited-1** (or another number, if you've edited this image several times) is added to the original filename, creating a separate file so that you do not overwrite your original or other edited copies in the version set. (See **45** **About Editing Images**.)

- **ICC Profile.** Select this option to include the *ICC color profile* being used by your system, along with the other image data, in the image file. Knowing the name of this profile will help your printer or other computers render the image as you are seeing it now, rather than making color adjustments you don't want. See **103** **About Color Management**.

- **Thumbnail.** Select this option to save an image preview. Normally, this option is always on, but if you've changed your file-saving preferences so that image previews are not automatically created when you save, you'll be able to optionally save or not save a preview for particular images. Not saving a preview makes the image file smaller; however, having a preview enables you to view an image's content in the **Open** dialog box before you actually open the file, for example.

- **Use Lower Case Extension.** Select this option to use lowercase letters in the filename extension—something that might be important if you intend to use the image on the Web or on a Linux computer, or if you're burning the image to a CD so it can be read on a computer with a different operating system (such as a Mac). By default, this option is enabled, and it's typically best to leave it like that.

NOTES

To change your preferences for saving files (such as whether image previews are created), choose **Edit, Preferences, Saving Files** from the menu.

Not all image formats support the inclusion of thumbnails. For those formats, the **Thumbnail** option is not available.

To save additional changes to a file you've already saved, click the **Save** button on the **Shortcuts** bar or choose **File, Save** from the menu. To change any of these options for a previously saved image (for example, to save a completed PSD file in TIFF format), choose **File, Save As** from the menu.

48 Save an Image in Photoshop Format (PSD)

After copying files from a digital camera onto your computer, or scanning images using a scanner, your first step should be to perform some type of backup. Typically, this involves burning copies of the image files onto a CD-R. See **5** **Import Images from a Digital Camera** for how to bring images into the *catalog* from your camera, and **14** **Back Up the Organizer Catalog** for help on making the backup copies of the catalog and its images.

After importing an image into the catalog, backing it up, and beginning work on any touchups, you will most likely want to open the image in the *Editor* and save it in the Photoshop image format (PSD). Doing so ensures that you have access to all of the Editor's features, such as *layers*, transparency, *vector* objects, and *masking*, while also preserving the integrity of your original image's data. As you work on an image, you might want to save it at various stages to which you can return later on.

Before You Begin

✔ **47** About Saving Images

See Also

→ **49** Save an Image in TIFF Format

→ **50** Compress an Image Using GIF Format

→ **51** Compress an Image Using JPEG Format

→ **52** Save an Image in PNG Format

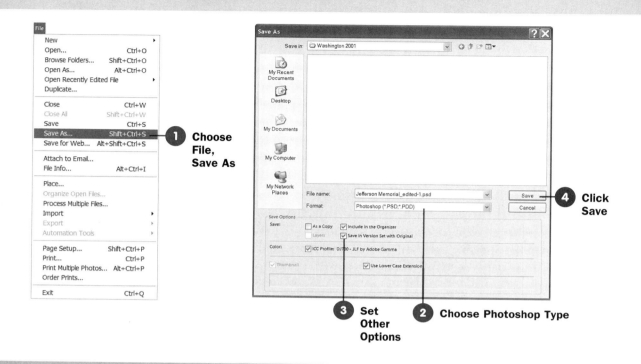

① Choose File, Save As

② Choose Photoshop Type

③ Set Other Options

④ Click Save

💡 TIPS

Photoshop Elements fully supports *EXIF*, which means that you will not lose important digital camera data when you save your original file in Photoshop format.

Although you can undo any work while a file is still open, saving intermediate stages of a final work enables you to easily return to a branching-off point, even days later. To save your work at some particular stage, choose **File, Duplicate** from the Editor menu. Type a name for the new file if you like, or accept the name the Editor suggests. Continue making changes to the new file (which is actually only a temporary file at this point), and when you save it, you'll be able to add it to the *Organizer* and stack it in a *version set* with the image's previous stages.

Instead of using the **File, Duplicate** command to create versions of your working image as you continue to edit, you can choose **File, Save As** and enable the **As a Copy** option.

① Choose File, Save As

After opening an image in the Editor, and before making any changes, choose **File, Save As** from the menu bar. The **Save As** dialog box appears.

② Choose Photoshop Type

From the **Format** drop-down list, choose **Photoshop** (*.PSD;*.PDD).

③ Set Other Options

Select other options as needed. For example, to save this edited copy with a different filename and group it with the original file in the catalog, enable the **Save in Version Set with Original** check box. See **47** **About Saving Images** for help in selecting options.

If desired, change the filename displayed in the **File name** text box. Normally, you do not have to do this because the file will automatically have a different file extension than the original file (the file extension changes because you've chosen a different file type).

④ Click Save

Click the **Save** button. If you see a note reminding you that you're saving this image as part of a version set, click **OK** to continue. The image is saved in PSD format. Make your changes to the image and save the file again. Before printing, emailing, uploading to the Internet, or using in a creation, you should probably convert the PSD image to a format that's smaller, easier to work with, and compatible with its ultimate purpose. See **49** **Save an Image in TIFF Format**, **50** **Compress an Image Using GIF Format**, **51** **Compress an Image Using JPEG Format**, or **52** **Save an Image in PNG Format**.

NOTE

As you periodically save the changes to the image that you've already saved once in Photoshop format, when you choose **File, Save** from the menu or click the **Save** button on the **Shortcuts bar**, the Editor responds by silently resaving your image and not bothering you with any other dialog boxes. Resaving an image in this manner does not create a new version, but simply overwrites the current file. If you're working in PSD format, that's what you want, unless you want to save a version of the working file at some stage, as explained in the introduction to this task.

TIP

If you have several photos that are similar to one another—especially if you shot a grouping of the same subjects at approximately the same time—you can have the Editor make the same corrections to all of them simultaneously, and automatically save the results (using PSD format, if you like). See **61** **Rename, Resize, Reformat, and Retouch a Group of Images** for details.

49 Save an Image in TIFF Format

Before You Begin

✔ **47** About Saving Images

See Also

→ **61** Rename, Resize, Reformat, and Retouch a Group of Images

NOTES

Although layered TIFF format is pretty universally accepted, there are no guarantees that a program will be able to open your image if you save it in that format. So always save your working copy in PSD format.

Turning off the **Layers** option automatically turns on the **As a Copy** option; that's just a protection against your accidentally overwriting a file that contains layer information.

If desired, change the filename displayed in the **File name** box. Normally you do not have to do this because the file will automatically have a different file extension than the original file (the file extension changes because you've chosen a different file type).

As you learned in **47** About Saving Images, TIFF format is a great format for photographic images because it offers *lossless compression*, meaning that your image data is not discarded during the compression process. In fact, some cameras use TIFF format when saving images in high-quality mode. You should start out by saving an image in Photoshop Elements in PSD format to create a working copy (see **48** Save an Image in Photoshop Format (PSD)). After making all your changes to the image, save the image in a format that's easier to share, such as TIFF.

TIFF format allows you to retain the various separate *layers* you might have created during the editing process, although you'll probably not want to do so because the layer data is already safely stored in your PSD file. If, however, you are planning to continue your edits on a computer that does not have a program that reads PSD format (such as Photoshop Elements or Photoshop), you can use the layered TIFF format to save your work in progress.

① Choose File, Save As

In the *Editor*, open the file you want to convert to TIFF format. The file is probably a PSD-formatted copy of an image to which you've already made changes. Choose **File**, **Save As** from the menu bar. The **Save As** dialog box appears.

② Choose TIFF Format

From the **Format** drop-down list, choose **TIFF**.

③ Select Save Options

Select options as needed. For example, if you're resaving a PSD file to TIFF format because you're through making changes, you will most likely want to disable the **Layers** check box. This action merges the layers together into a single-layered image, and does not save the layers separately. Because the layers are preserved in the PSD file, you won't need the separate layers in the TIFF file as well.

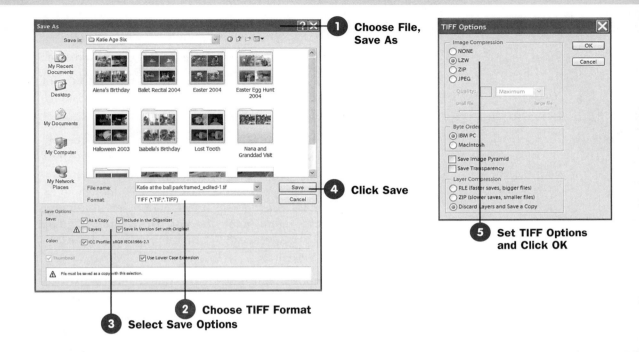

1 Choose File, Save As

4 Click Save

5 Set TIFF Options and Click OK

2 Choose TIFF Format

3 Select Save Options

To save the TIFF copy in the *catalog* and add it to the *version set* that includes the edited PSD copy and the original file, enable both the **Include in Organizer** and **Save in Version Set with Original** check boxes. See **47** **About Saving Images** for help in selecting other options.

4 **Click Save**

Click the **Save** button. If you see a note reminding you that you're saving this image as part of a version set, click **OK** to continue. The **TIFF Options** dialog box appears.

5 **Set TIFF Options and Click OK**

Select an **Image Compression**. Compressing a file reduces its size; however, as long as you choose LZW or ZIP, you can compress your file without sacrificing image data. Between the two, TIFF-LZW compression is probably more universally accepted; TIFF-ZIP compression might not be compatible with older programs. If you choose JPEG compression, select a **Quality** level from the drop-down list and drag the slider to fine-tune the level of compression.

Select a **Byte Order**. You can usually leave this set to **IBM PC**, but if you know that this image is destined for use on a Macintosh, you should select **Macintosh** instead.

To save multiple *resolutions* of your image in the TIFF file, enable the **Save Image Pyramid** option. Some programs might then be able to display your image in the resolution you select when it's opened; Photoshop Elements simply displays such an image at its highest resolution. If the image has transparent pixels in it and you want to preserve them, enable the **Save Transparency** option. TIFF transparency is not compatible with all programs, so you might not want to use it.

In the **Layer Compression** frame, the **Discard Layers and Save a Copy** option is normally enabled. However, if you enabled the **Layers** option in the **Save As** dialog box, you can choose how those layers are saved in the TIFF file. Select **RLE** to create a file that's quicker to save yet larger; select **ZIP** for a smaller file that takes a bit longer to save. When you're satisfied with your selections, click **OK**.

The file is saved. If the **As a Copy** option was enabled in the **Save As** dialog box, your original PSD file is still open; the TIFF copy is saved to disk and closed automatically. Click **Save** on the **Shortcuts** bar to make sure that your final edits are preserved in the PSD file, then click the **Close** button on the PSD image to close it as well.

---

50 Compress an Image Using GIF Format

Before You Begin

✔ **47** About Saving Images

✔ **63** Change Color Mode

See Also

→ **61** Rename, Resize, Reformat, and Retouch a Group of Images

As you learned in **47** About Saving Images, GIF format is used with images that contain a *palette* of 256 or fewer colors—typically images with large patches of one color, line art images such as cartoons and illustrations, and images that contain transparent backgrounds. You'll also find the GIF format used to create simple animations such as a flag waving in the breeze.

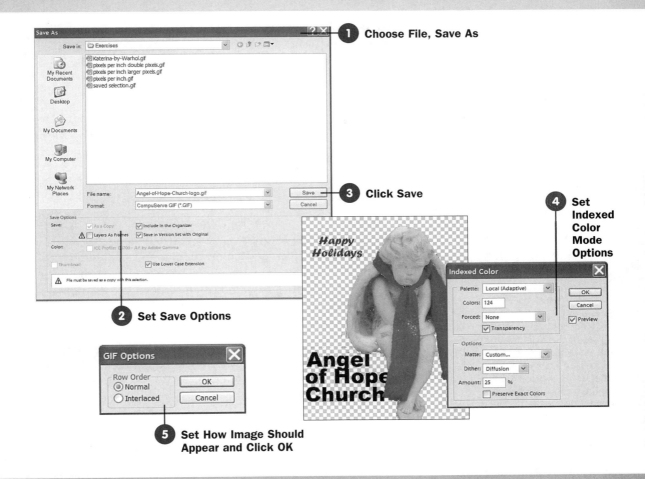

1 Choose File, Save As

2 Set Save Options

3 Click Save

4 Set Indexed Color Mode Options

5 Set How Image Should Appear and Click OK

Saving a file in GIF format gives you a number of options, such as the total number of colors you want to use (a factor that determines ultimate file size), how you want to simulate colors not in the limited color palette (using a process called *dithering*), and whether you want transparency. The latter is a sticky issue, not only because there are so many ways you might have varied the transparency within your image (reducing the opacity of a *layer*, *feathering* the edge of a selection, or using a brush with a lower opacity setting), but also because GIF supports transparency only in an all-or-nothing manner. (To retain variable transparency, or *alpha transparency*, save your image in PNG, JPEG 2000, or PSD format.) If you choose not to have transparency in your GIF image,

KEY TERM

Dithering—A technique for simulating a color whose value does not appear in an image's palette by mixing pixels of the two closest available shades, in either a predefined or mathematical pattern.

you can choose a color to convert the transparent pixels to. Semi-transparent pixels are blended with this color to make them opaque, whether or not you retain transparency.

① Choose File, Save As

In the *Editor*, open the file you want to convert to GIF format. This file is probably a PSD-formatted copy of an image to which you've already made changes. Choose **File**, **Save As** from the menu bar. The **Save As** dialog box appears.

② Set Save Options

From the **Format** drop-down list, choose **CompuServe GIF**. If the image contains multiple *layers*, you can have them appear in order, one after the other, in a simple animation by enabling the **Layers as Frames** check box. Imagine a book of pictures that seem to move as you flip the pages, and you'll get the idea of an animated GIF. Here, the "pages" are the separate layers in your image.

To save the GIF copy in the *catalog* and add it to the *version set* that includes the edited PSD copy and the original file, enable both the **Include in the Organizer** and **Save in Version Set with Original** check boxes. See **47** About Saving Images for help in selecting other options.

If desired, change the filename displayed in the **File name** box. Normally you do not have to do this because the file will automatically have a different file extension than the original file (the file extension changes because you've chosen a different file type).

③ Click Save

Click the **Save** button. If you see a note reminding you that you're saving this image as part of a version set, click **OK** to continue. The **Indexed Color** dialog box appears.

④ Set Indexed Color Mode Options

In the **Indexed Color** dialog box, select the options you want to use to reduce the number of colors in this image. You'll find a full description of each of these options in **63** **Change Color Mode**. Enable the **Preview** check box in the **Indexed Color** dialog box to change the image in the Editor window based on your selections. When you're satisfied with the results, click OK. The **GIF Options** dialog box appears.

5 Set How Image Should Appear and Click OK

In the **GIF Options** dialog box, choose how you want the image to appear on a user's system when it's downloaded from the Web. To have the GIF file appear one line at a time from the top down, select **Normal**. To have it appear in several cycles, with details filled in gradually, selected **Interlaced**. Click **OK** to convert the image. The GIF version of your image is saved to disk, and your original image is left open in the Editor. Click **Save** on the **Shortcuts** bar to make sure that your final edits are preserved in the PSD file, then click the **Close** button on the PSD image to close it as well.

NOTE

Even if you're not creating an animation, you can use the **Save For Web** dialog box to create your GIF image by choosing **File, Save for Web** from the menu. There a few less compression options there, but you'll find some tools that allow you to zoom in and out, compare the original and the compressed image side by side, view the current file size and download times, and preview the image in your Web browser. If you use the **Save for Web** command, however, you will not be given an opportunity to save the file in the Organizer or create a version set with the original image.

51 Compress an Image Using JPEG Format

In **47** **About Saving Images**, you learned that JPEG images are typically photographs or other complex images with lots of colors or variations in tone. Among the chief purposes for the creation of the JPEG format was to achieve very small file sizes for such images; however, the degree of compression you apply to a JPEG image is variable—from none at all to a level so high you can no longer tell what the image is. The most important point to remember about the JPEG format is that you should not use it for a working file. Instead, use JPEG to save a PSD image in a shareable format only when you're done making changes. Constantly changing and resaving a JPEG file can generate *artifacts* and other degradations to the image.

Before You Begin

✔ **47** About Saving Images

See Also

→ **61** Rename, Resize, Reformat, and Retouch a Group of Images

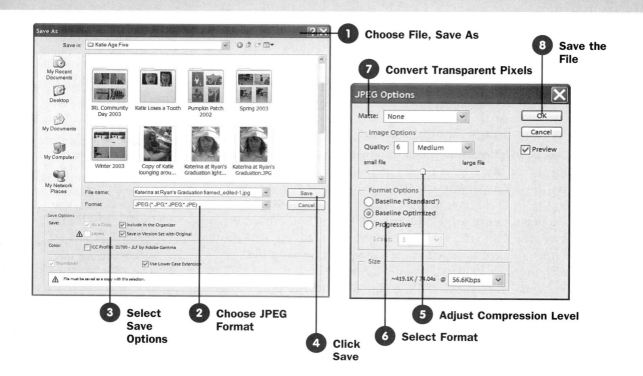

1 Choose File, Save As

8 Save the File

7 Convert Transparent Pixels

3 Select Save Options

2 Choose JPEG Format

4 Click Save

5 Adjust Compression Level

6 Select Format

NOTE

If your photograph contains added text, you'll get better results if you compress the image using JPEG 2000 format. With JPEG format (especially at middle to high compression levels), a lot of artifacts are created around the edges of the text. Yet at these same compression levels, a *photograph* saved with JPEG format looks fine.

1 **Choose File, Save As**

In the *Editor*, open the file you want to convert to JPEG format. The file is probably a PSD-formatted copy of an image to which you've already made changes. Then choose **File, Save As** from the menu bar. The **Save As** dialog box appears.

2 **Choose JPEG Format**

From the **Format** drop-down list, choose **JPEG**.

3 **Select Save Options**

Select options as needed. For example, to save the JPEG copy in the *catalog* and add it to the *version set* that includes the edited PSD copy and the original file, enable both the **Include in the Organizer** and **Save in Version Set with Original** check boxes. See **47** **About Saving Images** for help in selecting other options.

If desired, change the filename displayed in the **File name** box. Normally, you do not have to do this because the file will automatically have a different file extension than the original file (the file extension changes because you've chosen a different file type).

④ Click Save

Click the **Save** button. If you see a note reminding you that you're saving this image as part of a version set, click **OK** to continue. The **JPEG Options** dialog box appears.

⑤ Adjust Compression Level

Select the level of compression from the **Quality** drop down list, such as **High**. Fine-tune the amount of compression by dragging the slider left (to increase compression and reduce quality) or right (to decrease compression and increase quality).

⑥ Select Format

From the **Format Options** frame, select a format for the file. Your choice not only affects how the image appears on a user's system when it's downloaded from the Web, but also the final file size. To have the JPEG file appear one line at a time from the top down, select either the **Baseline ("Standard")** or **Baseline Optimized** option. With **Baseline**, the image is compressed in its entirety; **Standard** uses the original JPEG compression algorithm; **Optimized** uses a newer algorithm that might not be compatible with the NCSA Mosaic Web browser (which is all but extinct). The **Baseline Optimized** option produces the smaller file of the two options.

⑦ Convert Transparent Pixels

The JPEG format does not support transparency. If the original image file contains transparent pixels, select a color to change them to from the **Matte** drop-down list. Semi-transparent pixels are blended with the color you select to create fully opaque pixels. You can choose **Foreground Color, Background Color, White, Black, 50% Gray,** or **Netscape Gray** (a lighter gray) from the list, or select your own color by choosing **Custom** from the **Matte** drop-down list and using the **Color Picker** that appears to select a color to use. To choose a color from the image, just click in the image

 TIPS

Before you begin, adjust the image view so that you can clearly see any area of the image you want to preserve after the conversion is made to the limited color palette. For example, you might zoom in on a face, a curved object or bit of text, or any other critical area.

You can also use the **Save For Web** dialog box to compress your JPEG image by choosing **File, Save for Web** from the menu. There are a few less compression options there, but you'll find some tools that allow you to zoom in and out, compare the original and the compressed image side by side, and preview the image in your Web browser. If you use the **Save for Web** command, however, you will not be given an opportunity to save the file in the Organizer or create a version set with the original image.

 NOTE

Enable the **Preview** check box in the **JPEG Options** dialog box to change the image in the Editor window based on your selections.

TIP

At high compression levels, you might not only experience a loss of quality, but also introduce artifacts and other anomalies.

TIPS

As you make selections, the file size and download times are displayed at the bottom of the **JPEG Options** dialog box.

Typically, you'll want to set the **Matte** color to the same color as your Web page so that the nontransparent part of your image can "float" on top of the background seamlessly.

with the **Eyedropper** tool. If you choose **None** from the **Matte** drop-down list, semi-transparent pixels are blended with white while transparent pixels are simply made white.

8 Save the File

When you are satisfied with your choices, click **OK** to convert the image. The JPEG version of your image is saved to disk, and your original image is left open in the Editor. Click **Save** on the **Shortcuts** bar to make sure that your final edits are preserved in the PSD file, then click the **Close** button on the PSD image to close it as well.

 Save an Image in PNG Format

Before You Begin

✔ **47** About Saving Images

See Also

→ **61** Rename, Resize, Reformat, and Retouch a Group of Images

 TIP

Because transparency is one of the features not universally supported by Web browsers, you might not want to use transparency in your PNG image. In particular, the alpha channel in a PNG file allows you to store pixels of varying degrees of transparency regardless of color; however, this feature is not supported by Internet Explorer.

As you learned in **47** About Saving Images, the PNG file format is compatible with certain Web browsers, but not all. Because it isn't uniformly accepted as a Web format, you might not want to use PNG images on your Web site. PNG format, like GIF and JPEG formats, offers a variable amount of compression, depending on the choices you make. Unlike JPEG, PNG offers a lossless compression method. Like GIF, PNG offers transparency, but unlike GIF, PNG supports *alpha transparency*.

PNG format follows two compression schemes: PNG-24 and PNG-8. Both formats are lossless, but PNG-8 increases compression by reducing the number of colors an image displays onscreen. PNG-8 format is similar to GIF, and requires you to select the optimal color palette for best display. PNG-8 files are typically much smaller than GIF files. PNG-24 files are similar to JPEG but larger; however, PNG-24 files use lossless compression which JPEG files do not.

1 Choose File, Save As

In the *Editor*, open the file you want to convert to PNG format. The file is probably a PSD-formatted copy of an image to which you've already made changes. Then choose **File, Save As** from the menu bar. The **Save As** dialog box appears.

2 Choose PNG Format

From the **Format** drop-down list, choose **PNG**.

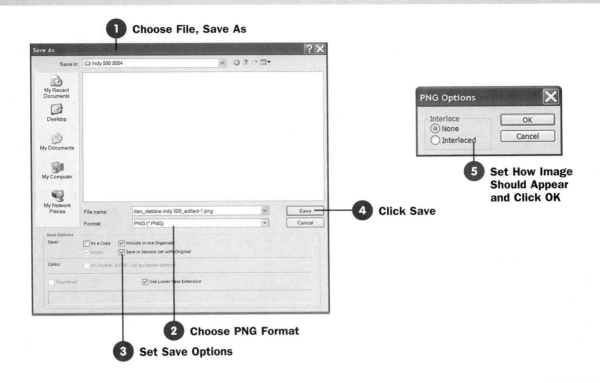

1 Choose File, Save As

5 Set How Image Should Appear and Click OK

4 Click Save

2 Choose PNG Format

3 Set Save Options

3 Select Save Options

Select options as needed. For example, to save the PNG copy in the *catalog* and add it to the *version set* that includes the edited PSD copy and the original file, enable both the **Include in the Organizer** and **Save in Version Set with Original** check boxes. See **47** About Saving Images for help in selecting other options.

4 Click Save

Click the **Save** button. If you see a note reminding you that you're saving this image as part of a version set, click **OK** to continue. The **PNG Options** dialog box appears.

NOTE

If desired, change the file-name displayed in the **File name** box. Normally, you do not have to do this because the file will automatically have a different file exten-sion than the original file (the file extension changes because you've chosen a different file type).

TIP

The method shown in this task results in a PNG-24 file. To compress the file even more using PNG-8 format, choose **File, Save for Web** to display the **Save For Web** dialog box. You'll find options for selecting an 8-bit color palette, along with tools that allow you to zoom in and out, compare the original and the compressed image side by side, and preview the image in your Web browser. If you use the **Save for Web** command, however, you will not be given an opportunity to save the file in the Organizer or create a version set with the original image. For help in selecting a color palette and choosing other options related to PNG-8, see **63** Change Color Mode.

5 Set How Image Should Appear and Click OK

In the **PNG Options** dialog box, choose how you want the image to appear on a user's system when it's downloaded from the Web. To have the PNG file appear one line at a time from the top down, select **Normal**. To have the image appear in several cycles, with details filled in gradually, select the **Interlaced** option.

Click **OK** to convert the image. If the **As a Copy** option was enabled in the **Save As** dialog box, your original PSD file is still open; the PNG copy is saved to disk and closed automatically. Click **Save** on the **Shortcuts** bar to make sure that your final edits are preserved in the PSD file, then click the **Close** button on the PSD image to close it as well.

7

Performing Basic Image Tasks

IN THIS CHAPTER:

53 About Image Information

54 Arrange the View of Multiple Images in the Editor

55 Zoom In and Out with the Zoom Tool

56 Zoom In and Out with the Navigator Palette

57 Scroll a Large Image

58 Magnify Your Work

59 About Size and Resolution

60 Change Image Size or Resolution

61 Rename, Resize, Reformat, and Retouch a Group of Images

62 Increase the Area Around an Image

63 Change Color Mode

This book is designed around you, the busy user, enabling you to quickly jump to whatever topic you're interested in at the moment. However, it seems that no matter what kind of image you're working on—a Web button, an old black-and-white photo, or pictures from your child's recent birthday party—you'll find yourself performing some of the same tasks. In this chapter, you'll learn how to accomplish the most common tasks, such as displaying image information, zooming in and out, scrolling, magnifying an area so that you can perform detail work, resizing an image, and changing the number of colors you can work with.

53 About Image Information

See Also

→ **60** Change Image Size or Resolution

→ **105** Ensure That What You See Is What You Get

When needed, the *Editor* can display information about the basic characteristics of an image—its file type, *resolution*, size, and data specific to the conditions under which it was taken. To display this metadata (so-called because it's stored at the top of the image file) for any image open in the Editor, select **File, File Info** from the menu bar. A dialog box opens, loaded with information about the current image.

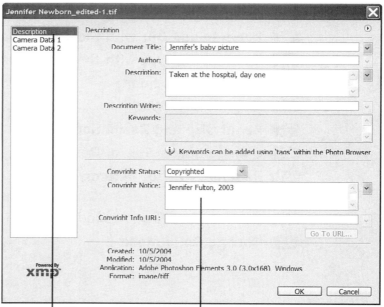

Click a Category to Display Its Page   You Can Enter Some Metadata Manually

*The **File Info** dialog box contains lots of information about your image.*

On the left, you'll find a list of categories of information stored within the image file. Click a category to display its page of information. For example, click the **Camera Data 1** category to find out what the flash setting was when you took this photograph. Some metadata can be entered by you, simply by clicking inside any of the white boxes. For example, you might enter your name under **Author** or type in a **Copyright Notice**. Metadata you can view but not change is shown in gray. This kind of metadata is typically *EXIF* data that your camera recorded when the image was taken, such as shutter speed and f-stop.

You can also change some of this metadata through the *Organizer*. For example, if you click the **Description** category on the left, you'll see the text *caption* you entered in the Organizer (shown here as the **Description**) and any *tags* or *collection* markers you attached to the image (shown here as **Keywords**).The metadata you enter manually is stored in the *alpha channel* of the image. Metadata you enter through this dialog box is permanently saved *only* if you store the image in PSD, TIFF, PNG, GIF, or JPEG format. At the bottom of the **Description** page, you'll find basic information about the image, such as the *file date, modified date*, and file type.

You can add a copyright notice on the **Description** page by changing the **Copyright Status** drop-down list to **Copyrighted**, and typing your copyright text in the **Copyright Notice** text box. You can add your Web page address in the **Copyright Info URL** box. Note, however, that copyright data such as this is of limited use because anyone with a program capable of reading image metadata can change or remove it. Better to protect your images with a copyright that can't be removed—see **191 Add Copyright Information** for help.

As I mentioned earlier, metadata your digital camera recorded when the shot was taken—such as the camera type, date the photo was taken, and shot conditions such as f-stop, shutter speed, and focal length—can be found on the **Camera Data 1** and **Camera Data 2** pages in the **File Info** dialog box. Some of this data can be used by an EXIF-compatible printer to print your photo more accurately, with better color and brightness matching. To make sure that you don't lose this valuable EXIF data, save your digital camera file using an EXIF-compatible program (Photoshop Elements just happens to be one), in an EXIF-compatible format (Photoshop PSD or JPEG). See **105 Ensure That What You See Is What You Get** for more information.

NOTES

You can also view and change a file's metadata on the **Metadata** palette within the **File Browser**. In the Editor, choose **File, Browse Folders** to display the browser. In the Organizer, you can view an image's metadata on the **Properties** pane. Choose **Window, Properties** from the Organizer menu, then click the **Metadata** button at the top of the **Properties** pane.

Some metadata, such as an image's size and resolution, is added or changed by Photoshop Elements when you edit an image and save changes. So even if you have an image that started out as a scan of a printed photo, there might be information for you to view in the **File Info** dialog box.

KEY TERM

Alpha channel—Data saved with an image for reuse when needed, such as selections, *masks*, and creator information.

NOTE

If you use the **Save for Web** command to compress an image for use on the Web, as part of its compression process, the *Editor* will strip all EXIF metadata from the image. So you'll definitely want to save your compressed image as a *copy*, and save your original image and your changes in a PSD-formatted file. See **50** **Compress an Image Using GIF Format, 51** **Compress an Image Using JPEG Format**, and **52** **Save an Image in PNG Format** for a safer method of compressing images for size and speed.

TIPS

The **Properties** pane normally appears over top of the thumbnails in the catalog. Drag it by its title bar to move it out of the way, or park it in the **Organize Bin** by choosing **Window, Dock Properties in Organize Bin**. Select this command again to make the **Properties** pane "float" in the work area once more.

You can display the **Properties** pane while using **Date View**, but you can't dock it because the **Organize Bin** is not displayed.

You can resize the **Properties** pane to make its data easier to read. Just drag a side or corner to resize.

Also on the **Camera Data 2** page, you'll find the image's current size in pixels, resolution, and *ICC color profile* (listed here as **Color Source**).

In the Organizer, the **Properties** pane can provide you with further information about the currently selected image. To display the **Properties** pane, click the **Show or Hide Properties** button on the **Options** bar, or choose **Window, Properties**. Although the **Properties** pane also displays EXIF data, it includes other information that you won't find in the **File Info** dialog box. In the **Properties** pane, you'll find information about where the image is stored, its file date, text caption, audio caption, and any notes you attached on the **General** tab. Markers you might have attached to an image are listed on the **Tags** tab. The file date, modified date, *import date* and related information can be found on the **History** tab, and EXIF and other metadata is located on the **Metadata** tab. To display a condensed version of the metadata, select the **Brief** option; to display all the metadata, select the **Complete** option instead.

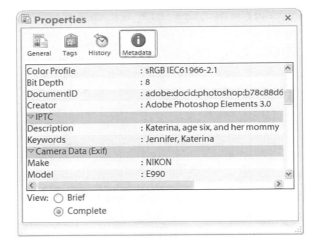

*The **Properties** pane enables you to access image information from within the Organizer.*

54 Arrange the View of Multiple Images in the Editor

As you work on an image, you might find it convenient to open a similar image at the same time. For example, perhaps you're copying data from one image into the other. Or perhaps you're trying to match the brightness or contrast levels in both images. In any case, the *Editor* provides commands that will help you not only arrange multiple images so that you can review them both easily, but also to zoom in on the same location within each image, such as the upper-right corner.

As you learned in **43** About the Editor, *Multi-window mode* enables you to arrange open images in either a tiled fashion (in which images are placed in similarly sized windows, right to left, like ceramic tiles) or in a cascade (in which images slightly overlap each other, like a deck of cards). Because the cascade arrangement does not allow you to really compare two images, you'll use the tiled arrangement in this task. After you've arranged your two images in a tiled fashion, you can zoom in at the same level and even scroll to the same location within the image windows, as explained in this task.

Before You Begin

✔ **43** About the Editor
✔ **46** Open an Image for Editing

See Also

→ **55** Zoom In and Out with the Zoom Tool

❶ Open Multiple Images

In the *Organizer*, click the *thumbnail* of the first image you want to work on, then press **Ctrl** and click the second one. Then on the **Shortcuts** bar, to open the Editor and display the images, click the **Edit** button, and from the menu that appears, choose **Go to Standard Edit**.

❷ Tile the Images

If the **Automatically Tile Windows** button (the "four squares" icon at the right end of the Editor's menu bar) is pushed in, the two images will be automatically tiled for you. If not, click the **Automatically Tile Windows** button to enable it, or choose **Window, Images, Tile** to arrange the two images in a tiled pattern.

▲ NOTES

You can arrange multiple image windows only while using **Standard Edit**. This task does not work while you are in **Quick Fix** mode.

If the Editor is already open and you are working on other image(s), minimize those image windows or save and close them (if you're done working on them) before beginning this task.

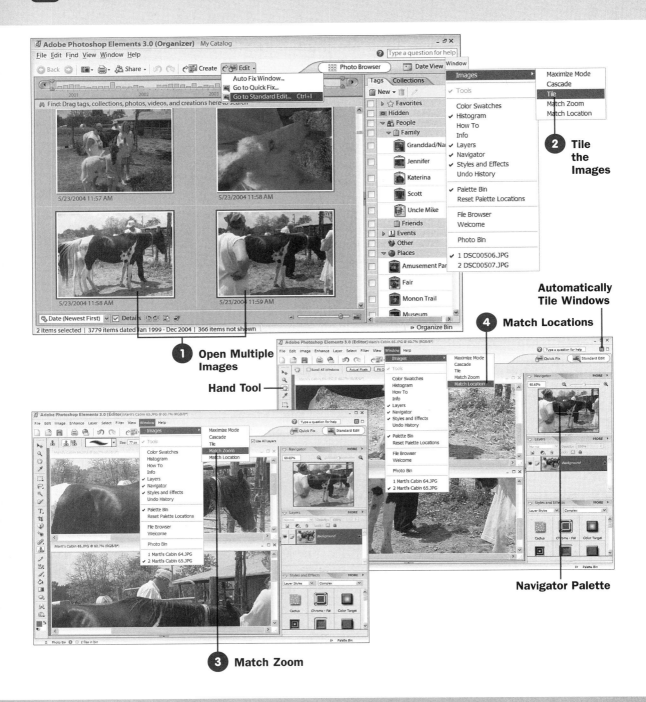

2 Tile the Images

Automatically Tile Windows

4 Match Locations

1 Open Multiple Images

Hand Tool

Navigator Palette

3 Match Zoom

③ Match Zoom

To zoom in both images by the same amount, click one image window to make it active. Then adjust the zoom using the **Navigator** palette. See **56** **Zoom In and Out with the Navigator Palette** for help.

Choose **Window, Images, Match Zoom.** The second image is zoomed to the same level as the active image.

④ Match Locations

Whether or not you match the zoom between the two images, you can scroll to the exact same location within each image window. To do that, click one image window to make it active. Then scroll to the portion of the window you want to see. You can use the scrollbars, the **Hand** tool, or the **Navigator** palette, as explained in **57** **Scroll a Large Image.**

Choose **Window, Images, Match Location.** The second image is scrolled to the exact same location as the first image. Here, I opened two similar images, arranged them, and then zoomed them to the same level and the same location so that I could clone the horse's head from one image into the other, essentially erasing the person on the right from the second image.

NOTES

Do not adjust the zoom using the **Zoom** tool, or the two windows might become untiled. If that happens, repeat step 2 to retile the windows.

To make more room for the two tiled windows, you might want to hide the **Photo Bin** by clicking its button on the **Status** bar.

TIP

You can continue to match the locations within the two images, even as you scroll. Just click the **Hand** tool in the **Toolbox** and enable the **Scroll All Windows** option in the **Options** bar. Then click in one window and scroll using the **Hand** tool. The second window is scrolled by that same amount.

---

55 Zoom In and Out with the Zoom Tool

Whether you're making changes to a photograph or some artwork you've created yourself, you must be able to view the image clearly to make precise changes. Typically, this means zooming in on some area that doesn't look right so that you can discern the problem, and later zooming back out again to see whether the change you made looks right when the image is viewed at its regular size. To zoom in on an image and back out again, use the **Zoom** tool.

① Select the Zoom Tool

Open an image in the *Editor* and then click the **Zoom** tool in the **Toolbox**.

See Also

→ **56** Zoom In and Out with the Navigator Palette

→ **58** Magnify Your Work

---

① Select the Zoom Tool

Zoom In
Zoom
Out

② Choose a Zoom Amount

③ Or Click to Zoom

④ Or Zoom to a Set Size

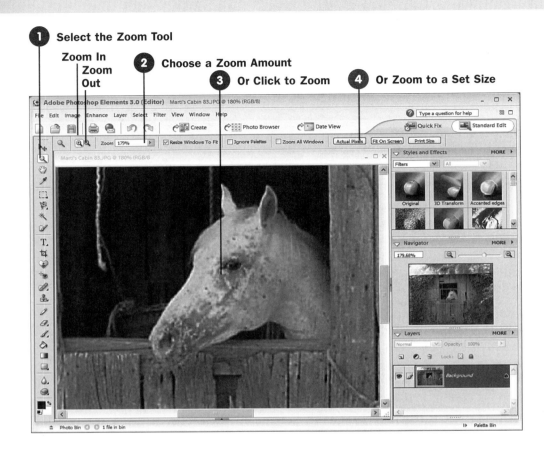

② Choose a Zoom Amount

The **Zoom** tool provides many ways in which you can zoom. To view an image at a particular zoom level (such as 50%), select the correct percentage from the **Zoom** box on the **Options** bar, type a new percentage, and press **Enter.** You can also use the slider on the **Zoom** box to select a zoom amount by dragging the slider left or right.

TIP

To zoom in and out without actually selecting the **Zoom** tool first, press and hold **Ctrl+Spacebar** and click the image to zoom in. Press and hold **Alt+Spacebar** and click the image to zoom out.

3 Or Click to Zoom

You can zoom by a predetermined amount toward a particular point within an image. First, click the **Zoom In** or **Zoom Out** button on the **Options** bar to determine the direction of the zoom. Then click the point you want to zoom in on (or away from) within the image window.

To zoom in on a particular area of an image, simply drag with the **Zoom In** tool to select the area you want to see up close. The selected area is enlarged to fit the size of the image window.

4 Or Zoom to a Set Size

To view the image at 100% (based on roughly 72 PPI, or optimum screen resolution), click the **Actual Pixels** button on the **Options** bar. You can also double-click the **Zoom** tool in the **Toolbox** to view the image at 100%. Assuming that a user's screen resolution is the same as yours, this option displays an image in the same size it will look on somebody else's screen.

To zoom the image as large as possible to fill the workspace, click the **Fit On Screen** button. You can also double-click the **Hand** tool in the **Toolbox** to fit the image to the workspace, and center the image within the window.

To zoom the image to the approximate magnification it will be when you print it (based on the current image resolution), click the **Print Size** button.

 TIPS

When you're zooming an image in or out to any percentage, you can change the size of the image window to fit the image, up to the available workspace, by first enabling the **Resize Window to Fit** option on the **Options** bar. To allow the image window to expand below free-floating *palettes* that might be in the workspace, enable the **Ignore Palettes** option. (To temporarily hide free-floating palettes, press **Tab**; press **Tab** again to make them reappear.) To zoom all open image windows by the same amount, enable the **Zoom All Windows** option. This option works only if you zoom using the **Zoom In** or **Zoom Out** buttons, and not the **Zoom** slider.

---

56 Zoom In and Out with the Navigator Palette

In the preceding task, you learned how to zoom in and out using the **Zoom** tool and its options. However, if the **Navigator** *palette* is displayed, you can use it to zoom in and out without changing to the **Zoom** tool first.

See Also

→ **55** Zoom In and Out with the Zoom Tool

→ **58** Magnify Your Work

1 Display the Navigator Palette

2 Enter a Zoom Amount

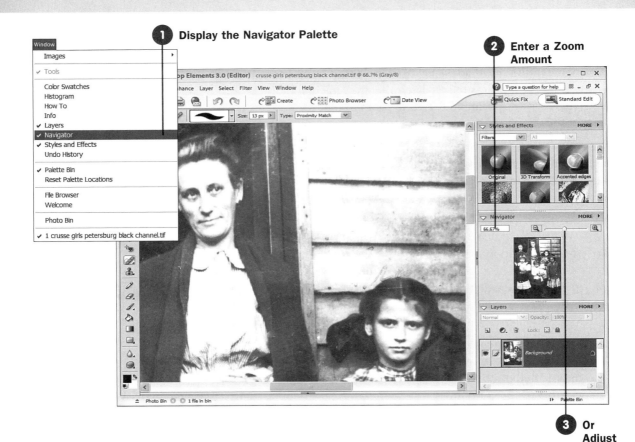

3 Or Adjust Zoom Slider

1 Display the Navigator Palette

Open an image in the *Editor*. If the **Navigator** palette is not displayed, choose **Window, Navigator** from the menu bar.

2 Enter a Zoom Amount

To view an image at a particular zoom level (such as 50%), select the correct zoom percentage from the box on the left side of the palette. Then type a new zoom percentage and press **Enter**.

③ Or Adjust Zoom Slider

You can also drag the slider on the **Navigator** palette to zoom. Drag the slider to the left to zoom out; drag it to the right to zoom in.

TIP

To zoom by a predetermined amount, click either of the **Zoom** buttons, located on either side of the slider. The minus button zooms out, whereas the plus button zooms in.

57 Scroll a Large Image

If an image is being shown with a magnification larger than the image window can display, parts of that image will be obscured from view. If you want to make changes on a part of the image you can't currently see, you'll have to scroll to view that part of the image. To do that, use the **Hand** tool, the scrollbars, or the **Navigator** *palette*.

① Select the Hand Tool

Open an image in the *Editor* and click the **Hand** tool in the Toolbox.

② Drag with the Hand Tool

Click the mouse in the image window and drag with the hand pointer to display the portion of the image you want to view. For example, drag down with the **Hand** tool to view a part of an image that's hidden just above the currently displayed portion.

③ Or Drag Navigator Rectangle

You can also reposition the viewable portion of the image by dragging the red rectangle within the **Navigator** palette. (If the **Navigator** palette is not displayed, choose **Window, Navigator** from the menu bar.) The rectangle encompasses the portion of the image you're actually seeing in the workspace; when it frames the entire thumbnail, you're actually seeing the entire image.

④ Make Small Adjustments

Click the scroll arrows on the horizontal/vertical scrollbars or press the arrow keys on the keyboard to move the viewable portion of the image by a small amount.

See Also

→ **55** Zoom In and Out with the Zoom Tool

→ **56** Zoom In and Out with the Navigator Palette

TIPS

A quick way to activate the **Hand** tool without actually clicking it in the **Toolbox** is to simply hold the **Spacebar** as you drag inside the image window.

The **Navigator** palette has several advantages over the other scrolling methods. Most notably, you can scroll quickly in the direction you want, and you can see what you're about to do before you do it.

To scroll to a particular point within an image, click that point in the image preview shown on the **Navigator** palette. The red rectangle moves to center itself on that point, and the image is scrolled by that same amount.

4 Make Small Adjustments

3 Or Drag Navigator Rectangle

1 Select the Hand Tool

2 Drag with the Hand Tool

58 Magnify Your Work

See Also

→ **55** Zoom In and Out with the Zoom Tool

→ **56** Zoom In and Out with the Navigator Palette

Some changes you'll want to make to an image will involve working in a small confined area. For example, perhaps you want to remove a small mole or other distraction from a person's face. To do that, you can use the **Clone Stamp** tool, but what if you can't see the area you want to fix all that clearly? You could zoom in, of course, but it might be nice to be able to view the changes as you make them using a more zoomed-out view. Of course, there's always the **Navigator** *palette* and its small image *thumbnail*, but your tiny changes might not be noticeable in that window. What you need is the ability to quickly zoom in on your work while still maintaining the big-picture view of your changes. To accomplish this task, you use a duplicate image window.

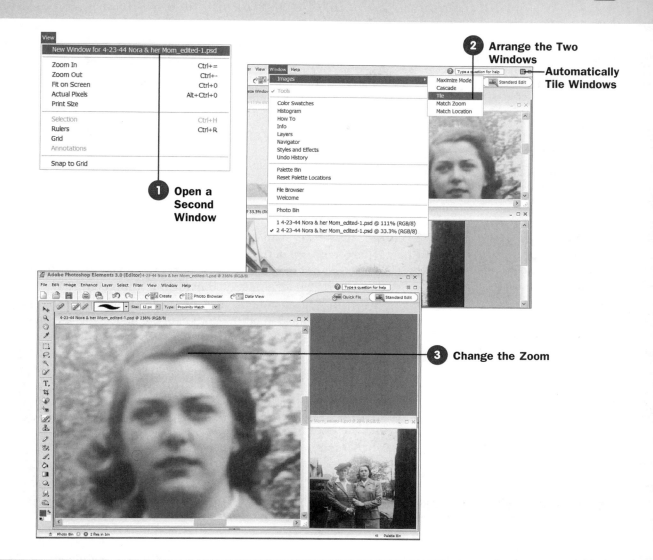

2 Arrange the Two
Windows

— Automatically
Tile Windows

1 Open a
Second
Window

3 Change the Zoom

1 Open a Second Window

Open an image in the *Editor* and increase the zoom so that the
area you want to work on is magnified and easy to see. To open a
second window that displays the same image, choose **View, New
Window for XXX**, where XXX is the name of the image file.

NOTE

If you don't want to open a second window on an image, you can quickly zoom in and out of an already open image window by pressing **Ctrl+Spacebar** and clicking the image window to zoom in, or pressing **Alt+Spacebar** and clicking the image window to zoom back out.

TIP

To create a larger working area, hide the *Palette Bin* and the **Photo Bin** temporarily by clicking their buttons on the **Status** bar.

To save time, instead of resizing the second (smaller) window and then zooming it, click the window, click the **Zoom** tool, and on the **Options** bar, enable the **Resize Window to Fit** option. Then drag the window to the exact small size you need.

❷ Arrange the Two Windows

Click the **Automatically Tile Windows** button (the four-tiny-squares button at the right end of the **Shortcuts** bar) or choose **Window, Images, Tile** from the menu to arrange the two windows on top of the other. Drag the border of the first window so that you can see the area you want to work on comfortably. Then drag the border of the second window that it doesn't take up too much room in the workspace (the second window will be smaller). You can use the first window as the work window, and the second, smaller window as a magnifier window.

❸ Change the Zoom

Change the zoom level of the second window so that the entire image fits within its boundaries: click the second image window to make it active, click the **Zoom** tool, and use the **Option** bar to adjust the zoom. You should now have two windows: one window that's larger and zoomed in on the portion of the image you want to work on, and a second window that's fairly small, which depicts the image in its entirety.

Here, I was working on an old photo of my mother and grandmother. Like most old photos, it had some spots and scratches that needed repair. So, I zoomed in on my mother's face and began work with the **Healing Brush** tool. To make sure that the changes I made to her face were subtle, I opened a second window so that I could view the photograph in its entirety as I worked.

59 About Size and Resolution

See Also

→ **60** Change Image Size or Resolution

→ **62** Increase the Area Around an Image

Two of the most common changes you'll make to an image are to adjust its *size* and to change its *resolution*. By *size*, I'm referring to an image's dimensions when printed, not its size onscreen. An image's resolution is determined by the number of pixels (dots) per inch.

To compute an image's print size, the *Editor* looks at the number of pixels in an image and their relative size (the number of pixels per inch). Take a look at the first figure here, which depicts an image that's ten pixels wide by five pixels high, using an imaginary scale of four pixels per inch. Based on the size of these pixels, the printed image will be about 2.5" wide by 1.25" high.

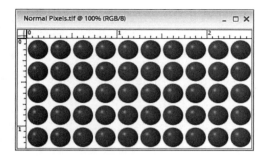

Figure 1: An (imaginary) image that's ten pixels wide by five pixels high.

 TIP

You can display an image onscreen in the same size it will be when printed by clicking the **Zoom** tool on the **Toolbox** and clicking the **Print Size** button on the **Options** bar. To display the image in the size it will appear on a user's screen set to the same screen resolution as you, click the **Actual Pixels** button instead.

To compute the resolution of an image, you simply count the number of pixels per inch. Luckily, Photoshop Elements does that for you, and you can view the image size (such as 2048 x 1536 pixels), resolution (such as 300 DPI), and print size (such as 6.827" × 5.12", which is calculated by taking the image size and dividing it by the resolution) of an image in the **Image Size** dialog box (choose **Image, Resize, Image Size** from the menu bar). You'll learn how to use this dialog box to change the size or resolution of an image in **60** **Change Image Size or Resolution**.

If you never plan to print a certain image, the image won't need a high resolution (a great number of pixels) to look good onscreen. But to print an acceptable image, you need the highest number of pixels you can get—the more the better. As I explain in **64** **About Printing Images**, you must have an print resolution of 200–300 *DPI* (dots per inch) to create a high-quality print using your home printer; for prints sent off to a lab, 150 DPI usually does just fine.

An image's print size and its resolution are interdependent; changing one without changing the other affects the image's print quality. For example, maintaining the same number of pixels in an image while trying to force it to print in a larger print size decreases the number of pixels per inch and, as you can imagine, inflates the size of each pixel to compensate. If the pixels become too large, a mosaic effect called *pixelation* might distract you from seeing the image as a whole.

Imagine for a moment that the first figure represents all the pixels in an image whose total resolution is 10 × 5 pixels. As shown in the second figure, if you change the size of the pixels to make them twice as big (in this case, by keeping the same number of pixels while increasing the print size), you'll get a much larger rectangle, but the pixels will be

NOTE

High resolution (more than 200 pixels per inch) is unnecessary for an image destined to be displayed on a computer monitor or a television screen because NTSC standard TV resolution (transposed to the average monitor size) is 72 dots per inch, computer screen resolutions average 102 pixels per inch. (Just so you know, the theoretical resolution for HDTV—high-definition—is 162 PPI.)

much more apparent. When printed, the rectangle might look more like a mesh of dots than a solid rectangle, which is probably not the effect you're going for. The same is true of any graphic image: If you print the image at something larger than its native print size without also increasing the number of pixels (the image resolution), the pixels will become bigger and more evident in the final print. This is what can happen if you choose to rescale an image "on the fly," using options in the **Print Preview** dialog box (in the Editor) or the **Print Selected Photos** dialog box (in the Organizer).

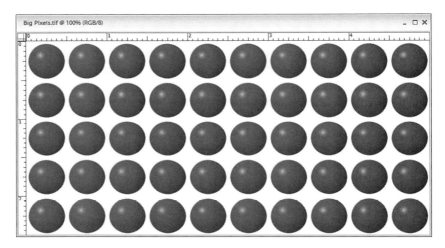

Figure 2: Enlarging the pixels increases the image size while decreasing its quality.

> ### NOTE
>
> **Just because you increase resolution on an image, you do not necessarily increase quality. Obviously, you can't add detail that wasn't there in the original image, so when you increase resolution (using resampling to add pixels and improve print quality), you do so at a possible loss of background detail.**

Suppose that, instead of changing the size of the pixels, you maintain their relative size but double their number. In other words, you double an image's resolution (increase the number of pixels) from 150 to 300 PPI, for example, while also doubling the print size of an image. The print quality will remain the same because the pixels will remain the same size, but you'll get a much bigger print, as shown here by comparing the first figure (10 – 5 pixels) with the third figure (20 – 10 pixels). The sizes of the pixels are the same in both figures, but the second one is bigger because it has twice as many pixels. Don't need a larger print size, but want better quality? Just increase the resolution (number of pixels) while maintaining the same print size. If you compare figure 2 to figure 3, that's exactly what I've done. The images are the same size, but figure 3 has more pixels and, therefore, more detail and better quality.

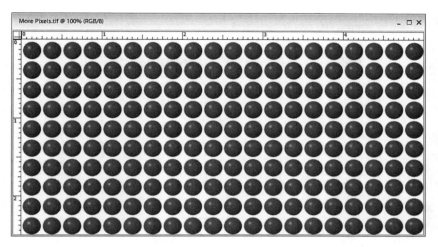

Figure 3: You can enlarge an image, and perhaps improve print quality, by increasing the number of pixels.

TIPS

To increase the size of an image without changing its resolution, resample it. *Resampling* uses one of a choice of five complex mathematical formulas to compute the color and brightness of new pixels added to an image to increase its size. See **60** Change Image Size or Resolution.

You do not have to use resampling when *reducing* the resolution or print size of an image, although you might because the resampling process mathematically decides which pixels to remove from the file.

---

60 **Change Image Size or Resolution**

As you learned in **59** About Size and Resolution, an image's size is tied directly to the number of pixels in the image as well as the relative size of the pixels. When you create images with a digital camera or scan printed images with a scanner, you choose the *resolution* you want to use—for instance, 300 pixels per inch. The resolution you choose also determines the resulting print size. For example, an image that's 2048 pixels wide by 1536 pixels tall (the typical dimensions of an image taken with a 3 megapixel camera), whose resolution is 300 pixels per inch, will print at 6.827" by 5.120".

Before You Begin

✔ **59** About Size and Resolution

See Also

→ **6** Import a Scanned Image

→ **62** Increase the Area Around an Image

→ **66** Print an Image

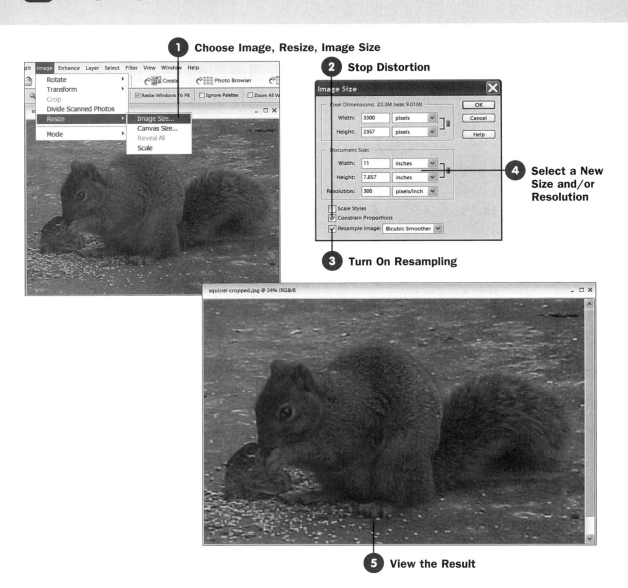

1 Choose Image, Resize, Image Size

2 Stop Distortion

4 Select a New Size and/or Resolution

3 Turn On Resampling

5 View the Result

So what do you do if you want to print your image at a different size—larger or smaller—while maintaining or even increasing its resolution to, say, 300 *DPI?* Answer: You use resampling. When you use *resampling* to increase an image's print size and/or its resolution, new pixels are inserted between existing ones. The Editor determines the colors for these new pixels by sampling the color value of each surrounding pixel, calculating a value within the sample range, and assigning that value to that new pixel. Conversely, when you reduce an image's print size, resampling removes pixels from the image then adjusts the colors of the pixels remaining in the image by approximating the blended color values of the pixels that were removed.

Because resampling is based on best-guess estimation, using it to change an image's size or resolution by more than 20% often produces poor results. You can resize or change an image's resolution without resampling by telling the *Editor* that you want to turn resampling off, and therefore maintain the relationship between the size and the resolution. In this manner, you can double an image's print resolution by cutting its print size in half (the image will contain as many pixels as it did before, but the pixels will be smaller, and there will be more of them per inch). Onscreen, you won't see any apparent change at all.

1 Choose Image, Resize, Image Size

In the Editor, open the image you want to resize or whose resolution you want to change, and save it in Photoshop (*.psd*) format. Then choose **Image, Resize, Image Size** from the menu bar. The **Image Size** dialog box appears.

To resize a group of images in one step, see **61** **Rename, Resize, Reformat, and Retouch a Group of Images**.

2 Stop Distortion

If you want to make sure that the image is not distorted during the resizing process, enable the **Constrain Proportions** check box.

If you've applied a *layer style* to the image and want the pattern of that style to be resized as the image is resized, enable the **Scale Styles** option as well. Note that the **Scale Styles** option does not affect the size of patterns formed by *effects*, so you might want to apply such embellishments after resizing the image.

NOTE

To calculate the print dimensions of an image yourself, take the image size in pixels and divide it by the number of pixels per inch. To display an image in its print size, click the **Zoom** tool on the **Toolbox** and then click the **Print Size** button on the **Options** bar. To view an image's size in pixels, resolution, and print size, display the **Image Size** dialog box by choosing **Edit, Resize, Image Size**.

KEY TERM

Resampling—The mathematical process applied during image resizing that evaluates the content of the pixels in the image in order to calculate the value of new pixels (when enlarging) or neighboring pixels (when reducing), and which re-interprets the result to minimize loss of detail.

TIP

One fast way to remove *moiré patterns*, fuzziness, and spots created when you scan an image is to scan at 600 DPI and then reduce its resolution to 300 DPI *while maintaining its print size*. See **128** **Restore Quality to a Scanned Photograph**.

TIPS

If you want to print an image in some size other than its normal print size, you can "rescale" the image on the fly when you print it. If you print an image in a larger size than normal, however, the resolution is decreased proportionately to compensate (pixels are not added). If the resulting resolution falls below acceptable levels of quality, you'll see a warning, so that you can choose a different print size. Regardless, with this method, the original resolution and print size of the image are left unchanged. If you get the warning, it's best to abandon printing and then resize and resample the image to the print size you want, by following the steps in this task.

Why would you ever choose *not* to resample an image? When you make your image larger or smaller, the rescaling process can introduce artifacts or patterns that resampling can eliminate. However, in smoothing out any possible artifacts or unwanted patterns, resampling after you resize can result in loss of detail, especially in the background or in small areas. So limit the number of times you resample an image to *once*; if you have detail in the background you don't want to risk losing, do not resample.

③ Turn On Resampling

To have the Editor mathematically re-evaluate and re-render the content of the image when you change its print size or resolution, enable the **Resample Image** option and select a sampling formula from the list. Here's a brief description of the formulas:

- **Bicubic.** Estimates each new pixel's color value based on the values of the 16 pixels nearest to the new pixel's location relative to the original image, in a 4×4 array. This method is best used when enlarging an image.

- **Bicubic Smoother.** Similar to the **Bicubic** formula, except that the tendency of Bicubic resampling to create halos around highly contrasting edges is reduced. Best used when enlarging an image.

- **Bicubic Sharper.** Similar to the **Bicubic** formula, except the edges are sharper with even higher contrast. Best used when reducing the size of an image.

- **Bilinear.** Estimates each new pixel's color value based on the values of the four pixels nearest to the new pixel's location relative to the original image. This method is best used when reducing an image.

- **Nearest Neighbor.** Estimates each new pixel's color value based on the values of all the pixels that fall within a fixed proximity of the new pixel's location relative to the original image. Here, the pixel residing in the same proportionate location in the original image as that of the new pixel in the resized image is given the extra "weight" when estimating the new color value. This method is best used when reducing the size of an image, but only for those images with edges that have not been anti-aliased.

④ Select a New Size and/or Resolution

If you know what size you want the final image to be, type a value in the **Document Size Width** box; the **Height** value changes proportionately (or vice versa).

You can also change an image's size by adding or removing pixels. When you add pixels while maintaining the same resolution, you make the image bigger. For example, if you want the image to be twice as big, in the frame marked **Pixel Dimensions**, for either **Width** or **Height**, type **200** in the text box, and from the adjacent drop-down list, choose **Percent**. This increases the number of pixels without affecting their size (assuming that **Resample Image** is on).

To change the resolution, type a value in the **Resolution** box. Altering resolution in this manner does not change the image's print size unless you entered new values for **Document Size** earlier. Click **OK**. Because the **Resample Image** option is selected, new pixels are created as needed to meet your print size and resolution requirements.

⑤ View the Result

After you're satisfied with the result of the resizing process, make any other changes you want and then save the final image in JPEG or TIFF format, leaving your PSD image with its *layers* (if any) intact so that you can return at a later time and make different adjustments if you want.

Even though I increased the size of this photo by quite a lot (from 5" × 7" to 11" × 7.857"), the quality (resolution) was maintained because I selected **Bicubic Smoother** resampling.

🖎 NOTE

To avoid resampling an image, disable the **Resample Image** option and change either the **Height/Width** or **Resolution** values in the **Document Size** area of the **Image Resize** dialog box. Just keep in mind that if you increase the **Resolution** without resampling, the image will be resized smaller.

🔧 TIP

Because resampling often leaves an image a bit fuzzy, it's best to follow up by treating your resampled image to an **Unsharp Mask**. See **149** Sharpen an Image.

---

61 Rename, Resize, Reformat, and Retouch a Group of Images

It's easier than you might think to collect hundreds, if not thousands, of digital photos before you realize it. Managing these photos can become a full-time job if you don't establish a method for dealing with common tasks that are part of the process. Establish a routine for processing new images that includes copying the files to your computer, backing them up onto CD-R or similar media, and converting those you want to work with to PSD format or some other lossless format, such as TIFF. You should follow a similar process for images you copy to the computer using your scanner.

Luckily, the *Editor* provides a method for easily converting a group of files from one format to another *all at once*. In addition, you can rename the files (which you might want to do if they use generic names such as **DSC01982.jpg**), resize them (and even increase their *resolution*), and automatically adjust their brightness, contrast, and *saturation*.

Before You Begin

✔ **47** About Saving Images

✔ **59** About Size and Resolution

✔ **109** Apply a Quick Fix

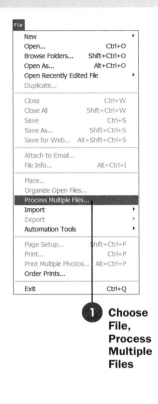

1 Choose
File,
Process
Multiple
Files

6 Enter New Filenames

2 Select Files to Process

3 Select Destination Folder

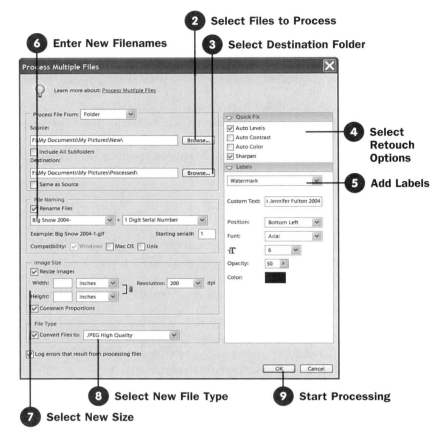

4 Select
Retouch
Options

5 Add Labels

8 Select New File Type

9 Start Processing

7 Select New Size

TIP

You can rename a single file in the *Organizer* by selecting the image and choosing **File, Rename**. You can resize a single image in the Editor by choosing the **Image, Resize, Image Size** command. To save a single image in a different format, with a different filename, or in a different folder using the Editor, choose

① Choose File, Process Multiple Files

If you want to process selected files in a folder (rather than all of them), open the **File Browser** (choose **Window, File Browser**) and select those files first. In the Editor, choose **File, Process Multiple Files** from the menu bar. The **Process Multiple Files** dialog box opens.

② Select Files to Process

To import images from your scanner, digital camera, or a PDF document for processing, from the **Process Files From** list, choose **Import**. Then select the source you want to use from the **From** list.

To process all the files that are currently open in the Editor's workspace, from the **Process Files From** list, choose **Opened Files**.

If the **File Browser** is open, and you have already selected the files you want to process, from the **Process Files From** list, choose **File Browser**.

To process all the images in a folder (and perhaps its subfolders), from the **Process Files From** list, choose **Folder**. Click the **Browse** button under **Source**, select the folder that contains the files you want to process, and click **OK**. You're returned to the **Process Multiple Files** dialog box. If you want to include images stored in subfolders of the folder you selected, enable the **Include All Subfolders** option.

③ Select Destination Folder

If you want to save the processed files in the same folder in which they are now, enable the **Same as Source** option. If you choose this option, be sure to rename the files as well so that you don't overwrite your originals (see step 6). Otherwise, click the **Browse** button under **Destination**, select the folder in which you want to save the converted files, and click **OK**.

④ Select Retouch Options

If you want to retouch the images automatically, select the adjustments you want to apply (such as **Auto Levels**) from the **Quick Fix** pane on the right side of the **Process Multiple Files** dialog box.

⑤ Add Labels

You can add a *watermark* or caption to identify your personal images and to protect them from being used without your permission. To create a watermark, select **Watermark** from the drop-down list at the top of the **Labels** pane. Enter the text you want to use in the **Custom Text** box. Adjust the font, size, opacity, and text color as desired.

💡 TIP

If you are processing files that are already in the *catalog*, you will need to update their *thumbnails* (if you retouch the images) and update their catalog information (if you rename them). If you copy the processed files to a new folder and prefer to use the new files over the ones already in the catalog, you must let the Organizer know their new location. After you've processed the files, in the Organizer, choose **File, Reconnect, All Missing Files**. See **⑬ Locate Moved Files**. To update just the image (when you haven't moved or renamed a file), see **⑳ Update an Image in the Catalog**.

📝 NOTES

The **Opened Files** option is the only way you can process multiple files located in different folders, where one is not a subfolder for the other. The **File Browser** method is the best way to process selected files from the same folder.

If the options under **Quick Fix** or **Labels** are not fully displayed, click the left arrow in front of **Quick Fix** or **Labels** to display the options.

KEY TERM

Watermark—Slightly transparent text placed over the key part of an image, not only to identify its creator but also to protect the image from being used illegally.

TIP

To enter the copyright symbol into the **Custom Text** box, press and hold **Alt** as you type **0169** on the numeric keypad.

NOTE

If you're using a serial number as part of the filename, you can change the starting number by changing the value in the **Starting serial#** text box.

To add a caption, select **Caption** from the drop-down list at the top of the **Labels** pane. Then select the text you want to include in the caption: **File Name, Description**, and/or **Date Modified**. You can choose as many of these text elements as you like—each will appear on its own line in the image. The **Description**, by the way, is the same description you can enter on the **Description** page of the **File Info** dialog box, or as an image caption in the Organizer. See **53** **About Image Information** and **31** **Add a Text Caption or Note**. Select a **Position** for the caption (such as **Bottom Right**), and adjust the font, size, opacity, and text color as desired.

6 Enter New Filenames

Digital photos straight from the camera have non-descriptive filenames such as **MVC-413G.JPG**. You can rename digital camera files to give them more understandable names. You can rename files from other sources as well. First, enable the **Rename Files** check box.

Below the **Rename Files** check box are two properties lists. By selecting items from one or both of these lists, you can use the existing properties of an image to create a unique filename. For example, you can use an image's date as part or all of its new name. You can also enter some text such as **Jan's Birthday** and add a sequence number, creating a unique filename for each image—**Jan's Birthday 01, Jan's Birthday 02**, and so on.

Start by choosing a property you want to use from the first list box in the **File Naming** area. To enter some text for use in the filename (such as **Jan's Birthday**), simply type that phrase into the first list box. Choose a second property (such as **2 digit serial number**) from the second list box if desired.

If you plan to use the converted files on a computer with a different operating system, select that system in the **Compatibility** area.

As you make your selections, a sample filename appears in the **Example** area.

7 Select New Size

If you want to resize these images or change their resolution, enable the **Resize Images** option. Then enter new **Width** and

Height values. *Resampling* will take place during resizing. To make sure that the images are not distorted as they are resized, enable the **Constrain Proportions** option. Enter a new **Resolution** if desired. See **60** **Change Image Size or Resolution** for more information.

8 Select New File Type

If you want to convert these images to a different file type (such as from GIF to PSD), enable the **Convert Files to** option, and then open the drop-down list and select the file type to which you want to convert the selected files.

9 Start Processing

When you're satisfied with your choices, click **OK**. Each image appears briefly in the Editor window as it is being processed.

To save any error messages that appear during processing in a text file that you can review later, enable the **Log errors that result from processing files** option before clicking **OK**. This log file is saved to the destination folder you identified in step 3.

NOTE

The **Document Name** property simply refers to the image's current filename. Selecting that property will enable you to use the existing filename and add something to it by selecting an additional property from the second list. This way, for instance, you can change the filename **DCX0304987.jpg** to **Walt and Saundra's Wedding - DCX0304987.jpg** if the original filename is important to you. Also, if you select **document name** from the list and the file is currently named **BBQ Party.jpg**, the file will be renamed **bbq party.jpg**; if you select **DOCUMENT NAME**, the file will be renamed **BBQ PARTY.JPG**, and so on.

62 Increase the Area Around an Image

Each image has a *canvas*—essentially the image background. The benefit of thinking of an image's *background layer* as a canvas is that it helps you conceive how that *layer* can be stretched to change the size of the area on which you can paint, draw objects, and insert text. For a newly imported digital photo, the image is "painted," if you will, to fill the canvas. You can expand the background layer (the canvas) of an image such as a photograph, for example, to make room for a frame, and fill the new area with color and apply a *filter*, style, or effect. Or you might simply want to expand the canvas to create more room in which to add a clip from another image, an object, or some text.

When you expand the canvas of an image, you add new pixels around its edges. Every photo imported from a digital camera or scanner has a background layer. When you use the **Canvas Size** command, the extra pixels are given the color you select. If an image has no background layer—for example, if you created the image using the **File**, **New** com-

See Also

→ **60** Change Image Size or Resolution

→ **113** Select a Color to Work With

KEY TERM

Canvas—The working area of an image, as defined by the image's outer dimensions.

mand and made the bottom layer transparent, or you converted the original **Background** layer to a regular layer using the **Layer, New, Layer from Background** command—then the new pixels are made transparent. Every layer above the base layer—whether it's a background layer or a regular layer—is expanded by the same amount.

❶ Choose Image, Resize, Canvas Size

In the *Editor*, open the image whose canvas size you want to adjust, and save it in Photoshop (*.psd) format. Choose **Image, Resize, Canvas Size** from the menu bar. The **Canvas Size** dialog box is displayed.

❷ Enter New Dimensions

The current dimensions of the image are displayed at the top of the **Canvas Size** dialog box. If you want to simply *add* a certain amount to the outer dimensions of the image, enable the **Relative** option. If the option is disabled, the dimensions you enter reflect the *total* width and height of the image.

In the **New Size** pane, select a unit of measure such as inches or pixels from one of the drop-down lists next to the **Width** and **Height** boxes (the other will change automatically). Then type values in the **Width** and **Height** boxes.

❸ Select Anchor Point

Normally, the anchor point is in the center of the **Anchor** pad. This means that the added canvas is placed equally around the image. If you want to add canvas to just one side of the image, you can tell the Editor where to position the image in relation to the canvas by clicking the appropriate arrow on the **Anchor** pad. For example, to add canvas only on the left side of the image, click the → arrow, located to the right of the center white button. This action tells the Editor to position the image in the right-center position and to place the additional canvas width to the left. To add space to the left and below the image, click the ↗ arrow (located in the upper-right corner of the **Anchor** pad) instead.

TIP

There are methods other than just resizing the canvas you can use to create a frame around an image. See **166** **Frame a Photograph**.

NOTE

You can reduce the canvas size of an image. If you do, although all the layers are reduced in size, data is not removed from the upper layers—it's just placed off the canvas where it is not seen in the final image. You can then use the **Move** tool to move the data on these non-background layers to display exactly the portion you want. Data from the bottom layer is clipped and cannot be retrieved. But if you increase the canvas size later on (even after saving and closing the image), you'll see that the data on upper layers is now visible again. See **99** **Move, Resize, Move, or Distort a Layer**.

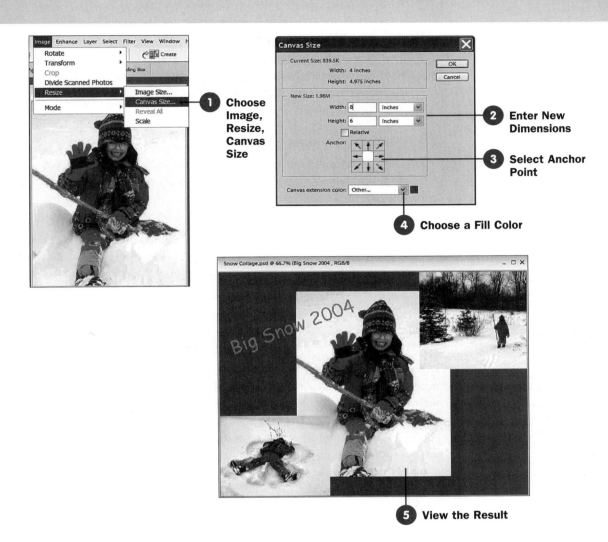

① **Choose Image, Resize, Canvas Size**

② **Enter New Dimensions**

③ **Select Anchor Point**

④ **Choose a Fill Color**

⑤ **View the Result**

④ Choose a Fill Color

If the bottom layer of the image is not a **Background** layer, the added canvas will be transparent. If the bottom layer is the **Background** layer, the added canvas will be opaque. You can choose a color to fill the extra canvas space. Open the **Canvas extension color** list and select an option such as **Background**

 TIP

To display the **Color Picker** without choosing **Other** from the **Canvas extension color** list, just click the box to the right of the list.

(which applies the current *background color*). If you choose **Other**, the **Color Picker** appears, and you can choose a color from it. With the **Color Picker** displayed, you can also click anywhere in the image to pick up that color with the dropper. Click **OK** to complete the operation.

⑤ View the Result

After expanding the image canvas, make any other changes you want and then save the final image in JPEG or TIFF format, leaving your PSD image with its layers (if any) intact so that you can return at a later time and make different adjustments if you want.

In the sample figure, the canvas was expanded around the central image, text was added, and several new images were pasted into the new space, creating a photo collage of a snowy day. Look for this image in the Color Gallery.

63 Change Color Mode

See Also

→ **44** Create a New Image

→ **176** Change a Color Photograph to Black and White

One of the key factors affecting the size of an image file is the maximum number of colors it can include. If a file is theoretically capable of including a large number of colors—even though it may actually contain very few—the file's size will be large to ensure that capacity. If you're working on an image to be shared over the Internet, small file size is often a high priority. One way you can reduce a file's size is to change its *color mode*—the number of colors an image can contain, even if it doesn't actually contain that many. However, reducing the number of colors an image can use might lead to striation and patchiness in areas you think should be a single, solid color.

A full-color image in RGB color mode generally does not actually contain all 16 million-plus colors that standard video cards support. (For RGB color mode, each color channel—Red, Green, and Blue—must be capable of "counting" to 256 for each pixel. 256 times 256 times 256 = 16,777,216.) To reduce the file size in a color image, the *Editor* gives you the option of switching to an indexed color mode similar to the encoding scheme for GIF images. With an indexed color mode, the entire image uses only 256 colors, although these colors are selected from all the 16,777,216 hues the standard video card produces. If your image is black and white, or black and white plus gray, there are other modes you can use to make your image file even smaller. How perceptible the difference is, when changing to a lower color mode, depends on the image you're working with. For this reason, the Editor makes it possible for you to sample different color reduction modes, enabling you to choose the least detrimental mode for your image.

If file size is your main priority, you can compress an image into GIF, JPEG, or PNG format (for example), a process that also reduces its color palette a bit more scientifically than the method discussed here. You can also convert an image to grayscale to reduce its color palette. See **50** **Compress an Image Using GIF Format**, **51** **Compress an Image Using JPEG Format**, or **52** **Save an Image in PNG Format**.

1 Choose Image, Mode

In the Editor, open the image you want to convert, and save it in Photoshop (***.psd**) format. Choose **Image, Mode** from the menu bar. Select the color mode you want to convert to from the submenu that appears:

- **Bitmap.** 1-bit color in black and white; suitable for images in black and white only, with no gray tones.

- **Grayscale.** 8-bit color in 256 shades of gray.

- **Indexed Color.** 8 bits per pixel, in 256 colors, selected from the entire color *gamut*. Perfect for use with GIF images.

- **RGB.** 24-bit color, with 8 bits per color channel. Here, 24 bits are used to encode the color value for each pixel. Compare to **Indexed Color** which uses 8 bits per pixel and you'll understand why RGB images provide the most detail.

If you're increasing color depth, the image itself is not changed, but more colors become available for your use. If you're reducing color depth, a dialog box appears from which you must choose options. Continue to step 2, 3, or 4.

2 If Indexing Colors, Choose Options and Click OK

If you're reducing colors in an image with **Indexed Color** mode, select how you want the Editor to choose the colors for the palette by choosing from various options in the dialog box that appears. Before you begin making selections, enable the **Preview** option so that you can see how your selections affect the actual image. From the **Palette** list, choose one of the following options:

NOTE

Because some commands are available only for images that use RGB or grayscale mode, you might sometimes find yourself temporarily *increasing* an image's color mode (from grayscale to RGB, for example). This won't, however, improve the *resolution* or quality of a low-resolution image—increasing an image's color *palette* simply makes more colors available for use; it does not tell the Editor where to use them in an image to boost detail and clarity.

NOTE

Technically speaking, the number of *bits* (binary digits) required for an image to encode the color value for one pixel is the base-2 logarithm of the maximum number of colors. In other words, 2 raised to that power equals the maximum number. It takes 8 bits to encode up to 256 values, and 24 bits to encode up to 16,777,216 values—thus the arithmetic behind the phrase *24-bit color*.

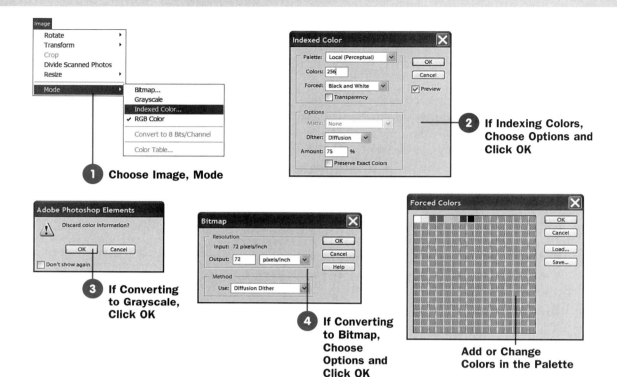

1 Choose Image, Mode

2 If Indexing Colors, Choose Options and Click OK

3 If Converting to Grayscale, Click OK

4 If Converting to Bitmap, Choose Options and Click OK

Add or Change Colors in the Palette

 NOTE

If the image already uses 256 colors or less, the **Palette** option is automatically set to **Exact**, which means that all colors in the image are added to the palette. You do not have to make a selection.

- **System (Mac OS)** uses the 256 color palette developed for the first color Macintosh computers. Select this palette to generate small files best displayed on Macs.

- **System (Windows)** uses the 256 color palette developed for Windows 3.0, which has been used as the backup palette for 8-bit color mode ever since.

- **Web** uses a 216 color palette (the last 40 index values are reserved) recommended for use in generating images for Web pages because these are the 216 values that the Mac and Windows have in common. Choosing this option ensures that the image will appear the same on both a Windows and a Mac computer.

- **Uniform** calculates 216 colors from equidistant positions in the RGB color gamut by rotating color index values from all white to all black. This setting ensures that your image uses colors sampled from throughout the image's color spectrum.

- The three **Local** options direct the Editor to create a palette based solely on the colors found in the currently open image.

- The three **Master** options instruct the Editor to create a palette based on the colors found in all the images currently open in the Editor.

  Among the **Local** and **Master** options, **Adaptive** instructs the Editor to select 256 colors that are mathematically most similar to the colors in the original image.

  Perceptual takes the 256 colors generated by the **Adaptive** algorithm and alters the selections slightly to favor colors that the human eye would tend to notice if they were changed—typically throwing away more colors in areas with the least amount of contrast, while favoring colors in areas with high contrast because the eye would notice that more.

  Selective takes the 256 colors refined by the **Perceptual** algorithm and then weights the values to more closely resemble the **Web** spectrum, while also favoring broad areas of color within the image.

- Select **Custom** to make changes to any colors in the palette that the Editor is currently preparing to adopt. When the **Color Table** dialog box appears (which looks similar to the **Forced Colors** dialog box shown here), double-click the color in the palette you want to change. Select a new color from the **Color Picker** dialog box and click **OK**. To add a color to the palette, click an empty spot and then select a color to add. Repeat for any other palette colors you want to change or add, and click **OK** when finished. You're returned to the **Indexed Color** dialog box.

- Choose **Previous** to load the previously used custom color palette. Use **Previous** to convert a series of images to indexed color mode, using the same color palette.

TIP

To reduce your file size even further, set **Colors** to a value less than 256 (to reduce file size *significantly*, select a value less than 128).

The options in the **Forced** list instruct the Editor to override some or all of its palette color choices and to include specific color values, some of which you can choose yourself from the **Forced Color** dialog box that appears. These "forced" choices may or may not be represented in the actual image, but they are included in the image's palette:

- **Black & White** forces the Editor to include pure black and pure white as two of the colors in the palette.

- **Primaries** forces the Editor to include the first eight colors of the old IBM Extended Graphics palette: red, green, blue, cyan, magenta, yellow, black and white. This allows a large measure of downward compatibility (if you really need it) with some of the first images ever produced for display on PCs.

- **Web** forces the Editor to include the entire 216-color Web palette (essentially the same as choosing **Web** from the **Palette** list).

- Choose **Custom** to enable you to change or add colors to the palette. Double-click a palette color. Select a new color from the **Color Picker** dialog box and click **OK**. To add a color, click an empty spot, select a color, and click **OK**. Repeat for any other palette colors you want to add or change and click **OK** when finished.

 NOTE

If you choose **None** from the **Matte** drop-down list, semi-transparent pixels are simply changed to fully opaque ones and are not blended with anything. Transparent pixels are made white.

If the image has transparency but you don't want to retain it, disable the **Transparency** option. Then select from the **Matte** drop-down list a color to change the transparent pixels to. Semi-transparent pixels are blended with the color you choose to make them fully opaque. You can choose **Foreground Color, Background Color, White, Black, 50% Gray,** or **Netscape Gray** (a lighter gray) from the list, or select your own color by choosing **Custom** from the **Matte** drop-down list and using the **Color Picker** that appears to select a color to use. To choose a color from the image, just click in the image with the **Eyedropper** tool.

If the image contains transparent pixels and you want to retain them, enable the **Transparency** option. If the image contains semi-transparent pixels, open the **Matte** list and choose a color to blend with them to make them fully opaque.

To reduce the side effects caused by using a smaller number of colors than the original image contained, select the *dither* pattern you prefer from the **Dither** list:

- **Diffusion** instructs the Editor to apply an *error diffusion* algorithm to blend dissimilar colors by dividing the differences between them mathematically and spreading that difference to neighboring pixels, hiding the transition. When you make this choice, enter the relative percentage of error diffusion in the **Amount** text box. Enable the **Preserve Exact Colors** option to instruct the Editor not to dither any colors it encounters in the original image whose values exactly match any of those in the current reduction palette.

- **Pattern** applies a geometric dithering pattern, which might be noticeable in photographic images but is permissible in more patterned images such as original drawings.

- **Noise** scatters dithered pixels randomly.

- **None** turns off diffusion and causes the Editor to substitute the closest color in the palette for any color not in the palette.

To finalize your choices, click **OK**.

③ If Converting to Grayscale, Click OK

When you're converting a color image to various hues of gray (grayscale), click **OK**; if the image has multiple layers, you'll be asked whether you want to flatten all layers before proceeding. Click **Merge**.

④ If Converting to Bitmap, Choose Options and Click OK

When converting an image to pure black-and-white (**Bitmap** mode), the Editor could simply make relatively dark pixels black and the relatively light ones white. However, the result might not be desirable, so you might want to apply dithering.

First, let the Editor convert your image to grayscale by clicking **OK**. It's easier for the Editor to convert grays to black-and-white than to convert colors directly to black and white. If there are multiple layers, the Editor warns you to flatten them first; click **OK** to have it

KEY TERM

Error diffusion—Any of several mathematical techniques that attempt to compensate for large error values (differences between the intensities of an original pixel and its replacement in a reprocessed image) by dividing this difference into parts and distributing it to neighboring pixels, thus masking the obvious inaccuracy.

NOTES

Because it uses a mathematical formula, error diffusion (when used in images with a very limited color palette or large blocks of color, such as comics art) can sometimes generate *artifacts* in a color blended area, more so than using an ordered dither method such as **Pattern**.

If the color layers currently in the image use blend modes other than **Normal** to create its current appearance—especially if that appearance depends on how the *color* of one layer interacts with the *colors* of the layers beneath it—then these effects will probably be completely lost if the image is flattened while converting it to grayscale. To preserve the layers and their blend modes, click **Don't Merge** in step 3.

do that and continue. In the **Bitmap** dialog box that appears, in the **Resolution** area, make sure that your image is set for the resolution of your output device. At first, this is set to the image's current resolution. To ensure best appearance, you might have to adjust resolution—and thus, size—accordingly. For on-screen use, choose *72 PPI*; for printing, choose 150–300 *DPI*. Altering this setting resizes the image, both in print and on-screen.

In the **Method** area, choose how you want the Editor to apply dithering. The **50% Threshold** option applies no dithering whatsoever—light pixels are made white, and dark ones are made black. The **Pattern Dither** option applies a geometric dithering pattern, which might be adequate if your original image is a simple drawing—such as a corporate logo—rather than a photograph. **Diffusion Dither** applies an error diffusion pattern, distributing vast differences in brightness value over wider areas—which is generally more appropriate for photographs.

To finalize your choices, click **OK**.

After changing the color mode of your image, make any other changes you want and then save the final image in JPEG or TIFF format, leaving your PSD image with its layers (if any) intact so that you can return at a later time and make different adjustments if you want.

TIP

If you're curious about what color mode your image is currently using, simply look at the title bar, after the image filename.

8

Printing Images

IN THIS CHAPTER:

64 About Printing Images

65 Set Print Options

66 Print an Image

67 Print a Contact Sheet

68 Print a Picture Package

69 Print Images Using an Online Service

NOTE

To print a single image, use the Editor; to print a group of images or multiple copies of one image, use the Organizer.

In Photoshop Elements, printing is the final step you take in rendering a picture, a group of pictures, or a printed *creation*. When you start the printing process, you should have already corrected the brightness, *saturation*, contrast, and sharpness of an image. If you're printing a photo album, card, or other printed creation, you should have already completed the layout process and reviewed the result. Printing is the *coup de grace*. If you've set up your printer properly and calibrated its output with the color you see on your monitor (see **103** About Color Management and **104** About Adobe Gamma for instructions), what you see onscreen in Photoshop Elements will soon become what you get on paper.

 NOTE

You can print an existing creation from the Organizer by selecting it and clicking the **Print** button on the **Shortcuts** bar and then selecting **Print** from the menu that appears. You can also print a creation after creating or editing it by clicking the **Print** button on the **Step 5: Share** page of the **Creation** wizard.

There are, however, a few steps you must complete before you click that **Print** button—whether you initiate the process from the *Editor* or the *Organizer*. You should, for example, change the print options so that your printer is aware that you're using photo paper or heavy bond paper (if you're printing a card, for example). And then, if you're printing photos, there are the endless choices you can make about what to print: multiple copies of the same image, single prints from a group of images, a set of prints in standard photo sizes, or small *thumbnails* of each image you can use as a reference. You can also reverse the image on-the-fly when printing onto iron-on transfer paper. As a final option, you might choose not to print your images at all, but to upload them to an Internet printing service instead. In this chapter, you'll learn how to complete all these tasks.

 About Printing Images

Before You Begin

✔ **105** Ensure That What You See Is What You Get

See Also

→ **66** Print an Image

→ **67** Print a Contact Sheet

→ **68** Print a Picture Package

→ **69** Print Images Using an Online Service

After working on an image and perfecting its beauty, there are several things you should consider before printing it.

- **What size do you want the image to be when printed? Is this size the same as the image is now?** As you'll learn in **66** Print an Image, you can make quick adjustments to the size of the image when printing *without changing the image file's actual size*. For example, you can choose to print an image at 43% its actual size if you like. Still, it's nice to have an idea of the image's final size when making modifications—you don't have to be as picky with image quality for a wallet-size photo as you do with an 8" × 10", for example. If you want to resize an image to the size you want to use for printing, do that before editing it, if possible. See **60** **Change Image Size or Resolution.**

Note that if you print an image in a larger size than normal by rescaling it in the **Print Selected Images** dialog box (in the Organizer) or the **Print Preview** dialog box (in the Editor), the *resolution* is decreased proportionately to compensate. In other words, pixels are not added as they would be if you resized the image using the **Image Size** command described in **60** **Change Image Size or Resolution.** If the resulting resolution falls below acceptable levels of quality, you'll see a warning telling you so; you can choose a different print size. Also note that, with this method, the resolution and print size of the original image is left unchanged; only the resolution of the printout changes.

- **What kind of quality do you expect?** Is this just a quick print to see roughly how something looks, or is this a keeper? As you can when printing documents from other programs, you can change the print quality of an image just before printing. For test prints, choose your ordinary ink jet or laser paper and draft quality; for final prints, choose a glossy or matte photo paper and best quality print speed. See **65** **Set Print Options.**

Color management helps your monitor and printer regulate the appearance of color through ICC profiles. Your monitor requires a color profile for your video card to display the colors in an image the way the Editor sees them. Your printer requires a separate color profile for the Editor to know what combination of inks faithfully reproduce the hues in your images' palettes. And now, there are color profiles for *paper* that can match the paper's capability to hold ink to the specific printer you use. In **103** **About Color Management,** you'll learn how to make your computer system manage color properly.

If you want to save a few bucks and buy your paper online, consider only those sources that provide *ICC profiles* that match your printer *and* their respective paper types. ICC profiles are customized to match the capabilities of your printer to the brand and paper type you buy, creating prints of high quality. You'll learn how to select the ICC profile to use in **66** **Print an Image;** to learn how to install a profile, see **105** **Ensure That What You See Is What You Get.**

NOTE

You need to match the print size of an image as shown in Photoshop Elements with the size of the paper you're printing. For example, if you're using 4" × 6" photo paper, you'll need to adjust the print size of your image to exactly 4" × 6" or *smaller* so that the image doesn't print off the edge of the paper.

TIP

For best results, use photo paper made by the same manufacturer as your printer because the printer's ink and paper are designed to work together—much like one brand of shampoo and conditioner.

WEB RESOURCE

This online photo paper store also offers free ICC profiles that match their paper types with Canon and Epson Stylus Photo printers.

www.pictorico.com

- **Do you need more than one copy of the image or want to print multiple images at one time?** As you can with other programs, in the *Organizer*, you can select the number of copies you want of a printed image. However, the Organizer has one feature many other programs don't have: the capability to arrange multiple images (or copies of the same image) on a single sheet of paper, like the photo sheets you get from a professional photographer. So, if you decide you want to share your photos, you won't have to waste a lot of paper printing each copy on its own sheet. See **68** **Print a Picture Package** for more information.

- **Will you be printing the image on a home printer or taking it to a lab for professional printing?** If you're printing at home, enhance the final quality of your prints by buying photo paper for photos you intend to frame or place in an album and high-quality paper for greeting cards, calendars, business cards, and reports. If they are available for your printer, buy high-quality inks that resist fading (archival inks).

TIP

You can directly upload images to the Ofoto Web site for printing, from the Organizer. See **69** **Print Images Using an Online Service**.

If you plan on taking the image to a professional service bureau or photo kiosk for printing, make sure that you know exactly what that service expects from you: specifically, the media type (CD, floppy, memory stick) and image type (JPEG, TIFF, Kodak Picture CD, and so on). For example, the Kodak Picture Maker machines in many retail stores accept most digital camera memory card format, Kodak Picture CD format, or JPEG format only. If your local choices are too limited, try the Internet. There are any number of high-quality photo labs on the Internet that will accept images sent by email or FTP.

Prepare an Image for Printing

Whether you plan to print a photograph locally or with a service, here are some tips for preparing the image properly:

- **Start with enough pixels.** Typically, you'll want your final print resolution to be 200 to 300 *DPI*. So, make sure that you scan at that resolution, if you're scanning a photo into your system for printing later. If you plan to resize and *resample* the image to remove *moiré patterns* caused by the scanning process, scan at double that resolution—400 to 600 *PPI*. If you're shooting an image with a digital camera, *always use the camera's highest resolution.* You can always reduce the print size of an image later by reducing the printout's DPI or by compressing the image, but you can never increase an image's resolution after it has already been shot.

- **Check the print size and resolution.** The dimensions of the original image, when viewed using the *Editor*'s **Image, Resize, Image Size** command, must correspond to the final print size you want to achieve, or you'll have to *resample* the image to add pixels, resulting in a loss of print quality. For example, if you want to print an image in 6" × 4" format at 600 DPI—which, for some basic inkjet printers, is "best quality"—the image file's dimensions shown in the **Image Size** dialog box must be least 3600 × 2400 pixels (600 pixels per inch times 6 inches by 600 pixels per inch times 4 inches). You can usually achieve acceptable quality print results at 300 DPI, and for that, the dimensions of your original image must be at least 1800 × 1200 pixels.

The highest quality images produced by a 3.1 megapixel (Mp) camera are stored at 2048 × 1536 (2,048 times 1,536 = 3,145,728 pixels, or 3.1 Mp). Dividing by 300 DPI minimum print resolution, you'll discover you can print 5" × 7" images at home, but if you want to print larger images, you must resample. If you own a 2.1 Mp camera, its highest quality images are stored at 1600 × 1200 resolution, which means that you can print good quality images at 300 DPI up to 4" × 6" without resampling.

- **Save the image using a lossless format such as Photoshop PSD or TIFF.** JPEG format allows for invisible, or semi-visible, selective reductions in image quality to achieve smaller file sizes. If you plan to use an outside photo service that requires JPEG format, edit your image first, making sure that you save changes in Photoshop PSD or TIFF format. When you're completely done with the image, save a *copy* as JPEG, using as low an amount of compression as your photo lab allows. If the lab accepts TIFF format, use it instead because TIFF files are certain to provide higher-quality prints.

NOTE

Makers of scanners, digital cameras, and the imaging community at large typically refer to an image's resolution in terms of *pixels per inch*, or PPI. Printer manufacturers refer to print resolution in terms of DPI, or *dots per inch*. Don't let yourself get too confused; they mean essentially the same thing—so many dots/pixels per inch of paper/screen.

TIP

Online services typically require images of only 150 DPI to achieve good quality prints (because they use higher quality printers, better inks, and Kodak paper). Many services such as Adobe's Ofoto make available *archival quality prints*, which are laser etchings made directly onto silver halide photo paper. These etchings use absolutely no ink, so there's no medium to degrade over time, and the paper actually captures a broader range of the film's color spectrum than inks or dyes are capable of reproducing. So if you don't like the results you get on your home printer, try sending your image to a film lab instead. See **69** Print Images Using an Online Service.

TIP

The **Layers** palette lists all the layers in an image that you can presently see on-screen by placing an "eye" icon next to each visible layer's listing. This icon also designates which layers will print. So to print just some of the layers in an image, on the **Layers** palette, turn off visibility for those layers you *don't* want to print. See **91** About Layers and the Layers Palette for details.

TIP

In the Editor, you can crop an image to an exact size such as 4" × 6" for example, simply by selecting that preset from the **Preset Options** list on the **Options** bar after choosing the **Crop** tool. A crop rectangle of that exact size appears; you can move it around the image to select the best portion to crop. You can also resize the crop rectangle by dragging from a corner without losing the aspect ratio.

- **Merge layers before printing.** If you plan to print from the Editor an image that has multiple *layers*, to save time, you should merge the layers of that image before printing. Save your working (***.psd**) image first, then merge your layers and save the result in JPEG or TIFF format. (See **47** About Saving Images for details.) Then print the resulting JPEG or TIFF image. Believe it or not, although the print process merges layers in memory before printing anyway, this process takes far longer than if you merge the layers before you print.

- **Size the image to fit the photo size you want.** If you are printing the image yourself, you can adjust its print size on the fly in the **Print Preview** or **Print Selected Images** dialog box to approximate the proper photo size, although, as noted earlier, this might cause a loss of print quality if the resulting resolution becomes too low. This can also result in areas of the image being cropped (not printed) as Photoshop Elements adjusts its size to fit your print needs.

  If you plan to turn the image over to a photo lab, limit how much the photo lab might have to crop your uploaded image by making sure its aspect ratio (its height to width ratio) *exactly* matches the photo size you want. For example, the aspect ratio of a 4" × 6" print is 1:1.5; a 5" × 7" print is 1:1.4; and an 8" × 10" print is 1:1.25. An unedited digital image typically has an aspect ratio of 1:1.33, which is the same as a computer screen. You can change the aspect ratio of a photo by cropping or resizing/resampling. Resizing an image to fit your print needs can also offer you benefits at home because you can retain or even increase your resolution or print quality when you need to, and you can ensure that your image size is always exactly what you want when you print it. You also avoid blowing up your pixel size to fit your new print size, which is what happens when you rescale an image on-the-fly. Just follow the steps in **60** Change Image Size or Resolution.

65 Set Print Options

Before printing, you should use **Page Setup** to set various print options. Photoshop Elements presents **Page Setup** in two parts. The first dialog box is fairly simple and governs general print options for the application such as paper size and print orientation: *portrait orientation* or *landscape orientation*. The second dialog box enables you to set specific printer options such as paper type and quality. These settings affect jobs sent to the printer by Photoshop Elements *during this Photoshop Elements session only*, so don't worry that your Microsoft Word documents might suddenly start printing in photo quality. You should check, however, to make sure that these printer settings are still in place before printing a second time from Photoshop Elements; some printers reset these selections with each print job whereas other printers do not.

① Choose File, Page Setup

Open the image you want to print in the *Editor*, or select the image in the *Organizer*. In either the Organizer or the Editor, select **File, Page Setup** from the menu bar. The **Page Setup** dialog box for Photoshop Elements appears.

② Choose Paper Size and Click Printer

In the **Page Setup** dialog box, the only change you typically make is to choose a different paper size from the **Size** list, which you might do if you are printing on 4"×6" paper, for example. You can also change the **Orientation** of the page if you like, and the **Source**, which tells the printer which paper tray to use (if your printer has more than one).

After making selections (if any) from this first **Page Setup** dialog box, click the **Printer** button. A second **Page Setup** dialog box appears.

Before You Start

✔ **103** About Color Management

✔ **104** About Adobe Gamma

See Also

→ **66** Print an Image

→ **67** Print a Contact Sheet

→ **68** Print a Picture Package

🔍KEY TERMS

Portrait orientation—A page printed across its shortest edge.

Landscape orientation—A page printed across its longest edge.

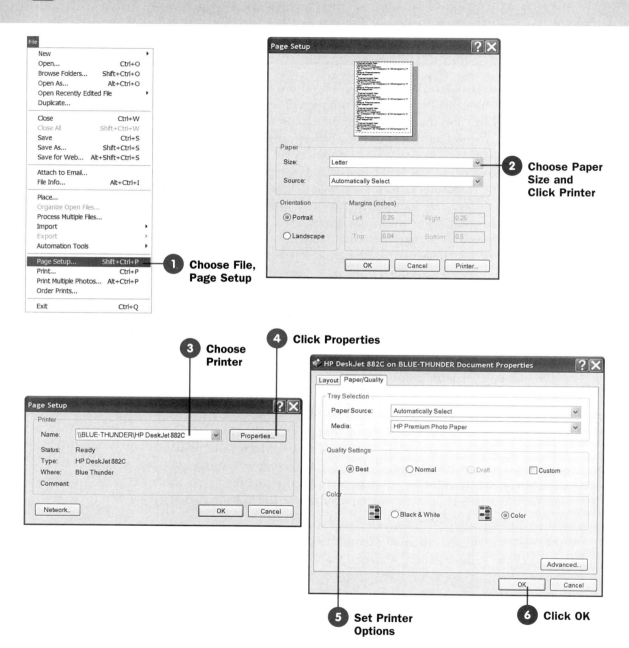

1 Choose File, Page Setup

2 Choose Paper Size and Click Printer

3 Choose Printer

4 Click Properties

5 Set Printer Options

6 Click OK

③ Choose Printer

In the second **Page Setup** dialog box, choose your printer from the **Name** drop-down list (if necessary). If, for example, you have both an inkjet and a photo printer, make certain that the printer named here is the one you intend to use for printing your image(s).

④ Click Properties

Click the **Properties** button. The **Properties** dialog box specific to your printer appears.

⑤ Set Printer Options

Because the **Properties** dialog box that appears is specific to your printer, what you see might only look similar to what's shown here. Consult your printer's manual for specific instructions regarding your printer's options. (The example shown here is for an HP DeskJet printer.) For my printer, I click the **Paper/Quality** tab and open the **Media** list to select the paper type I plan to use, such as glossy photo paper. I can change the **Quality** settings as well; for example, I select **Best** quality when printing photos.

Many printer dialog boxes include an **Advanced** feature, usually attainable through a button or tab. When you click this button or tab, all the printer's major options are listed *categorically* on one screen. Click the name of the category to see all the options for that category, such as **Paper/Output** for the size and thickness of paper you intend to use, or **Graphic** for *resolution* and color management options. If the **Advanced** settings are located on a separate dialog box, click **OK** to finalize your changes and return to the main **Properties** dialog box.

Some printers allow you to rescale an image to a different size for printing by specifying the size you want in the printer's **Properties** dialog box. However, you'll get better results if you rescale the image using the **Print Preview** or **Print Selected Images** dialog boxes provided by Photoshop Elements. Do not use both the printer's and Photoshop Elements' rescaling features, or you'll scale the image *twice*. Also, as noted earlier, you can achieve the best results by rescaling the image to the print size you want before printing. See **60** Change Image Size or Resolution.

See **60** Change Image Size or Resolution.

💡 TIPS

When you use *color management* (see **103** About Color Management and **104** About Adobe Gamma for how), the colors you see in your Photoshop Elements images are adjusted to approximate the colors and tones your printer is capable of reproducing. However, if you have more than one printer or printer driver, color management adjusts onscreen colors only for the current printer—which is either the Windows default printer or the one most recently used. If your photo printer isn't the default, and you intend to use it to print images in Photoshop Elements, follow these steps to change printers *while still editing*, so that images onscreen look as they will when printed.

You can print several images on one sheet of 8.5" × 11" paper using the Organizer. Even though these images might be printed in 4" × 6" size, for example, *do not change the* **Paper Size** *in the* **Page Setup** *dialog box* because you are using standard letter-sized paper.

6 Click OK

To finalize your printer settings, click **OK** to close the **Properties** dialog box. Then click **OK** to exit the second **Page Setup** dialog box, and **OK** again to finalize your choices from the first **Page Setup** dialog box.

Now that you've specified the printer and options you intend to use for this Photoshop Elements printing session, you can select the images you want to print. For most printers, these printer options will remain in effect until you exit Photoshop Elements; some printers reset these options with each print job, so check them each time you prepare to print.

 Print an Image

Before You Start

✔ **65** Set Print Options

✔ **105** Ensure That What You See Is What You Get

See Also

→ **68** Print a Picture Package

→ **69** Print Images Using an Online Service

NOTE

Printing low-resolution images in a large size results in poor quality (grainy) photos. If you took the photos using a low-resolution setting on your digital camera (or scanned them using a low resolution setting), choose a small print size for best print results.

After you're through making changes, you can print an image from the *Editor*. You'll be able to scale the image to fit a particular size (such as 5" × 7"—a process that may result in portions of the image being cropped or not printed). In addition, as I mentioned earlier, scaling the size of an image within the **Print Preview** dialog box may also reduce print *resolution* (quality), so avoid doing that if you can; instead, resize the image using the steps in **60** Change Image Size or Resolution. For prints that are smaller than the paper you're using, you can adjust *where* on the paper the photo prints (which may help you trim the print). You'll be able to add a colored border around the image, print the image filename and text *caption*, and select the specific *ICC printer profile* you want to use. Before printing, you can preview your selections to see how your image will look.

1 Click Print

Open the image you want to print in the Editor and save it in Photoshop (*.psd) format. Make any changes you want, including resizing the image to fit the print size you need, then save the result in JPEG or non-layered TIFF format, leaving your PSD image with its *layers* intact so that you can return at a later time and make different adjustments if you want.

Click the **Print** button on the **Shortcuts** bar, or select **File**, **Print** from the menu. The **Print Preview** dialog box appears.

❷ Select Print Size

If you need to change the paper size you've selected for use during this work session, click the **Page Setup** button to display the **Page Setup** dialog box. Select the size of paper you want to use from the **Size** list and click **OK** to return to the **Print Preview** dialog box. See **65** **Set Print Options** for more help.

The photo normally prints at its actual size which is shown next to the words, **Actual Size**, in the **Print Size** list box. (Here, "actual size" is based on the image size in pixels divided by the resolution of the image in dots per inch.) If the image's actual size is larger than the paper size you've chosen, parts of the image will be cropped (not printed). If you want to scale the photo to print at a different size, open the **Print Size** list and select the photo size you want to use, such as 5" × 7". The **Fit to Page** option from this list makes the photo as large as possible, while still fitting the paper size you chose. For best results, use these last two options only when the print size you select is *smaller* than the actual print size. To print in a size larger than the image's actual print size, resize the image as described in **60** **Change Image Size or Resolution**.

To scale the photo to fit the print size you select (not **Actual Size**), the Editor may crop (not print) portions of the image. To prevent this cropping, disable the **Crop to Fit Print Proportions** option. With this option turned off, the image will print at the largest size possible within the **Print Size** dimensions you've chosen.

❸ Adjust Scale and Position

After you select a photo size from the **Print Size** list, the Editor adjusts the photo as best it can to fit that size. Still, you can fine-tune the **Height** and **Width** values as desired.

TIPS

If you want to print more than one copy of an image or multiple images on a single photo sheet, use the *Organizer*. See **68** Print a Picture Package. If you've already displayed an image in the **Print Preview** dialog box discussed here, click the **Print Multiple Images** button at the top of the dialog box to change to the Organizer, where you can print multiple copies of your image or print this image along with other images on the same page.

You can print a photo in a custom size by selecting the **Custom Size** option from the **Print Size** drop-down list and entering the **Height** and **Width** dimensions. Alternatively, if the **Show Bounding Box** option is enabled, you can resize the image by dragging the corners of the *bounding box* that surrounds the image in the preview window. You can also reposition the image on the page by disabling the **Center Image** option and then dragging the image inside the preview area.

1 Click Print

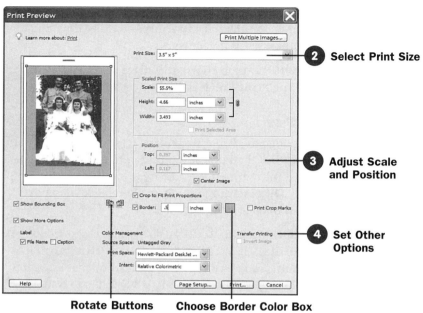

2 Select Print Size

3 Adjust Scale and Position

4 Set Other Options

Rotate Buttons   Choose Border Color Box

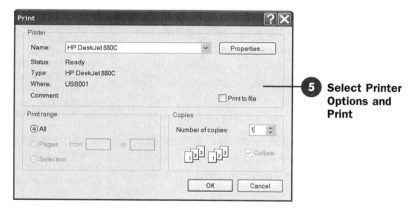

5 Select Printer Options and Print

Typically, the photo prints in the center of the page. To position the photo along the side (so that you can easily cut it) or anywhere else on the paper, disable the **Center Image** option and enter values in the **Position** frame that place the image relative to the **Top** and upper **Left** corner of the paper. A 1 inch **Top** value, for example, places the image 1" from the top of the page; –.5 places the image 1/2" above the top of the page, essentially cropping off the top of the image and not printing it.

The **Scale** setting shows the magnification of the image being sent to the printer, relative to the original size of the image. It's best to scale your image to the desired print size *before* you start the print process, to both save time and prevent printout degradation. If you do enter a setting here, keep in mind that degradation can be minimized by choosing percentage values that make for less awkward fractions. For example, 50% (1/2) or 75% (3/4) scale has less chance for degradation than 95% (19/20) or 98% (49/50).

④ Set Other Options

Enable the **Show More Options** check box to display all options related to printing, then select from among these additional options:

- Add a border around your image by enabling the **Border** option, setting the size, and then clicking the **Choose border color** box to select a color using the **Color Picker**. You can choose a color from the image by clicking anywhere within the image window (you may have to move the **Print Preview** dialog box out of the way to see the actual image).

- To print crop marks (tiny **X**s at the corners) that can help you trim the image after it's printed, enable the **Print Crop Marks** check box.

- Print the image **File Name** or text **Caption** just below the photo by selecting the corresponding options. See **31** **Add a Text Caption or Note.**

- Be sure to choose the ICC color profile you want your printer to use from the **Print Space** list. If you have installed an ICC color profile made just for your printer or for the paper you're using, you should see best results by choosing that ICC profile from this list and disabling printer color management through the printer driver, whose icon is located in the Windows **Control Panel**. In the absence of a printer color profile, your next best bet is choosing **Printer Color Management**, which assumes that your printer driver has its own color management routine (most photo printers do) and that it's turned *on*. If you don't like these results, try choosing

TIPS

If you make a selection before printing an image, you can enable the **Print Selected Area** option in the **Scaled Print Size** frame to print just that area. You must use only the **Rectangular Marquee** tool to select the area, there must be only one rectangle in the selection (not more than one joined), and the selection must not be feathered. See **72** **Select a Rectangular or Circular Area** for more about making this specific kind of selection.

To rotate the image on the paper, click the **Rotate 90° Left** or **Rotate 90° Right** button just below the preview window. When you do this, even though the upper-left corner of the *image* might be shifted to a different corner, the **Position** of the image remains relative to the upper-left corner of the *area* being printed.

Whatever you do, *do not* choose your monitor's color profile (the one you created using Adobe Gamma) from this list because you are trying to select the color spectrum intended for your *printer* and not your monitor. See **105** **Ensure That What You See Is What You Get** for more information about ICC color profiles.

Adobe RGB, again with the printer driver's color management turned off.

- To flip the image so that you can print it backwards onto iron-on transfer paper, enable the **Invert Image** option in the **Transfer Printing** frame. This way, when you iron the image onto your t-shirt, sweatshirt, or other material, the image will look correct.

5 **Select Printer Options and Print**

Click the **Print** button to display the **Print** dialog box. If you have more than one printer, select your photo printer from the **Name** list.

If you haven't set your paper type and print quality for this work session as described in **65 Set Print Options**, then click the **Properties** button to display the properties for your photo printer, make your selections, and click **OK** to return to the **Print Preview** dialog box. When you're ready, click **OK** to print the image.

67 Print a Contact Sheet

Before You Start

✔ **65** Set Print Options

See Also

→ **23** Change Image Date and Time

→ **66** Print an Image

✐ KEY TERM

Contact sheet—A printout of a group of images, along with identifying labels, as a collection of miniatures. The term originates from film photography, where contact sheets are often produced to record the contents of a roll of film.

After importing a new batch of images into the *Organizer*, you may want to print a *contact sheet* so that you can decide which images are worth saving, which ones need working on, and which ones are ready to print. A contact sheet is a printout of miniature photos or *thumbnails*, similar to the index sheet you get when you have photos commercially printed. Under each image, you can print its filename, text *caption*, and *file date*. Such a reference can make it easy, for example, to verify that the captions, filenames, and dates for your images make sense. You can use a contact sheet to quickly mark any information that seems wrong or incomplete so that you can later change it in the *catalog*.

You can select any number of images from the photo well to print on a contact sheet. The images do not have to belong to the same import batch or have the same *tag* or *collection* markers (although that might be one reason to print them together). If you don't make a selection, all the currently displayed images in the photo well are prepared for printing, along with any video thumbnails.

1 Select Images to Print

In the Organizer, press **Shift** and click the first image in the group you want to print, and then click the last image in the contiguous group. Alternatively, click the first image then press **Ctrl** and click each additional image you want to print.

2 Click Print Photos Button

Click the **Print photos** button on the **Shortcuts** bar and click **Print** from the menu that appears. You can also select **File, Print** from the menu. You may see a warning telling you that your selection contains creations and audio files that will not be printed; click **OK.** You may also see a warning box listing images or video thumbnails of low *resolution*, and therefore, low print quality. Click **OK** to dismiss the warning and continue. The **Print Selected Photos** dialog box appears.

3 Set Up Printer

If you have more than one printer, select your photo printer from the **Select Printer** list. Then click the **Show Printer Preferences** button to display the **Properties** dialog box for your printer. From this dialog box, you can select the type of photo paper you're using and the print quality you desire. See **65 Set Print Options** for help. Click **OK** after making your selections to return to the **Print Photos** dialog box.

To select the *printer ICC profile* you want to use for printing, click the **More Options** button in the **Print Selected Photos** dialog box and select the profile from the **More Options** dialog box that appears. If you have installed an ICC color profile made just for your printer or for the paper you're using, you will see best results by choosing that ICC profile from this list and disabling printer color management through the printer driver, whose icon is located in the Windows **Control Panel**. In the absence of a printer color profile, try choosing **sRGB**, again with the printer driver's color management turned off. Whatever you do, *do not* choose your monitor's color profile (the one you created using Adobe Gamma) from this list because you are trying to select the color spectrum intended for your *printer* not your monitor. See **105 Ensure That What You See Is What You Get** for more information about ICC color profiles. Click **OK** to return to the **Print Selected Photos** dialog box again.

TIP

Organizer prints all currently displayed images and video thumbnails. If you want to display a group of related images, such as all the images of your son or daughter, use the **Find** bar first. (See **33 About Finding Items in the Catalog.**) If the catalog is sorted by batch or folder, you can click the gray bar above a group to select all the items in that group. With either of these two methods, you might also end up selecting audio and *creation* files, but they'll be automatically excluded from the print job.

NOTE

If you don't want to include a low-resolution image on the contact sheet, you can remove it from printing in step 4, or you can **Cancel** printing altogether. For the most part however, the warning about low-resolution images can simply be ignored, because a contact sheet is typically only for image identification and not for sharing or hanging on a wall.

TIP

Because contact sheets are typically for your reference only, you might want to use less-expensive paper when printing them. Just make sure that the paper type you plan to use is selected in your printer's **Properties** dialog box before printing.

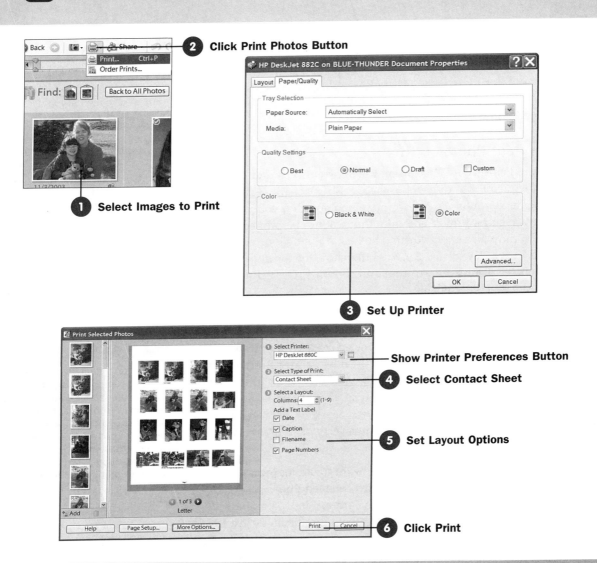

2 Click Print Photos Button

1 Select Images to Print

3 Set Up Printer

Show Printer Preferences Button

4 Select Contact Sheet

5 Set Layout Options

6 Click Print

If you use a PIM-enabled printer, and if the image you want to print contains PIM data (presumably because you captured the image using a PIM-enabled digital camera), enable the **PRINT Image Matching (P.I.M.)** option and/or the **Exit Print** option (see your printer manual for more information on which options to choose).

4 Select Contact Sheet

Open the **Select Type of Print** drop-down list and select **Contact Sheet**. The selected images are arranged as small thumbnails on as many pages as needed to meet the other options you select. To review the images on other pages, use the left and right arrows below the preview window.

If you accidentally included an image you don't want to print or if you want to exclude a low-resolution image, select it from the pane on the far left side of the **Print Photos** dialog box and press the **Delete** key or click the **Remove Selected Items** button (the trash can). This action does not remove the image from the catalog, just from the contact sheet you are setting up to print.

5 Set Layout Options

Control the size of each image by changing the number of thumbnails you want to appear in each row of the contact sheet using the box marked **Columns**.

Choose whether you want to display the **Date**, **Caption**, and **Filename** below each image by enabling the appropriate check boxes. You can also print the **Page Numbers** on each page of a multipage printout.

6 Click Print

To print the contact sheet using the options you have selected, click **Print**.

✎ NOTE

To add an image to the contact sheet for printing, click the **Add** button at the bottom of the left pane, check the images to add from the **Add Photos** dialog box, and click **OK.** You're returned to the **Print Selected Photos** dialog box, where the images you added are included in the left pane.

💡 TIP

Before printing, you can view and change an individual image's caption, filename, or file date using the **Properties** pane. See **31** Add a Text Caption or Note and **23** Change Image Date and Time for help.

---

68 Print a Picture Package

When you order prints from a professional photo lab, you're generally offered package deals where you can choose from multiple sizes of prints. To make the deal more economical, the lab lays out the different photo sizes on as few sheets of photo paper as possible, minimizing waste. The *Organizer* gives you similar options—the difference here being, of course, that you'll be doing the printing yourself. A *picture package* enables you to make maximum use of store-bought premium photo paper (generally 8 1/2" × 11") so that you can print wall-, table-,

Before You Start

✔ **65** Set Print Options

See Also

→ **66** Print an Image

KEY TERM

Picture package—Multiple copies of one or more photographs, printed on a single sheet of paper, using standard print sizes such as 8.5" × 11", 5" × 7", and wallet.

TIP

Organizer prints all currently displayed images and video *thumbnails*. If you want to display a group of related images such as all the images from your last vacation, use the **Find** bar first. (See **33** **About Finding Items in the Catalog**.) If the catalog is sorted by batch or folder, you can click the gray bar above a group to select all the items in that group. With either of these two methods, you might also end up selecting audio and *creation* files, but they'll be automatically excluded from the print job.

NOTES

If you don't want to include a low-resolution image in the picture package, you can remove it from printing in step 4, or you can **Cancel** printing altogether.

To avoid accidentally printing images with low-quality, resize them if needed to fit the print size you want to use. See **60** **Change Image Size or Resolution.**

and wallet-size photos of the same image or of multiple images, all at the same time. Some sizes may be rotated 90 degrees on the printed page to make room for other sizes. The program leaves enough margin between photos for you to cut between them with scissors.

① Select Images to Print

In the Organizer, press **Shift** and click the first image in the group you want to print, and then click the last image in the contiguous group. Alternatively, click the first thumbnail, then press **Ctrl** and click each additional image you want to print.

② Click Print Photos Button

Click the **Print photos** button on the **Shortcuts** bar and click **Print** from the menu that appears. You can also select **File**, **Print** from the menu. You might see a warning telling you that your selection contains creations and audio files that will not be printed; click **OK**. You might also see a warning box listing images or video thumbnails of low *resolution*, and therefore, low print quality. Click **OK** to dismiss the warning and continue. The **Print Selected Photos** dialog box appears (for a better look at this dialog box, check out the Color Gallery).

③ Set Up Printer

If you have more than one printer, select your photo printer from the **Select Printer** list. Then click the **Show Printer Preferences** button to display the **Properties** dialog box for your printer. In this dialog box, you can select the type of photo paper you're using and the print quality you desire. See **65** **Set Print Options** for help. Click **OK** after making your selections to return to the **Print Photos** dialog box.

To select the *ICC printer profile* you want to use for printing, click the **More Options** button and select the profile from the **More Options** dialog box that appears. If you have installed an ICC color profile made just for your printer or for the paper you're using, you will see best results by choosing that ICC profile from this list and disabling printer color management through the printer driver, whose icon is located in the Windows **Control Panel**. In the absence of a printer color profile, try choosing **Adobe RGB**, again with the printer driver's color management turned off.

Whatever you do, *do not* choose your monitor's color profile (the one you created using Adobe Gamma) from this list, because you are trying to select the color spectrum intended for your *printer*, not your monitor. See **105** **Ensure That What You See Is What You Get**. Click **OK** to return to the **Print Photos** dialog box again.

4 Select Picture Package

Open the **Select Type of Print** drop-down list and select **Picture Package**. The selected images are arranged in the standard package: one 5" × 7", two 2.5" × 3.5", and four wallet prints, on as many pages as needed to print all the images you've selected. To review the images on other pages, use the left and right arrows below the preview window.

If you accidentally included an image you don't want to print such as a low-resolution image, select it from the pane on the far left side of the dialog box and press the **Delete** key or click the **Remove Selected Items** button (the trash can). This action does not remove the image from the catalog, just from the current print job. To add an image for printing, click the **Add** button on the bottom of the left pane, check the images to add from the **Add Photos** dialog box, and click **OK**. You're returned to the **Print Selected Photos** dialog box, where the images you added are included in the left pane.

5 Set Layout Options

To select a different picture package, open the **Select a Layout** list and choose the picture package layout you want to use. This list features all the layout possibilities for your current printer paper size. Each entry in the list shows the quantity and size of the images that will be printed per page. For example, if your paper size is listed as 4" × 6", you might see entries such as 2.1" × 2.8" or 4" × 6".

You can add a picture frame border around each image by choosing one from the **Select a Frame** list.

To print each photo multiple times, using the picture package layout you've chosen, check the **One Photo Per Page** option.

TIP

You can drag and drop images from the strip on the left side of the dialog box to fill any vacancies in the picture package layout. If a picture was placed on the layout in a size you don't want it to be, just drag a different photo onto that location in the preview window.

NOTE

If you choose a print size larger than your paper size (for example, if you choose 5" × 7" print size when you're using 4" × 6" paper), the image will be enlarged to the print size you select and then cropped to fit the paper size. The selected images are automatically laid out to fit the size and positions described in the picture package you choose.

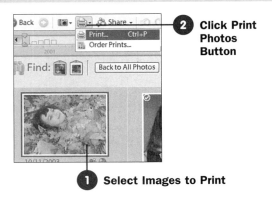

2 Click Print Photos Button

1 Select Images to Print

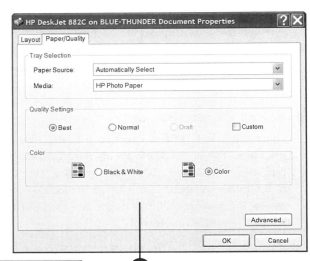

3 Set Up Printer

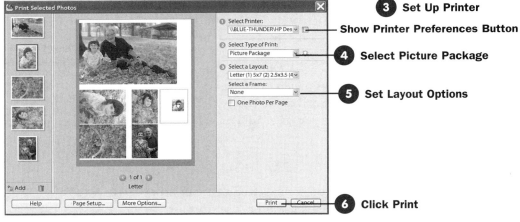

Show Printer Preferences Button

4 Select Picture Package

5 Set Layout Options

6 Click Print

NOTE

The Organizer crops equal amounts of content from opposite sides of an image where necessary for certain sizes to make that image fit the proportions of that size. For certain packages, you might notice that some sizes are cropped more than others.

To crop photos so that they exactly fit the photo sizes you've selected, check the **Crop to Fit** option. (This option is not available with all layouts.)

6 Click Print

To print the photos using the package options you've selected, click **Print**.

69 Print Images Using an Online Service

If you don't have a photo printer or a printer capable of printing on photo paper, you can still make wonderful, high-quality photo prints directly from the *Organizer*, *right now*. Using your Internet connection, you can link directly from the Organizer to an *online service*, upload your images, have the service print the images (perhaps with professional corrections), and ship you the results—in some cases, by next-day air!

Before printing, however, you should prepare your images properly. Select each image in the *Organizer*, send it to the *Editor*, save the file in PSD format, and make any necessary improvements to the image's color, contrast, saturation, and sharpness. Resize the image as needed to ensure that its print size matches the size you want to use when printing, and that it has a high-enough resolution to produce a good quality print. See **60** **Change Image Size or Resolution** for help. Finally, save a copy of your image in a shareable format you can upload to an online service, such as TIFF or JPEG.

1 Select Images to Print

After you've prepared each image for printing, in the Organizer, press **Shift** and click the first image in the group you want to upload for printing, and then click the last image in the contiguous group. Alternatively, click the first image, press **Ctrl**, and click each additional image you want to upload for printing.

2 Click Print Photos Button

Click the **Print photos** button on the **Shortcuts** bar and click **Order Prints** from the menu that appears. You can also select **File**, **Order Prints** from the menu. The **Adobe Photoshop Services** dialog box appears.

3 Log On to Service

If this is your first time using the service, you'll be asked to set up an account. Enter the required information. Read the **Terms of Service** by clicking its link and enable the check box to indicate

See Also

→ **158** Share Images Using Email

→ **160** Share Images Using an Online Service

→ **161** Send Image to a Mobile Phone

NOTE

To complete this task, you need a working Internet connection—dial-up is fine, broadband is better. This task also assumes that you have chosen Ofoto as your preferred print service (see **159** **Select an Online Service**. If you've chosen a different print service, the steps will be similar to those shown here, but not exactly the same.

**WEB RESOURCE**

http://www.ofoto.com

See Ofoto for special offers, which often include free prints.

NOTE

You can print a creation already saved to the catalog using an online service by simply following the steps given here. You can also print a creation after creating or editing it by clicking the **Order Online** button on the **Step 5: Share** page of the **Creation** wizard. Certain creation types (such as a slideshow) cannot be uploaded to an online service for printing.

TIP

Organizer uploads for printing all currently displayed images. If you want to display a group of related images, such as all the images from your last vacation, use the **Find** bar first. (See **33** About Finding Items in the Catalog.) If the *catalog* is sorted by batch or folder, you can click the gray bar above a group to select all the items in that group. With either of these two methods, you might also end up selecting video and audio files, but they'll be automatically excluded from the print job.

NOTE

Your Ofoto account is only accessible using the e-mail address and password you supply—from the computer where you first registered it.

that you agree with the terms. Enable the **Remember my password** check box to have the Organizer enter this data for you the next time you print using this service.

If you're already an Ofoto member and requested that your password be remembered, skip to step 4. Otherwise, enter your email address and password now. If you want your password remembered and you forgot to indicate that initially, select the **Remember my password** option when you log in. Click the **Next** button at the bottom of the dialog box.

4 Select Print Sizes

The **Order Prints** process is organized like a wizard, with the current step number highlighted at the top of the dialog box; click **Next** to continue to the next part of the order process or click **Back** to return to a previous step.

Here, the first step is to enter the quantities for the various print sizes you want next to the image *thumbnails* that appear on the left. A running total based on your current selections appears in the **Order Summary** frame. Use the scroll bars to select print sizes for each image. At the bottom of the listing, enable the **Zoom and Trim** option to let Adobe Photoshop Services (Ofoto) trim your images as needed to fit the print sizes you select. Click **Next** to continue.

5 Select Recipients

On the **Step 2 Recipients** screen, choose where you want your prints delivered. A list of people you've previously sent photos to appears on the left. Enable the check box in front of the person to whom you want these prints delivered. If you select more than one person, your order is duplicated that many times so that each person receives the number of prints you choose in step 4.

To add a new address, click the **Add New Address** link, enter the address data, and click **Next** to return to this screen. If a person's name is grayed out, you must complete their information by clicking **Edit** next to their name, entering the rest of the address data, and clicking **Next**. To replace the address listing with the data already stored in your Organizer Contact Book (see **157** Manage Contacts), click the **Import Addresses** button.

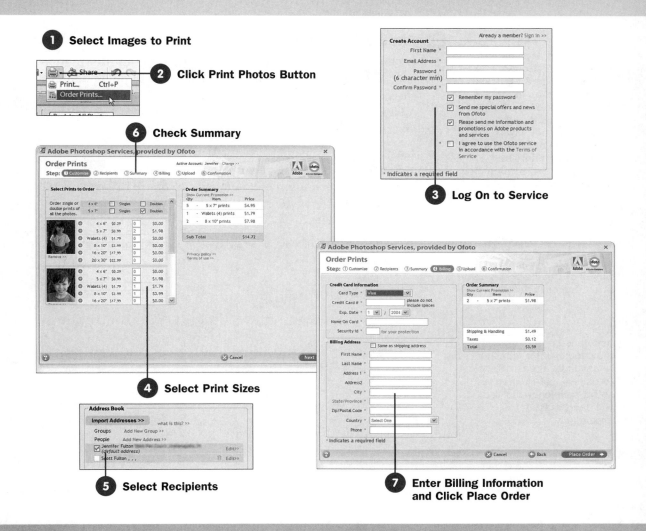

① **Select Images to Print**

② **Click Print Photos Button**

③ **Log On to Service**

⑥ **Check Summary**

④ **Select Print Sizes**

⑤ **Select Recipients**

⑦ **Enter Billing Information and Click Place Order**

⑥ **Check Summary**

On the **Step 3 Summary** screen, verify the **Order Details**. Select how you want the photos shipped from the **Ship Via** list. The cost of shipping your prints using this method is calculated and added to your total, displayed on the right. Verify this total and click **Next** to continue.

TIPS

A green icon appears next to each print size that's appropriate for a particular image based on its image size and resolution. A red icon indicates that the image does not have a high-enough resolution to support that print size; selecting one of these print sizes will result in a less-than-quality print.

To order single or double prints for all images in either 4" × 6" or 5" × 7" size, enable the appropriate **Single** or **Double** check box at the top of the image list on the left.

Even if you plan on shipping these prints to multiple people, enter only the total you want each person to receive. Later, when you select recipients, this total will be increased accordingly.

 Enter Billing Information and Click Place Order

On the **Step 4 Billing** screen, enter your **Credit Card Information**. Enter a **Billing Address**, or enable the **Same as shipping address** check box to ship the prints to the same address listed in the Address Book. Click the **Place Order** button to upload the images and place your order with the online service.

After the images are uploaded, the **Confirmation** screen appears, displaying your order number and an order summary. Click the **Print this Confirmation** button to print a copy of this page. You'll also receive an email message confirming your order and providing a delivery date.

Now simply wait for your selected delivery service to deliver your prints!

9

Selecting a Portion of an Image

IN THIS CHAPTER:

70 About Making Selections

71 Make Areas of an Image Easier to Select

72 Select a Rectangular or Circular Area

73 Draw a Selection Freehand

74 Select a Straight-Edged Area

75 Select an Object by Tracing Its Edge

76 Select Areas of Similar Color

77 Paint a Selection

Many of the modifications you make to an image in PhotoShop Elements are applied to only a portion of the image. For example, you might want to delete an item from the background or change the color of part of the image. To make modifications to any portion of an image, you must first select the area to change. Selecting an area enables you to make modifications to only that portion of the image without affecting the rest of the image.

In this chapter, you will learn how to make selections using the different selection tools available in PhotoShop Elements. You will see that the tool you choose to make selections is based on the type of selection you want to make. You will learn to select geometric portions of the image (such as a rectangle or an oval) or to select specific objects by tracing the object's borders (such as selecting only the light post in front of a house). You will also learn how to select specific portions of the image based on their color, such as selecting only the red balloons in a balloon bouquet. You will learn how you can use the **Selection Brush** tool to paint the area of the image you want to select. Or you can use that same tool to paint a sort of *mask* overlay, in which everything *except* what you paint is selected. Regardless of how you select a portion of the image, after you have made a selection, all the editing commands you then make affect only that portion. So, you can change the color of only the red balloons to blue or use the **Dodge** tool on just the light post without affecting the house. For more information about some of the image-editing commands available to you after making a selection, see **86** About Copying, Cutting, and Pasting Data Within a Selection.

70 About Making Selections

See Also

→ **71** Make Areas of an Image Easier to Select

→ **72** Select a Rectangular or Circular Area

→ **73** Draw a Selection Freehand

→ **74** Select a Straight-Edged Area

→ **75** Select an Object by Tracing Its Edge

→ **76** Select Areas of Similar Color

→ **77** Paint a Selection

Selecting a portion of an image is the first basic step in nearly all the photo editing you do in PhotoShop Elements. By selecting the desired portion of the image first, you then can apply the desired edits to just the selection. Any portion of the image not included in the selection is unaffected by the commands you use on the selection. Nearly every edit command in PhotoShop Elements can be applied to a selection. Most commonly, selections are used to identify portions of an image you want to copy somewhere else, delete, rotate, resize, or move. But you also can perform tasks such as applying filters or effects to the selection.

When you select a portion of an image, a scrolling line, or *selection marquee*, appears around your selection. This visual aid enables you to quickly identify the portion of the image that is selected.

Marquee Tool
|Lasso Tool
|Magic Wand Tool
|Selection Brush Tool

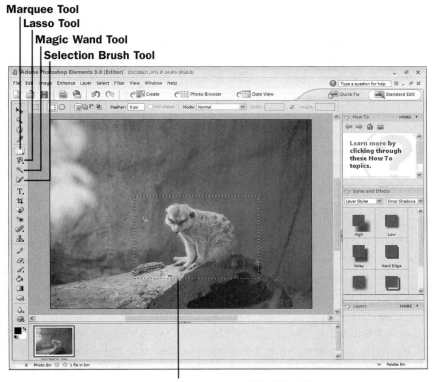

Rectangular Selection Marquee

The selection marquee identifies the selected portion of the image.

You find the tools for making selections on the **Toolbox** on the left side of the screen. PhotoShop Elements provides four different types of selection tools, but each of these tools has additional options you can manipulate on the **Options** bar. For example, if you select the **Marquee** tool, you can use the **Options** bar to select between the **Rectangular** and **Elliptical Marquee** tools. You can use these marquee tools to draw a rectangular or circular selection on the image. See **Select a Rectangular or Circular Area** for more information on using the marquee tools.

If you want to create an outline around a specific portion of the image, you can use the **Lasso** tools. PhotoShop Elements provides three different **Lasso** tools you can select from the **Options** bar. For example, you can use

NOTE

When you make a selection, you're selecting pixels on the current layer only. The exception is with the **Magic Wand** tool, which provides an option you can select to include all visible pixels, on all layers within an image.

the **Magnetic Lasso** tool to follow the outline of an object, selecting that object perfectly. See **75** **Select an Object by Tracing Its Edge**. With the **Lasso** tool, you can draw a selection area of any shape; see **73** **Draw a Selection Freehand**. To draw a straight-edged selection such as a hexagon, use the **Polygonal Lasso**. See **74** **Select a Straight-Edged Area**.

If you want to select areas of the image that are the same color, you can use the **Magic Wand** tool. When you use this option, you click the desired color in the photo, such as a patch of green grass, and PhotoShop Elements selects all the areas in the photo that match the color you clicked. See **76** **Select Areas of Similar Color** for more information on making selections based on similar color.

The other method for making selections is to use the **Selection Brush** tool to paint your selection. When you use this tool, you create a selection using a paint brush tool. You can specify the width of the brush using the **Options** bar. See **73** **Paint a Selection** for more information on using the **Selection Brush** tool.

For all the selection tools but the **Selection Brush**, you have the option of what you want to happen if a selection already exists: You can create a new selection, add to or subtract from the existing selection, or have the existing selection reduced to the area where it intersects the next selection you draw. Buttons that control what happens to an existing selection appear on the **Options** bar, as shown here. Just click the button you want to use *before* creating another selection when one already exists in the image. By the way, you can modify a selection (by adding or subtracting from it, for example) using any combination of selection tools. So, always choose the best tool for what you want to select at the time, and don't be afraid to use several selection tools if it helps you select whatever you're after quickly.

These buttons control how a new selection will affect an existing one.

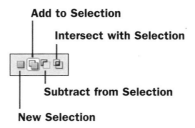

Add to Selection

Intersect with Selection

Subtract from Selection

New Selection

If you want to make edits to everything but the current selection in an

> **NOTE**
>
> With your selection made, any commands you perform are applied to only the selected portion of the image. For example, if you select part of the image and then press the Delete key, that selected portion of the image is deleted, but the unselected portion remains.

image, you can invert the selection. When you invert a selection, everything that wasn't selected before is now selected. For example, if you select a portion in the center of the image, when you invert the selection, everything *except* the center of the image is now selected. When a selection is inverted, you'll typically see two selection marquees: one around the outer edge of the image and another around the originally selected portion. See **83** **Select Everything But the Current Selection** for more information on inverting a selection.

When you invert the selection, the previously unselected portions are

Inverted Selection Marquees

selected.

When you apply a selection to an image, that selection remains until you unselect it. If you want to remove the marquee so that you can edit the entire image again, choose **Select, Deselect** to remove all selections from the image. To reselect the most recent selection, choose **Select, Reselect**.

In some instances, you might want to remove the marquee only temporarily so that you can view the entire image. If this is the case, you want to hide the marquee but maintain the selection. To hide the marquee, select **View, Selection**. Keep in mind that even though the marquee is not visible, it still is in effect. Any changes you make with the marquee hidden

 TIPS

To redisplay a selection that is hidden, choose **View, Selection** again. You will see a check mark next to the **Selection** option on the **View** menu when the selection is visible.

You can save selections in an image and recall them later when needed. See **84** **Save a Selection for Reuse**.

still apply only to the current selection.

If you copy or cut the data within a selection, the edges surrounding the pasted data can seem a little abrupt, especially if you paste the cropped image into another image. In some instances, you might want to create softer edges on your image so that the pixels around the edges of the selection can more easily blend with the existing pixels in the area to which you paste your data. You might also want to soften the edge of a selection to blend the change you make in that area with the unchanged portions of an image. You soften the edges of a selection through a process called *feathering*. When you feather the edges of the selection, you indicate the number of pixels from the edge that you want to use to soften the transition. For example, if you specify a feathering value of **5px**, the edge of the image is softened using a 5-pixel border around the outside edge of the selection. For more information on feathering the edge of a selection, see **82** Soften the Edge of a Selection.

Non-Feathered Data   **Feathered Data**

Feathering can help blend copied data with existing data in a new location.

You can modify an existing selection in many ways. Earlier, I mentioned the **Options** bar buttons that enable you to add to or subtract from an existing selection or to create a new selection using the area where two selections intersect. However, you can still modify a selection after it has been fully created. Using commands on the **Selection, Modify** submenu, you can expand a selection outward or shrink it inward by a certain amount. You can also add similar pixels to a selection, smooth out the jagged edge of a curved selection, or soften it with a nice feathered edge.

You'll even learn how to reposition the selection if you find that you've accidentally drawn it in the wrong spot on a layer. The details on how to do all these things and more are covered in upcoming tasks.

When desired, you can select the selection marquee (as it were), and even expand that selection by a bit, creating a border area. For example, you could create a circular selection. Then you could select the selection border and expand it by several pixels. You would then have a donut-shaped selection you could fill with color if you wanted. To do this, first, make a selection. Then choose **Selection, Modify, Border**. In the dialog box, enter the number of pixels you want to modify the selection by and click **OK**. On either side of the existing marquee, the selection is expanded by the amount you entered, creating a selection that's feathered on both sides. So, if you enter **5** for the border width, it's really 10, but pixels on either side of the original position of the marquee move from full selection in the center of the border to partial selection on the outer edges.

71 Make Areas of an Image Easier to Select

Sometimes it is difficult to see the edges of the area you want to select in an image. For example, if the lighting was not good when you took the photo, the subject might blend into the background. Or you just might have an image where there is no contrast between the objects and the background. Without enough contrast between your subject and the background, you'll find it difficult to use the **Magnetic Lasso** to trace its edge. If you're trying to select an area based on color, and that area doesn't contrast well enough with the surroundings, that can make using the **Magic Wand** tool difficult if not impossible to use. If this is the case, you can use different *filter* adjustments to change the area you want to select and make the selection easier.

Four specific filter adjustments work well for making an image easier to select. You can try each to find the one that works well with your particular image. You are looking for one that makes the part of the image you want to select easier to identify. For example, you can apply the **Threshold** adjustment to convert the image to black and white. With the **Threshold** effect, the light areas of the image are converted to white and the dark areas are converted to black; there are no grays. You can specify the **Threshold** level for the image. Everything darker than the specified threshold is converted to black, and pixels lighter than that value are converted to white. When you're looking at the image in black and white, the subject or object you want to select should be much easier to identify.

Before You Begin

✔ **70** About Making Selections

See Also

→ **75** Select an Object by Tracing Its Edge

→ **76** Select Areas of Similar Color

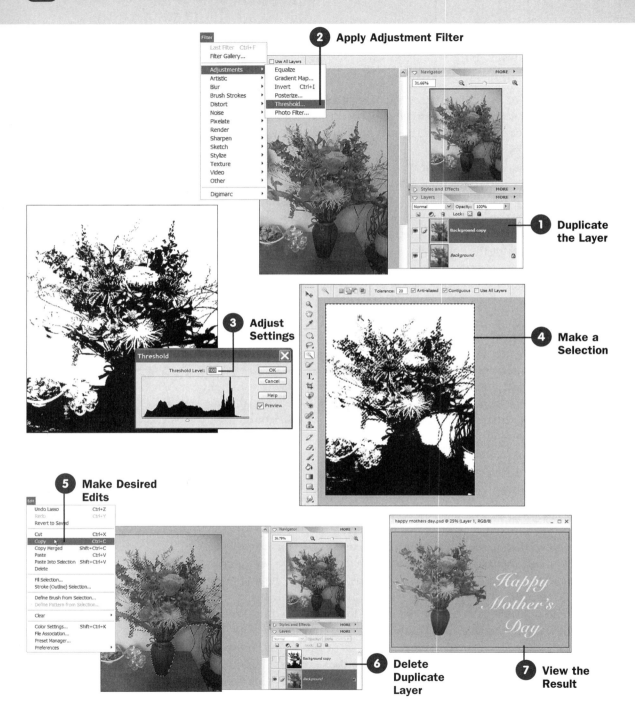

2 Apply Adjustment Filter

1 Duplicate the Layer

3 Adjust Settings

4 Make a Selection

5 Make Desired Edits

6 Delete Duplicate Layer

7 View the Result

Another adjustment you can make is to group the levels of brightness in the image using the **Posterize** adjustment. When you select this option, you specify the number of tones or brightness levels you want, and the brightness of pixels in the image are changed so that each pixel belongs to one of the specific groups you specified. If you want to make the selection look like a photo negative, you can select the **Invert** adjustment. Finally, if you want to convert the selection to grayscale, you can select the **Gradient Map** adjustment. With any of these filters applied to the image, the area you want to select should be easier to grab using the appropriate selection tool.

If you want to use one of the available filter adjustments to make a portion of the image easier to select, first copy the image to another *layer* and then apply the desired filter to the copy of the layer. After you make your selection on the original layer, you can remove the duplicate, filtered layer. See **91** **About Layers and the Layers Palette** for more information on working with layers in PhotoShop Elements.

❶ Duplicate the Layer

Open an image in the *Editor* in **Standard Edit** mode and save it in Photoshop (**.psd*) format. In the **Layers** palette, select the layer that contains the data you want to select. If you're working with a single-layer image, this layer is called, by default, the *Background layer*.

Select **Layer, Duplicate Layer** from the menu. A new layer is added to the **Layers** palette. If you're working with a single-layer image, the original layer is called **Background**; the copy of that layer is given the name **Background copy**. Although you can rename this layer, you're using it in this task only temporarily, so renaming it isn't worth the effort. See **92** **Create a New Image Layer** for more information on duplicating layers of an image.

❷ Apply Adjustment Filter

Apply the adjustment that helps isolate the area you want to select: Select **Filter, Adjustments** from the menu, and then choose **Threshold, Gradient Map, Invert,** or **Posterize.**

 TIP

If you don't like the results of an adjustment filter after applying it, select **Edit, Undo** to revert to the previous settings for the image.

3 Adjust Settings

When you select an adjustment filter, a dialog box opens in which you can specify the settings for the filter. For example, with the **Threshold** adjustment filter, you can specify the threshold level. Everything lighter than that level remains white, and anything darker becomes black.

If you selected the **Gradient Map** filter, on the **Gradient Map** dialog box, select the gradient pattern you want to use. The filter maps the color range of the image to the range of colors within the selected gradient.

If you selected the **Posterize** filter, on the **Posterize** dialog box, select number of levels of brightness you want. If you specify **4**, for example, the brightness of each pixel is adjusted to match one of those four levels. You can specify a value between **2** and **255**. See **182 Make a Photograph Look Like Andy Warhol Painted It** for more information on the **Posterize** filter.

As you manipulate the settings for an adjustment filter, a preview of the settings displays in the Editor window. Continue tweaking the settings until the outline or area of the object you want to select becomes obvious. In this image of a flower arrangement, I played with the **Threshold Level** setting until the outlines of the black flowers against the white background were very clear. See **136 About an Image's Histogram** for more information about the **Threshold** filter.

Click the **OK** button to close the dialog box and apply the adjustment to the selected layer.

4 Make a Selection

With the duplicate layer still active, use one of the selection tools described in **70 About Making Selections** to select the portion of the image you want. For example, you can trace the edges of an object using the **Magnetic Lasso** tool (see **75 Select an Object by Tracing its Edge**). If the area you want to select is all one color or close to it, use the **Magic Wand** to select the area instead (see **77 Select Areas of Similar Color**).

TIP

If you select the **Invert** filter, a dialog box does not appear. The colors within the layer are inverted to create the appearance of a photo negative.

TIP

With some images, even these filters will not make selecting a certain object with a few clicks a perfect operation, just quicker. After using the filter to help make the selection, if you find when you view the selection on the image that you've accidentally captured something you didn't want (like the shadow behind the vase in this photo), use the **Lasso** or another tool to quickly deselect that area.

⑤ Make Desired Edits

With the portion of the image you want selected, change to the original layer by clicking it on the **Layers** palette. If your image had only one layer, you'll want to select the **Background** layer.

Make the desired edits. Because you've selected the image layer and not the duplicate layer, changes you make occur only on that layer and within the selection marquee. You can make any changes you want, such as applying a filter, image adjustment, or cutting/copying the data. For this example, I copied the flower vase from its tabletop background and pasted it into a new, blank document as the start of a new composite image I had planned.

⑥ Delete Duplicate Layer

You can return to the duplicate layer to select other portions of the image for adjustments. But when you're through with it, it's safe to remove it from the image. In the **Layers** palette, select the duplicate layer (the **Background copy** layer) you created in step 1 and click the **Delete Layer** button (the trash can icon near the top of the **Layers** palette) or choose **Layer, Delete Layer** from the menu to remove the layer.

⑦ View the Result

After you're satisfied with the result, make any other changes you want and save the PSD file. Resave the result in JPEG or TIFF format, leaving your PSD image with its layers (if any) intact so that you can return at a later time and make different adjustments if you want.

View the results of edits you made using the selection. In this example, you can see the new document I opened and into which I pasted the flower vase selected from the original image. For options about making the elements you paste into another document more compatible with their new locations, see **169** **Create a Composite Image**.

 NOTE

To make the changes you are going to make to the image layer easy to see, hide the top layer (the duplicate layer you made the adjustment to). To hide the duplicate layer, click its eye icon on the Layers palette.

72 Select a Rectangular or Circular Area

Before You Begin

✔ **70** About Making
    Selections

See Also

→ **73** Draw a Selection
    Freehand

→ **74** Select a Straight-
    Edged Area

→ **78** Expand or Shrink a
    Selection

You can use the **Marquee Selection** tools to select any rectangular or elliptical area in an image. You can select between the two shapes of marquees in the **Options** bar. Typically, these selection tools are used to specify the portion of the image that you want to cut or crop. Because the shapes they select are prescribed, these selection tools are rarely used to make organic, curved selections for the purpose of adjusting colors or highlighting objects. See **75** **Select an Object by Tracing Its Edge** for tips on selecting curved shapes.

1 **Select the Marquee Tool**

Open an image in the *Editor* in **Standard Edit** mode and save it in Photoshop (***.psd**) format. In the **Layers** palette, click the layer that contains the data you want to select.

Click the **Marquee Selection** tool on the **Toolbox**.

2 **Select the Tool Shape**

On the **Options** bar, click the **Rectangular Marquee** tool button to create a rectangle-shaped selection area or click the **Elliptical Marquee** tool to create an oval area.

When you select the **Elliptical Marquee** tool, Photoshop Elements automatically enables the **Anti-Aliased** option in the **Options** bar. This ensures that the edges around the selection are rounded and not jagged looking.

NOTES

You will see either the **Rectangular Marquee** icon or **Elliptical Marquee** icon on the **Toolbox**. PhotoShop Elements remembers the last **Marquee** tool you used and displays it in the **Toolbox**.

You can select the exact tool you want in one step: Click the **Marquee Selection** tool, hold the mouse button down and, when the pop-up menu appears, choose either the **Rectangular Marquee** or **Elliptical Marquee** tool from the list.

3 **Set Options**

Set the desired options for the **Marquee** tool on the **Options** bar, such as the amount of **Feather**. Click the **New Selection**, **Add to Selection**, **Subtract from Selection**, or **Intersect with Selection** button as desired.

The default **Mode** setting is **Normal**, meaning that the selection size is based on how you drag it. If you want to create a selection of a specific size, select the **Fixed Size** option from the **Mode** drop-down list. With this option selected, you must then specify the size of the selection by providing the width and height in pixels, inches, or centimeters. You can also set a specific height-to-width ratio by selecting the **Fixed Aspect Ratio** mode.

2 Select the
Tool Shape

3 Set Options

New Selection Button

1 Select the
Marquee
Tool

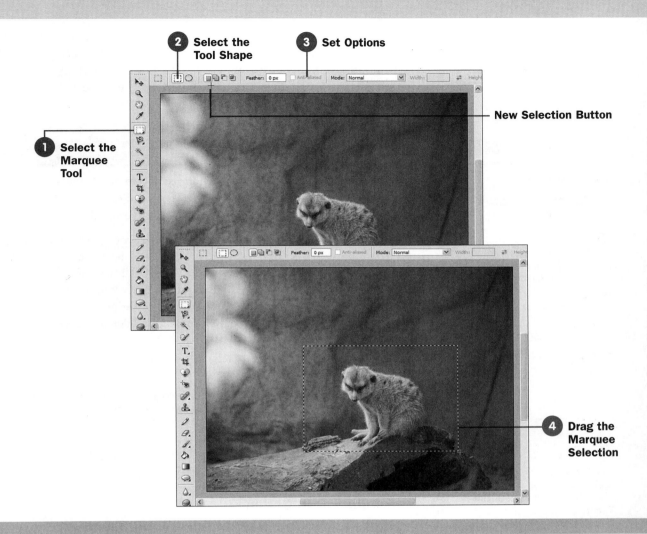

4 Drag the
Marquee
Selection

4 Drag the Marquee Selection

With the left mouse button, click the location on the image where you want to start the selection, hold down the mouse button, and drag to expand the selection to the desired size. If you've set a **Fixed Size**, just click and do not drag.

In this example, you can see that I've dragged a rectangular selection around the meerkat. Make changes to the area within the selection, copy or cut it to another image or layer, or delete the

 TIPS

If you want to create a perfectly square or circular selection instead of a rectangular or elliptical selection, press and hold the **Shift** key as you drag to create the selection.

To select a circle from the center out, press **Alt+Shift** as you drag.

data. After you're satisfied with the result, make any other changes you want and then save the PSD file. Resave the result in JPEG or TIFF format, leaving your PSD image with its layers (if any) intact so that you can return at a later time and make different adjustments if you want.

73 Draw a Selection Freehand

Before You Begin

✔ **70** About Making Selections

See Also

→ **72** Select a Rectangular or Circular Area

→ **74** Select a Straight-Edged Area

→ **75** Select an Object by Tracing Its Edge

→ **77** Paint a Selection

TIP

You can select the exact tool you want in one step: Click the **Lasso** tool on the **Toolbox**, hold the mouse button down and, when the pop-up menu appears, choose the **Lasso** tool from the list.

The **Lasso** tool enables you to create a freehand selection of elements within your image. For example, you can use this tool to draw a border around the head of a person or an animal lying on the ground.

To use the **Lasso** tool, you drag it around the area you want to select. The process is similar to freehand drawing in that everything you draw the selection around is selected. Intricate shapes can be difficult to trace with the **Lasso** tool. For more difficult shapes, you might want to use the **Magnetic Lasso** tool, which automatically snaps to the edges of objects you drag near. See **75** **Select an Object by Tracing Its Edge** for more information on using the **Magnetic Lasso** tool.

1 **Select the Lasso Tool**

Open an image in the *Editor* in **Standard Edit** mode and save it in Photoshop (***.psd**) format. In the **Layers** palette, click the layer that contains the data you want to select.

Select the **Lasso** tool from the **Toolbox**. The icon for the last **Lasso** tool you used is the icon displayed in the **Toolbox**.

2 **Select the Lasso Option**

If it's not already selected, select the **Lasso** tool on the **Options** bar.

3 **Set Options**

Set the desired options for the **Lasso** tool on the **Options** bar such as **Anti-aliased** or the amount of **Feather**. Click the **New Selection, Add to Selection, Subtract from Selection,** or **Intersect with Selection** button as desired.

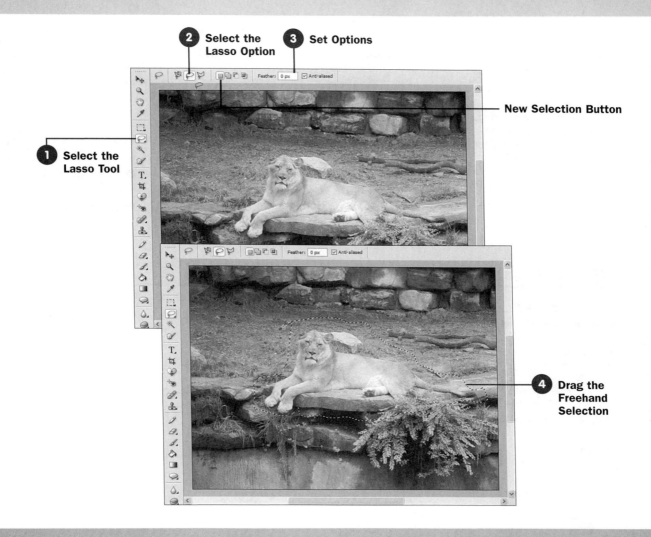

2 Select the Lasso Option

3 Set Options

New Selection Button

1 Select the Lasso Tool

4 Drag the Freehand Selection

4 Drag the Freehand Selection

Click the location on the image where you want to start your selection. Continue holding down the left mouse button and drag the mouse pointer around the edge of your selection. When you release the mouse button, Photoshop Elements completes the selection by connecting the start and end of your selection. Make changes to the area within the selection, copy or cut it to another image or layer, or delete the data.

⚠ NOTE

Make sure that you draw your selection so that it ends at the same point you started. When you release the mouse button, PhotoShop Elements drags a straight line to connect the starting and ending pixels of the selection.

After you're satisfied with the result, make any other changes you want and then save the PSD file. Resave the result in JPEG or TIFF format, leaving your PSD image with its layers (if any) intact so that you can return at a later time and make different adjustments if you want.

In this example, I drew a wavering line around this lion. Notice that the selection includes a little of the background as well. Had I wanted to select just the lion without any background, I could have used an adjustment layer as described in **71** **Make Areas of an Image Easier to Select**, and then traced the edge of the lion using the **Magnetic Lasso** as described in **75** **Select an Object by Tracing Its Edge**.

74 Select a Straight-Edged Area

Before You Begin

✔ **70** About Making Selections

See Also

➔ **72** Select a Rectangular or Circular Area

➔ **73** Draw a Selection Freehand

➔ **75** Select an Object by Tracing Its Edge

If you want to create a selection using straight lines, you can use the **Polygonal Lasso** tool. With this tool, you mark points along the edge of the image that you want to select, and PhotoShop Elements automatically connects the points with straight lines. This type of selection works well when you want to select the perimeter of an object with straight sides, such as a box or a house.

1 **Select the Lasso Tool**

Open an image in the *Editor* in **Standard Edit** mode and save it in Photoshop (***.psd**) format. In the **Layers** palette, click the layer that contains the data you want to select.

Select the **Lasso** tool on the **Toolbox**. The icon for the last **Lasso** tool you used is the icon displayed in the **Toolbox**.

2 **Select Polygonal Lasso**

If it's not already selected, select the **Polygonal Lasso** tool on the **Options** bar.

💡 TIP

You can select the exact tool you want in one step: Click the **Lasso** tool on the **Toolbox**, hold the mouse button down and, when the pop-up menu appears, choose the **Polygonal Lasso** tool from the list.

3 **Set Options**

Set the desired options for the **Polygonal Lasso** tool on the **Options** bar such as **Anti-aliased** or the amount of **Feather**. Click the New Selection, **Add to Selection**, **Subtract from Selection**, or **Intersect with Selection** button as desired.

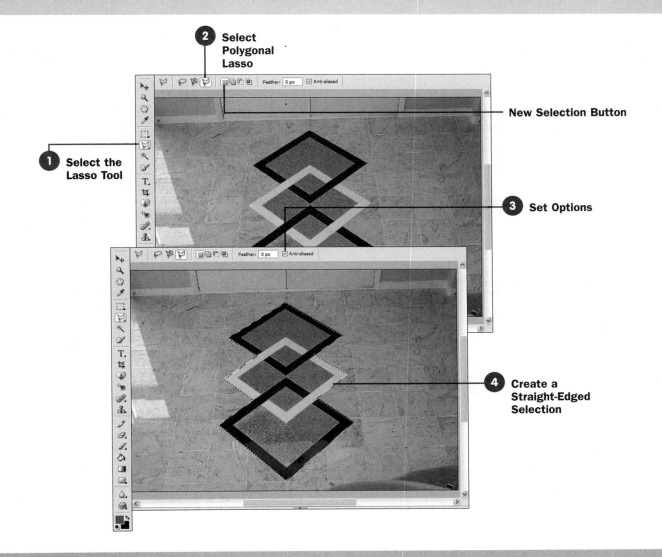

2 Select Polygonal Lasso

New Selection Button

1 Select the Lasso Tool

3 Set Options

4 Create a Straight-Edged Selection

4 Create a Straight-Edged Selection

Click the location on the image where you want to start your selection, move the mouse pointer to where you want to create a corner in the selection, and click the left mouse button again. As you reposition the mouse pointer, a springy line extends between the last anchor point and the mouse pointer so that you can see how the selection line will lay against the area you are selecting.

You must complete all sides of the selection by clicking again on the original selection point (the mouse pointer change to a lasso with a small o under it when you reach the beginning point), pressing the **Enter** key, or double-clicking the left mouse button.

Continue clicking to create points until you have surrounded the entire area. Make changes to the area within the selection, copy or cut it to another image or layer, or delete the data.

After you're satisfied with the result, make any other changes you want and save the PSD file. Resave the result in JPEG or TIFF format, leaving your PSD image with its layers (if any) intact so that you can return at a later time and make different adjustments if you want.

In this example, I used the **Polygonal Lasso** tool to outline the geometric tile design my husband had created in our front entry. After I selected the design, I could crop the image so that only the interlocking-square design appears in the image.

75 Select an Object by Tracing Its Edge

Before You Begin

✔ 70 About Making Selections

See Also

→ 72 Select a Rectangular or Circular Area

→ 73 Draw a Selection Freehand

→ 74 Select a Straight-Edged Area

→ 76 Select Areas of Similar Color

If you want to select an object that is irregularly shaped—such as a person sitting on a chair or an animal—by outlining its edges, you accomplish this goal using the **Magnetic Lasso** tool. With this tool, you mark points along the edge of the object, and PhotoShop Elements connects those points with lines that follow the closest edge.

When you use the **Magnetic Lasso** tool, you must specify settings that help PhotoShop Elements locate the edges of your object. For example, you can indicate a pixel **Width** value to define the width of the area near where you drag; Photoshop Elements looks in this area to locate the object edge. Photoshop Elements places the selection line along the edge it finds in that search area. To make an object easier to select, increase the contrast along its edge. See 71 **Make an Area of an Image Easier to Select** for suggestions on how to do this.

1 Select Lasso Tool

Open an image in the *Editor* in **Standard Edit** mode and save it in Photoshop (***.psd**) format. In the **Layers** palette, select the layer that contains the data you want to select.

Select the **Lasso** tool on the **Toolbox**. The icon for the last **Lasso** tool you used is the icon displayed in the **Toolbox**.

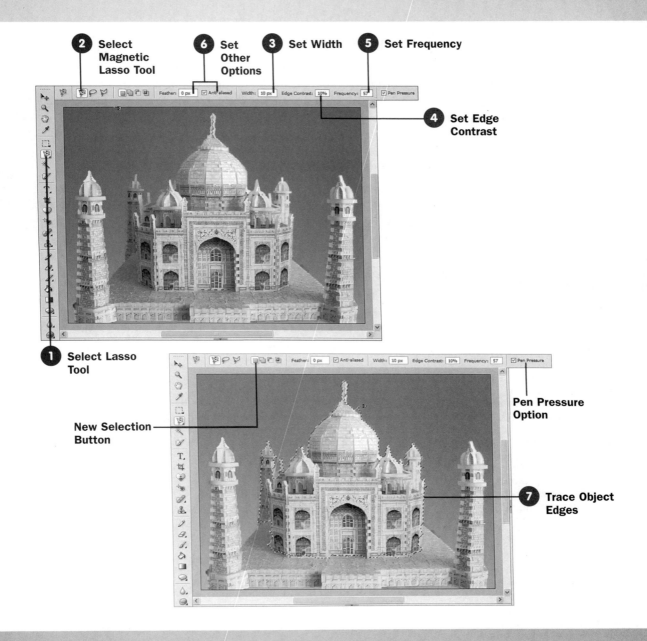

2 Select
Magnetic
Lasso Tool

6 Set
Other
Options

3 Set Width

5 Set Frequency

4 Set Edge
Contrast

1 Select Lasso
Tool

New Selection
Button

Pen Pressure
Option

7 Trace Object
Edges

2 Select Magnetic Lasso Tool

If it's not already selected, select the **Magnetic Lasso** tool from the
Options bar.

TIP

You can select the exact tool you want in one step: Click the **Lasso** tool on the **Toolbox**, hold the mouse button down and, when the pop-up menu appears, choose the **Magnetic Lasso** tool from the list.

 NOTES

If you have images with edges that are clearly defined, set both the **Width** and **Edge Contrast** values high. In images with high-contrast edges, you can roughly trace the border of the object, and Photoshop Elements will locate the actual border.

If the edge of the object is less defined, lower the **Width** and **Edge Contrast** values so that Photoshop Elements doesn't look too far afield from where you drag for the object's edge. With objects that have less-defined edges, you must typically be more precise when you trace the edges.

 TIP

If you are using a pen and drawing tablet, select the **Pen Pressure** option. When this option is enabled, if you increase the pen pressure, the **Width** value increases for the selection.

③ Set Width

On the **Options** bar, specify a number between **1** and **256** for the **Width** option to indicate the number of pixels around the point you drag in which Photoshop Elements will look to locate the edge of the object. The higher the value, the more likely Photoshop Elements will locate the actual edge of your object.

④ Set Edge Contrast

For the **Edge Contrast** option, specify a value between **1%** and **100%** to indicate the amount of contrast in the pixels that make up the edge of the object. If your object has low-contrast edges, use a higher value.

⑤ Set Frequency

For the **Frequency** option, specify a value between **0** and **100** that indicates the rate at which you want the lasso to set the anchor points along the object's edge as you drag. Use a higher value to set the border more quickly.

⑥ Set Other Options

Set any other options such as **Anti-aliased** or the amount of **Feather**. Click the **New Selection**, **Add to Selection**, **Subtract from Selection**, or **Intersect with Selection** button as desired, to create a new selection or add to an existing one.

⑦ Trace Object Edges

Click the location where you want to start the selection. Drag along the edge of the object you want to select. As you move the mouse pointer, a springy selection line extends between the mouse pointer and the last selection point to help you see where the selection line will land along the area you want to select. Fastening points are dropped along the edge as you drag, at the rate indicated by the **Frequency** value. Along edges that aren't so well defined, you might want to add your own points by clicking instead of dragging. If the edges of the object are straight, you need selection points only at the beginning and end of each edge. Edges that are more complex, such as a jagged or rounded edge, require more selection points to identify the edge.

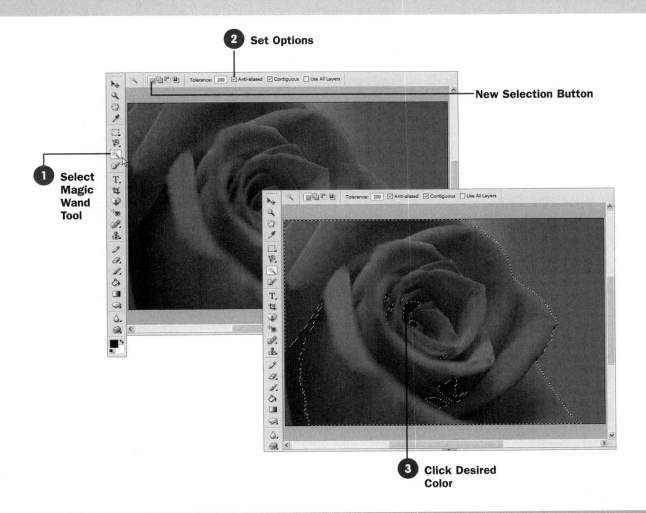

2 Set Options

New Selection Button

1 Select Magic Wand Tool

3 Click Desired Color

If you want to base your color selection using all the layers in the image, enable the **Use All Layers** option. Otherwise, Photoshop Elements makes the selection using only the pixels in the current layer.

3 **Click Desired Color**

Click the desired color on the image. Photoshop automatically selects all other pixels that match the selection based on the **Tolerance** and **Contiguous** options you have specified.

TIP

You cannot use the Magic Wand tool with a 16-bit color image. If you want to use this tool, you must first choose Image, Mode, Convert to 8 Bits/Channel from the menu bar to convert the image to 8-bit color.

Make changes to the area within the selection, copy or cut it to another image or layer, or delete the data. After you're satisfied with the result, make any other changes you want and save the PSD file. Resave the result in JPEG or TIFF format, leaving your PSD image with its *layers* (if any) intact so that you can return at a later time and make different adjustments if you want. In this example, I wanted to select the deep-red rose. Because I planned to use the selection to change the rose's color from red to coral, I increased the **Tolerance** setting to **200** to include as many of the varieties of red as possible. After I clicked a medium red on the edge of the front petal, note that, even with the **Tolerance** set this high, there are still areas of the rose that fall outside this color selection. If I want to select the entire rose, I'll have to increase the **Tolerance** setting and click again to broaden the selection even further.

After I have selected the entire red rose, I can use the **Enhance, Adjust Color, Replace Color** command to replace the red of the rose with a lovely coral color, or perhaps a golden yellow. As an alternative to recoloring an object with the **Replace Color** dialog box, you can use the **Color Replacement** brush, as described in **182** **Make a Photograph Look Like Andy Warhol Painted It**.

 **Paint a Selection**

Before You Begin

✔ **70** About Making Selections

See Also

→ **72** Select a Rectangular or Circular Area

→ **73** Draw a Selection Freehand

→ **75** Select an Object by Tracing Its Edge

→ **76** Select Areas of Similar Color

You can paint your selection on an image using the **Selection Brush** tool. When you paint a selection, you continue to click and drag the brush until you have selected the entire area. This method can be used to select any type of object. But unlike other selection methods where you are simply outlining the selection, with this method you paint every pixel that you want to select. And because you're using a brush to make the selection, you can partially select pixels by painting with a brush that uses less than 100% opacity.

The **Selection Brush** tool actually provides two different modes. With the default **Selection** mode, every pixel you paint becomes part of the selection. Any edits you make after painting your selection affect only the areas you painted. In this mode, the usual *selection marquee* marks the area that's selected.

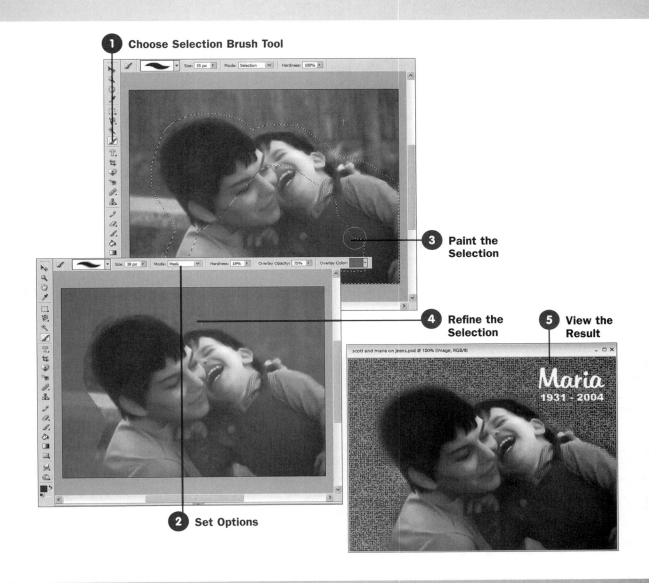

1 Choose Selection Brush Tool

3 Paint the Selection

4 Refine the Selection

5 View the Result

2 Set Options

The **Mask** mode works just the opposite way. If you select this mode, you paint a mask (a red overlay) over the areas of the image you *do not* want to edit. You can switch between **Mask** and **Selection** modes by simply changing the **Mode** option. If you switch from the **Selection** mode to the **Mask** mode, all selected pixels in the image become masked (appear in red).

**NOTES**

Although the process is similar, the mask you create here is not the same kind of *mask* you paint to protect lower layers from the effects of a fill or adjustment layer. It is also different from a *clipping mask*, which you can use to block parts of an upper layer from covering lower layers.

If you want to see the currently unselected areas of an image as a red overlay, you can switch to the **Selection Brush**'s mask mode after making a selection with any other tool.

TIP

You can quickly increase the size of the brush incrementally by pushing the] (right bracket) key. To decrease the brush size, press the [(left bracket) key. For example, if the brush size is between 1 and 10 pixels, the size changes by one pixel each time you press either the [or] key. If the brush size is 10 to 100 pixels, the size changes in increments of 10 pixels. You can increase the size of the brush on-the-fly as you paint.

① Choose Selection Brush Tool

Open an image in the *Editor* in **Standard Edit** mode and save it in Photoshop (*.psd) format. In the **Layers** palette, click the layer that contains the data you want to select. Select the **Selection Brush** tool on the **Toolbox**.

② Set Options

On the **Options** bar, select a brush tip and **Size**. A soft round brush works well in most cases. See **111** **About Tool Options** for more information about the available brush types.

By default, the **Selection** mode is selected in the **Mode** drop-down list. This means that everything you paint is treated as a selection. If you want, choose the **Mask** mode to paint areas you don't want selected. In this mode, unselected pixels are overlaid with the mask color fully; partially selected pixels are overlaid by the mask partially. Use **Mask** mode when you want more of a visual clue about what's included in your selection.

The mask overlay is usually red, but you can select a different mask color from the **Overlay Color** list. Typically, you select a color that will stand out against the image so that you can easily identify the masked area.

In the **Hardness** field, specify a value between **0%** and **100%** that indicates the hardness of the center of the brush tip. Typically, you will want to maintain a hardness value of **100** when painting a selection so that you can create crisp edges for the mask. By reducing the hardness value, the edges of the brush become softer, and pixels at the edge of your stroke become partially selected.

③ Paint the Selection

Paint over the area you want to select with short, quick strokes until you have selected all the desired area. Keep in mind that you are not just outlining the object in your image; you must paint the selection across the *entire area* you want to select or unselect, not just around the edge of the object.

④ Refine the Selection

To refine your selection, change to **Mask** mode by choosing that option from the **Mode** list on the **Options** bar. When working in **Mask** mode, remember that the goal is to paint the areas *you do not want selected*. Drag the brush over areas you want to exclude until your selection includes only what you want.

⑤ View the Result

Make changes to the area within the selection, copy or cut it to another image or layer, or delete the data. After you're satisfied with the result, make any other changes you want and save the PSD file. Resave the result in JPEG or TIFF format, leaving your PSD image with its *layers* (if any) intact so that you can return at a later time and make different adjustments if you want. In this example, I quickly selected the little boy and his mother and then refined the edge of the selection using **Mask** mode. After it was selected, it was easy to copy the data and paste it into a new image using **File, New, Image From Clipboard**. I added a pattern fill layer and a blue fill layer below to create the rough blue-jean-looking background. (See **Create a Layer Filled with a Color, Gradient, or Pattern**.) I lowered the **Opacity** of the pattern layer so its pattern would display on top of the blue fill layer, and not completely obscure it. After I added some text, the final image becomes a lasting remembrance of a wonderful lady and her son. Look for this image in the Color Gallery.

💡 TIP

You can create a straight-line selection by clicking at the desired starting location, holding down the **Shift** key, and then clicking the ending position.

10

Modifying a Selection

IN THIS CHAPTER:

78 Expand or Shrink a Selection

79 Add Areas Similar to the Current Selection

80 Smooth a Jagged Selection Edge

81 Move the Selection Marquee

82 Soften the Edge of a Selection

83 Select Everything But the Current Selection

Even with the variety of selection tools Photoshop Elements provides, sometimes it is difficult to select all the parts of the image you want with one selection maneuver. Fortunately, you can modify your selection by changing its size and location. You can even change the selection to select everything *except* what you originally selected.

In this chapter you will learn how to make changes to a selection. Not only can you change the selection size, you can also move the *selection marquee* to select a different area of the image. You can add additional areas to the selection by selecting other portions of the image that are similar to the current selection.

78 Expand or Shrink a Selection

Before You Begin

✔ **70** About Making Selections

See Also

→ **79** Add Areas Similar to the Current Selection

→ **81** Move the Selection Marquee

→ **83** Select Everything But the Current Selection

After making an initial selection, you can modify it in a variety of ways. You can expand or contract a selection by a specific number of pixels. For example, you could select an object, expand the selection by a few pixels, and after adding a new layer, fill the new expanded selection with some color. Assuming that the new layer is below the layer containing the selected object, you now have an object with a border around it.

1 Make Initial Selection

Open the image you want to select in the *Editor* in **Standard Edit** mode and save it in Photoshop (***.psd**) format. In the **Layers** palette, choose the layer that contains the data you want to select, and then use any selection tool to make the initial selection in the image.

2 Choose Expand or Contract

Choose **Selection, Modify, Expand** to expand the selection, or **Selection, Modify, Contract** to shrink it. The **Expand Selection** or **Contract Selection** dialog box appears; both are remarkably similar.

3 Enter Pixel Amount and Click OK

In the **Expand Selection** or **Contract Selection** dialog box, enter the number of pixels you want to expand or contract by, and then click **OK**. The selection is immediately modified.

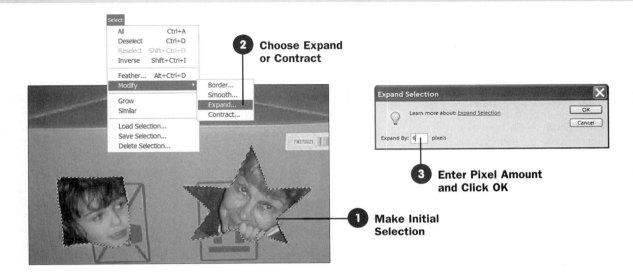

2 Choose Expand or Contract

3 Enter Pixel Amount and Click OK

1 Make Initial Selection

4 View the Result

---

4 **View the Result**

After you're satisfied with the selection, make changes to the area within the selection, copy or cut its data to another image or layer, or delete the data within the selection. Save the PSD file and then resave the file in JPEG or TIFF format, leaving your PSD image with its *layers* (if any) intact so that you can return at a later time and make different adjustments if you want.

TIP

You can refine a selection by adding to or subtracting from it, or by creating a new selection from the intersection of two selections, using the buttons on the **Options** bar for most of the selection tools (**Selection Brush** excluded). To build a selection, you can switch from selection tool to selection tool freely, using each tool to your advantage when trying to snag a particular area.

TIP

Suppose that you've applied one of the frame effects to an image, and you decide after the fact that you want to add a mat. You could undo everything and follow the steps in **166** Frame a Photograph to add a mat and a frame in sequence, or you could press **Ctrl** and click the image thumbnail in the **Layers** palette, which selects the image area. Save this selection by following the steps in **84** Save a Selection for Reuse. Then shrink the selection by the width of the mat you want, add a feather, and finally subtract this new

I loved how my daughter and her Grandma Ria looked peeking out of this cardboard box, and I couldn't resist trying to make something of it. So, I selected them and copied them to a new image (**File, New, Image from Clipboard**.) I returned to the original image, expanded the selection and filled it with red, and then copied and pasted the red selection to the new image (**Edit, Paste**). The red selection appeared on its own layer, which I moved to the bottom of the layer stack on the **Layers** palette. This action placed a nice red border around my two "girls." I added a gradient fill layer, placed that layer on the very bottom of the layer stack and added some text. Finally, I added a drop shadow *layer style* to the text and the red layer, making everything pop off the gradient background.

79 Add Areas Similar to the Current Selection

Before You Begin

✔ **70** About Making Selections

See Also

→ **78** Expand or Shrink a Selection

It is often difficult to select all the pixels that make up the area you want to select. For example, you might want to select the blossom of a firework explosion. Although you can use one of the **Lasso** tools to select the bloom, tracing around all the tendrils of the explosion of light can be tedious. Fortunately, Photoshop Elements provides tools that enable you to expand a selection to include pixels that match those in the current selection.

You have two options for expanding the current selection by adding similar pixels: If you want to select all the pixels in the image that match the current selection, choose the **Select, Similar** command. In a photo of a troop of costumed dancers in which you have selected a portion of a single blue costume (maybe using the **Lasso** tool and selecting an area quickly and well inside the borders of the costume), this command selects not only the rest of the original blue costume, but all similarly colored blue costumes in the image (and any other blue pixels, which you can usually quickly deselect by lassoing them). If you want to select only the pixels adjacent to the current selection (for example, only the remainder of the single blue costume), choose the **Select, Grow** command instead. You can use this process for a selection you intend to invert—for example, to quickly select a similarly colored background around an object.

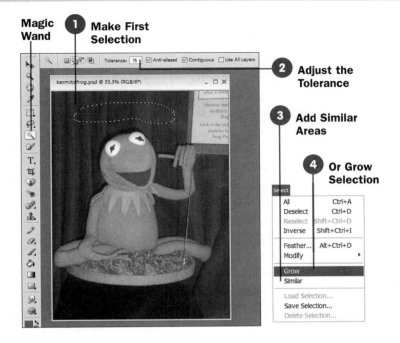

Magic Wand

1 Make First Selection

2 Adjust the Tolerance

3 Add Similar Areas

4 Or Grow Selection

5 View the Result

1 Make First Selection

Open the image you want to work with in the *Editor* in **Standard Edit** mode and save it in Photoshop (***.psd**) format. In the **Layers** palette, choose the layer that contains the data you want to select and then use any selection tool to make the initial selection in the image. You can use any of the selection tools to select the area containing the pixels you want to match. For example, you can use the **Elliptical Marquee** tool to select a circular area containing the pixels you want. The colors and tone in this selection will be used to find matching pixels in the image.

NOTE

You control how closely pixels must match the pixels in the current selection with the **Tolerance** setting, available with the **Magic Wand** tool. Basically, before using the **Similar** or **Grow** commands, you change to the **Magic Wand** tool (even if you didn't use that tool to create the selection), and adjust the **Tolerance** to a level that describes what kind of a match to the current selection you're looking for. See **76** **Select Areas of Similar Color** for more information on using the **Magic Wand** tool. Keep in mind that you want a low **Tolerance** level to most closely match the current selection. Specify a higher **Tolerance** value to include pixels with a wider range of colors and tone.

TIP

If these commands cause too much of the image to be selected, undo them and try reducing the **Tolerance** setting and then applying the **Grow** or **Similar** command again. Alternatively, increase the **Tolerance** value to include a broader range of colors in the selection.

2 Adjust the Tolerance

Select the **Magic Wand** tool on the **Toolbox** and adjust the **Tolerance** value on the **Options** bar to suit your needs. Remember that a higher **Tolerance** allows the Editor to add pixels to your selection that don't match the pixels in your original selection all that closely. See **76** **Select Areas of Similar Color**.

3 Add Similar Areas

Choose **Select, Similar** to select all areas in the image that are similar in color and tone to the area you selected in step 1.

4 Or Grow Selection

Alternatively, choose **Select, Grow** to expand the current selection to include only *neighboring pixels* of similar color and tone.

5 View the Result

When you have correctly adjusted the **Tolerance** value, all the matching pixels are selected. After you're satisfied with the selection, make changes to the data within the selection, copy or cut the data to another image or layer, or delete the data within the selection. Save the PSD file and then resave the file in JPEG or TIFF format, leaving your PSD image with its *layers* (if any) intact so that you can return at a later time and make different adjustments if you want.

I wanted to select this photo of Kermit the Frog for a birthday card I was designing, taken while visiting a recent exhibit at a children's museum. I tried to select him using the **Magic Wand**, but even at a high **Tolerance** setting, it didn't want to easily grab all those green pixels in the rug. And I wasn't looking forward to trying to use the **Magnetic Lasso** to outline Kermit, given all those fingers and the tiny pole his hand was sitting on. So, I made a quick selection of the red curtain behind him, set the **Tolerance** to 75, and used the **Select, Grow** command to grab similar neighboring pixels. It took a few seconds more to grab a few stray pixels, and then I inverted the selection and selected Kermit.

80 Smooth a Jagged Selection Edge

After you've used the **Magic Wand** tool to select a region from an image, there's a good chance the selection will have a number of pits and bumps. In some circumstances, this might be fine; but suppose that your project requires your clippings not to appear as though they were ripped out of a magazine and rubbed by sandpaper. Photoshop Elements' **Smooth** command enables you to iron out the boundaries of any selection so that the perimeter appears to flow fluidly and easily from point to point, as though it were drawn by hand.

With this form of smoothing, the *Editor* uses ordinary geometry to derive a series of simple curves whose paths most closely fit the more irregular pattern of the selection border. It's quite possible that, after smoothing, some portion you might have meant to exclude could end up being included, and other portions you meant to include could end up excluded. That's because the **Smooth** command actually changes the selection marquee here and there, smoothing out jagged ins and outs. The purpose of this kind of smoothing is not to create precise selection areas but more general ones—areas that appear more naturally cut out, especially when pasted into another image.

1 Make Initial Selection

Open the image you want to work with in the *Editor* in **Standard Edit** mode and save it in Photoshop (***.psd**) format. In the **Layers** palette, choose the layer that contains the data you want to select and then use any selection tool to make the initial selection in the image.

2 Choose Smooth

To include the stray pixels around the current selection, choose **Select, Modify, Smooth** from the menu bar. The **Smooth Selection** dialog box displays.

Before You Begin

✔ **70** About Making Selections

See Also

→ **82** Soften the Edge of a Selection

NOTE

Although *feathering*, *anti-aliasing*, and *smoothing* might appear to be synonymous, each actually refers to a different concept. Feathering a selection's border (covered in **82** Soften the Edge of a Selection) enables pixels along the very rim to be partly selected, for a fuzzy border. This involves adjustments being made to these pixels' *opacity*. Anti-aliasing adjusts the *color* value of pixels along the border— not their opacity—to help a selection look less jagged along the edges. Smoothing adjusts the geometry of the line used to select a region, removing stair-steps and pockets. This affects the selection's *shape*.

Before Smoothing

After Smoothing

4 **View the Result**

3 Set Sample Radius

In the **Sample Radius** field, specify a number between **1** and **100** that indicates the maximum number of pixels that the Editor will add or subtract on either side of the existing selection border to smooth out any jagged ins and outs it finds. This number represents how much change you'll allow to the existing selection perimeter. With a high value, your selected region could conceivably become much smaller. On the other hand, pockets of unselected pixels in the original region could become selected when smoothed because the **Smooth** command doesn't look just outside a selection for similar pixels, but inside as well. Click **OK** to proceed.

④ View the Result

After you're satisfied with the selection, make changes to the area within the selection, copy or cut its data to another image or layer, or delete the data within the selection. Save the PSD image and then resave the file in JPEG or TIFF format, leaving your PSD image with its *layers* (if any) intact so that you can return at a later time and make different adjustments if you want.

In this example, I used the **Magnetic Lasso** to select an old tractor I had seen at our state fair. I planned on using the tractor in a calendar for my brother, who's a big fan of old farm equipment. The **Magnetic Lasso** did a pretty good job, but the curves on the tractor wheels were still too jaggedy! A quick smoothing rounded out those curves easily.

 TIP

Because higher-resolution images have pixels that are closer together (more dense), you might have to set the **Sample Radius** value higher than you would in a lower-resolution image to get the same result.

---

81 Move the Selection Marquee

If you decide you don't like the positioning of the *selection marquee*, you can easily move it within the image. For example, if you've drawn a rectangular selection around some data, for the purpose of copying that data to another image or to start building a frame around that part of a photograph, after creating the selection you might decide that the result would be oh-so-much-better if you could just nudge the marquee a bit to the left. Or maybe you're painting a selection using the **Selection Brush**, creating a freehand heart shape or butterfly selection; although the shape of the selection looks pretty good, it no longer fits perfectly over the data you want to select. In such a case, moving the selection marquee is the solution.

When you move a selection, you are simply repositioning the borders of the selection marquee; you are *not* moving the data within the selection. If you want to do that, see **86** **About Copying, Cutting, and Pasting Data Within a Selection**. To move a selection marquee, you can drag it with any selection tool (except the **Selection Brush** tool). You can even move the selection to another image if you like.

Before You Begin

✔ **70** About Making Selections

See Also

→ **78** Expand or Shrink a Selection

→ **79** Add Areas Similar to the Current Selection

→ **80** Smooth a Jagged Selection Edge

→ **83** Select Everything But the Current Selection

New Selection Button

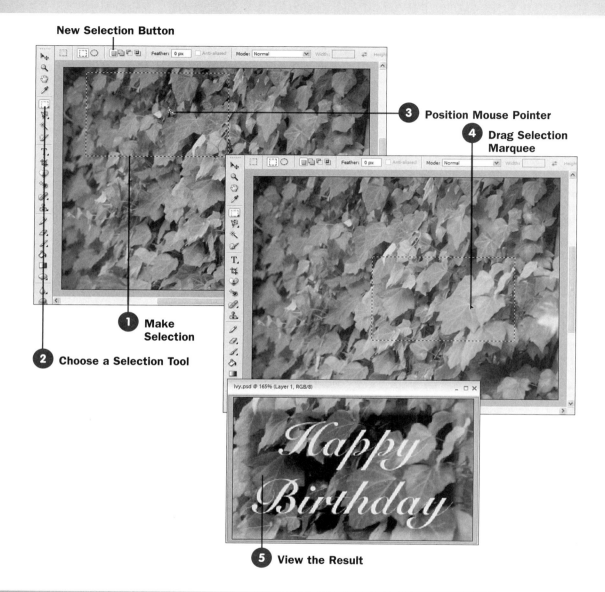

3 Position Mouse Pointer

4 Drag Selection Marquee

1 Make Selection

2 Choose a Selection Tool

ivy.psd @ 165% (Layer 1, RGB/8)

5 View the Result

1 Make Selection

Open the image you want to mask in the *Editor* in **Standard Edit** mode and save it in Photoshop (***.psd**) format. In the **Layers** palette, choose the layer that contains the data you want to select

---

and make an initial selection in the open image. You can use any of the selection tools (or any combination of tools) to create the initial selection.

2 Choose a Selection Tool

On the **Toolbox**, choose any selection tool except the **Selection Brush**. On the **Options bar**, make sure that the **New Selection** button is enabled.

3 Position Mouse Pointer

Move the mouse pointer so that it is positioned inside the selection marquee. Notice that the mouse pointer changes to a white arrow with a white rectangle under it when it is positioned inside the selection marquee.

4 Drag Selection Marquee

Click and drag the selection marquee to the desired location within the image or into another image window. As you drag the selection marquee, the mouse pointer changes to a solid black arrow.

5 View the Result

When the selection marquee is positioned in its new location, release the mouse button to drop it. After you're satisfied with the selection, make changes to the area within the selection, copy or cut its data to another image or layer, or delete the data within the selection. Save the PSD file and then resave the result in JPEG or TIFF format, leaving your PSD image with its *layers* (if any) intact so that you can return at a later time and make different adjustments if you want.

In this example, I created a rectangular selection around an area of green ivy leaves that I intended to use as the background for a birthday card I was creating in another image; then I decided to select a different area of ivy. After I placed the selection marquee in the desired position, I copied the selection so that I could paste it into the new image (see **86** **About Copying, Cutting, and Pasting Data Within a Selection**).

TIP

You might also move the marquee to select the same-sized area multiple times in one or more photos to create Web buttons, similarly sized photos for a locket or refrigerator magnet, or some similar purpose.

TIP

To move the marquee in small increments of a single pixel, use the arrow keys instead of the mouse. To move the marquee by ten-pixel increments, press **Shift** and the appropriate arrow key.

82 Soften the Edge of a Selection

Before You Begin

✔ **70** About Making Selections

See Also

→ **78** Expand or Shrink a Selection

→ **79** Add Areas Similar to the Current Selection

→ **80** Smooth a Jagged Selection Edge

NOTES

Setting the **Feather** value in the **Options** bar when you make the initial selection with the **Lasso** or **Marquee** tools does the same thing as opening the **Feather Selection** dialog box after the selection has already been made. See **70** About Making Selections for more information on making selections.

The **Magic Wand** and **Selection Brush** tools do not allow you to specify feathering on the **Options** bar, although the **Selection Brush** does enable you to lower the **Hardness** of its tip, which creates the same effect as feathering. For the **Magic Wand**, however, you must add feathering after the fact by following the steps in this task.

You can modify a selection to include a fuzzy border along the edge using the **Feather** command. When you feather a selection, the edge of the image appears to be almost transparent in contrast to the background. *Feathering* a selection is often preferable when you intend to copy the selection and place it on a different background, or to fade the edge of a selection gradually to white or black, creating a old-fashioned photographic vignette. Feathering is also preferred when you intend to change the color or tone of the data or apply a filter or effect, and you want the resulting data to blend into surrounding pixels. By feathering the edges of the selection, the edges seem softer and appear to fade into whatever background on which you place the object.

When you feather the selection within your image, you will not see the feathering in the selection itself. For example, if you feather the edge of a selection by 10 pixels, the marquee will shrink by that amount to surround only the area of fully selected pixels. If you copy or cut the data and then paste the selection into another image or onto another layer however, you'll notice that the copied data includes the partially selected pixels outside the marquee where the feathering occurred.

1 Make First Selection

Open the image you want to mask in the *Editor* in **Standard Edit** mode and save it in Photoshop (***.psd**) format. In the **Layers** palette, choose the layer that contains the data you want to select and use any of the selection tools (the **Marquee**, **Magic Wand**, **Lasso**, or **Selection Brush**—or any of their variations) to select an area in the open image.

2 Choose Feather

Choose **Select, Feather** from the menu bar to display the **Feather Selection** dialog box.

3 Set Feather Radius

In the **Feather Radius** field, type a value larger than **0** to indicate the number of pixels inside the marquee that will be used to create a fuzzy border around the selection. Click the **OK** button to close the **Feather Selection** dialog box.

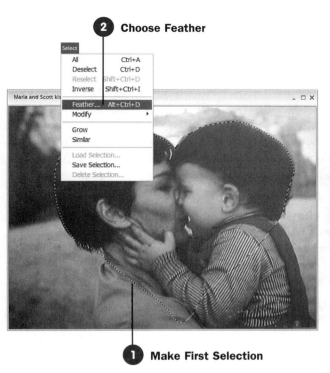

2 **Choose Feather**

1 **Make First Selection**

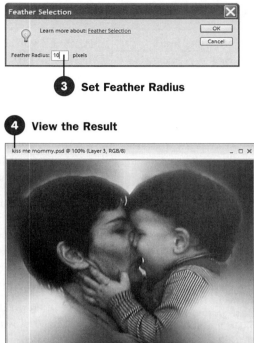

3 **Set Feather Radius**

4 **View the Result**

4 View the Result

After you're satisfied with the selection, make changes to the area within the selection, copy or cut its data to another image or layer, or delete the data within the selection. Save the PSD file and then resave the file in JPEG or TIFF format, leaving your PSD image with its *layers* (if any) intact so that you can return at a later time and make different adjustments if you want.

In this example, I created a heart-shaped selection and then opened the **Feather Selection** dialog box and used a **Feather Radius** value of **10** pixels. After setting the feathering, I copied the selection by selecting **Image, Copy** and then opened a new image with a white background where I pasted the selection (**Edit, Paste**) to create a traditional photographic vignette effect. I applied the **Red, White, Blue Contrast** *layer style* to the white layer to jazz it up a bit. Notice that the edges of the selection appear to blend into the background.

83 Select Everything But the Current Selection

Before You Begin

✔ **70** About Making
Selections

See Also

→ **77** Paint a Selection

 TIP

To capture everything in an image within the selection marquee (and not just the data on that layer), choose **Edit, Copy Merged**. You can then use the **Edit, Paste** or **New, Layer, Background from Layer** to paste the data onto a new layer in the same or another image.

At times, you might want to make changes to everything in an image except for one specific selection. For example, you might want to soften the background in a photo of an animal to make the animal stand out a bit more. To accomplish this, you can select the animal easily enough and then invert the selection so that everything *except* the animal is selected. If your purpose is to select the animal, and he happens to be in front of a neutral background, you could attempt to select the background first (using the **Magic Wand** would make the task simple), and then invert the selection to select the animal.

When you use the **Inverse** command, Photoshop Elements deselects everything that is currently selected on that same layer and selects everything that was not originally selected. Basically, this command gives you the inverse, or opposite, of the original selection.

1 **Make First Selection**

Open an image in the *Editor* in **Standard Edit** mode, and save it in Photoshop (*.psd) format. In the **Layers** palette, choose the layer that contains the data you want to select, and then use any selection tool to make the initial selection in the image.

2 **Invert the Selection**

Choose **Select, Inverse** from the menu bar to invert the *selection marquee*. The selection marquee is changed to select everything in the image *except* what was previously selected.

3 **View the Result**

When you're satisfied with the selection, make changes to the area within the selection, copy or cut its data to another image or layer, or delete the data within the selection. Any edits you make at this point affect only the new inverted selection. The data within your original selection is not affected. After you're satisfied with the result, make any other changes you want, and then save the PSD file. Resave the result in JPEG or TIFF format, leaving your PSD image with its *layers* intact (if any) so you can return at a later time and make different adjustments if you like.

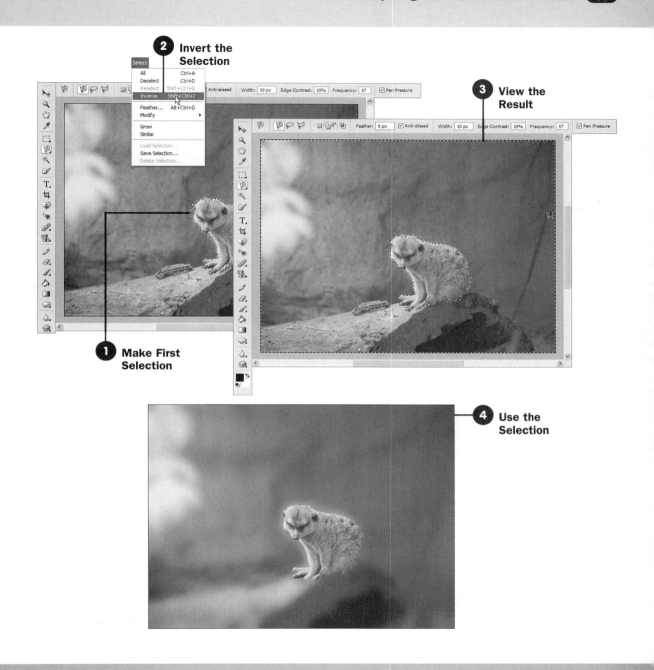

2 Invert the Selection

3 View the Result

1 Make First Selection

4 Use the Selection

TIPS

You can choose **Select, Inverse** a second time to switch back to your original selection.

You can't invert a selection with the *Selection Brush*, but you can use it to paint either what you want to select, or what you don't. See **77** **Paint a Selection**.

④ Use the Selection

In this example, I wanted to blur the background around the meerkat. To do this, I used the **Magnetic Lasso** tool to select the meerkat and then inverted the selection. When everything but the meerkat was selected, I applied a **Gaussian Blur** *filter* to the selection. See **151** **Blur a Background to Create Depth of Field** for more information on using the **Gaussian Blur** filter.

11

Using Selections to Edit Images

IN THIS CHAPTER:

84 Save a Selection for Reuse

85 Reload a Previously Saved Selection

86 About Copying, Cutting, and Pasting Data Within a Selection

87 Create a New Image from a Selection

88 Create a New Layer from a Selection

89 Rotate the Data in a Selection or Layer

90 Copy Data into a Selected Area

In previous tasks, you learned how to create and modify selections within an image using the different selection tools available in the *Editor*. In this chapter, you will learn how to save selections and then reuse those selections to edit the image. You will learn how selections can be used to create a new image or *layer*. You will see how the **Move** tool enables you to not only move the selected portion of the image, but also to rotate the data in a selection. You will also see how data can be pasted directly into a selection.

84 Save a Selection for Reuse

Before You Begin

✔ **70** About Making Selections

See Also

→ **85** Reload a Previously Saved Selection

→ **86** About Copying, Cutting, and Pasting Data Within a Selection

🔑 TIPS

You can reload a selection only from the image in which it was saved, but after it is reloaded, you can move the selection to another image if you need it for your work there. See **81** **Move the Selection Marquee**.

A selection can be used to select pixels on the current layer only, unless you create the selection using the **Magic Wand** tool and its **Use All Layers** option.

If you think you might want to work with a selection again later, you can save the selection. When you save a selection, the *Editor* remembers the exact position and shape of the selection marquee, and whether it had any feathering, anti-aliasing, or smoothing at its edges. You might want to save a selection you've worked hard at making, just in case you need it later on during editing—even after you've closed the image or selected something else. Saved selections are also useful for creating *masks*, frames, or for making the same-shaped selection in several images.

After you save a selection, you can reload it at any time, from within the image where you saved it. You can reload the saved selection to the same layer or to another layer. You can even add or subtract the saved selection from a current selection, creating a complex selection such as an oval frame. You build complex selections like these by making the outer selection, saving it, shrinking the selection, and subtracting this modified selection (the "hole") from the first selection ("the outer border"), leaving a selection "rim." See **85** **Reload a Previously Saved Selection** for more information on loading saved selections.

① **Make the Selection**

Open an image in the Editor in **Standard Edit** mode and save it in Photoshop (***.psd**) format. Use any of the selection tools to create your selection. When the selection is perfect, save it so that you can recall it again whenever you might need it in your work.

② **Save the Selection**

Choose **Select**, **Save Selection** to display the **Save Selection** dialog box.

2 Save the Selection

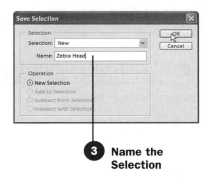

1 Make the Selection

3 Name the Selection

---

3 Name the Selection

In the **Save Selection** dialog box, choose **New** from the **Selection** drop-down list. In the **Name** field, type the name you want to assign to the selection. You can use any combination of characters to name the selection, but the selection name cannot be longer than 32 characters. Click **OK** to save the selection to the image's *alpha channel*.

After you've saved the selection, you can keep on working as usual. For example, you could make changes to the area within the selection, copy or cut its data to another image or layer, or delete the data within the selection. You can make other changes and even make another selection without fear of losing the original saved selection, which can be recalled when needed. When

NOTE

You can save multiple selections within the same image. To save a selection in an image, the image must be saved in PSD, TIFF, or JP2 format.

NOTE

You can modify an existing selection by making a selection and redisplaying the **Save Selection** dialog box. Select the name of the existing selection from the **Selection** drop-down list and then select the desired type of modification from the **Operation** area and click **OK**. For example, if you choose the **Add to Selection** operation, the current selection is added to the saved selection you chose from the **Selection**

you're satisfied with all your changes, save the PSD image. Resave the result in JPEG or TIFF format, leaving your PSD image with its *layers* (if any) and selections intact so that you can return at a later time and make different adjustments if you want.

After working for a few minutes to select the zebra closest to the car, I decided I should save it. Next, I'll select the other zebra and then reload this selection so that both zebras are selected. At that point, I can improve the contrast and tone of both zebras, and sharpen them a bit. By sharpening just the zebras, I can make them the central focus of my photo. I'll probably also blur everything else just slightly by inverting the selection and applying a light blur.

Reload a Previously Saved Selection

Before You Begin

✔ Save a Selection for Reuse

See Also

→ About Copying, Cutting, and Pasting Data Within a Selection

After you have saved selections for an image, you can reload those selections at any time when working with that same image (even if you close the image and open it later on). When you reload a selection, the *Editor* reselects the pixels in the area of the original selection. Remember that it's the selection marquee you are reloading, not any saved data. You can reload the selection onto a different layer if you like, although that really doesn't matter because you can move from one layer to another even after reloading a selection, and know that only the data on the current layer is selected.

NOTE

Selections can be saved only in PSD-, JP2-, and TIFF-formatted files. So, if you saved a selection in a file with one of these formats, and then resaved that image in a different format (such as JPEG), the selection will not be contained in the JPEG file and you won't be able to reload it. The selection should still be in the original PSD, JP2, or TIFF file—assuming that you saved that file again after saving the selection.

① Choose Select, Load Selection

Open the image in which you've already saved a selection in the *Editor* in **Standard Edit** mode and resave it in Photoshop (***.psd**) format. In the **Layers** palette, choose the layer that contains the data you want to select (this can be a different layer than the one on which you created the original selection).

Make a new selection if you like (you can add or subtract from this new selection, using the outline of the saved selection), and then choose **Select, Load Selection** to display the **Load Selection** dialog box. If the **Load Selection** command is grayed out on the **Select** menu, the current image does not contain any saved selections.

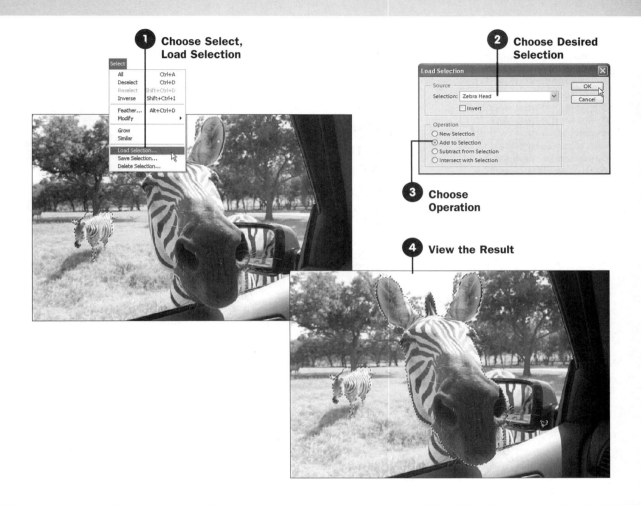

① **Choose Select, Load Selection**

② **Choose Desired Selection**

③ **Choose Operation**

④ **View the Result**

② **Choose Desired Selection**

From the **Selection** drop-down list, choose the name of the previously saved selection you want to load. If you want to select everything *except* the saved selection, enable the **Invert** check box.

③ **Choose Operation**

If you did not create another selection before you performed step 1, the only operation you can select is **New Selection**.

If you have selected another area of the image when you load a saved selection, you can choose an operation to perform when loading the selection:

- **New Selection.** Deselects any existing selections and loads the specified saved selection. Only the pixels in the reloaded selection are selected.

- **Add to Selection.** Adds the selection you reload to the current selection so that all pixels in both selections are selected.

- **Subtract from Selection.** Subtracts the pixels in the reloaded selection from what is currently selected. Only the pixels that are *not* part of the reloaded selection remain selected.

- **Intersect with Selection.** Selects only the pixels that are common in both the current selection and the reloaded selection. Any pixels that do not exist in both selections are not selected.

Click the **OK** button to load the selection with the specified options.

④ View the Result

After loading the selection, make changes to the area within the selection, copy or cut its data to another image or layer, or delete the data within the selection. When you're satisfied with the result, make any other changes you want and save the PSD file. Resave the result in JPEG or TIFF format, leaving your PSD image with its *layers* (if any) and selections intact so that you can return at a later time and make different adjustments if you want.

In this example, I selected the zebra in the background before I opened the **Load Selection** dialog box. I wanted to reload the **Zebra Head** selection that I had previously saved so that I could work on both zebras at once to make similar adjustments to color, contrast, and sharpness. I chose the **Add to Selection** operation to add the **Zebra Head** selection to the current selection. When I clicked **OK**, both the background zebra selection and the **Zebra Head** saved selection were active. If I had selected the **New Selection** operation instead, the **Zebra Head** selection would have been selected and the background zebra would have been deselected.

86 About Copying, Cutting, and Pasting Data Within a Selection

As with any other Microsoft Windows program, you can cut, copy, and paste the contents of a selection within the *Editor*. As I am sure you remember, when you use the **Edit, Cut** or **Edit, Copy** command to place a selection on the clipboard, you can then use the **Edit, Paste** command to paste the contents of the clipboard onto another *layer*, either in the current or a different image. The **Paste** command is the only one you can use to transfer data from the Clipboard, so you must use it to paste data from an outside source or from another image into the current image.

You can also use the **Paste** command to paste data from one layer to another in the same image, although there's an easier way: If you're working within a single image, you can bypass the Clipboard and copy or cut data in one step. Just make a selection and choose either **New, Layer, Layer via Copy** or **New, Layer, Layer via Cut**.

When you copy the data within a selection in the Editor, you can either copy the data on the current *layer* only (using the **Edit, Copy** command), or on all visible layers of the image (by selecting **Edit, Copy Merged**). When you use the **Copy Merged** command, the Editor actually creates a merged copy of the data in all the layers visible in the image. Because the data in the visible layers is merged when you **Paste** the copied selection, the selection is pasted to a single layer (instead of the multiple layers the data was in when you copied it).

Suppose that you have an image with multiple layers that include both image layers and text, such as the Happy Birthday image shown in this figure. If you choose **Edit, Copy** with the **Ivy** layer active, only the contents of that layer are copied, even if you have selected data on multiple layers using various selection tools. If you paste what you've copied, you'll only get data from the **Ivy** layer. If you choose **Edit, Copy Merged** instead, it doesn't matter what layer is current or if you've selected data on only the current layer; everything within the selection (data on all visible layers) is copied. When you paste what you have copied, the contents of all layers—in this example, the **Ivy** layer, the text layer, and the layer being used as a text background—are all merged into one layer that is pasted onto the new layer or selection.

Before You Begin

✔ **70** About Making Selections

See Also

→ **87** Create a New Image from a Selection

→ **88** Create a New Layer from a Selection

→ **90** Copy Data into a Selected Area

NOTES

Pasted data is always placed on a new layer *above the current layer*, regardless of whether you use the **Paste** or the **Layer, New** command. If, however, you paste data into a selection, or onto a new, completely empty layer, the data is placed *on* the current layer and a new layer is not created.

Data is always pasted at its original resolution. Thus, if you want to copy data from one image to another, you should adjust the source image so that its resolution matches the resolution of the destination image. See **60** Change Image Size or Resolution.

NOTES

In this example, the text is simplified (converted to bitmap) before it is pasted, whether you use the **Copy** or **Copy Merged** command. This means the text will not be editable when it's pasted in its new home. You can, however, copy a text layer into another image by dragging it from the **Layers** palette and dropping it in the other image window.

The **Copy Merged** command selects data on all visible layers; to exclude data on a particular layer, hide that layer temporarily by clicking the layer's eye icon on the **Layers** palette.

You can quickly select all the data on a layer by pressing **Ctrl** and clicking the layer's thumbnail on the **Layers** palette.

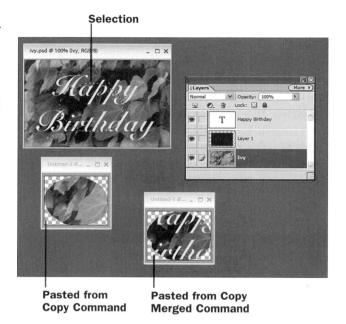

Selection

Pasted from
Copy Command

Pasted from Copy
Merged Command

The Copy command copies data on the current layer only; the Copy Merged command copies all visible pixels within the selection.

As you are aware, when you cut or copy data using the **Edit**, **Copy** or **Edit**, **Copy Merged** command, that data is placed on the clipboard for storage. Photoshop Elements has its own clipboard, separate from the Windows Clipboard. This means that data you cut or copy within Photoshop Elements is available to be pasted only within Photoshop Elements. Fortunately, Photoshop Elements does provide the ability to paste data into other programs, but you must enable the **Export Clipboard** option on the **Preferences** dialog box if the option is not already on (which it typically is). To display the **Preferences** dialog box so that you can check, from the *Editor*, choose **Edit**, **Preferences**, **General**. Enable the **Export Clipboard** option and click **OK** to save your changes.

The Photoshop Elements clipboard can hold only one selection at a time. Therefore, when you copy or cut a selection, that selection replaces any previous contents in the clipboard. The contents remain in the Photoshop Elements clipboard until you close Photoshop Elements, which clears the clipboard. The next time you open Photoshop Elements, the clipboard will be empty.

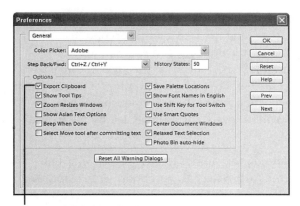

Export Clipboard Option

*Enable the **Export Clipboard** option in the **Preferences** dialog box if you want to use data you copy in the Editor in other Windows programs.*

If you have enabled the **Export Clipboard** option in the **Preferences** dialog box, the situation changes slightly. When you **Cut** or **Copy** a selection in the Editor, the selection is automatically copied to both the Photoshop Elements clipboard and the Windows Clipboard. If you close Photoshop Elements, the selection remains in the Windows Clipboard until you copy something else into that Clipboard from another Windows program. With the data safely stored on the Windows Clipboard, you can continue to paste a selection from an Editor image into other applications, even if you close Photoshop Elements.

You can also paste data you've copied to the clipboard (from the same image, a different image, or even a different Windows application) into a selection you've made in the image using the **Paste Into Selection** option. For example, in an image of a tree trunk, you can make a heart-shaped selection in the trunk and then paste a snapshot of you and your boyfriend you've copied from another image into that heart. Regardless of the size the snapshot was originally, it is reduced to fit into the heart-shaped selection, although it is resized proportionately, so it might not fill the selection. See **90 Copy Data into a Selected Area** for more information on pasting clipboard data into a selection.

When you make a selection, instead of cutting and pasting the data in it, you can move the data around on the layer using the **Move** tool on the **Toolbox**. Just click inside the *bounding box* with the tool and drag to move the data around on the layer. You can copy instead of moving by pressing **Alt** as you drag. You can move or copy data into another image

 TIP

The **File, Place** command helps you bring an image from a *PDF document*, Adobe Illustrator, or EPS (Encapsulated PostScript) file into an Editor image. Using **File, Place** rather than **Edit, Copy** and **Edit, Paste** causes the Editor to automatically convert the incoming data's resolution and size to fit the image into which you copy the data.

NOTE

Using the **Move** tool, you can copy or move data on the active layer only. If you make a selection that includes the contents of other layers, anything in those layers is ignored.

by dragging the selection into the other image window. If you move data on the *background layer* (and not a regular layer) or a layer that does not support transparency (the option is turned off), the location where the selection was originally positioned on the layer becomes the *background color*. For example, if the background color for the current image is set to white, the location where the selection was originally located is also white. On regular layers, the vacancy left by the moved data becomes transparent.

Normally, only selected data on the current layer is moved with the **Move** tool. If you enable the **Auto Select Layer** option on the **Options** bar, data on the topmost layer on the **Layers** palette—which is also located under the **Move** tool when you begin dragging—is the data that's moved, even if that data is not located on the current layer.

There are two different types of moving you can perform using the **Move** tool. You can either move the selection marquee, or you can move the contents of the selection. See **81** **Move the Selection Marquee** for more information on moving a selection marquee.

Move Mouse Pointer

Move Tool

Background Color

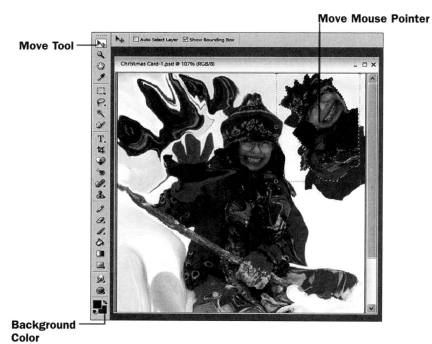

Use the Move tool to move data in the current selection to a new location on the layer or into another image file.

If you want to remove a specific portion of an image, you can select that area and then delete the selection by either pressing the **Delete** key on the keyboard or selecting **Edit, Delete**. You will also notice with this option that the location of the selection is replaced with the current background color if you remove data from the background layer or a layer that does not support transparency. Otherwise, the vacancy is filled with transparent pixels. Like the **Move** command, the **Delete** command removes data on only the current layer, even if the selection includes data on other layers, too.

87 Create a New Image from a Selection

You can create new images within the *Editor* by using selections from other images. For example, you might want to create a new image that contains only a portion of the original image, such as the head and shoulders of a person taken from a full-length photo of that person. When you have copied the selection to the new image, you can make modifications to the new image without affecting the original image.

When you create a new image by copying a portion of another image, you use the Clipboard. First select only the portion of the image you want to use and copy that selection to the Clipboard. When you issue the **File, New, Image from Clipboard** command, the Editor creates the new image using the contents of the Clipboard.

1 Copy the Selection

Open the image you want to copy data from in the *Editor* in **Standard Edit** mode. From the **Layers** *palette*, choose the *layer* whose contents you want to copy—in whole or part—into a new image. Make your selection using the tool of your choice.

From the menu bar, select **Edit, Copy** to copy the selection to the Clipboard. To copy all visible pixels within the selection, regardless of what layer they are on, choose **Edit, Copy Merged** instead. See **86** **About Copying, Cutting, and Pasting Data Within a Selection** for help.

2 Create the New Image

Select **File, New, Image from Clipboard** to create a new image from the contents of the clipboard. The new image is sized to match the actual size of the data within the clipboard. In other words, if the selection was 400×400 pixels in size, that will be the size of the new image.

Before You Begin

✔ **70** About Making Selections

✔ **86** About Copying, Cutting, and Pasting Data Within a Selection

See Also

→ **88** Create a New Layer from a Selection

→ **90** Copy Data into a Selected Area

🖌 NOTE

When you're copying data from one image to another, you're using the Elements clipboard. If you have enabled the **Export to Clipboard** option in the **Preferences** dialog box, data on this clipboard is also copied to the Windows Clipboard for use in other programs—the purpose of that option is to help you get data *out of Elements*; thus, that option does not have to be on for this task to work, even if you want to create a new image from data copied from another program (the option has nothing to do with data coming *into* Elements).

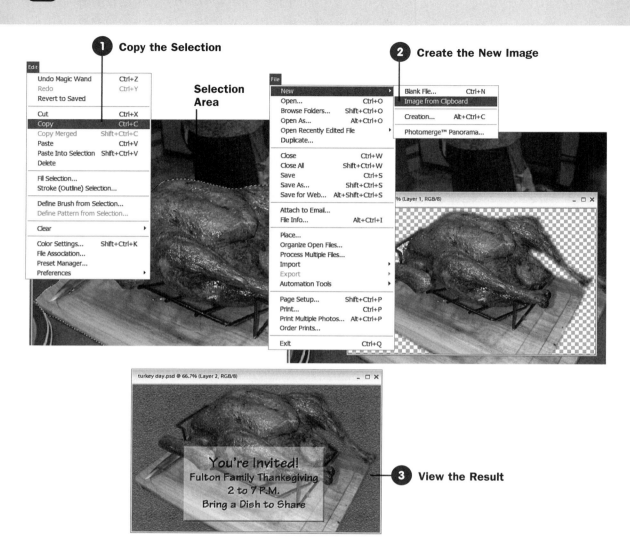

① Copy the Selection

② Create the New Image

Selection Area

③ View the Result

NOTE

You can create a new image from anything you have copied to the Windows Clipboard, even data that was copied from another Windows application.

When you create a new image file, the existing image file from which you copied the selection remains open. (You can see the open files in the **Photo Bin** at the bottom of the screen.) The Editor indicates the selected image file by outlining it in blue.

③ View the Result

Save the new image in Photoshop (***.psd**) format. Make any changes you want and save the PSD file again. Resave the final result in JPEG or TIFF format, leaving your PSD image with its *layers* (if any) intact so that you can return at a later time and make different adjustments if you want.

In this example, I created a new image using a roasted turkey copied from the original photo.

NOTE

To create an image using data you capture from your computer screen, arrange the monitor display to show the programs or elements you want to capture and press the **Print Screen** key. Return to the Editor and select **File, New, Image from Clipboard** to create a file containing whatever data was displayed on your computer monitor.

88 Create a New Layer from a Selection

One of the powerful features available in the *Editor* is the ability to create and work with different *layers* of an image. When you use layers, you can isolate portions of an image and make changes to only that portion. If you create a selection of your family from a larger image taken in front of your house, you can create a new layer with just your family on it. Now you have two layers: your family on one layer and your house plus your family on another. The composite image still shows your family in front of your house because the copy of your family, when initially pasted to the new layer, is in exactly the same location on that layer as it was on the original layer—in effect, there are two copies of your family, one directly on top of the other. You can do a lot of things now. You can move the family on the top layer over to one side, and have two families show up in the photo. Because the family is isolated on its own layer, you can adjust the brightness and contrast of just the family; select a *blend mode* on the top layer that causes the families to blend in such a way that makes the family appear more saturated, darker, or artfully colored; blur the entire bottom layer and make the duplicate family (which remains sharp on its own layer) stand out better against the background; resize the top family and move it to one side so they appear as a miniature with themselves; or you can replace the layer containing your house with an image of the White House. Just that easily, you've taken your family on "vacation" to Washington DC. The tricks begin, however, by first selecting the family and getting that selection on another layer in the same image, and that's what you'll learn to do in this task. (See **91** **About Layers and the Layers Palette** for more information on working with layers.)

Before You Begin

✔ **70** About Making Selections

✔ **91** About Layers and the Layers Palette

See Also

→ **87** Create a New Image from a Selection

→ **90** Copy Data into a Selected Area

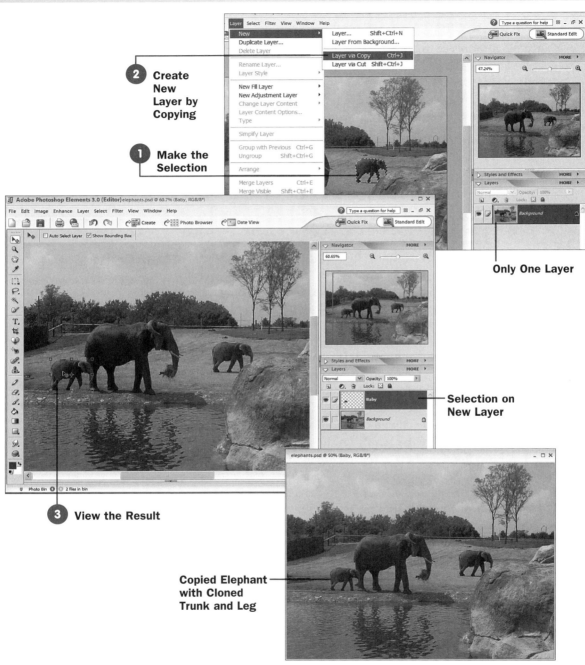

2 Create New Layer by Copying

1 Make the Selection

Only One Layer

Selection on New Layer

3 View the Result

Copied Elephant with Cloned Trunk and Leg

1 Make Selection

Open an image in the *Editor* in **Standard Edit** mode and save it in Photoshop (***.psd**) format. In the **Layers** palette, choose the layer that contains the data you want to select and make a selection using your favorite selection tools.

2 Create New Layer by Copying

Select **Layer, New, Layer via Copy** to copy the current selection to a new layer within your image. This new layer appears above the current layer in the **Layers** palette. The selection appears in the same location on the new layer as it occupied in the original layer.

You can also select **Layer, New, Layer via Cut** to cut the current selection from its existing layer and paste it in a new layer. If used in this example, the selected baby elephant would be cut from the **Background** layer and pasted on the new layer. A hole would be left in the **Background** layer where the baby elephant was originally located, and that hole would be filled with the *background color*, or transparent pixels (if the *background layer* has been converted to a regular layer, such as **Layer 0**).

3 View the Result

Make changes to the data on the new layer—move it around, resize it, adjust its brightness or contrast, apply *filters*, effects, layer styles, and so on. When you're satisfied with the result, make any other changes you want and save the PSD file. Resave your final result in JPEG or TIFF format, leaving your PSD image with its *layers* intact so that you can return at a later time and make different adjustments if you want.

In this example, I used the **Magnetic Lasso** tool to select the walking baby elephant. I then used the **Layer via Copy** command to move just the baby elephant onto a new layer all to himself. I wanted to make the photo a bit more interesting by adding another elephant, but to disguise that fact, I resized him slightly and moved him closer to his mother. See **99 Move, Resize, Skew, or Distort a Layer**. I had to clone in the missing trunk and leg that was hidden behind the rock on the original elephant. See **125 Repair Minor Tears, Scratches, Spots, and Stains**. I still have some more work to do, adding a shadow and a reflection in the water, but even now the effect is pretty convincing.

NOTE

In this task, you use the **Layer via Copy** command to create a new layer in the current image, with selected data from another layer. To paste selected data *from a different image* onto a new layer *in the current image*, use **Edit, Paste**.

NOTE

Note that you do not have to use the **Edit, Copy** command before completing step 2 in order to copy your selection to a new layer in the same image.

89 Rotate the Data in a Selection or Layer

Before You Begin

✔ **70** About Making
Selections

See Also

→ **86** About Copying,
Cutting, and
Pasting Data
Within a Selection

→ **90** Copy Data into a
Selected Area

◣NOTES

If the data you've selected is surrounded by non-transparent pixels, when you rotate the selection, you'll leave a hole. If you don't want to leave a hole where the original selection was located, you should paste your selection into a new layer before rotating it. See **88** Create a New Layer from a Selection.

If you want to rotate a selection on the **Background** layer and have the hole it leaves filled with the background color, click the background color swatch on the **Toolbox** and select that color first before rotating. If you rotate a selection surrounded by colored pixels on any other layer, the hole will be filled with transparent pixels. You can then fill the hole by cloning the surrounding data.

It is not uncommon to have to rotate the data in a selection or layer. You might have just pasted your daughter's pretty face onto a layer and want to rotate it just a bit so that it faces your son, who is located on another layer. Or you might want to rotate a shape that's on the same layer as another shape, or to rotate some text. No matter what the goal, the rotation process is basically the same in all instances: Select the data or layer to rotate and use the **Move** tool to spin it around.

This task teaches you what is essentially free rotation, meaning that you have the freedom to rotate a selection or layer by whatever amount you choose. If you want to rotate by 90° left or right, or by some exact amount you already know (such as 120°), or if you want to flip the data rather than rotate it, you can follow the steps in **106** **Rotate an Image or Layer** (rotating a selection in this manner follows the same basic procedure). If your goal is not rotation, but resizing, moving, or somehow distorting the data in a selection, see **99** **Move, Resize, Skew, or Distort a Layer** (again, the procedure for a selection is the same for a layer).

When you rotate a selection on a layer, the original location is filled with the *background color* if that layer is the *Background layer*. For example, if the background color is white, when you rotate an animal that you selected, the hole where the selection was originally located is filled with white. If, however, your selection is located on a regular layer (a background layer that's been simplified, an inserted layer, fill layer, adjustment layer, text layer, or shape layer), the hole is filled with transparent pixels.

1 Make a Selection or Choose a Layer

Open an image in the *Editor* in **Standard Edit** mode and save it in Photoshop (***.psd**) format. In the **Layers** palette, choose the layer that contains the data you want to rotate. If you want to rotate a selection, use any of the selection tools to select the portion of the image you want to rotate. To rotate text or a shape, continue to step 2, where the text or shape will be selected by the **Move** tool automatically.

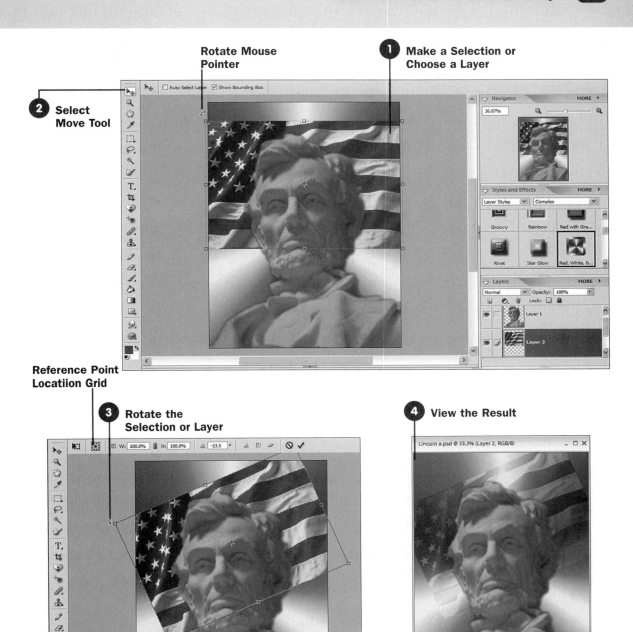

Rotate Mouse
Pointer

1 Make a Selection or
Choose a Layer

2 Select
Move Tool

Reference Point
Locatiion Grid

3 Rotate the
Selection or Layer

4 View the Result

② Select the Move Tool

If you're rotating an entire layer rather than a selection, maximize the image window and adjust the zoom so that the image is smaller than the window itself. This will give you the space you need in step 3 to grab the layer and rotate it.

Select the **Move** tool on the **Toolbox**; the mouse pointer changes to a solid black arrow. Enable the **Show Bounding Box** option. A *bounding box* surrounds the data in the selection or the chosen layer.

③ Rotate the Selection or Layer

Position the mouse pointer just outside a corner *handle* on the bounding box. If you're rotating all the data on a layer, the corners of the bounding box are located at the corners of the layer. As you move the mouse pointer over a corner handle, the pointer changes to a curved arrow like the one shown. Drag in the direction you want to rotate. When you rotate selected data, the area formerly occupied by the selection is made transparent or is filled with the background color (if you're moving data on the **Background** layer). You can also use any of the following techniques to rotate:

- To rotate a copy of the selection, press **Alt** as you drag. This technique cannot be used to rotate and copy a layer.

- To rotate by 15-degree increments, press **Shift** as you drag.

- To alter the reference point around which rotation takes place, first choose **Image, Rotate, Free Rotate Selection** or **Image, Rotate, Free Rotate Layer** from the menu. Then click the reference point you want to use in the **Reference Point Location** grid on the **Options** bar.

When you're done rotating the selection or layer, click the **Commit** button (the check mark) on the **Options** bar. To cancel your adjustment, click **Cancel** (the circle-with-a-slash icon) instead.

④ View the Result

When you're satisfied with the results, make any other changes you want and save the PSD file. Resave the result in JPEG or TIFF format, leaving your PSD image with its *layers* (if any) intact so that you can return at a later time and make different adjustments if you want.

I wanted the flag to appear diagonally behind ol' Abe, so I rotated the layer containing just the flag image. To get the see-through effect, I changed the flag layer's *blend mode* to **Soft Overlay**.

90 Copy Data into a Selected Area

Sometimes you want the data you paste to conform to a particular shape, such as an oval, heart, eagle, or frame. You can even paste data so that it conforms to the shape of some text. The secret behind this trick is to create a selection in the shape you want and then to paste data into that selection using the **Paste Into Selection** command. The *Editor* resizes the data as best it can to fit within the selection. If the data doesn't fit in its entirety, you can move the data within the selection to display exactly the portion you want. You can even resize the data further if that better suits your needs. For example, you could create a circular selection and paste your son's face onto a volleyball, or paste your daughter's face into a heart shape. The possibilities are endless, and limited only by your skill to create a selection in the shape you need.

When you use **Paste Into Selection**, the Editor pastes whatever is located in the Clipboard into the area you select. Thus, you can use these same steps to paste data from any Windows program into a selection. One thing you should keep in mind however: Whenever you use the **Paste Into Selection** command, data is pasted into the selection *on the current layer*. This makes manipulating the pasted data later on in your editing session a bit difficult. So, before you paste, be sure to first create a new layer.

1 Select Data to Copy

Open an image in the *Editor* in **Standard Edit** mode. In the **Layers** palette, choose the layer that contains the data you want to paste and use any of the selection tools to select what you want to copy. Because this data will be adjusted in size to conform to the shape of the selection in the other image, you can make a quick and easy rectangular or elliptical selection if you want.

Make any necessary adjustments to the selection to ensure that it contains only the portion of the image you want to paste. You can even move the selection marquee if necessary; see **81** Move the Selection Marquee. You will want to eliminate any unwanted background from the selection.

Before You Begin

✔ **70** About Making Selections

✔ **86** About Copying, Cutting, and Pasting Data Within a Selection

TIPS

To create a selection in an odd shape, such as the shape of a deer, I open an image that contains a deer and make a selection (often using the **Magnetic Lasso** to trace the object's edge). I then move the selection into the other image as described in **81** Move the Selection Marquee. Sometimes I just go ahead and copy and paste the deer into the other image (because that action creates a new layer automatically), keeping the deer selected so that I can then fill the selection shape with something else.

If you want the data pasted into the selection to blend into the layer below, retaining that object's reflections, shadows, and texture, paste the data onto a new layer and adjust that new layer's *blend mode*. Try using **Hard Light**, **Soft Light**, or **Overlay** for best results; don't forget to adjust the layer's **Opacity** as well.

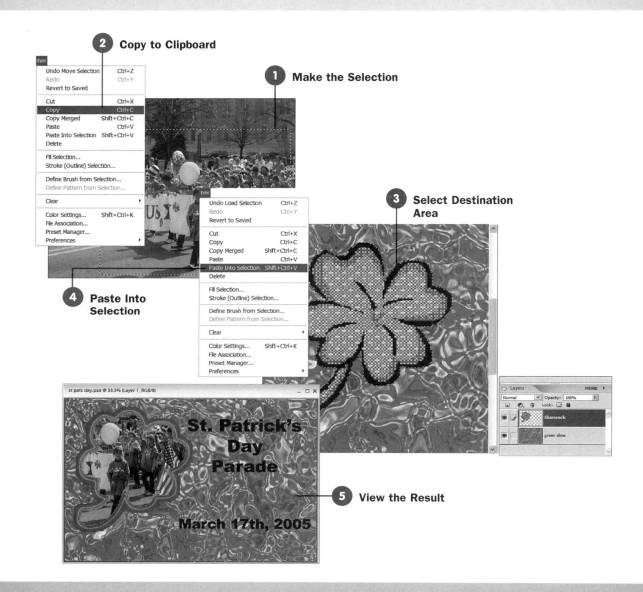

2 Copy to Clipboard

1 Make the Selection

3 Select Destination Area

4 Paste Into Selection

5 View the Result

TIP

To paste data into a selection in the shape of some text, use the **Horizontal** or **Vertical Type Mask** tools as described in **190** Fill Text with an Image.

2 Copy to Clipboard

Select **Edit, Copy** to copy the selection to the Clipboard. To copy all visible pixels within the selection, choose **Edit, Copy Merged** instead.

3 Select Destination Area

Open the image into which you want to paste the selection and save it in Photoshop (***.psd**) format. On the **Layers** palette, choose the layer that contains the shape you want to select and use the appropriate selection tool to select it. You can then paste the selection onto a different layer using this selection shape, or you can paste new data over top of the data already in the selection.

4 Paste into Selection

If you want to paste onto a new layer, create that layer *now*. Then select **Edit, Paste Into Selection** to paste the clipboard data into the selected area on the current layer.

Now you can use the **Move** tool to adjust the location or size of the data within your selection and to distort it to fit the shape of the selection better. See **99** **Move, Resize, Skew, or Distort a Layer** for more information on using the **Move** tool. If you want to use the **Move** tool to rotate the data, see **89** **Rotate the Data in a Selection or Layer**.

5 View the Result

When you're satisfied with the result, make any other changes you want and save the PSD file. Resave the result in JPEG or TIFF format, leaving your PSD image with its *layers* (if any) intact so that you can return at a later time and make different adjustments if you want.

Here I used the **Rectangular Marquee** tool to select a rectangular portion of a photo of a St. Patrick's Day parade. I wanted to make a flyer advertising this year's parade, so I pasted the parade people into a shamrock shape. I added some text and a green background. To the shape, I applied a **Radioactive Outer Glow** *layer style*. I also expanded the selection and used it on another layer to create a black border around the shamrock shape, to help it stick out more against the marbled green background.

NOTE

The **Magnetic Lasso** tool works well for selecting the area you want to paste into because it's great at outlining a shape. See **75** **Select an Object by Tracing Its Edge**.

12

Using Multiple Layers to Edit Images

IN THIS CHAPTER:

91 About Layers and the Layers Palette

92 Create a New Image Layer

93 Create a Layer Filled with a Color, Gradient, or Pattern

94 Create an Adjustment Layer

95 Convert a Background Layer to a Regular Layer and Vice Versa

96 Simplify a Layer

97 Erase Part of a Layer

98 Apply a Layer Style

99 Move, Resize, Skew, or Distort a Layer

100 Mask an Adjustment or Fill Layer

101 Group and Organize Layers

102 Merge or Flatten Layers into One

The use of *layers* to edit an image is the most powerful feature in Photoshop Elements. Using multiple layers, you can isolate each element of the image, in the same way a cartoonist isolates each element of a scene by placing them on sheets of clear acetate. You could put the sky and a roadway on the bottom layer, a race car on the next layer, and your son on the top layer. Separating your image into layers gives you the ability to make adjustments to any one of the objects within the image—such as the location, size, color and tone of the race car— without affecting the background or the other objects. When elements in an image are separated, you can apply effects, filters, and *layer styles* to specific objects without applying them to the entire image.

In this chapter, you learn about the different layer types available in Photoshop Elements and how to create them. You look at ways to work with the different layer types to produce the desired effects within your image. You learn how to work with layers in the **Layers** palette and how the order of the layers in the layer stack affects the look of your photo. Finally, you learn how to merge all layers of the image back into one layer so that the image can be saved in a file format that's compatible with many applications and the Internet.

91 About Layers and the Layers Palette

See Also

→ **92** Create a New Image Layer

→ **93** Create a Layer Filled with Color, Gradient, or Pattern

→ **94** Create an Adjustment Layer

→ **163** Mask an Image Layer

All images in Photoshop Elements have at least one *layer*, the *Background layer*. You will see this layer with any new image that you open in Photoshop Elements, including photos that you import from a digital camera. The **Background** layer is always locked, which means that you cannot change the stacking order, *blend mode*, or opacity of the **Background** layer in an image. You also cannot delete pixels on the **Background** layer and make them transparent. If you try, those pixels are filled with the current *background color*. If you want to make any of these changes to that layer, you must first convert the **Background** layer to a regular image layer.

By adding additional layers to the image, you can stack elements of the image to create a more complex image. Each layer you add to your image is stacked on top of the previous layer. For example, if you have an image of your daughter in her Easter outfit on the **Background** layer, you can place a little white bunny in front of her feet by just putting the white bunny on the layer above the **Background** layer. If you have a layer above the white bunny that contains a brown bunny, you can position the brown bunny so that he sits in front of the white bunny. If you change the order of the layers, the white bunny appears in front of the brown bunny.

— **The Brown Bunny on the Upper Layer**

— **The White Bunny on the Upper Layer**

The objects on the uppermost layer appear in front of whatever is on the lower layers.

You keep track of the layers in your image using the **Layers** palette. But first, let me explain the types of layers you might find there:

- **Background layer.** As mentioned, the **Background** layer is created automatically when you open a new image. When present, it is always the bottom layer of the image, although it can be converted to a regular image layer to allow for more editing capability.

  If you do not have a *background layer* (because you converted it), you can make any layer the bottom layer. You can also convert the bottom layer into a background layer, thereby locking it from editing. See **95** **Convert a Background Layer to a Regular Layer and Vice Versa**.

- **Image layers.** Each layer of the image that contains a portion of an image, or just pixels (applied by the **Brush**, **Pencil**, or other painting tool, for example), is an image layer. See **92** **Create a New Image Layer** for information on creating new layers within your image.

- **Fill layers.** Fill layers contain a color *gradient*, a solid color, or a pattern, See **93** **Create a Layer Filled with a Color, Gradient, or Pattern** for more information on creating fill layers.

- **Adjustment layers.** You can create a layer that controls the color, contrast, brightness, saturation or similar adjustment of the layers it is linked to, which always appear below the *adjustment layer* in the **Layers** palette. In addition, the adjustment can be *masked* to prevent the adjustment from affecting particular portions of the linked layer(s). See **94** **Create an Adjustment Layer** for more information.

- **Type layer.** When you add text to an image, the Editor automatically places the text on a separate **Type** layer within your image. You can fine-tune the placement of the text on the layer using the same techniques you use to move data on regular image layers. You can also edit the text and change text properties (such as font size) as often as you like. See **183** **Add a Text Caption or Label** for more information on adding text to an image.

- **Shape layer.** When you draw a shape such as a square or circle on your image, it is placed on a shape layer. Keeping the drawn shape on a separate layer allows you to make adjustments to the shape (such as resizing or moving it) without affecting the rest of your image.

NOTES

When a layer is converted to a background layer, the transparent areas in the layer are filled with the current background color.

If you've converted your original **Background** layer into a regular layer, you can name another layer "Background," but it won't act like a **Background** layer unless you convert it.

TIP

To make particular changes to a text or shape layer (to apply certain filters and effects, for example), you must convert the text or shape layer into a regular layer—a process that's called *simplifying the layer*. Basically, this process converts the vector data of the text or shape into raster data. See **96** **Simplify a Layer**.

These various types of layers are listed in the **Layers** palette in the order they are stacked in your image, from bottom to top. If the image contains a **Background** layer, you will always see the **Background** layer on the bottom of the list because it is the first layer in your image. If you've converted a **Background** layer to a regular layer, it might appear with the name **Layer 0** in the **Layers** palette. After it has been converted, the former **Background** layer can be moved up in the layer stack to appear in front of the layers below. It can also be renamed to reflect its contents.

The layer that is highlighted in the **Layers** palette is the layer you are currently working on; it is called the *active layer*. Typically, the changes you make affect only that layer of the image. You can switch between layers in the image by clicking the desired layer in the **Layers** palette. You change the order of the layers in the palette by clicking a layer and dragging it up or down within the **Layers** palette.

Each layer in the **Layers** palette contains information about that particular layer. A layer is visible in the image when the **Visible** icon (the eye) displays in the left column. Keep in mind that, even though the layer is marked as visible, you might not see its contents if an upper layer contains data that blocks all or part of the lower layer.

The **Edit** icon (a paintbrush icon) displays next to a layer when you click the layer on the **Layers** palette; it indicates that the layer is ready for editing. If a layer is fully locked, the **Lock** icon displays to the right of a layer's name. The **Background** layer is always fully locked (until you convert it to a regular layer). When the layer is fully locked, you cannot change its blend mode, opacity, or *layer style*. You also can't make any changes to the layer or remove it from the image. You fully lock a layer by clicking the **Lock All** button at the top of the **Layers** palette. Click the icon again to unlock the layer.

You can also lock just the transparency of a layer. When a layer is partially locked, you can edit only the fully opaque pixels on that layer—you cannot modify the semi-opaque areas or change their opacity level. Text layers and shape layers are partially locked by default, and you can't change their transparent pixels unless you simplify the layer first (convert it to *raster data*.) The **Lock Transparency** icon looks like a small *X* and appears in the same place the **Lock All** icon would appear if the layer were fully locked. To partially lock a layer, click the **Lock Transparency** button at the top of the **Layers** palette. Click the icon again to unlock the layer.

NOTE

You can add layers to your image in various ways: You can create new image, fill, or adjustment layers; you can create a layer from a selection or from data copied from another image; you can copy a layer and its contents; or you can use a **Text** or **Shape** tool (which creates a text or shape layer automatically). You learn how to perform each of these functions in various tasks throughout this book.

TIPS

You can hide a layer in your image by clicking the **Visible** icon. Click the icon again to redisplay the layer.

Hidden layers are not included when an image is printed. So, if you want to print various versions of an image, you can quickly hide particular elements right before printing.

TIP

To quickly select all the opaque pixels on a layer, press **Ctrl** and click that layer's thumbnail in the **Layers** palette.

NOTE

You can link a regular layer with a *clipping mask* layer to prevent part of that layer from blocking data on the layers below it. See **163** Mask an Image Layer.

When you select a layer in the **Layers** palette, any layers linked to the active layer display the **Link** icon (chain). When layers are linked, they work together as a group. You can make adjustments to all linked layers simultaneously. You can also move, copy, rotate, resize, skew, or distort the linked layers as if they were one. See **101** Group and Organize Layers for more information on linking layers and organizing them within the **Layers** palette.

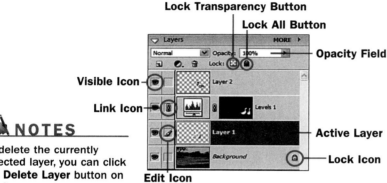

The Layers palette uses various icons to show which characteristics apply to each layer in the image.

NOTES

To delete the currently selected layer, you can click the **Delete Layer** button on the **Layers** palette or choose **Layer, Delete Layer**.

To rename a layer, double-click its name on the **Layers** palette or choose **Layer, Rename Layer** from the menu, type a new name, and press **Enter**.

To duplicate a layer and its contents, select the layer and choose **Layer, Duplicate Layer**, type a name for the layer, and click **OK**. You can also use this command to copy a layer and place it in another image. You can quickly duplicate a layer by dragging it onto the **Create New Layer** button on the **Layers** palette. To copy a layer into another image quickly, drag the layer with the **Move** tool from the **Layers** palette and drop it in the other image window.

At the top of the **Layers** palette are some buttons that provide shortcuts to common layer commands. You've already learned about the **Lock** and **Lock All** buttons; the other three buttons enable you to create a new image layer, add an adjustment or fill layer, or delete the selected layer. New layers are inserted above the current (active) layer in the palette, so always check to see which layer is active before clicking one of these buttons.

When you add a layer to your image, you have the option of setting the **Opacity** of the layer. The **Opacity** setting appears on the **Layers** palette and indicates how opaque or transparent the contents of that layer are. For example, if the layer has a default **Opacity** value of **100%**, anything in that layer completely covers contents in layers below (assuming that the contents on that layer are completely opaque—if they are partially opaque, the **Opacity** of the layer effectively lowers the pixel opacity even more). If you want to make a layer more transparent so that it will only partially cover the pixels on layers below, reduce the **Opacity** value of the layer by dragging the slider on the **Layers** palette.

Another way you can change how an upper layer's data affects the layers below it is through that layer's *blend mode*. By default, the blend mode for each new layer is set to **Normal**, which means that layer's pixels block data, but do not blend with the data on layers below. You can change a layer's blend mode by activating that layer in the **Layers** palette and selecting the blend mode you want to use from the **Mode** list at the top of the **Layers** palette. See **111** **About Tool Options** for a description of each blend mode and how it causes the pixels on the layer to blend with pixels below.

92 Create a New Image Layer

You can add a new image *layer* to just about any image you have open in the Editor. Because an image layer can hold any type of *raster data*, you might insert an image layer so that you can paint or draw on it, make a selection on the new layer and copy data into that selection, create a *clipping mask* to partially block data on another layer, or fill the layer with a filtered rendering of clouds. However, you don't have to create an image layer if your plan is to copy data from some other layer or image into this image; the Editor will paste the data on a new layer automatically.

When you add the new layer, you must first determine the location for the layer within the layer stack. To specify the layer location, select the layer *below* where you want the new layer (in other words, the new layer is added above the current layer). For example, to insert a new layer at the top of the layer stack, you select the top layer in the **Layers** palette. If the only layer is the **Background** layer, the new layer will always be placed on top of the **Background** layer because the **Background** layer is always at the bottom of the layer stack.

1 Select Layer Position

Open an image in the Editor in **Standard Edit** mode and save it in Photoshop (*.psd*) format. In the **Layers** palette, select the layer you want to be *below* the new layer you are adding. Photoshop Elements will insert the new image layer directly above the selected layer.

Before You Begin

✔ **91** About Layers and the Layers Palette

See Also

→ **93** Create a Layer Filled with a Color, Gradient, or Pattern

→ **94** Create an Adjustment Layer

NOTES

You cannot add layers to images that are using bitmap or indexed color mode. To change color modes, see **63** Change Color Mode.

If the image has only one layer (the **Background** layer), the new layer will be created above that layer. You cannot place any layers below the **Background** layer—unless you first convert the **Background** layer to a regular layer. See **95** Convert a Background Layer to a Regular Layer and Vice Versa.

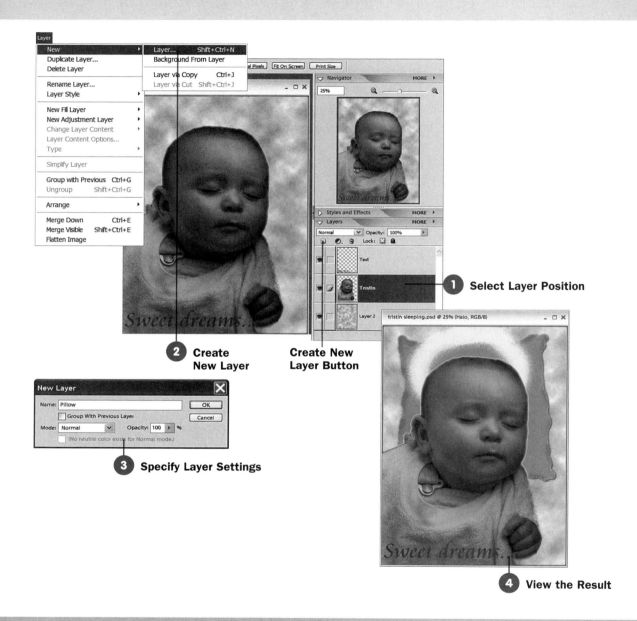

1 Select Layer Position

2 Create New Layer

Create New Layer Button

3 Specify Layer Settings

4 View the Result

2 Create New Layer

To create a new layer above the selected layer, select **Layer**, **New**, **Layer** from the menu bar. The **New Layer** dialog box opens.

③ Specify Layer Settings

In the **New Layer** dialog box, specify the settings for the new layer. Type a **Name** for the new layer (I usually use a name that reminds me of the layer's content or purpose), or accept the default name the Editor suggests, which is typically something like **Layer 1**.

The *blend mode* of a layer specifies how the pixels on that layer mix with pixels in the layer(s) below. The blend mode for a new layer is set to **Normal** by default. To select a different blend mode, open the **Mode** list and select the one you want to use. See ⑪ **About Tool Options** for more information on blend modes.

The opacity of a new layer is set to 100% by default. To reduce the overall opacity of the new layer, adjust the **Opacity** value. The lower the **Opacity** setting, the more transparent that layer's pixels will appear. If you add semi-transparent pixels to this new layer, the **Opacity** setting will reduce their overall transparency even more.

Click the **OK** button to close the **New Layer** dialog box and create the new layer using the specified settings. The new layer appears on the **Layers** palette above the layer you selected in step 1.

④ View the Result

After you have created the layer, it is ready for you to add data to it. A new image layer is filled with transparent pixels so that, at least initially, it does not block any layers below it. However, as you add opaque pixels, they *will* block the data below (or blend with them, if you selected a blend mode other than **Normal**). When you're satisfied with the image, save the PSD file. Then merge the layers together and resave the result in JPEG or TIFF format, leaving your PSD image unflattened so that you can return at a later time and make different adjustments if you want.

I started this image with data copied from another—of my great-nephew sleeping peacefully. I added some text, and then inserted a new layer and used the **Clouds** filter to create a puffy cloud background. I moved this layer to the bottom of the layer stack so that it would be behind the baby and not on top of him. Then I

 NOTES

You can create a *clipping mask* by grouping this new layer with the layer you selected in step 1, using the **Group with Previous Layer** option in the **New Layer** dialog box. See ⑯③ **Mask an Image Layer**.

TIPS

You can click the **New Layer** button on the **Layers** palette to create a new layer above the current layer. Photoshop Elements automatically assigns a default name to the layer, an **Opacity** level of 100%, and a blend **Mode** of **Normal**.

After creating the new layer, you can change the **Mode** and **Opacity** settings on the **Layers** palette by selecting the layer and then using the controls at the top of the palette.

You can duplicate the contents of a layer by dragging that layer onto the **Create New Layer** button on the **Layers** palette, or by selecting the layer and choosing **Layer, Duplicate Layer**.

If you select an object from another layer and copy and paste it onto your new blank layer, the copied data is placed on that layer. In other words, unlike normal **Copy** and **Paste** operations, a new layer is *not* created when data is pasted onto an empty layer.

TIP

You can make a selection and create a new layer above the current layer by choosing **Layer, New, Layer Via Copy** from the menu bar. A new layer is created instantly, and the data in the selection is placed on the layer.

inserted the **Pillow** layer and used the **Brush** tool to paint him a pillow. I locked the transparency on this layer so that I could brush soft texture along the edges of the pillow, giving it some dimension. To this I added a shadow. Next I inserted the **Halo** layer, on which I painted a yellow halo. I added an **Outer Glow** *layer style* to complete the effect.

---

93 Create a Layer Filled with a Color, Gradient, or Pattern

Before You Begin

✔ **91** About Layers and the Layers Palette

See Also

→ **92** Create a New Image Layer

→ **94** Create an Adjustment Layer

→ **100** Mask an Adjustment or Fill Layer

 TIP

Another neat thing about fill layers is that they can be used to instantly fill any selection with a color, gradient, or pattern. The selection in this case is not *actually* filled, but its shape is used on the fill layer's mask to block the layer's fill from appearing anywhere else but within the confines of your selection. In this manner, you can fill with a gradient text you created using the **Horizontal** or **Vertical Text Mask** tool—something you can't do using the ordinary text tools.

If you want to create a *layer* that contains a color, a *pattern*, or a *gradient*, you can create a fill layer. With a fill layer, the new layer is filled entirely with the one color, pattern, or gradient you select. However, unlike an image layer that you can indeed fill with a color or pattern (using the **Paint Bucket** tool) or a gradient (using the **Gradient** tool), a fill layer can be *masked*. This means that you can control what the fill layer covers up on the layers below the fill by masking portions of the fill layer. Initially, the mask doesn't prevent any data from flowing through from the fill layer—in other words, when you create a fill layer, it initially acts just like an image layer, covering up everything below. After creating the fill layer, however, you can paint on the mask to change it so that only portions of the fill layer are viewed. (See **100** **Mask an Adjustment or Fill Layer**.)

You can use fill layers for different effects in your image. For example, you can create a fill layer, mask out the center and create an instant frame for the image on the layer below. You can place the fill pattern layer over another layer, lower its opacity, and to use it to give that layer a "texture." You can also insert a fill layer and paint freely on the mask, creating a free-form shape or scribble that's filled with whatever color, pattern, or gradient you chose. And better yet, you can go in after the fact and exchange the fill you originally used for something else until you find just the right look.

1 **Select the Layer**

Open an image in the Editor in **Standard Edit** mode and save it in Photoshop (***.psd**) format. In the **Layers** palette, select the layer *below* where you want the new fill layer to be. The Editor inserts the fill layer directly above the selected layer.

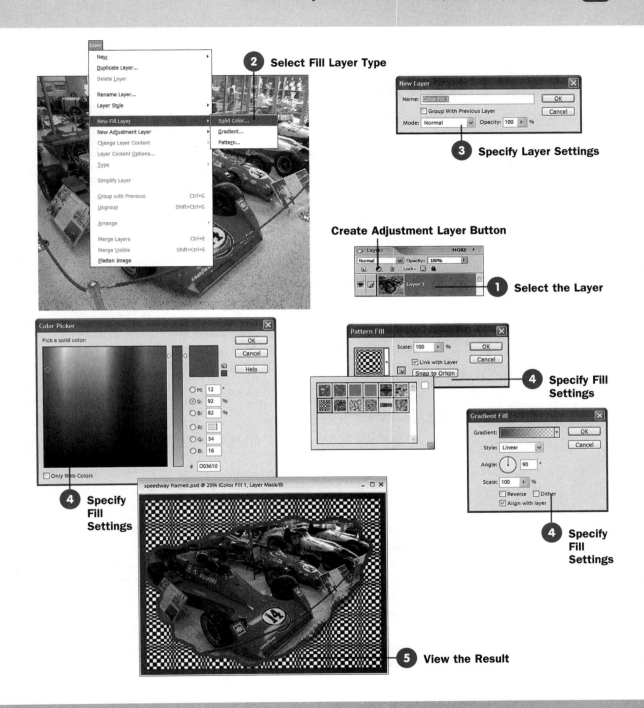

2 Select Fill Layer Type

3 Specify Layer Settings

Create Adjustment Layer Button

1 Select the Layer

4 Specify Fill Settings

4 Specify Fill Settings

4 Specify Fill Settings

5 View the Result

To create a fill layer that automatically fills only the area within a selection, make that selection *first* in step 1.

You can also add a fill layer by clicking the **Create Adjustment Layer** button on the **Layers** palette and selecting **Solid Color, Gradient**, or **Pattern** from the menu that appears.

2 **Select Fill Layer Type**

Choose **Layer, New Fill Layer, Solid Color** to add a fill layer that is all one solid color; **Layer, New Fill Layer, Gradient** to add a fill layer using a gradient color pattern; or **Layer, New Fill Layer, Pattern** to create a fill layer using a pattern.

3 **Specify Layer Settings**

On the **New Layer** dialog box, in the **Name** field, specify the desired name for the layer. Adjust the **Opacity** and blend **Mode** if desired. Click **OK**.

If you enable the **Group with Previous** option in the **New Layer** dialog box, you'll create a *clipping mask*, and your chosen fill will fill only the opaque pixels in the layer directly below and not other lower layers. If you change those pixels (erase some of them or paint more of them on the lower layer), the fill changes its shape to be visible only where the opaque pixels in the lower layer appear.

You can limit where the fill layer appears within this opaque pixel area, through its fill *mask*. See **163** **Mask an Image Layer** for more on clipping masks. See **100** **Mask an Adjustment or Fill Layer** to learn how to change the fill layer mask.

4 **Specify Fill Settings**

Depending on the fill type you selected in step 2, you will get a different dialog box. If you selected a **Solid Color** fill layer, the **Color Picker** dialog box displays so that you can select the appropriate fill color. See **113** **Select a Color to Work With** if you need help in choosing a color. Click **OK**.

If you selected a **Gradient** fill layer, the **Gradient Fill** dialog box displays. Select a **Gradient** from the list box. Choose a gradient **Style** and adjust the **Angle**, which controls the direction in which the gradient transitions from one color to the next. By lowering the **Scale**, you can have these transitions occur more often. Enable the **Reverse** option to reverse the colors in the gradient. Enable **Dither** to reduce jagged transitions, especially in lower-resolution images. Enable **Align with Layer** to use the layer's outer perimeter to calculate the gradient. Click **OK**. See **119** **Fill an Area with a Gradient** for more help in selecting a gradient.

If you selected a **Pattern** fill layer, the **Pattern Fill** dialog box displays. Select a pattern and adjust its **Scale**. Click the **Snap to Origin** button to reposition the pattern so that it's aligned with the image borders. Enable the **Link with Layer** option so that you can click in the image and move the pattern on the layer until you get its position just right for your purposes. Click **OK**.

⑤ View the Result

The new fill layer is created using the color, pattern, or gradient option that you selected. You will notice that in the **Layers** palette there are two icons for the layer. The first icon shows the type of fill that was added. For example, if you created a color fill, the icon contains the color that was used. The second icon shows the *mask*. It's white where the fill shows through to other layers and black where the fill is blocked. Unless you made a selection in step 1, you'll notice that the mask is initially white, meaning that the fill completely shows through at the moment, covering all data on the layer below. You'll learn how to edit the mask to block the effects of the fill in ⑩⓪ **Mask an Adjustment or Fill Layer**.

When you're satisfied with the image, save the PSD file. Then merge the layers together and resave the result in JPEG or TIFF format, leaving your PSD image unflattened so that you can return at a later time and make different adjustments if you want.

In this example, I took a photo of some race cars and devised a unique frame for it using fill layers. First I created a selection using the **Selection Brush**, marking the area where I wanted the photo to show through. I inverted this selection to mark where I wanted the fill pattern to appear, and then inserted a fill layer. The layer was instantly masked, and showed through only where I had selected. The photo seemed to need something at the outer edge, so I created a rectangular selection, inverted that, and filled that selection with dark red using another fill layer. The result is a unique frame that fits the racing car theme better than any of the premade frames the Editor offers.

 TIPS

Keep in mind that several gradient patterns use the current *foreground color*. Before creating a gradient fill layer, select the desired foreground color to make finding the right gradient easier. See ⑪③ **Select a Color to Work With** for more information on selecting the foreground color.

If you want to make modifications to a fill layer later on, click the fill thumbnail on the **Layers** palette. The corresponding dialog box displays so that you can adjust the fill's settings. For example, if I clicked the fill thumbnail on a gradient fill layer, the **Gradient** dialog box would display, showing the current settings for the fill layer. Make the desired adjustments and click **OK**.

94 Create an Adjustment Layer

Before You Begin

✔ **91** About Layers and the Layers Palette

See Also

→ **92** Create a New Image Layer

→ **100** Mask an Adjustment or Fill Layer

KEY TERM

Adjustment layer—A special layer that allows you to make a specific color or contrast adjustment to the layers underneath it.

NOTE

Because its effects are easy to change or remove, an adjustment layer is always preferable to applying that same adjustment directly to a layer. In addition, using the adjustment mask, you can easily limit the adjustment to particular portions of the layers below, *and even change your mind on which portions* you want affected, any time you want.

If you want to make adjustments to the color, contrast, brightness, and saturation of the *layers* in your image, you can add an *adjustment layer*. An adjustment layer changes the appearance of the layers below it in the layer stack without affecting the actual contents of those layers. This enables you to try out various adjustments without making any permanent changes to the image layer(s). If you don't like the result, you can open that adjustment dialog box again and make other changes, which is the same as if you had clicked Undo and had started over. However, in this case, you can change your mind at any time, even way down the editing process! You can also remove the adjustment layer and its effects completely.

There are several types of adjustment layers you can create:

- **Levels.** Allows you to adjust the highlight, midtone, and shadow values for each color channel or the entire tonal range. You can also remove a color cast using **Levels**. See **138** **Improve a Dull, Flat Photo**.

- **Brightness/Contrast.** Allows you to decrease or increase the general amount of brightness and contrast for all pixels on the affected layers. See **137** **Improve Brightness and Contrast**.

- **Hue/Saturation.** Allows you to adjust the hue, saturation, and lightness of all pixels on the affected layers. See **146** **Adjust Hue, Saturation, and Lightness Manually**.

- **Gradient Map.** Applies the colors in the gradient you select to the pixels in the affected layers, based on their brightness value. See **71** **Make Areas of an Image Easier to Select**.

- **Photo Filter.** Allows you to apply an effect that simulates the use of a particular photo filter to the affected layers. For example, if you want your image to have a sepia appearance, apply the **Sepia** photo filter.

- **Invert.** Changes the pixels on the affected layers so they are reversed in color and tone. See **71** **Make Areas of an Image Easier to Select**.

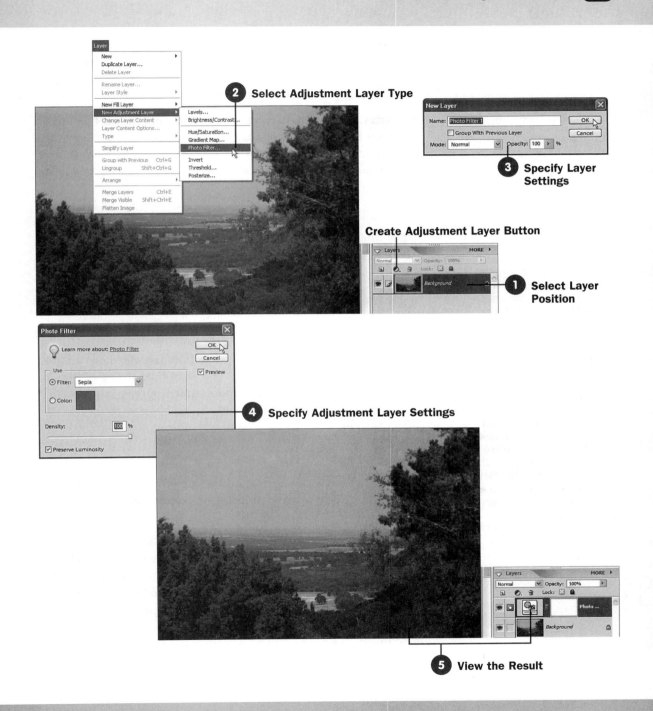

2 Select Adjustment Layer Type

3 Specify Layer Settings

Create Adjustment Layer Button

1 Select Layer Position

4 Specify Adjustment Layer Settings

5 View the Result

- **Threshold.** Allows you to convert the pixels in the affected layers to either black or white. Light areas are converted to white and dark areas are converted to black, depending on the threshold you select. See **71** **Make Areas of a Photo Easier to Select**.

- **Posterize.** Allows you to control the number of tones in the affected layers by specifying the number of brightness levels you want. The brightness of each pixel is then adjusted to fit within one of these tonal levels. See **71** **Make Areas of a Photo Easier to Select**.

TIP

To create an adjustment layer that automatically adjusts only the area within a selection (and not the entire layer), make that selection *first* in step 1.

NOTE

You can also create an adjustment layer by pressing **Alt,** clicking the **Create Adjustment Layer** button on the **Layers** palette and selecting the appropriate adjustment layer type. (The **Alt** button causes the **New Layer** dialog box to display, so you can change its settings as desired; if you don't press **Alt,** the layer is added using the default values.)

1 Select Layer Position

Open an image in the Editor in **Standard Edit** mode and save it in Photoshop (*.psd) format. In the **Layers** palette, select the lowest layer you want to be affected by the adjustment layer. The adjustment layer will appear in the **Layers** palette above the layer you select and will affect all layers below.

2 Select Adjustment Layer Type

Choose **Layer, New Adjustment Layer** from the menu bar and then select the type of adjustment you want from the menu that appears. Regardless of the type of adjustment layer you selected, the **New Layer** dialog box opens to request basic information about the new layer.

3 Specify Layer Settings

On the **New Layer** dialog box, in the **Name** field, specify the desired name for the layer. Adjust the **Opacity** and blend **Mode** if desired. Click **OK**.

If you enable the **Group with Previous** option in the **New Layer** dialog box, you'll create a *clipping mask* and your chosen adjustment will apply to only the opaque pixels in the layer *directly below* (and it will not affect other layers below the next lowest layer). You can limit the adjustment even within this opaque pixel area, through its *mask*. See **163** **Mask an Image Layer** for more on clipping masks. See **100** **Mask an Adjustment or Fill Layer** to learn how to change the adjustment layer mask.

4 Specify Adjustment Layer Settings

Depending on the type of adjustment layer you create, a different dialog box displays. For example, if you select the **Levels** adjustment layer type, the **Levels** dialog box displays. Make the appropriate selections for the adjustment layer you want to create. For example, on the **Photo Filter** dialog box, select the default filter or color you want to use to filter the layers. Then specify the density level for the filter.

When you have specified the appropriate settings for the type of adjustment you want to make, click the **OK** button to apply the adjustment filter.

5 View the Result

Unless you created a clipping mask, the adjustment you choose is applied to all layers below the adjustment layer. You will notice that in the **Layers** palette there are two icons for the layer. The first icon shows the type of adjustment that was added. The second icon shows the *mask*. It's white where the fill shows through to other layers, and black where the fill is blocked. Unless you made a selection in step 1, you'll notice that the mask is initially white, meaning that the adjustment completely shows through at the moment, affecting all data on the layer below. You'll learn how to edit the mask to block the effects of the adjustment so that it only affects portions of the layers below in **100** **Mask an Adjustment or Fill Layer**.

When you're satisfied with the image, save the PSD file. Then merge the layers together and resave the result in JPEG or TIFF format, leaving your PSD image unflattened so that you can return at a later time and make different adjustments if you want. In this example, I created a **Photo Filter** adjustment layer. I then applied the **Sepia** filter and set the **Density** level to **100**. Although this alteration is difficult to appreciate in the black-and-white images shown here, this adjustment made the photo look like it was taken with an old camera, changing all the colors in the image to various shades of brown.

 TIPS

The adjustment layer you create affects only the layers below it in the layers stack (unless you create a clipping mask). If you don't want a layer affected by the adjustment layer, you can move that layer above the adjustment layer by dragging it in the **Layers** palette.

If you want to make modifications to an adjustment layer later, click the adjustment thumbnail on the **Layers** palette. The corresponding dialog box displays. For example, if I clicked the adjustment thumbnail for my Photo Filter adjustment layer, the **Photo Filter** dialog box would display showing the current settings for the adjustment. Make the desired changes and click **OK**.

95 **Convert a Background Layer to a Regular Layer and Vice Versa**

Before You Begin

✔ **91** About Layers and the Layers Palette

See Also

→ **92** Create a New Image Layer

→ **97** Erase Part of a Layer

NOTES

When you convert another layer to the **Background** layer, the Editor automatically fills in any transparent portions of that layer with the current background color (shown in the swatch at the bottom of the **Toolbox**). Therefore, you should select the desired background color before converting a layer to the **Background** layer. See **113** Select a Color to Work With for information on setting the background color.

If you just want to lock the transparency, opacity, blend mode, and other attributes of a layer, you don't have to convert it to a **Background** layer, which must also occupy the lowest position in the layer stack. See **91** About Layers and the Layers Palette.

Photoshop Elements automatically makes the first *layer* in a new image the *Background layer*, and it is fully locked. This means you cannot change its *blend mode* or opacity, or move it up in the layer stack. In addition, you cannot make any of its pixels transparent. If you want to do any of these things (for example, if you have a nice photograph of the Lincoln Memorial up close, want to remove the pixels from around Lincoln and place him on another background), you won't be able to do that until you convert the **Background** layer into a regular layer. Conversely (assuming that your image no longer has a **Background** layer), you can make any regular image layer (one that contains *raster data* and not *vector data* such as shapes and text) the **Background** layer. You might do this, for example, to lock that layer against certain accidental changes.

1 **Select Layer to Convert**

Open an image in the Editor in **Standard Edit** mode and save it in Photoshop (***.psd**) format. In the **Layers** palette, select the layer you want to convert. To convert the **Background** layer, select it; to make a regular layer a **Background** layer (again, assuming that the image doesn't already have one), select it instead.

2 **Convert Layer**

To convert a regular image layer to the **Background** layer, select **Layer, New, Background from Layer** from the menu bar. The current image layer is renamed **Background**, placed at the bottom of the layer stack, and locked fully. Notice that the lock symbol appears next to the **Background** layer on the **Layers** palette.

If you are converting the **Background** layer to an image layer, select **Layer, New, Layer from Background** from the menu bar. The **New Layer** dialog box appears; type a **Name**, adjust other settings as desired, and then click **OK**. See **92** Create a New Image Layer for more information about using the **New Layer** dialog box.

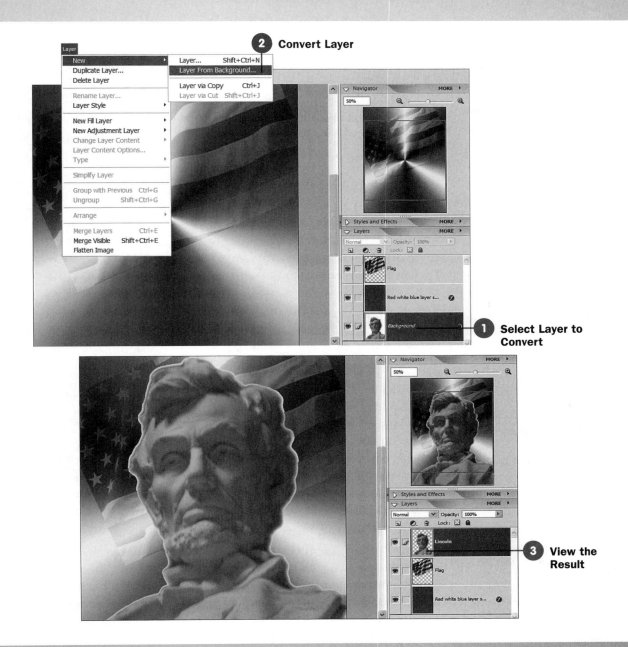

2 Convert Layer

1 Select Layer to Convert

3 View the Result

TIPS

To quickly convert a **Background** layer to an image layer, double-click the **Background** layer in the **Layers** palette and type a new name for the layer.

If you flatten the layers of an image, all the layers are merged together into a **Background** layer.

③ View the Result

When you're satisfied with the image, save the PSD file. Then merge the layers together and resave the result in JPEG or TIFF format, leaving your PSD image unflattened so that you can return at a later time and make different adjustments if you want.

For this example, I wanted to place Lincoln on a new background. I worked on the background first, pasting in a flag, positioning it an angle, and adding a red, white, blue layer style to the layer below. When I was satisfied with the background, it was time to move Mr. Lincoln. I converted the **Background** layer into a regular layer, naming it **Lincoln**, then moved him to the top of the layer stack. Of course, he now blocked everything, but it was easy to remove his all-white background and make it transparent, allowing his new background to shine through.

96 Simplify a Layer

Before You Begin

✔ **91** About Layers and the Layers Palette

See Also

→ **120** About Drawing Shapes

→ **183** Add a Text Caption or Label

 TIP

After you convert a shape layer to a simplified layer, you can no longer use the shape-editing tools to modify the shape you've drawn. The same is true with a text layer; the text-editing tools are no longer available for the simplified layer. Before you simplify a vector layer, make sure that it looks exactly as you want it to appear in your final image.

When you create text and shapes, they are placed on their own layers. Text and shapes are made of *vector data*, which allows them to remain easily editable because they are rendered onscreen using a formula. This formula allows the Editor to easily redraw the text or shape if you change the text font or size or rotate a shape, for example. This flexibility has its limits however. Because text and shape layers contain vector data, you can't apply filters, effects, and layer styles that work by manipulating individual pixels. For example, you can't apply the **Glowing Edges** filter to some text until that text has been simplified, a process that converts the vector data into *raster data*, or simply a series of pixels.

You can't do other things to text and shape layers as well, such as using the painting, drawing, and retouching tools to modify their content. For example, you can't use the **Smudge** tool to smudge the lower portions of some text, making it look like it's dripping. Nor can you erase portions of a circle shape to create the eyes of a Halloween pumpkin, or add the stem and leaf tendrils by simply painting them (but you could paint those details on the layer above the pumpkin circle shape.) The key is to simplify the layer first before making these types of pixel-based changes.

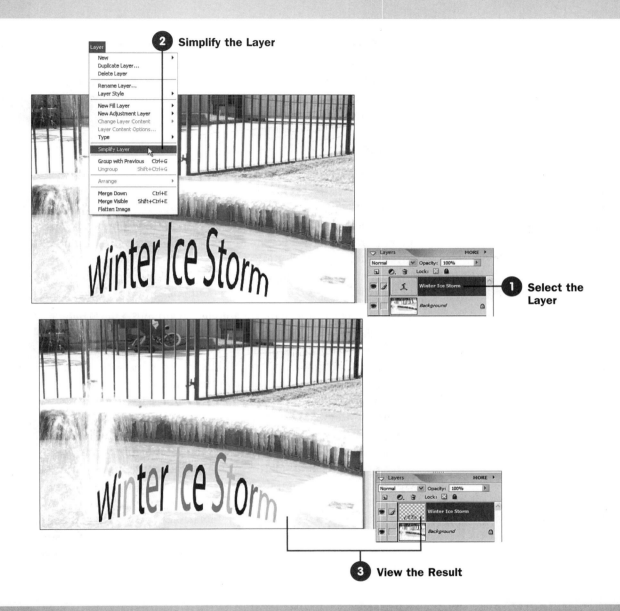

2 Simplify the Layer

Layer
New ▸
Duplicate Layer...
Delete Layer

Rename Layer...
Layer Style ▸

New Fill Layer ▸
New Adjustment Layer ▸
Change Layer Content ▸
Layer Content Options...
Type ▸

Simplify Layer

Group with Previous Ctrl+G
Ungroup Shift+Ctrl+G

Arrange ▸

Merge Down Ctrl+E
Merge Visible Shift+Ctrl+E
Flatten Image

1 Select the Layer

3 View the Result

1 Select the Layer

Open an image in the Editor in **Standard Edit** mode and save it in Photoshop (***.psd**) format. In the **Layers** palette, select the text or shape layer you want to simplify. In this example, I selected the layer containing the text *Winter Ice Storm*.

2 Simplify the Layer

Choose **Layer, Simplify Layer** from the menu.

TIP

If you are creating a shape layer and you still have the **Shape** tool selected, you can click the **Simplify** button on the **Options** bar to convert the layer instantly.

3 View the Result

When you simplify the layer, the layer thumbnail on the **Layers** palette changes to reflect the fact that the layer is now an image layer instead of a vector layer. For example, simplifying a text layer changes the thumbnail from the **Text** layer icon to a thumbnail of the actual text on a transparent background.

When you're satisfied with the image, save the PSD file. Then merge the layers together and resave the result in JPEG or TIFF format, leaving your PSD image unflattened so that you can return at a later time and make different adjustments if you want. In this example, I simplified the text layer so that I could use the **Paint Bucket** tool (after selecting the letters I wanted to paint, using the **Magic Wand** tool and its **Contiguous** option) to change the color of different letters in the text. If you want to change the color of the text in a text layer, you must set the color before typing each letter, or go back and select each letter and change its color on the **Options** bar. If you simplify the layer, you can paint the color on each letter by locking the transparency and being careful to brush over each letter separately and not its neighbor. You can also select the same colored text quickly with the **Magic Wand** tool after simplifying it and then apply a gradient fill to create instant rainbow text, something you can't do with the **Text** tool.

97 Erase Part of a Layer

One advantage of using layers is the ability to isolate changes to various elements in an image, such as applying a contrast adjustment to just a person and not the entire image. Another advantage of using layers is that you can easily add and remove data from a layer without affecting the other layers in your image. In fact, when you erase data from a layer using one of the eraser tools, the pixels are changed to transparent ones, and the contents of the layers below become visible "through" the area you just deleted.

If you attempt to "erase" data from a layer that has transparency locked (such as the **Background** layer), the pixels are not made transparent but are instead filled with the current *background color*.

To erase part of a layer, you use the eraser tools. There are different types of eraser: the regular *Eraser*, the **Background Eraser**, and the *Magic Eraser*. The **Eraser** works just as you might expect, making transparent the pixels the brush passes over. The **Background Eraser** works a little differently. As you drag the **Background Eraser** tool, pixels under the brush that match the pixel in the center of the brush tip crosshair are made transparent. How closely these pixels must match is controlled by the tool's **Tolerance** level, which is set on the **Options** bar. With the **Magic Eraser** tool, you erase matching pixels by clicking a sample pixel. Pixels that match the sample you clicked are erased from the layer. Again, the **Tolerance** option controls how closely this match must be before pixels are erased (made transparent). This works well if there is a lot of difference between the pixels you want to erase and the portion you want to remain. To remove a background with lots of different colors, it's easier to use the **Background Eraser** because you can drag and not click each color to remove. You'll learn how to use the **Eraser** and the **Magic Eraser** in this task; to learn how to use the **Background Eraser**, see **164** **Replace a Background with Something Else.**

1 Select Eraser Tool

Open an image in the Editor in **Standard Edit** mode and save it in Photoshop (*.psd*) format. On the **Toolbox**, select the **Eraser** tool.

Before You Begin

✔ **91** About Layers and the Layers Palette

See Also

→ **95** Convert a Background Layer to a Regular Layer and Vice Versa

→ **163** Mask an Image Layer

→ **164** Replace a Background with Something Else

EY TERMS

Eraser—A tool that allows you to erase (change to transparent) the pixels under its brush.

Magic Eraser—A tool that allows you to click on a pixel and instantly erase matching pixels. This tool, and a similar tool called the **Background Eraser** (which works by dragging and then erasing pixels similar to those under its crosshair), enable you to easily erase the background behind your subject (make the background transparent).

💡 TIP

You can also erase data by making a selection and pressing the **Delete** key.

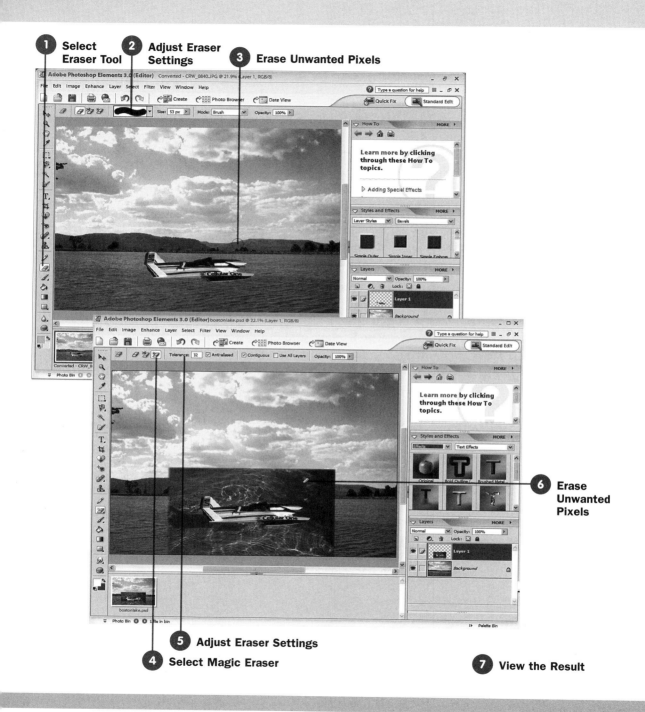

1 Select Eraser Tool

2 Adjust Eraser Settings

3 Erase Unwanted Pixels

6 Erase Unwanted Pixels

5 Adjust Eraser Settings

4 Select Magic Eraser

7 View the Result

② **Adjust Eraser Settings**

On the **Options** bar, select the **Mode** (**Brush**, **Pencil**, or **Block**), which determines the shape of the brush tip. For the **Brush** and **Pencil** options, you can further refine the tip by selecting an option from the drop-down list. Set the **Size** and **Opacity**. If you lower the **Opacity**, for example, the eraser only partially erases (it makes the pixels partially transparent instead of fully transparent).

③ **Erase Unwanted Pixels**

Drag with the tool; pixels under the tip are erased (made transparent).

④ **Select Magic Eraser**

Select the **Magic Eraser** on the **Toolbox** (if the **Eraser** tool is already selected, just click the **Magic Eraser** icon in the **Options** bar).

⑤ **Adjust Eraser Settings**

Set the **Tolerance** to a value that tells the Editor how closely you want pixels to match the one you click before they are erased. A low **Tolerance** level indicates that only pixels that are very similar to the pixel you click will be erased. The higher the **Tolerance** value, the broader the range of pixels that will match.

⑥ **Erase Unwanted Pixels**

Click a pixel that matches the ones you want to erase. Pixels that match closely enough (based on the **Tolerance** setting) to the one you click are erased. Continue the process until you have removed the unwanted portion of the layer. The portion of the layer you erased no longer blocks any data on the layers below, and that data becomes visible.

⑦ **View the Result**

When you're satisfied with the image, save the PSD file. Then merge the layers together (if any) and resave the result in JPEG or TIFF format, leaving your PSD image unflattened so that you can return at a later time and make different adjustments if you want.

NOTE

Set other options as well. Enable the **Anti-Aliased** check box to make sure that the edges are smooth around the area that is erased. Enable the **Contiguous** check box to erase only pixels that are adjacent to the pixel you click. If you clear the check box, Photoshop Elements will find all pixels in the layer or selection that match the pixel you click. Enable the **Use All Layers** check box to remove pixels on the current layer, based on the visible color and brightness of the blended pixel that you click. Again, adjust the **Opacity** to only partially erase matching pixels.

In this example, I pasted an image of my husband's model boat, taken in a backyard pool, into a larger image of a mountain lake. (The boat image was pasted in on a separate layer, making it easy for me to resize the image layer before I did anything else.) I wanted to remove the pool water from around the boat so that it would look like it was sitting on the lake. To accomplish this, I used the **Magic Eraser** tool to remove the pool water around the edges of the boat. I clicked on areas of the water, and the matching pixels were erased. Because there were several different shades in the water, I had to click several times.

Using the **Magic Eraser** enabled me to erase water pixels without accidentally erasing the boat. After the pixels near the boat were erased, I could work quickly with a large **Eraser** to remove the outer remains of the layer, by simply dragging over them indiscriminately. In the resulting image, my husband's model boat sits convincingly on the lake, looking for all the world like a full-sized boat. I have a bit more work to do to make the illusion perfectly convincing, such as lowering the brightness of the boat a bit to match the conditions of the water, and adding a shadow, but I'm nearly there.

98 Apply a Layer Style

Before You Begin

✔ **91** About Layers and the Layers Palette

✔ **92** Create a New Image Layer

See Also

→ **96** Simplify a Layer

Photoshop Elements provides several different *layer styles* you can use to customize the appearance of your *layers*. For example, you might want to simulate fog by applying a **Fog** layer style to an eerie photograph. When you apply a style to a layer, it affects *everything* currently within that layer (the opaque pixels). If you later change the layer's content, the layer style adapts to this new information and changes accordingly, applying itself to the new data. For example, if you drew an *X* on a layer with the **Brush** and then applied the **Toy** layer style to it, the *X* would be filled with a brightly colored rainbow. If you later painted a circle on the layer around the *X*, the circle would be filled with the rainbow style as well. Layer styles are also cumulative, so the order in which they are applied to a layer is often important because that order can produce different results.

You apply layer styles using the **Styles and Effects** palette. The layer styles are divided into two basic groups, with edge styles (which affect only the edges in a layer where high contrast occurs) listed first on the second drop-down list box, and filler styles (which fill objects on the layer with the style) appearing last.

① Select Layer

Open an image in the Editor in **Standard Edit** mode and save it in Photoshop (***.psd**) format. In the **Layers** palette, click to select the layer to which you want to apply the layer style. Because layer styles are applied to all opaque pixels on a layer, making a selection before you begin is pointless.

② Select Layer Styles Option

In the **Styles and Effects** palette, click the down arrow next to the first list box and select the **Layer Styles** option.

③ Select Style Type

From the second drop-down list, choose a layer style category, such as **Bevels**. After you select the type of layer style you want to apply, icons for each style in the selected type appear on the **Styles and Effects** palette.

If icons for the styles do not appear, you're using **List View**. To change to **Icon** view, click the **More** button at the top of the **Styles and Effects** palette and choose **Icon View** from the list that appears.

④ Apply Layer Style

Click the icon on the **Styles and Effects** palette that corresponds to the style you want to apply to the layer. If you're using **List** view, click the name of the style you want to apply.

If you have the **Background** layer selected, you will be prompted to convert it to a regular layer before applying the style. You cannot apply styles to the **Background** layer.

When a layer style is added to a layer, a small cursive *f* appears next to the layer's name on the **Layers** palette. Double-click this **f** to display the **Style Settings** dialog box, which enables you to make small changes to the layer style such as lighting direction and glow style. Right-click the **f** and select **Clear Layer Style** to remove the layer style altogether.

NOTE

If you choose a filler layer style and apply it to a regular layer (and not a shape or text layer), the filler style might replace all content on that layer with the style. If the layer contains image content, it's replaced; if it contains only pixels you painted onto the layer, only those pixels are changed—in other words, opaque pixels are replaced by the filler style and transparent ones are left alone.

TIP

You cannot apply a style to the **Background** layer. If you want to apply a style to that layer, you need to convert the **Background** layer to a regular layer. See **95** Convert a Background Layer to a Regular Layer and Vice Versa for more information on converting the **Background** layer. If you've just created a layer and want to apply a layer style to it, that layer must have some opaque pixels or you won't see the style after it's applied. So, fill the layer with a color (any color will do) or paint on the layer to add some opaque pixels.

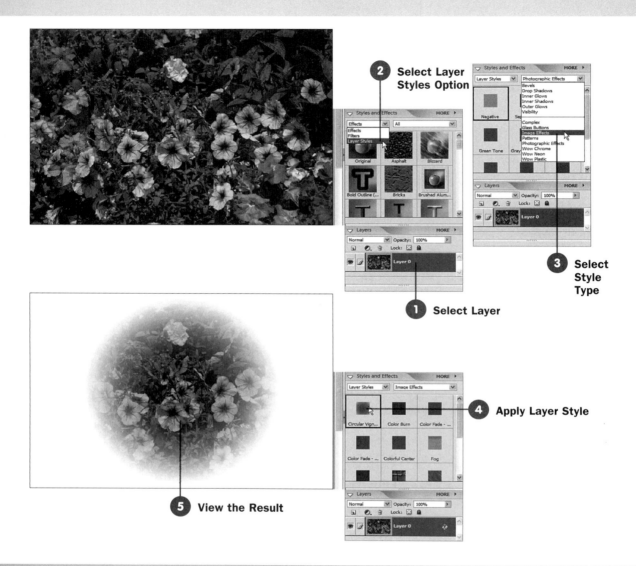

2 Select Layer Styles Option

3 Select Style Type

1 Select Layer

4 Apply Layer Style

5 View the Result

NOTE

You can remove the layer style at any time by right-clicking the layer in the **Layers** palette and selecting **Clear Layer Style** from the menu.

5 View the Result

The selected style is applied to the current layer. When you're satisfied with the image, save the PSD file. Then merge the layers together (if any) and resave the result in JPEG or TIFF format, leaving your PSD image unflattened so that you can return at a later time and make different adjustments if you want.

In this example, I selected the **Image Effects** style type and then applied a **Circular Vignette** style to the layer showing a bed of petunias. This style calculates a circle, using the area of opaque pixels on the layer as its guide to size. Because the style is applied to all nontransparent pixels in the layer, the size of the vignette was calculated using all the pixels on this layer. The vignette was created in the center of the layer, and those pixels were left untouched. Given the width of this image, that left a lot of petunias on the side. From the outer edge of the vignette circle to the edge of the layer, the image pixels were changed gradually to white. If I want to show more of the flowers in the circle, I only have to expand the canvas to make the image more square, and then fill the expanded area with any color (opaque pixels). The expanded canvas causes the style to be recalculated, making the transparent area in the center bigger, and more flowers show up.

 TIP

You can adjust the scale of a layer style after applying it if you don't like the result. For example, if you apply the **Puzzle** layer style and want the puzzle pieces to look smaller, choose **Layer, Layer Style, Scale Effects**. Then choose a percentage (less than 100% makes the pattern smaller; more than 100% makes it bigger).

99 Move, Resize, Skew, or Distort a Layer

One advantage of *layers* is that you can move, resize, *skew*, or *distort* the contents of each individual layer without affecting the data on other layers. For example, you might decide to reduce the size of a layer so that its contents fits better with the proportions of the contents of the other layers. This is common procedure after pasting data onto a new layer taken from a different image. For example, if you paste your dog into a family photo, you'll probably need to move and resize him so that he doesn't look out of proportion with the rest of the family members. You can skew or distort data to tilt or stretch it—sometimes just for fun, and sometimes to correct for perspective. For example, if you take a photo of a tall object while looking up, the base looks wider than the top, even if the object (such as a building) is the same size all the way up. Through distortion, you can pull the base of the building inwards, eliminating the illusion of a wide base.

You can move, resize, skew, or distort a layer using the **Move** tool. You can also perform these same functions on a shape or text object, or on a selection. When you move, resize, skew, or distort the data in a selection, however, the hole that is left by the selection's former location is filled with transparent pixels (if the layer supports transparency). For the **Background** layer, which does not allow transparency, the hole left by the altered selection is filled with the current *background color*.

Before You Begin

✔ **91** About Layers and the Layers Palette

✔ **92** Create a New Image Layer

See Also

→ **89** Rotate the Data in a Selection or Layer

→ **106** Rotate an Image or Layer

KEY TERMS

Skew—To tilt (slant) a layer right, left, up or down.

Distort—To stretch a corner of a layer in any one direction.

TIP

You can also transform the contents of a layer using the options on the **Image, Transform** menu. For example, to skew a layer, you select **Image, Transform, Skew**.

 **NOTES**

If the data you've selected is surrounded by nontransparent pixels, when you alter the area, you'll leave a hole. If you don't want to leave a hole where the original selection was located, you should paste your selection in a new layer before altering it. See **88** Create a New Layer from a Selection.

You can enter a percentage in the **W** and **H** boxes on the **Options** bar after beginning to drag. The selection or layer is then instantly scaled by that amount.

1 Select the Layer

Open an image in the Editor in **Standard Edit** mode and save it in Photoshop (***.psd**) format. In the **Layers** palette, select the layer you want to modify. If you want to alter a portion of the layer, make that selection now.

2 Select the Move Tool

On the **Toolbox**, select the **Move** tool. On the **Options** bar, enable the **Show Bounding Box** option. To automatically grab whatever object or layer under the mouse pointer is highest in the layer stack, enable the **Auto Select Layer** option as well.

The mouse pointer changes to a solid black arrow, and a **bounding box** appears around the edges of the selection or layer. If the layer is a shape or text layer, the bounding box appears around the edges of the shape or text object.

3 Resize the Layer or Selection

If you're altering an entire layer rather than a selection, maximize the image window and adjust the zoom so that the image is smaller than the window itself. This will give you the space you need to grab the layer handles properly.

To resize the contents of the layer or selection, position the mouse pointer over one of the handles on the edge of the bounding box until it changes to the **Resize** pointer (a straight line with arrows on each end). Drag to resize the layer or selection.

If you drag a corner handle and hold down the **Shift** key, you keep the proportions of the layer as you resize; if you drag a center handle, the image changes size in only one direction. If you begin resizing and then realize that the object is out of proportion, stop dragging and click the **Maintain Aspect Ratio** button that appears on the **Options** bar. The object's size is adjusted to fit its original proportions, and if you start dragging again, these proportions are maintained.

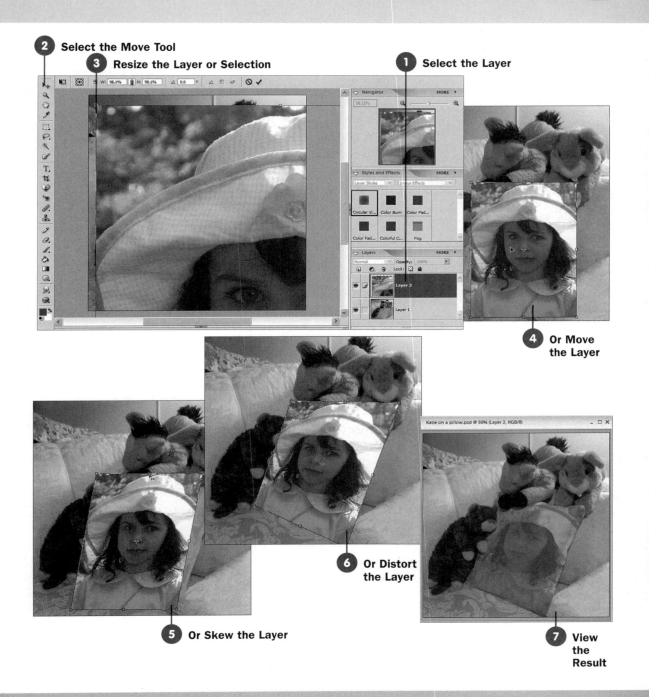

2 Select the Move Tool

3 Resize the Layer or Selection

1 Select the Layer

4 Or Move the Layer

6 Or Distort the Layer

5 Or Skew the Layer

7 View the Result

NOTE

If you want to alter a selection on the **Background** layer and have the hole it leaves filled with the background color, click the background color swatch on the **Toolbox** and select that color first, before altering. If you alter a selection surrounded by colored pixels on any other layer, the hole is filled with transparent pixels. You can then fill the hole by cloning the surrounding data.

TIPS

If pressing **Ctrl+Shift** is too hard to remember, you can also skew by first clicking the **Skew** button on the **Options** bar (it might not be showing yet; it appears when you begin to resize, skew, or distort) or by selecting **Image, Transform, Skew** and then dragging any side handle in the direction you want to skew.

To undo the last action by the **Move** tool (as opposed to all alterations this session), choose **Edit, Undo**.

If pressing **Ctrl** is too hard to remember, you can also distort by selecting **Image, Transform, Distort** and then dragging any handle the direction you want to stretch.

④ Or Move the Layer

To simply move the layer or selection, click in the center of the bounding box and drag the contents of the layer or selection to the desired position within the layer. You can use the arrow keys on the keyboard to move a selection. To move in one-pixel increments, press the arrow keys. To move in 10-pixel increments, hold down the **Shift** key while you press the arrow keys.

⑤ Or Skew the Layer

If you want to skew the layer or selection (tilt it horizontally or vertically in one direction), press **Ctrl+Shift** and then position the mouse pointer on a side (not a corner) handle. The mouse pointer changes to a gray arrow with a small double-headed arrow beneath it. Drag left or right to skew horizontally; drag up or down to skew vertically.

⑥ Or Distort the Layer

If you want to distort the layer or selection (stretch one corner), hold down the **Ctrl** key and position the mouse pointer on a corner or side handle. The mouse pointer changes to a gray arrow. Drag the handle of the bounding box inward or outward.

⑦ View the Result

When you're satisfied with your changes, click the **Commit** button on the **Options** bar. To undo all changes made with the **Move** tool this session, click the **Cancel** button instead.

Make any other changes you want in the image and save the PSD file. Then merge the layers together (if any) and resave the result in JPEG or TIFF format, leaving your PSD image unflattened so that you can return at a later time and make different adjustments if you want.

100 Mask an Adjustment or Fill Layer

Unless you made a selection when you created an adjustment or fill layer, the layer initially "flows through" to the layers below, affecting all of them. That's because the *mask* for the layer (the thing that controls what portions of the layers below are affected) is *all white*. White on a mask tells you that the pixels on layers below are being filled by a color, pattern, or gradient, or are being affected by the adjustment.

You might decide after inserting an adjustment or fill layer that you do not want its effect to be applied to your entire image. For example, if you created an adjustment layer and selected the **Brightness and Contrast** adjustment, you might want to apply the adjustment to just your subject and not the entire image layer below. To prevent adjustment and fill layers from affecting areas of an image, you must edit the mask for that layer—basically painting parts of the mask *black*, which causes the mask to block the effect in that area of the layers below. You can use any painting tool to accomplish this, such as the **Brush**, **Pencil**, or **Paint Bucket**. You can also apply a black-to-white gradient, for example, to fade the effect in one direction. You can apply any filter or effect that works on grayscale images, and use the **Text** or **Shape** tools to draw the area you want to block. If you use gray, the effects of the adjustment or fill layer are only partially blocked.

You can paint on the mask whether or not it's displayed in the image window; the thumbnail for the mask always appears next to the fill or adjustment layer on the **Layers** palette. However, for the most part, painting on the mask with it showing in the image window is the best way to go.

Before You Begin

✔ **91** About Layers and the Layers Palette

→ **93** Create a Layer Filled with a Color, Gradient, or Pattern

✔ **94** Create an Adjustment Layer

See Also

→ **116** Paint an Area of a Photo with a Brush

KEY TERM

Mask—The part of an adjustment or fill layer that acts as a filter, blocking the adjustment or fill from affecting the other layers that lie beneath it in the layer stack.

1 Select Layer

Open an image in the Editor in **Standard Edit** mode and save it in Photoshop (***.psd**) format. In the **Layers** palette, select the adjustment or fill layer whose mask you want to edit.

2 Display the Mask

Press **Alt**, and on the **Layers** palette, click the mask thumbnail for the adjustment or fill layer (the thumbnail on the right) to display the mask for that layer in the image window. If you haven't edited

TIPS

You can copy data into the mask (as long as the mask is displayed), and use that data as your mask. For example, you could select a portion of your image or another image, and paste that onto the mask. The data appears in grayscale; the black pixels (represented by the darkest parts of the image you pasted) block the fill or adjustment layer, and the lighter gray pixels only partially block it.

If you need to reposition the mask on the fill or adjustment layer, you must unlink it first by clicking the link icon (the chain), located between the layer thumbnail and the mask thumbnail. Use the **Move** tool to reposition the mask, and then click the link icon again to re-link the mask to the fill/adjustment layer.

 TIP

You can temporarily turn off a mask (and let the fill or adjustment flow through freely) by pressing **Shift** and clicking the mask thumbnail for the adjustment/fill layer on the **Layers** palette.

the mask, the entire mask layer will be white (indicating that the adjustment or fill layer is affecting all the pixels on the layers below it in the layer stack).

3 Edit Mask

Click one of the painting tools in the **Toolbox**, set the foreground color to black, and paint on the mask in the area where you want to block the layer's effect. Paint with gray to partially block the layer's effects. Paint with white again to let the layer's effects flow through.

You can use any tool, filter, effect, or command that works with grayscale images to edit the mask, such as the **Gradient** tool, **Text** tool, **Shape** tool, **Paint Bucket** tool, **Brightness/Contrast** or **Levels** command, or **Posterize** filter.

4 Hide Mask Again

To view the image again and hide the mask, press **Alt** and click the mask thumbnail on the **Layers** palette. Notice that the mask thumbnail has been updated to reflect your changes to the mask.

5 View the Result

When you're satisfied with the image, save the PSD file. Then merge the layers together (if any) and resave the result in JPEG or TIFF format, leaving your PSD image unflattened so that you can return at a later time and make different adjustments if you want.

In this example, I first applied a **Levels** adjustment to improve the contrast in my niece and great-nephew's face. But I didn't like what it did to the background—made it too bright and distracting. So, I displayed the mask and copied the image layer onto the mask to act as a guide as I painted the background black (to stop the adjustment layer's effect) and painted my subjects white (to let the **Levels** adjustment affect only that area). The result is a subtle yet striking difference.

**White Indicates Where
Layer Shows Through**

Black Blocks the Layer

3 Edit Mask

1 Select Layer

2 Display
the
Mask

Before

4 Hide
Mask
Again

5 View the
Result

101 Group and Organize Layers

Before You Begin

✔ **91** About Layers and the Layers Palette

✔ **92** Create a New Image Layer

See Also

→ **96** Simplify a Layer

→ **102** Merge or Flatten Layers into One

 TIP

In addition to linking layers together, you can group them. The purpose of grouping, however, is not the same as linking—you group two or more layers together for the sole purpose of creating a *clipping mask*. The purpose of a clipping mask is to block the data on a particular layer or layers from blocking the data on the layers below. See **163** Mask an Image Layer.

To remove a layer from an image, select it in the **Layers** palette and then click the **Delete layer** button at the top of the **Layer** palette or choose **Layers, Delete**.

If you have multiple layers that are related and that require similar adjustments, you can group (link) the layers together in the image. When layers are linked, you can move their contents as a unit using the **Move** tool. You can also resize, skew, and distort the layers as if they were a single layer (again, using the **Move** tool). See **99** **Move, Resize, Skew, or Distort a Layer**. For example, you might want to resize several layers, each containing a single person, so that the group of people is more proportional with the background scene. If the layers containing the people are linked, you can focus on resizing the group as if they were one layer. You can also copy and paste linked layers as if they were one. Layers that are linked together do not have to reside next to each other in the layer stack.

Whether or not layers are linked, you can still work on them as separate elements of your image. As you know, layers on the top of the layer stack block the data on layers below. So arranging layers properly in the **Layers** palette is critical to the way your final image looks. For example, a tree on the layer below a layer with a group picture can be made to appear *in front* of the group if you move the tree layer above the group layer in the **Layers** palette. You can move any layer except the **Background** layer, because it is locked. (To move the **Background** layer up in the layer stack, convert it to a regular layer. See **95** **Convert a Background Layer to a Regular Layer and Vice Versa**.)

➊ Move Layers in the Layers Palette

Open an image in the Editor in **Standard Edit** mode and save it in Photoshop (***.psd**) format. On the **Layers** palette, click a layer to select it and drag it up or down the stack until it is placed in the desired location.

As you drag a layer in the **Layers** palette, a location line displays to show where the selected layer will be inserted in the layer stack when you drop it. When the layer is located in the stack where you want it to be, release the mouse button.

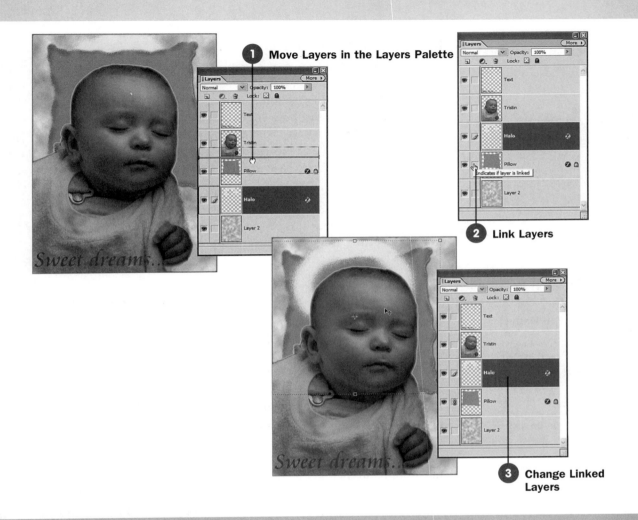

Move Layers in the Layers Palette

② Link Layers

③ Change Linked Layers

② Link Layers

Click to select a layer in the **Layers** palette. Click in the column to the immediate left of the layer icon for the layer you want to link to the currently selected layer. A **Link** icon (a chain) appears next to the linked layer indicating it is linked to the active layer. You can click the **Link** icon in front of any other layer to add it to this linked group.

 TIP

To unlink layers that are linked together, click either layer in the **Layers** palette. The **Link** icon appears on the other layer(s) it is linked to. Click this **Link** icon on any of the linked layers to turn off linking.

3 **Change Linked Layers**

With layers linked together, you can perform group functions on them. You can move, resize, skew, or distort the linked layers and even copy or paste their data as one. See **86** **About Copying, Cutting, and Pasting Data Within a Selection**, **99** **Move, Resize, Skew, or Distort a Layer**, and **106** **Rotate an Image or Layer**. Here, I linked the **Halo** and **Pillow** layers together so that I could move them as a unit beneath the baby's head.

When you're satisfied with the image, save the PSD file. Then merge the layers together and resave the result in JPEG or TIFF format, leaving your PSD image unflattened so that you can return at a later time and make different adjustments if you want.

102 Merge or Flatten Layers into One

Before You Begin

✔ **91** About Layers and the Layers Palette

✔ **92** Create a New Image Layer

See Also

→ **101** Group and Organize Layers

Unfortunately, the PSD format supported by both Photoshop and Photoshop Elements is one of the only image format that supports layers (the TIFF format also supports layers, although for various reasons, it is not the prime choice for your working image). Before you can save the image as another format, all the image layers must be merged together—in other words, the image must be flattened into a single layer. You can do this yourself or you can let the *Editor* do it. Typically, it's better to perform the merging process yourself, just before resaving the PSD image in another format so that you can see the result and make sure that the final merged image is what you want. When layers are merged, the Editor simplifies any vector layers (text and shape layers) by converting them to raster data (pixels), and then it blends the pixels together based on the order of the layers in the layer stack, the **Opacity** and blend **Mode** settings of each layer, and any fill/adjustment *masks* or *clipping masks*.

◣NOTE

After resaving your merged PSD image in another, more shareable format such as JPEG or unlayered TIFF format, click **Undo** on the **Shortcuts** bar to undo the merge. Then save your unflattened PSD image with its layers intact, so that you can return to work again on it at any time.

Before completing your work and saving it in a flattened format such as JPEG or unlayered TIFF, you might decide that you want to merge just a couple of layers together because you're done working with their contents separately. Not only does this action make your image easier to work with, it also makes the file *smaller*. For example, if you have manipulated a giraffe on one layer so that it is positioned above the location in a jungle-scene layer where you want it to live permanently, you can merge the giraffe layer into the jungle-scene layer. The layer stack is therefore less complex to work with, and the giraffe is now treated as one with the jungle.

❶ Merge Down

Open an image in the Editor in **Standard Edit** mode and save it in Photoshop (***.psd**) format.

You can merge layers by merging *neighbors*—two layers that lie next to each other on the layer stack. In the **Layers** palette, position the two layers you want to merge so that one is directly above the other in the layer stack. Select the top layer of the two layers you want to merge, then select **Layer, Merge Down**. Note that the two merged layers take on the name of the lower layer.

❷ Merge Visible

Another way you can merge layers is to merge just the ones that are currently visible. On the **Layers** palette, click the **Visible** icon (the eye) to hide any layers you don't want to merge, or to redisplay hidden layers you do want to merge. Select one of the visible layers in the **Layers** palette and choose **Layer, Merge Visible**. This time, the merged layers take on the name of the uppermost layer.

❸ Merge Linked

On the **Layers** palette, if you select a layer, any layers it is linked to appear with the **Link** icon (chain). Choose **Layer, Merge Linked** and the linked layers are merged. The merged layers take on the name of the lowest level.

❹ Flatten the Image

You can flatten the image when all modifications are complete. You will probably flatten the image right before you save it in any other file format (such as GIF or JPEG). Select **Layer, Flatten Image** to merge all the layers in the image together. The remaining layer is named **Background**.

❺ View the Result

When you flatten the image, all unmasked data on the merged layers is blended based on the **Opacity** and blend **Mode** settings for each layer. All layers, including adjustment, fill, type, and shape layers are merged. Any hidden layers or data are deleted. The opacity of the merged layer is 100%.

TIP

You can also merge only the linked layers in the image when needed. For example, if you linked layers together to resize and move them but continued to make minor adjustments to each layer separately, when each layer looks as you want it, you can merge the linked layers into a single layer you can still work with.

NOTES

You can't merge down if the lower layer is a fill or adjustment layer.

After an image has been flattened, saved, and closed, you cannot revert back to the separate layers. Make sure that you undo the flattening process in your PSD working image file before you save and close it.

TIP

In your working PSD file, you should keep the image with the layers unmerged, if possible, so that you can easily make changes to the image at a later time. After layers have been merged, it is more difficult to make changes to the individual image elements.

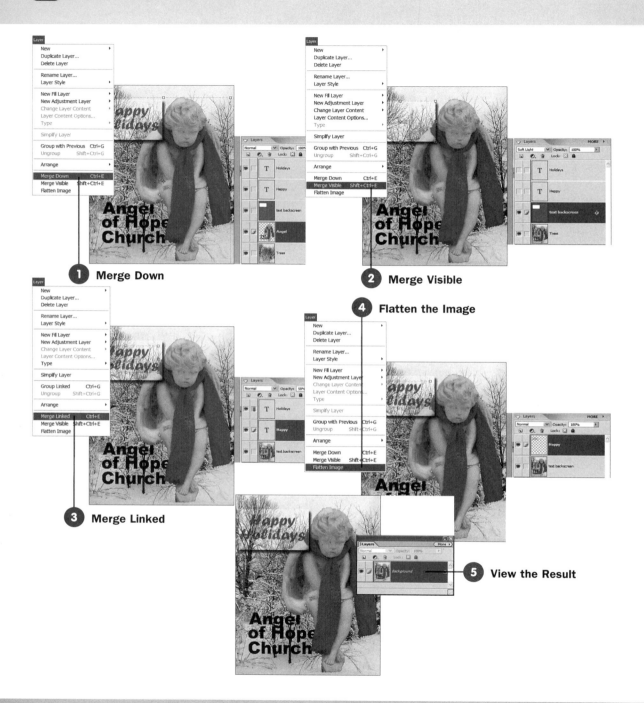

1 Merge Down

2 Merge Visible

3 Merge Linked

4 Flatten the Image

5 View the Result

PART III

Editing Images

IN THIS PART:

CHAPTER 13   Making Quick Corrections to a
Photograph   375

CHAPTER 14   Retouching Photos with the Tools   405

CHAPTER 15   Reparing Photographs   453

CHAPTER 16   Improving Portraits   477

CHAPTER 17   Correcting Brightness and Contrast in a
Photograph   499

CHAPTER 18   Correcting Color and Saturation   533

CHAPTER 19   Controlling Sharpness and Clarity   547

13

Making Quick Corrections to a Photograph

IN THIS CHAPTER:

103 About Color Management

104 About Adobe Gamma

105 Ensure That What You See Is What You Get

106 Rotate an Image or Layer

107 Crop a Portion of an Image

108 Straighten an Image

109 Apply a Quick Fix

Using the *Editor*, you can easily make adjustments to your photographs before printing them. For example, you might want to rotate or straighten an image, or crop it to remove distractions from around your subject. If the image is pretty good, you might want to give it only a quick fix (a series of simple, automated adjustments to an image's brightness, contrast, *saturation*, and sharpness), rather than a more complex, manual editing job. You'll learn how to perform all these simple, easy corrections in this chapter. For images that require a bit more work before you can print them, see upcoming chapters for help.

The *Organizer* provides two ways for you to make automatic improvements to a selected image without invoking the Editor. The **Edit, Auto Smart Fix** command makes automatic adjustments to color and tone *without any input from you*. The **Edit, Auto Fix Window** command brings up the **Auto Fix** dialog box, which allows you to select the automatic adjustments you want the Organizer to apply. However, you'll most likely prefer the results you get with the Editor's **Quick Fix** tool, which allows you to select not only the type but the amount of the automatic adjustment you want to apply. See **109** Apply a Quick Fix.

103 About Color Management

See Also

→ **66** Print an Image

→ **104** About Adobe Gamma

→ **105** Ensure That What You See Is What You Get

What you see onscreen when you view an image is often very different from what you get when you print an image on paper. Not only do your monitor, printer, and even your scanner use different methods to render color images, each device works with its own separate range of possible colors (also called a *gamut*). What this means is that, when representing an image onscreen, your monitor might display a grayish red for an area of an image, which is not reproducible by your printer as *an exact* match. The printer, in such a case, simply substitutes a *close* match to the grayish red from similar colors in its gamut. So, when the image is printed, you get something that's close to what it looked like onscreen, but not exactly. The best way you can deal with this messy situation is to create an environment that simulates onscreen (as nearly as possible) what an image will look like when it's finally printed. To do that, you use *color management*.

Why Manage Colors?

One of the tasks of color management is to match the gamut of colors your monitor uses with the gamut of colors your printer is capable of reproducing so that, in the best of all worlds, what you see onscreen as a "pale shade of greenish-blue" approximates that shade when printed. If the color of your son's shirt is a bit off when you print a photo, you might not even notice, but if his skin tone carries a slight greenish cast, it'll stick out like a sore thumb and the whole image will look "off."

— Onscreen Image

— Printed Image Shows a Shift in Color and Contrast

When what you see onscreen is not what you get when an image is printed, you need color management (in this example, the girl's skin tone, hair color, and even the color of the tractor is different). See the Color Gallery to compare these two images.

TIP

Because paper plays a critical role in the quality of photos printed at home, manufacturers of paper for inkjet and photo printers are now releasing ICC color profiles for their various grades and bonds of paper. How you use one of these profiles depends on how your printer driver manages color. Newer printer drivers can incorporate separate paper profiles along with their existing printer profiles. Some printer manufacturers' brands of paper—for instance, HP and Epson—provide color profiles that override the existing profiles for their older models of printers (those that don't manage paper profiles separately), thus becoming combination "printer + paper" profiles.

NOTE

Adobe Gamma creates an ICC color profile of its own, using information provided by the video card through Windows. The resulting profile is what Photoshop Elements uses to represent colors onscreen. You'll learn how to make adjustments to the choices Adobe Gamma makes in **105** **Ensure That What You See Is What You Get.**

Microsoft Windows has the unenviable task of translating colors from one device to another using specific ICM (Image Color Management) profiles for the devices involved—commonly called *ICC color profiles*. All devices that use color should have one of these profiles installed (your monitor, printer, and scanner). Typically, the profile is located on the manufacturer's disc, and you install it at the time you install the device driver and other software. With a profile installed, Windows shifts its color gamut to match the device's specifications, so that "rosy red" shows up as exactly that on your monitor, printer, and scanner.

In the absence of an ICC color profile for a device (if you haven't installed one for your printer, for example, or you simply couldn't find one on a disc or at the manufacturer's Web site), Windows uses its own color gamut instead. The video card then takes over the job of trying to represent colors on the screen with accuracy—basically by overriding the Windows default gamut with the one in the monitor's ICC profile. Photoshop Elements takes this one step further by making minor adjustments to these colors with some help from a program called Adobe Gamma.

Digital Cameras, Printers, and EXIF Data

Photoshop Elements uses information from separate camera ICC color profiles, when they are available. But both the *Editor* and the *Organizer* typically rely on EXIF information embedded within each of the images being imported, about how the camera perceived color *at the time it took the picture*. It is this information, specifically, that describes the camera's *gamut*. This is why proper photographic practices, including white balancing, are so important: When white looks the way it should for your digital camera, a calibrated monitor will precisely re-create that shade of white so that you won't make color adjustments to photos that might not really need them. For most digital cameras, the gamut used is sRGB. If you turn color management on within the Editor, the gamut used by the digital camera (and included in an image's EXIF data) is then used to translate that same information to the screen. For images that don't have a gamut listed in their EXIF data, you can choose which gamut to use. Again, sRGB is the gamut typically used by most digital cameras, so it's a good choice for use in the Editor when opening an image.

The color gamut information attached to image files follows a standard adopted by all major camera manufacturers (and some scanner

CHAPTER 14
111 About Tool Options

Top layer of test pattern.

Bottom layer of test pattern.

*Layered test pattern in **Normal** blend mode.*

The Editor's Blend Modes

Dissolve

Darken

Multiply

Color Burn

Linear Burn

Lighten

Screen

Color Dodge

Linear Dodge

Overlay

Soft Light

Hard Light

Vivid Light

Linear Light

Pin Light

Hard Mix

Difference

Exclusion

Hue

Saturation

Color

Luminosity

16 Review Images

*Using the Organizer's **Photo Review**, you can review a group of new photographs, make quick adjustments, add tags and collection markers, and mark photos for printing or deletion from the catalog.*

19 Stack Images

To keep your catalog small, you can group similar photos under one thumbnail in the Organizer catalog, and then expand the thumbnail when needed to display all the photos in the group.

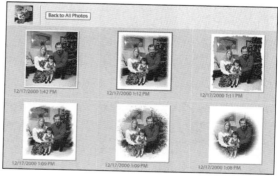

33 About Finding Items in the Catalog

After marking the items in the catalog, you can easily locate items with similar characteristics, such as images that include your wife and daughter.

COLOR GALLERY

CHAPTER 5

38 Find Items with the Same Date

Using the Organizer's Calendar View, you can quickly locate photos taken on the same day.

CHAPTER 7

62 Increase the Area Around an Image

By expanding the canvas around the central image, it was easy to insert other photos, creating this quick photo collage.

CHAPTER 8

68 Print a Picture Package

The Organizer can help you print multiple photos in multiple sizes, on a single page.

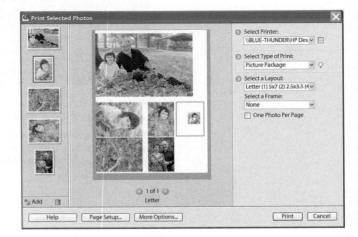

CHAPTER 9
77 Paint a Selection

*Paint a selection using the **Selection Brush** to quickly select the area behind this mother and child and replace it with something else, such as a simulated denim background.*

CHAPTER 23

178 Colorize a Photograph

Colorize your old grayscale images to give them a genuine hand-painted look.

CHAPTER 23

179 Make a Photograph Look Like an Oil Painting

I took a snapshot of birds playing in the water, and applied various techniques to make it look almost as convincing as this photograph of my mother's original oil painting, "Bird Dance."

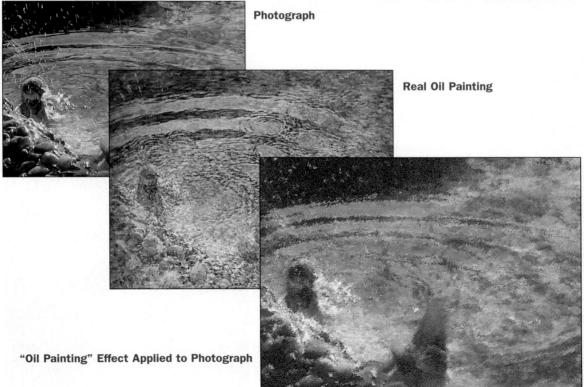

Photograph

Real Oil Painting

"Oil Painting" Effect Applied to Photograph

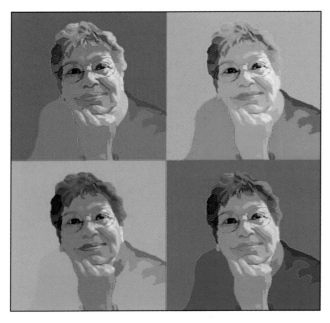

CHAPTER 23

182 **Make a Photograph Look Like Andy Warhol Painted It**

My mother-in-law, Maria, was a free spirit who embraced life, music, and most of all, her art. It's that spirit that I wanted to capture in my version of "Maria by Warhol."

CHAPTER 23

181 **Make a Photograph Look Like It Was Drawn**

and

CHAPTER 24

190 **Fill Text with an Image**

I made a selection in the shape of text and used it to copy the face of this little girl and insert it into a photograph I had changed to make it look like a drawing.

manufacturers) called Exchangeable Image File Format (*EXIF*). EXIF data helps Photoshop Elements (and other *graphics editors*) determine where the camera's interpretation of "pure" red, green, and blue (the optical primary colors) are located on a theoretical chart of all visible colors. Photoshop Elements can then compare these coordinates to where its own "pure" primary colors are located on the same theoretical chart. After the program knows how to adjust these three pure colors, it can mathematically determine how to adjust *all the other colors* so that it displays onscreen what your camera saw when the image was recorded. The EXIF data is in turn used by most photo printers when an image is printed, so again, you get a pretty good printout of what the camera saw when the photo was taken.

NOTES

If you want the **Adobe Gamma** profile to be used by other programs, make that selection from the **Color Management** tab of your video driver: double-click the **Display** icon in the **Control Panel**, click the **Advanced** button on the **Settings** tab, click the **Color Management** tab, and select the **Adobe Gamma** profile.

Some newer models of digital cameras have their own color profiles. An application that supports a camera color profile can use this information to help accurately translate color from the camera to the monitor. The goal of the digital camera ICC profile is to minimize information loss during the color translation from camera to monitor as much as possible.

As explained in **53** **About Image Information**, you can view the EXIF data for an image by displaying the **File Info** dialog box (in the Editor) or by looking on the **Metadata** tab of the **Properties** pane (in the Organizer).

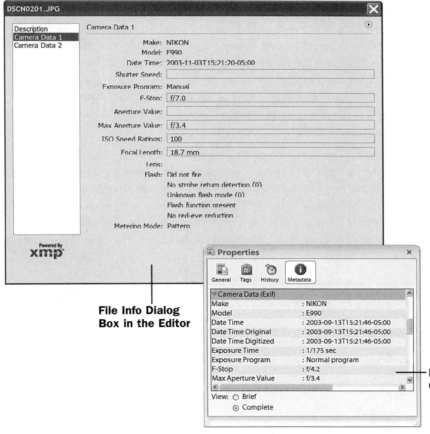

File Info Dialog Box in the Editor

Properties Pane in the Organizer

You can view the EXIF data attached to an image using the Editor or the Organizer.

NOTE

Some cameras tag their images with the sRGB color space (gamut), even if that is not the actual gamut used by the camera. This causes a noticeable color cast in all the camera's images when viewed onscreen (when Photoshop Elements assumes that sRGB was actually used, and uses that gamut to display the image onscreen). When your digital camera is pretending to use sRGB and it really isn't, you'll want to ignore the EXIF data when saving an image and have Adobe Gamma provide the color space data instead. Simply choose **Edit, Preferences, Saving Files** from the Editor menu, enable the **Ignore Camera Data (EXIF) Profiles** check box, and click **OK**.

Some printers do not interpret EXIF data. Instead, they rely on Windows to provide them with a standard set of colors to use when printing an image that has EXIF data. This set of colors, by the way, has been re-interpreted at least once by the imaging program (such as Photoshop Elements) that imported the image file from the camera. This system is pretty good, but printer manufacturer Epson decided to do it one better.

Recently, Epson has engineered a system for its inkjet and photo printers that gives the printer the EXIF data for an image directly, by way of a bypass driver. Epson calls its system Print Image Management (PIM), and it enables its printers to see with a high degree of accuracy (albeit through two translators) what a PIM-enabled digital camera saw when it recorded an image. This way, "black" in the digital image (which optically is comprised of no red, green, or blue whatsoever) translates into "black" on the printed page (which, for pigment, generally involves a mixture of black ink with equal parts of cyan, magenta, and yellow inks). Essentially, PIM—and its successor, PIM II—ensure that both the Epson printer and the PIM-enabled digital camera interpret color and present EXIF data in the same way. If you plan to use the PIM feature of your printer as it was intended, you should purchase or use a digital camera that explicitly supports PIM as well—and thankfully, many do, but you *do* have to look.

When PIM is involved, the color management scheme changes. Software called the *PIM plug-in* bypasses Windows color management and the ICC color profile, presenting EXIF data from an image directly to Photoshop Elements. The status of the PIM coalition changes often; as a result, other printer brands (such as Canon) might also be PIM enabled. Consult your printer's documentation to learn whether it is PIM enabled.

104 About Adobe Gamma

Keeping your monitor calibrated is the best way for you to reduce the likelihood that what you see when viewing an image in Photoshop Elements becomes something other than what you print. Using Adobe Gamma, you should calibrate your monitor (as explained in **105** **Ensure That What You See Is What You Get**) at least twice per year, plus every time you replace your video card or update your video drivers. Monitor calibration affects not just Photoshop Elements but everything you see and use in Windows—especially your imaging applications.

Selecting the Right Chromaticity

Photoshop Elements includes a tool for calibrating your monitor called Adobe Gamma. You'll learn how to use Adobe Gamma in **105** **Ensure That What You See Is What You Get**. Before you jump to that task, however, there are some technical terms you must understand to complete the steps, and the first one is called *monitor chromaticity*. Basically, every monitor has its own idea of how to display pure red, green, and blue, and that information is stored in the monitor's *ICC color profile*. The particular definition of pure red, green, and blue is called the monitor's chromaticity.

Before You Begin

✔ **104** About Color Management

See Also

→ **106** Ensure That What You See Is What You Get

NOTE

Proper calibration of color on your screen has a direct effect on how sharp your text looks in your word processor. How do colors affect contrast? Windows uses an anti-aliasing technique to make black letters look smooth on a white background. It's an optical illusion that involves "lacing" the stair-stepped notches in curves and diagonal lines with blue and orange dots (optical opposites) so that your mind actually blanks out the notches. If your monitor isn't calibrated, these colored dots become more evident, enhancing an illusion of *low* contrast rather than one of *high* contrast.

KEY TERM

Monitor chromaticity—A particular monitor's definition of pure red, green, and blue. A monitor's chromaticity is stored in its ICC color profile.

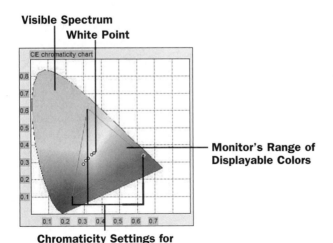

Visible Spectrum
White Point

Monitor's Range of Displayable Colors

Chromaticity Settings for Pure Red, Green, and Blue

A monitor's chromaticity chart based on its ICC color profile, as produced by a program called ICC Inspector.

A CRT monitor's profile contains this chromaticity data—the precise hues of red, green, and blue produced when its phosphors are struck by only one electron gun, at any one point, at full intensity. If you were to spread out your monitor's chromaticity color chart over your dining room table, it would look like a full-color version of the potato-chip shape pictured here. You could make three marks on that chart, and say that "pure" red, green, and blue for your monitor are "here," "here," and "here."

When all three of your CRT monitor's electron guns are directed toward the same point, the monitor produces white. So, the chromaticity of the light at that point on the chart is the *white point*. In the chromaticity chart shown here, the white point is always somewhere in the middle of the triangle that defines your monitor's *gamut*, but not necessarily in the geometric center. The five white dots represent the relative location of white points within the color gamut, for the five most commonly used light temperatures.

An LCD monitor produces its color in an entirely different manner, although its three optical primaries are also red, blue, and green. A crystalline compound whose physical state is described as "more liquid than solid," circulates between a pair of glass substrates. Light from a fluorescent source is shone through these substrates, which act as polarizing filters. In its natural state, the crystal also polarizes the light along the same axis as the glass. Certain points along the substrate have been tinted red, green, and blue. As some of these points are electrified, the crystal twists, blocking the passage of light and producing color. The precise hues produced can be plotted on the same chromaticity chart as for the CRT monitor.

Because white is produced on a CRT by red, green, and blue put together, the chromaticity of those three points directly affects the white point. But on an LCD, white is produced by red, green, and blue *taken away*. So, the white point there depends only on the wavelength of light produced by the fluorescent source behind the LCD screen.

The chromaticity of your monitor is not something you adjust, as you can with brightness or contrast. In the **Adobe Gamma** dialog box, you can set the exact chromaticity (selected from the **Phosphors** list) and white point (set in the **White Point** frame) for your monitor, and you can help it calibrate your entire color system so that what you see onscreen is what you get when you print an image. This might sound easy—and it is, as long as you've located and installed the appropriate ICC profile for your monitor. If you can't locate the ICC profile (either on the manufacturer's disc or its Web site), you must enter *some*thing, and here are some clues to help you:

- When your color is more than just a tiny bit off, but not completely wrong, *and* if you know for certain that your CRT is a Trinitron—especially if it was manufactured by Sony, but also if your manufacturer licenses Sony's technology—select **Trinitron** for your chromaticity setting.

- If your CRT is not a Trinitron, try the sRGB setting, which Adobe Gamma calls **EBU/ITU**. In Wizard mode, you can test your **Before** and **After** settings against one another to see whether the results look right to you. Of all the possibilities, **EBU/ITU** is the most likely to yield acceptable results if you have a non-Trinitron CRT.

- If the **EBU/ITU** setting doesn't result in true colors, and neither your monitor manufacturer nor the Internet can help you locate your chromaticity settings, your best course of action is to cancel Adobe Gamma and make *gamma* and white point adjustments to your video driver's chromaticity settings directly. In the Windows **Control Panel**, double-click the **Display** icon. Click the **Settings** tab and click the **Advanced** button. Click the tab for your video driver (such as GeForce or nVIDIA), and then adjust the gamma settings for each channel or for all channels simultaneously. The nVIDIA ForceWare driver panel shown here enables you to load a monitor profile (including chromaticity data and white points) into the video driver software directly (from the **Custom Color Settings** list), overriding Windows' own color management. You might find this to be a blessing or a curse, but in my experience, never anything in-between.

NOTE

Although Adobe Gamma allows you to do so, you should never attempt to guess at the chromaticity settings by manually entering a string of numbers.

TIP

In some cases—especially if your monitor is more than a few years old—the **EBU/ITU** (sRGB) chromaticity setting might look somewhat better than even your monitor's own designated profile settings. You do not risk damage to your monitor if you use chromaticity settings other than those specified by the manufacturer. But for the sake of image quality, do not override the ICC color profile unless the results look preferable to your own eyes.

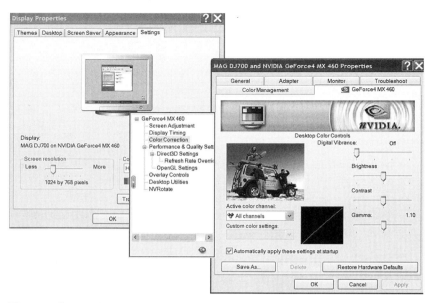

*The monitor calibration panel supplied with a recent version of nVIDIA's ForceWare video card driver. Go here to manually calibrate a monitor if choosing **EBU/ITU** as your chromaticity (**Phosphors**) setting produces less than optimal results.*

 TIP

If you decide to adjust the color correction settings of your video driver, make sure that you do so *after* making whatever changes you want to make to the ICC color profile using Adobe Gamma. Because the video driver's color corrections are applied over top of whatever the ICC color profile is telling the monitor to display, you'll want to make video driver adjustments last.

If, no matter what happens, the color on your monitor always looks wrong, consider upgrading your video card driver software. Whatever your card's manufacturer is, check its manual to see who produces its internal video chipset (most likely, nVIDIA or ATI). You can also look for the chip name on the video card, or try looking in the **Properties** dialog box for your monitor, which will contain a tab for the video card: Double-click the **Display** icon in the **Control Panel**, click the **Advanced** button on the **Settings** tab, click the tab for your video card, and look for a logo for nVIDIA or ATI. After determining who makes the chipset for your video card, go to that manufacturer's Web site and download its latest *benchmark* drivers. These drivers use the latest technology and are generally updated far more frequently than the brand-specific drivers for your video card. They are probably better drivers than what you're using now and will probably reset your chromaticity settings to sRGB specifications, or something at least remotely pleasing. Even so, you can tweak the results of using this new driver by changing the color correction settings of the video driver as explained earlier.

Adjusting Monitor Gamma

Another term you must be familiar with before calibrating your monitor is *gamma*. Because a monitor's gamma affects the brightness of images displayed on that monitor, you'll find this term used a lot in *graphics editors* such as Photoshop and Photoshop Elements. Because a monitor does not respond in a linear fashion to changes in brightness in an image (its response looks more like a sharp curve), by properly adjusting the gamma value on your monitor (the point where its luminance curve begins to bend), you can create a near 1:1 relationship between the tonal values in an image and their brightness onscreen. In other words, when the monitor gamma is set correctly, the brightness and contrast of the *midtones* within an image will also appear correct.

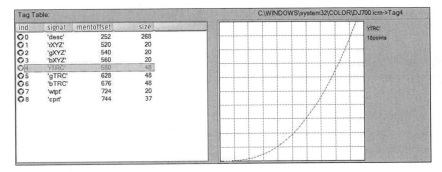

The increase in power needed to display colors ranging from pure black up to pure white is a gentle curve known as the monitor's gamma.

To properly calibrate a CRT or LCD monitor, you must adjust the gamma for each color channel individually. In Adobe Gamma, you adjust these gamma points by sight. Luckily, because of the way this adjustment is accomplished, *you can actually be color blind* and still make the proper choices. Adobe Gamma presents you with red, green, and blue squares. Each square is framed with a region of thin horizontal stripes, alternating between full color intensity and black. In the center is a block of color plotted at half intensity. As you squint at each square (so that you're looking at it fuzzy rather than in focus), you adjust a slider to minimize the distinction you see between the striped region and the solid center. If you consider "half intensity" to be a blend of "full intensity" and black, squinting provides you with a reasonable specimen of how half intensity should appear. (If you're color blind and can't see

NOTE

Software manufacturers don't make this very clear, but for any one monitor setup, you might actually have to deal with *three* different sets of gamma curves—one each for red, green, and blue. Windows has a basic curve of its own, whose gamma point is set at 2.20. Adobe Gamma enables you to adjust this starting value and also set gamma variations that pertain to the three color channels individually. Your video card driver might include a *separate* gamma setting that pertains to color correction for your monitor; it does not affect the choices you make in Adobe Gamma or the values saved in the resulting profile. The video card gamma is simply an additional adjustment to the profile *result*; typically this gamma is left at a neutral setting of 1.0 so that it does not affect color management.

red, green, or blue, you can still compare the striped shade you do see with the solid shade.)

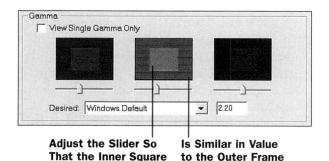

Adjust the Slider So   **Is Similar in Value**
That the Inner Square   **to the Outer Frame**

In Adobe Gamma, you adjust the gamma of each color channel using these three squares.

---

105 Ensure That What You See Is What You Get

Before You Begin

✔ **103** About Color Management

✔ **104** About Adobe Gamma

See Also

→ **66** Print an Image

KEY TERM

ICC color profile—Also known as an ICM profile, this file helps Windows translate colors between two imaging devices, such as the monitor and printer, so that the colors delivered by the devices match up as much as possible.

To ensure that what you see onscreen when viewing an image is what you get after printing that image on paper, you must properly calibrate your monitor. When you use the Adobe Gamma program for monitor calibration, you rely on your own eyes as the best gauge for what looks right. First, your monitor should be warm and stabilized so that colors and contrast don't appear washed out. For best results, leave your monitor running and active (that is, not in standby mode) for at least 30 minutes before running Adobe Gamma. When you're ready to begin, turn down any lights near your computer.

Adobe Gamma has two operating modes. The **Wizard** mode leads you by the hand, step by step, with each option presented in its own individual panel. The **Control Panel** mode displays all options in a single window, without description. This task shows you how to use the **Control Panel** mode to make your selections and to save them in a new *ICC color profile*.

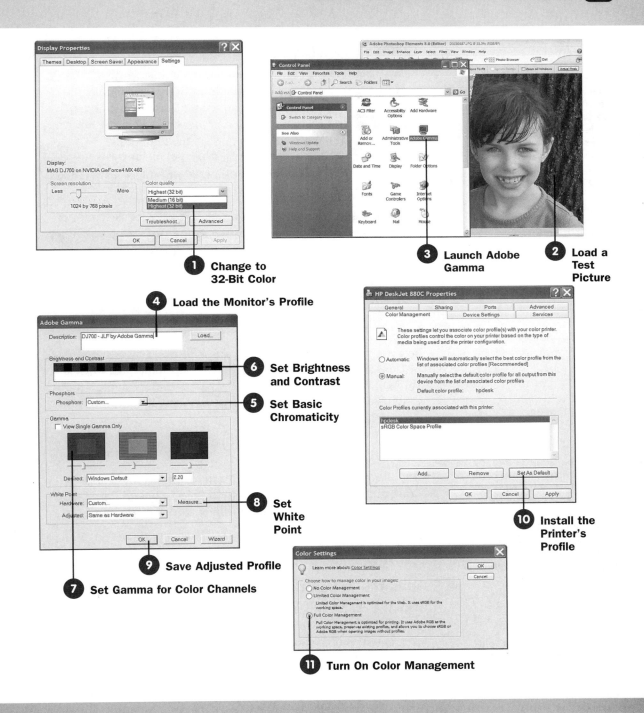

1 Change to 32-Bit Color

2 Load a Test Picture

3 Launch Adobe Gamma

4 Load the Monitor's Profile

6 Set Brightness and Contrast

5 Set Basic Chromaticity

8 Set White Point

10 Install the Printer's Profile

9 Save Adjusted Profile

7 Set Gamma for Color Channels

11 Turn On Color Management

TIP

If you've enabled any color correction features in your video card driver (for example, nVIDIA's **Digital Vibrance** option), be sure to disengage those features or reset them to their defaults before beginning monitor calibration with Adobe Gamma. You should make any video driver adjustments (if needed) *after* creating an Adobe Gamma profile.

NOTE

Has Adobe Gamma already been installed on your computer? Check your Windows **Control Panel** screen for the **Adobe Gamma** icon. If it's not there, install Adobe Gamma by copying the **Adobe Gamma.cpl** file from the **Adobe Gamma** folder of the Photoshop Elements CD-ROM to the **Windows****System** folder (for Windows 98, 98SE, and Me) or the **Windows****System32** folder (for Windows NT, 2000, and XP). You can then launch the program from the **Control Panel** as described in step 3.

① Change to 32-Bit Color

Before beginning work with Adobe Gamma, install the ICM color profiles for your monitor and printer (if they are available). If you have profiles for your scanner and digital camera, install them too. You might find them on the disc that came with the hardware or on the manufacturer's Web site. Save the files to the **Windows****System****Color** folder for Windows 98, 98SE, or Me; save the profiles to the **Windows****System32****Color** folder for Windows NT, 2000, or XP.

Right-click the Windows Desktop and choose **Properties** from the context menu to display the **Display Properties** dialog box. Click the **Settings** tab. Open the **Color quality** drop-down list and choose **Highest (32 bit)**. If this option isn't available, it's because your system does not have enough video memory to support it; in that case, choose the highest setting you can. Click **OK**.

② Load a Test Picture

You won't be able to tell whether the settings you're about to make are "right" unless you have a real-world test pattern whose colors you're familiar with. In the *Editor*, open an image you've already printed out so that you can compare its onscreen version with its printed version as you work.

③ Launch Adobe Gamma

After it's installed, the **Adobe Gamma** tool is located in the **Control Panel**. Click the **Start** button, select **Control Panel**, and double-click the **Adobe Gamma** icon to start the program.

If prompted, select the **Control Panel Mode** option and click **Next**. The **Adobe Gamma** dialog box appears.

④ Load the Monitor's Profile

If an ICC color profile for your monitor has been installed on your computer, load it now: Click the **Load** button, locate the file, and click **Open**. You'll probably find the profile in the **Windows****system32****spool****drivers****color** or **Windows****system32****COLOR** folder. The file will use the *extension* **.ICM**, and its filename will probably contain your monitor's model number. Adobe Gamma immediately applies those settings to your monitor. Although they might already be the optimal settings, you should test each setting to be sure.

If you don't have an ICC color profile for your monitor already loaded on your computer (because you couldn't find one), Adobe Gamma has to start from scratch rather than allowing you to adjust the profile settings. In any case, after you're done here, Adobe Gamma will create a separate monitor profile for you. So that you can easily switch between the profile you're creating and the existing profile (in case you ever want to return to your original settings), enter a unique name for the profile in the **Description** box. Preferably, include the model number of your monitor.

5 Set Basic Chromaticity

If you have a monitor profile installed, the **Phosphors** list shows the **Custom** option, which means that Adobe Gamma is reading the profile and loading the *monitor chromaticity* settings. Skip to step 6.

If you do not have monitor profile installed, use the guidelines presented in **104** **About Adobe Gamma** to determine the selection you should make from the **Phosphors** list.

6 Set Brightness and Contrast

The sample black and white bars in the **Brightness and Contrast** pane are presented as test patterns for your monitor. If you look closely, you'll notice that the black bar is actually made up of jet black and very dark gray boxes, alternating with one another. If you don't notice this, you will after you complete this section of the calibration.

Use the physical controls on your monitor (not on Adobe Gamma) to set your **contrast** to 100%, or as high as it will register. Next, set the **brightness** control on your monitor to as *low* a setting as possible where you can still distinguish the very dark gray blocks from the black ones. The moment they become indistinguishable, you're too low.

TIP

You might be able to determine whether a particular profile was designed for use with your monitor by right-clicking the profile file and choosing **Properties** from the context menu.

NOTE

The white bar in the **Brightness and Contrast** pane is there to make the test fair. It's easier to distinguish dark gray from black when they're alone; it's harder when they're adjacent to white.

7 **Set Gamma for Color Channels**

In the **Gamma** pane, from the **Desired** drop-down list, choose **Windows Default** (the other choices are **Macintosh Default** and **Custom**). The Windows default is always a good starting point for achieving best results. Then disable the **View Single Gamma Only** check box to see the test squares for all three color channels. With your eyes squinting, for each square, move the slider until the solid block in the center blends as closely as possible with its striped frame.

8 **Set White Point**

> **NOTE**
>
> The **Adjusted** list normally shows the setting, **Same as Hardware**. If your monitor's manufacturer has provided you with coordinates for its white point, in the **White Point** pane choose **Custom** from the **Adjusted** drop-down list. In the dialog box that appears, enter the white-point coordinates provided by the manufacturer and click **OK**. If your manufacturer has specified the white point in terms of temperature, select the appropriate temperature from the **Adjusted** list.

Most likely, you'll want to set the *white point* manually, rather than enter some values in the **Adjusted** text box. Click the **Measure** button. In the directions panel that opens, click **OK**. Your screen will go black, and then you'll see three gray squares. The warmer of these shades *in terms of temperature* (thus, the bluer shade) is on the left; the cooler shade (the redder one) is on the right. Study the middle shade carefully. Use the left and right arrow keys to rotate through the shades of gray until the middle square appears as *unbiased* or as neutral as possible (not bluish, not reddish). When you've found that shade, press **Enter**. The **Hardware** list in the **Adobe Gamma** dialog box now displays the word **Custom**.

9 **Save Adjusted Profile**

Repeat steps 6 through 8 as necessary until your test image looks as true to its printed counterpart as possible. When you're ready to save your settings, click **OK**. The **Save As** dialog box appears. In the **File name** text box, enter a unique name for the ICC color profile you've just created. Click **Save**.

At this point, all your Adobe programs and most of your Windows programs should start displaying images using the settings you've just saved in the new profile. The notable exception here is Paint Shop Pro, which must be told to use the new profile. Choose **File**, **Preferences**, **Color Management**, and then click **Enable Color Management** and select the **Monitor Profile** from those listed.

⑩ Install the Printer's Profile

Click the Windows **Start** button and choose **Printers and Faxes** or open the **Control Panel** and double-click the **Printers and Faxes** icon. Right-click the printer icon and choose **Properties** from the context menu. In the **Properties** dialog box that opens, click the **Color Management** tab.

Select the **Manual** option. A list of profiles associated with your printer appears. Select the profile that matches your printer and click **Set As Default**.

If the list is empty, click **Add**. The **Add Profile Association** dialog box appears. Select the ICC color profile supplied by your printer manufacturer—you should find it in the **\Windows\system32\ COLOR** or **\Windows\system32\spool\drivers\color** folder which automatically appears. If no printer profile is available, either on your driver installation disc or from the manufacturer's Web site, search this folder for a file named **sRGB Color Space Profile** and, if present, select it. Click **Add**. Make sure that the new profile is selected and click the **Set As Default** button.

Click **OK** to install the printer profile.

⑪ Turn On Color Management

To enable the Editor to embed the Adobe RGB ICC profile in your images so that the printer can properly translate their data, choose **Edit, Color Settings** from the Editor menu. In the **Color Settings** dialog box that appears, enable the **Full Color Management** option and click **OK**.

If you don't want to turn on full color management, you can embed a color profile in an image just before printing; see **66** **Print an Image** for help. As explained in **103** **About Color Management**, turning on full color management also affects how images appear in the Editor, whether or not you print them. As long as an image includes its color gamut in its EXIF data, that gamut is used to translate the image for display. If an image doesn't specify a color gamut, the **Full Color Management** option enables you to select one when the image is opened in the Editor. You can experiment to see what produces the best results, but you'll typically want to use the sRGB gamut for display. Then

TIP

To test your new profiles and the monitor calibration, print your test image from your newly recalibrated printer and compare it to what you see on your newly recalibrated monitor. The result should be fairly close to a true match.

when saving the image before printing, embed either the printer's ICC profile or the Adobe RGB profile, which is optimized for printing.

106 Rotate an Image or Layer

Before You Begin

✔ **45** About Editing Images

See Also

→ **108** Straighten an Image

→ **109** Apply a Quick Fix

NOTE

Rather than rotating an image or layer, try flipping it. Rotating pivots the image or layer around its center point, like a spinning top. Flipping pivots the image or layer along its central vertical axis, like the pages in a book, or along its central horizontal axis, like a gymnast rolling over a bar. On the other hand, when you flip text rather than rotate it, the text becomes reversed and might be illegible.

TIP

Although you can rotate an entire image in the *Organizer*, you can't rotate a single layer alone from the Organizer. In the photo well, click the image's thumbnail and then click either the **Rotate Left** or **Rotate Right** button located on the **Options bar**.

The single most common fix you'll ever perform on digital photos is to rotate them right-side up. Images freshly imported from a digital camera are always wider than they are tall—in other words, in *landscape orientation*. When you tilt your camera 90 degrees for a tall shot using *portrait orientation*, your camera doesn't recognize the different orientation (not even in the *EXIF* data), so Photoshop Elements doesn't know that the image is on its side. Thus, when you import such an image into the *catalog*, or open it directly into the *Editor*, it's sideways. To fix the problem, rotate the image as described in this task.

When desired, you can rotate a single *layer* rather than a whole image. For example, you might have text on a layer that you want to place diagonally across an image. By following this task, you can select the text layer and rotate it. You can also rotate layers that contain other data, such as drawn objects, or image data (such as a portion of a photograph you copied from another image file).

1 Open Image and Select Layer

Open the image you want to rotate in the Editor in **Standard Edit** mode and save it in Photoshop (***.psd**) format. If you want to rotate a single layer, switch to **Standard Edit** mode (if needed) by clicking the **Standard Edit** button at the end of the **Shortcuts** bar. Then click the layer's name on the **Layers** *palette* to select it. The selected layer is highlighted in blue.

2 Choose Image, Rotate

Select **Image, Rotate** from the menu bar. From the submenu that appears, select the type of rotation you want to perform on the selected image:

- **90° Left, 90° Right, 180°.** These commands rotate the image at its center point, to the left or right.

2 Choose Image, Rotate

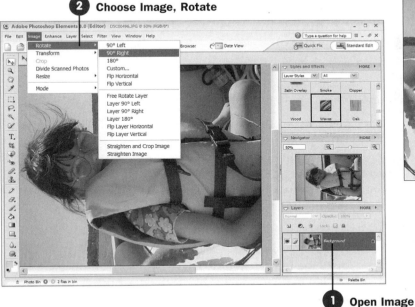

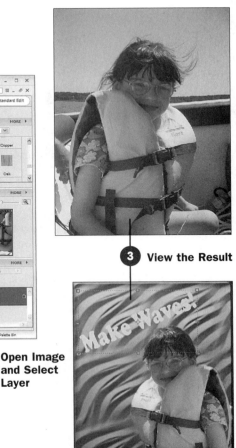

3 View the Result

1 Open Image
and Select
Layer

- **Custom**. This command displays the **Rotate Custom** dialog box so that you can enter an exact degree of rotation in the **Angle** box. Select the rotation direction—**Right** or **Left**—and click **OK**.

- **Flip Horizontal, Flip Vertical**. These commands flip, rather than rotate, the image. **Flip Horizontal** flips the image from left to right, over its central vertical axis. **Flip Vertical** flips the image top to bottom, over its central horizontal axis.

NOTE

To learn how to use the **Image, Rotate, Free Rotate Layer** command to rotate, move, or stretch a layer, see **99** Move, Resize, Skew, or Distort a Layer.

TIP

You can rotate an image (not a single layer separately from that image) while using the **Quick Fix** edit tool by clicking the **Rotate photo 90° clockwise (right)** or **Rotate photo 90° counterclockwise (left)** button on the **Quick Fix** pane. See **109** Apply a Quick Fix.

• **Layer 90° Left, Layer 90° Right, Layer 180°, Layer Flip Horizontal, Layer Flip Vertical**. These commands do exactly what the image commands do, but they rotate or flip only the currently selected layer.

③ View the Result

After you're satisfied with the image, save the PSD file. Then merge the layers (if any) together by selecting **Layer, Flatten Image** and resave the result in JPEG or TIFF format, leaving your PSD image unflattened so that you can return at a later time and make different adjustments if you want.

To capture this image of my daughter during a recent boating trip, I turned the camera 90 degrees. Because a digital camera saves all images in landscape orientation, I needed to rotate the photo before printing it. The **Image, Rotate, 90° Right** command did the trick.

To create the second image, I selected Katie from the first image. Then I used the **Image, Rotate, Layer Flip Horizontal** command to flip her left to right (so that she's facing the other way). I filled the *Background layer* with the **Waves** *layer style*, which I rescaled to make larger. Then I added the text, *Make Waves!* and used the **Image, Rotate, Free Rotate Layer** command to set the text at an angle. See **98** Apply a Layer Style for more about layer styles and **183** Add a Text Caption or Label for more about adding text layers. Look for this image in the Color Gallery.

---

107 Crop a Portion of an Image

Before You Begin

✔ **45** About Editing Images

See Also

→ **60** Change Image Size or Resolution

→ **168** Create a Scrapbook Page

To ensure a quality photograph that uses good composition, it's important to properly frame a photograph before you shoot. Whenever possible, you should crop in the lens, when taking the photo. Doing so prevents the loss of quality (*resolution*) that occurs when you have to manually crop an image after the fact. However, even with careful planning, unwanted objects sometimes appear along the border of otherwise perfect images—including my personal favorite, my *thumb*. In such cases, careful cropping after the fact can help eliminate the unwanted distractions. Cropping, by the way, is a process that cuts away the outer portions of an image that you no longer want to keep. Cropping not only eliminates distractions from your subject, it can also create a stronger composition by concentrating the image on your subject rather than the background.

Using the Editor, you can crop an image to any size you want. However, if you intend to print the image, you might prefer to crop the image to a particular print size, such as 4" × 6". To ensure that you maintain proper quality after cropping, you can also specify the resolution you want to use. If necessary, the Editor automatically generates extra pixels (using *neighboring pixel* colors as a guide) so that the final image matches the desired resolution. As you crop, a rectangle appears on the image; portions of the image outside this rectangle are discarded when the cropping is complete.

You can crop an image in the *Organizer* using **Auto Fix**. Choose the image you want to crop from the photo well, and then from the Organizer's menu bar, select **Edit**, **Auto Fix Window** to bring up the **Auto Fix** dialog box. Click the **Crop** button, select a size from the **Aspect Ratio** list, move the cropping rectangle around the image as needed to select the area to crop, and then click **Apply**.

❶ Click Crop Tool

Open the image you want to crop in the Editor in **Standard Edit** mode and save it in Photoshop (***.psd**) format. Then click the **Crop** tool in the **Toolbox**.

❷ Set Crop Dimensions

You can crop the image to any specific size you want, if you happen to know that size beforehand. If you want to draw the exact cropping area yourself, skip this step. To specify an exact size, open the **Preset Options** list on the **Options** bar and select a size. To flip the dimensions (to specify 4" × 6" for example instead of 6" × 4 ") click the **Swap height and width** button on the **Options** bar. If you can't find a preset that matches the exact size you want to crop the image to, enter the dimensions you want to use in the **Width** and **Height** boxes.

Enter the **Resolution** you want to use. For images you intend to print (photo prints), use a resolution setting of 200 to 300 *PPI*; for images meant to be seen on-screen only (for instance, in Web pages), use a resolution of 72 *DPI*.

NOTES

You can crop a single *layer* of an image, or crop an entire image, using a shaped border (such as a heart or an arrow) rather than a rectangular-shaped border. See `168` **Create a Scrapbook Page.**

If you've got a lot of photos to scan, you can scan them all at the same time (place multiple photos on the scanner glass at the same time) and then use the *Editor* to crop out each image automatically and place them in separate files. See `7` **Import and Separate Multiple Scanned Images.**

TIPS

If you want to crop the image to the same dimensions as another image, open that image, click the **Crop** tool, and then click the **Front Image** button on the **Options** bar. The dimensions of the current image appear in the **Width, Height,** and **Resolution** boxes. Change back to the image you want to crop, and continue to step 3.

If you've used the **Rectangular Marquee** tool (with no feathering) to select a single rectangular area of your image, and you want to crop specifically to the edges of that selection, choose **Image, Crop** from the menu bar.

Swap height and width button

2 Set Crop Dimensions

1 Click Crop Tool   **5** Crop Image

6 View the Result

4 Make Adjustments   **3** Draw Area to Crop

3 Draw Area to Crop

Click on the image in the upper-left corner of the area you want to keep. Drag downward and to the right to draw the cropping rectangle. The portions of the image within this rectangle are kept, and portions outside the rectangle (shown in a darkened color) are discarded.

Normally, the areas of the image to be cropped away appear through a partially black overlay. To change the color of this overlay, click the **Color** box that appears on the **Options** bar after the cropping rectangle is drawn, and choose a color to use from the **Color Picker**. Use the **Opacity** slider on the **Options** bar to adjust the overlay's opacity. To hide the overlay, disable the **Shield** check box.

4 Make Adjustments

To move the cropping rectangle around the image, click inside the rectangle and drag. To resize the rectangle while maintaining the same dimensions you specified in step 2, drag a corner handle inward to make the rectangle smaller or outward to make it bigger.

To *rotate* the rectangle (place the rectangle at an angle), move the mouse pointer a slight distance from any outer edge of the rectangle, until the mouse pointer changes to a curved two-headed arrow. Then drag in a clockwise or counter-clockwise direction to rotate the rectangle.

5 Crop Image

When the cropping rectangle is positioned as desired, click the **Check Mark** button on the **Options** bar to crop the image. The outer portions of the image are cropped. If the image contains layers, all the layers are cropped to this same size. To cancel the cropping operation, click the **Cancel** button (the slashed circle) instead.

6 View the Result

After you're satisfied with the image, save the PSD file. Then merge the layers (if any) together by selecting **Layer, Flatten Image** and resave the result in JPEG or TIFF format, leaving your PSD image unflattened so that you can return at a later time and make different adjustments if you want.

Cropping this informal portrait of my husband and his family improved its composition. I then added a blue-gray wooden frame using a technique discussed in **166** **Frame a Photograph**. Look for this image in the Color Gallery.

108 Straighten an Image

Before You Begin

✔ **45** About Editing Images

See Also

→ **106** Rotate an Image or Layer

→ **107** Crop a Portion of an Image

→ **125** Repair Minor Tears, Scratches, Spots, and Stains

→ **126** Repair Large, Holes, Tears, and Missing Portions of a Photo

💡 TIP

After straightening an image, empty spots will appear along the sides of the image; you might want to crop to remove these areas. As an alternative, you can use the techniques discussed in **125** Repair Minor Tears, Scratches, Spots, and Stains and **126** Repair Large Holes, Tears, and Missing Portions of a Photo to fill the empty areas with colors and details copied from other parts of the photograph.

Straightening an image is simply the process of rotating it by just a few degrees. The main reason for straightening an image is to draw the viewer's attention away from distractions such as a sidewalk running downhill, a slanting horizon, a pole that's leaning to one side, and so on. You might also use this technique to deliberately place an image on a slant to make it more interesting for use on a greeting card, Web page, scrapbook page, and so on.

Unfortunately, although the *Editor* provides you with both an **Image, Rotate, Straighten Image** and an **Image, Rotate, Straighten and Crop Image** command, neither one works very well or makes the same automatic choices that you would have made. Even applying these commands multiple times doesn't seem to really straighten an image because the changes are so small. So, to straighten a crooked image, you must rotate it manually and then crop the result.

① Choose Image, Rotate, Free Rotate Layer

Open the image you want to straighten in the Editor in **Standard Edit** mode and save it in Photoshop (***.psd**) format. If the image contains more than one *layer*, select the layer you want to straighten from the **Layers** palette.

Choose **Image, Rotate, Free Rotate Layer** from the menu bar. If the image contains a single *background layer*, you'll be asked whether you want to convert it to a regular layer that can be manipulated however you like. Click **OK** to continue. The **New Layer** dialog box opens; enter a new name for your newly promoted layer in the **Name** box and click **OK** again to continue.

If you want to straighten all the layers in a multilayered image, you must link the layers together first. Click the bottommost layer, and then click the **Link** icon on the upper layers you want to link together. When you rotate the bottom layer, the layers it's linked to rotate as well. See **91** About Layers and the Layers Palette.

14

Retouching Photos with Tools

IN THIS CHAPTER:

110 About the Toolbox

111 About Tool Options

112 About Preset Manager

113 Select a Color to Work With

114 Select a Color Already in Your Image

115 Draw on a Photo with a Pencil

116 Paint an Area of a Photo with a Brush

117 Paint an Area of a Photo with the Airbrush

118 Fill an Area with a Pattern

119 Fill an Area with a Gradient

120 About Drawing Shapes

121 Add Thought Bubbles to a Photo

Sometimes you might have to repair a damaged photograph or reinvigorate one that is old and faded. But often you'll just want to retouch an image that is not too bad but still could be better.

The Photoshop Elements *Editor* has several tools you can apply to retouch an image. Naturally enough, you'll find many of them on the **Toolbox**: brushes, pens and pencils, and the means to add *patterns*, shapes, and *gradients* to your images. The **Toolbox** is divided into sections; most of the retouching tools are in the fourth section from the top. In this group, you'll find the **Pencil**, **Eraser**, and **Brush** tools, the **Paint Bucket**, the **Gradient** tool, and shape tools. Several other tools can be used for retouching as well.

Each tool comes with an assortment of options. For example, if you want to use a brush, you can select from an assortment of brush sizes and stroke patterns. You make adjustments to the tool you're using in the **Options** bar displayed near the top of the screen.

NOTE

Locations of the **Toolbox**, **Options** bar, and palettes are described in **43** **About the Editor**.

Separate *palettes* and dialog boxes expand the options. For example, if you want to apply a particular color, you can select it from a Color Picker, from a palette of color swatches, or from an existing illustration.

110 About the Toolbox

Before You Start

✔ **70** About Making Selections

✔ **91** About Layers and the Layers Palette

See Also

→ **111** About Tool Options

→ **112** About Preset Manager

The **Toolbox** is the work center of Photoshop Elements. Nearly everything you do begins here. For example, if you want to crop an image, the first thing you do is to select the **Crop** tool from the **Toolbox**.

Selecting a tool from the **Toolbox** determines what the mouse pointer will do when you move it over an image. To use the **Crop** tool example again, when you move the pointer over a picture, the mouse pointer takes on the distinctive shape of the crop pointer. This tells you Photoshop Elements is ready for you to crop out part of the image and throw away the rest.

Some of the **Toolbox** buttons have small arrows in their lower-right corners. This means the buttons lead to groups of related tools, only one of which is displayed on the button. For example, when the **Rectangle** shape tool is visible, it hides a host of other shape-drawing tools including the **Ellipse**, **Polygon**, **Line** and **Custom Shape** tools. Click and hold to see a menu of all the hidden tools under that button. You can select any tool on this menu. When the tool opens, its various settings and options are displayed on the **Options** bar, along with a complete presentation of all the alternative tools for the chosen **Toolbox** tool. For example, if you click and hold the **Eraser** tool, you'll see a menu from which you can select the **Background Eraser** tool. After you've done that, the options for the **Background Eraser** tool appear on the **Options** bar, where you can set how big the tool is, what method it uses, and how strong it will be. Also note that the three eraser tools are shown on the left end of the **Options** bar—the **Eraser**, **Background Eraser**, and **Magic Eraser** tools—and you can select any of these alternative tools from the group at any time.

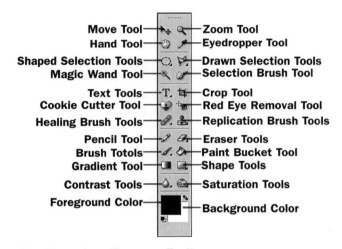

Move Tool — Zoom Tool
Hand Tool — Eyedropper Tool
Shaped Selection Tools — Drawn Selection Tools
Magic Wand Tool — Selection Brush Tool
Text Tools — Crop Tool
Cookie Cutter Tool — Red Eye Removal Tool
Healing Brush Tools — Replication Brush Tools
Pencil Tool — Eraser Tools
Brush Totols — Paint Bucket Tool
Gradient Tool — Shape Tools
Contrast Tools — Saturation Tools
Foreground Color — Background Color

The Photoshop Elements Toolbox.

Most tools in the **Toolbox** have parallels, or near-parallels, with tools you'd use in the real world in drawing, painting, retouching photographs, or drafting. Here are the classes of tools in the toolbox, from top to bottom:

- The **Move** tool lets you grab floating elements of an image, such as a small layer or a shape, and position them where you want them to appear. This tool also gives you options that let you alter, rotate, or *distort* any portion of an image that it can grab. It's featured in **99** Move, Resize, Skew, or Distort a Layer.

- The **Zoom** tool lets you change the magnification of the image you're editing so that you can see any part of it up close; later, you can zoom back to see the whole image. This tool is featured in **55** Zoom In and Out with the Zoom Tool.

TIPS

You may never perform every task in this book. That means you may not become familiar with the full contents of the Photoshop Elements **Toolbox**. So take a moment now to familiarize yourself with the available tools. To see the name of a particular tool, point to it with the mouse. If the tool's name appears in colored, underlined text, click that text to see the Help file that describes how to use the tool.

You also can select a **Toolbox** item by typing its keyboard shortcut. More accurately, each keyboard shortcut is associated with a slot in the **Toolbox** for a specific category of tool. The shortcut keys include **N** for the **Pencil**, **E** for the active eraser tool, **K** for the **Paint Bucket**, **G** for the **Gradient** tool, and **U** for the active shape tool. To cycle through the tools in a slot, repeatedly press its shortcut key. For example, if you repeatedly press **U**, you cycle through a variety of shape-drawing tools.

NOTE

The **Hand** tool lets you reposition an image in its window, just like you're scooting a paper on top of your desk. This tool is featured in **57** **Scroll a Large Image**.

TIP

You can pick up a color in an image for use with any tool by pressing **Alt** to change the mouse pointer into an eyedropper, and clicking that color in the image.

TIP

The **Crop** tool is one of the most frequently used tools among all Photoshop Elements users. It does exactly what you think it does—cuts an image to a smaller rectangular size. This tool is featured in **107** **Crop a Portion of an Image**.

- The **Eyedropper** tool samples the color of any point in your image and lets you apply that color to any other tool that uses color. This tool is featured in **114** **Select a Color Already in Your Image**.

- The shape selection tools, such as the **Rectangular Marquee** tool, let you designate a four-sided or an elliptical area of the image, as the region where you can make changes (leaving the rest of the image intact). You learn to use these tools in **72** **Select a Rectangular or Circular Area**.

- The drawn selection tools, such as the **Lasso** tool, let you draw a border around the area of the image where you want changes to be made (leaving the rest of the image intact). You see how to use these tools in **73** **Draw a Selection Freehand**.

- The **Magic Wand** tool lets you select a region of your image where you want to make changes based on the color of pixels in that image. This way, you can select "that bluish zone over there." This tool is featured in **76** **Select Areas of Similar Color**.

- The **Selection Brush** tool lets you designate a region of your image that you want to change as though you could paint that region with a watercolor brush loaded with water alone, and the water could fill in that region. There are wonderful effects you can create with this tool, as explained in **77** **Paint a Selection**.

- The text tools, such as the **Horizontal Type** tool, let you add captions and labels to your images and then bend or shape them to your whims. Chapter 24 covers the entire range of text tools, and the **Horizontal Type Tool** is featured in **183** **Add a Text Caption or Label**.

- The **Cookie Cutter** tool lets you take any image or any layer of an image and cut it into a common shape, such as a heart or star or arrow. You'll see this tool put to use in **168** **Create a Scrapbook Page**.

- The **Red Eye Removal** tool is almost self-explanatory. You use it to select the irises of your portrait subjects and watch as it removes the dramatic red glare caused by the direct flash of the camera. See **130** **Correct Red Eye** for details.

- The **Healing Brush** tools—one of which, appropriately enough, is named the **Healing Brush** tool—are used most effectively to hide or erase blemishes, cuts, insect bites, and other unwanted defects on a photograph. These tools are featured in **123** **Remove Scratches**.

- The replication brush tools, such as the **Clone Stamp** tool, absorb or sample material from one area of an image—or from a different image entirely—and apply that material to another area. This way, for example, you can remove an unwanted logo from a shirt by sampling a different area of the shirt where there's no logo and brushing that area over the logo, completely obscuring it. These tools are featured in **162** **Remove Unwanted Objects from an Image**.

- The eraser tools, which include one called **Eraser** tool, removes unwanted pixels from a layer of an image. This is important for a reason *other* than just getting rid of stuff: By taking away pixels, an eraser tool trims or cuts out portions of a layer, leaving contents beneath that layer to show through. This is demonstrated in **97** **Erase Part of a Layer**.

- The brush tools, such as the **Impressionist Brush** tool and the **Brush** tool, apply color directly to an image. One of the many places in this book that the **Brush** tool is discussed is **125** **Repair Minor Tears, Scratches, Spots, and Stains**. The Color Replacement tool in this set can apply one color only to spots where another specific color resides. This trick is demonstrated in **182** **Make a Photograph Look Like Andy Warhol Painted It**.

- The **Paint Bucket** tool spills paint into an area, starting at the spot you click and extending to areas of a different color, or the borders of a selection or of the image itself. This tool is featured in **118** **Fill an Area with a Pattern**.

- The **Gradient** tool creates an interesting backdrop you can use for an image with multiple layers, generally by painting a large wash that graduates between one color and another. You see this demonstrated in **119** **Fill an Area with a Gradient**.

- The shape tools, such as the **Rectangle** tool and the **Polygon** tool, don't just create pictures of filled geometric shapes in the middle of your image. They create objects that reside on their own layers, that you can bend and mangle and shape to build beautiful graphic enhancements, such as an embossed brass title plate or a transparent floating callout. You learn all about these tools in **120** **About Drawing Shapes**.

NOTE

The **Pencil** tool is used to apply color directly to an image. The key difference between the **Pencil** and the **Brush** tool is subtle: Although the **Pencil** tool is capable of using the same "brush tips" as the **Brush** tool, it only applies hard-edged strokes to an image; the **Brush** tool can apply soft-edged strokes. The **Pencil** tool is featured in **115** **Draw on a Photo with a Pencil**.

NOTE

The **Info** palette displays color and position information about the pixel under the tool pointer. This is helpful in identifying an image color or using a tool more precisely. By default, color data is displayed in Web notation. To display RGB or HSL color data instead, click the **Eyedropper** icon on the **Info** palette. By default, inches are used as the unit of measurement. To change it, click the **Crosshair** icon on the palette.

- The contrast tools, such as the **Blur** tool and the **Sharpen** tool, can help create the illusion of fuzzier or sharper focus, respectively, to *small selected parts* of an image. This way, you can de-emphasize part of a photo so that it stops taking attention away from your subject, or create added contrast along an otherwise unimportant edge to help draw attention. The **Sharpen** tool is featured in **149** **Sharpen an Image**, while the **Blur** tool is demonstrated in **150** **Blur an Image to Remove Noise**.

TIPS

Many users are already familiar with the Windows **Color** dialog box, which is already used in many Windows functions—for instance, choosing a background color for the Desktop. Some users have stored some favorite color swatches in the **Color** dialog box for easy recall whenever they need them. If you prefer to use the Windows **Color** dialog box rather than the Adobe **Color Picker**, that can be arranged. From the Editor's menu bar, select **Edit, Preferences, General**. Then choose your preferred color choice tool from the **Color Picker** list.

Some *color modes* limit the number of colors in an image, and thus restrict the number of colors you can select from the **Color Picker** or save in the **Color Swatches** palette. See **63** **Change Color Mode**.

- The *saturation* tools—namely, the **Sponge** tool, **Dodge** tool, and **Burn** tool—apply some of the same tricks to a color image that a professional film developer would use in a darkroom to alter the color saturation and brightness at specific spots in an image. The **Sponge** tool is featured in **147** **Adjust Saturation for a Specific Area**, while the **Dodge** and **Burn** tools are both demonstrated in **140** **Lighten or Darken Part of an Image**.

At the bottom of the **Toolbox** are swatches that represent the two solid colors that your tools can put to use in applying color to an image. The reason there are *two* color swatches is that the swatch behind the first box, called the *background color*—is often used in blending or in removing one color to reveal another. The *foreground color*—the swatch on top—is used predominantly by the **Brush, Pencil, Paint Bucket**, and other tools to apply color directly to an image. To select a different color for either swatch, click that box. Then choose a color from the **Color Picker** that opens. (Choosing colors is the subject of **113** **Select a Color to Work With**.)

If you've chosen a color you'd like to reuse, you can add it to the **Color Swatches** palette. Select **Window, Color Swatches**. The **Swatches** palette opens. Scroll down if necessary and point to an empty square. The pointer turns into the **Eyedropper** tool. Click the square. The foreground color is added to the palette, and a dialog box asks you to provide a name so that you can retrieve it later. Enter a name and click **OK**. See **113** **Select a Color to Work With** for information on how to apply the newly added color.

111 About Tool Options

In the real world, you have hands to prepare a drawing or painting utensil—for instance, to attach a nib to it or apply a color or medium to it—and then you have your own motor skills to help tilt the brush in just the right direction, or to make a smooth or jagged stroke. In the virtual world of digital painting, not every variety of brush or pencil stroke can be simulated with just a click-and-drag operation of the mouse. To set up your painting tools in precisely the right way, Photoshop Elements gives you *options*. When you pick up a tool from the **Toolbox**, the horizontal **Options** bar near the top of the screen displays the options specific to that tool.

Some tools share identically named options, such as **Mode** and **Opacity**. For example, the **Brush** and **Impressionist Brush** tools are similar, so each has nearly the same set of options including a drop-down list of preset brush designs. Thankfully, the Editor never uses the same term to mean two or more different things for two or more different tools. So **Opacity** for the **Brush** tool is the same as **Opacity** for the **Impressionist Brush** tool, as well as for the **Paint Bucket** tool.

Other tools have options exclusive to them. For example, only the **Pencil** tool offers an **Auto Erase** option, which instructs the **Pencil** to apply the background color whenever you start drawing on an area that already contains the foreground color—the color you'd normally draw with. Imagine if your real-world pencil could apply a second, auxiliary color to an area whenever it "knew" it was drawing on top of matching graphite-colored paper. It's a unique feature, which is why **Auto Erase** is a unique option.

The **Pencil** tool draws freehand lines, so the **Options** bar displays more line-drawing options than you might have known existed. The **Brushes** menu near the left end of the tool's **Options** bar lets you select from a variety of preset pencil tips. This list gives you the choice of selecting one of several hundred unique pencils; the regular brush tools, the healing brush tools (for repairing spots), the replication brush tools (for cloning areas), and the eraser tools all have similar lists in the same place in the **Options** bar.

Before You Begin

✔ **110** About the Toolbox

See Also

→ **112** About Preset Manager

→ **113** Select a Color to Work With

 TIP

After you have set options for using a tool, you can return to its original settings. Click the tool symbol at the far left end of the **Options** bar, and from the pop-up menu that opens, select **Reset Tool**.

Brush Tool Options

Brushes Menu

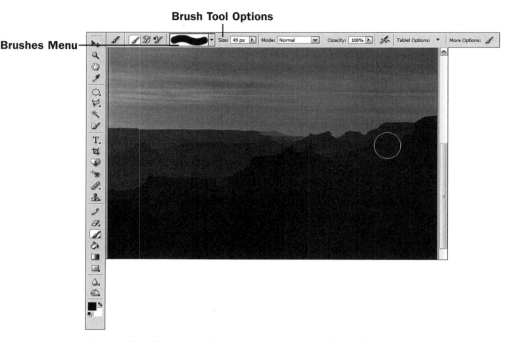

Few tools offer a broader range of options than the **Brush** tool. You can select from a variety of brush sizes and styles, and you have the opportunity to design your own brush. You can vary the opacity of a brush stroke from a thin film to total coverage. And you also have the advantage of two dozen *blend modes* that determine how the colors you add affect those that are already in the picture.

The most common options you will find among the Editor's tools are the following:

NOTE

You can often control the effect of a tool by specifying a low opacity, then repeating the application with multiple strokes. This approach is particularly effective when you use the **Airbrush** option of the **Brush** tool.

- **Brush style and size.** Open the **Brushes** menu on the **Options** bar to select brush tips of different sizes and styles. Some brush tips are solid; others have *feathered* edges. Different groupings or *libraries* of brush tips are available from the **Brushes** drop-down list on the **Brushes** menu. Here, you'll find special-purpose tips such as those that paint butterflies or maple leaves, or emulate faux finishes.

- **Opacity.** This setting determines the relative transparency of the paint you apply. Opacity is expressed as a percentage. A 100% opacity totally covers the surface you are applying it to; a 50% "coat of paint" lets about half the underlying picture show through. The **Brush, Pencil, Eraser, Paint Bucket,** and **Gradient** tools all have **Opacity** settings.

- **Tolerance**. When a tool that is working within an area of one color comes up against an area of a different color, the **Tolerance** setting governs how much of that difference is to be treated as significant, and how much is to be ignored. For example, the **Paint Bucket** tool is designed to spread paint over a large area—often an area of *roughly* the same color. Here, the **Tolerance** setting determines exactly what the tool considers to be "the same color." A high **Tolerance** setting covers areas of similar color, such as the varied tones of a sky. A low **Tolerance** setting covers only the selected color and those very close to it: If you apply the tool to a dark blue in the sky, the paint will not flow onto lighter blues.

- **Feather**. When you apply a color, you sometimes want a sharp edge. At other times, you might want to blend the color into its surroundings. A feathered edge helps you make that blend; the larger the **Feather** setting, the more gradual the blend. Some tools let you set the amount of feathering; with others, you can select a feathered brush.

- **Anti-Aliased**. This selection smoothes edges by averaging the colors at the boundary. Because digital images are made up of square pixels, sometimes you don't want boundaries to look like they're made up of stacked squares. *Anti-aliasing* provides the illusion of smoothness by varying the opacity of the blocks along the edges that show the sharpest corners. The final effect, up close, looks like blunting a serrated knife.

- **Use All Layers**. This instructs the Editor to sample the contents of an image not only from the layer on which you're currently drawing or painting or making selections, but from every layer in the entire image. This way, if there's a yellow border on an otherwise bluish background you want your tool to pay attention to, but you're painting on the layer with the bluish background and that yellow border exists on a different layer, **Use All Layers** instructs the tool to pay attention to the yellow border. With this option turned off, the tool ignores that border.

- **Aligned**. When you're using one of the replication tools or the **Healing Brush** tool, you're copying a pattern from one spot of an image to the spot directly beneath your brush. You generally want the location of the spot you're copying *from* to move in tandem with the spot you're copying *to*. But for in-between brush strokes, you might want the "from" spot to continue to follow your tool, or

NOTE

The **Size** setting for a brush tip is expressed in *pixels*, which means that size may vary depending on the resolution of the image you're drawing on. For instance, by default, when you create a new image from scratch in the Editor, it assigns a resolution of 72 *PPI*. With that low resolution, a 10-pixel-wide brush tip might be fairly thick. But when you load an imported digital photo, whose resolution can range from 200 to 600 PPI, the same brush tip can produce a very fine point.

you might want it to snap back to where it started. With the **Aligned** option enabled, the "from" spot always follows your brush, which is important when you're cloning *objects*. With the option disabled, the "from" spot snaps back to its origin at the end of a brushstroke, which is important when you're copying *shades of color*. You see the differences demonstrated in **162** **Remove Unwanted Objects from an Image**.

KEY TERM

Neighboring pixels—Pixels that physically touch each other. When trying to judge which pixels will by affected by a change, only pixels that match the criteria *and* that touch the original pixel you click or another matching pixel are included.

- **Contiguous**. When a tool operates on areas of an image with the same or similar color, the **Contiguous** option designates whether such areas must be comprised of *neighboring pixels* (which happens when the option is enabled), or of all pixels of the same or similar color throughout the entire selection or the entire image (which happens when the option is disabled).

Blend Modes

The **Mode** option is one of the most powerful—and yet underused—features of Photoshop Elements. You'll find that most editing procedures at some point are comprised of *putting something new on top of something old*. This is true whether you're applying new paint to an old background, moving a new layer on top of an old layer, or creating a new shape to fit on top of an existing element of a photo. When you put something on top of something else, Photoshop Elements wants to know what it should do to create the result: Does the new stuff replace the old stuff completely? Does the new stuff represent a transparency that lets some of the old material show through? And if so, what old material shows through and what gets replaced? Or does the new stuff represent a pattern for what parts of the old stuff get changed somehow? And if so, what constitutes the change? All these questions are answered through one major setting: **Mode**.

KEY TERM

Blend modes—Settings that govern the way colors interact when placed on top of each other. Some modes darken, others lighten, and others combine the colors in varying proportions. Blend modes can be applied with any of several tools when colors are combined. Common situations include applying a brush to an existing picture and correcting colors by blending layers.

Open the **Mode** drop-down list in the **Options** bar and select from two dozen different *blend modes*. When you apply color with a brush or other tool, the blend mode determines how the color being applied alters the colors already in the image.

The best way to describe how blend modes work is to show each one in action. To do this, I assembled two test patterns. One is the *source*, containing the layer to be copied. The other is the *target*, on top of which the copied layer will be placed. The source pattern is made up of four corners, labeled S, K, L, and J. The source's background is made up of a *gradient* that fills, left to right, from black to white. At corners K and L, opacity was reduced to 50%; at corners S and J, opacity was left at 100%. Three horizontal gradient stripes appear in the middle of the source image, graduating from red to yellow, cyan to green, and blue to magenta. All colors in these stripes are at full intensity. You can see the colors more clearly in the example reproductions in the Color Gallery. The target pattern is Abe's head from the Lincoln Memorial, set against a gradient background that graduates from top to bottom, blue to green to red. The background colors here are at *half* intensity.

TIP

The brush tools include two extra blend modes (not shown here, and not *really* blend modes) that do not apply to copying layers or selections: The **Behind** mode paints only on the transparent part of a layer. Using this mode is like painting on the back of transparent areas of a sheet of acetate. The **Clear** mode paints transparency onto an area, as if transparency were a paint. Neither mode works when painting on top of the **Background layer**, which has no transparent base, so no part of it can be made transparent.

Source

Target

The source image is a combination of colors and opacities. The target image is a photo with a gradient as a background.

With that setup out of the way, here are the blend modes used by Photoshop Elements:

- **Normal.** Source pixels *replace* target pixels. The **Opacity** setting of the source pixels determine the extent to which that replacement is made: totally (**Opacity** = 100) or partially (**Opacity** < 100). With **Opacity** set to less than 100, a percentage of source colors equal to 100 minus the **Opacity** setting is mixed with target colors. In square K, notice how the half-opaque light pixels brighten Abe's forehead and the background behind it, and in square L, how the half-opaque dark pixels darken that area. **Normal** is the default blend mode for all painting and all layer copying operations.

- **Dissolve.** Gives you the opportunity to apply some visual effects and relies entirely on the **Opacity** setting. When you set **Opacity** to less than 100, rather than making the blend color partially transparent, **Dissolve** removes pixels from the source at random locations to let target pixels show through. So if you're using a brush tool, your tool color might or might not overwrite the target pixel—the lower the **Opacity** value, the less likely your tool will do so. When you're laying one layer atop another, **Dissolve** covers up some pixels in the next layer entirely, while letting others show through; the higher the **Opacity** setting, the fewer of the lower-layer pixels show through. In the example, notice how the half-opaque squares K and L look fuzzy, while S and J were copied at full opacity.

- **Darken.** Source pixels are blended with target pixels only when they are *darker* than the target pixels. If you're using a brush tool to apply the blend color, **Darken** adds the color only when the result is *darker* than the existing color. The **Opacity** setting determines the extent of the darkening effect. Notice in the example that bright pixels in squares K and J have little or no effect on the right side of Abe's head, while squares S and L darken their respective target regions.

- **Multiply.** Compounds the darkness of source pixels with the darkness of target pixels so that the result is always darker. This blend mode most closely simulates the effect of laying one color transparency over another and projecting one light through both. What distinguishes **Multiply** from **Darken** mode is that, with **Multiply**, *all* pixels from the source darken all pixels in the target, to the extent that they are dark. With **Darken**, when a source pixel isn't darker than the target to begin with, its effects are discarded; with **Multiply**, if a source pixel is one unit darker than bright white, it darkens the corresponding target pixel by one unit. This is why you can see the faint K" and "J in the **Multiply** example, while they're almost invisible in the **Darken** example.

- **Color Burn.** A complex blend mode that also takes contrast adjustment into account. Dark and highly saturated (richly colored) pixels in the source darken pixels in the target, increase their saturation (technically, brightening them), and transfer their color value to the target. But also, pixels in the source with low saturation (blacks, grays, and whites) but high opacity borrow color data from *surrounding* pixels and apply that data to the target area, darkening it in the process. This expands areas of rich saturation from surrounding areas, resulting in higher-contrast areas where differing or opposite colors collide with, or come closer to, one another. Opaque, light, unsaturated pixels can *darken* opaque, dark, saturated ones. Notice in the example how the bright pixels in square J *darken* Abe's cheek. Up close, you can see how the highlight on his cheekbone in square J is pinker—the saturation there has been increased.

- **Linear Burn.** Applies a similar burn technique as **Color Burn**, but the difference here involves opacity. With **Linear Burn**, the pixels in the target are both darkened and saturated by exactly as much as the source pixels are *opaque*. So in the example, in square S, the dark and unsaturated pixels in the source not only darken Abe's forehead but add pinks and browns. Although square J has lighter pixels in its source, they too darkened and saturated the target by exactly as much as square S did. But squares K and L, which are 50% opaque, left Abe's face closer to its original saturation. Meanwhile, the richly saturated color stripes in the source not only transferred their hue value to the target, but compounded the saturation. So while **Color Burn** left Abe's nose white, **Linear Burn** turned it as blue-green as the center of the source.

- **Lighten.** Applies the source or target color, whichever is *lighter*, as the result color. Pixels darker than the blend color are replaced, and pixels lighter than the blend color do not change. The result is always the lightest of the two, although its brightness value is unchanged. Notice in the example how none of the dark pixels in squares S and L translated to the target. Square J is mostly lighter than the target, so it mostly occluded the target. Meanwhile, the 50% opaque square K lightened the right side of the target without overwriting it entirely.

- **Screen.** Compounds the lightness of the source pixels with the lightness of the target pixels, so the result color is *always* lighter. The effect is similar to projecting light from two photographic slides onto the same "screen," thus the title. With **Screen**, all pixels from the source lighten all pixels in the target to the extent that they are light. So in the example, even the very slight brightness of the gray pixels in square S brightens pixels near the bridge of Abe's nose.

- **Color Dodge.** A complex blend mode that involves borrowing color value from surrounding pixels. Light and highly saturated (richly colored) pixels in the source lighten and brighten pixels in the target and transfer their color value to the target. But also, pixels in the source with low saturation (blacks, grays, and whites) but high opacity borrow color data from *surrounding* pixels and apply that data to the target area, brightening it in the process. Areas of rich saturation are expanded into nearby light areas, introducing new areas of direct and sharp contrast. Notice in the example how the light gray letter *L* brings in red values from the gradient and from Abe's face, rendering the formerly green area bright yellow. And notice also how the lighter areas in squares K and J make the right edge of the target bright cyan and yellow, respectively. Meanwhile, the full color value of the three color bands is transferred to the target, leaving white areas white but rendering dark areas bright with color. The dark pixels at the left of the source have no effect on the target.

- **Linear Dodge.** Applies a similar dodge technique as **Color Dodge**, but the difference here is that **Linear Dodge** brightens and saturates pixels in the target by as much as the source pixels are both bright and opaque. Dark, opaque pixels have little effect on the target, but opaque *midtones* brighten the target by the degree of their opacity. This is how the dark-ish letter *K* in the example makes a light mark on Abe's hair, even though the half-opaque pixels in the source are actually lighter than the *K*. This is also why the equally opaque letter *S* brightens its target area, while its dark surroundings have no effect. Meanwhile, the full-intensity color bands brighten the dark zones in Abe's face, leaving the white zones white.

- **Overlay.** Applies the formula for the **Multiply** mode to dark target pixels and the formula for the **Screen** mode to light target pixels. The result is that lights compound with lights and darks compound with darks. The result includes more stark contrasts with fewer middle values. The **Overlay** mode is one way to create a ghostly image of one layer on top of another, especially at less than full opacity.

- **Soft Light.** A different combination of the **Multiply** and **Screen** modes, with similar results except with less augmented saturation. To compound both brightness and darkness, the source and target pixels are both blended using **Multiply**, then the product is multiplied back into the inverse of the source. Separately, both source and target are blended using **Screen**, with the result multiplied back into the source. The two interim results—darker darks and lighter lights, but with less dramatic saturation—are then added together, resulting in more natural saturation. As you can see in the example, the differences between **Soft Light** and **Overlay** are subtle, but noticeable.

- **Hard Light.** Applies the formula for the **Multiply** mode to dark *source* pixels (as opposed to **Overlay**, which tests the *target* pixels), and the formula for the **Screen** mode to light source pixels. The result with **Hard Light** is that the source (what you're adding) becomes more prominent than the target; with **Overlay**, the target (what you're adding *to*) remains prominent.

- **Vivid Light.** A blend of **Color Dodge** and **Color Burn** modes, applying the dodge formula to light target pixels and the burn formula to dark target pixels. The result contains either very highly saturated bright pixels or highly unsaturated dark pixels. Middle gray values in the source make the least impact on the target. Whereas the bright whites in squares K and J in our example leave the right side of the target bright cyan and yellow, the gray values from the source leave the subtle midtones in Abe's face largely untouched.

- **Linear Light.** A blend of **Linear Burn** and **Linear Dodge** modes, applying the burn formula to dark pixels in the target and the dodge formula to light pixels in the target. The result has greater impact on the overall lightness of pixels than on their saturation. Notice in the example how the patterns in the color bands are less graduated. For instance, in Abe's beard, the darkest darks were made more prominent by adding blue (the color from the dark side of the source, if you will); whereas the lightest lights were made more prominent by adding magenta from the light side.

- **Pin Light.** Uses a combination of the **Lighten** and **Darken** formulas. In essence, when pixels from the source are already significantly darker than the target, the **Darken** formula is applied to blend those dark pixels with the target; when pixels from the source are already significantly lighter than the target, the **Lighten** formula blends them with the target. But there's a notable bias against middle values, such as 50% gray. In the example, notice how the middle gray value on the right side of square S did *not* darken the center of Abe's forehead, and the same middle gray value on the left side of square J did *not* brighten the shadow under Abe's nose. So middle luminance values in the source are always tossed out of consideration; only extreme values apply.

- **Hard Mix.** Uses simpler mathematics to come up with a psychedelic, posterized result: When the source and target are combined, the hue components of the result are reset either to full strength (255) or no strength (0). The result is comprised only of basic primary colors (red, green, blue), secondary colors (cyan, magenta, yellow), black, and white. In the example, the only reason some middle tones remain in squares K and L is because the opacity for those squares at the source was 50%.

- **Difference.** Subtracts the RGB color values of the source pixels from those of the target pixels. The result is often a completely different color than the original target color. How different that is, is proportional to the difference between the source and target colors—thus, the name of the blend mode. It helps to remember these rules: First, black is considered "zero," and subtracting zero from anything leaves you with what you had to begin with. Second, subtracting a color from itself results in black. Third, subtracting double a color's value results in that same value, so medium gray minus white equals medium gray. Notice in the example how the half-opaque whites in square K ended up making the background of that square entirely middle gray from top to bottom, whereas the bright whites in square J made the background behind Abe's neck graduate from pink to cyan (as opposed to green to blue).

- **Exclusion.** In some ways the opposite of **Difference**, but with a twist: Unlike **Difference**, **Exclusion** mode *adds* the RGB color values of the source and the target pixels. But to bring the result back to the reality range of 0–255, twice the average of the source and target values are subtracted from the sum. **Exclusion**'s results are similar to **Difference**'s when the differences between the source and target are extreme. But as the example shows, when the differences are more negligible, the result is a middle value. Notice how the middle grays actually blur into one another in the center of Abe's head with **Exclusion** mode, whereas they created stark contrasts for **Difference** mode.

- **Hue.** Substitutes the hue component of the target pixels with that of the source pixels, leaving saturation and luminance intact. In the example, Abe's hair, the bridge of his nose, and his beard are all now slightly tinted. But the unsaturated portions of all four squares did create noticeable color *noise* behind Abe's head. This is because grayscales are all considered "Hue #0," so the unsaturated pixels' hue value is being applied to the target even when there's no color in those pixels.

- **Saturation.** Substitutes the saturation component of the target pixels with that of the source pixels, leaving hue and luminance intact. In the example, the fully opaque squares S and J removed all saturation from the target, so the result is as unsaturated as the source. The half-opaque squares K and L let some original color show through. But the fully opaque, fully saturated color bands "went to town" with the middle values in Abe's face. The light pixels look untouched because white is considered fully saturated, while any fully saturated hue ends up translating to white anyway. So the white on the bridge of Abe's nose, where it was white before, is actually "very light green."

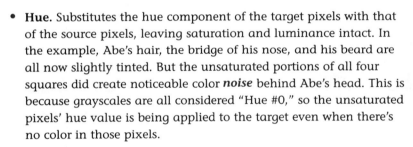

- **Color.** Substitutes the hue and saturation components of the target pixels with those of the source pixels, leaving the luminance component intact. Result pixels, therefore, are as light or as dark as they were before, but they might be colored. Technically, "color" is achieved by mixing hue and saturation (consider that there is no hue that represents shades such as russet, cobalt, and aquamarine). In the example, squares S and J are now unsaturated, as they were in the source. But as color is added by the color bands, the contrasts in Abe's face remain as they were.

- **Luminosity.** Substitutes the luminance (or "luminosity") component of the target pixels with that of the source pixels, leaving the hue and saturation components intact. This leaves target pixels colored as they were before, but made blacker or whiter by the source. Notice in the example how the color bands lent nothing but their brightness to the result.

112 About the Preset Manager

Before You Begin

✔ **110** About the Toolbox

✔ **111** About Tool Options

See Also

→ **113** Select a Color to Work With

Photoshop Elements can present a bewildering variety of *presets*: brushes, swatches, gradients, and *patterns* you can use when painting directly onto an image. The Preset Manager helps you keep track of them. It serves as a console for gathering all the materials you use in painting and drawing into accessible groups or *libraries* that you can easily recall from the **Options** bar. This way, you never lose a brush tip or the perfect gradient pattern in the endless sea of choices.

To open the Preset Manager, from the *Editor*'s main menu, select **Edit, Preset Manager**. Here, you can collect your favorite brush tips and save them in a library you can reload when you want to use them. You also can choose from libraries of brushes, swatches, gradients, and patterns. Open the **Preset Type** list to select one of these options.

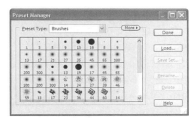

*The **Preset Manager** dialog box.*

Preset Manager already compartmentalizes several libraries. To choose one and open its contents, click the **More** button and choose the library's name from those listed in the last section on the menu.

You can select part of a picture and save it as a brush. Select the area you'd like to use—perhaps a round, button-shaped object like an animal's eye or the headlight of a car. Then select **Edit, Define Brush from Selection**. In the dialog box that opens, enter a name for the brush and click **OK**. The brush is included in of the current brush library. You can use it as you would any other brush tip.

To save the current brush settings, such as those for the **Brush** tool, open the **Brushes** menu on the **Options** bar, select the brush library you want to add your brush to from the **Brushes** drop-down list, click the right arrow button, and choose **Save Brush**. Type a **Name** and click **OK**.

 TIP

In the upper section of the **More** menu, choose how you want the presets displayed in the **Preset Manager**. For example, you can display the presets using **Large Thumbnails** or in a **Small List** (with small thumbnails and the preset name).

Select part of a picture such as the headlight of this hot rod and save it as a brush.

TIPS

You can also load a library by clicking the **Load** button in the **Preset Manager** window. For example, you might load a library of presets you've created yourself. Instead of replacing the current library, this option *adds* the new library to the presets that are already there. The combined library is available as long as it remains open. If you want to save it permanently, click **Save Set** and save it under a new library name.

The **Replace** menu option on the **More** menu enables you to load the presets stored in a separate library.

You also can select a preset and click the **Delete** button to delete a preset from the library. But it is usually better to leave the current library intact and to exclude the unwanted preset when you select items for a custom library

Suppose that you have a custom brush or two you have created and also some standard brushes you use often. You can save them in a new library that you can recall whenever you want to use these brushes. From the *Editor's* main menu, select **Edit, Preset Manager**. The **Preset Manager** opens and displays the brushes in the current library. Select the brushes you want to place in the new library then click the **Save Set** button. Give the new library a name and click **Save**. You can find this library again by clicking the **More** button.

You can save a custom preset library in any folder you want. However, if you save it in the Photoshop Elements **Presets** folder with other presets of its type (for example, save a brushes library in the **Brushes** subfolder), the custom library will be listed when you click the Preset Manager's **More** button.

With the **Brush** tool, when you open the **Brushes** menu on the **Options** bar, a list of **Default Brushes** appears. If you prefer the **Calligraphic Brush** tips instead, you can use the Preset Manager to make those tips appear by default, for all the brush tools such as the **Selection Brush**, **Clone Stamp**, and **Pencil**. Just select the library you want use from the **More** menu. Then open the **More** menu again and choose **Replace Brushes** to set the current library to the default.

If a preset has a name that doesn't suit you, change it to something more descriptive. Click the preset in the listing and then click the **Rename** button. In the **Name** dialog box that appears, enter the new name you want to use and then click **OK**. You're returned to the Preset Manager.

To restore the original library that was shipped with Photoshop Elements, select **Reset** on the **More** menu.

113 Select a Color to Work With

Before You Begin

✔ **110** About the Toolbox

✔ **111** About Tool Options

See Also

→ **63** Change Color Mode

→ **114** Select a Color Already in Your Image

→ **115** Draw on a Photo with a Pencil

At the bottom of the **Toolbox** is the foreground/background color control. Use it to set both foreground and background colors. Photoshop uses the *foreground color* to paint or fill selections and the *background color* to fill in the erased areas of the *background layer*. These colors are also used jointly by the **Gradient** tool as well as by some *filters* such as the **Clouds** filter.

By default, the foreground color is black and the background color is white. You can select a new foreground or background color from the **Color Picker** or the **Color Swatches** *palette*. You can also pick up the color to use from the image, with the **Eyedropper** tool. See **114** **Select a Color Already in Your Image**.

Within the foreground/background color control are two small icons. To return to the original black-and-white selections, click the small squares in the lower-left corner, or press the **D** key on your keyboard. To swap the foreground and background colors, click the curved arrow in the upper-right corner or press **X**.

1 **Click Foreground/Background Color Swatch**

Open an image in the *Editor* in **Standard Edit** mode and save it in Photoshop (***.psd**) format. In the **Layers** *palette*, select the layer you want to work on. Select a tool from the **Toolbox**.

Click the foreground color swatch or the background color swatch at the bottom of the **Toolbox**. The **Color Picker** opens. Unless you have made another selection, it is the Adobe **Color Picker**. You use this dialog box to select a color by choosing from a color spectrum or by defining colors numerically.

2 **Select a Color Visually**

In the middle of the **Color Picker**, the currently chosen color's components are displayed as two groups of three components each: **HSB** and **RGB**. Beside each component is an option button. When you click one of these buttons, the vertical **color slider** in the middle of the dialog box displays the complete spectrum of possible settings for that component, in the context of the current settings for the other components. The big, square **color field** on the left of the dialog box displays all the possible variations you can make to the *other two* components in the chosen triplet.

For example, when you enable **H** (hue), the **color slider** reveals the full spectrum of hues at full intensity. You can click one of these hues in the slider to set the **H** value. Meanwhile, the **color field** changes to show all possible shades—light and dark—of the hue you've chosen. You can also click a spot in the **color field** to pick a color. This action changes the **S** and **B** values as well. If you proceed from here and enable **S** (saturation), the **color slider** changes to reveal the entire spectrum of saturation choices, while the **color field** reveals your array of choices with the same saturation, but with different hues (horizontally) and brightness (vertically). Your current hue choice is indicated by a circle in the **color field**.

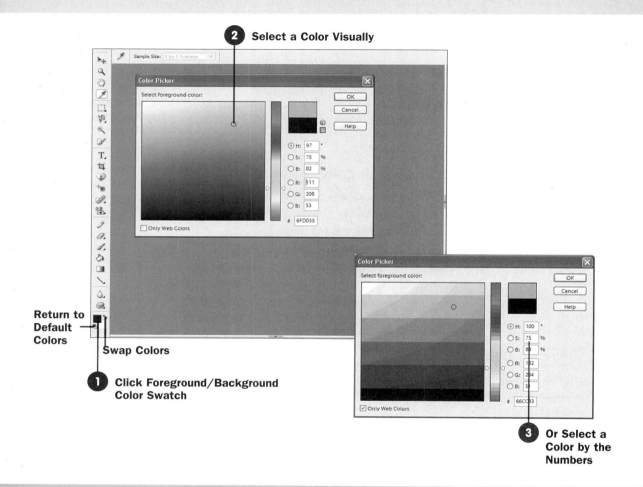

② Select a Color Visually

Return to
Default
Colors

Swap Colors

① Click Foreground/Background
Color Swatch

③ Or Select a
Color by the
Numbers

You might notice a stacked pair of colored rectangles in the upper-right corner of the **Color Picker**. The lower rectangle shows the original *foreground color* or **background color** at the time you opened the dialog box; the upper rectangle shows the new color you have selected. This allows you to compare the two colors, which can be an important consideration if you are choosing a color as an adjustment to an existing color you've absorbed with the **Eyedropper** tool. See **114** **Select a Color Already In Your Image** for details on absorbing existing colors.

The Editor recognizes a small subset of the color palette—specifically, 216 combinations—as *Web-safe colors*. These are the hues that
can be accurately reproduced by both Windows and Macintosh
Web browsers, when either system is set to display only the minimum of 256 colors. (The 40 colors that do not translate well are
excluded.) There are two ways you can address the problem of
choosing colors that might not translate accurately to low-color
systems:

NOTE

The foreground color
swatch is on the left; the
background color swatch is
on the right.

- To have the **color field** show only shades from this limited
  palette, enable the **Only Web Colors** check box in the lower-
  left corner of the **Color Picker**. Instead of the infinite spectrum that was previously available, the **Color Picker** displays
  only what are known as *Web-safe colors*. If you already chose
  a color, that choice is changed to the nearest Web-safe alternative.

- Next to the sample rectangle for the **original color** (the foreground color chosen at the time you opened this dialog box),
  you might see an **Alert Cube**. This symbol serves as a gentle,
  if unintuitive, indication that you have not chosen a Web-
  safe color. If your objective is *not* to make certain this image
  can be seen by the few remaining users of NCSA Mosaic on a
  Macintosh II, you can safely ignore this warning.

NOTE

The number of colors in the
Color Picker is limited by
the number of colors in the
image. To change color
modes—and the number of
colors allowed in an
image—see **63** Change
Color Mode.

❸ Or Select a Color by the Numbers

You can specify a color by entering its description on one of three
numerical scales in the right side of the **Color Picker**:

- **RGB.** Enter the values of red, green, and blue that make up
  the color, using a scale of 0 to 255 for each component. For
  example, a pure red is R255, G0, B0. A medium orange has
  the values R228, G135, B42.

- **HSB.** Here, the three values you enter to define a color indicate hue, *saturation*, and brightness. The hue is indicated by
  the number of degrees in a standard color wheel, the saturation and brightness by percentages of their maximum values.
  On this scale, orange has the values H30, S82, B89.

- **HTML.** HTML color codes are used in hypertext markup language, the programming language of the World Wide Web.
  This is a single value, using six digits preceded by a pound

TIP

You also can pick a color from the **Swatches** palette. To display this palette, from the Editor's menu bar, select **Window, Color Swatches**. To set a new foreground color, click that color; to set a background color, **Ctrl**+click that color.

sign. The digits express the RGB values on a hexadecimal scale. The first two digits contain the red value, the second two the green value, and the final two the blue. In this notation, lime green color appears as #6FD035.

Enter the values you want to use on any of the three scales. The other scales automatically display their versions of the values you just entered.

To finalize your color choice, click **OK**.

Select a Color Already in Your Image

See Also

→ **113** Select a Color to Work With

Suppose you need to duplicate a color from an existing image. You might want to duplicate the exact shade of blue in a corporate logo or the bright plumage of a rare bird. You can try to emulate the color using a **Color Picker**, or you might try to find it in a color swatch. There is a quicker and more accurate alternative: select the color directly from the picture.

KEY TERMS

Sample size—The area from which a color is derived by computing the average color of the pixels in that area.

Neighboring pixels—Pixels that physically touch each other.

Select the **Eyedropper** tool, point to the picture, and click the shade you want to duplicate. It's nearly as simple as that. You do have one decision to make, though: the size of the sample the tool should retrieve. The **Eyedropper** offers three options. If you choose **Point Sample**, the **Eyedropper** tool picks up the color of the specific pixel you click. That's fine if you are selecting from an area of solid color such as a logo. It's not so fine if you are selecting from an area of varied color such as the feathers of a bird. There's a good chance that the specific pixel you select will not accurately represent the overall color of the bird. You might click in a shadow and pick up a dull color instead of the bright hue you were hoping for. To compensate, you can adjust the sample size to average the colors of several *neighboring pixels*. Open the **Sample Size** drop-down list in the **Options** bar and choose either **3 by 3 Average** or **5 by 5 Average**.

❶ Select the Eyedropper Tool

Open the image in the *Editor* in **Standard Edit** mode and save it in Photoshop (***.psd**) format. In the **Layers** *palette*, select the layer that contains the color you want to pick up from the image and use.

Click the **Eyedropper** tool in the upper section of the **Toolbox**.

1 **Select the Eyedropper Tool**

3 **Select the Color**

2 **Select a Sample Size**

2 Select a Sample Size

On the **Options** bar, select the **Sample Size** you want to use. This option affects whether the tool samples the specific color from one point or samples the average of all colors in a three- to five-pixel radius from that point.

3 Select the Color

Click in the image to sample a pixel or pixels, and make that sample the foreground color. To sample for the *background color* instead, press Alt as you click the image.

Make changes using the color you've picked up and your tool of choice. After you're satisfied with the result, make any other changes you want, then save the result in JPEG or TIFF format,

 TIP

To quickly borrow the **Eyedropper** while you're busy with one of the drawing tools, don't switch tools from the **Toolbox**. Instead, just hold down the **Alt** key. Your pointer becomes the **Eyedropper**. Click any point on *any* open image (not just the one you're drawing on) to absorb a new foreground color. Then release the **Alt** key and continue painting.

leaving your PSD image with its *layers* (if any) intact so that you can return at a later time and make different adjustments if you want.

In this example, I sampled the orange in the bird's head and used it as the color for the text I added to label this image of an oriole. See **183** Add a Text Caption or Label for more about adding simple captions like this one to an image.

115 Draw on a Photo with a Pencil

See Also

→ **111** About Tool Options
→ **112** About Preset Manager
→ **120** About Drawing Shapes

The **Pencil** and **Brush** tools are close cousins. You can use either to draw on a picture. The main difference is that the **Brush** tool is intended to create often fluffy strokes of color; the **Pencil** is designed to create hard-edged lines. You might use the **Brush** to add a swath of color or *pattern* across an image. A typical use of the **Pencil** would be to annotate a picture, such as pointing to a critical element.

1 Select the Pencil Tool

Open the image in the *Editor* in **Standard Edit** mode and save it in Photoshop (***.psd**) format. In the **Layers** palette, select the layer on which you want to draw.

In the **Toolbox**, select the **Pencil** tool. You can click the tool's icon, or you can press the keyboard shortcut **N**.

2 Select Options

The **Pencil** tool draws freehand lines, so the **Options** bar lets you select from a variety of preset pencil lines and patterns. You also can select a blend **Mode** and **Opacity** setting. These settings are explained in **111** About Tool Options.

To choose a pencil tip, open the first drop-down list in the **Options** bar. In the palette that appears, from the **Brushes** list, choose a library or leave the current library set to **Default Brushes**. Scroll the list to see examples of each tip and choose one by clicking directly on the example. Here, I selected the second preset from the top, which was indicated by a tiny, hard point and the number **3**. This selection results in a pencil tip that applies a line three pixels wide.

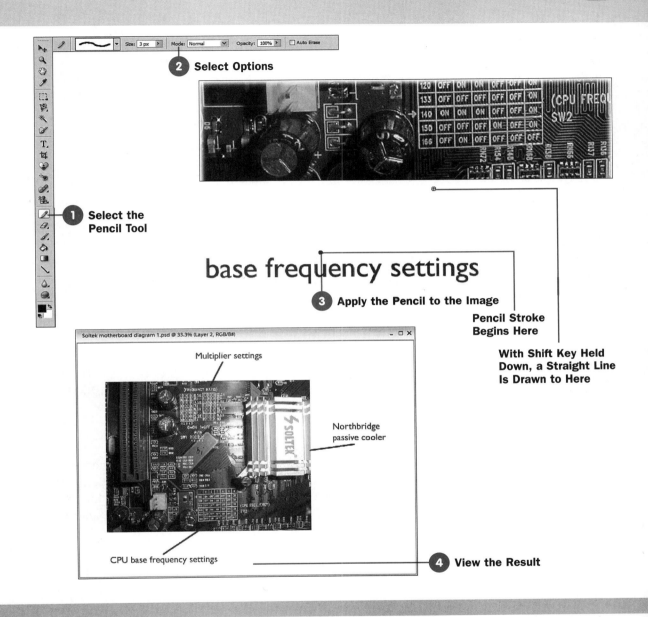

Select Options ②

Select the Pencil Tool ①

Apply the Pencil to the Image ③

base frequency settings

Pencil Stroke Begins Here

With Shift Key Held Down, a Straight Line Is Drawn to Here

Soltek motherboard diagram 1.psd @ 33.3% (Layer 2, RGB/8#)

Multiplier settings

Northbridge passive cooler

CPU base frequency settings

View the Result ④

When you select a preset, other options in the **Options** bar are adjusted as necessary to reflect the selection. For example, selecting a three-pixel preset automatically sets the **Size** option to 3 pixels.

NOTE

The **Brushes** list obviously shows preset options that apply to the brush tools as well as to the **Pencil** tool. Among these options are several soft and fuzzy strokes, which appear to contradict the definition of the **Pencil** tool as a device for hard-edged lines. You can choose a soft-edged brush tip for the **Pencil** tool; however, when you apply it, you'll note that none of the softness of that tip is applied to the **Pencil**. A chosen tip might be as wide or as spotty as shown in the list, but never as soft when used with the **Pencil**.

TIP

To draw a straight line between points, release the mouse button. For a pen tablet, lift the pen. Move the pointer to where you want the end of the line (or, to be geometrically accurate, the "line segment") to appear. Press **Shift** and then click this point. You can continue drawing from here—either a freehand mark or another straight line segment.

Your image might have many layers whose contents simultaneously occupy a single point on an image. While you're drawing, if you need to see a list of all layers that have contents at a given point, hold down **Ctrl** and right-click that point. A pop-up menu lists the names of all layers at that point. Select a layer from this list and continue.

The **Auto Erase** option is unique to the **Pencil** tool. When this option is enabled, the **Pencil** paints the background color whenever the pencil stroke begins on a spot containing the *foreground color*. If you carefully select the foreground and background colors, you can use this option to replace one color with another.

3 **Apply the Pencil to the Image**

Begin the pencil stroke by clicking and holding the mouse button where you want to start drawing. For a pen tablet, position the pointer by hovering the pen, then tap and hold the pen where you want the stroke to begin.

To draw a freehand stroke, continue holding the button down as you drag the mouse. The mark you draw will follow your pointer.

To draw a straight horizontal or vertical line, press **Shift** now and continue dragging the mouse. The Editor senses whether you intend for the line to move up, right, left, or down, by the general direction in which you're moving the mouse—it doesn't have to be exact.

To change pencil tips at any time, right-click the image. The **Brush Presets** palette appears. Choose a new tip from the **Brushes** list then click the **X** button to dismiss the palette.

4 **View the Result**

After you're satisfied with the result, make any other changes you want, then save the PSD image. Resave the result in JPEG or TIFF format, leaving your PSD image with its layers (if any) intact so that you can return at a later time and make different adjustments if you want.

Here, I used the **Pencil** tool to help create some basic callouts for a diagram. The textual callouts, of course, were produced with the **Horizontal Type** tool; but once those text passages were in place, I was able to select the **Pencil** tool, choose a foreground color, pick up a nine-pixel wide tool tip (which is actually quite narrow for an image with high *resolution*), click next to the text, hold down **Shift**, and click what I wanted the callout text to point to. The entire job took just seconds.

116 Paint an Area of a Photo with a Brush

The **Pencil** draws lines; the **Brush** works in smoother, softer, and more variable strokes. For that and many other reasons, you probably will find the **Brush** a much more versatile tool. You can use it to fix someone's hair or darken their eyelashes. You can paint a flowery or leafy border around an image.

Among the **Brush** tool's host of options are the standard settings for the brush tip preset, which takes care of the tool's **Size**, **Mode**, and **Opacity**. These options can be set separately (see **111** **About Tool Options**). Also on the **Options** bar, the **More Options** button reveals just what it promises: a collection of *brush dynamics options* you can apply to the brush before you paint onto a picture. The dynamics settings are not critical, nor do you need to concern yourself with them every time you pick up the brush. Instead, they come into play when you want to have fun making a quintessentially unique tool that you can perhaps save in a library and use later. (See **112** **About Preset Manager** for details on creating and saving presets.) Among the dynamics options are settings for the rate at which a brush stroke fades out, and the rate at which patterns repeat themselves or change color.

1 Select the Brush Tool

Open an image in the *Editor* in **Standard Edit** mode and save it in Photoshop (***.psd**) format. In the **Layers** *palette*, select the layer you want to paint on. Select the **Brush** tool in the **Toolbox**. You can click the tool's icon, or you can press the keyboard shortcut **B**.

2 Set Tool Options

Select a brush tip, adjust its **Size**, and set other options such as **Mode** and **Opacity** as desired. Set the *foreground color* swatch at the bottom of the **Toolbox** to the color you want to apply with the brush.

3 Specify More Options

To indulge yourself with settings that create unique and imaginative tools, click the **More Options** button on the **Options** bar to display **Additional Brush Options**. Adjust the settings for the following options to get the effect you're looking for:

Before You Begin

✔ **110** About the Toolbox

✔ **113** Select a Color to Work With

See Also

→ **115** Draw on a Photo with a Pencil

1 Select the Brush Tool

2 Set Tool Options

3 Specify More Options

4 Apply Brush to the Image

5 View the Result

- **Spacing.** All brush strokes are actually made up of repeated points of an applied pattern. The appearance of a smooth and uninterrupted stroke is actually an illusion. For all brush strokes, the Editor determines how far the tool must travel on the image before it deposits another spot of paint. Each deposit is called a *step*. The **Spacing** setting expresses the gap between steps as a percentage of the brush's current **Size** setting. At 100%, for example, the pointer will leave gaps that are the same diameter as the brush **Size**. At a lesser percentage, the steps are spaced more closely together; and at a *much* lesser percentage, the spotting becomes unnoticeable. At 500%, the stroke leaves gaps that are five times the size of the brush **Size**. This might be what you want if you need an instant dotted line or a string of cloud puffs.

- **Fade**. This setting enables a brushstroke to "run out of steam," like a paint brush going dry. It is expressed as the number of steps before the brush runs out of paint. With a high **Spacing** value, set **Fade** low to be noticeable; if **Spacing** is set low, more steps will take place for any given brushstroke length, so set **Fade** higher to avoid running out of paint early. When **Fade** is set to **0**, the brush never runs out of paint.

- **Hue Jitter.** This setting enables the brushstroke to vary the shade of each step, on occasion or often, between the foreground and background colors. When set to 100%, the brush frequently alternates between these two colors. At a lower percentage, the brushstroke varies less frequently; and at *much* lower percentages (but still above 0%), the brush occasionally applies subtle blends between the foreground and background colors.

- **Hardness**. Expressed as a percentage, **Hardness** governs the relative amount of each brushstroke step that is devoted to *pure tone*. The remainder is used for blending the paint color with its surroundings. For example, a 33% setting designates that the core one-third of the step is devoted to pure, unblended color. This is important, because if you choose a hollow brush tip such as an unfilled star, in order for some portion of each brush step to be pure color, the **Hardness** setting must be extended past the area of hollowness. At a 100% setting, no part of the brush stroke is made up of blended color (making the brush tip the equivalent of using the **Pencil** tool); at 0%, no part is made up of pure color.

- **Scatter**. Expressed as a percentage, the **Scatter** setting governs the maximum relative amount of displacement each step of the brushstroke can assume from the tip of the brush. Set at a high value, steps dance around the center of the tool. With an unusual brush tip pattern, such as stars, balloons, or blades of grass, a high **Scatter** setting lets you create instant pointillism and frivolity.

- **Angle**. This setting governs the tilt of the brush tip in degrees. Its range is −180° to +180°, with a positive setting twisting the brush tip counter-clockwise from straight east. With a round brush tip, this setting is inconsequential. For a

NOTE

The **Airbrush** option of the **Brush** tool changes the meaning of the **Spacing** dynamics setting. Although the range of values remains the same, it changes to refer not to distance between points on the page, but to *intervals of time*. The **Airbrush** applies paint for as long as you hold the mouse button down. So if you hold it down and move the pointer slowly, the **Airbrush** determines how long a period of *time* to wait to deposit the next step, based on how high **Spacing** has been set to. See **117** Paint an Area of a Photo with the Airbrush for details.

wedged tip, however, the **Angle** setting enables you to tilt the brush the way you'd tip the nib of a calligraphy pen, enabling such effects as thin side-to-side strokes and thick downstrokes.

- **Roundness.** A deceptively named setting. Expressed as a percentage, it actually governs the height of the brush tip (measuring from bottom to top). More accurately, it's an expression of the relative "un-flatness" of the brush tip. For a round brush tip, a high **Roundness** setting does make the tip more circular, but for a different shape (even one that isn't round), a high setting doesn't make the tip any rounder but does make it *taller*. A low setting makes the tip flatter. You can create a perfect rectangular calligraphy tip using a square brush tip preset with an **Angle** setting of –30° and a **Roundness** setting of 40%.

To use the same dynamics settings for any new brush tip you choose, enable the **Keep These Settings for All Brushes** check box. When you change to a new tip, and with this option enabled, all your scattering, jitter, fade, and other dynamics are retained.

④ Apply Brush to the Image

Begin the brushstroke by clicking and holding the mouse button where you want to start painting. For a pen tablet, position the pointer by hovering the pen, then tap and hold the pen where you want the brushstroke to begin.

To paint a freehand brushstroke, continue holding the button down as you drag the mouse. The brushstroke you paint follows your pointer.

To paint a straight horizontal or vertical line, press **Shift** now and continue dragging the mouse. The Editor senses whether you intend for the line to move up, right, left, or down, by the general direction in which you're moving the mouse—it doesn't have to be exact.

To paint a straight line between points, release the mouse button. For a pen tablet, lift the pen. Move the pointer to where you want the end of the line to appear. Press **Shift** then click this point. You can continue painting from here—either a freehand brushstroke or another straight line.

TIP

The changes you make to the dynamics of any brush tip are *not* automatically saved to the slot in the **Brushes** palette from which you originally loaded the brush tip. To save a brush tip you like and want to use again, use the **Preset Manager**. See ⑫ **About Preset Manager** for a description.

To change brush tips at any time, right-click the image. The **Brush Presets** palette appears. Choose a new tip from the **Brushes** list and click the **X** button to dismiss the palette.

Your image might have many layers whose contents simultaneously occupy a single point on an image. While you're painting, you can change from layer to layer as needed to see a list of all layers that have contents at a given point, hold down **Ctrl** and right-click that point. A pop-up menu lists the names of all layers at that point. Select a layer from this list and continue painting.

5 **View the Result**

After you're satisfied with the result, make any other changes you want, then save the result in JPEG or TIFF format, leaving your PSD image with its layers (if any) intact so that you can return at a later time and make different adjustments if you want.

For most applications of the **Brush** tool, even with heavy dynamics settings such as **Hue Jitter** and **Scatter**, your brushstroke will be recognizable as a brushstroke. This isn't generally the tool you'll use to make a mark on your photo that's *unnoticeable*; when you want to not be noticed, use the **Clone Stamp** tool or one of the healing brushes instead. With that said, the maple leaves I've drawn here blend nicely with the leaves in the photo, giving you the impression of looking out across the lawn through a leaf-filled window. Again, this isn't a maple-leaf picture frame but a leaf-shaped brush tip with high **Scatter** and high **Hue Jitter** settings.

NOTE

If you use a soft brush tip and hold the brush still while depressing the mouse button, paint will slowly fill out to the edges of the tip, which gives the appearance of "building up."

Set **Step** and **Fade** to a low value to get an airbrush that fades away at the end of the stroke.

---

117 **Paint an Area of a Photo with the Airbrush**

There is one subtle difference between using the **Brush** tool with the **Airbrush** setting and using it without the setting. It is an *extremely* subtle difference, but you can learn to use this subtlety to your advantage: Without the **Airbrush** option, the **Brush** tool applies paint to an image *as you move the mouse pointer*. With the **Airbrush** option turned on, the **Brush** tool applies paint to an image *as long as you hold the mouse button down*. You can move the pointer slowly to make the **Airbrush** deposit its "steps of paint" more closely together.

Despite what you might read from any number of sources, the effect of the **Airbrush** is not cumulative within the same stroke. If you hold the pointer down over one spot, for instance, the tool doesn't build up paint to any greater level than your **Opacity** setting. This is exactly the same behavior as the **Brush** tool. You can, of course, accumulate paint over an area by making multiple strokes of the **Airbrush** at low opacity. But you can do that with the **Brush** tool as well. So the reason for using the **Airbrush** is to "motorize" the tool, if you will, so that fast strokes are more thinly spaced than slow ones, therefore more closely approximating the effect you'd get from using a real motorized paint gun or a spray paint can. You might use the **Airbrush** to apply digital makeup, as explained in **135** **Brighten a Face with Digital Makeup**.

Before You Begin

✔ **110** About the Toolbox
✔ **113** Select a Color to Work With

See Also

→ **116** Paint an Area of a Photo with a Brush

2 Enable the Airbrush Option

3 Set Options

1 Select the Brush Tool

4 Apply the Color   **5** View the Result

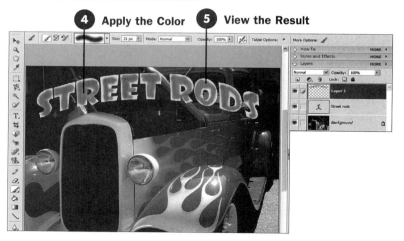

① Select the Brush Tool

Open an image in the *Editor* in **Standard Edit** mode and save it in Photoshop (***.psd**) format. In the **Layers** *palette*, select the layer you want to paint. Select the **Brush** tool from the **Toolbox**. You can click the tool's icon or press the keyboard shortcut **B**.

2 **Enable the Airbrush Option**

Click the **Airbrush** icon on the right side of the **Options** bar.

3 **Set Options**

Select a brush tip, **Size**, **Mode**, and **Opacity** from the **Options** bar. No single stroke of the **Airbrush** can build up paint beyond the amount specified in the **Opacity** setting; single **Airbrush** strokes are not cumulative within themselves. From the **Toolbox**, set the *foreground color* to the color you want to apply.

To set brush dynamics options, including **Spacing**, click the **More Options** button on the **Options** bar. Here, the **Spacing** setting becomes relative, referring to the interval of time the **Airbrush** waits between steps (paint deposits). Descriptions for all other dynamics settings appear in **116** **Paint an Area of a Photo with a Brush**.

> **TIP**
>
> Test the brush size by passing it over the picture without pressing the mouse button. A circle indicates the area the brush will cover.

4 **Apply the Color**

Begin the brushstroke by clicking and holding the mouse button where you want to start painting. For a pen tablet, position the pointer by hovering the pen, then tap and hold the pen where you want the brushstroke to begin.

To paint a freehand brushstroke, continue holding the button down as you drag the mouse. The brushstroke you paint follows your pointer. Paint is continually applied for as long as you hold down the mouse button (for pen tablet users, as long as the pen touches the tablet). If you hold the mouse pointer over an area with the button still pressed, paint appears to spill outwards from the tip. This is a result of repeated applications of a soft tip, when several soft-edged steps are applied on top of one another over time.

To paint a straight line between points, release the mouse button. For a pen tablet, lift the pen. Move the pointer to where you want the end of the line to appear. Press **Shift** then click this point. Here, the **Airbrush** mimics the behavior of the **Brush** tool, so how much paint is applied between the two points is governed by the **Spacing** dynamics setting, just as it is for the **Brush** tool. You can continue painting from here—either a freehand brushstroke or another straight line.

> **TIP**
>
> To paint a straight horizontal or vertical line, press **Shift** now and continue dragging the mouse. The Editor senses whether you intend for the line to move up, right, left, or down by the general direction in which you're moving the mouse—it doesn't have to be exact.

5 **View the Result**

After you're satisfied with the result, make any other changes you want and save the result in JPEG or TIFF format, leaving your PSD image with its *layers* (if any) intact so that you can return at a later time and make different adjustments if you want.

In this example, I wanted the label to emulate the flame paint job of this hot rod from a local car show. I used a novelty typeface to create a text label and took the color from a light area of the car's fender (See **114** **Select a Color Already in Your Image**.) The **Text** tool created its own new layer; I then added a new layer on which to paint so that I could erase any mistakes and so that I wouldn't have to simplify my text before I could paint on the text layer. I selected the **Airbrush** tool and a soft brush and used it to apply a darker color from the fender over the type.

118 Fill an Area with a Color or Pattern

Before You Begin

✔ **70** About Making Selections

✔ **110** About the Toolbox

✔ **112** About Preset Manager

See Also

→ **116** Paint an Area of a Photo with a Brush

→ **119** Fill an Area with a Gradient

The **Brush** tool—particularly its **Airbrush** subspecies—is a tool to be used with finesse. Use the **Brush** tools to fill constrained areas, often with *feathered* edges. The **Paint Bucket**, on the other hand, is more like throwing a bucket of paint at the side of a barn. It fills large areas with a color or pattern and does it with a single click.

Of course, there are limits on the **Paint Bucket's** barnside behavior; in fact, you'll probably want to apply some limits. Left to its own devices, the **Paint Bucket** identifies the color of the pixel on which you click and throws paint on every pixel of a similar color. The most important restraint is to adjust the tool's idea of what constitutes a "similar color." Do this with the **Tolerance** setting. The greater the tolerance, the greater the range of colors the tool will cover; a lower tolerance limits the color range. For example, you might want to change the color of someone's shirt. Folds and shadows create variations on the base color. Set the **Tolerance** to cover this range. Then, you can select the shirt, the whole shirt, and nothing but the shirt.

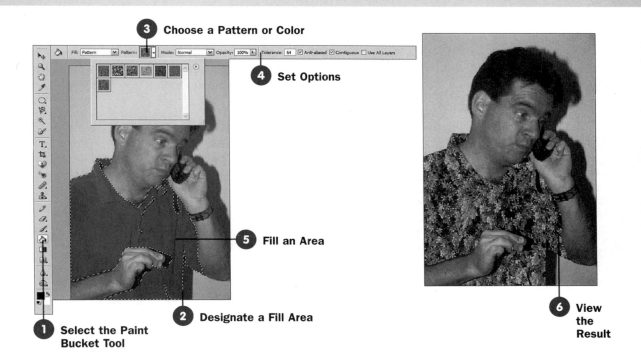

③ **Choose a Pattern or Color**

④ **Set Options**

⑤ **Fill an Area**

② **Designate a Fill Area**

① **Select the Paint Bucket Tool**

⑥ **View the Result**

The **Contiguous** setting is also an important restraint on the **Paint Bucket**. When you enable this option, the **Paint Bucket** changes only *neighboring pixels* of similar color to those it has already changed. This is important if you want to restrain the area where the **Paint Bucket** is applied. With this option disabled, the tool searches the entire layer for similar colors and change every instance it finds. The results are unpredictable. The **Paint Bucket** also has **Mode** and **Opacity** settings that work as described in ⑪ **About Tool Options**.

The **Paint Bucket** is not limted to sloshing paint. Open the **Fill** list in the **Options** bar and select the **Pattern** alternative. Then open the **Pattern** list just to the right and select a *pattern*. Instead of slopping on a single color, you can fill an area with the selected *pattern*. Patterns are useful ingredients of many illustrations. For example, you could use a pattern as a background or to set off an area of an illustration.

 TIP

Another way to prevent the **Paint Bucket** from going to excess is to first select the area where you want to apply the new color. Use any of the selection tools described in ⑦⓪ **About Making Selections**. When you then apply the **Paint Bucket**, it affects only the selected area.

KEY TERM

Pattern—A design that repeats at regular intervals, like wallpaper.

1 Select the Paint Bucket Tool

Open an image in the *Editor* in **Standard Edit** mode and save it in Photoshop (***.psd**) format. In the **Layers** *palette*, select the layer you want to fill. Click the **Paint Bucket** tool on the **Toolbox.**

TIP

To prevent transparent pixels from being filled, lock the layer's transparency by selecting the layer in the **Layers** palette and then clicking the **Lock transparent pixels** button at the top of the palette.

2 Designate a Fill Area

To limit the area affected, select the area you want to fill using any selection tool. The fill operation cannot extend beyond the area you've selected. **70 About Making Selections** explains how the selection tools work and how they can be useful in the context of filling areas.

3 Choose a Pattern or Color

On the **Options** bar, select **Foreground Color** or **Pattern** from the **Fill** drop-down list. If you choose **Foreground Color**, be sure to set the *foreground color* swatch at the bottom of the **Toolbox** to the color you want to use for the fill. If you choose **Pattern**, open the **Pattern** drop-down list and select the pattern to use for the fill.

4 Set Options

On the **Options** bar, set the **Mode, Opacity**, and **Tolerance** you want. The **Tolerance** value controls how similar pixels must be to the one you click in order to also be filled. A low **Tolerance** value means that pixels must be very close in color to the one you pick in order to be filled. A high **Tolerance** value fills more pixels— even fairly dissimilar ones to the pixel you click.

If you chose **Anti-aliased**, pixels along the edge of the filled area will be only partially filled with the color or pattern in order to soften the edge and make it less jagged. The **Contiguous** option allows you to fill pixels that are non-*neighboring pixels*. If you enable the **Use All Layers** option, even pixels on other layers will be filled if they are similar to the one you click.

NOTE

You can define your own patterns and add them to the pattern libraries. Create a pattern with the tools, *filters*, *effects*, or *layer styles*, or pick one up from an image. Make a rectangular selection of the pattern with no feathering. Then choose **Edit, Define Pattern from Selection** from the menu bar. Name the pattern and click **OK** to add the pattern to the current library. See **112 About Preset Manager** for help in managing the patterns you create.

5 Fill an Area

In the layer, click on a pixel you want to fill. The **Paint Bucket** fills similar pixels with the color or pattern you chose based on the options you set in step 3.

6 View the Result

After you're satisfied with the result, make any other changes you want and save the result in JPEG or TIFF format, leaving your PSD image with its layers (if any) intact so that you can return at a later time and make different adjustments if you want.

In this example, I used the **Magic Wand** to select what was originally a red shirt. This eliminated some juggling with the **Paint Bucket's Tolerance** setting to make sure that the paint covered only the shirt. Then I selected a pattern from the drop-down list in the **Options** bar and dumped it into the selected area. The man is suddenly wearing a brightly patterned shirt.

119 Fill an Area with a Gradient

A *gradient* is a transition from one color to another—often between several colors. You can use a gradient as a backdrop for an image or to fill a frame around an image.

The simplest gradient is a selection that gradually fades in linear fashion from the *foreground color* to the background color. More complex gradients make the transition outward from the center, at angles, and across multiple colors.

There are many preset gradients you can choose from with the **Gradient** tool. If you don't find what you want, click the **Edit** button on the **Options** bar to create your own gradient.

1 Select Gradient Tool

Open an image in the *Editor* in **Standard Edit** mode and save it in Photoshop (***.psd**) format. In the **Layers** *palette*, select the layer you want to change. To put the gradient on a new layer, create one by clicking the **Create a new layer** button on the **Layers** palette. To limit the gradient to a specific area, make a selection now.

Because a lot of gradients use the *foreground* and *background colors*, set the foreground and background colors to the colors you want to use, as explained in **114** **Select a Color to Work With**. Then click the **Gradient** tool on the **Toolbox**.

Before You Begin

See Also

✔ **110** About the Toolbox

→ **118** Fill an Area with a Pattern

→ **183** Add a Text Caption or Label

🔑 **KEY TERM**

Gradient—A gradual transition between two colors, sometimes by way of a third (or more) color.

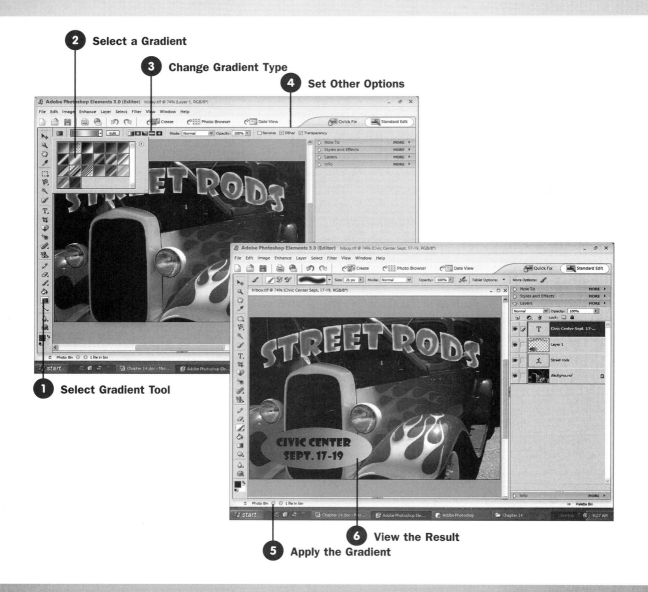

2 Select a Gradient

3 Change Gradient Type

4 Set Other Options

1 Select Gradient Tool

6 View the Result

5 Apply the Gradient

2 Select a Gradient

On the **Options** bar, open the **Gradient Picker** drop-down list and select a gradient. To change to a different set of gradient styles, click the right arrow on the palette and choose a gradient set from those listed at the bottom of the menu that appears.

③ Change Gradient Type

Make a selection from one of the five gradient styles displayed on the **Options** bar. The gradient styles define how the gradient will fill the area you select:

- **Linear** applies a straight-line gradient from one color to the next.

- **Radial** applies the gradient outward in all directions from the center of the selected area.

- **Angle** applies the gradient in a 360° sweep starting at a designated angle, resulting in an effect that looks like an old air traffic control radar.

- **Reflected** applies the gradient in bands on either side of the center of the selected area.

- **Diamond** applies the gradient in a diamond shape, radiating from the point where you click to begin the gradient.

④ Set Other Options

Set the **Mode** and **Opacity** as desired. You can reverse the order of the colors in the gradient by enabling the **Reverse** option. To reduce a possible banding effect where colors blend when the gradient is printed, enable the **Dither** option. To retain transparent areas of a gradient, enable the **Transparency** option. If you turn this option off, then the transparent areas are filled with the colors from the gradient.

⑤ Apply the Gradient

Click and drag across the area you want to fill with the gradient *in the direction* you want the gradient to transition. For example, drag from the upper-left corner of the layer to its lower-right corner to have the gradient transition in that direction. The gradient is applied to the selection.

⑥ View the Result

After you're satisfied with the gradient, make any other changes you want and save the result in JPEG or TIFF format, leaving your PSD image with its layers (if any) intact so that you can return at a later time and make different adjustments if you want.

NOTE

When you drag to create the gradient, keep in mind that gradient bands often appear in the opposite direction. For example, if you drag from upper-left to lower-right to create a **Linear** gradient, the bands appear in diagonals that bend from the lower-left to the upper-right. The color in the gradient bands, however, changes as it moves from upper-left to lower-right.

TIP

To create a gradient with an angle that's an exact multiple of 45 degrees, press and hold **Shift** as you drag to create the gradient.

In this example, I used the **Elliptical Marquee** tool to drag an oval-shaped selection over the picture. Then I applied the gradient I created using some colors already in the picture. I then used this gradient-filled oval as the background for a text block. (See **183** **Add a Text Caption or Label**.)

120 About Drawing Shapes

Before You Begin

✔ **110** About the Toolbox

See Also

✔ **99** Move, Resize, Skew, or Distort a Layer

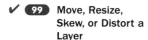

NOTES

A layer style applies special effects such as beveled edges, chrome effects, or color overlays to the contents of a layer. See **91** About Layers and the Layers Palette.

If you want to draw a shape from the center out, instead of from one corner to the other, select the **From Center** option on that shape's **Options** palette.

You can add shapes to an image such as a rectangle, circle, or even a star. You might add a circle, for example, to frame some text, or a star to adorn a favorite photo of your son. You can draw these basic shapes using the versatile **Shape** tool in Photoshop Elements. You can change the form of this adaptable tool to draw a rectangle, a rectangle with a rounded corners, an ellipse, a line, or a polygon with the number of sides you select. There is also a **Custom Shape** tool with which you can apply a variety of irregular shapes such as a heart, flower, butterfly, or pawprint.

To draw a shape, first click the **Shape** tool on the **Toolbox**. If necessary, select the shape to draw (such as a rounded rectangle) from those shown on the left end of the **Options** bar. On the **Options** bar, change other settings as desired. For example, you can change the color for the object you're about to draw by selecting a new *foreground color*, or by chosing a color from the **Color** list. You can apply a *layer style* to the shapes on this layer by selecting a **Style**.

In addition, each shape has its own options that you can change before drawing the shape. Some of these options appear on the **Options** bar. For example, if you chose the **Polygon** tool, you can change the number of sides on your polygon by adjusting the **Sides** value. Adjust the roundness of the corners of the **Rounded Rectangle** by changing the **Radius** value. The larger the **Radius**, the more round the corners. Adjust the thickness of the **Line** by changing its **Weight**. Select the shape you want to create with the **Custom Shape** tool by choosing one from the **Shape** list.

You can access additional options for each shape on its **Options** *palette*. Just click the down arrow at the end of the shapes list on the **Options** bar to display the options for your chosen shape. For example, you can enter the aspect ratio (proportions) of the rectangle you want to draw, and your shape will be constrained to those proportions automatically.

Options Palette

Shape Tool

*You can draw shapes on your photos with the **Shape** tools.*

Click to establish the upper-left corner of your shape then drag down and to the right. The shape appears on its own layer. If you draw another shape, it's typically placed on its own layer, too. But there are buttons on the **Options** bar that allow you to add the new shape to the current layer and control how they interact.

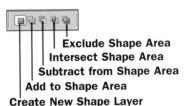

Exclude Shape Area
Intersect Shape Area
Subtract from Shape Area
Add to Shape Area
Create New Shape Layer

*These buttons on the **Shape** tool's **Options** bar let you specify where to place a new shape.*

- To place this shape on its own layer, click the **Create New Shape Layer** button.

- To add this shape to any existing shape it intersects, click the **Add to Shape Area** button.

TIP

To draw a regular shape, press the **Shift** key as you draw the shape. Depending on the tool you have selected, you can draw a perfect square, a perfect circle, or a perfectly straight line at a 45-degree angle.

 TIP

You can change the color and layer style of a shape right after you create it if you like. Because shapes are vector data, you can change them as often as you like. To make certain changes however, such as applying a filter to the shape layer, the shape must be simplified first (that is, converted to raster data).

 KEY TERMS

Bounding box—A rectangle that describes the boundaries of a drawn object, cropping border, or selection.

Handles—Small squares that appear along the perimeter of the bounding box surrounding a drawn object, cropping border, or selection marquee. By dragging these handles, you can resize the object, border, marquee, or bounding box.

- To remove from an existing shape the area where it overlaps the new shape, click the **Subtract from Shape Area** button. The new shape is not filled; its shape is used only to take a "bite" out of an existing shape.

- To display only the area where the existing shape overlaps the new shape, click the **Intersect Shape Area** button. Neither shape is filled in this scenario; only the overlap area is filled.

- To subtract the area where the existing shape overlaps the new shape, click the **Exclude Shape Area** button. In this scenario, both shapes are filled, but the overlap area is not.

Shapes you draw are *vector objects*, which means they can be resized, moved, and otherwise manipulated after they are created. To select a shape so that you can change it, click the **Shape** tool on the **Toolbox**, and then click the **Shape Selection** tool on the **Options** bar. Click a shape in the image; *handles* appear around the perimeter of the shape's *bounding box*. Resize a shape by dragging a handle inward (to make the shape smaller) or outward (to make it bigger). To move the shape, drag it from the center. You can *skew* or *distort* an object in the same way you can a layer; see ⑨⑨ **Move, Resize, Skew, or Distort a Layer.** You can rotate a shape in the same way you rotate a layer; see ⑩⑥ **Rotate an Image or Layer.**

Shape Selection Tool   **Bounding Box**

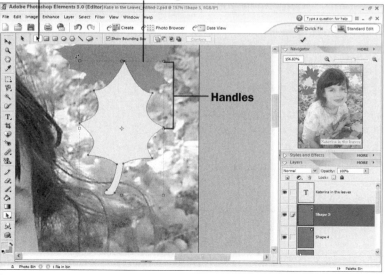

You can move, resize, or transform a shape.

121 Add Thought Bubbles to a Photo

You can use small variations on basic shapes to add interest to any photo. For example, you could use circles and ellipses to add cartoon-style text balloons and thought bubbles to a picture. Even easier, you could delve into the **Custom Shape** tool's Smithsonian-scale shape inventory and find some talking-style balloons you can use or readily adapt.

1 Select a Thought Balloon

Open an image in the *Editor* in **Standard Edit** mode and save it in Photoshop (*.psd) format. In the **Layers** palette, select the image layer. The shape layer you're about to create will appear above this layer in the **Layers** palette, which will make the "thought balloon" sit on top of your image.

In the **Toolbox**, select the **Custom Shape** tool. In the **Options** bar, click the small arrow on the right edge of the **Shape** window. The menu that opens includes a long list of shape libraries from which you can choose. Near the bottom of this list, select **Talk Bubbles**. A library of cartoon balloons opens. For a typical thought bubble, select **Thought 1**. To apply white bubbles, open the **Color** drop-down list in the **Options** bar and select white.

2 Apply the Balloon

Click and drag in the picture to draw a rectangle where you want the balloon to appear. The balloon appears on its own new layer called **Shape 1**.

If you need to move or resize the balloon, select the **Move** tool. The balloon appears in a bounding box with adjustment handles around its edges. Use these handles to adjust the balloon so that it fits neatly within the picture.

3 Add Some Dimension

Whether in champagne or a picture, bubbles should not be flat. In the **Custom Shape** tool's **Options** bar, the **Styles** drop-down list offers a host of options for adding bevels, shadows, glows, and other ways to add dimension to a shape.

Before You Begin

✔ **110** About the Toolbox

✔ **120** About Drawing Shapes

💡 TIP

The trick here is to draw a shape large enough for the text you want your subject to "say." Then you can adjust the shape's dimensions and orientation so that the small bubbles point to the subject. Finally, add text over your talking balloon shape, and apply a drop shadow or some other layer *effect* to give the balloon some substance. *Voila!* Your subject is talking to you.

💡 TIP

You probably will have to adjust the balloon somewhat to fit the picture. For example, the bubbles may point away from the subject instead of toward it. Make sure that the **Shape 1** layer is selected in the **Layers** palette. From the main menu, select **Image, Rotate, Flip Layer Horizontal** to flip the orientation of the bubbles.

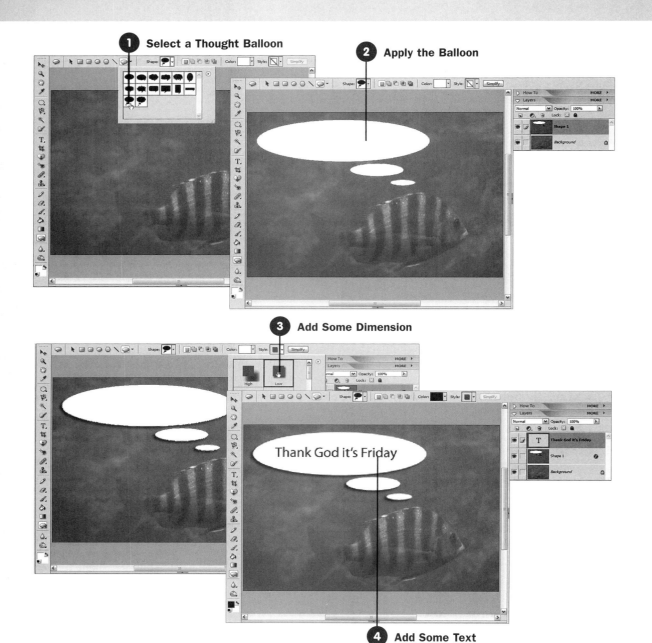

1 Select a Thought Balloon

2 Apply the Balloon

3 Add Some Dimension

Thank God it's Friday

4 Add Some Text

Again, make sure that the shape layer is selected in the **Layers** palette. In the **Options** bar, click the small arrow to the right of the **Styles** window. From the menu of types of styles that opens, select the library you'd like to apply. In this case, one of the **Drop Shadows** might do the job. After selecting that library, choose a shadow from the samples that appear. The shadow is applied to everything on the selected shape layer.

4 Add Some Text

Select the **Text** tool from the **Toolbox**. Select a typeface and size, and make sure that the color is different from that of the balloon. Click in the large bubble and type the text you want to attribute to the subject. If necessary, you can select the text and apply a different type size to make a good fit. You also can use the **Move** tool to center the text in the bubble.

15

Repairing Photographs

122 About Removing Scratches, Specks, and Holes

123 Remove Scratches

124 Remove Specks and Spots

125 Repair Minor Tears, Scratches, Spots, and Stains

126 Repair Large Holes, Tears, and Missing Portions of a Photo

127 Restore Color and Tone to an Old Photograph

128 Restore Quality to a Scanned Photograph

When people suffer a disaster, what are some of the first things they try to protect or recover? Family pictures. No doubt more than once you've seen heartbreaking stories on the news of people searching through the wreckage of their homes, looking for pictures that were dear to them. Short of disasters, the pictures from your past face a formidable hazard: old age. Even if you store them carefully in albums—not to mention throwing them into boxes—your cherished images tend to fade, bend, and decay.

Recognizing this, the makers of Photoshop Elements have packed up an extensive kit of tools to help restore old photographs. In this chapter, you'll learn how to remove scratches and specks and to repair tears, stains, and even holes. You'll also learn how to quickly restore color and contrast to an old photograph, and to repair any loss of quality when you scanned in the photograph. When you're finished, you might look at the results and decide the old homestead never looked better and that Uncle Ben was a surprisingly handsome guy.

122 About Removing Scratches, Specks, and Holes

Before You Begin

✔ **45** About Editing Images

✔ **70** About Making Selections

✔ **91** About Layers and the Layers Palette

See Also

→ **123** Remove Scratches

→ **124** Remove Specks and Spots

→ **125** Repair Minor Tears, Scratches, Spots and Stains

→ **126** Repair Large Holes, Tears, and Missing Portions of a Photo

It's not uncommon for photographs to acquire small scratches, spots, holes, and tears, even if the photos are not very old. If a photograph is not stored flat with its surface protected from damage, the photo can easily develop surface defects. The *Editor* offers many tools you can use to repair these scratches and other small anomalies:

- **Spot Healing Brush.** If scratches or spots are small, use the **Spot Healing Brush** to get rid of them quickly. The **Spot Healing Brush** samples pixels at the outer edge of the brush tip and uses them to replace the pixels under the center of the tip. In this way, the tool can be used to repair spots and small scratches. The **Spot Healing Brush** can also be set to sample all pixels under the brush tip, creating a blended patch for the center of the tip. In this way, the tool can be used to repair a textured area. See **123** **Remove Scratches**.

- **Clone Stamp.** This tool enables you to remove defects by cloning (copying) good parts of an image over top of small tears, scratches, spots, or stains. For example, if there's a small hole in someone's dress, you can copy a good part of the dress to make the repair. See **125** **Repair Minor Tears, Scratches, Spots, and Stains**.

- **Healing Brush.** Works like the **Clone Stamp** tool in that it copies pixels from a good area of an image. However, unlike the **Clone Stamp**, the **Healing Brush** *blends* the good pixels with existing pixels in the repair area, thus hiding the repair by matching the texture of the repair area. Use this tool instead of the **Clone Stamp** when you're cloning into an area with a texture, such as grass, wood, or a sweater. See **123** **Remove Scratches** and **162** **Remove Unwanted Objects from an Image**.

- **Smudge tool.** Uses either the current foreground color or the color under the brush tip at the beginning of a stroke to blend into existing pixels as you drag. This is sort of like finger painting. Use this tool to work color into damaged areas, fix some stray hairs, or soften a bad makeup job by smudging it.

- **Blur tool.** Softens hard edges to reduce contrast. Often, you can soften the impact of a defect by using this tool to blur the contrast between it and an unpatched area.

- **Brush tool.** Yes, you can even paint in a repair when needed. The trouble here is you're painting solid-colored pixels that do not blend well with the natural randomness of the pixels in a photo, so use this technique sparingly. I have used a very tiny **Brush** tool with a dark grayish purple to paint in eyelashes on occasion. Learn about other digital makeup wizardry in **135** **Brighten a Face with Digital Makeup**.

In addition to tools, the Editor provides the digital retouching artist with many useful filters to help make repairs:

- **Despeckle, Median, and Reduce Noise.** To remove a general scattering of dots or *noise* from a photograph, use one of these three filters (see **124** **Remove Specks and Spots**). The **Reduce Noise** filter is also helpful in removing noise caused by photographing in low light without a flash. See **141** **Improve a Nighttime Photo** and **143** **Fix a Flash That's Too Far Away**.

- **Dust & Scratches.** To remove small spots in a localized area, apply the **Dust & Scratches** filter. The **Dust & Scratches** filter is also good at repairing small scratches. Contrast at the edges of objects is preserved (see **123** **Remove Scratches**).

TIP

Like most changes you can make to an image, you can limit your retouching to either a layer or a selection.

KEY TERM

Noise—A random pattern of pixels that gives an image a grainy texture. Digital still cameras have the same picture-taking electronics as digital video cameras, so the noise that generally cancels itself out when viewed at 30 frames per second can't be ignored in a frozen frame (single image).

NOTE

Many of the tools you might use to remove scratches, specks, and holes require that your image use either **Grayscale** or **RGB Color** mode. See **63** **Change Color Mode**.

NOTE

All filters work on the current layer. Because these retouching filters work by either reducing contrast between pixels or blurring edges, it's best to make a selection first before applying any of the filters listed here or to copy the area you want to repair to its own layer. That way, important contrast (along the edges of objects, for example) is preserved and the detail in your photo won't be lost.

Remove Scratches

Before You Begin

✔ **122** About Removing Scratches, Specks, and Holes

See Also

→ **125** Repair Minor Tears, Scratches, Spots, and Stains

This small photo has been around since the 1940s and has had plenty of opportunity to acquire dust spots, scratches, and other flaws. Such a picture is a good candidate for a progressive approach: Start with a tool such as the **Dust & Scratches** filter to remove thin, short scratches and scattered dust spots in a small area. Then, move up to the **Healing Brush** to remove longer and wider scratches.

Like any old photo, there's typically several different ways to go about repairing the damage. In this task, you'll learn a method that's best applied when you have several small scratches and dust spots in the same area. If your photo has spots but no scratches, you can still use the method described here, but if the spots are in an area that's fairly even in tone, you'll want to see **124** **Remove Specks and Spots** for an alternative method that might work better. If your photo has isolated spots, scratches in areas of detail, or small tears and stains, see **125** **Repair Minor Tears, Scratches, Spots, and Stains**.

1 Choose Dust & Scratches Filter

Open an image in the *Editor* in **Standard Edit** mode and save it in Photoshop (***.psd**) format. Zoom in on an area of dust spots—it's easier to work with an enlarged view.

Using the **Lasso** tool, select an area that contains thin scratches or dust spots. Your selection will help contain the effect of the filter so that you don't lose important detail. Keep this area as small as possible while still including as many spots and scratches as you can. Choose **Filter, Noise, Dust & Scratches**. The **Dust & Scratches** dialog box appears.

2 Set Options and Click OK

The **Dust & Scratches** filter works by searching out pixels that contrast greatly with their neighbors and reducing this contrast, essentially removing the dust or scratch by camouflaging it. The **Radius** setting controls the area over which the filter searches for such differences. The larger the radius, the larger the area and the larger the spots the filter will correct. Ideally, you want to set the **Radius** to roughly the same size as the scratches or spots you're trying to remove.

NOTE

If you enable the **Preview** check box in the **Dust & Scratches** dialog box, the effects of your current settings appear on the actual image. If necessary, repeat steps 1 and 2 to select another area with spots and scratches and remove them. Assuming that most of the spots and scratches in the image are grouped in smallish areas, you can use this method to remove the majority of the spots and scratches in a photo in just a few minutes.

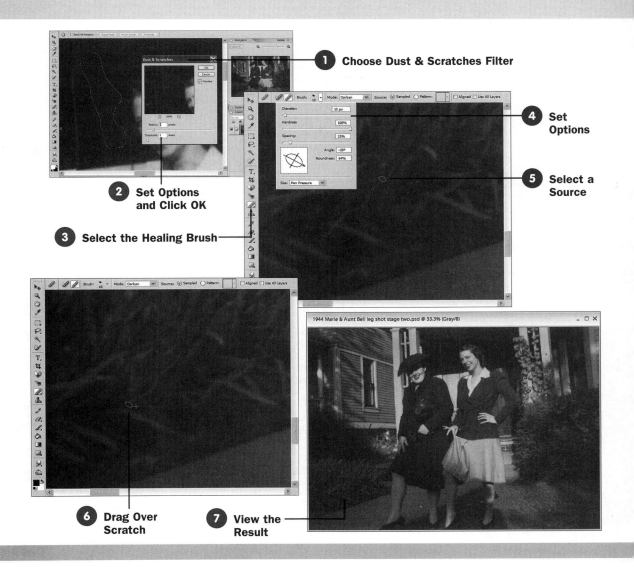

1 Choose Dust & Scratches Filter

4 Set Options

2 Set Options and Click OK

5 Select a Source

3 Select the Healing Brush

6 Drag Over Scratch

7 View the Result

You control the level of correction with the **Threshold** setting. If **Threshold** is set to a low value, the spot or scratch must contrast a lot with neighboring pixels before it will be removed. As you raise the **Threshold** little by little, you'll remove more spots at the risk of possibly losing some detail. When you find the right balance between the settings, click **OK** to apply them.

<img> TIP

To remove the next set of spots, select them and then reapply the **Dust & Scratches** filter using the same settings. Unless these spots or scratches are really different in size, the original settings should work fine on this new selection. To reapply the last filter you used, with the exact same settings, press **Ctrl+F**, or choose that filter from the very top of the **Filter** list, where it will continue to appear until you use a different filter.

<img> NOTE

With the **Aligned** option enabled, the relationship between the source point and the place where you begin cloning is maintained throughout the entire cloning procedure, regardless of how many times you stop and start. With **Aligned** disabled, pixels are always copied beginning at the original source point, and moving in the same direction you drag. If you begin a new stroke, the pixels are copied beginning at the original source.

③ Select the Healing Brush

When you have wider or longer scratches that seem to resist the **Dust & Scratches** filter, turn to the **Healing Brush** tool. Because the **Healing Brush** blends the cloned pixels with original pixels at the repair site, it preserves the original shading and texture of the picture while it overlays a repair. Thus, you should use the **Healing Brush** rather than the **Clone Stamp** whenever you want to repair scratches in a textured area, such as grass or wood. Select the **Healing Brush** from the **Toolbox**.

④ Set Options

On the **Options** bar, open the **Brush** palette and adjust the brush **Diameter** to the size of the scratch you're trying to repair. I typically reduce the **Roundness** setting to flatten the brush tip and adjust the **Angle** to match the scratch.

Enable the **Sampled** option. Because the scratch is lighter than the cloned pixels will be, select **Darken** from the blend **Mode** list. Set any other options as desired.

⑤ Select a Source

Press **Alt** and click the image to establish the source for the repair. I typically click very near the scratch so that the cloned pixels will match the repair area closely.

⑥ Drag Over Scratch

Drag the brush over the scratch to remove it. As you move the brush, the source point (the crosshair) moves with it. Pixels are copied from the source and blended with existing pixels, completing the repair. Because you selected **Darken** blend mode, the cloned pixels replace the source pixels completely if they are darker than the scratch. Repeat steps 3 to 6 to repair any remaining scratches.

⑦ View the Result

After removing the scratches and small spots grouped in the same area, make any other changes you want, and save the PSD file. Then resave the file in JPEG or TIFF format, leaving your PSD image with its *layers* (if any) intact so that you can return at a later time and make different adjustments if you want.

After less than five minutes, I had easily removed the majority of the spots and faint scratches on this photo. There are a few larger spots that remain, and I'll use the **Spot Healing Brush** described in the next task to remove them.

124 Remove Specks and Spots

Dust, scratches, and other "age spots" aren't the only kinds of damage a picture can suffer. Digital cameras and cell phone cameras can add their own kinds of spottiness in the form of *CCD noise*. This kind of *noise*, which occurs in a digital camera when you take a long exposure or overextend the digital zoom, takes the form of graininess or colored specks in areas that should be fairly uniform. Cell phone cameras introduce a certain level of noise naturally, simply because of the low quality of their images. Noise can also appear in scans of halftone images printed in a newspaper or magazine, in still images captured from video, or in images recorded under low-light conditions.

Three noise filters can help eliminate these specks. The **Median**, **Despeckle**, and **Reduce Noise** filters can easily remove the random pattern of dots caused by noise, regardless of the cause. Because it tends to average out the tones in a selection (changing pixels to the same average level of brightness as their neighbors), the **Median** filter is often a good choice when the noise affects large areas that are supposed to be even in tone. The **Despeckle** filter blurs pixels to smooth out areas of low contrast, leaving areas of high contrast (which are typically the edges of objects in a photo) untouched. The **Despeckle** filter is lousy at removing dust and speck type spots, but is good at removing low-contrast noise in a large area while preserving your edges.

The **Reduce Noise** filter again looks for pixels that contrast with their neighbors, and in a manner similar to **Median**, reduces their contrast by averaging out their brightness. Unlike **Median**, the **Reduce Noise** filter also evens out color by averaging the hue of each pixel with that of its neighbors. And like **Despeckle**, the **Reduce Noise** filter preserves the contrast along edges in your photo. After removing general noise (tiny specks that occur in a random pattern over a wide area), you'll learn how to use the **Spot Healing Brush** to remove spots that occur in isolated areas.

Before You Begin

✔ **122** About Removing Scratches, Specks, and Holes

See Also

→ **123** Remove Scratches

→ **125** Repair Minor Tears, Scratches, Spots, and Stains

→ **126** Repair Large Holes, Tears, and Missing Portions of a Photo

→ **143** Fix a Flash That's Too Far Away

⬤**K**EY TERM

CCD noise—Random distortions introduced into a photo by the CCD chip in a digital camera, cell phone camera, or scanner—its principal light detector. In a digital camera or cell phone camera, CCD noise during long exposures, occurs or at high ISO settings (film speed), and is magnified when electronic zoom is used to simulate a close-up of a subject at a distance. In a scanner, CCD noise happens naturally, but especially at low scanning resolutions.

2 Remove Noise with the Despeckle Filter

3 Or, Remove Noise with the Median Filter

Before

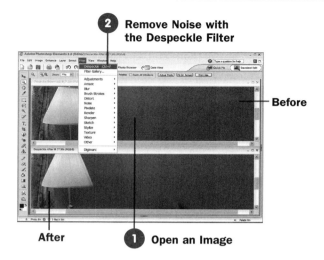

Before

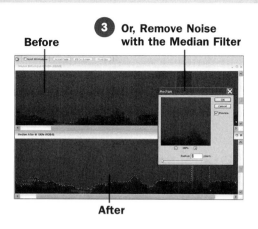

After

After

1 Open an Image

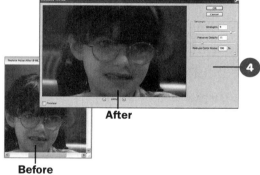

After

Before

4 Or Remove Noise with the Reduce Noise Filter

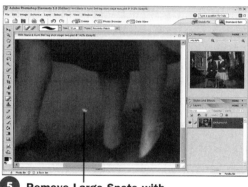

5 Remove Large Spots with the Spot Healing Brush

---

1 Open an Image

Open an image in the *Editor* in **Standard Edit** mode and save it in Photoshop (***.psd**) format. Then remove noise using any of the three **Noise** filters.

2 Remove Noise with the Despeckle Filter

To remove low-contrast noise from a photo, choose **Filter**, **Noise**, **Despeckle**. Although you could make a selection first, because **Despeckle** works only on low-contrast areas to remove noise, your edges will be preserved so there's typically no need to isolate the filter with a selection. The **Despeckle** filter works automatically, so you'll be able to judge its effectiveness right away.

This photo was taken to record the new paint job in our bedroom. Despite the sunshine coming through the window, the resulting photo had a lot of noise throughout. The **Despeckle** filter did a pretty good job of removing this low-contrast noise. I applied the filter multiple times to remove the noise completely, and yet the edges were preserved.

③ Or Remove Noise with the Median Filter

To apply the **Median** filter to an area of similar tone, first select the portion of the image you want to change. If necessary, on the **Layers** palette, change to the layer that contains the data to change. Then use your favorite selection tool to select the area that contains the noise you want to remove. Because the sky in this example is nearly a uniform color, I selected it with a few clicks of the **Magic Wand** tool (see **76** **Select Areas of Similar Color**). Zoom in on the image so that you can see your changes clearly. Choose **Filter**, **Noise**, **Median**. The **Median** dialog box appears.

Adjust the **Radius** value to a setting that removes the noise without removing too much natural texture. The **Radius** defines the area in which neighboring pixels are examined, to calculate an average value for the central pixel. Typically, a low value such as **2** or **3** is sufficient. Click **OK** to apply the filter.

I used the **Magic Wand** to select the sky in this nighttime photo of the Washington Monument. The low-light conditions caused the noise, but it was easily removed using a low **Radius** setting in the **Median** dialog box.

④ Or Remove Noise with the Reduce Noise Filter

The **Reduce Noise** filter combines the best of the **Despeckle** and **Median** filters, so it's a good one to try in their place. Choose **Filter**, **Noise**, **Reduce Noise**. The **Reduce Noise** dialog box appears.

First, lower the **Preserve Details** value or you won't see any effect. This value controls how much contrast a pixel must have with its neighbor before its brightness is lowered to bring it more in line

NOTE

To remove small spots in a specific area, it's typically best to use the **Dust & Scratches** filter rather than the **Median** filter because the **Median** filter tends to remove not only spots but detail as well, as it averages out the tone in a selection. The **Dust & Scratches** filter removes small spots in an area without removing detail; however, in some situations, such as areas of even tone that contain specks or spots caused by age, the **Median** filter can do a better job.

TIPS

The **Median** filter averages out the brightness of neighboring pixels, so make sure that you do not include high-contrast edges in your selection because you might lose that detail after applying the filter.

Enable the **Preview** check box in the **Median** dialog box so that you can see how the changes you make to the filter's settings affect the selected area in the image window.

with the "neighborhood average." Increase this value to preserve your edges; lower it to reduce noise even more. **Strength** controls the **Median** effect on qualifying pixels—in other words, the amount that a pixel's brightness might be changed. To change pixel hue values in a manner similar to the way the **Strength** value adjusts pixel brightness, increase the **Reduce Color Noise** value. The effect of your selections on the image appears in the large preview window on the left. When you're satisfied, click **OK** to apply the filter.

⑤ Remove Large Spots with the Spot Healing Brush

The **Noise** filters are great, but they do nothing to large spots on a digital image. The **Dust & Scratches** filter does a wonderful job of removing such spots, especially when they are grouped together, but you must be careful to apply the filter to a small area or you'll lose detail. To remove spots that are isolated or larger than a small dot, use the **Spot Healing Brush**.

You don't have to make a selection first; the effect is controlled by the size of your brush tip. Zoom in so that you can see the spot you want to remove, and then select the **Spot Healing Brush** on the **Toolbox**. On the **Options** bar, select a brush tip and adjust its **Size** to something slightly larger than the size of the spot you want to repair. Set the **Type** option to **Proximity Match**. This option analyzes the pixels around the edges of the brush to create a patch for the repair. Click the spot to remove it. Here, I returned to the 1940s photo and removed several large-to-medium spots with quick clicks of the **Spot Healing Brush**.

When you're satisfied with the results of the **Noise** filters and the **Spot Healing Brush**, make any other changes you want and save the PSD file. Then resave the file in JPEG or TIFF format, leaving your PSD image with its *layers* (if any) intact so that you can return at a later time and make different adjustments if you want.

TIP

If the area the spot is in has a definite texture, you can replicate that texture to a degree and create a more convincing patch than with the **Proximity Match** option. Just enable the **Create Texture** option on the **Options** bar instead, which analyzes all the pixels under the brush tip for both color and tone, and then uses that sampling to create a similar pattern.

125 Repair Minor Tears, Scratches, Spots, and Stains

Even cute pictures from the past are vulnerable to damage. Sometimes the damage is minor but annoying, such as a thin crease, small tear, scratch, spot, or stain. As you learned in **123** **Remove Scratches**, you can use the **Dust & Scratches** filter to remove thin scratches and small specks in the same general area, in one quick step. You also learned how to use the **Healing Brush** to clone data and texture from one area of a photo, repairing wider scratches in the process. In **124** **Remove Specks and Spots**, you learned that you can use the **Median** filter to remove larger specks within a selected area and use the **Spot Healing Brush** to remove isolated, large specks.

Sometimes the damage to the image is too much for the **Healing Brush** to correct. Although the **Healing Brush** works in a manner similar to the **Clone Stamp**, it *blends* copied pixels with those in the area you're repairing, and sometimes, blending is not what you want. For example, if you're repairing a tear that's fairly white, the **Healing Brush** blends the copied pixels (taken from an intact part of the picture) with the whiteness of the tear, creating an almost ghostlike effect. The same thing happens if you use the **Healing Brush** to repair a large hole; the whiteness of the hole will interfere with the cover-up job you're trying to achieve. In this task, you'll learn how to use the **Clone Stamp** effectively to clone missing data back into a photo. In **126** **Repair Large Holes, Tears, and Missing Portions of a Photo**, you'll learn an alternative technique that's quick and effective at filling in missing information. In this task, you'll also learn how to use the **Smudge** tool to blend out small blemishes and the **Sponge** tool to swab off stains.

➊ Smudge Out Spots

Open an image in the *Editor* in **Standard Edit** mode and save it in Photoshop (***.psd**) format. Select the **Smudge** tool from the **Toolbox**. In the **Options** bar, select a soft brush in a **Size** that will cover the spot you want to erase. Set other options as desired; because the first spot I wanted to correct was a dark spot on light-colored skin, I chose the **Lighten** blend **Mode** because it uses only pixels lighter than the spot to complete the repair.

Before You Begin

✔ **122** About Removing Scratches, Specks, and Holes

See Also

➔ **126** Repair Large Holes, Tears, and Missing Portions of a Photo

NOTE

In some situations, you can use the **Brush** tool to daub over small blemishes—if you can achieve an exact color match. Select the **Brush** tool on the **Toolbox** and press **Alt**; when the brush tip changes to an **Eyedropper**, use it to pick up the color you need from the image. Because the **Brush** delivers a solid bit of color, the patch often stands out from the blended pixels around it. The secret to using the **Brush** on a photo is to use it sparingly, with as small a tip as possible, and lower the **Opacity** setting.

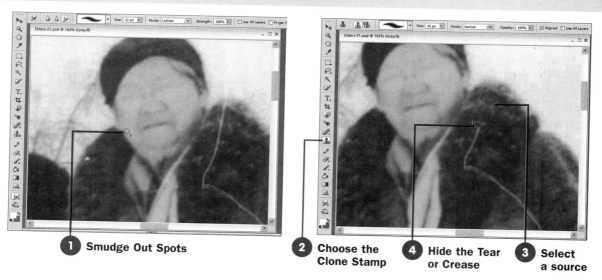

1 Smudge Out Spots

2 Choose the Clone Stamp

4 Hide the Tear or Crease

3 Select a source

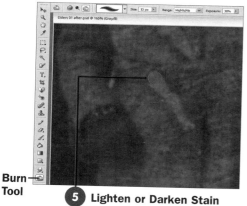

Burn Tool

5 Lighten or Darken Stain

Sponge Tool

6 Blend Stain Edges

Before

7 View the Result

Click a bit away from your spot and drag with the **Smudge** tool toward the spot. This action picks up nearby colors and blends them over the spot's color. Repeat this step to blend out other spots. If there are light spots in dark areas, change the **Mode** setting to **Darken** and click to correct those areas. Change the **Mode** to **Normal** to correct less-noticeable spots, such as lighter spots on a light background or dark dust specks on a darker background.

② Choose the Clone Stamp

Select the **Clone Stamp** tool from the **Toolbox**. Select a soft brush tip and set the **Size** just a bit larger than the flaw you want to repair. Because tears and creases are lighter than surrounding pixels, select the **Darken** blend **Mode**. That way, if your brush tip is a bit larger than the crease or tear in some spots, you won't replace good pixels with cloned ones because only light pixels are replaced with this mode. Enable the **Aligned** option, and set **Opacity** to 100% to fully replace the tear.

With the **Aligned** option enabled, the relationship between the source point and the place where you begin cloning is maintained throughout the entire cloning procedure, regardless of how many times you stop and start. That makes the **Aligned** option perfect for repairing a crease or large tear—the repair will match surrounding pixels perfectly. With **Aligned** disabled, pixels are always copied beginning at the original source point and moving in the same direction that you drag. If you begin a new stroke, the pixels are copied beginning at the original source point.

③ Select a Source

Press and hold the **Alt** key. Click in the image near the crease or tear to specify the source point—the "good pixels" you want the tool to clone to fix the flaw.

④ Hide the Tear or Crease

Click at the beginning of the tear or crease and drag slowly down the crease. The pixels you sampled in step 3 are copied over the flaw as you drag. As you work, the source point (marked by a crosshair) moves with the brush tip.

TIPS

Because the **Smudge** tool blends pixels into existing ones, I typically use a **Strength** setting at 100% to cover the spot completely. In cases where the spot is hardly there and I want to retain its color, I lower the **Strength** value.

Instead of smudging a color from the surrounding area, the **Finger Painting** option uses the current foreground color to smudge into the areas over which you drag. Although this is a fun option for playing around, it has limited use in photo repair because the color you'll want to use to cover up a spot is typically right next to the spot itself and so you can just smudge it over.

TIP

Because the **Clone Stamp** adjusts the source point as you drag, it allows for differences in color and tone as you drag over the tear or crease. The disadvantage is that the tool picks up and duplicates any flaws it encounters. This is why selecting your source point is important. As a rule, select the source as physically close to the flaw as you can. As the tear or crease changes direction, adjust the source point as well (by pressing **Alt** and clicking the image again) so that you can continue to match objects perfectly.

TIPS

You can also use the **Sponge** tool to saturate pixels, which you might do in a color image that's faded over time. Use the **Sponge** tool after adjusting for any color shifts in the image, which also occurs as photographs get older. See **127** Restore Color and Tone to an Old Photograph.

If the stain has occurred on a color photograph, the simplest method is to clone over the stain with good data (if available). If not, isolate the stain by selecting it and copying it to a new layer. Then you can try several methods for changing its color to the color it should be. You can invert the layer colors (**Filter**, **Adjustments**, **Invert**) and blend the result with the image layer by changing the copy layer's blend mode to **Color**. Or you can colorize the layer (**Enhance**, **Adjust Color**, **Hue/ Saturation**), enable the **Colorize** option, and adjust the **Hue** slider to change the color. Lower the **Lightness** value as well, because stains are darker than surrounding pixels.

⑤ Lighten or Darken Stain

Removing stains on color images can be tricky, but for grayscale images, it's fairly straightforward. The center of the stain will probably be lighter, especially if it's a water stain like the one shown here. To darken the pixels, select the **Burn** tool on the **Toolbox**. On the **Options** bar, adjust the **Size** of the tool to the width of the stain's *interior*. Set the **Range** to **Highlights** and the **Exposure** rate to a low value, such as **30%**. This setting prevents you from darkening the pixels too quickly. Brush over the stain's interior, darkening the lightest pixels. To darken the *midtones* as well, change the **Range** setting to **Midtones** and brush over the interior again.

If the interior of the stain is darker than the surrounding area, use the **Dodge** tool instead, because it lightens pixels. Set the **Range** to **Shadows** and then to **Midtones** to lighten the pixels in the center of the stain.

⑥ Blend Stain Edges

To hide the repair, use the **Sponge** tool to desaturate the pixels around the edge of the stain, where they are typically darker. This tool helps blend the edge of the stain with surrounding pixels. Change to the **Sponge** tool by clicking its icon on the **Options** bar. Select a soft brush tip and choose a **Size** that's slightly larger than the dark edge of the stain. Choose **Desaturate** from the **Mode** list. Lower the **Flow** to **50%** or less, so that the tool will lower the pixels' saturation slowly and not overdo the repair. Brush the tool over the edge of the stain, desaturating the pixels.

⑦ View the Result

This photo of three elderly aunts braving a snow storm was apparently stored in someone's pocket. It has many creases, spots, specks, and a few water stains. It took a little while to repair the damage, but as you can see, the result is a great improvement.

126 Repair Large Holes, Tears, and Missing Portions of a Photo

Photoshop Elements has retouching tools that can take care of most of the small defects in an old photo. They will even take care of some of the larger ones. But once in a while, a picture is missing a big chunk. At some time in the past, it might have been torn or have been mounted in an album with plastic tape (a sworn enemy of photo preservation). The photo might be missing a corner or have holes in it from being mounted on a bulletin board.

Repairing this kind of damage has the same purpose as using the **Clone Stamp** or the **Healing Brush** to repair smaller areas: The goal is to replace the bad section of a photo with a good section of the photo. However, when you must repair a large damaged area, using the **Clone Stamp** or **Healing Brush** to copy data is not only tedious (you have to move the source often to hide what you're doing) but often leads to poor results despite your best efforts. In this task, I show you a rather tricky approach to filling in big gaps in your photo.

1 **Copy Bottom Layer**

Open an image in the *Editor* in **Standard Edit** mode and save it in Photoshop (***.psd**) format. On the **Layers** palette, drag the layer onto the **Create a new layer** button or select **Layer, Duplicate** to create a duplicate of the original **Background** layer. Rename this new layer **Shifted.**

2 **Shift the Top Layer**

On the **Layers** palette, change the **Opacity** of the **Shifted** layer to 50%. This setting lets you see the **Background** layer as you shift the top layer. You're going to use good pieces of the **Shifted** layer to cover the holes and tears in the **Background** layer.

Click the **Move** tool on the **Toolbox.** Click the **Shifted** layer in the image and slowly move it left, right, up, or down until its good portion covers up the area on the **Background** layer that you want to fill in.

Before You Begin

✔ **91** About Layers and the Layers Palette

✔ **122** About Removing Scratches, Specks, and Holes

See Also

→ **125** Repair Minor Tears, Scratches, Spots, and Stains

💡 TIP

If the good information you want to use to repair the hole or tear is located in another image, open that image, and adjust its size and resolution to match the image you want to repair. See **60** Change Image Size or Resolution. Choose **Select, All,** and then choose **Edit, Copy.** Change to the image you want to repair, and choose **Edit, Paste** to paste the image with the good data onto a new layer. Rename this new layer **Shifted.**

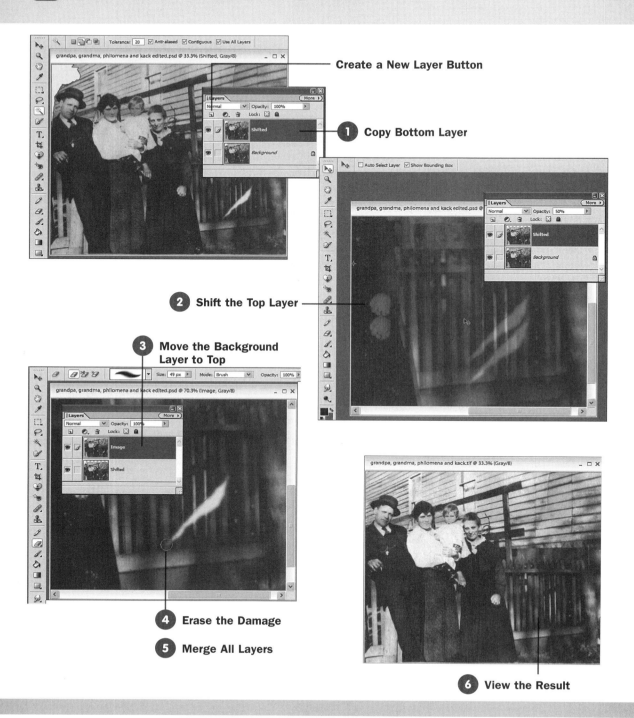

Create a New Layer Button

1 Copy Bottom Layer

2 Shift the Top Layer

3 Move the Background Layer to Top

4 Erase the Damage

5 Merge All Layers

6 View the Result

❸ Move the Background Layer to Top

In the **Layers** palette, reset the **Opacity** of the **Shifted** layer to 100%. Convert the **Background** layer to a regular layer (a process also known as "simplifying") by choosing the **Background** layer in the **Layers** palette and choosing **Layer, New, Layer from Background**. Name the converted layer **Image**. Simplifying the background layer allows you to move its position in the layer stack.

Click the newly created **Image** layer in the **Layers** palette and drag it above the **Shifted** layer. The **Shifted** layer is now on the bottom, with the **Image** layer on top. Notice that the hole in the original image is noticeable once again.

❹ Erase the Damage

On the **Layers** palette, select the **Image** layer. In the **Toolbox**, select the **Eraser** tool. In the **Options** bar, set the **Mode** option to **Brush**, select a soft-edged brush, and adjust its **Size** to fit the size of the hole or tear. Set **Opacity** to **100%**.

Start brushing over the damaged area, erasing the top image layer to reveal the undamaged area of the **Shifted** layer under it.

❺ Merge All Layers

If the shifted data happens to line up with another hole or tear, you can repeat step 4 to repair that damage as well. If not, you'll need to merge the layers, and then repeat steps 1 to 4 to repair any other damaged areas. To merge the layers, choose **Layer, Flatten Image**.

❻ View the Result

After you've made all necessary repairs to the holes and tears, make any other changes you want, such as removing small spots and creases. Save the PSD file, and then resave the file in JPEG or TIFF format, leaving your PSD image with its layers (if any) intact so that you can return at a later time and make different adjustments if you want.

This old photo of my grandparents and aunt has been through a lot, as you can see. There was a tear in the middle and in one corner; small specks and spots adorned various areas, and it had lost its tone. To repair the damage, I borrowed a good spot in the fence and, following the steps in this task, repaired it. I repeated the process to fix the missing section in the upper-left corner. After merging all layers, I adjusted the contrast and used the **Spot Healing Brush** on the specks. The result, as you can see, is much improved.

127 Restore Color and Tone to an Old Photograph

Before You Begin

✔ **136** About an Image's Histogram

See Also

➔ **137** Improve Brightness and Contrast

➔ **138** Improve a Dull, Flat Photo

➔ **146** Adjust Hue, Saturation, and Lightness Manually

The colors in this picture are a clue to the picture's age. As photos age, their colors fade. Inks fade at different rates, causing not only a loss in saturation, but a shift in color as well. The *Editor* has several automatic tools on the **Enhance** menu to correct the color and lighting of photos like this one, but they aren't always as precise as you might like. Try these commands on your photos, but be prepared to cancel them and try more precise, manual methods. In the case of this picture, using **Enhance**, **Auto Levels** or **Enhance**, **Auto Color Correction** was like using a sledgehammer when the situation called for a scalpel. In this task, I'll explain how to manually adjust the color saturation and tones in your image to improve its overall appeal.

① Open the Info Palette

Open an image in the Editor in **Standard Edit** mode and save it in Photoshop (***.psd**) format. In most old photos, the overall tone is medium and the contrast is not as sharp as it should be; when you display a histogram for the image, the graph doesn't meet either end of the scale. The first step in restoring an old photograph is to find the brightest and darkest points in the picture and place them at each end of the histogram to balance the overall tone.

Open the **Info** palette by choosing **Window**, **Info** from the menu bar. The **Info** palette provides data about whichever pixel is currently under the mouse pointer; you'll use this information to select the darkest and lightest points in the image. To make the **Info** palette show the HSB (hue, saturation, and brightness) values you'll need to complete this task, click the **Eyedropper** icon in the first pane and select **HSB Color** from the menu.

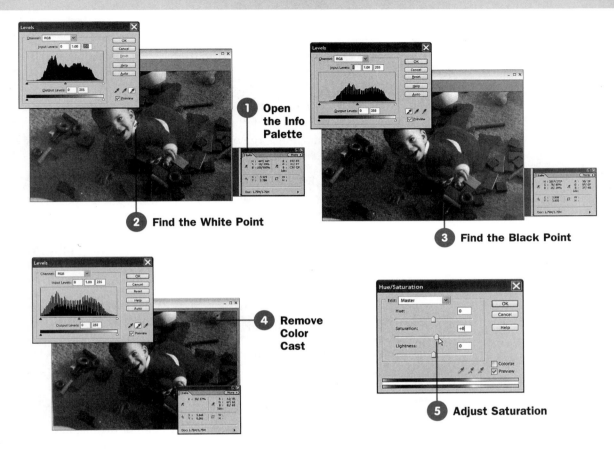

1 Open the Info Palette

2 Find the White Point

3 Find the Black Point

4 Remove Color Cast

5 Adjust Saturation

Before

After

6 View the Result

② Find the White Point

Choose **Enhance**, **Adjust Lighting**, **Levels** from the menu bar. The **Levels** dialog box opens to display the histogram. In the bottom-right corner of the dialog box is a trio of eyedroppers colored black, gray, and white. You use the black and white eyedroppers to pick the darkest and lightest tones in the image. After setting the black and white points, the overall contrast and tone of the image will be restored.

TIP

When selecting the whitest point in the image, ignore reflections. Extreme bright spots like these are called specular highlights and should not be considered when finding the true white point in an image.

Press **Alt** and click the white slider just below the right end of the histogram in the **Levels** dialog box. The image changes to display the lightest points in yellow. Memorize the general area of one of these points. Select the white dropper in the **Levels** dialog box. Move it over the image, in the same area you identified earlier as containing the lightest spot. Look for the highest **B:** reading in the **Info** palette. When you find the lightest pixel, click it.

The picture brightens considerably because the **Levels** dialog box uses the white point you just specified to adjust its histogram. The point you clicked becomes "absolute white" in the image, and the rest of the points along the histogram graph are adjusted to accommodate this shift.

③ Find the Black Point

Press **Alt** and click the slider below the left end of the histogram in the **Levels** dialog box, and make note of the darkest points in the image, shown on the main image in magenta. Select the black eyedropper in the **Levels** dialog box. As you move the mouse pointer over the image, look for the lowest **B:** value on the **Info** palette. When you find the darkest point in the image, click it.

④ Remove Color Cast

Assuming there's something in your photograph that's gray, you can use the gray eyedropper in the **Levels** dialog box to remove any color cast in the image. Otherwise, use the method explained in **144** **Correct Color Manually**.

First, click the eyedropper in the first panel on the **Info** palette and select **Grayscale** from the menu that appears. This selection will help you find a middle gray pixel in the image. Click the gray eyedropper in the **Levels** dialog box. As you move the mouse pointer over a gray area in the photo, look for a pixel that's roughly 50% gray in the **Info** palette. When you find a middle gray pixel, click it. The colors in the image shift; assuming that you've clicked a middle gray pixel, any color cast is removed. Click **OK** to close the **Levels** dialog box and accept the changes.

⑤ Adjust Saturation

Again, the automatic color adjustments that Photoshop Elements provides (**Auto Levels** and **Auto Color Correction**) are too heavy-handed for the purpose of improving this picture. Manual adjustment using the **Hue/Saturation** control provides more control.

Choose **Enhance, Adjust Color, Hue/Saturation** from the menu bar to display the **Hue/Saturation** dialog box. Drag the **Saturation** slider to the right to increase the intensity of the colors in a faded image. (For more information about the **Hue/Saturation** dialog box, see **146 Adjust Hue, Saturation, and Lightness Manually.**) Click **OK** to save your changes.

⑥ View the Result

When you're satisfied with the color and tone of the image, make any other changes you want and save the PSD file. Then resave the file in JPEG or TIFF format, leaving your PSD image with its layers (if any) intact so that you can return at a later time and make different adjustments if you want.

After improving the contrast and saturation in this old photo and removing the reddish color cast that seemed to make everything pink, I had just a few remaining issues to attend to. I used the **Spot Healing Brush** to remove a few isolated specks, and the **Median** filter to remove some noise (see **124 Remove Specks and Spots**). The final result is a much improved treasure.

TIPS

Sometimes the color in a photograph fades unevenly. You can increase the saturation in selected parts of an image using the **Sponge**. Click the **Sponge** tool on the **Toolbox**, set the **Mode** to **Saturate**, adjust the **Flow** as desired, and then drag the tool over the area you want to saturate.

You can also increase the saturation in an old photo by duplicating the image on another layer and setting the duplicate layer's blend mode to **Multiply**.

128 Restore Quality to a Scanned Photograph

See Also

→ **6** Import a Scanned Image

→ **60** Change Image Size or Resolution

→ **124** Remove Specks and Spots

→ **137** Improve Brightness and Contrast

→ **149** Sharpen an Image

KEY TERM

Moiré pattern—The optical illusion that occurs when one regular geometric pattern—such as a grid made up of dots—overlays another or similar pattern, when placed slightly askew. For example, two window screens placed on top of each other at an angle form a moiré effect.

TIP

For persistent noise, you might have to blur the image while preserving the edge contrast (sharpness). See **150** Blur an Image to Remove Noise.

Sometimes an image doesn't require a lot of restoration. There are no holes, scratches, big dust spots, or faded colors. It just lacks the sharpness and snap that make you want to look at it again. If the original photograph contained sharp edges and high-quality color, these subtle qualities sometimes can be lost when you scan the picture.

To improve your chances of getting a good scan, you might want to scan at double the resolution you're going to need for printing—600 DPI. After making the adjustments shown in this task, you can resize the image downward as a last step, a process that increases the quality of the scan by making the pixels in an image even smaller.

The worst type of photo to scan is a halftone photograph common to newspapers. In fact, scanning any type of printed material often results in a poor-quality digital image. If your scanner has a Descreen option, turn it on when scanning such photos; it can help remove the *moiré pattern* that often occurs.

Remove Moiré Pattern and Noise

Open an image in the *Editor* in **Standard Edit** mode and save it in Photoshop (*.psd) format. If your scan is of a halftone image, it might have moiré. Even if a scan is of a regular photograph, the scanning process might have introduced some *noise* that's more easily seen when the image is zoomed in.

In **124** **Remove Specks and Spots**, you learned how to remove noise from an image. You can start with the **Despeckle** filter by choosing **Filter, Noise, Despeckle** from the menu. If the noise persists, try the **Median** filter by choosing **Filter, Noise, Median**. In the **Median** dialog box that appears, adjust the **Radius** until the noise is removed. Because it combines the best of both filters, the **Reduce Noise** filter is often a very good choice: choose **Filter, Noise, Reduce Noise**. Adjust the **Strength**, **Preserve Details**, and **Reduce Color Noise** values as needed to remove the noise, and then click **OK**.

1 Remove Moiré Pattern and Noise

2 Adjust the Contrast

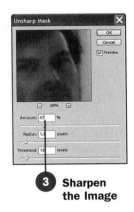

3 Sharpen the Image

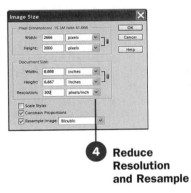

4 Reduce Resolution and Resample

2 Adjust the Contrast

Next, you should improve the scan's contrast and tone. There are various ways you can do that, but the easiest method is to use **Brightness/Contrast**, described in **137 Improve Brightness and Contrast**. Select **Enhance, Adjust Lighting, Brightness/Contrast**. The **Brightness/Contrast** dialog box appears. Drag the **Brightness** or **Contrast** slider to the right to increase it, or to the left to decrease it. When you're satisfied, click **OK**.

NOTES

③ Sharpen the Image

When making multiple changes to an image, it's generally recommended that you not do any sharpening until the final step because sharpening is really a process that adjusts the contrast between pixels. If you sharpen too early in the process, other changes you make can sometimes undo the effects of sharpening. The best tool for sharpening an image is the **Unsharp Mask**, explained in detail in **149** Sharpen an Image.

After performing any other repairs you want to perform on the image—such as removing creases, tears, specks, and such (see **122** About Removing Scratches, Specks, and Holes)—select **Filter, Sharpen, Unsharp Mask** from the menu bar. The **Unsharp Mask** dialog box opens. Adjust the **Radius** to set the size of the area around each pixel to be examined for contrast, and set the **Threshold** to a value that tells the filter what level of contrast must exist before a pixel is changed. Finally, set the **Amount** to the amount of contrast by which you want to increase qualifying pixels. When you're happy with the results, click **OK**.

④ Reduce Resolution and Resample

If you scanned the image at 600 DPI or higher, you can reduce the resolution without changing the image's print size, a process that will cause the Editor to pack the pixels closer together, creating a denser, more detailed image.

First, save the PSD file. Then resave the file in JPEG or TIFF format, leaving your PSD image with its *layers* (if any) intact so that you can return at a later time and make different adjustments if you want. Starting with a JPEG or TIFF speeds up the process of resampling, while preserving the resolution of your original scan.

Choose **Image, Resize, Image Size** from the menu. The **Image Size** dialog box appears. Enable the **Constrain Proportions** option, and type a value that's half the image's current resolution in the **Resolution** box. Select the type of resampling you want to use from the **Resample image** list and click **OK**. See **60** Change Image Size or Resolution.

16

Improving Portraits

IN THIS CHAPTER:

129 Create a Soft Focus Effect

130 Correct Red Eye

131 Remove Wrinkles, Freckles, and Minor Blemishes

132 Whiten Teeth

133 Awaken Tired Eyes

134 Remove Glare from Eyeglasses

135 Brighten a Face with Digital Makeup

Although a photograph is an accurate record of a specific moment in time, there's no particular reason why you have to "remember" the flaws your camera captured as well: the slightly yellow teeth, the blotchy skin, the wrinkles, and the wind that blew everyone's hair out of place. Using the *Editor*'s tools, you can erase these flaws or simply make them less noticeable. For example, you can remove *red eye*, erase freckles and blemishes, and remove glare from eyeglasses. You can even add a slight blush to a cheek or a bit of rouge to the lips. In this chapter, you'll learn how to perform these and other digital tricks while maintaining the essential loveliness and inner beauty of your subjects.

129 Create a Soft Focus Effect

Before You Begin

✔ **91** About Layers and the Layers Palette

✔ **97** Erase Part of a Layer

✔ **151** Blur a Background to Create Depth of Field

See Also

→ **63** Change Color Mode

To apply a soft, romantic look to an image, you can use the **Gaussian Blur** *filter*. This filter applies a soft blur to the entire *layer* or selection and is easy to use. The filter has only one option—the radius, which controls the amount of blur. The larger the radius, the greater number of pixels blurred together, and the more detail you lose. I like to control the effect somewhat by using it on a duplicate layer and then softly sharpening important features such as a person's eyes, nostrils, and mouth. In this task, you'll learn how to perform this same trick.

❶ Duplicate Image

Open the image in the *Editor* in **Standard Edit** mode and save it in Photoshop (***.psd**) format. If the image isn't using grayscale or RGB color mode already, convert it by selecting that option from the **Image, Mode** menu.

If the image has more than one layer, select the layer you want to soften from the **Layers** *palette*. Then drag the layer you want to blur onto the **Create a new layer** button on the **Layers** palette (to create a copy of it), or select **Layer, Duplicate Layer**. Name the new layer **Blurred**.

NOTE

The Editor comes with a **Soft Focus** *effect* you can try if you like, but the result is very, very subtle and produces a very soft overall blurring of the current layer.

❷ Select Gaussian Blur Filter

With the **Blurred** layer selected, select **Filter, Blur, Gaussian Blur** from the main menu or double-click the **Gaussian Blur** icon on the **Filters** list of the **Styles and Effects** palette. The **Gaussian Blur** dialog box appears.

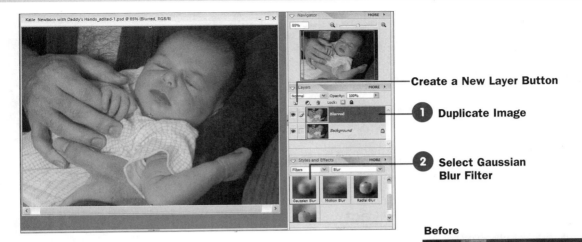

Create a New Layer Button

1 Duplicate Image

2 Select Gaussian Blur Filter

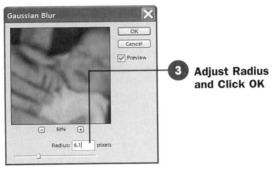

3 Adjust Radius and Click OK

Before

5 View the Result

After

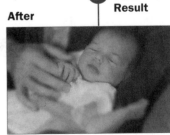

Eraser Tool

4 Sharpen Features

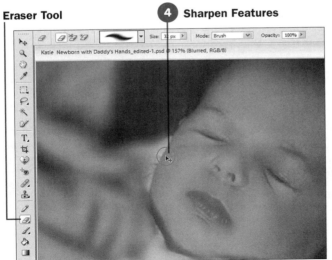

Diffuse Glow and Gaussian Blur Combined

③ Adjust Radius and Click OK

Adjust the **Radius** setting to a value that blurs the image enough to soften it, typically somewhere between **4** and **9**. You can type a value in the **Radius** text box or drag the slider. Keep an eye on the preview window to see how the **Radius** setting is affecting the image. To preview your changes in the real image, enable the **Preview** check box. Click **OK** to apply those settings.

④ Sharpen Features

The **Gaussian Blur** filter blurs everything on the current layer, including the features of your subject's face. This causes the image to lose impact because the viewer's eye depends on sharp features to distinguish a person. Select the **Eraser** tool from the **Toolbox**. On the **Options** bar, select a soft, small brush from the **Brushes** drop-down list. Lightly brush over the eyes, nostrils, and mouth areas of your subject. This action reveals the original, sharp layer underneath, bringing those features back into focus.

After you're satisfied with the image, save the result in the PSD file. Then merge the two layers together by selecting **Layer, Flatten Image** and resave the image in JPEG or TIFF format, leaving your PSD image unflattened so that you can return at a later time and make different adjustments if you want.

⑤ View the Result

I've always loved this photo of my daughter, lying contentedly in her Daddy's arms on the day she was born. But I thought a bit of soft focus might improve the image. So, I applied a Gaussian blur using a radius of 6.1 to blur the image. Then I sharpened her features just a bit, placing the focus clearly on her peaceful face. I also sharpened her hand because I considered it an intimate part of the photograph. Having just her hand in sharp focus made her father's hand look strange because it was blurred. But I didn't want to sharpen it because I didn't want her father's hand to dominate the photo which it could have because his hand was so much larger than she was at that time. So, I sharpened along the edges of two fingers only, using the **Eraser** set to half opacity. Look for this photo in the Color Gallery.

130 Correct Red Eye

When used properly, a camera flash can help lighten shadows and illuminate an otherwise dark image. Unfortunately, using a flash might sometimes have unintended effects, such as *red eye*. In nonhuman subjects such as dogs or cats, the result might be "glassy eye" rather than red eye. No matter; you remove it in the same way: with the *Editor*'s **Red Eye Removal** tool.

1 Zoom In on Eye

Open an image in the Editor in either **Quick Fix** or **Standard Edit** mode and save it in Photoshop (***.psd**) format. Zoom in on the first eye you want to correct so that you can see it better. To zoom in, click the **Zoom** tool in the **Toolbox**. Then select a **Zoom** amount on the **Options** bar or click the **Zoom in** button on the **Options** bar and drag a rectangle within the image around the eye you want to see more closely.

2 Click Red Eye Removal Tool

Click the **Red Eye Removal** tool in the **Toolbox**.

3 Set Options

If the *pupil* of the eye you want to correct is larger in area than 50% of the *iris*, change the **Pupil Size** setting on the **Options** bar to the correct ratio. If the **Pupil Size** ratio is way off, the Editor might not remove all the red eye, or it might paint in too much of the iris color, making the iris larger than it should be.

Typically, you won't have to adjust the **Darken Amount** on the **Options** bar. However, if the pupil is not darkened enough after you apply the **Red Eye Removal** tool, you can try the tool again after increasing the **Darken Amount**.

4 Select the Red Pupil

Drag the **Red Eye Removal** tool to select the red area of the pupil you want to correct. You don't have to be terribly precise because only red pixels will be affected; on the other hand, you don't want to select too big an area and accidentally remove the red from pixels you don't want to change. After you drag, red pixels within the selected area are changed to black or the iris color, depending on the **Pupil Size** you've set.

See Also

→ **133** Awaken Tired Eyes

🔍 **KEY TERMS**

Red eye—A reddening of the pupil caused by a reflection of the intense light from a camera flash against the retina in the back of the subject's eyes.

Pupil—The black center of the eye which adjusts in size based on the amount of ambient light.

Iris—The colored part of the eye; typically brown, blue, or green.

🛈 **TIPS**

When you're shooting your photograph, you can avoid giving your subjects red eye by separating the flash unit from the camera (if possible), or by telling your subjects to not look directly at the camera.

Some cameras have a red eye reduction feature, which causes the flash to go off several times. The first series of flashes at lower intensity cause the pupil to contract, thus blocking the reflection, while the final flash at full intensity illuminates the subject for the picture. Just be sure to warn your subject not to move until the second flash goes off.

Zoom In Button

1 **Zoom In on Eye**

Zoom Tool

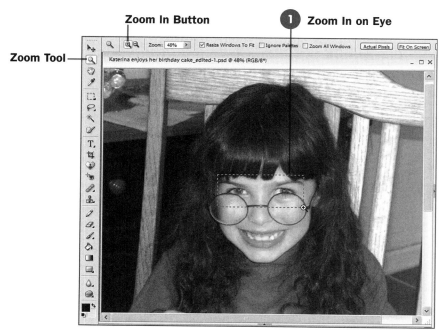

Katerina enjoys her birthday cake_edited-1.psd @ 48% (RGB/8*)

6 **View the Result**

3 **Set Options**

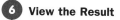
Pupil Size 50% | Darken Amount 60%

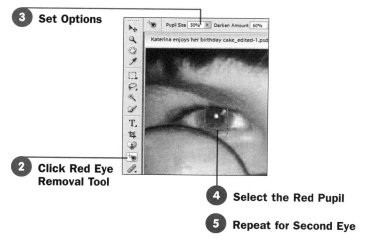

Katerina enjoys her birthday cake_edited-1.psd

2 **Click Red Eye Removal Tool**

4 **Select the Red Pupil**

5 **Repeat for Second Eye**

5 Repeat for Second Eye

Scroll the image if necessary so that you can see the second eye. Drag again to select the red area. The red pixels within that area are changed to black.

6 View the Result

After you're satisfied with the result, make any other changes you want to the PSD image then save it. Resave the result in JPEG or TIFF format, leaving your PSD image with its *layers* (if any) intact so that you can return at a later time and make different adjustments if you want.

This photo of a young "Hermione Granger" at her Harry Potter birthday party was marred only by a bit of red eye. Lucky for me, the problem was quickly fixed with the **Red Eye Removal** tool.

TIP

Instead of dragging to select the area to change, you can click anywhere within the red area of the pupil. Red pixels contiguous to the pixel you clicked are changed to black. If one method doesn't work for you, try the other and you might get better results.

131 Remove Wrinkles, Freckles, and Minor Blemishes

Almost everyone has certain…er…cosmetic distinctions that help identify and even glamorize a person. However, if they're the temporary kind, you might not want a permanent record of them. Sometimes a perfectly good photograph is marred by minor distractions such as a few blemishes, a mole, a cold sore, or a few wrinkles just beginning to show. Is it vain to want to fix nature? Perhaps, but don't let that stop you—especially when it's so easy to eliminate them.

As explained in **162 Remove Unwanted Objects from an Image**, you can use the **Clone Stamp** tool to paint away minor defects in a photograph by copying good pixels from some other area. For some very minor problem areas, you might try the **Spot Healing Brush** discussed in **124 Remove Specks and Spots** and an upcoming tip. But in either case, the process is tedious and often easily detectable unless the tools are used sparingly. In this task, you'll use a quicker method that involves one of the blur *filters*.

Before You Begin

✔ **91** About Layers and the Layers Palette

See Also

→ **132** Whiten Teeth

→ **133** Awaken Tired Eyes

→ **135** Brighten a Face with Digital Makeup

1 Duplicate Background Layer

Open an image in the *Editor* in **Standard Edit** mode and save it in Photoshop (*.psd) format. Then drag the *Background layer* onto the **Create a new layer** button on the **Layers** palette (to create a copy of it), or select **Layer, Duplicate Layer**. Name the new layer **Unblurred**.

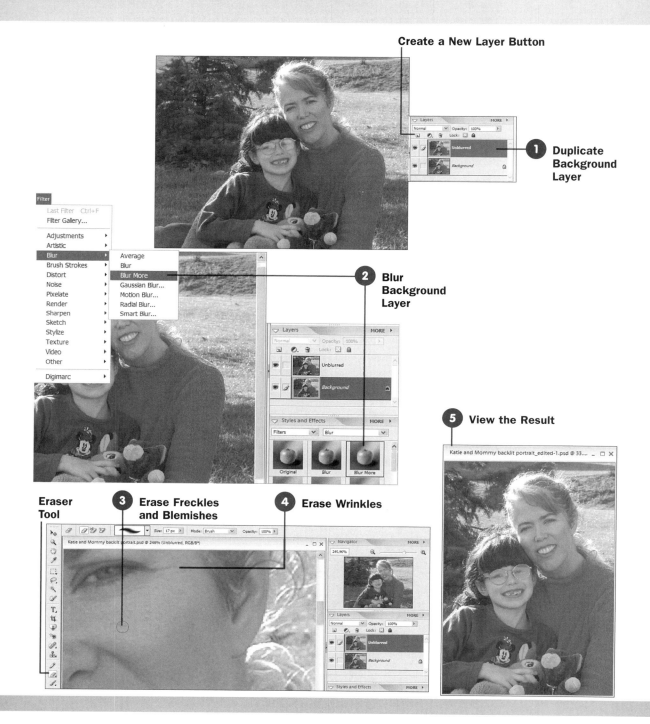

Create a New Layer Button

1 Duplicate Background Layer

Filter

Last Filter   Ctrl+F
Filter Gallery...

Adjustments   ▶
Artistic   ▶
Blur   ▶   Average
Brush Strokes   ▶   Blur
Distort   ▶   Blur More
Noise   ▶   Gaussian Blur...
Pixelate   ▶   Motion Blur...
Render   ▶   Radial Blur...
Sharpen   ▶   Smart Blur...
Sketch   ▶
Stylize   ▶
Texture   ▶
Video   ▶
Other   ▶

Digimarc   ▶

2 Blur Background Layer

5 View the Result

Eraser Tool

3 Erase Freckles and Blemishes

4 Erase Wrinkles

② Blur Background Layer

Change to the **Background** layer and select **Filter, Blur, Blur More** from the menu or double-click the **Blur More** icon on the **Filters** list of the **Styles and Effects** palette. The **Background** layer is blurred just a bit.

For very large images such as those at 1048 × 1478 *resolution*, the **Blur More** filter might not do enough to blur the layer. In such cases, try the **Gaussian Blur** filter (choose **Filter, Blur, Gaussian Blur**) or double-click the **Gaussian Blur** icon in the **Filters** list of the **Styles and Effects** palette.

③ Erase Freckles and Blemishes

On the **Layers** palette, change to the **Unblurred** layer. Click the *Eraser* tool on the **Toolbox**. On the **Options** bar, select a soft round brush. Adjust the **Size** value so that the eraser is slightly bigger than the blemish you want to remove. Click the freckle or blemish with the eraser, which erases that spot, revealing the blurred layer beneath.

④ Erase Wrinkles

Change the **Size** value on the **Options** bar to resize the **Eraser** tool so that it's just wider than the wrinkles you want to remove. Then drag the **Eraser** over any wrinkles to erase the wrinkle, revealing the blurred wrinkle on the **Background** layer.

⑤ View the Result

After you're satisfied with the image, save it in its PSD format. Merge the layers together by selecting **Layer, Flatten Image** and save the result in JPEG or TIFF format, leaving your PSD image unflattened so that you can return at a later time and make different adjustments if you want.

This photo of me and my daughter is just wonderful, but the small blemish and the wrinkles just beginning to show on my face made the photo less than perfect for me. A bit of blur and a few minutes with the **Eraser**, and I'm the person I see when I look in the mirror. Add a bit of judicious cropping and some work at removing the reflections from my daughter's glasses as described in **134 Remove Glare from Eyeglasses**, and I have a portrait worthy of my living room wall.

 TIP

To see the blurred **Background** layer, hide the top layer temporarily by clicking its eye icon on the **Layers** palette.

TIP

Another way you can remove blemishes and freckles quickly is to blend them away with the **Spot Healing Brush** tool. Set the **Size** so that the brush includes the clean area of skin around the blemish or freckle, set **Type** to **Proximity Match**, position the pointer over the blemish or freckle, and click to blend it away.

132 Whiten Teeth

Before You Begin

✔ **111** About Tool Options

See Also

→ **131** Remove Wrinkles, Freckles, and Minor Blemishes

→ **133** Awaken Tired Eyes

→ **135** Brighten a Face with Digital Makeup

NOTE

I always get good results with the **Dodge** tool, but if you don't like its effects, try selecting the teeth, choosing **Enhance, Adjust Color, Color Variations**, choosing **Highlights**, and clicking the **Increase Blue** and **Lighten** buttons. See **145** **Correct Color, Contrast, and Saturation in One Step**. You can also try choosing Enhance, Adjust Color, Adjust Hue/Saturation, and then increasing the lightness in the Master channel and decreasing the saturation in the Yellow channel. See adjust Hue and Saturation Manually

There are many products on the market you can use to whiten your teeth—gels, toothpastes, whitening strips, and bleaches—but none work as fast and as effectively as digital editing. It's not vanity to want to improve Mother Nature; in our culture today, a great importance is placed on having clean, white teeth, and if a photo will be used in a resume or to advertise a product, you'll want to give the best impression you can by making sure that your subject looks his or her best.

Whitening teeth is tricky, however; you don't want the effect to look obvious and artificial. You'll want to avoid the temptation to use *pure white* to paint over all your teeth, which results in a picket-fence effect that can look genuinely scary. The technique explained here uses the **Dodge** tool, which selectively lightens the brightness of the pixels over which it passes. You must be cautious, however, so that you don't burn out the color and create a fake whiteness.

❶ Select the Dodge Tool

Open an image in the *Editor* in **Standard Edit** mode and save it in Photoshop (***.psd**) format. Zoom in on the teeth so that you can see them clearly, and then select the **Dodge** tool in the **Toolbox**.

❷ Set Options

On the **Options** bar, choose a soft round brush. Adjust the **Size** of the **Dodge** tool so that the brush tip is about the size of one tooth. Set the **Range** to **Midtones** so that you affect only the *midtones*, and set **Exposure** to about **20%** so that you don't lighten the teeth too fast and accidentally burn out the color.

❸ Whiten the Teeth

Position the brush tip over the first tooth and click once. The tooth should get just a bit lighter. Click again to lighten a bit more, or move to the next tooth. Repeat until all the teeth are whiter. You can also drag the brush over the teeth.

Remove any remaining imperfections (such as uneven color or spots on the teeth) with the **Clone Stamp** tool. See **162** **Remove Unwanted Objects from an Image**.

① **Select the Dodge Tool**

② **Set Options**

Before

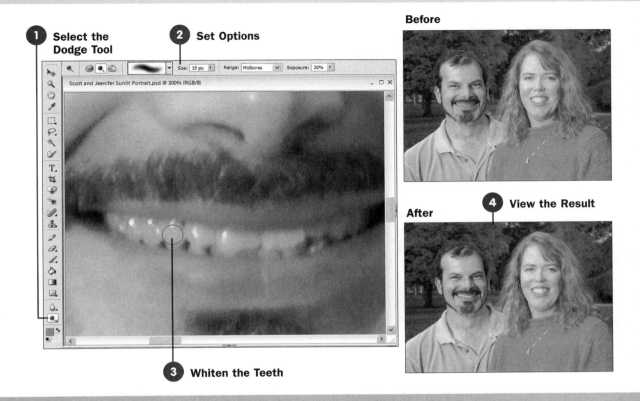

Scott and Jeenifer Sunlit Portrait.psd @ 300% (RGB/8)

③ **Whiten the Teeth**

After

④ **View the Result**

④ View the Result

When you're satisfied with the result, make any other changes you want and save the PSD file. Resave the result in JPEG or TIFF format, leaving your PSD image with its *layers* (if any) intact so that you can return at a later time and make different adjustments if you want.

In this portrait, the golden light of sunset made our teeth look yellowish. A few minutes with the **Dodge** tool fixed that easily. Compare the original to the whitened version; you can see that the teeth look better, and yet still natural. I also used the technique discussed in **131** **Remove Wrinkles, Freckles, and Minor Blemishes** to freshen my face a bit. The last things to address are the circles under my husband's eyes, caused mostly by the low angle of the sun. To fix that problem, I'll follow the steps in the next task, **133** **Awaken Tired Eyes**. Look for the final result in the Color Gallery.

TIPS

To isolate the effects of the **Dodge** tool, select the teeth before beginning. You might want to select the gums as well (if they are reddish and irritated) so that you can lighten them too.

Instead of using the **Dodge** tool to whiten teeth, you can try selecting them, choosing **Enhance, Adjust Color, Adjust Hue/Saturation**, and then increasing the lightness in the **Master** channel and decreasing the saturation in the **Yellow** channel. See **146** **Adjust Hue, Saturation, and Lightness Manually**.

133 Awaken Tired Eyes

Before You Begin

✔ **70** About Making Selections

✔ **111** About Tool Options

See Also

→ **130** Correct Red Eye

→ **131** Remove Wrinkles, Freckles, and Minor Blemishes

→ **132** Whiten Teeth

→ **140** Lighten or Darken a Portion of an Image

They say that the eyes are the window to the soul. It must be true because if a woman has dark circles under her eyes, we think she looks tired (even if the dark circles are a natural skin condition). By slightly lightening the skin under the eyes, you can take years off a face and brighten a person's outlook. And it's simple to do, using the **Dodge** tool.

Redness in the whites of the eyes caused by chlorine in swimming pools or lack of sleep can also make your subject look tired. To whiten the eyes, you'll remove the redness gradually and lighten them a little using the **Color Variations** command. One final thing that can make eyes look tired is a lack of sharpness. Eyes that are in sharp focus have a distinctive twinkle that makes their owner look alert, interesting, and beautiful. Eyes such as these invite a viewer to look a moment longer at the subject. To fix a problem with slightly out-of-focus eyes, you'll oversharpen a copy of the image on a new *layer* and use the **Eraser** to reveal only the sharpened eyes.

1 Select the Dodge Tool

Open an image in the *Editor* in **Standard Edit** mode and save it in Photoshop (***.psd**) format. Zoom in on the eyes so that you can see them clearly, and then select the **Dodge** tool in the **Toolbox**.

2 Set Options

On the **Options** bar, choose a soft round brush. Adjust the **Size** of the **Dodge** tool so that the brush tip is about the size of the area you want to lighten. In this case, I adjusted the size so that the brush was the same size as the crease under one eye.

Set the **Range** to **Shadows**, and **Exposure** to about **20%** so that you don't lighten the under-eye area too fast and accidentally burn out the color.

3 Lighten Under Eye

Drag the brush over the area you want to lighten. In my case, I drug the brush carefully over the under-eye crease. Repeat this step for the second eye.

💡 TIP

If you'd like more control over the **Dodge** tool, try duplicating the image layer and performing your lightening on the copy layer. You can then adjust the **Opacity** of the copy layer to lower the effect of the lightening if you accidentally apply too much.

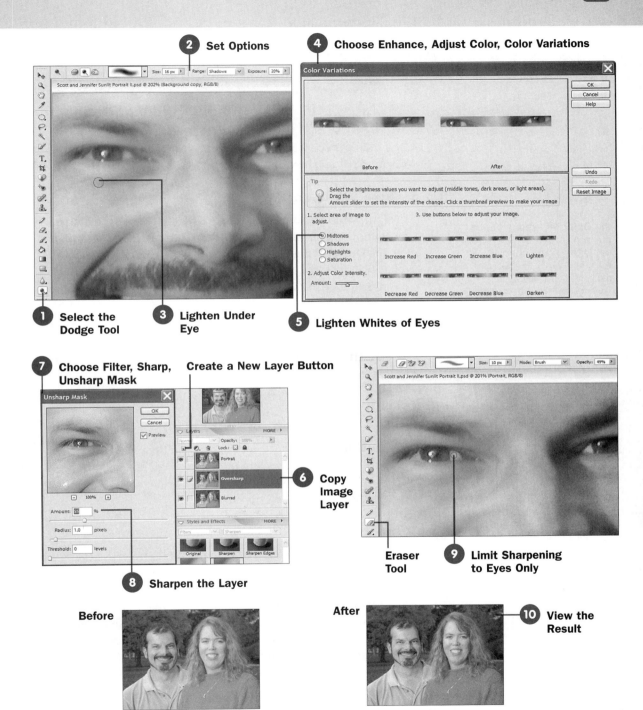

2 Set Options

4 Choose Enhance, Adjust Color, Color Variations

1 Select the Dodge Tool

3 Lighten Under Eye

5 Lighten Whites of Eyes

7 Choose Filter, Sharp, Unsharp Mask

Create a New Layer Button

6 Copy Image Layer

8 Sharpen the Layer

Eraser Tool

9 Limit Sharpening to Eyes Only

Before

After

10 View the Result

4 Choose Enhance, Adjust Color, Color Variations

If your subject's eyes are red or tired looking, select the white area of both eyes using your favorite selection tool. (I used the **Magic Wand** tool to select the whites of each eye, and the **Lasso** to snag any parts that didn't get selected.)

Choose **Enhance, Adjust Color, Color Variations**. The **Color Variations** dialog box appears.

NOTE

You can click the buttons in the **Color Variations** dialog box more than once to apply the same change multiple times. For example, you could click the **Decrease Red** button twice if your subject's eyes are particularly reddish.

5 Lighten Whites of Eyes

Select the **Midtones** option in the lower-left corner of the dialog box so that you affect only the *midtones* in the image, and then click the **Decrease Red** button to remove the redness from the eye area. Click the **Lighten** button to make the whites a little whiter. The **After** image at the top of the dialog box reflects the changes you're making. When you're through, click **OK**.

6 Copy Image Layer

To sharpen the eyes of your subject, drag the image *layer* onto the **Create a new layer** button on the **Layers** *palette* (to create a copy of it), or select **Layer, Duplicate Layer**. Name the new layer **Oversharp**.

NOTE

My original image is on a layer called **Portrait**; the **Blurred** layer at the bottom was added so that I could remove some wrinkles, blemishes, and the like. See **131** Remove Wrinkles, Freckles, and Minor Blemishes.

7 Choose Filter, Sharp, Unsharp Mask

With the **Oversharp** layer selected, choose **Filter, Sharpen, Unsharp Mask** from the menu or double-click the **Unsharp Mask** icon on the **Filters** list of the **Styles and Effects** palette. The **Unsharp Mask** dialog box appears.

8 Sharpen the Layer

In the **Unsharp Mask** dialog box, zoom in on one of the eyes and then adjust the settings for the *filter* until the eye is sharp and crisp. I typically leave the **Threshold** at a low value, set the **Radius** to somewhere between 1 and 2, and then play with the **Amount** until I get the effect I want. See **149** Sharpen an Image for more help. Check the other eye in the preview window of the dialog box (by dragging the image in the preview), and when you're satisfied with the look, click **OK**.

To make the eyes really sharp, reapply the **Unsharp Mask** settings one or two more times by choosing **Filter, Unsharp Mask**.

9 Limit Sharpening to Eyes Only

The effect right now is a too-sharp image, and we wanted to limit the effect to just the eyes. On the **Layers** palette, drag the **Oversharp** layer below your image layer. The sharpness will appear to go away, but really it's just hidden by the image layer above it.

To reveal the sharpened eyes, click the *Eraser* tool on the **Toolbox**. On the **Options** bar, select a small, soft brush. On the **Layers** palette, select the image layer. Then erase just the eyes, revealing the over-sharpened layer below.

10 View the Result

After you're satisfied with the result, make any other changes you want and save the PSD file. Resave the result in JPEG or TIFF format, leaving your PSD image with its layers (if any) intact so that you can return at a later time and make different adjustments if you want.

Although I had brightened our teeth and done some other minor retouching to this portrait of my husband and me, the circles under my husband's eyes and the tired look in both our eyes still bothered me. So I lightened the creases under his eyes and whitened both of our eyes just a bit, and then sharpened the eyes. Finally, I used the **Spot Healing Brush** to remove some shininess on our faces, ending up with a very special portrait. Look for this final result in the Color Gallery.

> **TIP**
>
> Because the **Oversharp** layer is below the image layer, you won't see the effects of the sharpening on your actual image at first. To view the sharpening, on the **Layers** palette, click off the eye icon on the image layer to hide that layer temporarily.

> **TIP**
>
> If your image is on the *Background layer*, you'll have to convert it to a regular layer before you can drag the **Oversharp** layer underneath it in the layer stack. To do that, select the **Background** layer on the **Layers** palette and choose **Layer, New, Layer From Background**.

134 Remove Glare from Eyeglasses

Probably the most difficult photographic repair you will ever attempt is to remove glare from a person's eyeglasses. What makes this repair so difficult is that no one method works every time. In this task, you'll learn a variety of techniques, one or two of which should work on your photograph.

Because glare is difficult to remove, it's best to try to eliminate it while *taking* the photograph. One way to remove glare is to use a *polarizing* filter—a special filter that you twist to bend the light so that the glare is not picked up by the camera lens. If you don't happen to have a polarizing filter with you, try moving your subject so that the light is coming at him or her from a different angle, moving your own position in relation to the subject, or simply having your subject remove his or her eyeglasses or look off to one side or slightly downward.

Before You Begin

✔ **70** About Making Selections

✔ **91** About Layers and the Layers Palette

See Also

→ **123** Remove Scratches

→ **125** Repair Minor Tears, Scratches, Spots, and Stains

→ **133** Awaken Tired Eyes

→ **140** Lighten or Darken a Portion of an Image

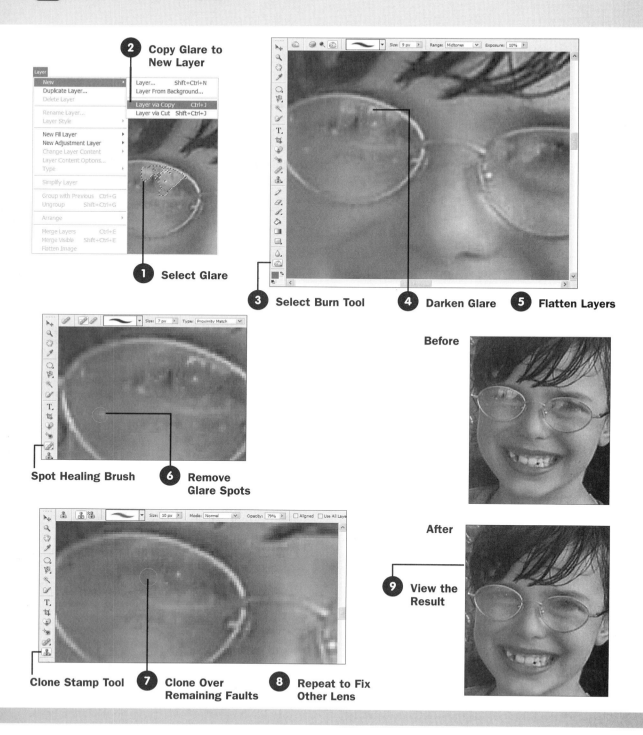

2 Copy Glare to New Layer

1 Select Glare

3 Select Burn Tool **4** Darken Glare **5** Flatten Layers

Spot Healing Brush **6** Remove Glare Spots

Before

Clone Stamp Tool **7** Clone Over Remaining Faults **8** Repeat to Fix Other Lens

After

9 View the Result

1 Select Glare

Open an image in the *Editor* in **Standard Edit** mode and save it in Photoshop (*.psd) format.

Because each eyeglass lens typically needs a slightly different adjustment, it's best to work on one eye at a time. It's also best to isolate what you're doing on another layer so that you can easily start over (by deleting the layer) if need be. Zoom in and then, using either the **Lasso** or **Magic Wand** tool, select the area of glare on the first lens.

2 Copy Glare to New Layer

To copy the selected area, choose **Edit, Copy** from the menu. To place the copy on a new *layer*, choose **Layer, New, Layer via Copy**. Name the new layer **Glare**.

3 Select Burn Tool

Click the **Burn** tool on the **Toolbox**. On the **Options** bar, choose a soft round brush. Adjust the **Size** of the **Burn** tool so that the brush tip is about the size of the area you want to lighten. Set the **Range** to **Highlights** so that you affect only the lightest areas of the image, and set the **Exposure** to a small value such as **10%** so that each stroke over the area darkens the pixels only slightly. These settings enable you to work slowly to remove the glare.

4 Darken Glare

Make sure that the **Glare** layer is selected on the **Layers** *palette*. Brush the **Burn** tool over the glare to darken it so that it better matches the surrounding area. If necessary, darken the midtones as well by setting the **Range** to **Midtones** in the **Options** bar. You might not be able to remove the glare entirely; your goal here is to bring out the detail of the eye behind the glare.

5 Flatten Layers

When you're satisfied that you've done all you can with the **Burn** tool, choose **Layer, Flatten Image** to merge the layers together.

Before you merge the layers, you might want to increase the *saturation* in the glare area because it might have been desaturated by the **Burn** tool. Select the **Sponge** tool from the **Toolbox**, set the **Mode** to **Saturate**, adjust the **Size** and **Flow** settings, and drag over the area to bring its colors back.

💡 TIP

If you wear eyeglasses, you can keep an old pair of frames (minus the lenses) on hand for picture-taking time. Without the lenses, you obviously won't get the glare, and the empty frames will help your face look more natural.

💡 TIP

If only one eyeglass lens is affected with glare, you can try another method to remove the glare. Try copying the good eye to another layer, flipping it, and *skewing* it to conform to the other eye space. Then flatten the layers and use the **Clone Stamp** tool to blend the eye into its new surroundings. You can also try copying an eye from a similar photograph that does not have any glare.

6 Remove Glare Spots

After merging the layers, if there are any sharp points of glare (as opposed to larger glare patches), you can remove them with the **Spot Healing Brush.** Click the **Spot Healing Brush** on the **Toolbox.** Set the **Type** to **Proximity Match** and adjust the **Size** so that the brush is slightly larger than the glare spot you want to remove. Then click the spot to remove it. Repeat this process as needed to remove any other glare spots.

7 Clone Over Remaining Faults

To fix the remaining problem areas, click the **Clone Stamp** tool on the **Toolbox.** On the **Options** bar, select a soft round brush, adjust the **Size,** and set the **Mode** to **Normal.** You might want to lower the **Opacity** as well to help disguise what you're doing. Press **Alt** and click the area you want to clone, and then drag the brush over the glare area to transfer the **Alt**-selected pixels to the new area. Repeat to repair any other flaws.

TIP

To clone a skin color from another portion of the face, you might want to turn off the **Aligned** option for the **Clone Stamp** tool in the **Options** bar so that you don't clone anything but that small area, and not the objects in that same vicinity.

8 Repeat to Fix Other Lens

After you're satisfied with the way in which the first eyeglass lens looks, repeat steps 1 to 7 to remove the glare from the second lens (if any).

9 View the Result

After you're satisfied with your changes, save the PSD image. Then resave the result in JPEG or TIFF format, leaving your PSD image with its layers (if any) intact so that you can return at a later time and make different adjustments if you want.

Even though this portrait of my daughter was taken under the shade of a large maple tree, the glare of the sunlight still caught her eyeglasses. After removing the glare, her wonderful eyes are now much more apparent. Look for this image in the Color Gallery.

135 Brighten a Face with Digital Makeup

As we age, we lose color from our skin, turning almost pale and lifeless in extreme cases. To combat this effect, most women wear some kind of makeup: some eyeliner to outline the eyes, eye makeup to add color and depth to the eyebrow area, a bit of blush to rosy up a cheek, and some lipstick to add color and definition to the lips. Even if your subject is not a woman, a bit of neutral color here and there can erase the sun's effect on the skin, leaving your subject more youthful. In this task, you'll learn how to apply makeup after the fact, or to touch up areas that simply wore off during a long day of festivities.

Before You Begin

✔ **91** About Layers and the Layers Palette

✔ **116** Paint an Area of a Photo with a Brush

✔ **117** Paint an Area of a Photo with the Airbrush

See Also

→ **178** Colorize a Photograph

1 Create Eyes Layer

Open an image in the *Editor* in **Standard Edit** mode, and save it in Photoshop (*.psd) format.

To create a *layer* for the eye makeup, click the **Create a new layer** button on the **Layers** *palette* or choose **Layer, New, Layer** from the menu. Name this new layer **Eyes**.

2 Apply Eye Makeup

Zoom in on one eye. Click the **Brush** tool on the **Toolbox**. On the **Options** bar, select a soft, round brush. Adjust the **Size** so that the brush is about the same width as the eyelid. Select the color you want to use as makeup; I pressed **Ctrl**, and when the mouse pointer on the **Brush** tool changed to an **Eyedropper**, I clicked on the image to pick up the subject's blue eye color. To add an almost metallic effect to the color, I set the *background color* to light gray, clicked the **More Options** button on the **Options** bar, and set the **Hue Jitter** to 15%. This setting causes the brush color to change between the *foreground color* and the background color as you brush.

Change the *blend mode* for the **Eyes** layer to **Soft Light**. Brush the eye makeup color over the eye lid of each eye. Adjust the effect by lowering the **Opacity** of the **Eyes** layer, or selecting a different blend mode such as **Hard Light, Hue, Color,** or **Overlay**.

NOTE

Although they don't need the extra color, this technique can also be used to create unique portraits of children. If you desaturate an image, for example, and then add touches of color to a child's cheeks, lips, and hair, you can create an angelic effect.

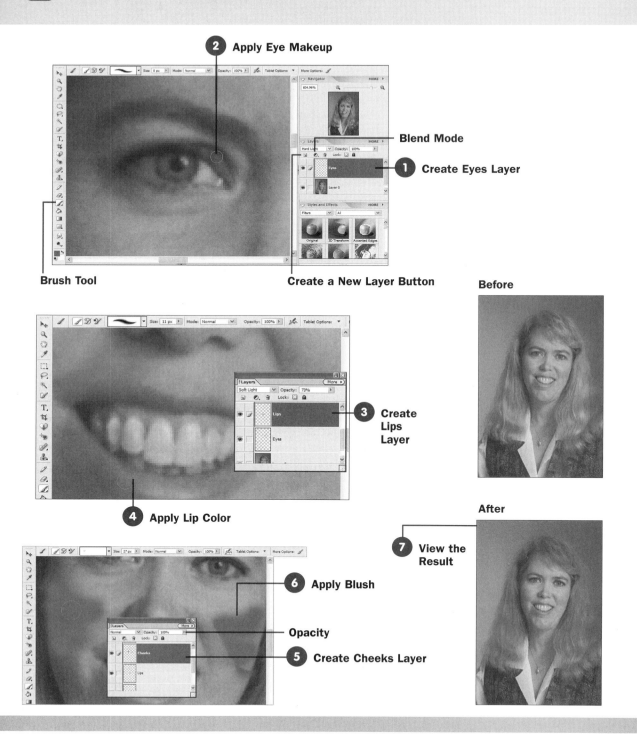

2 Apply Eye Makeup

Blend Mode

1 Create Eyes Layer

Brush Tool

Create a New Layer Button

Before

3 Create Lips Layer

4 Apply Lip Color

After

7 View the Result

6 Apply Blush

Opacity

5 Create Cheeks Layer

③ Create Lips Layer

To create a layer for the lip color, click the **Create a new layer** button on the **Layers** palette or choose **Layer, New, Layer** from the menu. Name this new layer **Lips**. Change the blend mode of the **Lips** layer to **Soft Light**.

④ Apply Lip Color

With the **Brush** tool still selected, set the *foreground color* to the lip color you want to use. On the **Options** bar, adjust the **Size** of the brush to fit the width of the lips, and then paint each lip carefully with the color you've chosen. Again, you can adjust the effect by changing the **Lips** layer's **Opacity** and blend mode. Try **Hard Light, Hue, Color, Vivid Light, Linear Light,** or **Overlay**.

⑤ Create Cheeks Layer

Create a layer for the cheek color by clicking the **Create a new layer** button on the **Layers** palette or choosing **Layer, New, Layer** from the menu. Name this new layer **Cheeks**. Change the blend mode of the **Cheeks** layer to **Soft Light**.

⑥ Apply Blush

With the **Brush** tool still selected, set the foreground color to the blush color you want to use. Alternatively, can press **Alt**, and when the brush tip changes to an **Eyedropper**, click the image to sample the existing cheek color. Click the foreground swatch at the bottom of the **Toolbox** and use the **Color Picker** to increase the sampled color's saturation (and add a bit more red if you like).

After choosing a blush color, on the **Options** bar, increase the **Size** of the brush to around 1/2 to 1/3 the size of one cheek. You might want to decrease the **Opacity** to around 30% so that you create a subtle effect. Click the **Airbrush** button on the left end of the **Options** bar and then click the **More Options** button and set the **Fade** setting to a low value such as **9** so that the paint will quickly fade away to nothing as you brush. This will help you apply the blush more naturally to the cheek. For help using the **Airbrush,** see **117 Paint an Area of a Photo with the Airbrush**.

Using short strokes that begin at the highest point of the cheek and move toward the outer edge of the face, paint the blush color onto

TIPS

If you're not sure what makeup color to use, you can view sample eye, lip, and cheek makeup colors on the Web, at various makeup manufacturers' Web sites.

If you want to add eyeliner, use a very small, hard brush set to 50% **Opacity**. Pick up the color of the skin just under the eye, and darken it (by lowering the brightness in the **Color Picker**) to create a natural eyeliner color that's not black (black will be too dark if you use it on a photo). You can use this same brush to stroke in thicker eyelashes if you like.

the cheeks. Do not apply blush closer to the nose than two of the subject's finger widths. Continue applying the blush, creating a small triangle of color on each cheek. Adjust the effect by reducing the **Opacity** of the **Cheeks** layer, or by selecting a different blend mode such as **Overlay** or **Hard Light**.

7 View the Result

After you're satisfied with the image, save the PSD file. Then merge the layers together by selecting **Layer, Flatten Image** and resave the result in JPEG or TIFF format, leaving your PSD image unflattened so that you can return at a later time and make different adjustments if you want.

I decided that I could improve this portrait a bit by adding a touch of makeup. I also used these same techniques to change my hair color—I always wanted to see what I'd look like as a redhead! Look for the before and after images in the Color Gallery.

TIPS

If this method does not produce the subtle effect you're looking for, erase everything on the **Cheeks** layer using the **Eraser** tool and try applying the cheek color again, this time with the **Brush** tool's **Opacity** set to **40%** or less.

If your subject has a nice blush on her cheeks already, but you want to bring it out more, use the **Sponge** tool to increase the saturation of color in the cheek area. See **147 Adjust Saturation for a Specific Area**.

17

Correcting Brightness and Contrast in a Photograph

IN THIS CHAPTER:

136 About an Image's Histogram

137 Improve Brightness and Contrast

138 Improve a Dull, Flat Photo

139 Lighten a Subject on a Snowy Background

140 Lighten or Darken Part of an Image

141 Improve a Nighttime Photo

142 Fix a Flash That's Too Close

143 Fix a Flash That's Too Far Away

Not all of us enjoy a professional level of reliability with our cameras. With the benefit of digital photography, though, you can use the computer to correct a great many defects in your photos. Correcting images works best, of course, when the defects are not too serious.

One of the easiest problems to overcome using a **graphics editor** is poor exposure. Your picture might be overexposed (too dark) or underexposed (too light). It might have too little contrast (too gray) or too much contrast (taken in bright sun and deep shadow). Within its extensive electronic darkroom, Photoshop Elements has a host of tools to correct exposure problems and "make it come out right."

136 About an Image's Histogram

See Also

→ **137** Improve Brightness and Contrast

→ **138** Improve a Dull, Flat Photo

KEY TERM

Histogram—A chart that depicts the relative distribution of pixels in an image that share the same characteristics, such as lightness, saturation, hue, or presence in a particular color channel (red, green, or blue). Use it to determine whether particular colors or brightness values disproportionately predominate, diminishing picture quality.

Business analysts and economists frequently create charts whose sole purpose is to confirm for their benefactors what they already know about their business or about the world in which they live. What they can't say out loud with spoken language about how expensive things are getting, how unproductive workers have become, and how few employees there seem to be on *this* continent can be conveyed briefly and simply in a chart that speaks volumes. One word for a type of chart that speaks volumes about a changing subject—any subject—is a *histogram*. Adobe uses the concept of the histogram in all its imaging tools, including Photoshop Elements, to refer to a chart that describes the progression of tones and of brightness in images. What is difficult to describe in words about what's right or what's wrong about an image, a histogram conveys in mere moments.

The characteristics that define the content of any one pixel in an image can be represented on either of two scales: one that represents relative quantities of red, green, and blue; and another that locates a particular pixel on a coordinate scale based on hue, saturation, and luminance. Perhaps you've noticed that all six of these key characteristics are represented on a scale from 0 to 255. This creates an interesting convenience: If you imagine a bar chart where the left side represents all the 0 values and the right side all the 255 values, you can plot all six characteristics on the same chart.

Red and Green Separate Here...

...And Here

An old Polaroid print whose yellows have faded.

Suppose that such a chart represented the relative *redness* of pixels throughout an image. All the pixels whose red component is 0 can line up in the leftmost column, all those pixels whose red is 255 can line up in the rightmost column, and all the intermediate values can fill in between the two. So, you now have a plot of dark reds on the left, bright reds on the right. Combine this with a plot of relative greens and relative blues, and the chart now gives you a complete picture of the distribution of all the colors in the available spectrum, throughout your image.

What do you learn from looking at such a chart? When you know there's something wrong with the appearance of a photograph but you just can't put your finger on what or why, the histogram helps to direct your finger to specifically what and why. For instance, old color photographs—especially Polaroid prints—tend to look dreary and muted. After you've scanned one, the histogram of its color channels will probably reveal a dip in its green levels on the right end of the graph. Red and green together, optically, produce yellow; and on a printed Polaroid photograph, yellow is the ink that tends to fade the soonest (cyan next, whereas magenta always seems to outlast the other

NOTE

Although yellows tend to fade first in old Polaroid prints, the cyan inks fade first in old Kodak prints, leaving the reds, pinks, and yellows.

two inks). A histogram of the same photo's brightness channel will probably also reveal deep chasms along both the left and right sides, indicating an image with neither sharp brights nor deep darks. Shifting the weight of these plots to restore balance to the green channel and to fill in the side gaps on the brightness channel can restore most, if not all, the original print's luster and brilliance. With the Photoshop Elements **Levels** command, you can restore an image by directly tinkering with the histogram; you can actually change the graph to alter the image.

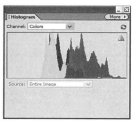

This histogram of a faded Polaroid print shows a classic separation between the channels.

Making the proper changes to an image can be as simple as adjusting the histogram so that the left side of the "mountain" touches the left edge of the graph, the right side touches the right edge, and the peaks are more toward the middle than to one side or the other. This is true if you're changing overall brightness—which affects all three color channels at once—or one color channel at a time. When you're working with individual color channels, making the proper changes can also involve moving one channel in the graph so that its peaks and valleys fall in line with the other two channels.

There is, however, one tricky point to histogram adjustment, and it involves neither the left side nor the right side, but the *middle*.

Specifically, where should the middle be? In optics, the richest or brightest color is *not* the lightest color, but instead what artists and engineers alike call the *midtones*. When Photoshop Elements is plotting a histogram for the **Histogram** *palette* or for the **Levels** dialog box, it's answering two questions: First, how soon is the image progressing from darks to midtones? Second, how much space remains for the progression between midtones and lights? This is important because the very lightest shades attainable for any color are all represented in the HSB scale by *white*. The whiter a shade is, the less saturated it is and—because all the other color channels use white as their lightest point as well—the more likely your eyes are to mistakenly perceive that shade as a color other than it truly is.

So, the most important point on a histogram is not the peak but the point that represents the midtone for all channels together, as well as for each channel separately. This point is called the *gamma*.

No single adjustment is more effective at restoring midtones to an image than repositioning the gamma point. When an image is first scanned in or imported from a digital camera, the *Editor* assumes a gamma for that image of 1.0. This value represents the bias that the Editor is applying to the image it's processing now; keep in mind that your camera might already have applied its own bias when it originally shot the photo. The adjustments you make to an image's gamma in the **Levels** dialog box affect the way the Editor reinterprets the image.

KEY TERMS

Midtones—Pixels with a luminance value near the middle of those allowed—a value of about 128. The midtones in an image are an object's true color, without shadows or highlights (reflected light).

Gamma—The measure of the contrast of an image or imaging device, such as a monitor. Adjusting the gamma of an image affects the contrast within the midtones without affecting the contrast within the shadow and highlight areas. If you plot the power needed by your monitor to produce a range of values from pure white to pure black, you'd see a curve. In mathematics, the gamma is the point at which the curve bends.

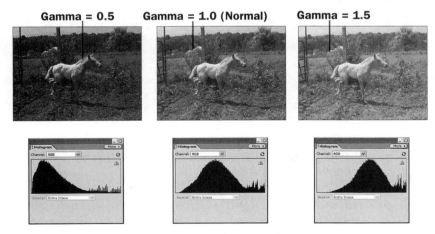

In the middle is the original image. On the left is a copy with gamma decreased; on the right is a copy with gamma increased.

With the **Levels** command, you can make the adjustments that restore the balance and continuity to a scene that your mind told you it had when you first received the impulse to take a picture of it. You can make the lights lighter and the darks darker, and in so doing, vastly improve the contrast of an image while losing none of the detail. Yet these types of changes are not at all the same as turning up or down the contrast and brightness knobs. Those other one-touch changes (one of which you'll see in **137 Improve Brightness and Contrast**) affect the whole picture equally and proportionally in all places. And as the histogram will demonstrate to you, they don't actually restore or create balance. Because everything is adjusted equally, these controls simply move the *imbalance* of an optical factor from one point to another, less noticeable point.

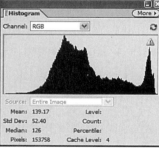

"Twin peaks" help illustrate the clear and natural contrast between midtones and highlights in this photo.

With histograms, you see the distribution of light and dark pixels throughout an image (or a selection of a portion of an image, or a particular *layer*). Boiled down to its technical underpinnings, *contrast* can be defined as the differentiation between light and dark elements. Thus, arguably, images with the sharpest possible contrasts would use only black and white pixels. The Editor would plot the histogram for such an image with high cliffs on the left and right, and a chasm in-between. More realistic images with very extreme light and dark contrasts would have relatively high peaks on the left and right, with a dip in the middle, suggesting a relative absence of midtones. To make such a pronounced image more pleasing to the eye, one type of histogram adjustment you might attempt is to blunt the peaks and fill up some of the valley. With histogram adjustment, you experiment with altering the image by tinkering with the geometry of the graph.

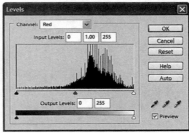
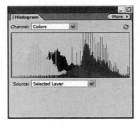

*With the **Levels** command, you can see whether brights and darks within a selection are pinched together or spread apart.*

Using the **Levels** command and the **Histogram** palette in conjunction with one another, you can learn why your composition works the way it does. For example, would you believe the smaller rose in this picture is *green*? From the computer's vantage point, what appears to be a red rose is actually comprised of strong, dark blue-green tones according to the **Histogram** palette. Why? Because blues and greens combine to form an optical opposite of red, and opposites are used in combination with pure colors to *darken* them. So, the dark parts of the rose are less saturated as a result. But notice that it's the bright reds (as you see isolated in the

NOTE

Astonishingly, a photograph that's mainly a portrait of a person's face reveals its own signature through its histogram: from left to right, a blue peak, followed by a green one, and then a red one. This is true for faces with any skin tone, dark or light; with lighter tones, the trio of peaks simply appears further to the right. African skin tones register on the histogram with their green peaks slightly to the right of the middle; Norwegian and other light skin tones register slightly to the left of the middle. In any case, the green peak falls between the other two. Knowing this, one way you can correct an apparent discoloration in someone's portrait is to examine the histograms of other well-balanced portraits of the same person and adjust the graphs of the red, green, and blue channels of the discolored photo so that the peaks fall mainly within the same areas.

Layers dialog box) that stand out on the right side of the histogram. It's this standing out that gives the entire rose its red appearance. If the red and green peaks were closer together on the right side of the graph, the little rose might look more like the big yellow rose at the top of the image. In **138** **Improve a Dull, Flat Photo**, you'll see how to use the **Levels** dialog box.

*The **Colors** channel reveals the telltale signature of human flesh tones: a blue peak, followed by green, followed by red.*

With the **Histogram** palette, you can view the current statistics for any open image—specifically, from any chosen layer in that image or from the current selection for a layer in that image. To display the palette, select **Window, Histogram** from the Editor's main menu. If it's convenient, you can keep this palette open at all times, either docked in the *Palette bin* or free-floating. You don't have to do anything more; from that point on, the palette shows the graph of your choice for whatever is currently selected.

You can use the **Histogram** palette to display information for the three color channels (red, green, and blue), either separately or as a whole.

Open the **Channels** drop-down list at the top of the **Histogram** palette and choose **Red**, **Green**, or **Blue**. The histogram curve changes to reflect the distribution of pixels in just that color channel. To get a clearer idea of how colors interact with one another, choose **Colors** from the **Channels** list. In this display, each color component is shown with its own natively colored curve. The histogram shows *cyan* where the blue and green curves intersect, *yellow* where the green and red curves intersect, *magenta* where the red and blue curves intersect, and *gray* where all three curves intersect with each other.

The histogram for the **Luminosity** channel displays an *evaluation* of the relative brightness of pixels in the image. There's a subtle difference between the **Luminosity** channel and the **RGB** channel of the **Histogram** palette: Commonly considered the primary histogram, **RGB** displays relative values of the Brightness (**B**) component of all the pixels in the image; whereas **Luminosity** is a result of a formula that evaluates the other two components of a pixel—Hue (**H**) and Saturation (**S**). Think of the **Luminosity** channel as representing the *richness* of color, as opposed to its brightness or *whiteness*. Don't confuse **Luminosity** with *luminance*, which is a term often used elsewhere to mean brightness, and in some color models, is used in place of Brightness (**B**).

As you make a change to all or part of an image using a tool such as the **Brightness/Contrast** dialog box (covered in (137) **Improve Brightness and Contrast**), when the **Preview** option is enabled, the **Histogram** palette shows you the extent of the change you're making *as you're making it*. For the currently displayed channel (except for **Colors**), the palette shows a gray curve with a bright peak, representing the current state of the image, along with a black curve representing the state of the image *if and when* you apply the changes. You can watch the black curve move away from the gray curve as you use the slider.

 TIP

The **Threshold** filter helps you find the brightest or darkest spots on an image. This knowledge can be valuable later in designating white points and black points for the **Levels** dialog box so that you can balance an image's brightness histogram (see (138) **Improve a Dull, Flat Photo**). Select **Filter, Adjustments, Threshold.** The current image changes to stark black and white, and a new histogram appears, called the *threshold*, with a slider at the bottom. The slider is initially set at the midpoint of the graph: **128.** Any portion of the original image detail that is darker than the position marked by the slider is rendered in black; anything lighter is in white. To find the image's darkest point, move the threshold slider to the left until only the fewest black spots are visible. These are the darkest parts of the picture. To identify the brightest spots, move the slider to the right until only a minimum number of white spots are visible.

(137) Improve Brightness and Contrast

If you grew up using a television set that had an old style of operating control called *knobs*, you'll recall there were two such gadgets, generally labeled *Brightness* and *Contrast*. And if you ever played with these knobs as a child—and survived with your wrists unscathed—you remember that Brightness made your picture *whiter* while Contrast made the blacks and whites in your picture stand out.

Before You Begin

✔ (136) About an Image's Histogram

See Also

→ (138) Improve a Dull, Flat Photo

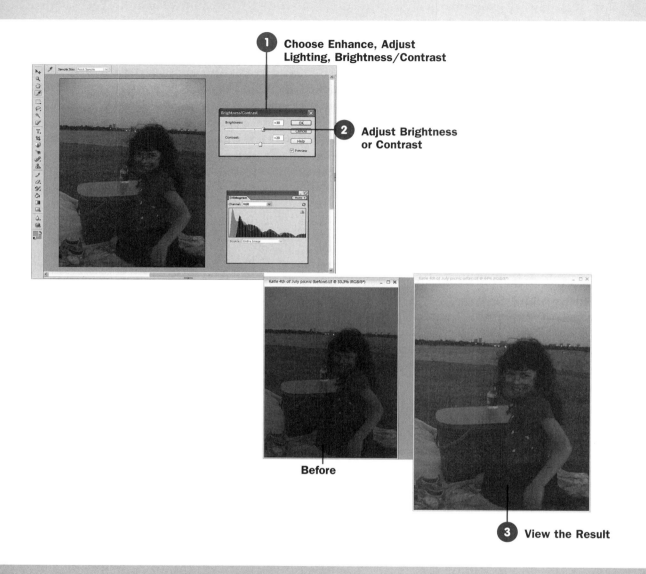

1 Choose Enhance, Adjust Lighting, Brightness/Contrast

2 Adjust Brightness or Contrast

Before

3 View the Result

With all due respect to Philco-Ford, Admiral, Magnavox, and the other great manufacturers of the past century, I'm going to show you here how to use Photoshop Elements' equivalent of the Brightness and Contrast knobs. And then I'm going to rap you on the wrists if you use them too much. Actually, I'm not kidding this time: Although it does help in some circumstances to restore a more natural appearance to an image, the **Brightness/Contrast** command, when used too liberally, can result in a washed-out look (too bright), a washed-*down* look (too dark), or an underexposed look (too much contrast). More importantly, because pixels cannot have a brightness value of greater than 255 or less than 0, when you brighten or darken pixels *too much*, you lose the distinguishing contrasts between the brightest or darkest pixels among them. Then when you try to get those contrasts back with a **Levels** adjustment, you can't. With the technique demonstrated here, you can use the **Brightness/Contrast** command effectively and safely, without losing information in your image.

① Choose Enhance, Adjust Lighting, Brightness/Contrast

Open the image you want to adjust in the *Editor* in **Standard Edit** mode and save it in Photoshop (***.psd**) format. To display the **Histogram** *palette* if it is not already showing, select **Window, Histogram**. From the palette's **Channel** drop-down list, choose **RGB**. If there is more than one layer in the image, choose the layer you want to adjust in the **Layers** palette. If you want to limit your adjustment to a region of the image, use a selection tool to select that region. See **70 About Making Selections** for an explanation.

Choose **Enhance, Adjust Lighting, Brightness/Contrast** from the menu bar. The **Brightness/Contrast** dialog box opens. Enable the **Preview** check box so that you can see the results of the adjustments you're making in the actual image.

In this example, the photo was taken at dusk without a flash. Although it does capture the moment, it's the worst time of day to take a digital photo for many cameras. If the flash had been turned on, the subject would have been well lit, but the sky would no longer be a dreamy blue but a dreary clay color. My goal here, for now, is to make the subject matter clearly visible while losing as little of the original color scheme as possible.

② Adjust Brightness or Contrast

To add brightness value to all the pixels in the designated region, slide the **Brightness** slider to the right, or enter a positive value in the **Brightness** text box. To reduce brightness in all the pixels in the designated region, slide the **Brightness** slider to the left, or enter a negative value in the **Brightness text** box.

⬛ NOTE

With the **Brightness/Contrast** command, brightness is added to an image (or to a layer or selection) by adding equal amounts to, or subtracting from, the **Brightness** component of *every pixel in the image.* So, although you might be restoring the natural brightness level of the midtones, natural darks might be washed out. By comparison, a contrast adjustment mathematically redistributes brightness across the entire image, flattening the image's *histogram* and reducing its peaks. However, the same danger of losing bright and dark values remains valid with contrast adjustment, except on both sides of the histogram instead of one.

NOTE

As you increase contrast for an image, you might notice that the black curve in the **Histogram** palette has "teeth" in it—specifically, evenly spaced vertical stripes. This is natural, and is an accurate depiction of the brightness values in an adjusted image. For the sake of argument, suppose that there were only 10 levels of brightness in a given image, ranging in value from 10 to 20. After the adjustment, suppose that they now ranged in value from 5 to 25. Because all pixels were adjusted—none are left behind—*there are still only 10 levels of brightness*. They've just been broken up, such that there are pixels with brightness of 5, 7, 9, and so on, but none with 6, 8, 10, and so on. Notice in the example how the contrast-adjusted image looks spotty, noisy, and unsmooth. What your eyes see is verified by the "teeth" in the contrast-adjusted histogram.

TIP

If you press the **Alt** key on your keyboard, the **Cancel** button changes to read **Reset**. Click that button to erase your changes to the image, leaving the dialog box open so that you can try again.

To add contrast between pixels in the designated region (making light pixels lighter and darks darker), slide the **Contrast** slider to the right, or enter a positive value in the **Contrast** text box. To reduce contrast between pixels in the designated region (bringing all brightness values together toward a middle gray tone), slide the **Contrast** slider to the left, or enter a negative value in the **Contrast** text box.

As you make adjustments, notice the instant change to the **Histogram** palette. The gray curve with the bright tip represents the image's existing *histogram*; the black curve represents the adjusted state as you see it in the preview. With a brightness change, the entire "mountain" of the graph shifts to the left or right. With a contrast change, the entire "mountain" is flattened, as if eroded by a rising tide. While you're making these changes, watch the **Histogram** palette, being mindful of two things:

- Don't adjust the image so much that pixels on either or both sides of the histogram fall off the edge. When that happens, you're losing vital information which, when saved, cannot be retrieved.

- In the interest of restoring one of the image's qualities to a natural or pleasing appearance—for example, distinguishing a little girl from her picnic basket—don't introduce negative qualities on the opposite end of the scale, such as a washed-out tone for the grass, or water that appears to glow as if it were emanating from a nuclear facility.

To finalize your adjustments, click **OK**.

③ View the Result

In the example, after adding **+30** to brightness and **+20** to contrast, the range of color now looks more natural. But the image has far to go before it's fixed. In the adjustment, I did lose some of the distinguishing bright values along the right side of the *histogram*, although not many.

138 Improve a Dull, Flat Photo

Perhaps the real revolution in computing has finally been realized with the introduction of color photocopying systems into the average home. Today, the everyday individual has it within her grasp to duplicate photographs and documents with astounding *resolution* and brilliance. But xerography is by no means a perfect science. In the act of copying a color photograph, so many translations of color tables and formulas take place that the initial product often ends up washed out, as if it had been left out in the sun for several weeks.

In this task, we'll restore some of a faded, scanned photograph's natural brilliance and contrast by narrowing the range of its input levels. A similar feat of restoration is demonstrated in **127** **Restore Color and Tone to an Old Photograph**, although the parts of the **Levels** dialog box we'll use here focus primarily on regulating the three primary color channels. When a photograph fades—as the one in this example did—not only does it take on a decided *color cast*, it loses its darkest darks. With the **Levels** command, this task demonstrates bringing those natural darks back, one channel at a time, paying attention to the *histogram* all the while, and relying on what you know about *what color things should be* to help you out.

1 Choose Enhance, Adjust Lighting, Levels

Open the image you want to adjust in the Editor in **Standard Edit** mode and save it in Photoshop (***.psd**) format. To display the **Histogram** *palette* if it is not already showing, select **Window**, **Histogram**. From the **Channel** drop-down list, choose **Colors**. If there is more than one layer in the image, choose the layer you want to adjust from the **Layers** palette. If you want to limit your adjustment to a region of the image, use a selection tool to select that region. See **70** **About Making Selections** for an explanation.

From the menu bar, select **Enhance, Adjust Lighting, Levels**. The **Levels** dialog box opens to display a histogram of the picture. Enable the **Preview** check box so that you can see the result of the adjustments you make in the actual image.

Before You Begin

→ **136** About an Image's Histogram

See Also

→ **127** Restore Color and Tone to an Old Photograph

→ **137** Improve Brightness and Contrast

→ **144** Correct Color Manually

 TIP

The scanner drivers shipped with many flatbed scanners tend to use their own automatic levels correction when scanning faded photos, especially black-and-whites. More often than not, these drivers tend to overestimate their own corrections and perform too much contrast adjustment. Rather than wrestle with undoing in the Editor the errors that your scanner driver caused, try turning *off* the automatic correction feature *before* you proceed with the scan, and then make the right corrections yourself with the **Levels** command. See **6** Import a Scanned Image for more about bringing an image into the Editor or the Organizer from a scanner.

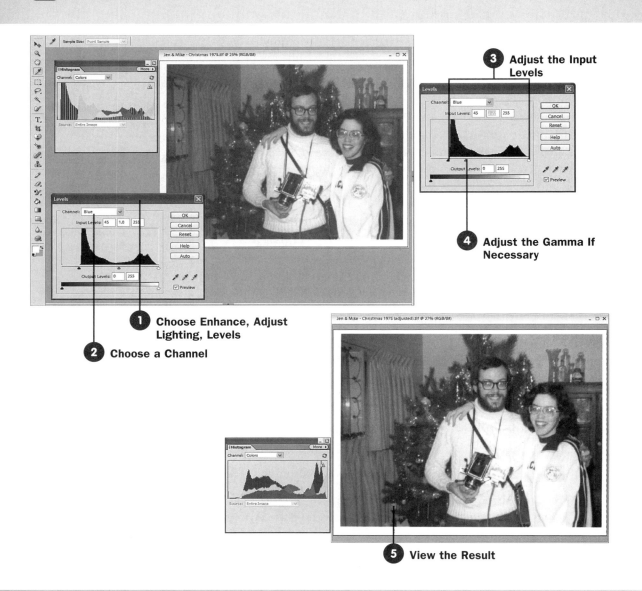

③ Adjust the Input Levels

④ Adjust the Gamma If Necessary

① Choose Enhance, Adjust Lighting, Levels

② Choose a Channel

⑤ View the Result

② Choose a Channel

From the **Channel** drop-down list, choose whether you want to adjust the **RGB** channel (the combined brightness of all three color channels) or the color value of the **Red**, **Green**, or **Blue** channel independently. For a grayscale image (especially a grayscale TIFF), this setting will read **Gray** and will have been made for you.

❸ Adjust the Input Levels

The histogram shown in the **Levels** dialog box represents a brightness scale, showing all *possible* brightness values in the image for the chosen channel, for all possible values between 0 and 255. A clear indication that an image can be lightened is when few or no pixels are registered in the rightmost region of the histogram.

The *white point* of an image represents the pixel or region of pixels that should be the brightest region, and therefore perhaps should be corrected to become pure white. The **Levels** dialog box begins by representing the theoretical white point as the white up-pointing arrow on the scale just below the histogram, on the far right side. To try brightening the image, slide the white point to the left, toward the right tail end of the charted pixels in the histogram. The white point on the histogram is like one side of a fence. Wherever you set it, all pixels represented on the histogram that are currently plotted at the white point *or higher*, will be altered to the maximum brightness level represented in the second box above the graph marked **Output Levels**. Then all the other pixels' brightness values from that point toward the left side are rescaled upward, rendering them brighter in the process. The **Histogram** palette shows the effects of this change the moment your preview of the image changes. No distinctions or contrasts between pixels are lost *unless* pixels on the histogram fall to the right of the white point.

The *black point* on the histogram is on the other side of the scale. When the **Levels** dialog box first appears, the black point (the black up-pointing arrow on the scale just below the histogram, on the far left side) is set at 0. To darken the image, slide the black pointer to the right. Wherever you set it, all pixels represented on the histogram that are currently plotted at the black point *or lower* will be altered to the minimum brightness level represented in the first box above the graph marked **Output Levels**. Then all the other pixels' brightness from that point toward the right side will be rescaled downward, rendering them darker in the process. No contrasts will be lost unless pixels on the histogram fall to the left of the black point.

KEY TERM

Black and white points— Pixels in a photo that should be pure white or pure black. By identifying these pixels, you can correct the color balance and tone throughout an image.

NOTE

Adjusting the *gamma* will give you weird results if you don't adjust the white and black points first. The gamma describes an important geometric point on a curve. The white and black points are at opposite ends of this curve. Adjusting the gamma is almost pointless if you intend to adjust the white and black points later, which will *move the curve*.

NOTES

Suppose that you are preparing an image for printing on a commercial press. You've been told that the press cannot reproduce detail in highlights where the amount of ink required is thinner than 5% of the maximum. You can use the white **Output Levels** slider to set the brightest point to 242—which, when rounded off, is 5% less than the maximum of 255. This setting ensures that the press will reproduce all your highlight detail. You can make a similar adjustment to allow for press characteristics in printing shadow detail.

You can use the eyedroppers in the **Levels** dialog box to select black, white, and neutral gray points. Click the black eyedropper in the dialog box and then click a point in the image to identify that point as the blackest. Click the white eyedropper and then click in the image to identify that point as the whitest point in the image. The adjustment that **Levels** makes creates a new brightness curve between the two points you select. For more about using eyedroppers to set black, gray, and white points, see **127** **Restore Color and Tone to an Old Photograph**.

By moving the white and black points, you're "fencing in" your photograph, ensuring that there is a black and a white *somewhere*. For most images, this is what you want.

4 Adjust the Gamma If Necessary

The gray pointer in the middle of the scale represents the degree of bias in determining how to rescale the brightness values of pixels between the black and white pointers. As you move the black or white pointer, notice that the gray pointer also moves, registering the same gamma bias applied to the relocated scale. A gamma of 1.0 implies no bias toward either brights or darks. To make more room for bright pixels—brightening the overall image and increasing the gamma—slide the gray pointer to the *left*, toward the dark side. This *reduces* the interval between the black and gray pointers, indicating less room for darks and more for brights. To make room for dark pixels—darkening the image and decreasing the gamma—slide the gray pointer to the *right*.

For this example, noting how red this photo had become, I started off by making adjustments to the **Blue** channel. I moved its black point to **44**, at the left cusp of the curve. I then tried several gamma settings before settling on a startlingly high **2.22** (up from the presumed normal setting of **1.00**). In judging whether these settings were right, I kept an eye on the **Histogram** palette, which shows the increased spread in brightness in comparison to the other two channels. I also took note of my wife's collar. (Yes, that's my wife, circa 1975. No, that's my brother-in-law.) I knew she was supposed to be wearing a white pullover jacket with patriotic blue and red trim. What I tried to do was bring back as much blue as possible without making the pine tree behind them look like a blue spruce.

5 View the Result

When you're satisfied with the result, make any other changes you want and save the PSD file. Then resave the result in **JPEG** or **TIFF** format, leaving your **PSD** image with its layers intact so that you can return at a later time to make new adjustments.

For this example, after restoring the **Blue** channel, I proceeded to the **Red** channel, raising its black point to **92** and its gamma to **1.50**. For the **Green** channel, I raised its black point to **46** and its gamma to **1.91**. Those numbers, in and of themselves, probably seem pointless on the surface; but take a look at the **Histogram** *palette* for the result figure. The three color channels now begin and end at basically the same point on the graph, and their peaks and valleys are more in sync with one another. The numbers I just rattled at you were the ones that put this histogram in sync. Now the pine tree is green, the blue jeans are blue, the silver garland isn't wine-colored, Mike's hair is...*there*, and my wife is a striking brunette.

139 Lighten a Subject on a Snowy Background

Typically, the sheer brightness of snow changes the way your camera handles light from darker objects—and on a snowy day, almost everything is darker than snow. Digital cameras are especially sensitive to bright light reflecting off snow, bleaching out the rest of the scene and causing subjects in the foreground, including people, to appear muted and dark. Furthermore, because many digital cameras tend to normalize their light input on-the-fly, even though the snow is the brightest thing in the image, the camera makes it gray, making your foreground subjects even darker to compensate.

In remedying an image that suffers from this problem, you could start by invoking the **Levels** command, but you know already that your bright whites are already going to command the right edge of the graph for the **RGB** channel. Besides, you might not want to change your *snow* at all, especially if it's bright enough. The technique you're about to see helps you easily separate your foreground subject from your background snow (which is, after all, mostly the same shade), so that you can restore the foreground despite the snow.

Before You Begin

✔ **136** About an Image's Histogram

→ **138** Improve a Dull, Flat Photo

See Also

→ **137** Improve Brightness and Contrast

1 Duplicate the Background Layer

Open the image you want to adjust in the *Editor* in **Standard Edit** mode and save it in Photoshop (***.psd**) format. To display the **Histogram** *palette* if it is not already showing, select **Window**, **Histogram**. From the **Channel** drop-down list, choose **Luminosity**.

In the **Layers** palette, choose the **Background** *layer*. From the menu bar, select **Layer**, **Duplicate Layer**. Name the new layer **Threshold**.

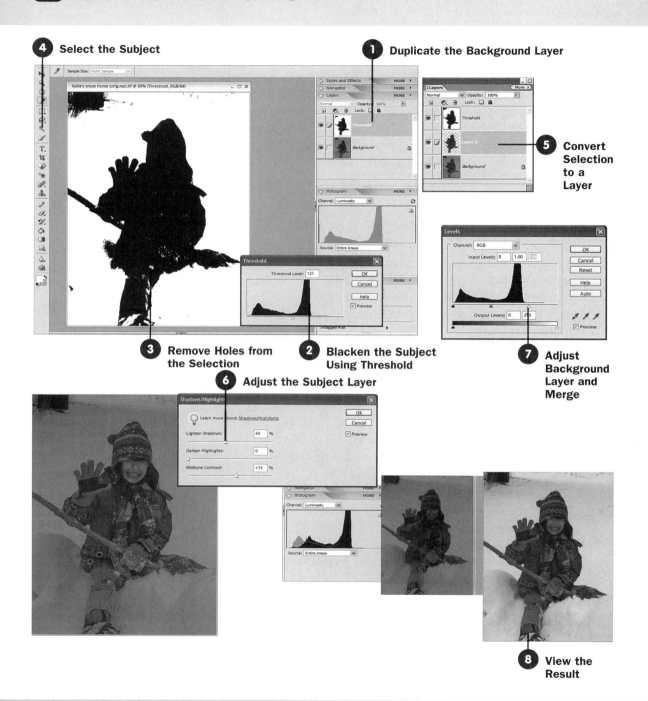

4 Select the Subject

1 Duplicate the Background Layer

5 Convert Selection to a Layer

3 Remove Holes from the Selection

2 Blacken the Subject Using Threshold

7 Adjust Background Layer and Merge

6 Adjust the Subject Layer

8 View the Result

2 Blacken the Subject Using Threshold

With the **Threshold** layer chosen, from the menu bar, select **Filter**, **Adjustments**, **Threshold**. In the **Threshold** dialog box, adjust the **Threshold Level** setting until the black area just covers your subject. You'll probably also blacken *some* of the shadows your subject is casting on the snow; don't worry, that's okay. Click **OK**.

3 Remove Holes from the Selection

Your subject should now be black and the background white, but that's only temporary. At this moment, your selection probably includes some specks of snow on your subject—especially if she's recently been in a snowball fight. These beads of snow will produce holes in your black subject area. The simplest way to remove them is using the **Brush** tool. In the **Toolbox**, click the **Brush** tool, and then click the **Default Colors** button in-between the *foreground color* and *background color* boxes. Choose a five-pixel-wide brush tip from the **Options** bar and apply that brush tip to the small holes in the black image. Choose a larger brush tip and sweep away the larger areas of dustier snow from the subject.

4 Select the Subject

From the **Toolbox**, click the **Magic Wand** tool. In the image, use the tool to select the subject. In this example, the selection included the girl, the big stick she was holding, and a portion of the shadow behind her back. It did not include the shadow of the air conditioning unit in the upper-left corner. Use of the **Magic Wand** tool is explained in **76** **Select Areas of Similar Color**.

5 Convert Selection to a Layer

In the **Layers** palette, change to the **Background** layer, and select **Layer**, **New**, **Layer via Copy** from the menu bar. Name this new layer **Subject**. Your subject is now isolated on its own layer, where you can make adjustments that bring out its own details without disturbing the snowy background. You can also adjust the snowy background by brightening it significantly, without in turn over-brightening the subject.

You no longer need the **Threshold** layer. In the **Layers** palette, choose the **Threshold** layer and select **Layer, Delete Layer** from the menu bar. Click **Yes** to confirm. For now, your image looks exactly as it did before.

⑥ Adjust the Subject Layer

In the **Layers** palette, choose the **Subject** layer. From the menu bar, select **Enhance, Adjust Lighting, Shadows/Highlights**. The **Shadows/Highlights** dialog box appears. You might have to reposition it to get a clear view of both your image and the **Histogram** palette.

With the **Histogram** palette open and visible, it's easy to get a clear read of what the **Shadows/Highlights** command does, and what your limits are with regard to safely using it. Sliding the **Lighten Shadows** setting forward clearly bunches up the *histogram* from the left side against the right edge. You gain brightness, but at the expense of contrast, so be careful not to trade off too much. Similarly, sliding the **Darken Highlights** setting forward bunches up the histogram from the right side against the left edge.

Sliding the **Midtone Contrast** to the left bunches up tones in the histogram toward the middle of the chart, whereas sliding it to the right splits tones into two humps. The simple rules of shaping a histogram (don't push tones off the edges; evenly distribute them whenever possible; don't segment tones into two equal humps like a camel's back) and the rules of adjusting an image (don't overcorrect for brightness; balance your lights, darks, and *midtones* whenever possible; don't sacrifice your midtones for darks and lights) correspond to one another. You'll be surprised how many corrections you can make "flying on instrumentation alone"—trusting the histogram to tell you how far to go, and when you're in danger of going too far.

For this example, the highlights were dark enough already. I needed to lighten the shadowy areas to give the picture more punch—especially to bring Katie's bright red glove toward you (because vivid colors tend to convey the illusion of dimension better). I adjusted **Lighten Shadows** significantly higher, and then added a little to **Midtone Contrast** to compensate.

To finalize your adjustments, click **OK**.

7 Adjust Background Layer and Merge

On the **Layers** palette, choose the **Background** layer. From the menu bar, select **Enhance**, **Adjust Lighting**, **Levels**. Using the method described in **138 Improve a Dull, Flat Photo**, reduce the *white point* until you've restored your snowy whites. Your subject will be unaffected. With this method, I significantly lowered the white point from 255 all the way down to 186 without losing any information about the crisp, clear, fresh snow.

To reduce the number of layers down to one, select **Layer**, **Flatten Image** from the menu bar.

8 View the Result

When you're satisfied with the result, make any other changes you want and save the PSD file. Resave the image in **JPEG** or **TIFF** format, leaving your **PSD** image with its layers intact so that you can return at a later time to make new adjustments.

My original photo suffered from a phenomenon common to digital cameras: The brightness of the snow overwhelmed the light detectors, even when the camera was set for bright outdoors. As a result, Katerina's colors were muted and dull. I made **Shadows/Highlights** adjustments to brighten her clothes, but had my image been one undivided layer, the same changes I made to her clothes and skin tones would have made the snow pink. By separating the snow from the foreground, I was able to shield the snow from the changes I made to the color channels, and then applied color-safe changes to the snow.

NOTE

If your digital camera includes a scene mode such as **Snow** or **Beach**, use it when taking a photo with a bright background, and your subject will not appear so dark in the resulting photograph.

140 Lighten or Darken a Portion of an Image

Before You Begin

✔ **136** About an Image's
        Histogram

See Also

→ **137** Improve Brightness
        and Contrast

→ **138** Improve a Dull, Flat
        Photo

→ **141** Improve a
        Nighttime Photo

→ **147** Adjust Saturation
        for a Specific Area

NOTE

Both the **Dodge** and **Burn**
tools have the side effect
of desaturating what they
touch. But they're not to be
confused with another tool
specifically designed for
desaturation (or re-
saturation): the **Sponge**
tool. The **Sponge** could conceivably darken an area by
compounding its native
color. And when desaturating a spot, the **Sponge**
doesn't lighten it; instead, it
removes the colored hue,
shifting it more toward
grayscale. The **Sponge** tool
is covered in **147** Adjust
Saturation for a Specific
Area.

To make a photographic print, the classic development technique is to project an image of the negative onto sensitized printing paper. To lighten an area, the developer can *dodge* it by placing an object, usually a small paddle, in the projected light. To darken an area, he would *burn* it by forming a sort of donut hole with his hands and directing extra exposure light to the target area.

The **Dodge** and **Burn** tool icons in Photoshop Elements depict these traditional tools. Their jobs are, in essence, to lighten a spot and to blacken a spot, respectively. But they don't do this by painting white and black; you could do that with a **Brush** tool. Instead, the **Burn** tool darkens whatever it touches using the same formula used in the **Burn** *blend modes*. The **Dodge** tool lightens using the **Dodge** blend mode formula. Because you apply these tools to your image using an adjustable brush tip, you can pinpoint your changes to a few pixels or make changes to broader areas of the image. The effect much more closely resembles the old darkroom technique.

❶ Click Dodge or Burn Tool

Open the image you want to adjust in the *Editor* in **Standard Edit** mode and save it in Photoshop (***.psd**) format. If there's more than one layer in the image, from the **Layers** palette, choose the layer containing the contents you want to compensate for. To protect any parts of the image you want to protect, select the region containing the spot you want to correct.

Select the **Dodge** or **Burn** tool on the **Toolbox**.

In the **Toolbox**, click the **Dodge** tool if you want to lighten an area; click the **Burn** tool if you want to darken an area.

❷ Set Tool Options

The **Options** bar offers several options that control the brush you'll use to apply the burn to the image. Open the brush presets dropdown list and select the type of brush you want to use. One with a feathered edge works best with these tools; hard-edged brushes can result in unnatural effects. In the **Size** text box, enter a brush size in pixels or select one using the slider. You can check the relative size by passing the tool over the picture without clicking; a circle shows the brush area that will be used.

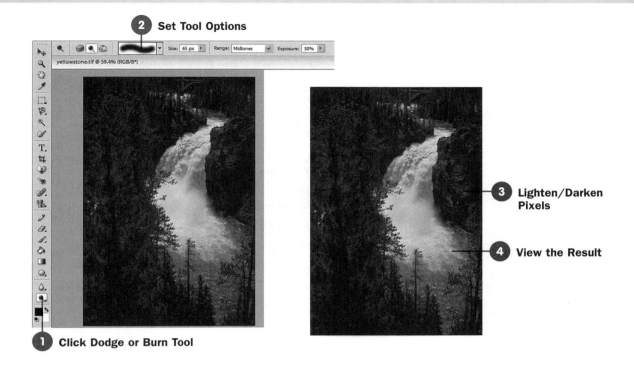

2 Set Tool Options

3 Lighten/Darken Pixels

4 View the Result

1 Click Dodge or Burn Tool

From the **Range** drop-down list, select whether to alter shadows, midrange tones, or highlights. This is an extremely important setting because it enables you to further protect those elements of your image that don't need correcting. For instance, you might not want to indiscriminately darken *everything* the **Burn** tool touches, so you might consider setting its **Range** to **Midtones**. Likewise, using the **Dodge** tool, you might not want to lighten the lightest tones, but only the **Shadows**. Choose the **Range** you want to change.

The **Exposure** scale enables you to set the strength of the effect. In general, stick to the standard **Exposure** setting of 50% or less. That way, you can make multiple passes that change the picture in small increments.

③ Lighten/Darken Pixels

Begin applying the tool by clicking and holding the mouse button where you want to start. For a *pen tablet*, position the pointer by hovering the pen, and then tap and hold the pen where you want the stroke to begin.

To draw a freehand stroke, continue holding the button down as you drag the mouse. The mark you draw will follow your pointer. As you continue applying the tool to an area, its effects are cumulative—which means you can continue applying the **Dodge** tool to the same area within the same stroke, and it will continue to lighten the area. The tool's effect within the same stroke are limited, however, to the extent of the **Exposure** setting.

To draw a straight horizontal or vertical line, press **Shift** now and continue dragging the mouse. The Editor senses whether you intend for the line to move up, right, left, or down, by the general direction in which you're moving the mouse—it doesn't have to be exact.

To draw a straight line between points, release the mouse button. For a pen tablet, lift the pen. Move the pointer to where you want the end of the line (or, to be geometrically accurate, the *line segment*) to appear. Press **Shift** and click this point. The line will be an application of the tool over the distance between the start and end points, relative to the tool's current **Exposure** setting. You can continue drawing from here—either a freehand mark or another straight line segment.

④ View the Result

When you're satisfied with the result, make any other changes you want and save the PSD file. Then resave the result in **JPEG** or **TIFF** format, leaving your **PSD** image with its layers intact so that you can return at a later time to make new adjustments.

This sample image is a natural candidate for dodging and burning. The spray at the bottom of the falls is overexposed; its details are washed out. The rocks just to the right of the spray are underexposed; detail there is obscured in shadow. The rest of the image, however, needs no serious correction. So, I used the **Burn** tool to correct the overexposure in the spray at the bottom of the falls;

TIP

To change brush tips for the **Burn** or **Dodge** tool at any time, right-click the image. The **Brush Presets** palette appears. Choose a new tip from the **Brushes** list, and then click the **X** button to dismiss the palette.

there's a bit more detail now than there was in the original image. I used the **Dodge** tool on the rocks just to the right of the spray to lighten up that area and reveal some additional detail.

141 Improve a Nighttime Photo

Nighttime photography is a particular challenge. When there's not much light to work with, even the best photographers sometimes misjudge the exposure. The perennial problem with photographing a scene at night is that there's never enough natural light to produce a proper exposure. Increasing the exposure time often ruins the picture's clarity, and using a flash generally bleaches out the colors of nearby subjects while drowning out background items in the distance.

In most nighttime photographs, however, the detail is there—hidden, dormant—and can be rediscovered not so much by increasing contrast but instead by compounding the *saturation* levels. The technique demonstrated here borrows a trick from the **Overlay** blend mode, using *white* as a signal to turn up the color volume.

❶ Create a Duplicate Overlay Layer

Open the image you want to adjust in the *Editor* in **Standard Edit** mode and save it in Photoshop (***.psd**) format. To display the **Histogram** *palette* if it is not already showing, select **Window, Histogram**. From the **Channel** list, choose **Luminosity**.

With the **Background** *layer* chosen in the **Layers** palette, from the menu bar, select **Layer, Duplicate Layer**. Name this new layer **Subject**. Click **OK**.

❷ Create a Gradient Adjustment Layer

In the **Toolbox**, set the *foreground color* to white and the background color to black. With the **Subject** layer still active, select **Layer, New Adjustment Layer, Gradient Map** from the menu bar. Name this new layer **White Shadow**. Set its **Mode** to **Overlay**, and its **Opacity** to **100%**. (It's a good guess to start out with.) Click **OK**.

In the **Gradient Map** dialog box, click the down arrow next to the **Gradient Used for Grayscale Mapping** strip, and choose **Foreground to Background** from the list of samples. Click **OK**.

Before You Begin

✔ **136** About an Image's Histogram

See Also

→ **138** Improve a Dull, Flat Photo

→ **140** Lighten or Darken Part of an Image

💡 TIP

The purpose of the *gradient* map is to provide the Editor with a roadmap of how the transitions between darks and lights in an image *should* occur. Because the **Foreground to Background** gradient runs from pure black to pure white, the Editor doesn't apply any colorization to the pixels that are adjusted by the adjustment layer. Instead, it reprograms the *midtones* of the image so that they're 50% as bright as the brightest tones—just like the gradient itself.

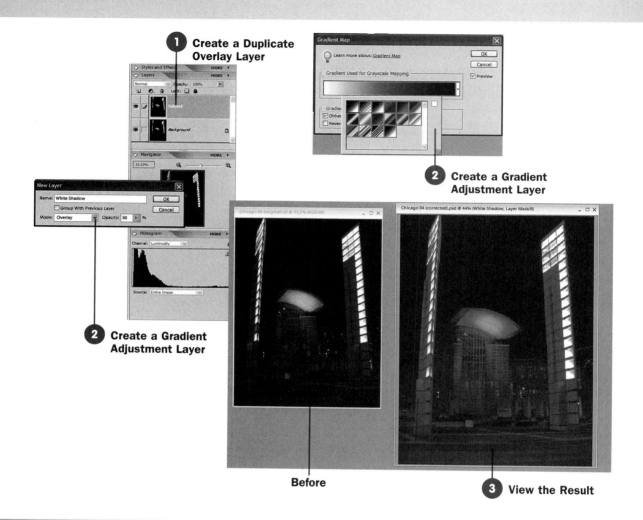

1 Create a Duplicate Overlay Layer

2 Create a Gradient Adjustment Layer

2 Create a Gradient Adjustment Layer

Before

3 View the Result

To reduce the number of layers down to one, from the menu bar, select **Layer, Flatten Image**.

3 View the Result

When you're satisfied with the result, make any other changes you want and save the PSD file. Then resave the result in **JPEG** or **TIFF** format, leaving your **PSD** image with its layers intact so that you can return at a later time to make new adjustments.

This was a quick snapshot taken after sundown, outside the McCormick Place Convention Center in Chicago. With the original image, it was difficult to discern what you were looking at—the outside of a building or a passing spaceship. Now you can easily identify the building's entrance and unloading area.

142 Fix a Flash That's Too Close

When you shoot a subject with the flash turned on at a very close distance, a strange thing happens to your photo that you can see in its *histogram*: The colors become bleached out and desaturated. The contrasts in the picture become too heavy, such that the histogram looks like a camel's back: a big clump of darks and a big clump of lights.

Restoring *midtones* isn't a difficult task in itself. But with an overlit photo, you run the risk of restoring too much *saturation* to peripheral elements of the image—things you'd rather not be the center of attention. This task demonstrates how to restore midtones, while at the same time, reducing the attention that the background receives—all without over-saturating the background.

1 Select Foreground Subject

Open the image you want to adjust in the **Editor** in **Standard Edit** mode and save it in Photoshop (**.psd*) format. To display the **Histogram** *palette* if it is not already showing, select **Window**, **Histogram**. From the **Channel** list, choose **Colors**.

With the **Background** *layer* chosen in the **Layers** palette, click the **Lasso** tool on the **Toolbox**. Use this tool (primarily) to draw a marquee border around the foreground subject. Include all clothes and as much hair as possible.

2 Create Foreground Layer

With the *selection marquee* showing in the active image window, select **Layer**, **New**, **Layer via Copy** from the menu bar. Name the new layer **Foreground**.

Before You Begin

✔ **136** About an Image's Histogram

✔ **138** Improve a Dull, Flat Photo

✔ **151** Blur a Background to Create Depth of Field

See Also

→ **144** Correct Color Manually

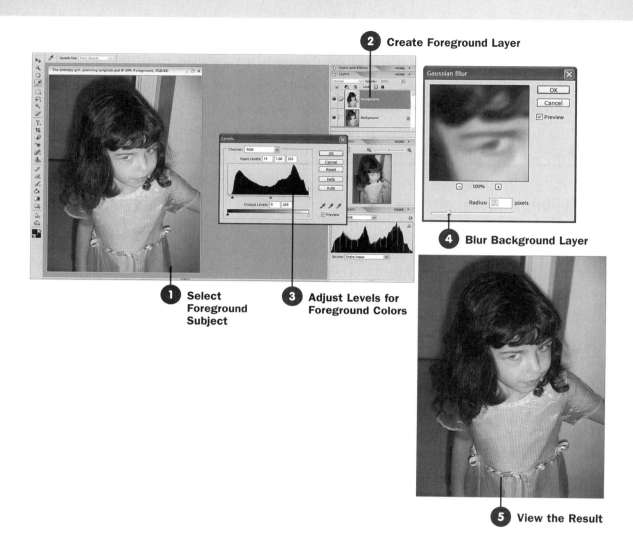

2 Create Foreground Layer

4 Blur Background Layer

1 Select Foreground Subject

3 Adjust Levels for Foreground Colors

5 View the Result

3 Adjust Levels for Foreground Colors

With the **Foreground** layer chosen, select **Enhance, Adjust Lighting, Levels** from the menu bar. The **Levels** dialog box appears. From the **Channel** drop-down list, choose **RGB**. Enable the **Preview** check box.

The histogram for the **RGB** channel should show definitive "twin peaks." In ⓭ **Improve a Dull, Flat Photo**, the **Levels** dialog box is explained in detail. In this particular circumstance, the most important adjustment you can make is to decrease the *gamma* for the **RGB** channel. Do this by sliding the gray pointer on the scale below the histogram to the *right*. It seems backward at first to slide right to turn it *down*, but what you're doing is pinching the gap between midtones and highlights, adding more midtones in the process. In the example, I raised the *black point* for Katerina just slightly from **0** to **14**, but then I dropped gamma significantly to **0.75**. To finalize your adjustments, click **OK**.

❹ Blur Background Layer

It's extremely likely that your background is as desaturated as your foreground, as a result of your over-bright flash. But you don't want to resaturate it because that will make it compete with the foreground you just rescued. What you want is to de-emphasize the background. Because it's on its own layer now, the easiest way you can accomplish this is by *blurring it*.

In the **Layers** palette, choose the **Background** layer. From the menu bar, select **Filter, Blur, Gaussian Blur**. In the **Gaussian Blur** dialog box, enter a small radius such as **4** (slightly higher if your image *resolution* is above 150 *PPI*). Don't worry if the sample makes it appear like you're about to blur your subject; Her blurred copy will be obscured by the **Foreground** layer when this is done. Click **OK**.

❺ View the Result

When you're satisfied with the result, make any other changes you want and save the PSD file. Resave the result in **JPEG** or **TIFF** format, leaving your **PSD** image with its layers intact so that you can return at a later time to make new adjustments.

One of the great three-dimensional illusions in all photography is that richer, clearer yellows and reds appear to "pull" toward the viewer, whereas desaturated colors appear to recede. In this example, from the angle at which this photo was originally taken, Katerina looks foreshortened, as though she were a giant being photographed by a passing miniature blimp. Bringing her midtones back down into the realm of richness and clarity with a

💡 TIP

When objects in the foreground and objects in the background are both bleached out by a nearby or overpowered flash, it might be difficult for you to select the foreground elements to isolate them. This is where you might need some practice with the **Lasso** tool—not the **Magnetic Lasso** or the **Polygonal Lasso**, but the one where you draw the border of a selection yourself. This skill is covered in ⓭ **Draw a Selection Freehand**. Because this is a skill, you might find yourself having drawn pockmarks or holes in the border of your foreground selection. In such a case, the **Selection Brush** tool, covered in ⓱ **Paint a Selection**, comes in handy.

📝 NOTE

If your subject is severely desaturated, you can increase the saturation of the **Foreground** layer only. See ⓲ **Adjust Hue, Saturation, and Lightness Manually**.

simple gamma adjustment makes her appear human again and not so much like a colossal statue. What do you suppose that this little girl was getting into at the time this photo was taken? Maybe her redder cheeks will give her away.

143 Fix a Flash That's Too Far Away

Before You Begin

✔ **136** About an Image's Histogram

✔ **137** Improve Brightness and Contrast

✔ **138** Improve a Dull, Flat Photo

See Also

→ **139** Lighten a Subject on a Snowy Background

NOTE

In this photo, my brother is fully illuminated, but not the other subject, the dartboard. So I'll lighten the background. You could use these steps to lighten just the foreground of your image.

A typical on-camera flash does well to carry across a medium-sized room—something to remember when you see a stadium full of winking flashbulbs that can't possibly affect the players on the stage or on the field.

Most cameras have light meters that read the reflected light from the flash unit and set the exposure accordingly. With older cameras, you had to set the exposure manually, and sometimes you set it wrong. Poorly exposed prints that have faded before you scan them in can make the problem more complex.

Photoshop Elements can do what the photographer did not: bring a proper scale of lighting values to an otherwise incorrectly exposed shot. The **Levels** command enables you to adjust the darkness levels for distant objects and increase the *gamma* so that the progression curve from dark to bright favors the brights a bit more and compensates for localized regions of glare. But you wouldn't want to apply these same changes on top of other subject matter in the near foreground. You'll want to separate the foreground and background matter and apply the gamma changes to the background only.

● **Select Foreground Subject**

Open the image you want to adjust in the *Editor* in **Standard Edit** mode and save it in Photoshop (*.psd) format. To display the **Histogram** *palette* if it is not already showing, select **Window, Histogram**. From the **Channel** drop-down list, choose **RGB**.

With the **Background** *layer* chosen in the **Layers** palette, click the **Lasso** tool on the **Toolbox**. Use this tool (primarily) to draw a marquee border around the foreground subject. Include all clothes and as much hair as possible.

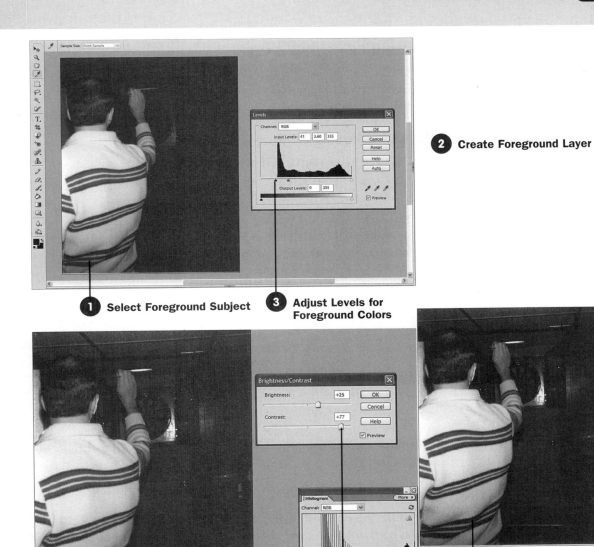

2 Create Foreground Layer

1 Select Foreground Subject

3 Adjust Levels for
Foreground Colors

5 View the Result

4 Adjust Background Layer

2 Create Foreground Layer

With the *selection marquee* showing in the active image window, from the menu bar, select **Layer**, **New**, **Layer via Copy**. Name the new layer **Foreground**.

3 Adjust Levels for Foreground Colors

With the **Foreground** layer chosen, select **Enhance**, **Adjust Lighting**, **Levels** from the menu bar. The **Levels** dialog box appears. Enable the **Preview** check box.

The problem with this layer should be obvious immediately through a check of the *histogram*: There's a great big hump on the left side. This confirms what you see: too many darks, relatively. On the other hand, the darks start at about a brightness level of 42 in this example, which is an indication of how much this scanned print has faded. You actually want the darkest tones darker than they are now, but when you're through, you want fewer of those dark tones overall.

To accomplish this goal, raise the *black point* of the histogram, and then compensate by lowering the gray pointer and increasing the *gamma*. For this example, I brought the *black point* to the cusp of the histogram at 41 and increased the gamma to a tremendous **2.66**. See **138** **Improve a Dull, Flat Photo** for precise instructions for using the **Levels** dialog box. Click **OK** to finalize your changes.

4 Adjust Background Layer

Unlike the case with **142** **Fix a Flash That's Too Close**, your background is already blurry enough. In this case, you want to restore it separately because the background—unlike your subject matter—has its own peculiar needs. As the **Histogram** palette confirms but you knew already, the **Background** layer is full of dark middle grays. Because their detail is critical only to set the scene for the subject matter, it's safe to use an easier—if more crude—correction tool to restore the background.

Select the **Background** layer in the **Layers** palette. From the menu bar, select **Enhance**, **Adjust Lighting**, **Brightness/Contrast**. In the

TIP

After restoring a wider spectrum of color to the subject matter in the **Foreground** layer, you might learn that your original selection wavered just a bit to include pixels that aren't part of your subject. In this example, I managed to include some ceiling tile when I selected Mike's hair. Luckily, because these adjustments are made to a separate layer, I can use the **Eraser** tool to trim off any unduly selected pixels. See **97** **Erase Part of a Layer** for details.

Brightness/Contrast dialog box, *increase* the brightness by a fair amount (for this example, I entered +25) and increase contrast by a *large* amount to compensate (for this example, +77). If you look carefully at the **Histogram** palette, you'll see the "Golden Gate Bridge" effect caused by breaking up the one solid tower of dark middle grays (represented on this chart by the gray hump hiding beneath the vertical stacks). There are still only a few tonal grades in this part of the photo, but because they represent distant elements, that actually doesn't matter much. Photos shot with far-away flashes leave the background blurry and spotty anyway, so at least you don't have to worry about blurring them yourself.

When you've adjusted brightness and contrast to the point where you can at least distinguish where the photo was taken, click **OK**.

5 View the Result

When you're satisfied with the result, make any other changes you want and save the PSD file. Then resave the result in **JPEG** or **TIFF** format, leaving your **PSD** image with its layers intact so that you can return at a later time to make new adjustments.

Although these adjustments have made an improvement, this project is far from done. There are numerous scratches and specks yet to be removed, and permanent fingerprint damage to the lower-right corner. Manual color correction could still be applied to the center of the dartboard, which I happen to know has vivid reds and yellows. The glare effect to the lower-right of the dartboard could be reduced.

But the results thus far have been dramatic. Who would have dreamt there was a bright yellow door to Mike's left? Magnified sharply enough, you can make out gold-wing darts propped up in the dartboard's shutters—and for that matter, shutters themselves, which no one could possibly make out in the original. By making corrections to the foreground and background separately, I managed to re-create the illusion of depth and distance. The reds in the sweater stripes pull *toward* the viewer, while the neutrals in the wood paneling recede.

18

Correcting Color and Saturation

IN THIS CHAPTER:

144 Correct Color Manually

145 Correct Color, Contrast, and Saturation in One Step

146 Adjust Hue, Saturation, and Lightness Manually

147 Adjust Saturation for a Specific Area

Color balance is one of those features that's difficult to explain (to borrow a phrase from the U.S. Supreme Court), but you know it when you see it. Your eyes are accustomed to seeing the full spectrum of colors for any scene you happen to be looking at, at any time. This is true even if you're standing in a yellow room with yellow walls, yellow carpet, near a yellow sofa with yellow pillows. Your eyes—literally—chemically manufacture the opposite color—purple—to compensate for the over-saturation of a narrow range of color frequencies. This is why you can still see a faint image of something you've stared at for a long period of time when you look away from it. When the scene you're viewing is biased toward one color, your eyes and even your mind know how to compensate.

But your camera doesn't. If one of your digital photos has a particular *color cast*, such as yellow or red, it will typically not have the color balance your eyes expect to see if you were looking at the same scene. For example, a red color cast can happen when a picture is shot without enough light (such as a photo taken at sunset) or if you are working with an old photograph. Because color cast happens frequently, Photoshop Elements provides several tools you can use to restore the color balance to an image.

144 Correct Color Manually

See Also

→ **145** Correct Color, Contrast, and Saturation in One Step

→ **146** Adjust Hue, Saturation, and Lightness Manually

→ **147** Adjust Saturation for a Specific Area

KEY TERM

Color cast—The unwanted predominance of a particular color throughout an image, caused by improper white balancing at the time the image was taken, or the fading of inks in an old printed image.

Although the eye is more sensitive to differences in lightness and contrast than it is to color, when the color spectrum in a photograph is out of balance, it stands out like a sore thumb. For example, old photographs can appear to have a red cast, and photos taken without enough light can have a yellow cast. Color casts happen when *all* the colors in an image tend to show a bias toward one frequency, rather than displaying no bias at all. Even an image that is predominantly green can have a red *color cast* as a result of aging, which drags both the greens (and the opposites that make them stand out) toward the *yellow* side of the color spectrum. You can use the **Remove Color Cast** option in Photoshop Elements to correct a color-cast issue.

After you've selected the **Remove Color Cast** option, you select a portion of the image that should be white, gray, or black. Photoshop Elements uses the area you designate to determine the color cast in the photo. Whatever color must be removed to make the selected area white, gray, or black is the color removed from the entire photo.

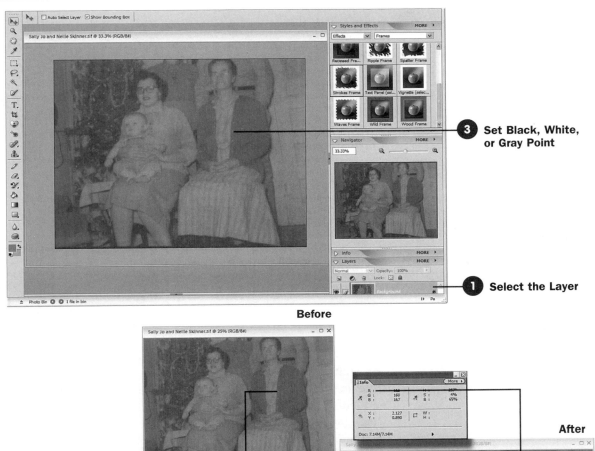

3 Set Black, White, or Gray Point

1 Select the Layer

Before

2 Choose Enhance, Adjust Color, Remove Color Cast

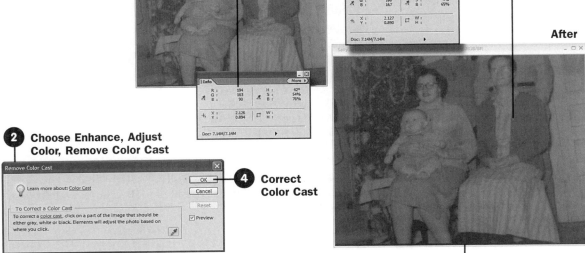

After

4 Correct Color Cast

5 View the Result

1 Select the Layer

Open the image you want to correct in the *Editor* in **Standard Edit** mode and save it in Photoshop (*.psd) format. You can correct the color cast in an image only one *layer* at a time. If your image has several layers, you must correct the color cast in each layer separately. If the **Layers** *palette* is not visible, select **Window, Layers**. In the **Layers** palette, make sure that the desired layer is selected. If there is only one layer in the image (the *Background layer*), click to select it.

TIP

Because determining the extent of color cast in an image relies on how *you* see color, it's a good idea to calibrate your monitor before you start this process to ensure that you're seeing color as you should. See **105** Ensure That What You See Is What You Get for details on monitor calibration.

2 Choose Enhance, Adjust Color, Remove Color Cast

Select **Enhance, Adjust Color, Remove Color Cast** from the menu to open the **Remove Color Cast** dialog box.

3 Set Black, White, or Gray Point

When the **Remove Color Cast** dialog box is displayed, the mouse pointer changes to the **Eyedropper** tool when you drag it over your image. Using this pointer, click an area of the image that should be white, gray, or black. Photoshop Elements relies on *your eyes* to identify the shades in your photograph that should have no color bias whatsoever. The program asks you to click a black, gray, or white area; more accurately, it could have asked you to click any area that should have no distinct color whatsoever. The extent to which the area you clicked *does* have color is measured as the amount of color cast in the entire image.

TIP

If the **Preview** check box is enabled on the **Remove Color Cast** dialog box, you can see how the image will be corrected before closing the dialog box. If you do not like the correction, click the **Reset** button to undo the correction and select a different gray point within the image.

4 Correct Color Cast

Click the **OK** button to close the **Remove Color Cast** dialog box and correct the color cast in the image.

The color cast correction does not actually occur in your image until you click the **OK** button. (If you do not want to make the correction, click the **Cancel** button to close the dialog box.) The color cast corrections are applied to your photo. This process might take a few seconds.

5 View the Result

When you're satisfied with the results, make any other changes you want and save the PSP file. Resave the result in JPEG or TIFF format, leaving your PSD image with its *layers* (if any) intact so that you can return at a later time and make different adjustments if you want.

This example features the undamaged part of a 50-year-old Polaroid. It needs a lot of work to bring it back, but the first step is obviously a removal of the greasy yellow color cast that's a result of the degradation of the plastic coating bonded to the print (more than the print itself). What in this photograph do we really *know* to be white? The best guess is the second button from the top on Great Grandmother Nellie's pullover sweater. That's the spot I used as the *white point* for this image. With the yellow color cast corrected, you can see there's still a lot of work to be done, but bringing the natural color spectrum back has gone a long way toward improving the image. Look for the final version of this photo in the Color Gallery.

145 Correct Color, Contrast, and Saturation in One Step

You can quickly correct the color, contrast, and *saturation* in a photo using the **Color Variations** command. With this command, you select the color correction for the image by simply clicking a *thumbnail* variation of the image. For example, if you want to reduce the red in your image, you click the **Decrease Red** thumbnail.

You can adjust the color variations within your image for the **Midtones**, **Shadows**, and **Highlights** tonal areas. The **Shadows** adjustments affect all the darker areas in the image. The **Highlights** adjustments affect the lighter areas, and the **Midtones** adjustments affect the middle values in the image.

You can also control the saturation of the colors in the image by selecting the **Saturation** option. Then you can click either the **Less Saturation** thumbnail to decrease saturation (making the color more muted) or the **More Saturation** thumbnail to increase it (making the color more vivid).

As you make changes to the color, contrast, and saturation of the image, the before and after previews display at the top of the **Color Variations** dialog box. These views of your image enable you to see your progress. At any time, you can restart the process by clicking the **Reset Image** button.

See Also

→ **144** Correct Color Manually

→ **146** Adjust Hue, Saturation, and Lightness Manually

→ **147** Adjust Saturation for a Specific Area

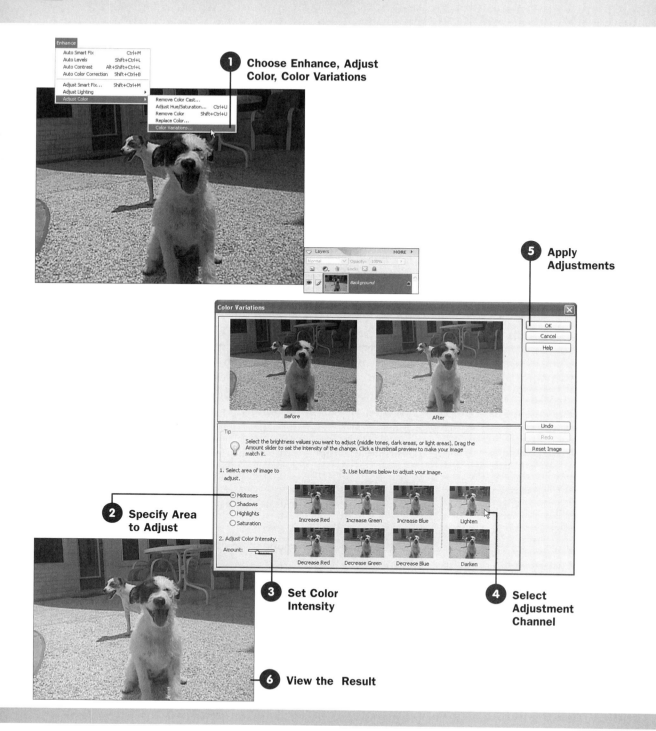

1 Choose Enhance, Adjust Color, Color Variations

5 Apply Adjustments

2 Specify Area to Adjust

3 Set Color Intensity

4 Select Adjustment Channel

6 View the Result

1 Choose Enhance, Adjust Color, Color Variations

Open the image you want to correct in the *Editor* in **Standard Edit** mode and save it in Photoshop (*.psd) format. In the **Layers** *palette*, choose the *layer* you want to correct.

From the menu bar, select **Enhance, Adjust Color, Color Variations** from the menu. The **Color Variations** dialog box appears.

2 Specify Area to Adjust

Select the radio button that corresponds to the tonal area of the image you want to adjust. For example, to adjust the middle range of colors, select the **Midtone** radio button.

3 Set Color Intensity

Set the color intensity for the adjustment by dragging the **Adjust Color Intensity** slider to the left to decrease the intensity or to the right to increase it. As you drag the slider, you will see the color intensity adjusted for the thumbnail images.

4 Select Adjustment Channel

Click the thumbnail image that corresponds to the type of color adjustment you want to make. For the **Midtones, Shadows,** and **Highlights** adjustment areas, the top row of thumbnails is devoted to *increases*, the bottom row to *decreases*. The group of adjustments on the left is devoted to individual color channels (red, green, and blue); on the right, **Lighten** and **Darken** apply changes to all three channels simultaneously. When you click a thumbnail, the changes are applied to the image in the right preview widow at the top of the dialog box. In addition, the thumbnail images at the bottom of the dialog box update to reflect the changes you just applied.

Repeat steps 2 through 4 to make adjustments for other areas of the image. As the adjustments are made to the image, you can view the result in the **After** preview window on the top-right of the **Color Variations** dialog box.

TIP

If you select the **Saturation** option, buttons appear to adjust the saturation. Click the **Less Saturation** button to reduce the saturation or the **More Saturation** button to increase it.

⚡ TIP

If you do not like the corrections selected, click the **Reset Image** button to switch back to the original version of the image.

⑤ Apply Adjustments

When you have made the desired adjustments, click the **OK** button to close the dialog box and apply the color variation selections to the image.

⑥ View the Result

When you close the dialog box, Photoshop Elements applies the selections to your image. This process might take a few seconds. When you're satisfied with the results, make any other changes you want and save the PSP file. Resave the result in JPEG or TIFF format, leaving your PSD image with its *layers* (if any) intact so that you can return at a later time and make different adjustments if you want.

For this example, I decreased the amount of red in the **Midtones** and lightened the image. This made the dog's coat look whiter and brightened the overall image considerably. Rather than panting in a shady spot (as looked to be the case in the original photo), the dog now appears to be sitting on a blazing hot patio, which was exactly where the photo was taken.

⑭⑥ Adjust Hue, Saturation, and Lightness Manually

See Also

→ ⑭④ Correct Color Manually

→ ⑭⑤ Correct Color, Contrast, and Saturation in One Step

→ ⑭⑦ Adjust Saturation for a Specific Area

→ ⑰⑧ Colorize a Photograph

A pixel's color value is defined by three components: hue, *saturation*, and lightness (or *luminance*, or *luminosity*). A pixel's hue represents its location on the color wheel, which is the entire spectrum of colors in the computer's *gamut* or colorspace. Saturation defines the relative power of that hue within a pixel—quantifying, for instance, the range between a clear red (full saturation) to a colorless gray (no saturation). Lightness defines the amount of white in a pixel, from black (no light) to white (all light) to somewhere in-between (light pink). To make individual adjustments to these components of pixels within a given region, use the **Adjust Hue/Saturation** command. For example, many images taken with digital cameras seem to lack saturation. A boost of saturation by even a few degrees can revive an otherwise dull image, infusing it with excitement and drama.

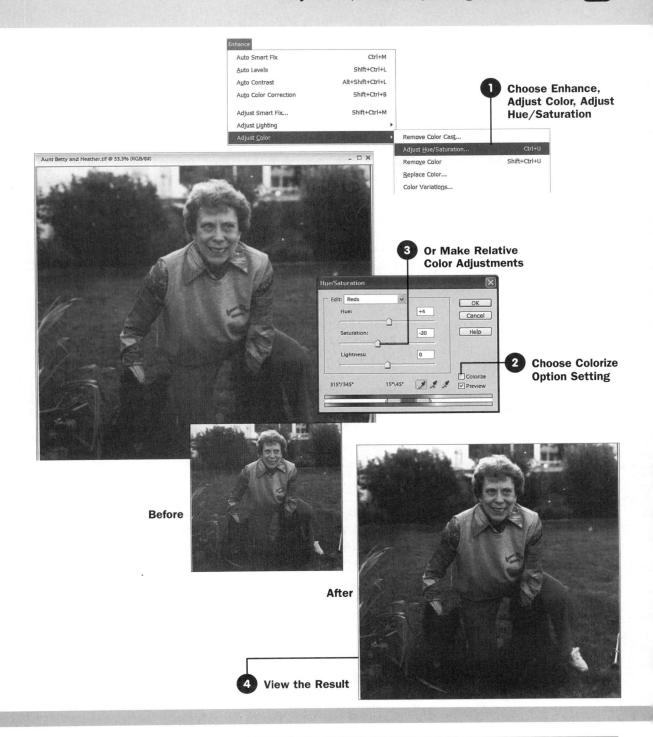

1 Choose Enhance, Adjust Color, Adjust Hue/Saturation

3 Or Make Relative Color Adjustments

2 Choose Colorize Option Setting

Before

After

4 View the Result

By reducing the saturation in a color image, you can create a black-and-white photo—often with better results than simply converting the image to grayscale. By adjusting the hue of a selected object, you can change its color from red to green, for example. By reducing the lightness of an image's background, you can make it fade into the distance—placing more importance on the subject of your image.

 KEY TERM

Saturation—The amount of a particular hue present in a pixel. A fully saturated red pixel is bright red; a less saturated red pixel has more gray and its reddish tone is more subtle.

1 Choose Enhance, Adjust Color, Adjust Hue/Saturation

Open the image you want to correct in the *Editor* in **Standard Edit** mode and save it in Photoshop (*.psd) format. In the **Layers** *palette*, choose the *layer* you want to adjust. To restrict your adjustment to a given region of the chosen layer, use a selection tool to select that region. See **70 About Making Selections** for an explanation of how selections can be used to restrict changes and adjustments to a designated region.

From the menu bar, select **Enhance, Adjust Color, Adjust Hue/Saturation** to display the **Hue/Saturation** dialog box. Enable the **Preview** check box to see examples of your choices in the image before making them final.

 NOTE

To see an example of colorizing layers to bring life to an old monochrome photo in the aquatint style, see **178 Colorize a Photograph.**

2 Choose Colorize Option Setting

This dialog box has two purposes: The *second* of these purposes is to give you a way to apply a single hue to the designated region. *Colorizing* a region in this way eliminates all the area's original color information, replacing it with the values designated by the **Hue** and **Saturation** settings. To colorize the designated region and *replace* color values rather than simply *adjust* them, enable the **Colorize** check box. When you do this, the meanings of the sliders change. The **Hue** slider represents an angle on the color wheel between **0°** and **360°**, theoretically encompassing all the colors of the rainbow. **Saturation** is a percentage representing how much of the chosen **Hue** to apply to the region, while **Lightness** remains a relative setting between **–100** and **+100**, governing how much white is added or removed. (Technically, sliding **Lightness** in either direction should remove saturation, but in this case, the **Saturation** slider remains stable.)

If you're colorizing the designated region, make your adjustment choices from these sliders and click **OK** to exit the dialog box and skip to step 4. Otherwise, continue to step 3.

3 Or Make Relative Color Adjustments

With the **Colorize** option disabled, the purpose of the
Hue/Saturation dialog box is to make *relative* adjustments to one,
two, or all three of the color channels in the designated region.

From the **Edit** drop-down list, select the color channels you want to
adjust. The **Master** option refers to all three (red, green, and blue)
in combination. The primary channels (**Reds**, **Greens**, and **Blues**)
are represented on this list, as well as the secondary colors
(**Yellows**, **Cyans**, and **Magentas**). **Yellows** refers to the red and
green channel, **Cyans** to the green and blue channel, and
Magentas to the blue and red channel.

At this point, the **Hue** slider represents an angle of adjustment
between **−180°** and **+180°**. When you adjust this setting, the **Hue**
component values of all pixels in the selected region are adjusted
by that amount on the color wheel. For example, a yellow pixel
when increased 180 degrees becomes blue.

The **Saturation** slider represents a percentage of adjustment
between **−100** and **+100**. Any non-zero setting represents a degree
of increase or decrease of color in the chosen channels. Drag the
Saturation slider to the right to increase the saturation of the designated region or to the left to decrease the saturation.

The **Lightness** slider represents a percentage of adjustment
between **−100** and **+100**. Any non-zero setting represents a degree
of increase or decrease of *whiteness* in the chosen channels. Drag
the **Lightness** slider to the right to increase the lightness of the
selected color range or to the left to decrease the lightness. If
you've chosen **Blues**, for instance, setting **Lightness** above zero
adds *white* to the blues in the selected region.

Click the **OK** button to close the dialog box and apply the adjustments to your image.

4 View the Result

When you're satisfied with the results, make any other changes
you want and save the PSP file. Resave the result in JPEG or TIFF
format, leaving your PSD image with its *layers* (if any) intact so
that you can return at a later time and make different adjustments
if you want.

TIP

Whereas the **Adjust
Hue/Saturation** command
applies changes to all or
part of a layer, you can create an *adjustment layer*
that applies a saturation
adjustment to several
underlying layers in an
image. See **94** **Create
an Adjustment Layer** for
details.

This example featured a scanned photograph that was damaged from exposure to sunlight for several years, probably clinging to the front door of the refrigerator. My first objective was to restore some of the warm skin tones to Aunt Betty's face. I did this by choosing the **Reds** channel, moving the **Hue** setting to +4 to restore some of the yellows that had faded (yellows always fade first from exposure to sunlight), and set **Saturation** to –20 to help balance her skin tones.

Next, I restored the radiant sunlight on the edges of Betty's sweater and hair by choosing the **Yellows** channel, setting **Hue** to +9, **Saturation** to a relatively high +41, and **Lightness** to a quite high +63. Now the subject matter looks bright and in the center of the picture once again. I used the **Magentas** channel as an opportunity to bring back contrast to Betty's face because the print was using magenta tones in the shadows. With the **Magentas** channel chosen, I set **Hue** to +11 (taking it more toward the red), **Saturation** to +9, and **Lightness** way down to –25. Now Betty's face truly is in the center of the picture.

These adjustments were far from enough to fix the overall picture. I tried to add saturation to the **Greens** channel, for instance, but the problem with this faded print is that too much of the grass and shrubbery color is made up of elements from the **Blues** channel. I'll need to make spot adjustments to the garden, perhaps with the **Color Replacement** tool. And nothing I do with the **Hue/Saturation** dialog box will help me restore contrast to Betty's two jet-black Scottie dogs. But I have Betty's warm, radiant face smiling at me again, and that's a very good start. Look for this image in the Color Gallery.

147 Adjust Saturation for a Specific Area

See Also

→ **144** Correct Color Manually

→ **145** Correct Color, Contrast, and Saturation in One Step

→ **146** Adjust Hue, Saturation, and Lightness Manually

If you want to adjust the *saturation* in specific areas of an image, you can do so quickly using the **Sponge** tool. With the **Sponge** tool, you drag the mouse pointer over the area of the image you want to change. It either adds saturation to the area or removes saturation.

Although it's called a sponge, you control this tool's shape and size as you do with any of the brush tools. You can select its brush type and size from the **Options** bar. The larger the brush size, the more area you can change at once. Photoshop Elements provides several different sizes and types of brushes you can select when using the **Sponge** tool.

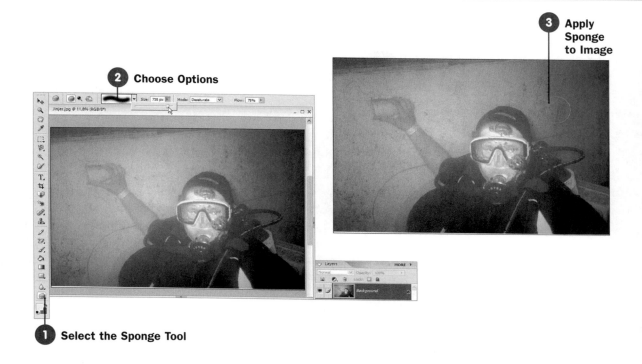

② **Choose Options**

③ Apply Sponge to Image

① **Select the Sponge Tool**

Imagine if the color in a photograph were liquid, like India ink held in place by black pixels. The **Sponge** tool either absorbs colored "liquid" from spots in the image or adds new "liquid" of the same color to spots in the image. From the **Options** bar, you instruct the tool to remove color (**Desaturate**) or add color (**Saturate**). The **Flow** setting is actually metaphorical: It designates how much color is removed or added to a spot for each brushstroke. This setting is comparable to the **Opacity** setting of the **Brush** and **Pencil** tools.

① **Select the Sponge Tool**

Open the image you want to correct in the *Editor* in **Standard Edit** mode and save it in Photoshop (***.psd**) format. In the **Layers** *palette*, choose the *layer* whose color you want to adjust. Select the **Sponge** tool from the **Toolbox**.

2 Choose Options

Click the down arrow next to the brush sample in the **Options** bar and select the desired brush tip for the **Sponge** tool. Select a brush with a feathered edge so that there is a gradual change between the areas where you use the **Sponge** tool and the adjoining pixels.

From the **Mode** drop-down list, select either **Saturate** or **Desaturate**. If you want to intensify the color in an area, select **Saturate**. If you want to dull the colors in an area, select **Desaturate**.

The **Flow** setting regulates the intensity of the **Sponge** tool. When **Mode** is set to **Saturate**, the **Flow** value represents how much saturation is added to a spot, relative to its current saturation. Theoretically, you could apply stroke after stroke until an area is saturated as fully as possible. When **Mode** is set to **Desaturate**, the **Flow** value represents how much saturation is *removed* from a spot. When set to **100%**, the tool removes all color from an area, leaving only grayscale pixels.

3 Apply Sponge to Image

Begin the "sponge stroke" by clicking and holding the mouse button where you want to start applying the **Sponge** tool. For a *pen tablet*, position the pointer by hovering the pen, and then tap and hold the pen where you want the stroke to begin.

To apply a freehand stroke, continue holding the button down as you drag the mouse. The tool follows your mouse pointer. To end the stroke, release the mouse button; with a pen tablet, lift the pen.

When you're satisfied with the results, make any other changes you want and save the PSP file. Resave the result in JPEG or TIFF format, leaving your PSD image with its *layers* (if any) intact so that you can return at a later time and make different adjustments if you want. In this example, the features on the diver's face were too saturated and looked overly red. I wanted to reduce that effect to make the image appear more balanced. To accomplish this, I selected the **Sponge** tool and chose **Desaturate** from the **Mode** drop-down list and set the **Flow** at 75%. I then used the **Sponge** tool on the face of the diver.

19

Controlling Sharpness and Clarity

IN THIS CHAPTER:

148 About Sharpness

149 Sharpen an Image

150 Blur an Image to Remove Noise

151 Blur a Background to Create Depth of Field

152 Create a Spin Effect

153 Soften Selected Details

154 Add Motion to an Image

One very important element of every image is its sharpness. The fuzzier the edges of the subject in your image, the less appealing the image becomes. When referring to *sharpness*, many people have a tendency to characterize it as a quality of *edges*, like the sharpness of a blade. In practice, that's inaccurate. The subject of a photograph looks sharp when all of its surface reflects light the way your eyes expect it to. If you sharpen every element of a subject, it will appear two-dimensional, like a frame in a comic book. An image looks sharp when a fuzzy subject—such as a cat—*appears* fuzzy but not overcompensated. A round object such as the globe of a streetlamp or a marble in a child's hand looks sharp when its deep, translucent interior looks just as hazy as the real thing. Sharpness is not to be confused with accuracy. If every element of a scene looked sharp in a photograph—perfectly in focus, nothing slightly blurred—it wouldn't look real. The proper processing of a digital photograph requires you to be *in control* of sharpness, so you get to say what's crystal clear and what's background *noise*.

The sharpness of an image can be affected by several factors, such as low-light conditions, an out-of-focus photograph, camera movement, or even movement of the subject.

In these tasks, you will learn how to use the tools available in Photoshop Elements to control the sharpness of your images. Not only will you see how to sharpen an image, you will also learn how blurring the background can help to increase the overall sharpness of the subject in your image. You will also look at the effects of softening and adding the appearance of motion to your image.

148 About Sharpness

See Also

→ **149** Sharpen an Image
→ **150** Blur an Image to Remove Noise
→ **151** Blur a Background to Create Depth of Field
→ **153** Soften Selected Details

Unfortunately, when you take photographs with either a standard film camera or a digital camera, the camera does not always capture a picture as sharp as what you are able to see with your eyes. The sharpness of the picture can be affected by multiple conditions, such as poor lighting, poor visibility, or even the fact that your digital camera is set to capture images at a lower *resolution*. The sharpness of a photo can also be diminished when you scan a photo into your computer. Fortunately, you can improve the sharpness of an image with Photoshop Elements.

Photoshop Elements provides several filters you can use to improve the sharpness of your image. You can apply the filter to the entire *layer* of the image or to just a selected portion of the layer. Each of the following filters uses a slightly different method of increasing the contrast of adjacent pixels to make the image appear sharper:

- **Sharpen.** Use this filter to increase the distinction between contrasting regions of an image by eliminating the appearance of blending along the edges of those regions. Think of the **Sharpen** filter as the *opposite* of *anti-aliasing*. To apply the **Sharpen** filter to your selection, select **Filter, Sharpen, Sharpen**.

- **Sharpen Edges.** Use this filter to sharpen the edges of objects within your selection or layer. This filter sharpens the edges by finding regions where there is a significant change in the colors between adjoining pixels. Those regions appear sharper by increasing the contrast between the pixels while the other areas in the image remain untouched. To apply the **Sharpen Edges** filter to your selection, select **Filter, Sharpen, Sharpen Edges**.

- **Sharpen More.** Use this filter when you want to create a stronger focus and more clarity to the selection than what is provided by the **Sharpen** filter. To apply the **Sharpen More** filter to your selection, select **Filter, Sharpen, Sharpen More**.

- **Unsharp Mask.** Although its name can be misleading, this filter actually enables you to create the most professional sharpening effect of all the sharpen filters. With the **Unsharp Mask** filter, you can adjust the contrast of the edge detail in your image to emphasize the edge by creating darker and lighter lines on each side of the edge. When you use this filter, you specify the amount of contrast used to compare the pixels that surround the edges by adjusting the **Threshold** level. You can specify the exact region around each pixel to compare by adjusting the **Radius** setting. You apply the **Unsharp Mask** filter by selecting **Filter, Sharpen, Unsharp Mask**. See **149 Sharpen an Image** for more information on using the **Unsharp Mask** filter to sharpen an image.

Another method for making part of an image look sharper is to blur the background or the noise in the photo. See **150 Blur an Image to Remove Noise** for more information. See **151 Blur a Background to Create Depth of Field** for information on blurring the background to make the subject stand out.

 TIP

You can use the **Sharpen** tool, available from the **Toolbox**, to sharpen specific portions of your image. With this tool, you paint the areas of the image you want to sharpen. This tool works well when you want to sharpen only a small portion of the image. See **153 Soften Selected Details** for more information on setting the **Options** bar settings for the **Sharpen** tool.

149 Sharpen an Image

Before You Begin

→ **148** About Sharpness

See Also

→ **150** Blur an Image to Remove Noise

→ **151** Blur a Background to Create Depth of Field

→ **152** Create a Spin Effect

→ **153** Soften Selected Details

→ **154** Add Motion to an Image

→ **163** Mask an Image Layer

NOTE

Why is the filter called unsharp mask if it sharpens content? As preposterous as it might sound, the way this filter works begins with the act of *blurring*. In the computer's memory, the filter creates a duplicate of the selected layer or region that you'll never see, and then blurs that duplicate. Mathematically, the product of the data from the duplicate is subtracted from the data in the visible image. The theory is that the remainder of the *mostly* blurred region combined with a *partly* blurred version of that same region will yield a cleaner, clearer, and sharper rendering of that region. Don't knock it; it works.

When you create an image, either by taking a photograph or drawing a picture, you always have a particular point in the image where you want the viewer to focus. This focal point is often referred to as the *subject* of the image. It is not unusual to take a photo of an object and find that the subject of the photo does not have the desired sharpness necessary to make it stand out from the background.

Improving the sharpness in your images can be a challenge. You often have to increase the contrast between the edges of the subject and the surrounding background. One tool that works well for sharpening an image is the **Unsharp Mask** filter. When you apply this filter to your image, it locates the pixels in the image that differ from the surrounding pixels and increases the contrast between those pixels. When you use this filter, you control the sharpening effect by specifying the amount of contrast, the number of pixels to sharpen around the edges, and the **Threshold**, or how different the target pixels need to be from the surrounding pixels.

You can apply the **Unsharp Mask** to an entire layer or to a selection. Keep in mind that everything within the selection will be affected by the filter. If you don't select a portion of the image, the entire active layer is sharpened. You might want to sharpen only the subject of the image, leaving its surrounding elements as they are so that the subject stands out. To accomplish this, select that subject using one of the selection tools and then apply the **Unsharp Mask**. See **70** **About Making Selections** for more information on using selection tools.

If you want to have more control over how the **Unsharp Mask** filter affects the final image, you can use an *edge mask* to apply the filter as explained in this task. In creating an edge mask, you sharpen an image so that the edges of its subject matter are well pronounced. You can then mask the image so that only the edges you select are actually visible to the viewer. For example, in this example of a koala, I want only the koala, and *not* the tree branches, to be sharp. By masking the koala, you can sharpen only those edges. This way, any background edges that were sharpened by the **Unsharp Mask** will not display in your final image.

Although Photoshop Elements allows you to create masking effects, you cannot create and save masks as you can with other photo editing software packages such as Adobe Photoshop. Masking works well for hiding portions of an image you don't want to be visible. See **163** **Mask an Image Layer** for more information on masking portions of an image.

1 Create Sharpening Layer

Open the image you want to adjust in the *Editor* in **Standard Edit** mode and save it in Photoshop (***.psd**) format. If it's not already showing, display the **Layers** *palette* by selecting **Window, Layers**. In the **Layers** palette, click to select the **Background** *layer* and choose **Layer, Duplicate Layer** from the menu bar to duplicate the *background layer*. On the **Duplicate Layer** dialog box, specify a name for the duplicate layer, such as **Sharpening**. The layer you are creating is where you will apply the **Unsharp Mask** filter. You want to create a separate sharpening layer so that you can mask out the edges you want visible in the image.

2 Apply Unsharp Mask Filter

With the **Sharpening** layer chosen in the **Layers** palette, select **Filter, Sharpen, Unsharp Mask**. The **Unsharp Mask** dialog box opens. Enable the **Preview** check box.

3 Specify Settings

In the **Amount** field, specify a value representing the amount you want to increase the contrast between the pixels. For these purposes, you'll want to choose a much higher value than you'd want for a layer you actually intend to keep, such as **200%** or higher.

In the **Radius** field, specify a value that indicates how many pixels around the vicinity of each pixel play a role in adjusting the color to appear sharper. The larger the number, the wider the band of pixels that are evaluated when sharpening each one.

The **Unsharp Mask** filter adjusts every pixel to some extent based on its evaluation of the color values of its *neighboring pixels*. The **Radius** setting determines how many neighboring pixels to evaluate for each pixel being evaluated. **Threshold** is a relative setting designating how much of a brightness difference between neighboring pixels constitutes a *meaningful* difference—in other words, how much contrast is a contrast that *matters*. Material contrasts are the ones that are enhanced, so a lower **Threshold** setting means that more contrasts (by lesser differences) are enhanced.

KEY TERM

Edge mask—A selection that encompasses only the edge pixels in an image, thus preventing unwanted sharpening to everything else.

NOTE

See **92** **Create a New Image Layer** for more information on adding layers to an image.

TIPS

Don't worry about over-sharpening the background. You are going to use a *mask* to display only the desired sharpened edges of the subject.

Use the − and + buttons to change the size of the image that displays in the preview window.

If you plan to print the image, you'll want the sharpening effects to be more dramatic. Images from printers are not as sharp as they appear on the screen.

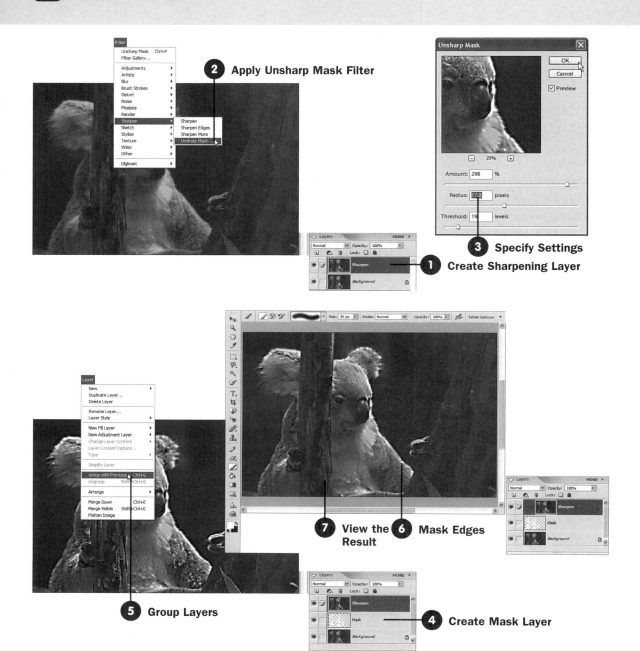

2 Apply Unsharp Mask Filter

3 Specify Settings

1 Create Sharpening Layer

7 View the Result **6** Mask Edges

5 Group Layers

4 Create Mask Layer

For the purposes of this task, you want to turn up the contrast along the edges of objects as much as possible. This generally means you should set **Radius** to a high value (above **50**) and **Threshold** to a low value to compensate. Take a good look at the preview and remember that you're looking for edges to be *overemphasized*. Click the **OK** button to finalize your choices.

4 Create Mask Layer

In the **Layers** palette, click the **Background** layer and then choose **Layer, New, Layer** from the menu bar to create a new blank layer. You can name this layer **Mask** because it is the layer where you will mask the sharpened edges of the image. You are going to create a mask that includes just the sharper edges of the image.

5 Group Layers

In the **Layers** palette, choose the **Sharpening** layer. Select **Layer, Group with Previous** from the menu bar to group the **Sharpen** layer with your new **Mask** layer.

Notice that the sharpening effects are no longer visible—now the image looks as it did in step 1. When you group layers, the top layer (in this case, the **Sharpening** layer) shows through only where there is content in the bottom layer (in this case, the as-yet empty **Mask** layer). When you paint on the **Mask** layer in the next step, however, you will allow only selected areas of the **Sharpening** layer to appear.

TIP

If you don't want some of the edges to appear as sharp, you can reduce the **Opacity** setting for the **Brush** tool in the **Options** bar before painting those edges.

6 Mask Edges

The next thing to do is to add content to the **Mask** layer where you want the edges of the image to appear sharpened. To accomplish this, you use the **Brush** tool.

In the **Layers** palette, choose the **Mask** layer, and then select the **Brush** tool from the **Toolbox**. On the **Options** bar, select a soft brush style and a brush size that matches the width of the edge you want to sharpen. Make sure that the **Opacity** setting is **100%**, and that **Mode** is set to **Normal**. It actually does not matter what you use for your *foreground color*, although you might want to choose black simply because your marks become more visible in the thumbnail for the **Mask** layer in the **Layers** palette.

In the image, paint along the edges of the subject where you want to sharpen. As you paint, the sharpened edges from the **Sharpen** layer will become visible.

To remove part of a sharpened edge, select the **Mask** layer and, using an *eraser* tool, remove the portion you do not want visible. You can also use any of the selection tools to delete part of the mask. For example, you can use the **Lasso** tool to select part of the mask, and then press the **Delete** key to remove the selection.

❼ View Results

When you're satisfied with the result, make any other changes you want and save the PSD file. Then resave the result in **JPEG** or **TIFF** format, leaving your **PSD** image with its layers intact so that you can return at a later time to make changes or additions.

The **Unsharp Mask** filter makes a number of positive corrections to the sharpness of a layer, along with a wide array of really wild and unwanted changes. But with masking, you can paint directly on top of those areas that reflect the **Unsharp Mask** changes you do want, and leave behind those areas of changes you don't want.

I had a picture of a koala that was taken through a glass window at the zoo. Because the glass made the koala blend into the background, I used the technique described in this task to sharpen the koala without sharpening the background or the tree branches in the foreground.

When I applied the **Unsharp Mask**, I set the contrast **Amount** value very high to make sure that the edges got a lot of contrast and so that the sharpness would also be apparent when I printed the image. Sharpening the image this way also made the trees in the foreground stand out, but I choose not to allow the sharp tree branches to carry over when I masked the image. I just wanted the koala to stand out as the main focal point.

When I created the **Mask** layer, I used a brush wide enough to create the desired edge for my image. Because it was a very high *resolution* photo, I had to use a fairly large brush size. I outlined the entire koala and also painted over the facial features to sharpen them as well.

150 Blur an Image to Remove Noise

If you have a grainy-looking image such as an old photograph you scanned in, you can blur portions of it to remove the graininess. Because graininess can contribute to a lack of sharpness in an image, blurring the graininess has the effect of sharpening the image. If you blur only the background of the image, you appear to sharpen the subject of the image. Keep in mind, you are creating the *perception* of sharpening the subject of the image by blurring the surrounding background.

When you blur an image or portion of the image, the pixels along color edges are blended with one another—sometimes using averaging—to create a softer edge. This averaging and blending of colors creates smoother transitions between different colored sections of the image, thus eliminating the appearance of tiny spots, often called *noise*, from the image.

With the **Blur** filter, noise is eliminated from the photo by averaging the color values of the pixels where transitions occur to create hard lines or shaded areas. The **Blur More** filter performs the same steps as the **Blur** filter, but the effect is much stronger. The most versatile filter for removing noise is **Smart Blur** because it enables you to control how the image is blurred. The **Smart Blur** dialog box enables you to specify custom **Radius** and **Threshold** settings. By specifying a **Radius** value, you indicate how far to search for pixels that don't match. You indicate the **Threshold** value to specify how different the pixels must be before they are blurred. This filter also enables you to select the blur quality and indicate the blur mode.

1 Select the Smart Blur Filter

Open the image you want to adjust in the *Editor* in **Standard Edit** mode and save it in Photoshop (***.psd**) format. If it's not already showing, display the **Layers** *palette* by selecting **Window, Layers**. In the **Layers** palette, click the *layer* you want to sharpen by blurring the graininess and select **Filter, Blur, Smart Blur**.

To limit your changes to a specific region of the image, use one or more selection tools from the **Toolbox** to draw a *marquee* around that region, protecting areas outside that region from being blurred. See **70** **About Making Selections** for more about making selections.

Before You Begin

→ **148** About Sharpness

See Also

→ **149** Sharpen an Image

→ **151** Blur a Background to Create Depth of Field

→ **152** Create a Spin Effect

→ **153** Soften Selected Details

→ **154** Add Motion to an Image

NOTE

To see an example of using the **Gaussian Blur** filter to blur a portion of a photo—specifically, a portion moved onto its own layer to protect it—see **142** Fix a Flash That's Too Close.

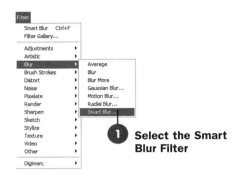

1 Select the Smart Blur Filter

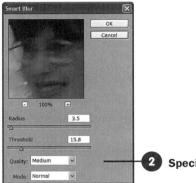

2 Specify Settings

Spotty, Over-Zoomed Original Image

3 View the Result

2 Specify Settings

In the **Smart Blur** dialog box, specify the settings for blurring your image. You can view a sample of how the image will be blurred in the preview window at the top of the dialog box.

In the **Radius** field, specify a value that indicates the number of pixels around each pixel that the **Smart Blur** filter will search for dissimilar pixels to blur.

In the **Threshold** field, specify a value between 0 and 100 that indicates, relatively, how different the pixels must be in tonal difference before they are blurred. The higher the **Threshold** level, the more pixels are blurred in your image.

In the **Quality** drop-down list box, specify the desired blur quality for the image. You can select from **Low**, **Medium**, or **High** quality. The higher the quality setting, the longer it takes to apply the filter, although a **Quality** setting of **High** produces the smoothest results. However, the higher the **Quality** setting, the more likely you will have banding when you print or view the image.

The **Mode** list box presents the different modes the filter uses to create the blur. The default selection, **Normal**, blurs the entire selection. Select **Edge Only** if you want to create pure white edges on a pure black background, like sketches made with a thin stylus on a blackboard. Select **Overlay Edge** to combine this white edge with the existing image contents for a special effect that divides contrasting regions of the image by a thin white boundary.

When the preview appears as you intend, click **OK**.

③ View the Result

When you're satisfied with the result, make any other changes you want and save the PSD file. Then resave the result in JPEG or TIFF format, leaving your PSD image with its layers intact so that you can return at a later time to make changes or additions.

This example features a digital photo of a ballet curtain call that suffers from many of the same problems faced by digital video photographers: It was taken at high digital zoom, using no tripod. So, the shakiness of the photographer's hand (mine), coupled with the artifacts created by the digital zoom, resulted in a nice moment compounded by the problems of modern technology.

Neither sharpening nor blurring restores focus to an image, but it can restore some sense of *composition*...or, at least, cover up some of my mistakes. This example actually shows two types of blurs at work: Along the edge of the photo, I used the **Elliptical Selection**

TIPS

Use the − and + buttons to adjust the zoom size of the preview window. As you point to the preview, the mouse pointer becomes the **Hand** tool. Use this tool to drag the image to see another portion.

Click and hold the preview window to toggle the effect off, and release to turn it back on. This enables you to compare the look of the image before and after the effect is applied.

TIPS

You can combine the **Smart Blur** effect with the edge mask technique discussed in **149** Sharpen an Image. To accomplish this, apply the **Smart Blur** to the **Background** layer after creating your **Sharpen** layer. Then create a mask layer and paint a mask for the portions of the blurred layer that you want visible.

To blur a small area, you can select the **Blur** tool from the **Toolbox**. With the tool selected, specify the desired brush type and brush size. Set the **Strength** to **100%** on the **Options** bar to create the most blur. Click and drag across the area you want to blur. See **153** Soften Selected Details for more information on setting the options for the **Blur** tool.

tool to create a *feathered*, vignette-shaped selection, copied that selection to a new layer, and then applied a mild **Gaussian Blur** (see **151** Blur a Background to Create Depth of Field). For the **Background** layer, I used the **Smart Blur** filter described here. I set **Radius** to a low value of **3.5** to preserve the shading of Katerina's face and to prevent posterization. I then set **Threshold** to **15.8**, which was a nice balance between blurring and losing her face altogether (higher) and returning to the original spottiness (lower).

The result shows how **Smart Blur** reconstructed an even tone to the subject of the image, thus restoring the illusion of sharpness; the **Gaussian Blur** technique compounded the illusion by taking the viewer's focus away from the edges and corners, without disrespecting the other fine performers in the production.

151 Blur a Background to Create Depth of Field

Before You Begin

→ **148** About Sharpness

See Also

→ **149** Sharpen an Image

→ **150** Blur an Image to Remove Noise

→ **153** Soften Selected Details

→ **154** Add Motion to an Image

One good method to make the subject of your image stand out is to blur the background of the image. When you do this, you can draw more attention to the actual subject and eliminate distractions. For example, you might have a picture of your child playing with other children. You can blur all the other children in the photo so that you child stands out. By blurring the background of the image, you create *depth of field*. Suddenly, all the other surrounding distractions in the image fade into the distance, and the viewer's eyes can concentrate on the subject, the situation, and the moment.

The best tool for blurring the background of your image is the **Gaussian Blur** filter. When you select this filter, you can create a hazy effect by controlling the level of blurring with the **Radius** value. The higher the **Radius** value, the hazier your selection will appear. The **Radius** value indicates the range of the scan, in pixels from each pixel in the currently selected region or layer. If any pixels within that range are dissimilar, the filter will blur them.

Because you want to blur only the background of the image, you must preserve the subject. One way to accomplish this is to create a duplicate copy of the **Background** *layer* and apply the **Gaussian Blur** filter to the **Background** layer only. Then switch to the unblurred copied layer and use the **Eraser** tool to erase the background portion of the layer, revealing the blurred **Background** layer.

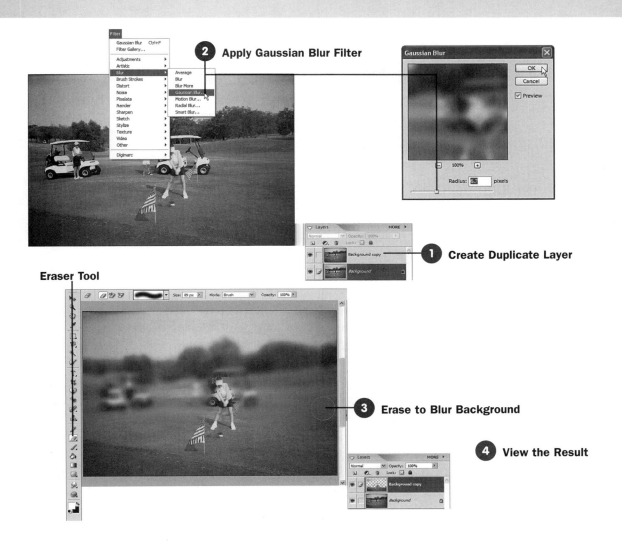

Apply Gaussian Blur Filter

2

Create Duplicate Layer

1

Eraser Tool

Erase to Blur Background

3

View the Result

4

① Create Duplicate Layer

Open the image you want to adjust in the *Editor* in **Standard Edit** mode and save it in Photoshop (***.psd**) format. If it's not already showing, display the **Layers** *palette* by selecting **Window, Layers**. In the **Layers** palette, select the **Background** layer and then choose **Layer, Duplicate Layer** from the menu bar to duplicate the selected layer.

2 Apply Gaussian Blur Filter

In the **Layers** palette, select the **Background** layer once again, and choose **Filter, Blur, Gaussian Blur**. In the **Gaussian Blur** dialog box, enable the **Preview** check box. Select a **Radius** value representing the extent of how much each pixel in the region is blurred, measured in terms of pixel length. For this technique, you'll want to set **Radius** quite high (**20** pixels or above), to the extent that you almost cannot make out the contents of the current layer.

Click **OK** to close the dialog box and apply the blur settings to the **Background** layer. You will not be able to see the effects of the blurring in the image window because the blurred **Background** layer is beneath the non-blurred copied layer.

3 Erase to Blur Background

Click the **Eraser** tool on the **Toolbox**. On the **Options** bar, set the **Opacity** of the tool to **100%**, and from the **Presets** list, choose a wide, soft brush tip you can easily work with. If **Opacity** is less than 100%, the copied layer will not be completely erased.

In the **Layers** palette, select the **Background Copy** layer. Use the **Eraser** tool to erase the background areas and reveal the blurred image underneath.

4 View the Result

When you're satisfied with the result, make any other changes you want and save the PSD file. Then resave the result in **JPEG** or **TIFF** format, leaving your **PSD** image with its layers intact so that you can return at a later time to make changes or additions.

I took a photo of a friend in a golf tournament. Because I wanted to make sure that the viewer's attention was focused on her, I blurred everything in the background, including the other two golfers and the golf carts. By blurring everything but her, she becomes the clear focus of the image, and everything else looks like it is in the distance.

152 Create a Spin Effect

One method of blurring the background is to create a spinning effect using the **Radial Blur** filter. With this filter, you can create two different effects: a **Zoom** or a **Spin**. With the **Zoom** option, your selected region is given the effect of the camera lens being zoomed-in fast during exposure. The **Spin** option has a circular whirlpool appearance, like rotating the whole camera along the axis of its own lens during exposure.

There are probably very few photos ever produced in the world that would benefit from being spun around *in their entirety* by the **Spin** option of the **Radial Blur** filter. In practice, you would use it to dress up a subject, to place that subject in imaginary space and spin it around. So, when you use this filter, make sure that the subject of the image is not affected by it. In this example, we'll create a copy *layer* of the background surrounding the subject and then spin that layer around in space exclusively.

Before You Begin

→ **70** About Making Selections

See Also

→ **107** Crop a Portion of an Image

→ **150** Blur an Image to Remove Noise

→ **153** Soften Selected Details

→ **154** Add Motion to an Image

1 Center Subject in the Image

Open the image you want to adjust in the *Editor* in **Standard Edit** mode and save it in Photoshop (***.psd**) format. If it's not already showing, display the **Layers** *palette* by selecting **Window, Layers**.

When you don't have an active selection, the **Radial Blur** filter performs its magic on the entire layer. For this technique to work accurately, the subject you're isolating should be in the general center of the image. (In a moment, her entire world will be spinning before her eyes.) For this example, I used the **Crop** tool to crop the image to a perfect square, with my subject in the center. I ensured a perfect square by holding down **Shift** as I dragged the tool from one corner to the other. I then kept **Shift** held down as I repositioned the *handles* until the crosshairs at the center of the *bounding box* touched the subject's face. See **107** **Crop a Portion of an Image** for more on the **Crop** tool.

2 Create a Circular Cutout Copy Layer

In the **Toolbox**, click the **Elliptical Marquee** tool. In the **Options** pane, set **Feather** to a fairly high amount, such as **40** pixels.

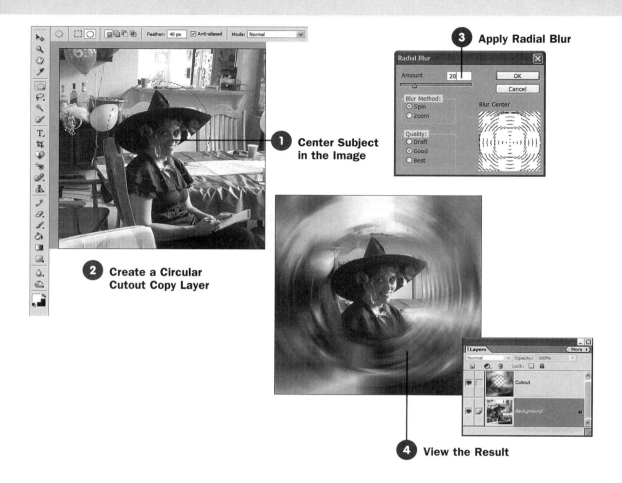

3 Apply Radial Blur

1 Center Subject in the Image

2 Create a Circular Cutout Copy Layer

4 View the Result

In the image, again with **Shift** held down, drag the pointer from one corner of the bounding box to the other, until the circle surrounds the subject matter perfectly. Choose **Select, Inverse** from the menu bar to invert the selection.

From the menu bar, select **Layer, New, Layer from Copy**. Name the new layer **Cutout**.

3 Apply Radial Blu

With the **Cutout** layer chosen, select **Filter, Blur, Radial Blur** from the menu bar. In the **Radial Blur** dialog box, specify the settings for the filter. Select the desired blur method, either **Spin** or **Zoom**. Specify the relative amount of blurring you want to apply to the image in the **Amount** field. As you change this setting, the diagram marked **Blur Center** changes to show the degree of alteration the blur will make to the image (there is no preview available). Here, the sweep of the arcs in the diagram represents the degree of change.

You can change the origin of the blur by dragging the wireframe pattern in the **Blur Center** pane. This origin is calculated relative to the center of the image, although the diagram appears to be square even when your image is not square.

The **Quality** setting determines whether **Radial Blur** takes its time to produce a less grainy, more believable effect. If you want to quickly apply the filter to see how it looks, click the **Draft** option. The **Draft** quality will be grainy, but it's quicker to produce. **Best** quality may take quite some time to render for images with very high *resolution*.

To finalize your choices, click **OK**. In a moment, the filter is applied to the chosen layer.

4 **View the Result**

When you're satisfied with the result, make any other changes you want and save the PSD file. Then resave the result in **JPEG** or **TIFF** format, leaving your **PSD** image with its layers intact so that you can return at a later time to make changes or additions.

It isn't every family that has a grandmother who is willing to volunteer for witch duty. This particular Nana was showered with roses on her granddaughter's sixth birthday—which is a whole lot better reward than, say, having a house dumped on you.

Conceivably, this photo could have been reserved for the task about removing a green *color cast*. Instead, we placed Nana in the center of the legendary Oz effect. All that was rotated in this image is the circular cutout of the dining room details surrounding our witch; by *feathering* the selection from which the layer was cut, you can't really tell where the real world ends and the **Radial Blur** effect begins.

TIP

Using **Best** quality can cause banding in the image when you print. In addition, the time required to apply **Best** quality is substantially longer than for other settings.

TIP

To experiment with a more subtle application of the **Radial Blur** filter, try applying a blend mode to the **Cutout** layer. The **Lighten** mode gives the pattern a more ethereal quality, like the beginning of a dream sequence ("There's no place like home"). The **Darken** mode is still soft, but more ashen; darkening itself softly toward the edges for what could conceivably be a romantic effect.

153 Soften Selected Details

Before You Begin

✔ **148** About Sharpness

See Also

→ **149** Sharpen an Image

→ **151** Blur a Background to Create Depth of Field

→ **152** Create a Spin Effect

If you want to soften specific details in your image so that they are not so obvious, you can do so with the **Smudge** tool. This tool absorbs colors from the point where you first touch it to the image and paints copies of those colors it absorbs as you apply the brushstroke. The tool continually absorbs new samples and applies those samples again as the stroke continues. The result is a smudge effect, as though your image were made of liquid pixels and you were dragging a cotton swab over it.

You select the settings for the **Smudge** tool on the **Options** bar. You can select any brush style or size. Typically, you select a brush size that matches the area of the image you want to smudge. You can also specify a **blend mode** for the smudge effect. See **111** **About Tool Options** for more information on setting brush styles, sizes, and blend modes.

1 Choose Smudge Tool

Open the image you want to adjust in the **Editor** in **Standard Edit** mode and save it in Photoshop (*.psd) format. If there's more than one **layer** in the image, choose the layer containing the contents you intend to smudge from the **Layers** **palette**. To protect any parts of the image you don't want to smudge, select the region containing the spot you want to correct.

From the **Toolbox**, click the **Smudge** tool.

2 Set Tool Options

Specify the settings for the **Smudge** tool on the **Options** bar. From the **Presets** list, choose a brush tip. Elsewhere on the **Options** bar, you can select the tool's size, blend mode, and strength. See **111** **About Tool Options** for more information. The blend mode determines how the colors in the pixels are blended together when you use the **Smudge** tool. Typically, the **Normal** mode works best when softening details in an image.

Typically, you want to keep the **Strength** of the smudge at around 50% so that the pixels will blend evenly to create a soft effect. You can adjust the strength by typing a value in the **Strength** field or by adjusting the slider.

NOTE

The **Smudge** tool shares the same location on the **Toolbox** as the **Blur** and **Sharpen** tools. If you do not see the **Smudge** tool, click the **Blur** or **Sharpen** tool and then select the **Smudge** tool from the **Options** bar.

 TIP

If you want to add the *foreground color* to your smudge, enable the **Finger Painting** check box. The foreground color (as specified in the swatch at the bottom of the **Toolbox**) will be blended into the image as you use the **Smudge** tool.

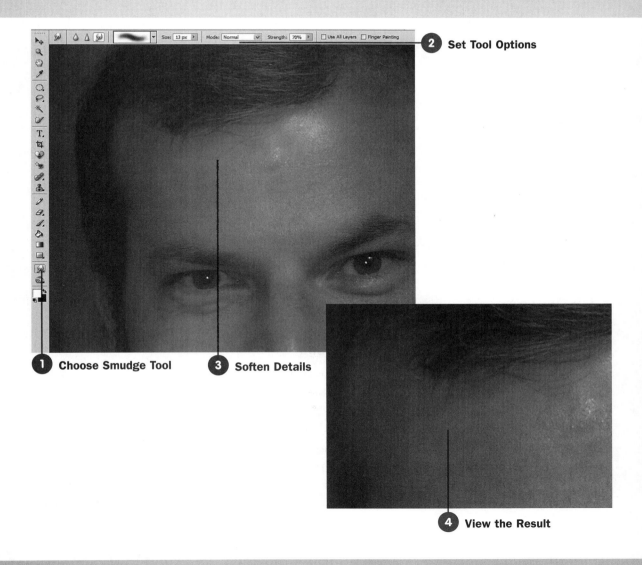

2 Set Tool Options

1 Choose Smudge Tool

3 Soften Details

4 View the Result

3 Soften Details

Begin applying the tool by clicking and holding the mouse button where you want to start smudging. For a **pen tablet**, position the pointer by hovering the pen, and then tap and hold the pen where you want the stroke to begin.

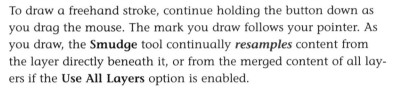

To draw a freehand stroke, continue holding the button down as you drag the mouse. The mark you draw follows your pointer. As you draw, the **Smudge** tool continually *resamples* content from the layer directly beneath it, or from the merged content of all layers if the **Use All Layers** option is enabled.

To draw a straight horizontal or vertical line, press **Shift** now, and continue dragging the mouse. The Editor senses whether you intend for the line to move up, right, left, or down by the general direction in which you're moving the mouse—it doesn't have to be exact.

To draw a straight line between points, release the mouse button. For a pen tablet, lift the pen. Move the pointer to where you want the end of the line to appear. Press **Shift**, and then click this point. The line will be an application of the tool over the distance between the start and end points, relative to the tool's current **Strength** setting. You can continue drawing from here—either a freehand mark or another straight line segment.

④ View the Result

When you're satisfied with the result, make any other changes you want and save the PSD file. Then resave the result in **JPEG** or **TIFF** format, leaving your **PSD** image with its layers intact so that you can return at a later time to make new adjustments.

It's enough that I have fewer hairs of my own these days without having to spend time going over my publicity photos to remove even more of it. ("Hairs," I've noted, is the only word in the English language where by using it in the plural, you imply *fewer* of them rather than more.) But here, alas, I have a stray hair. So, I smudge it out of existence with the **Smudge** tool.

The trick is to sample parts of the forehead and smudge them over to one side to cover up the hair. If I had applied all my strokes in one direction, I'd end up basically moving my hair to one side. So, I applied several very small strokes in varying directions. I use a soft, narrow brush tip because I don't want to obviously copy forehead patterns—the result will look too obvious...well, like a *comb-over*, and I already have one of those. In a moment, the unwanted hair is removed. (And all for three conveniently low, easy payments....)

TIP

To change brush tips for the **Smudge** tool at any time, right-click the image. The **Brush Presets** *palette* appears. Choose a new tip from the **Brushes** list, and then click the X button to dismiss the palette.

TIP

Repeated applications of the **Smudge** tool starting at the same point on an image results in the creation of a solid area of color. In an image of a person's face, this result could be confused with a sore or blemish.

154 Add Motion to an Image

If you want to add the appearance of background movement to your image, you can use the **Motion Blur** filter. When you use this filter, you make objects look like they are moving fast.

The **Motion Blur** filter blurs the image in the direction you specify. You can specify an **Angle** between –360 and 360 degrees. You can also control the "length" of the motion blur: The higher you set the **Distance** value, the more pixels are blurred to create the motion effect.

You can apply the **Motion Blur** filter to a selection or to the entire *layer*. A good approach to using the filter is to copy the **Background** layer and apply the filter to the **Background** layer. Then you can erase the top layer (the copied layer) at the locations where you want the motion to appear.

Before You Begin

✔ **148** About Sharpness

See Also

→ **149** Sharpen an Image

→ **150** Blur an Image to Remove Noise

→ **151** Blur a Background to Create Depth of Field

→ **152** Create a Spin Effect

❶ Create a Duplicate Layer

Open the image you want to adjust in the *Editor* in **Standard Edit** mode and save it in Photoshop (***.psd**) format. If it's not already showing, display the **Layers** *palette* by selecting **Window, Layers**. In the **Layers** palette, select the **Background** layer and then choose **Layer, Duplicate Layer** from the menu bar to duplicate the selected layer.

❷ Apply the Motion Blur Filter

In the **Layers** palette, choose the **Background** layer. Select **Filter, Blur, Motion Blur** from the menu bar to display the **Motion Blur** dialog box. Enable the **Preview** check box.

In the **Angle** field, indicate the number of degrees for the motion angle. You can see the motion direction on the circular button to the right of the **Angle** field. You can also change the **Angle** by clicking the button and dragging its handle—literally twisting it like an old TV channel changer—in the direction you want the motion.

In the **Distance** field, indicate the number of pixels over which the blur effect is to be applied. The larger the value in the **Distance** field, the longer the blur streak will be. Watch the preview window in the dialog box to get an idea how your settings will affect your image.

Add Motion to an Image

 Add Motion to an Image

154

TIP

Use the – and + buttons under the preview window on the **Motion Blur** dialog box to change the zoom settings of the preview.

Click **OK** to close the **Motion Blur** dialog box and apply the blur settings to the **Background** layer. The blurred layer is not visible at this point because the nonblurred layer is on top.

❸ Erase Portions to Add Motion Blur

Select the **Eraser** tool from the **Toolbox**. On the **Options** bar, set the **Opacity** of the tool to **100%**, and adjust the **Size** field to match the part of the background you want to blur.

In the **Layers** palette, select the unblurred **Background copy** layer. Use the **Eraser** tool to erase the areas you want to blur. Where you apply the **Eraser** tool, the unblurred area is erased, revealing the blurred **Background** layer underneath.

❹ View the Result

When you're satisfied with the result, make any other changes you want and save the PSD file. Then resave the result in **JPEG** or **TIFF** format, leaving your **PSD** image with its layers intact so that you can return at a later time to make new adjustments.

In this example, I used the **Motion Blur** filter to create a motion effect for the vehicle behind the giraffe. Because the movement of the vehicle was fairly horizontal, I kept the **Angle** setting at **0**. I increased the **Distance** setting to **283** pixels to create a fairly large amount of motion.

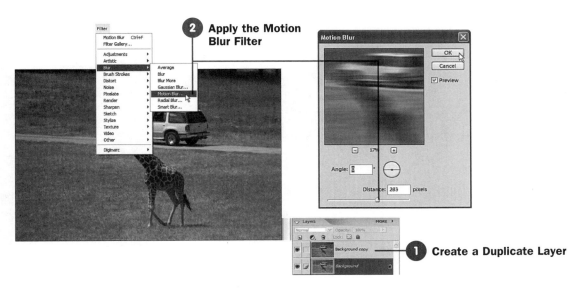

2 Apply the Motion Blur Filter

1 Create a Duplicate Layer

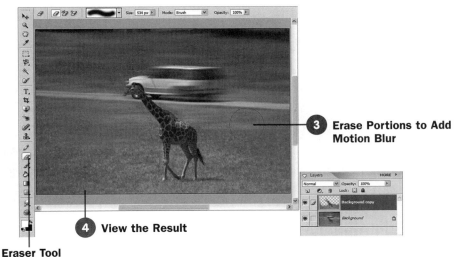

3 Erase Portions to Add Motion Blur

4 View the Result

Eraser Tool

PART IV

Sharing, Creating, and Having Fun

IN THIS PART:

CHAPTER 20 Sharing Images   573

CHAPTER 21 Improving a Photograph's Visual Impact 595

CHAPTER 22 Applying Visual Effects   629

CHAPTER 23 Creating Artistic Photographs   643

CHAPTER 24 Adding and Embellishing Text   683

20

Sharing Images

IN THIS CHAPTER:

155 About Emailing

156 Set Up Photoshop Elements for Emailing

157 Manage Contacts

158 Share Images Using Email

159 Select an Online Service

160 Share Images Using an Online Service

161 Send Images to a Mobile Phone

The long-running comic strip *Blondie* often depicts the Bumstead family looking through a photo album and commenting on some disreputable relative. In the twenty-first century, the photo album easily could be electronic, and the Bumsteads could share photos by email with all their relatives, including the disreputable ones.

Photoshop Elements is not an email program, but it can work in close partnership with the email software you *do* have. This chapter explains how to get your images from the *Organizer catalog* on your computer in Texas to Great-Uncle Henry over on the Emerald Isle (or wherever his travels might have taken him). In addition to individual pictures, you can email creations such as slide shows, photo albums, postcards, and calendars. You also can include sound and video files, but not automatically. You must manually attach them to the email message. If your friends and relatives have a slow connection to the Internet, you can share images using an online service. Not only does this make it quicker and easier for Grandma to view the latest photos of your daughter's birthday party, she can select the ones she wants to have copies of and have the service print and mail them directly to her. Of course, Adobe's online service, Ofoto, comes with built-in security so you don't have to worry about someone viewing your photos if you didn't invite them to.

155 About Emailing

See Also

→ **156** Set Up Photoshop Elements for Emailing

→ **157** Manage Contacts

→ **158** Share Images Using Email

KEY TERM

Email client—A program that sends and receives email. Popular email clients/programs include Outlook and Outlook Express.

In all likelihood, you have an electronic mail program on your computer. If yours is a Windows system, your email program is probably one of the two supplied by Microsoft. Outlook, part of Microsoft Office, is an email and contact manager designed for networked, corporate use. Outlook Express, supplied with Internet Explorer, is a less bulky counterpart intended for personal use.

Photoshop Elements works with the two Microsoft email applications plus Adobe's own email service (available through **www.adobe.com**). If you use an independent program such as Eudora or AOL Mail, it won't work directly, but you can still use Photoshop Elements to prepare your images for sending. Assuming that your particular email program is Outlook, Outlook Express, or Adobe E-Mail Service, it works with Photoshop Elements in the role of an *email client*, bridging the gap between Photoshop Elements and your email delivery system. When you want to email a few pictures, the *Organizer* manages the first steps of processing and preparing the photos for sending, collecting them, identifying them as email attachments, and even packaging them in a nice formatted email message with a fancy background if you like. It then hands off the process of emailing to your email program. Photoshop Elements is programmed to determine how to attach any photo item to an email client; the client then generates an email message with the photos included.

Whether you initiate the process of sending an open image from within the Editor or you select one from the Organizer *catalog*, it is the Organizer that does the work. The Organizer, luckily, is designed specifically to make this process fairly simple, first by keeping your pictures organized in its catalog. (See **24** **About Organizing Items**.) After marking photos with *tags* and *collection* markers, you can quickly display related photos in the catalog and initiate the email process. If you initiated the email process from within the Editor, or if you simply forgot to select all the photos you wanted to send, you can also select images from within the **Attach Selected Items to Email** dialog box, again using the tag and collection markers with which you organized them, to help you locate them for emailing.

You also use this dialog box to select who you want to send images to, and how compressed you want the photos to be. If you increase the quality, you lower the compression, making the files larger and a bit more difficult to send and receive. It's best to choose a happy median— slightly smaller files with acceptable quality. The Organizer can help you keep track of recipient's email addresses using its contact book, or you can skip the process of selecting recipients in the dialog box and use your email client's address book after the email message is packaged by the Organizer. See **157** **Manage Contacts**. Your final decision in this dialog box has to do with format—you can embed photos in a designer message, attach them to a plain-vanilla message, or convert them to a *PDF* slideshow for viewing on a computer.

You can send more than just photos from the Organizer. You can also send a creation, but just one at a time, please. Note that you cannot send photos at the same time you're sending a creation. You can, however, send photos, video files, and audio files in one message if you like. The **Attach Selected Items to E-mail** dialog box looks a bit different depending on the items you're sending, but the process is remarkably similar. It's described in **158** **Share Images Using Email**.

TIP

If, for some reason, you find that your email program doesn't work well with Photoshop Elements, you can still attach your pictures manually to the email message, using the instructions provided for your program.

NOTE

Some email programs transmit only text. If so, Photoshop Elements might not be able to embed pictures in email messages using its fancy collection of layouts and formats. It will, however, create email attachments and prompt you to attach the files manually to a text message.

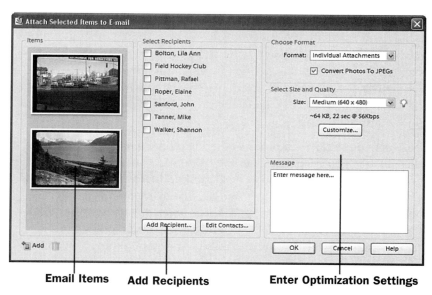

Email Items   **Add Recipients**   **Enter Optimization Settings**

Use this dialog box to prepare the items you want to send using your email client.

156 Set Up Photoshop Elements for Emailing

Before You Begin

✔ **155** About Emailing

See Also

→ **69** Print an Image Using an Online Service

→ **157** Manage Contacts

→ **158** Share Images Using Email

→ **160** Share Images Using an Online Service

Whether you initiate emailing from within the *Editor* or the *Organizer*, it's the Organizer that actually packages your items in an email message and passes that off to your email client. Before the Organizer can send photos or other items as email, however, it must be able to identify your *email client*. Accordingly, the first step in emailing photos is to set up the Organizer so that it makes the right connection with the right email program.

At the same time you tell the Organizer which email client to use, you can set your default email preferences, such as the amount of file compression. File compression is a method that mathematically makes a file smaller. Because data is often removed during file compression, the setting you choose directly affects the quality of the photos you send. Any selection you make during this setup process, however, can be overridden during the sending process if you decide you don't mind sending a larger image to make sure that it arrives looking good.

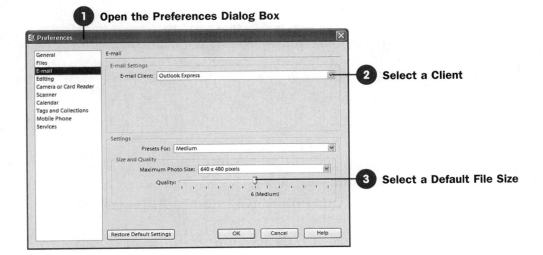

Open the Preferences Dialog Box

2 Select a Client

3 Select a Default File Size

① Open the Preferences Dialog Box

From the Organizer main menu, select **Edit**, **Preferences**, **E-mail**. The **Preferences** dialog box opens with the **E-mail** page selected.

You also can open this dialog box from the Editor by selecting **Edit**, **Preferences**, **Organize & Share**. When the dialog box opens, select **E-mail** from the list in the left pane.

② Select a Client

Open the **E-mail Client** drop-down list. It displays the email clients currently available on your system. Select the client you want to use.

If you choose **Adobe E-mail Service**, in the **Your Name** text box, enter your name as you want it to appear in your email messages. Enter your **E-mail Address** as well.

✎ NOTE

The amount of compression you set here, or later on during the email process, is used to make your images smaller so that they can be sent faster. The actual image files on your hard disk are not affected in any way, so you're in no danger of losing the quality of your saved images no matter which setting you chose. The only factor here is the quality at the receiving end, balanced against how long it might take for your intended recipient to download the image file.

TIPS

The **Setting** you choose for email preferences defines the maximum file size the Organizer will prepare uncompressed for email transmission. If your item is larger than the maximum, the Organizer prepares a copy and compresses it enough so that it doesn't go over the maximum file size. Your original remains intact, of course.

When resaving your edited PSD image files in a sharable format, try to select a low-enough compression that your picture files are as small as you can make them without losing quality. When you try to send a large file, the best-case scenario is that it takes a long time, perhaps longer than the recipient is willing to tolerate. The worst-case scenario is that any of the multiple links in the email system could reject the file as too large to handle. This is particularly likely with the high levels of Internet security now in effect.

If your email client is not listed here, it is not compatible with Photoshop Elements. In that case, select the **Save to Hard Disk and Attach Files Yourself** option. As the label suggests, when you send items in an email, they are actually compressed and saved in the folder you choose by clicking the **Browse** button. You can then use your email program to originate a message manually and attach the saved files.

3 Select a Default File Size

In the **Settings** pane, open the **Presets For** list and select a compression size preset, such as **Medium**. You can also leave this option set at **Leave as Is**, which means that your items are never compressed before sending.

After choosing a compression size, you can adjust its associated **Maximum Photo Size** and **Quality**. These default settings will be used next time you send items using email, unless you change them for an individual transmission.

You can also change the settings for the other options in the **Presets For** drop-down list by choosing them one at a time and making adjustments. Just be sure to go back and choose the preset you want to use most often so that it will be the default the next time you send items. Make your selections and click **OK**. You're now ready to send some email. See **158** Share Images Using Email.

At 72 pixels per inch (a standard setting for computer screen viewing), the **Small** size produces a picture about 4" × 3". That is often large enough for ordinary snapshots. A **Medium** picture is twice the size, and a **Big** setting is twice that size again, more than 14 inches in its longer dimension. A useful approach for many family photographers is to choose the **Small** setting as a default. If you expect the recipients to print the pictures, you might want greater size or quality. If so, you can manually increase the setting for that particular email message. See **158** Share Images Using Email.

157 Manage Contacts

If you regularly send photos to certain individuals or groups, you can keep track of their email addresses in the *Organizer* **Contact Book**. The **Contact Book** is an address book similar to those you might have in your email client or in other applications that use name and address information, such as Microsoft Word. When sending items using email, sharing them through an online service, uploading items for printing (and later sharing), or sending photos to a cell phone or other device, you can use the addresses already entered in your **Contact Book** to designate who should receive the photos or be notified that you want to share them online. Although you can always enter addresses through your email client after the associated email notifications have been created, it's a lot easier to set up at least the few people you regularly send items to in the **Contact Book**.

1 Open the Contact Book

From the Organizer menu, select **Edit**, **Contact Book**. The **Contact Book** dialog box opens. If you have already added contacts to the book, the names and email addresses of those people are listed in the dialog box in alphabetical order. The icons in the **Type** column tell you whether the contact is an individual or a group.

2 Click New Contact

To add a new individual to your **Contact Book**, click the **New Contact** button. The **New Contact** dialog box opens.

3 Enter Contact Information

On the **Name** page of the dialog box, type the contact's name, email address, and other contact information. Note that the dialog box asks you to enter the person's name on three separate lines: **First Name**, **Middle Name**, and **Last Name**. The **Contact Book** sorts your contacts alphabetically based on last name; if you want to sort your list by first name, enter the person's *entire* name in the **First Name** text box.

If you want, you also can click the **Address** tab and enter a street address. Click **OK**. You're returned to the **Contact Book** dialog box.

Before You Begin

✔ **155** About Emailing

See Also

→ **69** Print an Image Using an Online Service

→ **158** Share Images Using Email

→ **160** Share Images Using an Online Service

→ **161** Send Images to a Mobile Phone

NOTE

You can maintain individual addresses in the **Contact Book**, or you can assemble contacts into groups, each with its own name. When you want to send a message to all members of the group, you can do so by sending it to the group name.

TIP

If the contact has a separate email address for a mobile telephone, you also can enter that information here. You can use that email address to send pictures by email. (See **161** **Send Images to a Mobile Phone**.)

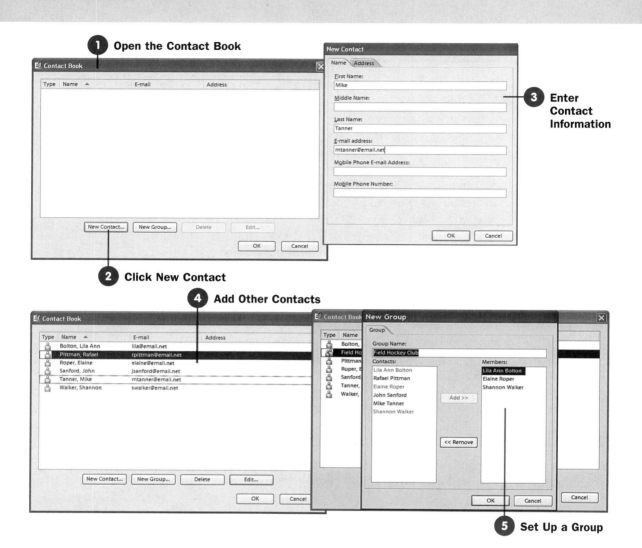

1 Open the Contact Book

2 Click New Contact

3 Enter Contact Information

4 Add Other Contacts

5 Set Up a Group

④ Add Other Contacts

The name and contact information are added to the **Contact Book**. Repeat steps 2 and 3 to add other names to the **Contact Book**.

⑤ Set Up a Group

To create a group of related email addresses, such as the addresses of your parents and siblings, click the **New Group** button at the bottom of the **Contact Book** dialog box. The **New Group** dialog box opens.

In the **Group Name** box, type a name for the group. Typical group names identify the purpose of the group and can be any name that makes sense to you, from **Lottery Investment Trust Team** to **Freeloading Relatives**.

All the names currently in your **Contact Book** appear in the **Contacts** list on the left side of the **New Group** dialog box. Select any or all of these names (press **Ctrl** or **Shift** to make multiple selections). Click the **Add** button. The names are added to the **Members** column on the right side of the dialog box, designating that they are now part of the group you are creating. When you're finished adding contact names to the group, click **OK**.

The group is added to the **Contact Book**. When sending a message, you can select an individual contact name to send the message to a single person or a group name to send the message to every member in that group.

TIPS

To upload images for printing and sharing, you'll have to add yourself to the **Contact Book** so that you can be notified that the images were uploaded successfully and are ready for viewing. If you intend to use Adobe's Ofoto service to print items, you'll have to add your mailing address as well. If you want to send prints to other people, be sure to enter their mailing addresses too.

If you need to change a contact's email address or other information, open the **Contact Book**, select the contact from the list, and click **Edit**. To delete a name from the **Contact Book**, select the name in the list and click **Delete**. To confirm your changes and deletions, click **OK**.

NOTE

Group names are sorted with individual contact names as a single list in the **Contact Book**, sorted alphabetically by last name.

158 Share Images Using Email

Before You Begin

✔ **155** About Emailing

✔ **156** Set Up Photoshop Elements for Emailing

✔ **157** Manage Contacts

See Also

→ **33** About Finding Items in the Catalog

→ **69** Print an Image Using an Online Service

→ **160** Share Images Using an Online Service

→ **161** Send Images to a Mobile Phone

TIPS

You might want to send a group of related images, such as the photos from a recent family outing. Use the **Find** feature to display them in the catalog (see **33** About Finding Items in the Catalog). When only these items are displayed, press **Ctrl+A** to select them all. If the catalog is sorted by batch or folder, click the gray bar above a group to select every item in the group.

You can send an image from within the Editor by saving it first and then choosing **File, Attach to Email**. The **Attach to E-mail** dialog box appears.

If you have an Internet connection and use Microsoft Outlook, Outlook Express, or Adobe E-mail Service, you can send anything you create in Photoshop Elements to anyone who has an email address. Even if you don't use a compatible *email client*, you can still use the *Organizer* to prepare your items for sending using email. After you've shown Photoshop Elements and your email client how to find and recognize each other (see **156** Set Up Photoshop Elements for Emailing), you can select what you want to send from the Organizer *catalog* or open an image in the Editor, decide who to send it to, add a message, and give the order to **Send**. And you can do all this without shutting down or minimizing the Editor or the Organizer window and switching to your email program. You do all the work in Photoshop Elements, and the application then hands off the message to your email client to process and send.

In addition to individual pictures, you can send creations such as slide shows, photo albums, postcards, and calendars. You also can include sound and video files with your photos, but not with creations. In addition, only one creation can be included in an email message, and you can't send it with any other item type.

1 Select Items to Send

In the Organizer catalog, select one or more items to send. To select contiguous items, click the first item, then press and hold the **Shift** key while you click the last item in the group. To select non-contiguous items, click the first item, then hold the **Ctrl** key while you click each additional item. Remember that you can send a mix of images, audio files, and video files, but you can only send an individual creation by itself. Blue borders around the thumbnails indicate the selected items.

2 Click Share

When the items you want to send are selected, click the **Share** button on the **Options** bar. From the menu that opens, select **Email**. The **Attach Selected Items to Email** dialog box opens. The items you selected to send are displayed on the left.

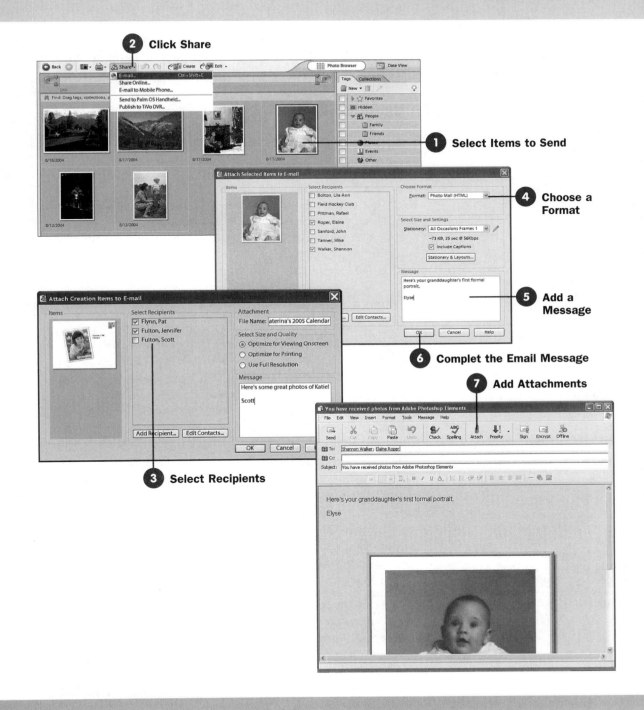

2 Click Share

1 Select Items to Send

4 Choose a Format

5 Add a Message

6 Complet the Email Message

7 Add Attachments

3 Select Recipients

TIPS

To send a creation immediately after making it, click the **Email** button in the last step of the wizard.

You do not have to designate recipients at this stage. If you haven't added people to the **Contact Book** yet, just skip step 3. You'll have a chance later to add them using the address book of your email client in step 6.

If you forgot an item you wanted to send, click the **Add** button at the bottom left. In the dialog box that appears, you can sort through the entire catalog listing, or narrow the display by selecting a *tag* or *collection*. Select the items to add to those already selected for sending and click **OK**.

NOTE

Aware that viruses are often planted in graphic files, some email systems strip the illustrations from HTML mail and send them as attachments instead. This ensures that the graphics are not automatically opened along with the message. Should you receive such a message, make sure that it's from someone you trust before you open the attachments.

Because some e-mail systems place limits on the file sizes they will handle, try to send small files whenever possible so that you do not exceed that limit.

③ Select Recipients

In the **Select Recipients** section of the dialog box, check one or more of the names in your **Contact Book** to identify those you want to receive the message.

If a recipient's name doesn't appear on this list, click the **Add Recipient** button to add the name to your **Contact Book**—and to the list you see in the **Attach Selected Items to Email** dialog box. See **157 Manage Contacts** for details of how to add a contact. If you want to update a recipient's listing, click the **Edit Contacts** button and change that person's name or email address.

④ Choose a Format

If you're sending images, audio files, or video files, open the **Format** list and choose a format for the email message you are going to send. If your recipients all have HTML mail service that allows them to receive photos embedded in their messages, select **Photo Mail (HTML)**. Open the **Stationery** list and select a background for the email message, or click the **Stationery and Layouts** button and select a design you can customize. Choose a stationery on the first page of the wizard that appears, click **Next Step**, and set options to customize the stationary (such as photo size and layout). Click **Enter message here** to type a personal message. Click **Done** to return to the **Attach Selected Items to E-mail** dialog box. If you have previously added *captions* to your selected items through the **Organizer**, you can enable the **Include Caption** check box to include that caption below its item in the message. A typical caption explains or identifies the item, such as **Cousin Mary at Yawning Gap**.

To combine the selected pictures and video items into an automated slide show that can be played on the recipient's computer, select **Simple Slideshow (PDF)**. The pictures and video files are packaged as an Adobe Acrobat *PDF* file; recipients can open the file in Acrobat or the Adobe Reader and scan through them one by one. Type a **File Name** for the file. Adjust the quality of the resulting slide show by selecting a **Size**.

Among the creations you can make through the Organizer is a custom slide show that can include sound and other forms of multimedia. You can create such a slide show separately and attach it to a message, but you cannot do so using the email wizard.

If any recipients have text-only email service, select the **Individual Attachments** option. Enable the **Convert Photos to JPEGs** option to have the Organizer compress the attachments using JPEG compression and the **Size** you choose. If you don't choose this option, the items are attached uncompressed. The items are prepared and attached to the resulting email message, rather than embedded in it. If you're sending video or audio files, they are normally sent as attachments.

If you are sending a creation, it will be converted to PDF format before sending. You will have to enter a **File Name** for the resulting file and set a **Size and Quality** option.

⑤ Add a Message

If you want to include a message to the people who are receiving the selected items, type it in the **Message** text box. This entry will become the text block of the email message.

⑥ Complete the Email Message

Click **OK**. Items are prepared for sending, the message is created, and it opens in your email program. The format of the email message form should be very familiar to you; you are now in your email client's native format.

At this point, you can do anything the email program allows, including adding or subtracting recipients and editing the message text. Because your email client's address book is undoubtedly more complete than your Photoshop Elements **Contact Book**, you can add names from your address book to the **To** or **CC** line in the email message form.

⑦ Add Attachments

If any items you selected were not embedded in the email message or attached for you, you can attach them yourself. Follow the steps for adding attachments using your particular email client. For example, both of the Outlook programs have an **Attach** button. Click it to select the files to attach.

NOTE

Photoshop Elements generates its own subject line. You might want to take this opportunity to replace it with something more personal.

See Also

→ **69** Print an Image Using an Online Service

→ **160** Share Images Using an Online Service

Using Adobe's associations with various providers, Photoshop Elements offers a way to take advantage of online imaging services. For example, you can upload images to a printing service associated with Photoshop Elements. The service prints the images and mails the prints back to you—just as if they'd come from the photo print shop down the street, and you don't have to leave home to take them or pick them up. You could also have your image printed on a t-shirt, cup, magnet, greeting cards, or postcards (see **69** **Print an Image Using an Online Service**). In North America, Adobe has partnered with Kodak Ofoto to provide you with fast, professional Kodak quality prints.

Another option some services offer (including Ofoto) is to post your images on the World Wide Web where your friends and relatives can see them (see **160** **Share Images Using an Online Service**). In North America, your only choice for either of these services is Adobe Ofoto. If you travel abroad, however, update your services list to find a local service that can deliver your prints, for example. In addition, you might want to download the latest creation types and set up the Organizer to notify you of sales and promotions.

NOTE

From time to time, Adobe adds service providers to the list of online service providers associated with Photoshop Elements. To make sure that your provider list is up to date, click the **Refresh** button in the **Preferences** dialog box. To have Adobe automatically check for new services and other updates to the program, enable the **Automatically check for updates** option at the top of the dialog box.

① **Open the Preferences Manager**

Make sure that your Internet connection is active. From the *Organizer*'s main menu, select **Edit**, **Preferences**, **Services**. If you are starting from the *Editor*, select **Edit**, **Preferences**, **Organize & Share**. Then click **Services** from the list on the left. The **Preferences** dialog box opens with the **Services** page selected.

② **Select a Location**

Click the **Choose** button in the **Location** frame. The **Choose Location** dialog box appears. Select your country from the **Country** list and click **OK**. This selection lets Photoshop Elements know where you live so that it can provide a list of service providers best suited to your current printing and sharing needs.

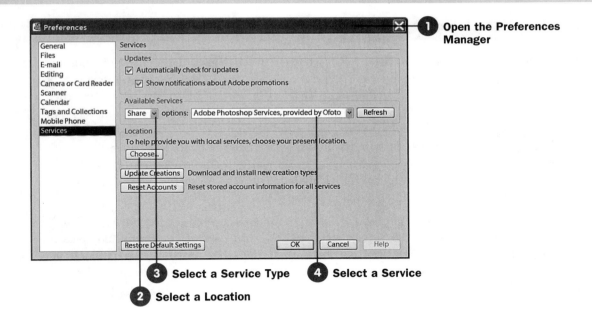

① **Open the Preferences Manager**

③ **Select a Service Type** ④ **Select a Service**

② **Select a Location**

③ Select a Service Type

Based on the location you selected in step 2, the **Available Services** list includes applicable online service options for which you can set up preferences. To locate an online service that can host a display of your images your friends and family can visit, select the **Share** option from the first drop-down list.

④ Select a Service

Open the **options** list (the second drop-down list). A list of available services for the service type you chose in step 3 appears. Select a service from those listed.

Repeat steps 3 and 4 for each online service type you want to use. For example, select **Print** from the **Available Services** list to select an online print service. When you're finished selecting the specific service you want to use for each online service type, click **OK** to close the **Preferences** dialog box and save your selections.

✎ NOTES

If you want to be notified from time to time about promotions related to your online services, enable the **Show notifications about Adobe promotions** option. A **Notification** icon appears on the status bar when there's a promotion; click this icon to view the promotion details.

To update your program with the latest creation types supported by your online service, click **Update Creations**.

160 Share Images Using an Online Service

Before You Begin

✔ **159** Select an Online Service

See Also

→ **69** Print an Image Using an Online Service

→ **161** Send Images to a Mobile Phone

 NOTE

This task also assumes that you have chosen Ofoto as your preferred share service (see **159** Select an Online Service). If you've chosen a different share service, the steps will be similar to those shown, but not exactly the same.

 TIP

If the images are grouped by date or folder, you can click the gray bar above a group to select the entire group.

 WEB RESOURCE

Visit the Ofoto site for special offers, which often include free prints.

You can use email to quickly send messages and photos to friends and family members. But as pointed out in **158** Share Images Using Email, emailed pictures must be small enough to travel through the Internet mail system without being rejected by an email server. Small files, particularly if they're compressed for transmission, often leave much to be desired in terms of quality. An additional problem with email is that not everyone has an email connection at home, and many people rely on the service they have available at work. Receiving your pictures on office email systems does not always go over well with employers.

An alternative is to post your pictures on the World Wide Web by way of an online service such as Adobe Ofoto. There, you can display pictures in larger sizes and higher *resolution*. Your recipients can check out your images at times convenient to them; using a Web browser to view images is much easier for most people than dealing with an email client.

1 Select the Images

In the Organizer, before you choose the images you want to share, review each one and edit it to look its best. You might also want to give each a text caption to help identify and explain it when people visit your online gallery (see **31** Add a Text Caption or Note).

Display your images in the *catalog*. To select a single image, click it. To select multiple images, click the first one, then press and hold the **Ctrl** key as you click each additional thumbnail. To select a range of contiguous images, click the first image, press and hold the **Shift** key, and then click the last image of the group.

http://www.ofoto.com

2 Click Share, Share Online

On the **Shortcuts** bar, click **Share**. From the menu that opens, select **Share Online**. The **Adobe Photoshop Services** dialog box appears.

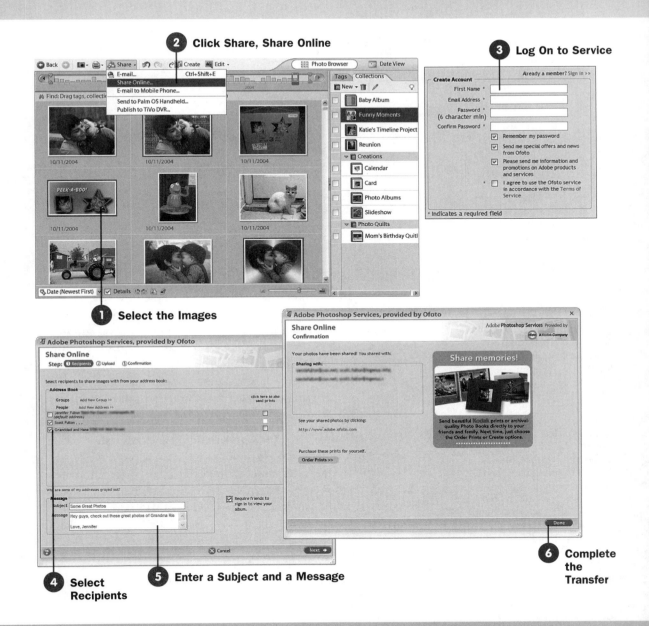

2 Click Share, Share Online

3 Log On to Service

1 Select the Images

4 Select Recipients

5 Enter a Subject and a Message

6 Complete the Transfer

3 Log On to Service

If this is your first time using the service, you'll be asked to set up an account. Enter the required information and select additional options (such as automatic notification of sales and other offers). Read the **Terms of Service** by clicking its link, and enable the check box to indicate that you agree with the terms. Enable the **Remember my password** check box to have the Organizer enter this data for you the next time you use this service.

If you're already an Ofoto member and you asked that your password be remembered, skip to step 4. Otherwise, enter your email address and password now. Click the **Next** button at the bottom of the dialog box.

4 Select Recipients

On the **Step 1 Recipients** screen, a list of people in your **Contact Book** appear on the left. Enable the check boxes in front of the persons with whom you want to share these photos. You can also order prints of the shared photos for each person you selected—just click the **click here to also send prints** check box to the right of their names. If you chose this option, a few extra pages in the wizard appear so that you can select the number of prints and their sizes. See **69 Print Images Using an Online Service**.

To add a new address to the **Contact Book**, click the **Add New Address** link, enter the address data, and click **Next** to return to this screen. If a person's name is grayed out, you must complete their information by clicking **Edit** to the right of their name, entering the rest of the email and address data, and clicking **Next** to return.

5 Enter a Subject and Message

Type a **Subject** and **Message** in the email notification form near the bottom of the dialog box. Click **Next**.

6 Complete the Transfer

To make each invitee join Ofoto and sign in to view the images, enable the **Require friends to sign in to view your album** option. Without this option, anyone who knows the link to your web page can view your photos. Click **Next** to upload the images.

NOTE

Your Ofoto account is accessible using the email address and password you supply—only from the computer where you first registered it.

If you want your password remembered and you forgot to indicate that initially, select the **Remember my password** option when you log in.

TIPS

If you simply have the email notification sent to you, you can use the addresses already in your email client's address book to forward the message onto your friends and relations.

If you want to see your own online photos, add your own email address to the address list and select your name as one of the recipients in step 4.

After the images are uploaded, the **Confirmation** screen appears, displaying the list of names with whom you shared the photos, and a link to the website.

If you ordered prints, the **Confirmation** screen will include an order summary. Click the **Print this Confirmation** button to print a copy of this page.

Click **Done**. The wizard closes, and you return to the catalog. Recipients will receive email invitations to look at your images.

161 Send Images to a Mobile Phone

Not long ago, it would have been hard to envision a telephone as a picture-taking tool. In recent years, though, a mobile phone has catapulted to become a multipurpose communication tool. One such purpose is to transmit and display pictures, and sometimes to take the pictures as well. The Organizer has the means to send a picture or a photographic creation to a mobile phone. It does so in the form of an email message. The mbile phone then can use its own communication capability to forward pictures to another mobile phone user.

Before You Begin

✔ **156** Set Up Photoshop Elements for Emailing

See Also

→ **157** Manage Contacts

→ **158** Share Images Using Email

❶ Select the Images

In the *Organizer*, select one or more pictures from the *catalog*. Click the first image, and then press and hold the **Ctrl** key and click to select multiple pictures; press and hold the **Shift** key and click the last image in a contiguous range of pictures.

❷ Click Share, E-mail to Mobile Phone

In the **Shortcuts** bar, click the **Share** button. From the menu that opens, select **E-mail to Mobile Phone**. The **Send to Mobile Phone** dialog box opens.

❸ Select Recipients

The items you selected in step 1 appear on the left side of the dialog box. The people in your Organizer **Contact Book** appear in the **Select Recipients** list in the center.

NOTE

Email service on a portable phone requires that the phone be equipped to send, receive, and display email. Such a phone has an email address assigned by the email service provider.

2 Click Share, E-mail to Mobile Phone

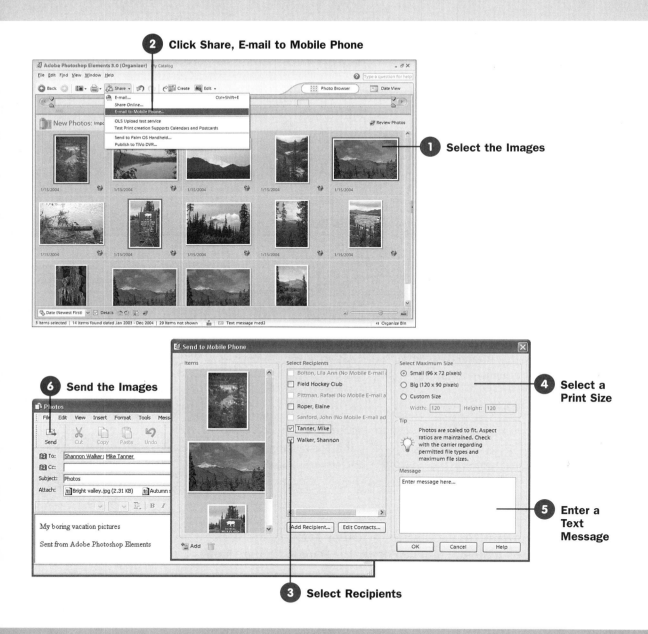

1 Select the Images

6 Send the Images

4 Select a Print Size

5 Enter a Text Message

3 Select Recipients

Those contacts for whom you have not yet entered a mobile phone email address are grayed out. Place check marks next to the names of people and groups to whom you would like to send pictures.

If you want to add a mobile phone email address to a recipient's entry in your **Contact Book**, click **Edit Contacts**. You then can select the contact and enter the new information. To enter a new recipient, click **Add Recipient**.

4 Select a Print Size

In the upper-right corner of the dialog box, you can select a maximum size: **Small**, **Big**, or a **Custom Size** of your own choosing. The size you select here controls the onscreen size and quality of the mobile phone image. It also controls the maximum size an image can be, before the Organizer is forced to compress it before sending.

Image size is relative when talking about viewing the images on a mobile phone. At 72 pixels per inch, a vertical **Big** image is only about an inch tall. A **Small** picture is only 0.8 inches high at 72 pixels per inch.

5 Enter a Text Message

In the lower-right corner of the dialog box, enter any message you want to send along with the picture.

6 Send the Images

Click **OK**. Your *email client* opens and displays the message addressed to the selected recipients. The pictures are added as attachments.

Click the **Send** button. The message is transmitted from your computer to the specified mobile phone's email service.

NOTES

Only the recipients for whom you entered mobile phone email addresses in your **Contact Book** are available in the **Select Recipients** list (see 157 **Manage Contacts** for more information about adding and editing contacts).

If you want, you can skip step 3; after the email message has been created and sent to your email client, you can select email addresses using the email client's address book.

To fit the size you select, pictures might be scaled proportionately, but they won't be stretched out of proportion.

21

Improving a Photograph's Visual Impact

IN THIS CHAPTER:

162 Remove Unwanted Objects from an Image

163 Mask an Image Layer

164 Replace a Background with Something Else

165 Fix a Bland-Looking Sky

166 Frame a Photograph

167 Blend Two Images into One

168 Create a Scrapbook Page

169 Create a Composite Image

170 Create a Panorama

Up until now, you have probably focused most of your attention on improving a photograph's contrast, color balance, and sharpness; repairing damage caused by old age or improper storage; and improving the look of your subject by removing blemishes and minimizing wrinkles. Now that you have improved your images to the point at which they look good, it's time to have some fun. In this chapter, you'll learn how to improve a photograph's visual impact by removing distractions (and fingers) from a photo, placing the subject on a new background, adding drama to a bland all-white sky, adding a picture frame, and combining images to create a blended image, a composite of several images, or a scrapbook page.

162 Remove Unwanted Objects from an Image

Before You Begin

✔ **111** About Tool Options

See Also

→ **125** Repair Minor Tears, Scratches, Spots, and Stains

→ **131** Remove Wrinkles, Freckles, and Minor Blemishes

→ **134** Remove Glare from Eyeglasses

→ **164** Replace a Background with Something Else

Using the **Clone Stamp** tool, you can easily remove unwanted objects from an image—such as telephone poles, wires, trash cans, a thumb that wandered in front of the lens, or a few stray hairs blown in the wind—simply by copying over these distractions with pixels located somewhere else in the image (or in another image). To use the **Clone Stamp**, you first indicate the source area, and then you click or drag to paint with pixels copied from the source. Be sure to "cover your tracks" and avoid creating a noticeable pattern as you copy. The best way to do that is to lower the **Opacity** of the tool or select a *blend mode* so that the pixels you clone blend with existing pixels, paint with single clicks or very short strokes, use a large brush to avoid copying multiple times to the same area (but a small-enough brush that you don't copy things you don't want), and vary the source area from which you're copying by re-establishing a new source point every so often.

The source you select for the **Clone Stamp** can be located within a different image, on a different *layer*, or on the same layer. For example, you might clone some hair from one side of a photo to repair a small rip or a bad hair day. Or, you might clone a squirrel from one photo onto the head of your brother in another photo to create a comic image.

The most important option that affects how the **Clone Stamp** works is its **Aligned** option. With the **Aligned** option enabled, the relationship between the source point and the place where you begin cloning is maintained throughout the entire cloning procedure, regardless of how many times you stop and start. For example, if you establish a source and begin cloning one inch to the right of the source, when you begin another stroke, data is copied from the image *one inch to the right* of where you began that stroke. This enables you to clone data in a manner that maintains the way pixels were originally aligned with each other. If you use the **Aligned** option to clone a squirrel onto your brother's head, the squirrel would be reassembled properly in the new location, no matter how many strokes you took or in which direction you brushed the tool—because the relationship between the source and where you first started cloning would be maintained. With **Aligned** disabled, pixels are always copied beginning at the original source point, and moving in the same direction that you drag. If you begin a new stroke, the pixels are copied beginning at the original source. If you cloned a squirrel with the **Aligned** option off, it might be reassembled with its nose on its belly, unless you place each stroke precisely.

The **Healing Brush** tool can also be used to copy pixels from one area to another, but it works differently than the **Clone Stamp** tool. The **Healing Brush** samples pixels from the source and blends them into the existing pixels (unless you use **Replace** mode, which copies the sampled pixels instead of blending them). You can only control this blending a little, by choosing a different blend **Mode** and reducing the **Hardness** of your brush. Use the **Healing Brush** when your main purpose is to blend data into existing image data (rather than covering it up) to remove some distraction or small imperfection, for example. The **Healing Brush** is especially useful if the image data you want to blend into is irregularly patterned, such as a street, sky, carpet, or grass. Use the **Clone Stamp** tool as described here when your main goal is to copy over image data (rather than blend it with other data) and to control the amount of coverage with each stroke through the **Opacity** setting. See **122** About **Removing Scratches, Specks, and Holes** for help with the **Healing Brush**.

TIPS

You might also be able to remove objects from an image in the same way you repair tears and holes. See **126** **Repair Large Holes, Tears, and Missing Portions of a Photo.**

You can remove small objects with the **Spot Healing Brush** by covering them up with pixels copied from the surrounding area. See **122** About Removing Scratches, Specks, and Holes.

1 **Select Clone Stamp Tool**

Open an image in the *Editor* in **Standard Edit** mode, and save it in Photoshop (***.psd**) format. Click the **Clone Stamp** tool on the **Toolbox.**

1 Select Clone Stamp Tool

2 Set Options

4 Paint with Brush **3** Establish a Source

Before

After **5** View the Result

② Set Options

On the **Options** bar, select a brush tip and enable the **Aligned** check box. Set other options as desired. For example, to copy visible pixels from a multilayered image, enable the **Use All Layers** check box; to enable more subtle and less obvious corrections, such as borrowing the general skin tone from one swatch to hide a blemish in another, lower the **Opacity** value. You can also blend the cloned pixels with the existing pixels you brush over by selecting a blend mode from the **Mode** list. See **111** **About Tool Options**.

③ Establish a Source

If you're cloning a region from another image, open that image in the Editor.

On the **Layers** palette, choose the layer containing the data you want to copy. If the image has multiple layers, enable the **Use All Layers** option to make sure it's set the way you want (see step 2).

Finally, press **Alt** and click on the image layer to establish the source point.

④ Paint with Brush

If needed, change to the image to which you want to copy. On the **Layers** palette, change to the layer on which you want to copy the data.

To begin copying pixels, click on the layer or drag with short strokes to sample pixels from the source and paint them under the brush tip. Note that a crosshatch pointer shows you the location of the source point, and that it moves as your painting point moves. Don't confuse one point with the other. Repeat until the repair has been made or until the undesirable object has been painted over.

⑤ View the Result

After you're satisfied with the result, make any other changes you want and save the PSD file. Then resave the file in JPEG or TIFF format, leaving your PSD image with its *layers* (if any) intact so that you can return at a later time and make different adjustments if you want.

TIPS

If you're cloning data from one image into another, it might be easier if you tile the images so that you can see them both at the same time, but you don't have to. The source point is maintained as you clone, even if you can't see the source image. To tile all the open images, choose **Window**, **Images**, **Tile** from the menu.

To hide your clone tracks, change the source often by pressing **Alt** and clicking a different source point (if you're cloning a texture such as skin rather than a specific object such as a nose).

When establishing your source point, be careful that you don't place it too close to objects you don't want to copy to the new area.

I liked this photo of my daughter's seventh birthday, but the more I looked at it, the more distracting the large white napkin in the foreground became. And no matter how I cropped the photo, that napkin still seemed to draw attention to itself. So, I cloned a bit of the same table from another photo taken at that same time and with the same lighting conditions, over top of the napkin, essentially removing the napkin from the photo. I didn't use the **Healing Brush**, even though it does a very nice job of cloning, because it also blends the cloned pixels with the existing pixels. If I had used the **Healing Brush**, it would have blended the table pixels with the white napkin pixels, creating a "ghostly napkin" effect.

163 Mask an Image Layer

Before You Begin

✔ **91** About Layers and the Layers Palette

See Also

→ **100** Make an Adjustment or Fill Layer

→ **164** Replace a Background with Something Else

→ **166** Frame a Photograph

→ **169** Create a Composite Image

KEY TERM

Clipping mask—Controls what portions of any upper layers grouped with the mask appear in the final image.

As you learned in **91** About Layers and the Layers Palette, a *mask* blocks data on a *layer* from covering up data on the layers below it. Masks are automatically created when you insert an adjustment or fill layer. For an *adjustment layer*, the mask blocks the adjustment from affecting certain areas of the layers below. For a fill layer, the mask simply blocks the fill from appearing in particular areas of the layers below.

But what do you do if you want to mask an image layer rather than an adjustment or fill layer? For example, suppose you want a flag to appear within the contours of an American eagle? You could use the **Cookie Cutter** tool to cut the flag into an eagle shape (if it had an eagle shape to use, which it doesn't). But even if the **Cookie Cutter** tool had the shape you wanted, you couldn't reposition the flag image within the eagle shape after committing the change. The simplest way to create what you want is to use a *clipping mask* in the shape of an eagle to control what portions of the flag appear in the final image. Unlike an adjustment or fill mask, in which black is used to block data and white is used to allow data on upper layers to show through, in a clipping mask, opaque pixels (regardless of their color) allow data to show through, and transparent or partially transparent pixels block data fully or partially.

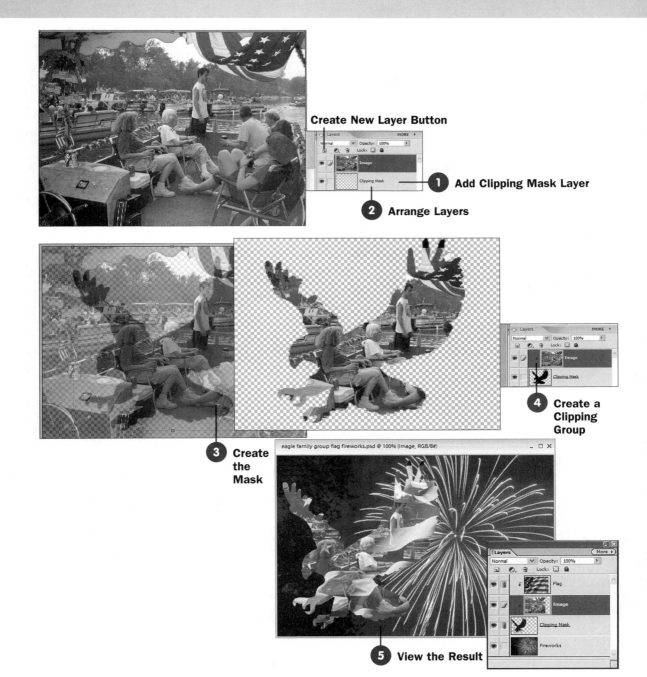

Create New Layer Button

1 Add Clipping Mask Layer

2 Arrange Layers

3 Create the Mask

4 Create a Clipping Group

5 View the Result

1 Add Clipping Mask Layer

Open the image you want to mask in the *Editor* in **Standard Edit** mode and save it in Photoshop (***.psd**) format. Insert a new layer for the mask by clicking the **Create new layer** button on the **Layers** palette, or choosing **Layer**, **New**, **Layer** from the menu bar. Name this new layer **Clipping Mask**.

2 Arrange Layers

The **Clipping Mask** layer must go beneath the layer(s) you want to mask. So, if necessary, in the **Layers** palette, drag the **Clipping Mask** layer into position under the layer you want to mask.

3 Create the Mask

On the **Layers** palette, select the **Clipping Mask** layer. To create a mask on this layer in the shape you want, you have the following choice of methods:

- Paint on the **Clipping Mask** layer with any color using the **Brush** tool, or draw with the **Pencil**. To create a feathered effect, select a soft brush to apply semi-transparent pixels to allow the upper layers to show partially through. Remember: Where you paint or draw, that portion of the image layer will show through in the final image. See **115** **Draw on a Photo with a Pencil** and **117** **Paint an Area of a Photo with a Brush**.

- Draw any shape you want onto the **Clipping Mask** layer, using any of the shape tools, such as the **Rectangle** tool or the **Custom Shape** tool. If you want more than one shape on the **Clipping Mask** layer, or if you want to create an object with a complex shape made up of several different shapes (such as a rectangle and two circles), draw your shapes with the **Add to shape area** button enabled on the **Options** bar. Again, the portion of the image layer that appears in the final image will be in the shape you draw. See **120** **About Drawing Shapes**.

- Fill the layer with a *gradient*, using the **Gradient** tool. The upper layers will be blocked only where the gradient is fully transparent, will show through partially where the gradient is partially opaque, and will show through fully where the gradient uses fully opaque pixels, so keep that in mind when selecting a gradient preset. See **119** **Fill an Area with a Gradient**. In a similar manner, you can fill

➤ NOTE

If you need to position the **Clipping Mask** layer below the *Background layer*, you must first convert the **Background** layer to a regular layer. In the **Layers** palette, click the **Background** layer and choose **Layer**, **New**, **Layer from Background**. In the **New Layer** dialog box that appears, you can name the converted layer **Image** if you like, so you'll remember what it contains.

💡 TIP

To help you position and size the clipping mask, lower the **Opacity** of the **Image** layer. After creating the clipping mask, move and resize it using the **Move** tool. See **99** **Move, Resize, Skew, or Distort a Layer**.

the **Clipping Mask** layer with a *pattern*. See **118** **Fill an Area with a Pattern**.

- Use the **Selection Brush** to create a selection in the shape you need; fill the selection with any color using the **Paint Bucket** tool. The image layer will show through only in the area you fill. If you feather the edges of the selection, the upper layers will show through at the edges, but only partially. This might enable you to blend the masked area more smoothly into the layers below. See **77** **Paint a Selection**.

- Type text, and then merge the text layer into the **Clipping Mask** layer by selecting the text layer in the **Layers** palette and choosing **Layer, Merge Down**. The upper masked layer(s) will then appear only within the outline of the text. See **183** **Add a Text Caption or Label**.

4 Create a Clipping Group

In the **Layers** palette, choose the **Image** layer and, if needed, return it to full opacity. Group this layer with the **Clipping Mask** layer by choosing **Layer, Group with Previous**. On the **Layers** palette, the **Image** layer is indented, indicating that the upper layer is being clipped (masked) by the layer below. Data on the **Image** layer is now masked by the **Clipping Mask** layer and shows through only where the **Clipping Mask** layer is partially or entirely opaque.

You've just created a clipping group. Now, if you'd like to clip other layers as well, you can add the layer just above the **Image** layer to the clipping group—there cannot be any other layers in between. In the **Layers** palette, select the layer above the **Image** layer and choose **Layers, Group with Previous** to group the layer with the clipping group. In this same manner, add as many other layers as you like to the clipping group.

5 View the Result

After you're satisfied with the result, make any other changes you want and then save the PSD file. Resave the result in JPEG or TIFF format, leaving your PSD image with its layers intact so that you can return at a later time and make different adjustments if you like.

To create this image, I used the shape of an eagle to mask two layers—one of my sister's family enjoying the Fourth of July on

TIP

You can create a **Clipping Mask** layer using any of the selection tools to select an object in another image that's in the shape you want to use and copying that object into your image, to a new layer below the image layer you want to clip. This process saves you from having to create a **Clipping Mask** layer manually because pasting data from a different image always results in a new layer. Skip the step here that creates a **Clipping Mask** layer, remove the **Clipping Mask** layer if you've already created one, or merge the layer you pasted into the image with the **Clipping Mask** layer so that there's just one layer. See **70** **About Making Selections**.

their pontoon boat, and another layer of an American flag. I blended these two layers together so that you can just see the ripple of the flag across the family photo, and the result was clipped by the eagle mask. On the bottom layer, I placed an image of the fireworks we enjoyed later that evening. By placing the fireworks layer on the bottom, its contents are obstructed by only the portion of the image layer that's clipped by the mask. Look for this image in the Color Gallery.

164 Replace a Background with Something Else

Before You Begin

✔ **111** Select Tool Options

See Also

→ **97** Erase Part of a Layer

→ **162** Remove Unwanted Objects from an Image

→ **165** Fix a Bland-Looking Sky

One of the simplest special-effects tricks you can pull off is to remove the background from around a subject and replace it with something else. For example, are you the only one who didn't make it to a recent family reunion? There's no reason you have to remember that fact forever—just use the **Background Eraser** to remove the background from a recent photo of yourself, and then replace the background with the reunion photo. After a few minutes' work, you'll be partying with your cousins. Of course, there are legitimate reasons for needing to replace an image background as well—for example, if you have a photo of someone in a black suit on a dark background, you won't be able to do much using the *Editor*'s contrast controls to separate them visually. Better to select the man and place him on a lighter background that provides more contrast.

The secret to using the **Background Eraser** tool is to *slow down* and watch where you're going. Its job is to erase colors that are similar to those at the center of the pointer. What gets erased are pixels with similar colors within the circular area of the brush tip. To control which pixels are similar enough to warrant erasure, adjust the tool's **Tolerance** and **Limits** options. When you set **Limits** to **Contiguous**, the **Background Eraser** tool samples the pixel under the *hotspot*, located at the center of the brush tip, and erases only those similarly colored pixels under the brush that touch the hotspot, or some other similarly colored pixel. **Contiguous** is typically your best bet, although **Discontiguous** erases any and all similarly colored pixels under the brush tip, regardless of their position. By default, the **Limits** value is set to **Contiguous**, but this setting might make it difficult to erase the background if it peeks through your subject (as the sky does through tree branches). Use **Discontiguous** in such a case.

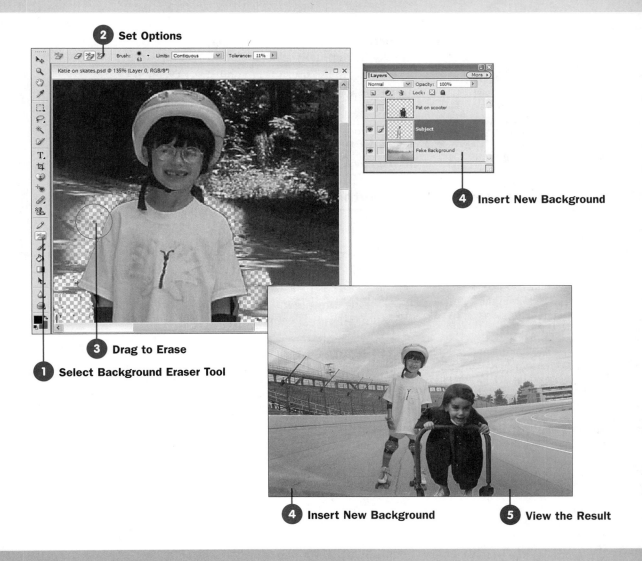

② Set Options

Katie on skates.psd @ 135% (Layer 0, RGB/8*)

Brush: 63 Limits: Contiguous Tolerance: 11%

Layers More ▶
Normal Opacity: 100%
Lock:
Pat on scooter
Subject
Fake Background

④ Insert New Background

③ Drag to Erase

① Select Background Eraser Tool

④ Insert New Background

⑤ View the Result

① Select Background Eraser Tool

Open an image in the Editor in **Standard Edit** mode and save it in Photoshop (***.psd**) format. On the **Toolbox**, click the **Background Eraser** tool.

TIPS

If you want to erase from this layer by sampling visible pixels from all layers, use the **Magic Eraser** tool and enable its **Use All Layers** option. You can also partially erase pixels with the **Magic Eraser** tool (by adjusting the **Opacity** setting). See **97** **Erase Part of a Layer**.

To prevent yourself from accidentally erasing something you don't want to, make a selection first—the **Background Eraser** erases only the pixels within the selection. For example, to erase the sky around a girl's face who also happens to be wearing a blue hat, draw the selection boundary omitting the hat so that it isn't mistaken for the background and isn't erased as you work at removing the background from around her face.

NOTE

If you want to place the original image on a Web page background or your Windows desktop, just skip step 4 and leave the background around the subject transparent. To retain the transparent pixels when you resave the completed PSD file, use **GIF**, **PNG**, or **JPEG 2000** format.

2 Set Options

On the **Options** bar, select the brush tip you want to use. Click the arrow next to the brush tip to adjust the **Diameter** (size), **Hardness**, and other options you want. See **111** **About Tool Options** for descriptions of these options.

3 Drag to Erase

In the **Layers** palette, change to the *layer* you want to erase—if you erase pixels from the *Background layer*, the Editor will automatically convert that layer to a regular layer after the end of your first stroke because the **Background** layer can't contain transparent pixels (which the **Background Eraser** creates).

Click and drag with the **Background Eraser** tool. Pixels that are a relative match for the pixel under the center of the brush tip (the hotspot, which is marked by the crosshair) are erased from the layer (made transparent). To keep things straight, you might want to rename this layer **Subject**.

4 Insert New Background

After erasing the background from around a subject, replace the background with something else. Open the image you want to use as the background, and if necessary, select the layer you want to use from the **Layers** palette. Choose **Select**, **All** to select all the pixels in your background image that reside on that particular layer, and choose **Edit**, **Copy** to copy them to the Clipboard.

Paste the new background into the image you're editing by activating its window again, and then choosing **Edit**, **Paste**. This action creates a new layer with the contents from the Clipboard (the new background you want to use). Rename the layer **Fake Background**.

In the **Layers** palette, drag the **Fake Background** layer below the **Subject** layer so that the new background appears in the holes the **Background Eraser** tool created. Resize and reposition the **Fake Background** layer if needed. See **99** **Move, Resize, Skew, or Distort a Layer**.

⑤ View the Result

After you're satisfied with the result, make any other changes you want, then save the PSD file. Resave the result in JPEG or TIFF format, leaving your **PSD** image with its layers intact so that you can return at a later time and make different adjustments if you want. For example, you might want to try out some different backgrounds and have some fun!

Last year, my sister Pat let me borrow an old picture of her pushing a walker around our driveway; when I looked at it, I couldn't help but imagine her racing someplace sportier. I just happened to have a photograph of the Indianapolis 500 track (taken while my husband was driving around on it in his sports car), so I merged the two to create a cute photo. This year, I did it one better by adding my daughter on roller skates. Now they can race each other to the checkered flag.

Because the walker image was in grayscale, I changed the image mode in my daughter's photograph to grayscale before copying the image of my daughters into the master PSD file. I then resized and positioned my daughter just behind my sister on her walker.

 TIP

To quickly copy a layer from one image to another, select that layer in the **Layers** palette and drag and drop it into the other image window. If the **Layers** palette isn't visible, you can drag and drop using the **Move** tool.

165 Fix a Bland-Looking Sky

Nothing can spoil an outdoor photo more than a boring, lifeless sky—overbright, cloudless, and lacking detail or interest. Not that the sky is the most important part of most outdoor photographs; frankly, in most cases, it *should* be a bit bland looking so that it doesn't steal attention away from your subject. The trouble is that our eyes are naturally drawn to light, so we seek out the lightest areas of a photograph first. So, if you have an outdoor photograph in which the sky is extremely light and lifeless, you might find that the sky steals the "thunder" from your subject, in some cases dominating a photograph. In this task, you'll learn how to quiet that light sky by cloning over it with a better-looking sky taken from another image.

① Select Clone Stamp Tool

Open the image with the bland sky you want to change in the *Editor* in **Standard Edit** mode and save it in Photoshop (*.psd) format. Click the **Clone Stamp** tool on the **Toolbox**.

Before You Begin

✔ **60** Change Image Size or Resolution

✔ **125** Repair Minor Tears, Scratches, Spots, and Stains

See Also

→ **164** Replace a Background with Something Else

 TIP

Another way to tame a light, attention-grabbing sky is to darken it a bit using the **Burn** tool. See **140** Lighten or Darken Part of an Image.

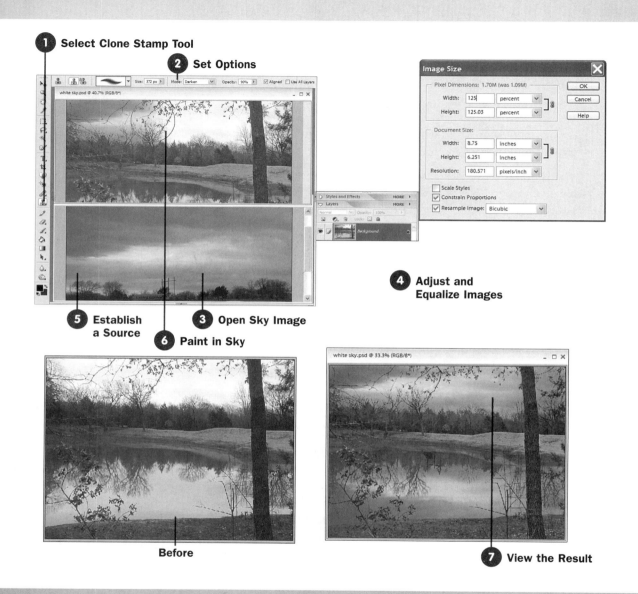

① Select Clone Stamp Tool

② Set Options

③ Open Sky Image

④ Adjust and Equalize Images

⑤ Establish a Source

⑥ Paint in Sky

⑦ View the Result

Before

② Set Options

On the **Options** bar, select a brush tip for the tool, and then enable the **Aligned** check box. Set other options as desired. For example, you might want to reduce the **Opacity** if you want to

blend the new sky with the old, and not change it that much. See
111 **About Tool Options**.

To make the cloning process easier, select the **Darken** blend mode
from the **Mode** list. This blend mode limits the cloning to pixels
from the source image (the "good sky") that are darker than corresponding pixels in the target image (the "bad sky"). Because tree
pixels are dark anyway, a lighter "good sky" color can't overwrite
them, so the trees in your "bad sky" image remain safe and
untouched.

3 Open Sky Image

Open the image that contains the sky you want to clone. If necessary, click the **Automatically Tile Windows** button at the right
end of the menu bar or choose **Window, Images, Tile** to tile the
two images so that you can see them both. Scroll both windows so
that you can see both skies.

4 Adjust and Equalize Images

Objects in a sky, such as clouds, help your mind establish perspective. If the clouds in your "good sky" image are too big or too
small to seem real within the framework of the "bad sky" image,
this whole illusion gets shot out of the, *um*, sky. This perspective
problem might be caused by one of three things: different zoom
factors for the lenses of the cameras that shot the two photos, different resolutions for the two images, and different photo sizes.

If necessary, change to the "good sky" image and match the resolution and/or size of the "bad sky" image you're editing with the
Image, Resize, Image Size command. See **60** **Change Image Size
or Resolution**. After resizing, you might have to scroll the "good
sky" image window again.

5 Establish a Source

Change to the "good sky" image if needed. Press **Alt** and click on a
reference point in the "good sky" image to establish a source. I typically click in a clear area on the left side of the "good sky" image
so that I can brush from far left to far right in the "bad sky" image
to paint in the new sky.

> **NOTE**
>
> With the **Aligned** option
> enabled, the source point
> follows the mouse pointer,
> even between strokes. This
> helps you copy the sky
> exactly, no matter how
> many strokes you take or
> in which direction. If the
> option is turned off, the
> source point follows the
> mouse pointer until you
> release the button, at
> which point the source
> snaps back to its original
> location.

TIP

You can create your own sky if you like. Just erase the bad sky using the **Background Eraser**, insert a new *layer* below the image layer, set the fore-ground color to the sky color you want, and the *background color* to the cloud color, and apply the **Render**, **Clouds** filter to the new layer.

6 Paint in Sky

Activate the "bad sky" image. Brush across the bad sky to clone in the new sky. Repeat until the sky has been replaced.

7 View the Result

After you're satisfied with the result, make any other changes and save the PSD image. Resave the result in JPEG or TIFF format, leaving your **PSD** image with its *layers* (if any) intact so that you can return at a later time and make different adjustments if you want. Close the "good sky" image without saving changes.

This photo, taken at "Granddad's Pond," was pretty good, but the sky seemed very white and less than fitting for this dramatic setting. So, I simply cloned in a sky taken later that same day (if you don't like the weather, just wait a minute…). Before I cloned the sky onto the water, I flipped the source image vertically so that it would look like a reflection of the sky I'd cloned above. Look for this image in the Color Gallery.

166 Frame a Photograph

Before You Begin

✔ 60 Change Image Size or Resolution

✔ 93 Create a Layer Filled with a Color, Gradient, or Pattern

✔ 163 Mask an Image Layer

After spending lots of time creating the perfect image, why not frame it? With the *Editor*, it's easy to add a frame—from brushed aluminum to rough wood—simply by applying a frame *effect*. Some frame effects require you to make a selection first, and then the frame is placed around this selection. One frame effect creates a simple frame using the current *foreground color*. Although applying a frame effect is quick and easy, it allows you no artistic freedom whatsoever. In this task, I'll show you how to create your own frame and mat.

1 Add an Inner Bevel

Open an image in the Editor in **Standard Edit** mode and save it in Photoshop (*.**psd**) format. If your image contains more than one *layer*, flatten the image so that it will be easier to add a frame and a mat by selecting **Layer**, **Flatten Image** from the menu bar.

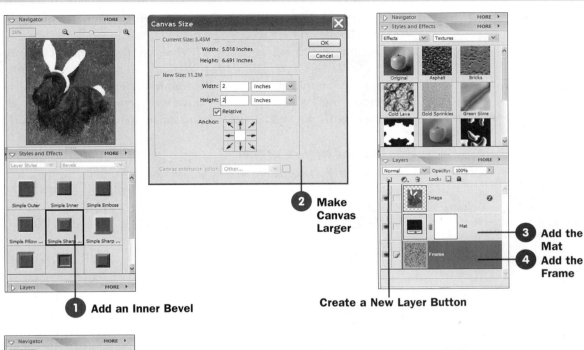

2 Make
Canvas
Larger

3 Add the
Mat

4 Add the
Frame

1 Add an Inner Bevel

Create a New Layer Button

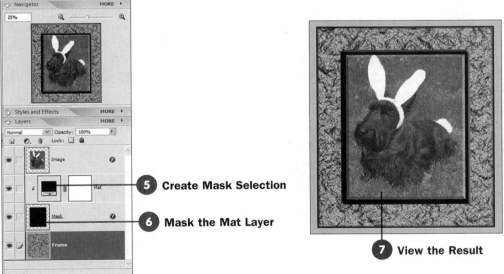

5 Create Mask Selection

6 Mask the Mat Layer

7 View the Result

 **NOTES**

Obviously, you won't take the trouble to add a graphic "frame" around an image that you intend to print and frame yourself, but you might add a digital frame to an image destined for a card, scrapbook, or Web page.

To apply a frame effect, select **Effects** from the first drop-down list on the **Styles and Effects** palette, and select **Frames** from the second list. Then, double-click any effect thumbnail to apply it to your image. You might be asked to flatten the image first; click **OK** to continue. If an effect's name contains the **{selection}** notation, you must make a selection first before applying that effect to the image.

 TIPS

If you change the **Foreground Color** swatch on the **Toolbox** to the color you want to use for your mat *before you begin step 3*, that color will be automatically chosen for you when the **Color Picker** appears, and it will be used to fill the new layer.

Add a texture to your mat by applying a texture filter or effect using the **Styles and Effects** palette.

Add an inner bevel to the image to simulate the bevel normally found along the inner edge of a photographic mat. On the **Styles and Effects** palette, select **Layer Styles** from the first drop-down list, and select **Bevels** from the second list. Double-click the **Simple Inner** or **Simple Sharp Inner** *thumbnail* to apply that style to the image. You might be asked if you want to convert the *Background layer* into a full layer. Click **OK** and name the new layer **Image**.

2 Make Canvas Larger

Increase the *canvas* to make room for the mat and the frame. Choose **Image, Resize, Canvas Size** from the menu. Enable the **Relative** option and click the center box in the **Anchor** pane. Type the same amount in the **Width** and **Height** boxes, and click **OK**. I usually add an amount that's slightly greater than 1/4 the largest dimension of the original image. For example, if your image is roughly 5" × 7" like mine, add 2 inches to the width and height.

3 Add the Mat

To add the mat, insert a fill layer below the **Image** layer. To create this new layer, choose **Layer, New Fill Layer, Solid Color** from the menu bar. Name the new layer **Mat**. *Do not enable the **Group With Previous Layer** option*. Choose the color you want for the mat from the **Color Picker**. Ideally, you can use the **Eyedropper** tool to choose a color already in your image (see **114 Select a Color Already in Your Image** for details). On the **Layers** palette, drag the **Mat** layer below the **Image** layer.

4 Add the Frame

To create the frame, do any of the following:

- Add a new fill layer and fill it with any color you want. (You're not going to actually see this color when you're finished; you're using the color only to make the layer opaque.) Name this new layer **Frame**. On the **Layers** palette, drag the **Frame** layer to the bottom of the layer stack. Then, apply a *layer style* that compliments your photo; the layer style replaces the color you chose earlier. On the **Styles and Effects** palette, with **Layer Styles** still selected in the first drop-down list, select **Patterns** from the second list. Then, double-click the thumbnail of the *pattern* you want to use for your frame. For example, you might choose **Batik**, **Manhole**, **Oak**, or **Dry Mud**. There are some options on the **Complex** list you might like, such as **Diamond Plate**, **Molten Gold**, **White Grid on Orange**, or **Red, White, and Blue Contrast**. Experiment until you find the perfect compliment to your photograph.

- Insert a new layer by clicking the **Create a new layer** button on the **Layers** palette or choosing **Layer**, **New**, **Layer**. Name this new layer **Frame**. On the **Layers** palette, drag the new layer to the bottom of the layer stack. Then, fill the new layer with a color or *gradient*, or simply paint or stamp a pattern on it with various colors taken from the photograph. You also could draw shapes using the **Custom Shape** tool, such as a paw print or a butterfly. If you like, add a *filter* to mix the colors to create a pattern or texture, or to achieve an artsy look.

- Choose an effect to create your frame. Because effects automatically add a layer to your image, you don't have to create the frame layer first. On the **Styles and Effects** palette, select **Effects** from the first drop-down list. Select **Texture** from the second list, and then double-click the thumbnail of a texture that complements your image. Drag the new layer to the bottom of the layer stack of the **Layers** palette. From there, you can rename this new layer **Frame**.

5 **Create Mask Selection**

Right now, with the **Frame** layer at the bottom of the layer stack, you can't see the frame at all because the **Mat** layer is covering it up. So, you need to mask the **Mat** layer using a *clipping mask* so that only part of it shows through. Press **Ctrl** and click the thumbnail for the **Image** layer on the **Layers** palette. This selects the image. Choose **Select**, **Modify**, **Expand** to increase the selection around the image by the amount you want the mat to show, roughly 1/4 the size of the frame.

You can repeat the **Expand** command if necessary to add more space for your mat. If you accidentally expand the selection by more than you want the mat to show, use the **Selection**, **Modify**, **Contract** command to shrink it a little.

TIP

Instead of creating a mat and frame, you can create a decorative edge for a photo by simply painting on a layer below your image layer (lower the opacity of the image layer to aid your work), and then creating a clipping mask using that layer. See **163** Mask an Image Layer.

6 Mask the Mat Layer

Insert a new layer below the **Mat** layer and above the **Frame** layer for the mask. To do this, select the **Frame** layer in the **Layers** palette and insert a new layer by clicking the **Create a new layer** button on the **Layers** palette or by choosing **Layer, New, Layer**. Name this new layer **Mask**.

Click the **Paint Bucket** tool on the **Toolbox**. On the **Options** bar, be sure that **Opacity** is set to 100% and **Mode** is set to **Normal**. Then, click within the *selection marquee* to fill the selection with any color. The mask layer thumbnail should show a rectangle just a bit larger than the size of your image, filled with the color you selected. To mask the **Mat** layer with this rectangle, select the **Mat** layer in the **Layers** palette and choose **Layer, Group with Previous**. The **Mat** layer appears indented in the **Layers** palette to indicate that it's being masked by the layer below. You should now see the frame.

7 View the Result

After you're satisfied with the result, make any other changes you want and save the PSD file. Resave the result in JPEG or TIFF format, leaving your **PSD** image with its *layers* intact so that you can return at a later time and make different adjustments if you want.

I wanted to frame this photo of Hattie, my Aunt Betty's Scottie dog, for use on a greeting card. I used a black mat and a frame created with the **Cold Lava** texture effect. I added a border outside the frame by **Ctrl**+clicking the thumbnail for the **Frame** layer on the **Layers** palette (which selected the **Frame** layer), choosing **Select, Modify, Border** and expanding the border selection by 25 pixels, and filling the selection with black using the **Paint Bucket** tool. Look for this image in the Color Gallery.

> **NOTE**
>
> If you want, you can add an inner bevel to help the **Mat** layer look more like a mat. Select the **Mask** layer on the **Layers** palette (yes, you add the bevel to the **Mask** layer, not to the **Mat** layer). Then repeat step 1 to add the inner bevel.

167 Blend Two Images into One

If you have two photographs with similar themes, you can blend them into one image using the *Editor*. For example, you could blend a portrait of a recent graduate with a snapshot of his school or diploma. By using the Editor's *layer* and *blend mode* features, you can create a ghostly image of one photo on top of the other. In this manner, the portrait of your graduate is enhanced by the second photo, which provides additional context—for example, the location of the graduation.

1 Open Background Image

Open the background image in the *Editor* in **Standard Edit** mode, such as an image of the Jefferson Memorial shown here. Save the image in Photoshop (***.psd**) format. Convert the *background layer* to a regular layer by choosing **Layer, New, Layer from Background**. This action enables you to reposition this layer and adjust its opacity if needed. Name this new layer **Background**. (Yes, it's okay to *name* the former background layer **Background**.)

2 Copy Main Image to a Separate Layer

Open the main image, such as a close-up of the Jefferson statue as shown here. Arrange the two image windows so that you can see both onscreen. Drag the *thumbnail* of the main image (Jefferson) from the **Layers** palette and drop in the window of the background image (the memorial). A copy of the main image appears on a layer above the **Background** layer. Name this new layer **Main**. Close the main image because it is no longer needed.

3 Resize and Position Main Image

In the **Layers** palette, select the **Main** layer. Click the **Move** tool on the **Toolbox**. Enable the **Show Bounding Box** option on the **Options** bar. Press **Shift** and drag a corner node to resize the new layer as needed. Pressing **Shift** as you drag ensures that you won't lose the proportions of your subject as you resize the image layer.

Before You Begin

✔ **91** About Layers and the Layers Palette

✔ **99** Move, Resize, Skew, or Distort a Layer

✔ **111** About Tool Options

💡 **TIP**

In choosing two photos to blend, the background photo typically works best as a landscape or other photo with minimal sharp detail (so that it doesn't distract from the main image); the main photo can be anything from a portrait to a detail shot. It also looks better if the main image is darker than the background image.

Move Tool **Maintain Aspect Ratio**

1 Open Background Image

2 Copy Main Image to a Separate Layer

4 Change Layer Blend Mode to Hard Light

3 Resize and Position Main Image

Eraser Tool

5 Clean Up Main Layer

6 View the Result

Click in the middle of the main image with the **Move** tool and reposition it as needed so that its location complements the background image. Click the checkmark button on the **Options** bar to accept your changes.

4 **Change Layer Blend Mode to Hard Light**

On the **Layers** palette, change the **Blend Mode** for the **Main** layer to **Hard Light**. The **Main** layer now appears as a ghost over the top of the **Background** layer.

5 **Clean Up Main Layer**

With the **Main** layer still chosen, remove any portions of the **Main** layer you don't want to use in the final image. For example, click the **Background Eraser** tool on the **Toolbox** to erase the background from around a person's portrait, so that the portrait blends more into the background image. For this example, I used the **Eraser** tool rather than the **Background Eraser** because I didn't want to erase the background, only soften it. With a soft brush and less than full **Opacity**, I used the **Eraser** tool to soften the hard edge of Jefferson's portrait so that it blended better with the memorial image.

6 **View the Result**

After you're satisfied with the result, make any other changes you want and save the PSD image. Resave the result in JPEG or TIFF format, leaving your PSD image with its *layers* intact so that you can return at a later time and make different adjustments if you want.

Blending these two photos taken during a trip to Washington, D.C. seems to enhance both images. The result is a unique portrait of one of our country's great leaders. Look for this image in the Color Gallery.

 TIP

Don't forget that you can flip the main image layer if needed. In this example, I used the **Image, Rotate, Flip Layer Horizontal** command to flip the statue so that Jefferson was facing inward, toward his memorial.

 TIP

If you want the **Main** layer to appear even more ghostly on top of the **Background** layer, on the **Layers** palette, lower the **Opacity** of the **Main** layer.

168 Create a Scrapbook Page

Before You Begin

✔ **44** Create a New Image

✔ **91** About Layers and the Layers Palette

See Also

→ **99** Move, Resize, Skew, or Distort a Layer

→ **106** Rotate an Image or Layer

→ **120** About Drawing Shapes

→ **183** Add a Text Caption or Label

TIPS

Use the scrapbook pages you create for greeting cards, post cards, or special scrapbook photo albums. You can have your scrapbook pages bound professionally into a hard cover book, by uploading the individual images to an *online service*. See **69** **Print an Image Using an Online Service.**

You also can create quick-and-easy photo album pages in the *Organizer*: Just select the photos to use and click the **Create** button on the **Options** bar. Choose **Photo Album Pages** from the **Select a creation type** list, and then follow the onscreen instructions.

Scrapbooking is a multimillion dollar industry, providing artists with a complete array of colorful papers, wavy-edged scissors, die-cut shapes, and small paper punches—tools designed specifically to help you create a unique presentation for your photographs. Without spending a dime on these special papers and tools, you can create beautiful scrapbook pages on your computer using the *Editor*. And best of all, with the **Type** tool, your "handwriting" will look perfect!

❶ Create New Image

Open the *Editor* in **Standard Edit** mode and set the *background color* to the color you want to use for the background of your scrapbook page. Then, click the **New** button on the **Shortcuts** bar to start a new image, or choose **File**, **New**, **Blank File**. The **New** dialog box appears.

Type **Scrapbook** in the **Name** text box. From the **Preset** list, select **8 × 10**. Select **Background Color** from the **Background Contents** list. Adjust any other options you like, such as the *Resolution*. Click **OK** to create a new image with the background color you choose. Save the new image in Photoshop (***.psd**) format.

❷ Define Areas

Break up the page by defining large areas for text and photos. Click the **Rectangle**, **Ellipse**, or other shape tool on the **Toolbox**, and use it to create one or two areas of various sizes and colors. Enable the **Create new shape layer** option on the **Options** bar so that each "area" will be on its own layer. This arrangement enables you to resize the areas that define the page as needed so that you can fine-tune the layout of your page. See **120** **About Drawing Shapes**. These areas will help to anchor the various elements on the page. Breaking a page into thirds or halves typically works best.

You can create unusual shapes for your page, such as the lightning bolt shown here, using any of the selection tools and then filling the selection with color using the **Paint Bucket**. I plan on using the lightning bolt shape to hold text later on, but you could use a shape to frame a photo. When creating shapes for photos, keep in mind that placing photos in odd-numbered groups (such as singly or in threes) helps to create more flow and interest on your page. Also, to avoid cluttering the page, try not to use too many photos.

③ Insert Photos

Bring in your photos one by one. To insert a photo, open the image and arrange the screen so that you can see the **Scrapbook** window too. Drag the photo's *thumbnail* from the **Layers** palette and drop it into the **Scrapbook** window. A new layer for the photo is automatically created.

Use the *bounding box* that appears around the shape to resize, rotate, skew, and reposition the image on the layer. See **99** **Move, Resize, Skew, or Distort a Layer**.

To set off the photo on the page, add a frame (see **166** **Frame a Photograph**), a drop shadow or outer glow *layer style*, or cut the image in a shape that complements your theme: Click the **Cookie Cutter** tool on the **Toolbox** and choose a shape from the **Shape** palette on the **Options** bar. To view other shapes, click the right-arrow button on the **Shape** palette and select the shape preset list you want to see from the menu that appears; select **All Elements Shapes** to see all available shapes in this list. Click the **Shape Options** button and set how you want the shape sized. For example, choose **Defined Proportions** to keep the original proportions of the shape and not make it fatter or taller. Add a **Feather** if you like, to soften the edges of the photo shape. Disable the **Crop** option. Drag on the image to draw the cookie cutter shape; again, you can use the bounding box that appears to move, resize, rotate, or skew the shape on the image before cutting. Click the **Commit** button (the checkmark) to cut the image to that shape.

With the **Crop** option disabled, the **Cookie Cutter** tool will crop only the current layer, which in this case is one of your images. If you enable the **Crop** option, all layers are cropped, making your entire scrapbook page that shape.

💡 TIPS

For ideas on what colors to use for your scrapbook pages, look to paint-set samples. The colors on each sample card are designed to go together, so if you use those same colors, you'll automatically have a complementary color scheme.

Add texture or a *pattern* to your background using the **Pattern Stamp**, a filter, layer style, or effect. You can even insert a photo above the background layer and meld it with the background color by changing to **Hard Light** blend mode on the photo layer.

To make the sides of one of your areas look like it's torn paper, select the shape layer you want to change and simplify it (**Layer, Simplify Layer**). Use the **Lasso** tool to draw your jagged edge, invert the selection, and then press **Delete**. Set the foreground color to the same color as the shape, and the background color to the color of the background the shape is lying on, or some contrasting color. Deselect the selection and apply the **Torn Edges** filter (**Filter, Sketch, Torn Edges**). Set **Smoothness** to 2 and **Contrast** to 20, and then play with the **Image Balance** setting until the torn edge appears. Because you have to simplify the layer first, apply this filter after you're sure that the area is the size you need it to be for your photos.

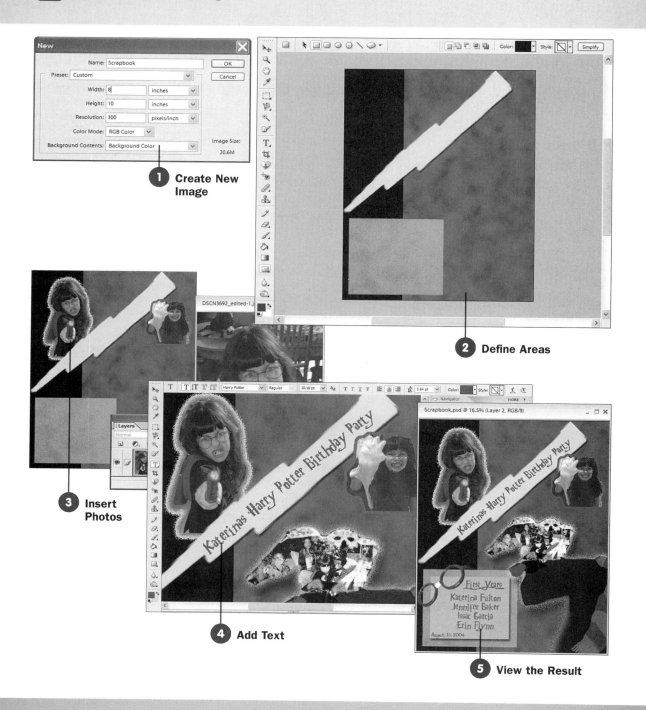

1 Create New Image

2 Define Areas

3 Insert Photos

4 Add Text

5 View the Result

4 **Add Text**

Click the **Horizontal** or **Vertical Type** tool on the **Toolbox**. On the **Options** bar, select the **Font, Font Style,** and **Font Size** you want to use. Select a **Color** and set any other options you want. Then type your text. See **183** **Add a Text Caption or Label** for help. Click the **checkmark** button on the **Options** bar to accept your changes.

To rotate the text to fit in a particular location on the page, click it with the **Move** tool. Then, drag just outside a corner *handle*, right or left, to rotate the text into position. Drag from the center of the text to move it on the layer. See **106** **Rotate an Image or Layer**.

5 **View the Result**

After you're satisfied with the result, make any other changes you want and save the PSD file. Resave the result in JPEG or TIFF format, leaving your PSD image with its layers intact so that you can return at a later time and make different adjustments if you want.

I had a lot of fun creating this scrapbook page of my daughter's recent birthday sleepover party. I have a lot more photos, so I might create a second page using the same colors and shapes so that the two look like they go together.

When I created the guest list for the lower-left corner, I remembered that I'd taken a photo of the glasses the kids wore, so I erased the background in the photo and hung the glasses over the sign. For the owl photo, I created my own owl and Harry's arm using the **Paint Brush** tool. I then placed a photo on the layer above the owl drawing, and used the **Layer, Group with Previous** command to create a clipping mask, which caused that image to be clipped in the shape of the owl I had drawn. I then changed the image layer's blend mode to **Vivid Light** so that the whitest areas of the owl shape I drew (such as its head and upper wing feathers) still appear, like a ghost on the image shape. That way, the faces of my daughter and her friends on the image layer appear to be casting a spell on the photographer. Look for this image in the Color Gallery.

169 Create a Composite Image

169 Create a Composite Image

Before You Begin

✔ **44** Create a New Image

✔ **97** Erase Part of a Layer

✔ **99** Move, Resize, Skew, or Distort a Layer

A composite image is made up of several related photographs, each on its own *layer*. Typically, the photographs overlap a bit, with their edges feathered to make the transition between the two images smooth and not jarring. You might add a background that peeks through where the photographs don't appear, and maybe even some text that pulls the theme together.

Unlike when you make a scrapbook page (see **168** **Create a Scrapbook Page**), each photo in a composite image is left unframed so that it can blend with the other photographs into a cohesive whole. If you're look-ing to blend two images and create an artistic impression of both pho-tos, see **167** **Blend Two Images into One**. In that task, two images are laid on top of each other, and a special blend mode creates a ghostly image of one on the other.

① Create New Image

Open the *Editor* in **Standard Edit** mode and set the *background color* to the color you want to use for the background of your com-posite image. Then, click the **New** button on the **Shortcuts** bar to start a new image or choose **File, New, Blank File**. The **New** dia-log box appears.

Type **Composite** in the **Name** box. Select the size for the final image from the **Preset** list, or enter **Width** and **Height** measure-ments. Select **Background Color** from the **Background Contents** list. Adjust any other options you like, such as the *Resolution*. Click **OK** to create a new image with the background color you choose. Save the new image in Photoshop (***.psd**) format.

② Insert the Main Photo

Insert your main photo by first opening the image and arranging the screen so that you can see the **Composite** window too. Drag the main photo's *thumbnail* from the **Layers** palette and drop it into the **Composite** window. A new layer for the photo is automat-ically created.

Move Tool   **Maintain Aspect Ratio Button**

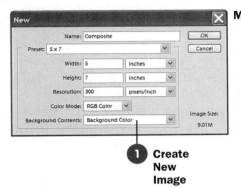

1 Create New Image

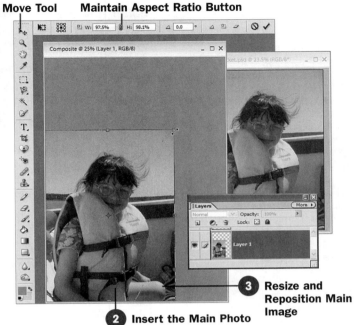

3 Resize and Reposition Main Image

2 Insert the Main Photo

4 Insert Other Photos

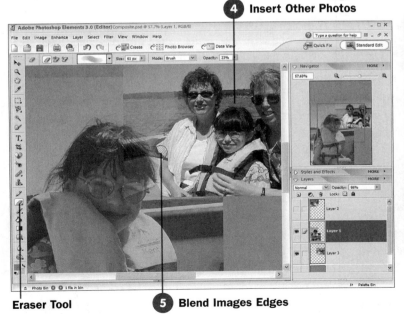

Eraser Tool

5 Blend Images Edges

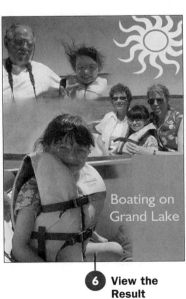

6 View the Result

Boating on Grand Lake

TIPS

To help you blend the edges of your images, reduce the **Opacity** of the top image in the **Layers** palette so that you can see the underlying image more easily. Now you can erase just enough of the top image so that the subject in the underlying image is not obscured.

You can also try using a clipping mask to blend two images together. Just fill a layer with a gradient that flows in the same direction as the two images flow from one to the other. Select a gradient that transitions from transparent to fully opaque back to transparent again, such as **Foreground to Transparent**. Enable the **Reverse** option on the **Options** bar, and use the **Radial Gradient**, **Reflected Gradient**, or **Diamond Gradient** type. Then place this layer below the top image and choose **Layer, Group with Previous** to create the mask. See **163** **Mask an Image Layer**.

③ Resize and Position Main Image

Click the **Move** tool on the **Toolbox** and use it to resize and reposition the main image. To move the image on its layer, click in the middle of the image and drag left, right, up, or down. To resize the image, press **Shift** and click it with the **Move** tool and drag a corner *handle*. Pressing **Shift** as you drag ensures that you don't distort the photo as you resize it.

④ Insert Other Photos

Repeat steps 2 and 3 to insert the other photos for the composite. Resize and position each one so that the photos slightly overlap.

⑤ Blend Image Edges

To make the effect softer, erase the edges of your photos so that they blend. In the **Layers** palette, select the inserted image you want to trim. Click the **Eraser** tool on the **Toolbox**. On the **Options** bar, choose a large, soft brush and adjust the **Opacity** so that you erase gradually, creating a smooth transition.

⑥ View the Result

After you're satisfied with the result, make any other changes you want and save the PSD file. Resave the result in JPEG or TIFF format, leaving your PSD image with its *layers* intact so that you can return at a later time and make different adjustments if you want.

I added a custom sun shape and some text to finish off my composite image of a fun day spent boating on a lake. Look for this image in the Color Gallery.

---

170 Create a Panorama

See Also

→ **168** Create a Scrapbook Page

→ **169** Create a Composite Image

If a landscape is too vast to capture in a single image, take several overlapping images instead and use the *Editor* to blend the images into a single, wide panorama. Good panoramas start with good images: First, set your camera on a tripod and make sure that the camera is level with the horizon. Then *white balance* the camera and adjust the exposure for the conditions in which you are shooting. If your digital camera has a feature called **Stitch Assist**, **Panorama**, or **AE Lock**, turn it on because that will help you get an even exposure throughout your series of images. If your digital camera also comes with **AF Lock**, turn it on as well because it will lock in the focus and make the *depth of field* consistent throughout your images. As you take your photos, be sure to overlap them by about 30%. After you copy the separate images to your computer, follow the steps in this task to stitch them together into a panorama.

① Open the Photomerge Dialog Box

Start the Editor in **Standard Edit** mode. Choose **File**, **New**, **Photomerge Panorama** from the menu. The **Photomerge** dialog box appears.

② Select Panorama Images

Click the **Browse** button, navigate to the folder that contains your panorama images, select the pictures to use, and click **Open**. You're returned to the **Photomerge** dialog box.

③ Start Photomerge Process

Click **OK** to begin the assembly process. The Editor opens each image and starts putting them in order. A second **Photomerge** dialog box appears.

④ Make Adjustments as Needed

The Editor arranges the images within the work window in order. If the Editor is unsure where an image should appear within the panorama, you'll see a message. Click **OK** to continue. Perform any of these adjustments:

- If an image can't be placed, the Editor leaves that image in the work area, to the left of the assembled panorama. Some unused images might also appear in the light box at the top of the window. If you don't want a particular image included, drag it into the light box. To include an excluded image, drag the image into place within the panorama.

- Drag to rearrange any image within the panorama. You can also drag an image right or left to adjust how it connects to an adjacent image.

 TIP

It helps if you can place a significant feature, such as a tree or shrub, within the overlap zone because any feature that appears in side-by-side images will help the Editor put those images together later on.

TIPS

If you have trouble dropping an image where you want it, turn off the **Snap to Image** option.

If you have trouble grabbing the image you want because it overlaps another image, press **Alt** as you move the mouse pointer over the image you want to grab. When the image you want appears with a red outline, click to select that image.

To zoom in, click the **Zoom** tool, and then click within the work area. To zoom back out, press **Alt** and click with the **Zoom** tool. You can scroll or use the **Hand** tool to adjust your view of the panorama within the **Photomerge** dialog box.

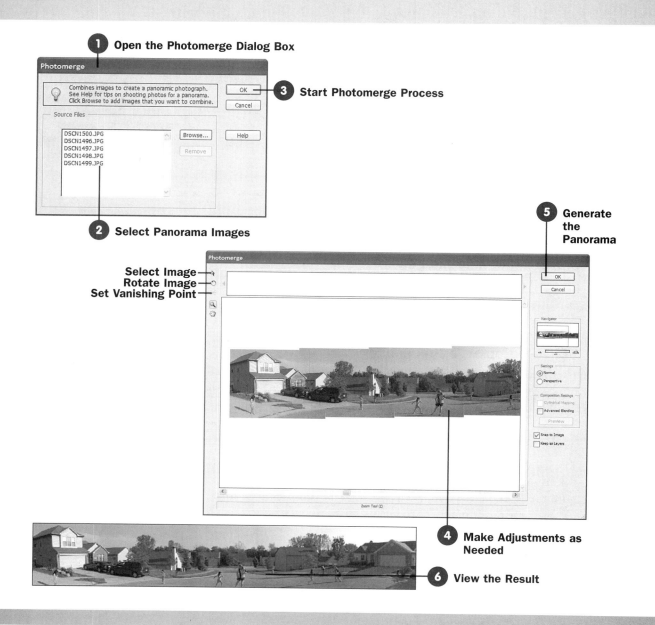

1 Open the Photomerge Dialog Box

3 Start Photomerge Process

2 Select Panorama Images

Select Image
Rotate Image
Set Vanishing Point

5 Generate the Panorama

4 Make Adjustments as Needed

6 View the Result

- To rotate an image, click the **Rotate Image** tool, click the image, and drag left or right.

- To change which image contains the highest point on the horizon (the vanishing point), click the **Select Image** tool if needed. Then click the image that contains the vanishing point. Enable the **Perspective** option to adjust the perspective using this new vanishing point image. With the **Perspective** option enabled, make a different image the vanishing point by clicking the **Set Vanishing Point** tool and then clicking that image. The image with the vanishing point is now shown with a cyan border. To return to a normal perspective, enable the **Normal** option.

- To reduce the differences between images taken with different exposures, enable the **Advanced Blending** option and click the **Preview** button to view it. To return to edit mode, click **Exit Preview**.

> **TIP**
>
> After applying a perspective adjustment, the panorama might bow inward in the middle. To even out the top and bottom edges, enable the **Cylindrical Mapping** option and then click the **Preview** button. To return to edit mode, click **Exit Preview**.

⑤ Generate the Panorama

If you think you might want to make some adjustments to the panorama after it's generated, enable the **Keep as Layers** option. When you're ready, click **OK** to create the panorama.

A new image is created, and if you chose the **Keep as Layers** option, the separate images that make up the panorama are placed on different *layers*. This arrangement enables you to make any final adjustments to contrast, color balance, *saturation*, sharpness, and other important features. If you did not enable the **Keep as Layers** option, a final, single layered image is generated.

⑥ View the Result

After you're satisfied with your panorama, save the image. If the image is still in layers, save it first in PSD format, and then after you've made any additional changes, save the result again. Resave the result in JPEG or TIFF format, leaving your PSD image with its *layers* intact so that you can return at a later time and make different adjustments if you want. If the image is not in layers, you can save it in any format you like, such as JPEG or TIFF.

Regardless of whether or not the layers are merged in your panorama, you'll have to perform at least one adjustment before you print the result: cropping. The images were aligned to create the panorama by matching their content, and not their top and bottom edges. To even those edges up, click the **Crop** tool on the **Toolbox**. Then drag from the upper-left corner of the panorama downward to the bottom right. Adjust the cropping rectangle as needed to keep as much of the panorama as possible. When you're satisfied, click the **checkmark** button on the **Options** bar to accept your changes.

My brother took a series of photographs while my daughter and I played in the cul-de-sac where we live. It took the Editor only a few minutes to arrange the separate images into a striking panorama. Look for this image in the Color Gallery.

22

Applying Visual Effects

IN THIS CHAPTER:

171 "Melt" an Image

172 Wrap an Image Around an Object

173 Create the Illusion of Snow or Rain

174 Simulate a Water Reflection

Now that you've gained some confidence in using the Editor to improve the look of your images, it's easy to take the next step and begin to create optical illusions. In this chapter, you'll learn how to melt and warp the objects in an image; wrap an image around a sphere, cube, or cylinder; add convincing rain or snow to an image; and even reflect an object onto a body of water.

171 "Melt" an Image

See Also

→ **99** Move, Resize, Skew, or Distort a Layer

→ **184** Bend Text

 TIP

There are many other distortion filters you can try, such as **Wave, Glass, Ocean Ripple,** and **Shear;** you'll find them on the **Filter, Distort** submenu. The filters work on a selection or a *layer*. In addition, you can have fun with the **Smudge** tool on the **Toolbox,** which acts like a finger smearing pixels of paint.

NOTE

To zoom in on the image, click the **Zoom** tool in the toolbox and click the image. To zoom back out, press **Alt** as you click the image with the **Zoom** tool. You can also select a zoom level from the list box in the lower-left corner of the dialog box. Drag with the **Hand** tool to scroll the image.

If you want to give parts of an image a Salvador Dali look—the famous artist who loved melting clocks, violins, and other household objects, surreal, almost faceless people, and leafless, lonely trees—the *Editor* provides you with the **Liquify** *filter*. With the tools the filter provides, you can paint various warp effects directly onto an image, swirling, pushing, and pulling pixels in any direction. That way, you can liquefy small areas of an image, or the entire image if you like.

The **Liquify** tools include **Warp** (pushes pixels in the direction you drag), **Turbulence** (slowly mixes up the pixels under the brush tip), **Twirl Clockwise** (rotates pixels clockwise around the center of the brush), **Twirl Counter-Clockwise** (the opposite of **Twirl Clockwise**), **Pucker** (pulls pixels inward), **Bloat** (the opposite of **Pucker**), **Shift Pixels** (pushes pixels in a direction that's perpendicular to the direction in which you drag), **Reflection** (copies pixels to the left or below the brush tip, to the place under the brush tip, creating a reflection), and **Reconstruct** (removes the **Liquify** filter's effect if it has not yet been applied, a little at a time, based on how long you hold the brush over a spot).

① **Choose Filter, Distort, Liquify**

Open an image in the *Editor* in **Standard Edit** mode and save it in Photoshop (**.psd*) format. In the **Layers** palette, select the layer you want to warp. You can limit the effect to a specific area by making a selection on the chosen layer first. Choose **Filter, Distort, Liquify** from the menu. The **Liquify** dialog box appears.

② **Select a Tool**

Click a tool from the toolbox on the left side of the **Liquify** dialog box.

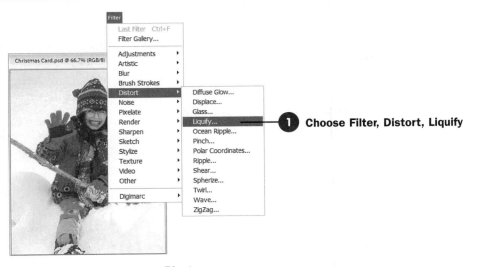

1 Choose Filter, Distort, Liquify

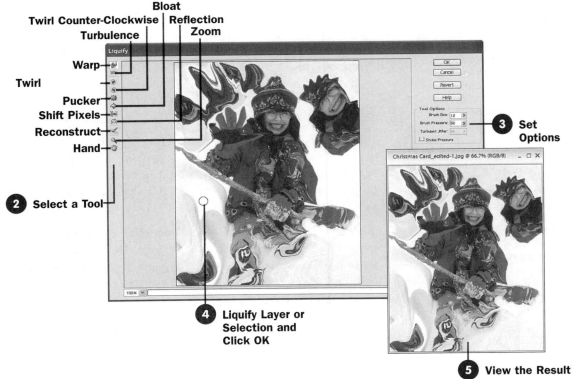

Bloat

Twirl Counter-Clockwise | Reflection
Zoom

Turbulence

Warp

Twirl

Pucker

Shift Pixels

Reconstruct

Hand

2 Select a Tool

3 Set Options

4 Liquify Layer or Selection and Click OK

5 View the Result

3 Set Options

In the **Tool Options** pane on the right side of the dialog box, adjust the **Brush Size** for the chosen tool as desired. To make changes gradually, lower the **Brush Pressure**. To make changes more rapidly, increase the **Brush Pressure**. If you're using a *pen tablet*, enable the **Stylus Pressure** option.

To increase the smoothness of the blending effect caused by the **Turbulence** tool, raise the **Turbulence Jitter** in the **Tool Options** pane.

4 Liquify Layer or Selection and Click OK

Position the brush over an area and click. The effect gets stronger the longer you hold the brush over the same area. With some tools, you must drag with the brush to liquefy. Change from tool to tool to apply different liquefy effects as desired.

When you've warped the image as you like, click **OK** to accept your changes. To abort your changes and close the **Liquify** dialog box, click **Cancel**. To abort your changes and keep the **Liquify** dialog box open so that you can try again, click **Revert**.

5 View the Result

After you're satisfied with the result, make any other changes you want and save the PSD file. Then resave the result in JPEG or TIFF format, leaving your PSD image with its *layers* (if any) intact so that you can return at a later time and make different adjustments if you want.

This photo of my daughter playing on a mound of snow after a recent blizzard was wonderful, but the snow was so white and bright that the background was a bit featureless. A few minutes with the **Liquify** filter helped me spark up the background and create an interesting portrait. I refrained from using any of the tools on her face so that she would be easy to distinguish from her liquid surroundings, although you can apply the tools on a face just as easily as you can a tree branch. Look for this image in the Color Gallery.

TIPS

The **Shift Pixels** tool normally pushes pixels to the left or downward; press **Alt** as you drag to push pixels right or upward.

The **Reflection** tool normally copies pixels to the left or below the brush; press **Alt** as you drag to copy pixels to the right or above the brush tip.

You can also use the **Liquify** filter to warp text, but the text layer must be simplified (changed to raster text) first. Select the text layer from the **Layers** palette and choose **Layer, Simplify Layer** to convert the text from vector data to raster (bitmapped) data that can then be liquefied.

172 Wrap an Image Around an Object

With the help of the **3D Transform** *filter*, you can wrap an image around a sphere, cube, or cylinder. Using a wireframe that represents the outer surface of the chosen 3D object, you can reposition the image on the 3D object and even bend the frame inward or outward at opposite points, creating your own unique 3D shapes. After applying your changes, the 3D object is rendered on top of an image (where the image acts as a background for the shape), or on top of a plain black background.

① Choose Filter, Render, 3D Transform

Open an image in the *Editor* in **Standard Edit** mode and save it in Photoshop (***.psd**) format. In the **Layers** palette, select the *layer* you want to transform. You can limit the effect to a specific area by making a selection in the chosen layer. Then choose **Filter, Render, 3D Transform** from the menu. The **3D Transform** dialog box appears.

② Set Options

Click the **Options** button. The **Options** dialog box appears. Adjust the **Resolution**. Higher *resolutions* produce better quality in spheres and cylinders, but require more time to render. The resolution has little effect on the quality of rendered 3D cubes. Select the level of *anti-aliasing* with the **Anti-aliasing** slider. Enable the **Display Background** option if you want to place the newly rendered 3D shape on top of the image. If this option is turned off, the 3D shape will appear on a black background. Click **OK** to return to the **3D Transform** dialog box.

③ Draw Shape

Click the **Cube**, **Sphere**, or **Cylinder** tool. Then drag on the image to create the wireframe which defines the outline of the shape.

④ Adjust Wireframe

Adjust the wireframe as needed:

- To adjust the wireframe's position on the image, click the **Selection** tool and drag the frame.

See Also

→ **99** Move, Resize, Skew, or Distort a Layer

→ **171** "Melt" an Image

→ **184** Bend Text

TIPS

For best results, before using the **3D Transform** filter, you'll want to skew your subject so that it begins to conform to the 3D shape you want to apply. For example, you might want to bend the top and bottom of the image inward to fit the image onto a *sphere*. See **99** Move, Resize, Skew, or Distort a Layer.

You can create your own distortions using any image in PSD format and the **Filters, Distort, Displace** filter. The image you start with is warped based on the light and dark areas of the PSD image you select. For example, you could select a waving flag image saved in PSD format, and warp another image so that it looks as if it's been pasted to the surface of the flag.

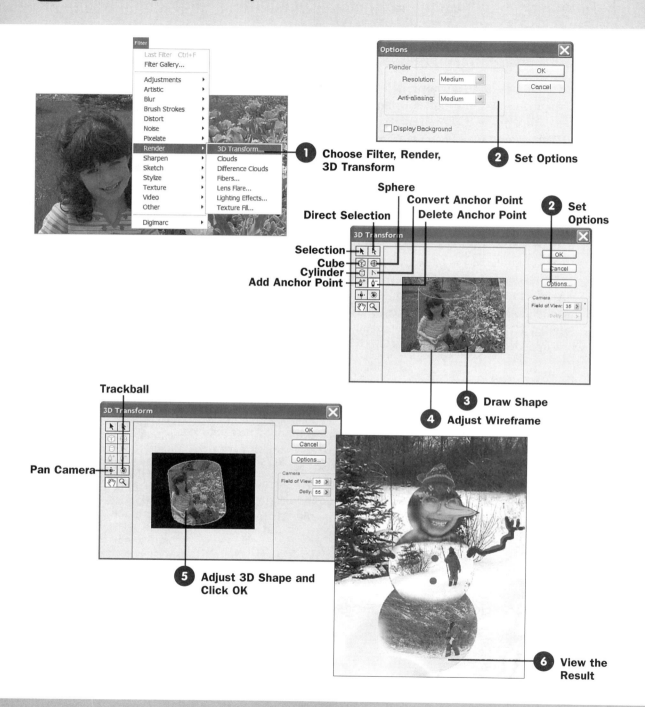

Filter
Last Filter Ctrl+F
Filter Gallery...

Adjustments ▸
Artistic ▸
Blur ▸
Brush Strokes ▸
Distort ▸
Noise ▸
Pixelate ▸
Render ▸   3D Transform...
Sharpen ▸   Clouds
Sketch ▸   Difference Clouds
Stylize ▸   Fibers...
Texture ▸   Lens Flare...
Video ▸   Lighting Effects...
Other ▸   Texture Fill...

Digimarc ▸

1 Choose Filter, Render, 3D Transform

Options
Render
Resolution: Medium
Anti-aliasing: Medium
OK
Cancel
☐ Display Background

2 Set Options

Sphere
Convert Anchor Point
Delete Anchor Point
Direct Selection

2 Set Options

Selection
Cube
Cylinder
Add Anchor Point

3D Transform
OK
Cancel
Options...
Camera
Field of View: 35
Dolly:

3 Draw Shape

4 Adjust Wireframe

Trackball

3D Transform
OK
Cancel
Options...
Camera
Field of View: 35
Dolly: 55

Pan Camera

5 Adjust 3D Shape and Click OK

6 View the Result

- To resize the wireframe, click the **Direct Selection** tool and drag a corner anchor point (otherwise known as a corner *handle*).

- To move an anchor point on a cylinder (and change the shape of the wireframe), click the **Direct Selection** tool and drag the anchor point along the frame.

- To bend the wireframe on a cylinder inwards or outwards (to create an hourglass shape, for example), add or remove anchor points. Anchors are added or removed in pairs. To add a pair of anchors, click the right side of the frame with the **Add Anchor Point** tool. Drag this right anchor in or out to bend the wireframe. To remove an anchor, click it with the **Delete Anchor Point** tool.

5 Adjust 3D Shape and Click OK

Make any of the following further adjustments as desired, then click **OK** to apply your changes:

- Move the 3D object within the image window by dragging it with the **Pan Camera** tool.

- Rotate the 3D object by dragging it right or left with the **Trackball** tool.

- Zoom the view of the 3D object in or out by adjusting the **Dolly** slider.

6 View the Result

After you're satisfied with the result, make any other changes you want and save the PSD file. Resave the result in JPEG or TIFF format, leaving your PSD image with its *layers* (if any) intact so that you can return at a later time and make different adjustments if you want.

I have several photos of my daughter playing in the snow last winter, and as I was messing around with the **3D Transform** filter, I suddenly got the idea of using the filter on three images to create three separate spheres. I then copied the results to a new image and assembled them into a snow girl. I painted arms and buttons on the snow girl using the **Brush** tool, pasted her hat from one of the original images and resized it to fit the snow girl's head, then

---

NOTES

Anchors are normally smooth, causing curves in the wireframe when you drag them inward or outward. To create a corner rather than a curve, convert the anchor by clicking it with the **Convert Anchor Point** tool. Click with the tool again to convert the anchor back to curve mode.

If the wireframe turns red, you've manipulated it in such a way that a 3D rendering is no longer possible. Abort your changes and try again.

Use the **Field of View** slider to adjust for the angle in which the photo was taken. Doing so might help the image better fit the 3D shape you've chosen.

TIP

You can create a nice half sphere by applying the **Filters, Distort, Spherize** filter to a circular selection. Apply the filter more than once to improve the effect.

---

used the **Liquify** filter to warp her nose, creating the traditional "carrot nose" effect. As a final touch, I airbrushed some snow on the snow girl to give her a bit more dimension. See **171** **"Melt" an Image**. Look for this image in the Color Gallery.

173 Create the Illusion of Snow or Rain

Before You Begin

✔ **92** Create a New Image Layer

✔ **110** About the Toolbox

See Also

→ **123** Remove Scratches

→ **154** Add Motion to an Image

→ **174** Simulate a Water Reflection

**NOTES**

To create rain instead of the snow effect described here, start with a suitably gloomy photo. Follow the same basic steps but when adding the *noise*, add less, around 70%. When blurring the rain, increase the **Distance** to about 60 pixels. Finally, to improve the effect, increase the contrast a bit.

To add snow quickly to a photograph, try the **Blizzard** effect. On the **Styles and Effects** palette, select **Effects** from the first drop-down list and **Image Effects** from the second. Double-click the **Blizzard** thumbnail to apply that effect. Although you don't have any control over the result, the effect is fairly nice.

With a *graphics editor* such as Photoshop Elements, you can improve the contrast, *saturation*, and sharpness of your images. But why stop at simply fixing reality when it's so easy to create believable illusions? For example, if a winter photograph is missing only a touch of snow to make it perfect, why not add some? And why scrap a gray, moody photograph just because it lacks the rain that might have made that day interesting? In this task, you'll learn how to create great photographs—come rain or snow.

❶ Add Snow Layer

Open an image in the *Editor* in **Standard Edit** mode and save it in Photoshop (*.psd) format. Add the snow *layer* above the image layer by clicking the **Create a new layer** button on the **Layers** palette or choosing **Layer, New, Layer** from the menu. Name this layer **Snow** and fill it with black using the **Paint Bucket** tool.

❷ Add Noise

You can add white dots for the snow with either the **Add Noise** or the **Pointillize** *filter*. With **Add Noise**, you get tinier flakes than with **Pointillize**. You might want to try both and compare the two images to see which one you like best. To add noise, choose **Filter, Noise, Add Noise**. The **Add Noise** dialog box appears. Enable both the **Gaussian** and **Monochromatic** options. Then increase the **Amount** slider until you get a fairly heavy snowfall. Click **OK** to apply the change.

To use the **Pointillize** filter instead of the **Add Noise** filter, choose **Filter, Pixelate, Pointillize**. The **Pointillize** dialog box appears. Adjust the **Cell Size** until the snowflakes (the white spaces between the black dots) are the size you want them to be. Click **OK** to accept your changes.

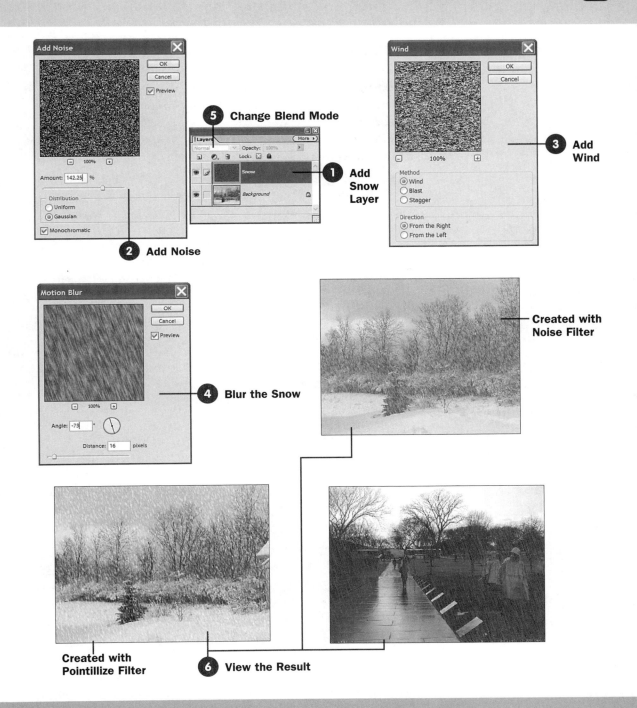

5 Change Blend Mode

1 Add Snow Layer

2 Add Noise

3 Add Wind

4 Blur the Snow

Created with Noise Filter

Created with Pointillize Filter

6 View the Result

3 Add Wind

If you applied the **Add Noise** filter in step 2, add some wind to create randomness in the snow pattern; otherwise, skip this step. Choose **Filter, Stylize, Wind.** Enable the **Wind** method. Select a **Direction** and click **OK.**

4 Blur the Snow

Right now, the snowflakes look too sharp and clear to be real, so to create the illusion of gently falling snow, add a motion blur. Choose **Filter, Blur, Motion Blur.** The **Motion Blur** dialog box appears. Change the **Angle** to the direction in which you want the snow to fall. Set the **Distance** value to a low number to create softly falling snow; use a higher number if a blizzard is more desirable. Don't blur the snow so much that you can no longer distinguish the individual snowflakes. Click **OK** to apply your changes.

TIP

To lessen the apparent amount of snow, adjust the contrast. Choose **Enhance, Adjust Lighting, Brightness/Contrast.** Then increase the **Contrast** slowly until you get the amount of snowfall you want. You can try decreasing the **Brightness** as well.

5 Change Blend Mode

To overlay your image with the newly created snow, on the **Layers** palette, change the **Blend Mode** for the **Snow** layer to **Screen** for a heavy downfall or **Lighten** for a very light snowfall.

6 View the Result

After you're satisfied with the result, make any other changes you want and save the PSD image. Resave the result in JPEG or TIFF format, leaving your PSD image with its *layers* intact so that you can return at a later time and make different adjustments if you want.

The snowy scene was taken after a heavy snow hit our area last winter. The addition of falling snow adds to the peacefulness of the scene. As you can see, you definitely get different results when you use the **Pointillize** filter instead of the **Add Noise** filter.

The photo of the Korean Veteran's Memorial in Washington, D.C. was actually taken after a rain. But it was easy to add the rain back, following the steps in this task. The grayness of the day and the puddles on the sidewalk add realism to the rain effect. Keep that in mind when selecting a suitable photo for the addition of fake rain. Look for these images in the Color Gallery.

174 **Simulate a Water Reflection**

Using a *graphics editor* such as Photoshop Elements, you can create lots of illusions. One of the most popular is simulating a reflection. When creating a simulated reflection, you should keep several things in mind: First, an object reflected in water is distorted by the angle of that reflection. Also, the object's reflection is distorted by the ripples in the water. Luckily, both of these distortions are easy to simulate in the *Editor*.

Before You Begin

✔ **91** About Layers and the Layers Palette

✔ **99** Move, Resize, Skew, or Distort a Layer

1 Add Reflection Layer

Open an image in the Editor in **Standard Edit** mode and save it in Photoshop (***.psd**) format. Using your favorite **Selection** tools, select the object or portion of the image you want to reflect and choose **Layer, New, Layer via Copy** to copy that portion of the image to a new layer. Name this new layer **Reflection**.

To create my illusion, I pasted in my house from another image, and put it on its own layer (**House**). I then selected this layer and duplicated it, creating the **Reflection** layer. If the object you want to reflect is isolated on its own layer, you don't have to select it first; just duplicate the layer as I did.

2 Flip Reflection

You must flip the portion of the image you copied so that it will appear as a reflection. To do that, make sure that the **Reflection** layer is selected on the **Layers** palette. Then choose **Image, Rotate, Flip Layer Vertical**.

3 Transform Layer

Click the **Move** tool on the **Toolbox**. Drag the reflection into place. *Distort* or *skew* the reflection as needed, using the **Image, Transform, Free Transform** command. See **99** **Move, Resize, Skew, or Distort a Layer**.

💡 TIPS

If you want to make some text look as if it's being reflected in water, try applying the **Water Reflection** effect on the **Styles and Effects** palette.

To create your own fake water, try setting the *foreground* and *background colors* to blue, one just a little lighter than the other. Choose **Filter, Render, Clouds**; then apply one of the ripple *filters* described here to stir the "water."

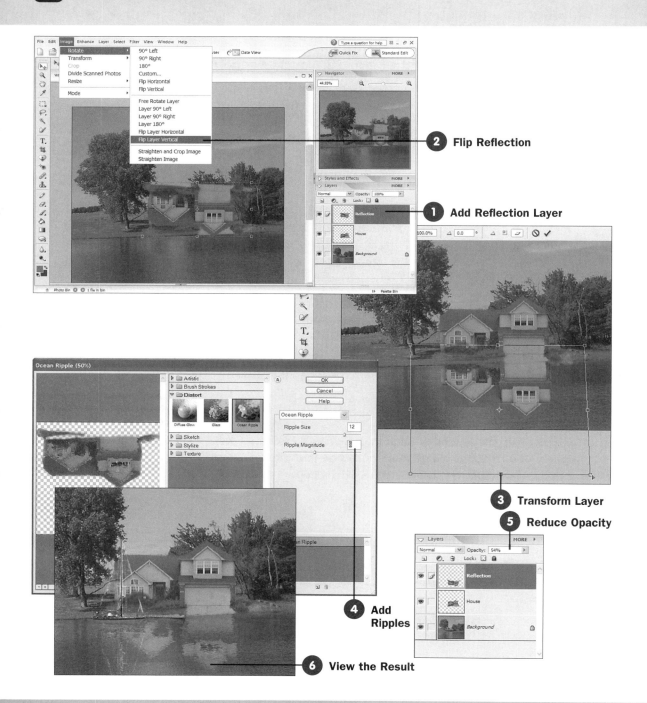

2 Flip Reflection

1 Add Reflection Layer

3 Transform Layer

5 Reduce Opacity

4 Add Ripples

6 View the Result

4 Add Ripples

If the object is being reflected in water, you should add some ripples to the reflection for realism. The Editor supplies you with a variety of filters you can use to apply the ripples. Try them all and choose the one that works best for your current image: Choose **Filter, Distort**, and then select **Glass, Ocean Ripple, Ripple** or **Zig Zag**.

5 Reduce Opacity

Finally, to allow the water to show through the reflection just a bit, lower the **Opacity** of the **Reflection** layer by adjusting that setting on the **Layers** palette.

6 View the Result

After you're satisfied with the result, make any other changes you want and save the PSD file. Resave the result in JPEG or TIFF format, leaving your PSD image with its layers intact so that you can return at a later time and make different adjustments if you want.

I've always wanted to see what it would look like if we owned a home on a lake. So I copied our house into a photo of a small lake and added a reflection of our house on the water to complete the illusion. There's no point in living lakefront without a boat—especially when you have a paved "boat ramp" (the driveway) and a boat house (the garage)—so I added one in—along with the boat's reflection.

One thing you have to be careful of when combining several images like this into a single photo is to match the weather conditions throughout. My house photo was a bit dark, being taken on an overcast day. So, I lightened the **House** layer a bit and increased the contrast to match the sunny conditions of the lake photo. Although the boat photo was taken on a sunny day, it was almost too sunny, so I reduced the brightness of the **Boat** layer just a bit. Look for this image in the Color Gallery.

TIP

With calmer water like the kind in my lakeside photo, none of these rippling filters did the job. So I tried a few of the **Brush Strokes** filters and found that the **Sprayed Strokes** filter worked best at producing those gentle horizontal waves evident in my final result. I set the **Stroke Direction** to **Horizontal** and used a fairly long **Stroke Length** and wide **Spray Radius**. You can also try **Filter, Stylize, Wind**.

23

Creating Artistic Photographs

IN THIS CHAPTER:

175 Make a Photograph Look Old

176 Change a Color Photograph to Black and White

177 Create a Negative Image

178 Colorize a Photograph

179 Make a Photograph Look Like an Oil Painting

180 Turn a Photograph into a Watercolor

181 Make a Photograph Look Like It Was Drawn

182 Make a Photograph Look Like Andy Warhol Painted It

The first step to creating a photograph that shines on its own as a work of true art is to capture the perfect composition. This isn't a task that Photoshop Elements can help you with; only you have the ability and skill to manipulate the light, steer the subject, anticipate the perfect moment, and produce a scene that attracts the adoration of people's eyes. But after you've done that, you can manipulate your composition so that it does appear—at least partly—to have been rendered by hand instead of by pixel. The *Editor* in Photoshop Elements can help you apply textures, *effects*, and optical illusions to give your composition the feel of a painting. If you yourself are inclined to painting with real paint on a real canvas, you might even become inspired, having seen your own photographs in prototype painted form.

175 Make a Photograph Look Old

Before You Start

✔ **72** Select a Rectangular or Circular Area

✔ **83** Select Everything but the Current Selection

✔ **85** Reload a Previously Saved Selection

✔ **93** Create a Layer Filled with a Color, Gradient, or Pattern

See Also

→ **166** Frame a Photograph

→ **176** Change a Color Photograph to Black and White

→ **178** Colorize a Photograph

At hardware stores, you can find cans or jars of something called "antique paint," which you can supposedly brush or spray on your curios to instantly make them look old. Although these paints often do have some crackling glazes in them, and some metallics that bunch up together, you can't expect to just spray it on something and instantly age it. By that same token, you can't expect to make any photograph you take look ancient simply by recasting it as monochrome or reducing its *saturation*. The earliest photographs are dated not just by their technology but also by the nature of their content: Because exposure in the nineteenth century was generally achieved either through extreme brightness or long shutter openings, early photos—especially Daguerreotypes—were *portraits*, usually of people holding painfully still. They were often overexposed and lacked detail. But unlike Polaroids, whose age many can easily guess down to the precise year by gauging the gradual reduction of blue tints, ancient photos (when well kept, of course) actually look much the same as they did when they first emerged from the developing room. So, what you're trying to do when making a photo look *vintage* (for instance, circa 1880) is to approximate the style and content of the photos of that era, rather than make the photo look like it's aged several generations.

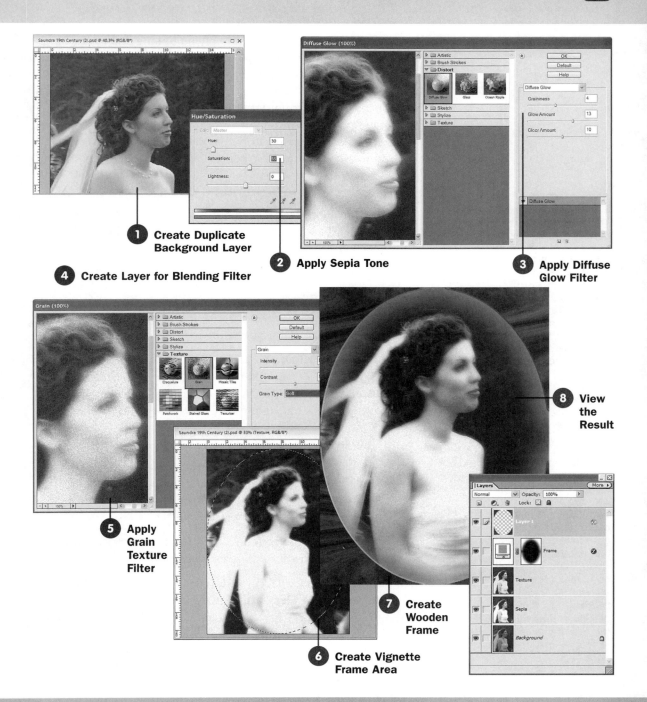

1 Create Duplicate Background Layer

2 Apply Sepia Tone

3 Apply Diffuse Glow Filter

4 Create Layer for Blending Filter

5 Apply Grain Texture Filter

6 Create Vignette Frame Area

7 Create Wooden Frame

8 View the Result

Adobe's *filters* are extremely adept at applying unique and captivating effects to images; but for you to capture a specific set of nuances—such as the appearance of an 1880's photograph—you should apply several filter effects in succession. For this example, we'll take a scene where the subject happens to be wearing clothing suitable for that era and also happens to be standing fairly still. We want to create an effect where the final product appears overexposed in the brighter areas and noisy or pixilated in the darker areas.

TIP

If the effect you're going for isn't the nineteenth-century Daguerreotype look, but instead a 1940s-era magazine color reproduction with the old *Look* magazine's warm, grainy style, try applying the **Film Grain** filter. Set **Grain** to **5** (lower than medium), **Highlight Area** to its minimum of **0**, and **Intensity** to its maximum of **10**.

NOTE

If you've ever held a mylar diffusion sheet—used in the photo development process and in the printing process for cardboard packaging—you know that it's smooth, evenly frosted, and very finely grained. One photo reproduction trick used in antiquing is to lay one of these diffusion sheets on top of a fully developed image and then reshoot the image. The **Diffuse Glow** filter is designed to approximate the use of one of these sheets for just that purpose.

① Create Duplicate Background Layer

Open the image in the Editor in **Standard Edit** mode and save it in Photoshop (***.psd**) format. With the **Background** layer selected in the **Layers** *palette*, select **Layer**, **Duplicate Layer**. Name the new *layer* **Sepia**.

② Apply Sepia Tone

With the **Sepia** layer selected, select **Enhance**, **Adjust Color**, **Adjust Hue/Saturation** from the menu bar.

In the **Hue/Saturation** dialog box that opens, check **Colorize**. Under **Hue**, enter **30** (the optimum sepia color) and under **Saturation**, enter **55**. Click **OK**. For the moment, this might look like *too much* sepia, but what you're about to do will compensate.

③ Apply Diffuse Glow Filter

In the **Toolbox**, click the **Default Colors** button that appears just below and to the left of the foreground and background color swatches. This action prevents the **Diffuse Glow** filter from being influenced by any other hues from the outside.

With the **Sepia** layer selected in the **Layers** palette, select **Filter**, **Distort**, **Diffuse Glow** from the menu bar.

The three variables the **Diffuse Glow** filter uses are **Graininess**, **Glow Amount**, and **Clear Amount**. You can experiment with the settings for these variables to some extent. You don't want a high value for **Graininess**, and you'll probably want an even smaller value for a lady's portrait, such as this one. For this example, I set **Graininess** to **4**, although I might have set it as high as **6** for the more rugged face of her groom.

Glow Amount, for these purposes, controls the extent of the over-exposure effect. The higher this setting, the more *white* is added to the lighter sections of the face. This diminishes the sepia effect only at the lightest areas, which is what you want. On the other hand, this can make your *midtones* a chalky brown, which you can compensate for with the **Clear Amount** setting. **Clear Amount**, in effect, is the opposite of **Glow Amount**, and can balance or even compensate for it. In this example, I wanted the bride's upper cheeks and forehead to glow, but I didn't want to lose the rich tones in her lower cheeks and neck. So, I set **Glow Amount** to **13**, and recovered the sepia in the midtones by setting **Clear Amount** to **10**.

To finalize your choices and apply the filter to the **Sepia** layer, click **OK**.

 TIP

In artistic terms, "clear" color is brighter, more vibrant color.

4 Create Layer for Blending Filter

To complete the illusion of an old photograph, we want to create a noticeable grainy pattern, beyond what the **Diffuse Glow** filter can provide. But filters generally apply their effects evenly throughout an entire image or a selected area of an image, and what we want is noticeable graininess *only in the medium-dark-to-dark regions*. This way, we antique the image without losing the gentle glow we've just achieved in the subject's face.

In the **Layers** palette, select the **Sepia** layer. Choose **Layer**, **Duplicate Layer** from the menu bar. Name the new layer **Texture**.

In the **Layers** palette, select the new **Texture** layer. From the menu bar, select **Enhance**, **Adjust Color**, **Adjust Hue/Saturation**. In the **Hue/Saturation** dialog box, enable the **Colorize** check box. For the **Hue** setting, enter **0**; and for the **Saturation** setting, enter **25**. Click **OK**. This creates a russet-hued undertone, which will later appear mostly in the darker regions; the midtones will retain the original sepia.

In the **Layers** palette, with the **Texture** layer selected, change its **Blend Mode** to **Multiply** and its **Opacity** to **50%**. The **Multiply** blend mode accumulates darks on darks, as though you were holding up two transparencies of the same image on top of one another. The light still shines through, but the darks are now more opaque.

⑤ Apply Grain Texture Filter

With the **Texture** layer selected in the **Layers** palette, select **Filter, Texture, Grain** from the menu bar. In the **Grain** dialog box that opens, set **Intensity** to **50%**, **Contrast** to **50%**, and **Grain Type** to **Soft**. In the preview pane of the dialog box, what you'll see is the effect this filter will have *on this particular layer*, not on the entire image. This is important because we've reduced this layer's opacity by half. By earlier setting its blend mode to **Multiply**, we're in effect telling the Editor to apply only the *dark* pixels of the grains we've just created to the darker areas of the layers beneath the **Texture** layer. Click **OK**.

The **Grain** filter achieves its effects partly by varying the colors of the original pixels, not just their brightness. So, some of the pixels on the **Texture** layer are now *greener* than they were before. From a distance, this creates a more natural, pointillistic effect. If you look at a true antique photo under a magnifying glass, you'll see that it isn't monochromatic by design, either. The varying colors in any small region are joined together by your eyes to produce a sepia tone at a distance.

⑥ Create Vignette Frame Area

To complete the full effect, we're going to set this image in an oval vignette frame. With the **Texture** layer still selected in the **Layers** palette, in the **Toolbox**, select the **Marquee** tool. The current tool is probably the **Rectangular Marquee** tool with the dashed rectangle icon; if so, in the **Options** bar, click the **Elliptical Marquee** tool to make that the current tool.

In the image, point your crosshairs to the absolute upper-left corner. Click and drag the pointer to the absolute lower-right corner. The area you're selecting includes everything within the oval, which should just graze the sides of the image.

Because we'll need this ellipse again later, save it to the image's *alpha channel*: Choose **Select, Save Selection** from the menu bar. In the **Save Selection** dialog box, under **Name**, type **Frame border** and click **OK**.

To give this selection a very soft edge, first choose **Select, Modify, Contract** from the menu bar. In the **Contract Selection** dialog

TIP

If your image contents tend to fall *outside* the boundaries of even the widest ellipse you can create, you might want to try instead a rounded rectangle. To make one, start by using the **Rectangular Marquee** tool to define the basic rectangle shape, or choose **Select, All** from the menu bar to select the entire image. Then choose **Select, Modify, Smooth** from the menu bar. In the dialog box, enter a large amount, such as **100**. Click **OK**.

box, enter **50** to reduce the selection size a bit, and then click **OK**. Then choose **Select**, **Feather** from the menu bar. In the **Feather Selection** dialog box, under **Feather Radius**, enter **50** to bring the selection boundaries in even further, but this time softly. Click **OK**.

Because our real objective is to create a frame that appears everywhere our current selection *is not*, we have to invert the selection. Choose **Select**, **Inverse** from the menu bar. Notice that the marquee now surrounds the edge of the image.

TIP

For images with relatively high resolution, such as above 300 PPI, try higher amounts for both contracting and feathering.

7 Create Wooden Frame

To add the wooden pattern as the vignette frame, select **Layer**, **New Fill Layer**, **Pattern**. In the **New Layer** dialog box that opens, under **Name**, type **Frame** and click **OK**.

In the **Pattern Fill** dialog box, click the down-arrow next to the pattern sample; from the array of swatches that appears, choose **Wood**. Enable the **Link with Layer** check box and click **OK**.

In the **Styles and Effects** palette, choose **Effects** and, from the samples, choose **Wood – Rosewood**. Don't be afraid. For a moment, you'll see nothing but the wood panel. What's happened is that you've created a new layer *on top* with just the rosewood panel. Here's where we bring back the oval selection. From the menu bar, choose **Select**, **Load Selection**. In the **Load Selection** dialog box, under **Selection**, type **Frame border** and click **OK**.

We want to cut the shape of the selection from the inside of the rosewood panel. But we don't want to make it look like we did this with a buzz saw. So, choose **Select**, **Modify**, **Smooth** from the menu bar. In the **Smooth Selection** dialog box, under **Sample Radius**, type **5** and click **OK**. Then select **Edit**, **Cut**. The interior of the rosewood panel is now extracted, revealing the photo beneath it.

Finally, from the **Styles and Effects** palette, in the left drop-down list, choose **Layer Styles**; from the right drop-down list, choose **Bevels**. From the sample thumbnails, choose **Simple Sharp Outer** to create a simple beveled edge along the oval cut-out.

8 View the Result

After you're satisfied with the result, make any other changes you want and save the PSD file. Resave the result in JPEG or TIFF format, leaving your PSD image with its layers intact so that you can return at a later time and make different adjustments if you want.

In this image of a modern-day bride made to look a bit more vintage, the lighter-colored wooden area beneath **Layer 1** now resembles the faded edges of a domed glass mounting, where an antique photo generally disintegrates, revealing the old wooden mounting beneath. The very last application of the **Simple Sharp Outer** bevel gives the rosewood a bit of depth, while also providing a slight and unobtrusive sheen to the photo area.

176 Change a Color Photograph to Black and White

Before You Start

✔ **92** Create a New Image Layer

✔ **136** About an Image's Histogram

✔ **149** Sharpen an Image

See Also

→ **138** Improve a Dull, Flat Photo

TIP

For comparison's sake, here's the one-step method for making any image monochromatic: With the image open in the Editor, select **Image, Mode, Grayscale** from the menu bar. Click **OK** at the warning. (Okay, *two* steps.) In many cases, what looked like perfectly distinguished shades in a color photograph become murky and muddled when the hue and saturation data is removed.

Although it literally takes one step to make any color image monochromatic in Photoshop Elements, there's no guarantee that the result will be an attractive black-and-white image. Professional photographers know there are special effects that can be achieved only with black and white; when you add color, your eyes are no longer drawn to the same points of drama and impact.

But you generally can't obtain a quality black-and-white image simply by removing the hue and saturation data from a color image. Your eyes naturally distinguish elements of the scene you're viewing now by contrasting their colors against one another; if you were to remove the color, the contrast would go away as well. The great cinematographers of the 1930s and '40s knew this, and would construct movie scenes with bold, surrealistic lights and shadows—in the real world, at least—that looked majestic and beautiful in monochrome. For you to obtain a similarly beautiful monochrome image from what might very well be a beautiful color image, you might have to generate some unrealistic contrasts *in color* that form dramatic but realistic contrasts *in monochrome*.

1 Create New Layer for Red Channel

Open the image in the *Editor* in **Standard Edit** mode and save it in Photoshop (***.psd**) format. With the *Background layer* selected in the **Layers** *palette*, choose **Layer, Duplicate Layer** from the menu bar. Name the new *layer* **Red**.

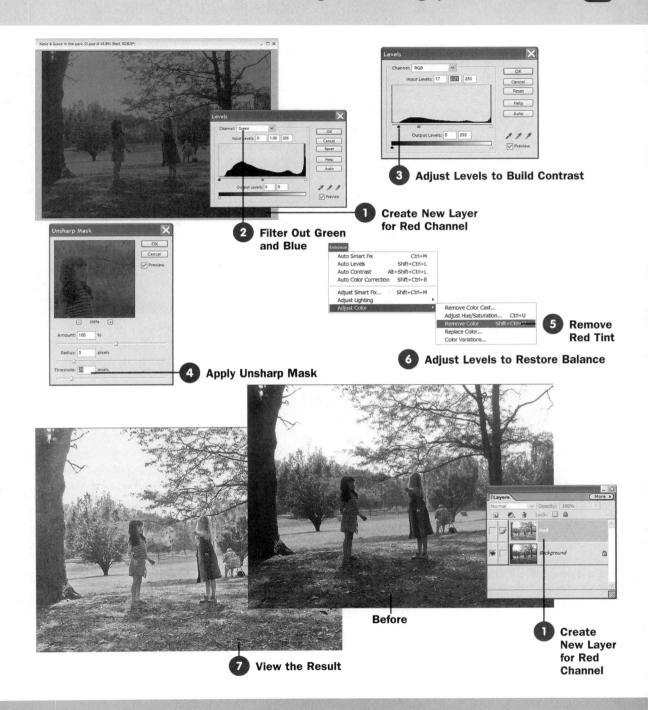

Katie & Grace in the park (2).psd @ 45.8% (Red, RGB/8*)

Levels

Channel: Green

Input Levels: 0 1.00 255

OK
Cancel
Reset
Help
Auto

Output Levels: 0 0

Preview

Levels

Channel: RGB

Input Levels: 17 2.31 255

OK
Cancel
Reset
Help
Auto

Output Levels: 0 255

Preview

3 Adjust Levels to Build Contrast

1 Create New Layer for Red Channel

2 Filter Out Green and Blue

Unsharp Mask

OK
Cancel
Preview

100%

Amount: 100 %

Radius: 3 pixels

Threshold: 0 levels

Enhance

Auto Smart Fix   Ctrl+M
Auto Levels   Shift+Ctrl+L
Auto Contrast   Alt+Shift+Ctrl+L
Auto Color Correction   Shift+Ctrl+B

Adjust Smart Fix...   Shift+Ctrl+M
Adjust Lighting   ▶
Adjust Color   ▶

Remove Color Cast...
Adjust Hue/Saturation... Ctrl+U
Remove Color   Shift+Ctrl+U
Replace Color...
Color Variations...

5 Remove Red Tint

6 Adjust Levels to Restore Balance

4 Apply Unsharp Mask

Layers

More ▶

Normal Opacity: 100%

Lock:

Red

Background

Before

1 Create New Layer for Red Channel

7 View the Result

TIP

For best results, consider making color corrections and levels adjustments to your color image to perfect it before you take the trouble to convert it to a black-and-white. See **138** Improve a Dull, Flat Photo for some ideas.

 NOTE

Why are we making everything red? Why aren't we filtering out everything except blue or green? As photographer Ansel Adams discovered early in his career, applying a red filter to his camera lens enabled him to capture daytime landscapes with either bright or highly variegated skies. In an Adams photo, skies often look very bright (at midday) or serenely dark (at sunrise or dusk). At any time of day, Adams could establish a bold contrast between his sky and his subject matter on the ground. Adjusting an image's red channel performs the digital equivalent of applying a red filter to your lens. For indoor portraits and scenes, if there's not enough detail in the red channel, you might have better luck with the blue or green channel instead.

2 Filter Out Green and Blue

With the **Red** channel selected in the **Layers** palette, select **Enhance**, **Adjust Lighting**, **Levels** from the menu bar.

In the **Levels** dialog box, enable the **Preview** check box so that you can see the effect the changes you are making have on the image. From the **Channel** drop-down list at the top of the dialog box, select **Green**. For the **Output Levels** settings, in the second text box (where it currently says **255**), enter **0**. Immediately, your image should look pink and purple.

From the **Channel** drop-down list, select **Blue**, and in the second **Output Levels** text box, enter **0**. You should now be seeing your image as though you were wearing red-tinted glasses.

3 Adjust Levels to Build Contrast

In the **Levels** dialog box (you didn't click **OK** yet, did you?), from the **Channel** drop-down list, select **RGB**. Looking at the *histogram* in the middle of the dialog box, adjust the black and white pointers, if necessary, so that they point to the edges of the graph.

Slide the gray pointer (the one in the middle of the histogram) on the graph to the *left*, and watch your image as you do. You should notice that the middle tones become lighter, while the brightest and darkest tones remain with little or no change. As you slide the pointer to the left, you increase the RGB channel's *gamma*—the rate at which the gradation from black to gray speeds up, and from which the gradation from gray to white slows down. With the gamma pointer more to the left, pixels in the image tend to become brighter *faster*. *Now* click **OK**.

4 Apply Unsharp Mask

To create sharper edges and brighter highlights that remain crisp without becoming blocky, use the **Unsharp Mask** *filter*. From the menu bar, select **Filter**, **Sharpen**, **Unsharp Mask**. In the **Unsharp Mask** dialog box, set **Amount** to **100%**. It can be more, but we don't want to create halos around the bounce-light areas. Set

Radius to **3.0** pixels. This setting brightens some of the brightest spots without making them *larger* or extending them into the mid-tones and shadows. Finally, set **Threshold** to **25** levels. This is a low setting—any lower, and we'd over-*darken* the shadows; any higher, and we'd lose detail in areas like the leaves of the trees. We don't want to convert them into big clubs. Click **OK**.

5 **Remove Red Tint**

Now let's start the process of removing the red tint from the image. From the menu bar, select **Enhance, Adjust Color, Remove Color**. For the time being, your image will appear to be murky gray.

6 **Adjust Levels to Restore Balance**

From the menu bar, select **Enhance, Auto Levels**. This command performs the same magic as balancing the histogram (**Levels**), restoring full luminance to the white points. What had been the brightest red on your earlier red-tinted layer is now the brightest white in your image.

7 **View the Result**

After you're satisfied with the result, make any other changes you want and save the PSD file. Resave the result in JPEG or TIFF format, leaving your PSD image with its layers intact so that you can return at a later time and make different adjustments if you want.

The best black-and-white images have clearly discernable bright and dark areas, even if the subject matter is a darkened room or a bright day in the park. Film developers understand this and apply their skills in the darkroom to give images the appropriate contrasts, even when the film lacks it. What you've done here is set the range of contrast from the darkest possible to the brightest possible shade of gray, made your middle hues brighter, and the contrasts between all three groups of shades crisper. All these elements generally define the best *technically* composed monochrome images.

 TIP

As you drag the gray pointer on the histogram, notice that you're creating three zones of relative brightness within your image—well-defined darks, well-defined brights, and midtones. The middle value under **Input Levels** increases as you slide left. You'll want to drop the gray pointer at a location far to the left of a realistic setting for an undamaged color image—probably at **2.00** or higher.

177 Create a Negative Image

Before You Start

✔ **46** Open an Image for Editing

✔ **91** About Layers and the Layers Palette

See Also

→ **176** Change a Color Photograph to Black and White

Why would you want a negative image? There are interesting photo effects you can achieve with a negative. For example, a negative of a black-and-white image of a subject's face can be filtered to create an embossed effect, which you can cut and paste on the top of a coin shape. (Imagine your son's head on the nickel!) Negative layers can also be combined with *layers* beneath using a subtractive *blend mode* such as **Difference**, for instance, to create effects where a ghost of a person appears in the sky. Being able to "negate" an image becomes a useful utility when you're working to create new and unique effects.

1 **Open the Image in the Editor**

Open an image in the *Editor* in **Standard Edit** mode and save it in Photoshop (*****.psd**) format.

2 **Select Layer to Negate**

In the **Layers** *palette*, click the layer whose image you want to make negative. If the image has only one layer, or has recently been imported from a digital camera or file, this should be the *Background layer*.

3 **Choose Invert**

From the menu bar, select **Filter**, **Adjustments**, **Invert**. Immediately, the Editor negates the pixels in the chosen layer. For a black-and-white layer, obviously, the light pixels become as dark as they were light previously, and vice versa. For a color layer, the resulting pixel colors are mathematical inverses of their original values. For example, if a pixel is entirely red (RGB {255, 0, 0}), the negated pixel becomes entirely cyan (RGB {0, 255, 255}). Mathematically speaking, the values of each of the pixel's existing color channels are subtracted from 255. So, a midtone such as RGB {135, 48, 201} becomes RGB {120, 207, 54}.

NOTE

You see more about how to use the **Gaussian Blur** filter in **151** **Blur a Background to Create Depth of Field**.

4 **View the Result**

After you're satisfied with the result, make any other changes you want and save the PSD file. Resave the result in JPEG or TIFF format, leaving your PSD image with its layers intact so that you can return at a later time and make different adjustments if you want.

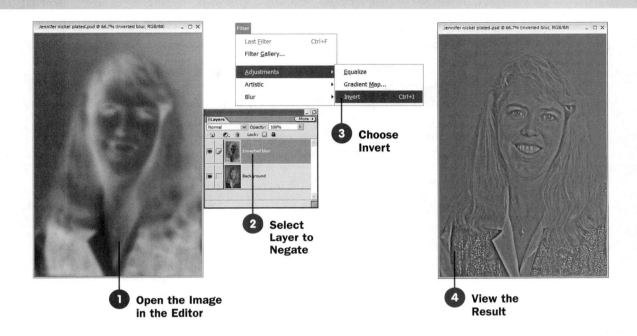

3 Choose Invert

2 Select Layer to Negate

1 Open the Image in the Editor

4 View the Result

Is there someone in your life whose face you think should be embossed on a coin? An inverted portrait might not on the surface look like something sculpted. But when you play with the lighting effects and use *blend modes* to merge the result back with the original photo, you can easily achieve a "nickel plating" effect.

Here's how I nickel-plated my wife: I took her publicity photo and made a duplicate layer. I then applied a heavy Gaussian blur to the duplicate layer only by selecting the duplicate layer in the **Layers** palette, selecting **Filter**, **Blur**, **Gaussian Blur**, choosing a **Radius** value that makes her look as she would if I were squinting at her (in this case, **10** pixels), and clicking **OK**. I then inverted the blurred layer by selecting **Filter**, **Adjustments**, **Invert**, as described in this task. Finally, with the inverted layer still chosen in the **Layers** palette, I set its blend mode to **Vivid Light**. The effect is to desaturate everything *except* those parts of the blurred layer that contrast with the untouched **Background** layer beneath it.

 NOTE

Because of the way the **Vivid Light** blend mode works when blending a layer with its own inverse (or, in this case, near inverse), a flat background like the one in this example is assured to have an average color of 50% gray (RGB {128, 128, 128}). This makes it easy for you to create a new image with a flat, 50% gray background (perhaps with a slight amount of noise added), and then in the newly embossed image, select the area around the head, feather the selection, cut it out, and paste it in the new image seamlessly.

178 Colorize a Photograph

Before You Start

✔ **76** Select Areas of Similar Color

✔ **84** Save a Selection for Reuse

✔ **94** Create an Adjustment Layer

✔ **150** Blur an Image to Remove Noise

See Also

→ **176** Change a Color Photograph to Black and White

NOTE

Every black-and-white photo you colorize will need some preparatory work before you proceed. One preparation I *avoided* was the *histogram* adjustment (handled in Photoshop Elements with the **Levels** command), which tends to make the lights lighter and darks darker. It's more difficult to colorize a white or black region than a middle gray region—or, more accurately, it's more difficult to notice the colorization.

There is no automatic method for colorizing a black-and-white photo. Neither Photoshop Elements nor any other program thus far constructed would be capable of discerning for itself just what you want to colorize and just what colors you want to apply. This is a task that requires extra measures of patience and skill on the part of the artist (that's you), although the process itself is relatively easy to explain.

That said, there's no perfect way to truly convert a black-and-white photograph—especially an old one—into an image that's both colorfully rich and colorfully accurate. So, you have to concede at the outset that what you're working on is an artistic interpretation. You know you're not going to achieve 100% photo-realism, so you try to chalk up the difference to artistic license. What you want to avoid, however, is a paint-by-number look that resembles having cut out translucent, colored acetate strips and taped them over the original image. Avoiding this look can be difficult because there is no single colorizing hue you can choose that represents "flesh tones" for everyone's color of skin.

1 Select the Region to Colorize

Open the image in the *Editor* in **Standard Edit** mode and save it in Photoshop (***.psd**) format. With the *Background layer* selected in the **Layers** *palette*, choose **Layer**, **Duplicate Layer** from the menu bar. Name the new *layer* **Colorized**.

With the **Colorized** layer selected, from the **Toolbox**, choose a selection tool. In the image, select and enclose a region of the image which should be primarily one color. This could be a solid-colored article of clothing, a portion of an object, or an exposed part of the body, such as the head and neck together, an arm, or a leg. Subtle color variations within these regions, or smaller regions such as eyes, teeth, lips, or jewelry that require major variations can be handled later. Right now, you're selecting the broader region that will receive general colorizing with a single hue.

To make it easier to make alterations to this same region should you require them later (or just so that you don't accidentally lose the selection), use the process discussed in **84** **Save a Selection for Reuse** to save the selection to the image's *alpha channel*.

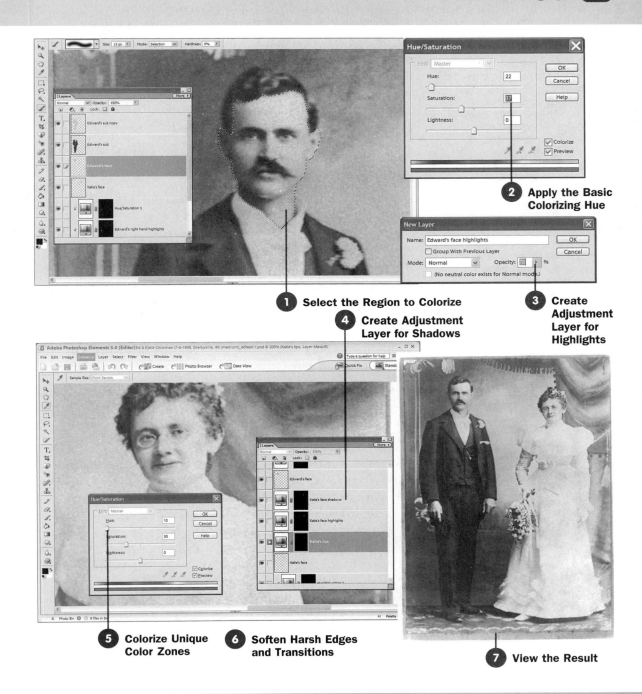

1 Select the Region to Colorize

2 Apply the Basic Colorizing Hue

3 Create Adjustment Layer for Highlights

4 Create Adjustment Layer for Shadows

5 Colorize Unique Color Zones

6 Soften Harsh Edges and Transitions

7 View the Result

TIP

For quickly selecting regions of similar skin tone within a subject's face, hands, or some other part of the body, you might find the **Magic Wand** tool the handiest. See **76** Select Areas of Similar Color for an introduction to this tool. But if you're colorizing a subject whose face is set against a background whose luminance value isn't much different from values at the edge of the face, you could end up selecting part face and part wall. To avoid this hassle, start by selecting the entire face with the **Lasso Tool** or **Magnetic Lasso Tool** first, and then cutting that selection into a new layer. Select the layer, and then use the **Magic Wand** tool to select portions of that layer. The wand cannot grab any pixels that are outside the current layer.

For selected regions that might later have extra color zones applied on top of existing colorization, you'll find it easier to promote those selections to full layers. With the region selected in the image window, select the **Colorized** layer in the **Layers** palette. From the menu bar, select **Layer, New, Layer via Copy**. In the **Layers** palette, double-click the name of the new layer (generally **Layer 1**), type a new name (such as **Edward's Face**), and press **Enter**.

② Apply the Basic Colorizing Hue

From the menu bar, select **Enhance, Adjust Color, Adjust Hue/Saturation**. In the **Hue/Saturation** dialog box that opens, enable the **Preview** check box so that you can see the effects of your changes in the actual image, and also enable the **Colorize** check box. This second check box converts the purpose of the dialog box so that the **Hue** value you choose refers to a specific color. In this rainbow system based on *geometric angular degrees* on the color wheel, **0** and values in the vicinity of **0** refer to reds, progressing to orange as values increase. Yellows are around **45**, vivid greens around **90**, cyans at **150**, deep blues at **220**, purples at **290**, before the cycle returns to pinks by **340** and vivid reds at **360**.

Set the **Hue** slider to the basic hue you want to apply to the region. Set the **Saturation** slider to a value representing how much of this hue to apply to the region.

What you're determining here is the object's basic "shade." There is no single hue that represents "flesh tones," although the **Hue** value you're searching for is probably from **10** to **18** for Caucasian skin tones, **16** to **26** for African and Middle Eastern skin tones, or **26** to **32** for Asian skin tones. Darker skin requires heavier *Saturation* values than lighter skin; usually, you need to saturate Caucasian skin by no more than **20**, whereas for African skin, you might require as much as **40**. There are exceptions to these scales, as was the case with this particular example, where I applied a ruddier brown hue to the man's skin shade—a **22** rather than an **18**. A very slight **Lightness** adjustment of no more than **+5** might be necessary when applying heavy saturation in a scene with direct sunlight.

When the image reflects the hue you want to apply to the selected area, click **OK**.

❸ Create Adjustment Layer for Highlights

For solid objects, fabric, or background elements, a single hue might be all that's required for the selected area. But for skin tones, to complete the illusion, you should adjust those portions that reflect the most light (what artists call the "light" areas) to imply more yellow, and the darker portions to tint downward to slightly cooler tones. The result of these manipulations gives the skin some shape and depth.

Here's how to use tinting to create the illusion of shape on a face: In the **Layers** palette, select the **Face** layer you created earlier. To select just the bright regions of the object you just colorized, from the **Toolbox**, choose the **Magic Wand** tool. On the **Options** bar, enable the **Anti-aliased** and **Contiguous** options and set the **Tolerance** option to a medium-low value above **0**—I do well with **16** for brightly lit faces, **8** or less for dimly lit ones. In the image window, click on just the brightest or chalkiest region of the object until the *marquee* encloses only the bright spots, not the middle values or shadows. These spots generally reflect the greatest amount of light—for a face, the sides of the cheek facing the sun, the tip of the nose, the front of the forehead. For a solid object, select the areas that reflect the most direct light or that include glares or streaks.

From the menu bar, select **Layer, New Adjustment Layer, Hue/Saturation** to create an *adjustment layer* that will modify the hue you just applied in the newly selected areas. In the **New Layer** dialog box, enter a unique and descriptive name for your adjustment layer, such as **Face highlights**. Set the blend **Mode** to **Lighten**, and **Opacity** to a value between **66%** and **100%**, proportional to how much light there is on the subject. (With the earliest photographs, subjects were often *extremely* brightly lit.) Click **OK**.

In the **Hue/Saturation** dialog box that opens, *disable* the **Colorize** check box. We want to change the tint of this region *relative to its current hue*, rather than choosing a specific hue from a color wheel. Depending on the strength of the light, set the **Hue** slider to a value from **16** to **21**. This will add a more yellow tint to the selected region. If necessary, *reduce* the **Lightness** value by setting it to a value no lower than **–3** to prevent the yellower patch from standing out too prominently. Click **OK**.

💡 TIP

If you're working with a low-resolution image, when you select a region with the **Lasso** tool, there's a greater possibility that the edges of your selection will be chunky or blocky. When you apply color, the result might look like you've painted the side of a staircase. However, when you set the **Feather** option of the **Lasso** tool to a value above **0** pixels, there's an equal possibility that selections along the edge of the subject's flesh might cause a foggy mist of color to be applied *outside* the flesh boundaries, or it might leave a foggy mist of gray border *inside* the flesh boundaries. For best anti-aliasing results, make sure that you enable the **Lasso** tool's **Anti-aliased** check box, but also use **Select, Modify, Smooth** to remove the chunkiness from your edges.

NOTE

You might be thinking, why not just use the **Eyedropper** tool to absorb skin tone colors from an image in the real world? That might make sense if everybody's skin were a flat color. For colorized images, everybody's skin *is* a flat color—but in the real world, skin tones are made up of combinations of pixel patterns that the eye blends to make flesh tones. If you were to apply the **Eyedropper** tool onto even a well-photographed image, there's a possibility you might pick up a shade that's strangely greener than you know skin to be.

TIP

When using a selection tool such as the **Lasso** to select more than one region of an image, you must make your selection in multiple parts. The best way to prevent your second selection from canceling out your first selection is by clicking the **Add to Selection** button in the **Options** bar for the selection tool. See **79** Add Areas Similar to the Current Selection for details.

4 Create Adjustment Layer for Shadows

Choose **Select, Deselect** from the menu bar to clear the current selection. To select the "shadow" regions—the dark parts of the skin that face away from the light—click the **Magic Wand** tool and leave its options as you set them in step 3. Click with the tool to select the darker regions of the colorized object. For a face, these would include the underside of the nose, the rim of the face, the unlit side of the cheeks, the shadows cast by sockets over the eyes and, most notably, the chin over the neck when the chin is prominent.

From the menu bar, select **Layer, New Adjustment Layer, Hue/Saturation** to create an adjustment layer that will modify the hue in the selected shadow areas. In the **New Layer** dialog box, enter a unique and descriptive name for the adjustment layer, such as **Face shadows**. Set the blend **Mode** to **Darken**, and leave **Opacity** set to **100%**. Click **OK**.

In the **Hue/Saturation** dialog box that opens, disable the **Colorize** check box. We want to tilt the hue on the color wheel so that it points to a color that has the opposite optical characteristics of the basic color you applied in step 2. For face colors, I've often found the optimum spot to be on or around the following: **Hue: +43** (slide the **Hue** slider to the right of **0**), **Saturation: –50** (slide **Saturation** to the left of **0**), and **Lightness: –5**. Click **OK**.

5 Colorize Unique Color Zones

Unique features such as blue eyes and red lips should be handled separately. With the **Colorized** layer active in the **Layers** palette, select the entire unique color zone with the **Lasso** tool and then select **Enhance, Adjust Color, Adjust Hue/Saturation** from the menu bar. In the **Hue/Saturation** dialog box, enable the **Colorize** check box. For eyeballs (excluding the *pupil*) and teeth, you can achieve the effect you want by reducing **Saturation** to a value *near but above* **0**. Natural lips generally require a **Hue** setting of about **10** for Caucasian and **14** for African and Asian; **Saturation** should be set to around **30**. Click **OK** to continue.

Repeat steps 1 through 5 for as many objects in your image as require colorization. Sometimes, you can get away with not colorizing every object in your image. In my example, for instance, some of the objects in the background didn't particularly warrant color. As far back as the 16th century, hand-painted aquatint lithographs of famous paintings originally done in oil often omitted any colorized pigment in certain regions of the print that were deemed less important. Surprisingly, faces were often left gray and barren, while the clothes or the chair on which the subject was seated were lovingly embellished with the finest transparent inks.

6 Soften Harsh Edges and Transitions

One of the unwanted side effects of colorizing elements that are adjacent to one another—for instance, a person's neck and a blouse's neckline—is the appearance of harsh borders. This can be easily eradicated with a quick and mild application of the **Blur** tool. See **150** **Blur an Image to Remove Noise** for instructions for using this tool.

7 View the Result

After you're satisfied with the result, make any other changes you want and save the PSD file. Resave the result in JPEG or TIFF format, leaving your PSD image with its *layers* intact so that you can return at a later time and make different adjustments if you want.

For this example, I scanned an original photograph of the newly wedded Mr. & Mrs. Edward Chrisman of Shelbyville, Indiana, taken in 1898. Here, I discovered that male and female skin tones, set next to one another, should perhaps vary to give the image maximum character. When two faces side-by-side with one another have exactly the same color, the mind naturally suspects something fishy, even if the subjects are twins. In the case of the dashing groom, I gave his basic skin shade a **Hue** value of **22**, which is more toward the *green* side of the color wheel than the beautiful bride, to whom I gave a **Hue** shade of **13**. But neither face looks realistic, or even well colorized, when these chosen hues are applied over the entire skin area. So, for the shadow areas, I applied hue adjustment layers on top of the basic skin shades.

Mr. Chrisman's suit proved to be a challenge. Supposedly, it's already black, but how do you colorize a black suit so that it looks *naturally* black instead of monochromatic—like it was cut out of a newspaper? The secret I employed is borrowed from the realm of impressionist painting: I colorized the layer with a gushing,

NOTE

An adjustment layer limits its effects to a specified region of an image by way of a tool Photoshop CS users know quite well: a *mask*. By creating a mask for itself, an adjustment layer cordons off areas of an image, preventing them from being adjusted. This is how adjustment layers such as **Face highlights**, in this example, restrict themselves to selected parts of an image. See **94** **Create an Adjustment Layer** for specific details on how to use this feature.

TIP

When using the **Hue/Saturation** dialog box to colorize the lips of a woman in your image, you might want to give her some lipstick. Ruby-red lipstick requires a **Hue** setting of around **5** and **Saturation** turned up to **40**. You can experiment with other shades at your leisure.

saturated *purple* tint, and then applied on top of it a duplicate layer of *bright orange* (purple's opposite) to pick up the brighter spots. I gave the orange layer the **Overlay** blend mode and an **Opacity** setting of **30%** so that no visible pixels actually ended up being orange. But the lighter colors of the suit are made warmer, while the medium colors remain icy cool. And because the two colors are optical opposites, the eyes cancel out most of their interplay with each other, with the exception of those tones that are warmer and cooler than the middle section. The result is a suit that looks like *black silk* rather than black coal. Look for this image in the Color Gallery.

179 Make a Photograph Look Like an Oil Painting

Before You Start

✔ **91** About Layers and the Layers Palette

✔ **92** Create a New Image Layer

✔ **102** Merge or Flatten Layers into One

See Also

→ **180** Turn a Photograph into a Watercolor

→ **181** Make a Photograph Look Like It Was Drawn

Adobe Photoshop Elements offers several *filters* that purport to make a digital photo look like it was hand-rendered, including some that simulate painting with oil or acrylics. Although these filters do mechanically simulate brushstrokes on canvas, the challenge is to use them to make a photo look like a painted *composition*.

I know more than a little bit about painting composition. As an artist myself, I was taught by my mother, Maria DeLaJuen, who was a professional artist and instructor for 47 years. Throughout my life, I witnessed literally hundreds of masterworks in the act of creation, from inception through the final application of varnish. So, I know how a painting is *composed*. My challenge is, could I come up with a method for giving any photo the illusion of professional composition? The way I discovered this method was using an original DeLaJuen painting and the real digital photo on which that painting was based. Applying Adobe filters to the photo, could I modify it to reasonably resemble a professional composition?

① Create Underpainting Layer

Open the image in the *Editor* in **Standard Edit** mode and save it in Photoshop (***.psd**) format. With the *Background layer* selected in the **Layers** *palette*, select **Layer**, **Duplicate Layer**. Name this new layer **Underpainting** and click **OK**.

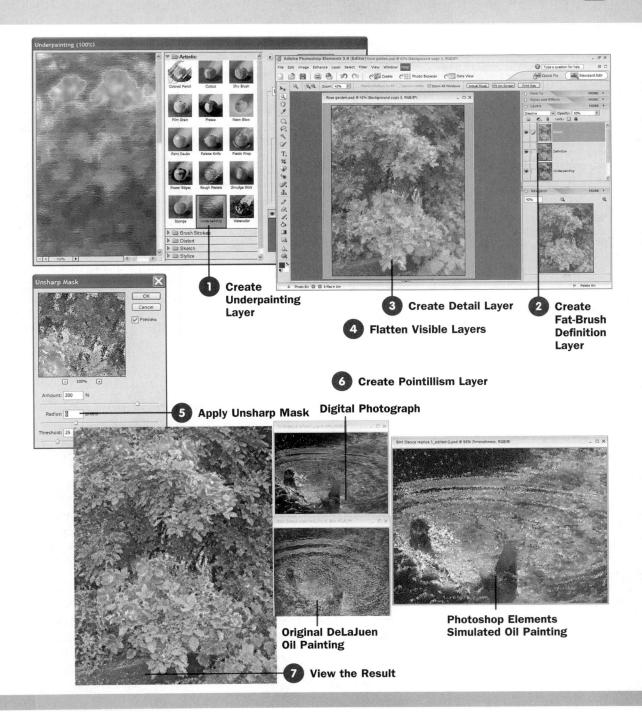

1 Create Underpainting Layer

3 Create Detail Layer

2 Create Fat-Brush Definition Layer

4 Flatten Visible Layers

6 Create Pointillism Layer

5 Apply Unsharp Mask

Digital Photograph

Original DeLaJuen Oil Painting

Photoshop Elements Simulated Oil Painting

7 View the Result

The **Underpainting** filter creates spotty areas where lighter, chalkier colors appear flat, whereas clearer, more transparent colors are given a simulated canvas texture. It's a clever idea because whiter colors are almost always "piled on" a painting using a white blending medium, and midtones such as Terre Verde green are usually brushed on with paint mixed with copal or thinned by turpentine.

Among the other options for the **Underpainting** filter are settings that determine how the simulated underlying texture should appear. I happen to like the default **Canvas** texture, although there's also **Brick**, **Burlap**, and **Sandstone**. All four textures are simulated digitally, not just with overlapping patterns. The **Scaling** setting is a percentage that governs the size of your texture's grain, whereas **Relief** is a relative value that varies the darkness used to imply the grain—a higher number darkens the texture, but too high a number interferes with the content. You also have a choice of **Light** source, expressed as a general direction (such as **Top**); the **Invert** option, for what it's worth, applies the opposite of the basic texture pattern, so that pits become heaps and vice versa.

One genuine method for producing a pointillistic oil painting is to start with applying what Maria would call a "soup" of slippery, wet, opaque paint in fat, general regions. Detail is something you apply *last*, which is why detail should look like it's painted *on top*. Underpainting is what the detail is on top of. I can mimic an underpainting layer by applying a filter to a duplicate of the **Background** layer; I'll add other layers to provide the detail I want in the final image.

With the **Underpainting** layer selected in the **Layers** palette, select **Filter**, **Artistic**, **Underpainting** from the menu bar. In the dialog box, set **Brush Size** to a low value, such as **7**, and set **Texture Coverage** to a middle value, such as **20**. From the **Texture** list, choose **Canvas**. The **Relief** setting affects how "soupy" your underpainting layer will appear. Experiment first with a low value for high "soupiness," such as **8**, and check the sample area at the left side of the dialog box for effectiveness. You'll want some of the canvas texture to show through, so a higher **Relief** setting will reveal more canvas but will also look like you're using a drier brush. Click **OK** to continue.

② Create Fat-Brush Definition Layer

With a real oil painting, after your underpainting is complete, one genuine composition method has you using a fat, loaded brush to add some distinct, defined brush strokes. Unlike underpainting, where you're painting "zones," here you want your brushstrokes to look like strokes. I can do that with the **Glass** filter.

To create a defined brushstroke layer, duplicate the **Background** layer once again. Name this new layer **Definition**. In the **Layers** palette, drag **Definition** and drop it above the **Underpainting** layer you filtered earlier. For now, this will obscure the layer you just edited; later, *blend modes* will let portions of that filtered copy show through.

Make sure that the **Definition** layer is selected and choose **Filter**, **Distort**, **Glass** from the menu bar. The ostensible purpose of the **Glass** filter is to simulate the appearance of your scene as through a glass block, or through an antique, handmade glass pane. For our purposes, it simulates the watery shimmer of a slippery coat of wet paint. In the dialog box, set **Distortion** to **3**, **Smoothness** to **3**, and choose **Canvas** from the **Texture** drop-down list. Any higher settings would make the layer look too much like glass, and not enough like wet paint. Click **OK**.

The key here is blending the **Definition** layer with the **Underpainting** layer so that elements of both show through effectively. There are two ways of doing this that produce genuine results, but your choice of methods depends on your approach to the composition. Here is where artistic license starts to come into play. With the **Definition** layer still selected in the **Layers** palette, you can do either of the following:

- Set the blend mode to **Overlay**. The result will be stark, bright contrasts, which can be lovely although they can also be startling. You could reduce the **Opacity** setting to **66%** or more to soften the effect of the definition layer.

- Set the blend mode to **Dissolve** and the **Opacity** setting to between **66%** and **75%**. These settings let the original color of the underpainting layer show through the definition layer in places, without creating extra brightness. Use this blend mode if you want to retain more of your original image's natural color. With the **Dissolve** blend mode, you get a grittier texture, which is quite believable. If you prefer this grittier texture but also like brighter colors, select **Enhance, Adjust Color, Adjust Hue/Saturation** from the menu bar. In the dialog box, set **Saturation** to **+40**. You can also experiment with raising the **Lightness** value up to **+26**. Click **OK**.

③ Create Detail Layer

Once again, duplicate the **Background** layer, and name this new copy **Detail**. In the **Layers** palette, drag the **Detail** layer and drop it above the **Definition** layer.

For the full effect, you want to skew the color of this layer a little bit. Select **Enhance, Adjust Color, Adjust Hue/Saturation**. In the dialog box, set **Hue** to **–8** (no more, no less), **Saturation** to a medium value such as **+50**, and **Lightness** up a few ticks, such as **+10**. Click **OK**.

Next, select **Filter, Brush Strokes, Sprayed Strokes** from the menu bar. In the dialog box, set the **Stroke Length** to **16**, **Spray Radius** to **7**, and **Stroke Direction** to **Right Diagonal** (or **Left Diagonal** if

NOTE

Well-composed oil paintings often include exaggerated bright tones, including *very* brightly colored brushstrokes whose impact on the viewer is softened when opposite colored strokes are placed next to one another.

TIP

In painting, "detail" is often the chalky whites that are piled on top of the definition layer to make edges more distinct and to help objects appear more distinguished from one another.

you'd rather simulate the work of a left-handed artist). Notice in the sample that the definition of this layer is not radically disturbed. We're trying to simulate the tendency for oil brushstrokes to have some direction independent of their content. This layer will demonstrate that tendency *too much*; but the plan is to blend this layer with the other layers so that the direction shows through only in larger patches of similar color. To finalize these filter choices, click **OK**.

In the **Layers** palette, with the **Detail** layer still selected, set the blend mode to **Dissolve** and **Opacity** to between **50%** and **66%**.

At this point, you might already have a very convincing simulated composition. *You could stop here.* But if you intend for your final product to look large, like a mural, rather than small and quaint, there are a few more steps you can take to achieve the room-size effect.

 TIP

If the **Dissolve** blend mode is leaving too many small dots for you to make out the image, here's an alternative that works with *some* compositions—not all, but especially scenes with bold contrasts, such as sunlit tree trunks: Set the blend mode for the **Detail** layer to **Soft Light** and leave **Opacity** at **100%**.

④ Flatten Visible Layers

From the menu bar, select **Layer**, **Flatten Image**. Your image might change slightly because you'll lose a small degree of the **Dissolve** effect, as the two dissolve blend modes are merged into one. Don't fret too much.

⑤ Apply Unsharp Mask

From the menu bar, select **Filter**, **Sharpen**, **Unsharp Mask**. This command removes some of the pixellation from the various **Dissolve** blend modes and also simulates the richer and more saturated colors of an oil painter, rather than the subtler and more photographic palette of the camera. In the **Unsharp Mask** dialog box, the setting you give the **Amount** value depends on whether you want to add or remove color contrast. To add contrasts and make the darks bolder and the lights more pastel, set **Amount** in the range between **100%** and **200%**. To reduce contrasts, letting the composition be quieter and gentler, set **Amount** between **50%** and **100%**.

 NOTE

Higher **Threshold** settings diminish the canvas effect and return the image to photorealism—which you actually don't want—whereas settings below **10** create too much contrast along the edges and introduce strange colors you might not want.

Set the **Radius** option to a value between **4** and **10** pixels, the higher setting creating a "fatter pile." Experiment with **Threshold** settings between **10** and **30** pixels. Click **OK**.

6 Create Pointillism Layer

With the **Background** layer selected in the **Layers** palette, select **Layer**, **Duplicate Layer**. No, we're not starting all over again. Name this new layer **Pointillism**. We need to add a touch of randomness to this composition.

From the menu bar, select **Filter**, **Brush Strokes**, **Accented Edges**. In the dialog box, set **Edge Width** to **2**, **Edge Brightness** to **32**, and **Smoothness** to **5**. This particular window of settings for this filter creates regions of color with bright surrounding edges, almost like paint flecks that are fading and chipping off. Click **OK**.

Now, you have a choice of blend mode effects depending again on what elements of this composition *you* feel are most important:

- With the **Pointillism** layer selected in the **Layers** palette, set the blend mode to **Dissolve** and **Opacity** to **25%**. These settings enable one-fourth of the points in this accented layer to show through at full strength, looking very much like tiny points applied by palette knife at the end of the composition.

- Set the blend mode to **Soft Light** and **Opacity** to **50%**. These settings result in a smoother effect, as though no palette knife were applied, but with the brush strokes fatter and more boldly defined.

- Set the blend mode to **Multiply** and **Opacity** to **50%**. These settings bring back many of the dark tones that might have been eliminated earlier, and might reintroduce some realistic variegation among the brush strokes that, for some compositions, will be more balanced and pleasing.

7 View the Result

After you're satisfied with the result, make any other changes you want and save the PSD file. Resave the result in JPEG or TIFF format, leaving your PSD image with its layers intact so that you can return at a later time and make different adjustments if you want.

The objective of this method is not to produce oil paintings by "fudging" photographs. Instead, it's to easily enhance a photo and commemorate the beauty of its subject matter by recasting it in a light reminiscent of a real oil composition.

In discovering the methodology for simulating components of a real oil painting as best I could, I had the benefit of owning an original painting of Maria's whose composition is based on a real digital photo she took in her backyard. The figure shows the digital photograph Maria took, the painting she made using that photo as inspiration, and the simulated oil painting I made with Photoshop Elements.

In the Color Gallery, you'll notice the effects much more readily, such as how the simulated oil painting manages to mimic the painter's oversaturated palette. Bright blues appeared in the water rings right where Maria put them, and the juxtaposition of the bright blue rings with the gold flecks reflecting the rocks from under the surface of the water reflects a pointillistic palette style that is *not* representative of the photorealistic palette in the example markeed **Digital Photograph**. The water splashes from the bird's wings follow the direction of the splash, which is unexpected.

What's missing from the simulation are *identifying details*. It's hard to see, for instance, the birds' eyes. Maria would add the eyes as solid entities, irrespective of the head patterns around them, so that the mind can more readily identify the subjects as birds. If the simulation can't isolate birds' eyes, you can imagine how it would also lose detail from human faces, even close up.

NOTE

Portraits are the most difficult subjects to simulate as oil paintings. The randomization that Adobe's filters use to produce simulated brush strokes can be excused when the subject matter is leaves or water, but people are usually painted more deliberately. Your mind will treat random brushstrokes in facial details as *errors*. So, the best candidates for painting simulations are landscapes, where the people—if any—are small, in the distance, and have their full bodies showing.

---

180 **Turn a Photograph into a Watercolor**

Before You Start

✔ **73** Draw a Selection Freehand

✔ **77** Paint a Selection

✔ **82** Soften the Edge of a Selection

✔ **93** Create a Layer Filled with a Color, Gradient, or Pattern

✔ **146** Adjust Hue, Saturation, and Lightness Manually

The secret to enabling Photoshop Elements to generate a simulation of a watercolor from a photograph is to present it with a photograph that looks like a watercolor to begin with. A snapshot of the family hugging Donald Duck in front of Epcot Center simply isn't a candidate, nor particularly are any photos where *people* are the predominant subjects. Instead, you want still, wistful scenes whose latent patterns—the effects beneath the surface—can be exploited by the paintbrush. The *Editor's* simulation of watercolor strokes is simply unconvincing for the everyday photograph, but can be striking when reprocessing an image that's prepared well ahead of time to receive the watercolor treatment.

Different watercolor techniques apply to differing styles of compositions. To make an image that convincingly looks like it was produced by a watercolor artist, your composition should look not only like watercolor *paint* was used to make it, but watercolor *technique* as well. The Asian watercolor technique is minimalist, and suits itself to very simple renderings such as a directly lit portrait against a neutral background, or in the case of the example used here, dark trees on very bright snow. This technique uses very few pigments—generally black, terre verde (green), raw umber (brown), perhaps cobalt blue (although not in this example), and very few others. The key here is to make the image look like it was *simply* produced, carefully and quietly, in places by dragging a tapered-tip brush through a patch painted ahead of time with clear water.

① Create Composition and Paper Layers

To begin, open the image in the Editor in **Standard Edit** mode and save it in Photoshop (*.psd) format. With the *Background layer* selected in the **Layers** *palette*, select **Layer, Duplicate Layer**. Name the new *layer* **Composition**. This layer is where the basic alterations will be made.

Select the **Background** layer again. This time, select **Layer, New Fill Layer, Solid Color**. In the **New Layer** dialog box, type **Paper** as the layer's name. Click **OK**.

New layers, by default, are transparent. For this **Paper** layer to be useful, it must be fully opaque—generally pure white, but perhaps a light pastel. Choose a paper color from the **Color Picker** that opens automatically and click **OK**.

② Remove Unwanted Elements

We need to remove any unwanted material that appears on the **Composition** layer, especially portions of things like halves of flowers or sides of barns. On the **Layers** palette, choose the **Composition** layer. From the **Toolbox**, click the **Lasso** tool. On the **Options** bar, set **Feather** to a reasonably high value, from **25** to **40** pixels for an image with 150 *PPI*, or higher if your image's resolution is higher. With your wrist loose and your elbow free in the air, make a sweeping loop around everything in your image that you want to *include*. When the loop is complete, choose **Select, Inverse** from the menu bar to invert the selection. Then press **Delete** to delete all the background elements, revealing the **Paper** layer beneath. The image should now have a fuzzy, white or pastel background.

See Also

→ **179** Make a Photograph Look Like an Oil Painting

→ **181** Make a Photograph Look Like It Was Drawn

NOTE

For true watercolor painting techniques, detail is reserved exclusively for the smallest possible areas of foreground matter, whereas the background is produced with iridescent washes. Rarely is every inch of the paper filled; often, the best watercolor compositions make good use of empty space to produce a pleasing, ethereal background.

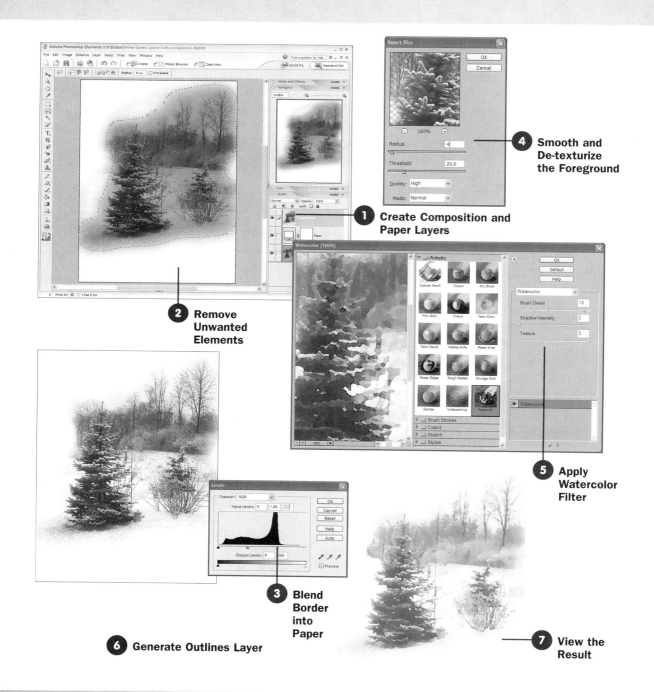

1 Create Composition and Paper Layers

2 Remove Unwanted Elements

3 Blend Border into Paper

4 Smooth and De-texturize the Foreground

5 Apply Watercolor Filter

6 Generate Outlines Layer

7 View the Result

③ Blend Border into Paper

Cancel any active selections you have open: Choose **Select**, **Deselect** from the menu bar. In the **Layers** palette, choose the **Composition** layer. From the menu bar, select **Enhance**, **Adjust Lighting**, **Levels**. In the **Levels** dialog box, slide the white pointer to the left until you can no longer detect the feathered border you generated when you created the **Composition** layer. Click **OK**.

④ Smooth and De-texturize the Foreground

The texture of the foreground matter must be eliminated, removing the photographic look and leaving a smooth, polished appearance. Choose the **Composition** layer and select **Filter**, **Noise**, **Dust & Scratches** from the menu bar. In the dialog box, set **Radius** to 2—a very low setting indeed, but you don't lose detail in the process—and **Threshold** to 35. Here, we're trying to isolate areas to make them look as though they could have been produced with single brushstrokes. Click **OK**.

For this Asian technique, the brushstrokes are generally more representative of *outlines* or *textures* rather than areas. So you don't have to reduce the texture too much to make the existing lines look as though they can be produced with contiguous strokes. From the menu bar, select **Filter**, **Blur**, **Smart Blur**. In the dialog box, set **Radius** to **4.0**, and set **Threshold** to **20.0**. These settings generate edges that are crisp and smooth—a higher **Threshold** setting would generate fuzzy edges, and a smaller **Radius** setting would result in the loss of some of the image's character. From the **Quality** drop-down list, choose **High**; from the **Mode** drop-down list, choose **Normal**. Click **OK**.

For this image of the trees, I discovered that the product of using these filters was a bit too dark. With the **Composition** layer chosen, I selected **Enhance**, **Adjust Lighting**, **Levels** and increased the layer's *gamma* to 1.25 by sliding the gray pointer to the left. Click **OK**.

⑤ Apply Watercolor Filter

The highlight of converting an image into a simulated watercolor is...as you might imagine...applying the **Watercolor** *filter*. Here is where the magic really happens. From the **Layers** palette, choose

---

NOTE

The background elements for your composition should have large segments that are relatively free of detail—if not a snowy hillside, perhaps a grassy knoll, a deep and calm ocean, or something as simple as a white wall. If your composition focuses on ground elements, your sky should be cloudless; if it focuses on the sky or has tremendous clouds, consider a serene and nondetailed desert for the ground elements. Whatever your background happens to be, you'll want to boost its levels to such a bright white that you no longer see the feathered border of the **Composition** layer.

TIP

If there's anything you have to "fudge" in the image, now's the time to do it— before you apply the **Watercolor** filer. I used the **Selection Brush** tool (featured in **77** Paint a Selection) to specify small areas of the composition that I wanted gone, such as my neighbor's outdoor sauna peeking through one of the trees. I then used the **Clone Stamp** tool (featured in **162** Remove Unwanted Objects from an Image) to extend a far-off hill in the distance.

---

the **Composition** layer. Then select **Filter, Artistic, Watercolor**.

For the **Watercolor** filter, the **Brush Detail** option should be set to a *high* value (from **12** to **14**) to preserve the clean, smooth edges you've already created. The **Shadow Intensity** value should be left at **0** to avoid the addition of simulated black inks that aren't necessary for this technique. Set **Texture** to its maximum value of **3** to simulate the effects of watercolor paper. Click **OK**.

6 Generate Outlines Layer

The icing on the cake, as it were, is the bordering effect. Bordering actually generates some of the pits where the powder in the pigment bunches up against the edges of the brushstroke, reinforcing the realism of the effect.

From the **Layers** palette, choose the **Composition** layer. From the menu bar, select **Layer, Duplicate Layer**, name the duplicate **Outlines**, and click **OK**.

Select **Filter, Brush Strokes, Accented Edges**. In the **Accented Edges** dialog box, set **Edge Width** to its minimum of **1**. You want a very thin border line along the edges of *some*, not all, of your brushstrokes. Set **Edge Brightness** to **44** (medium light), and **Smoothness** to the medium setting of **8** to eliminate much of the clumping. Our goal is to borrow the paper color (white) to create faint, light distinguishing borders around the brushstroke areas. You can experiment with a medium dark **Brightness** setting of around **12**, if you have a bolder composition; either way, you want some kind of border. Click **OK**; in the **Layers** palette, set the *blend mode* for the **Outline** layer to **Screen**, and **Opacity** to **50%**. (For a dark border, set the blend mode to **Darken** instead.)

7 View the Result

After you're satisfied with the result, make any other changes you want and save the PSD file. Resave the result in **JPEG** or **TIFF** format, leaving your **PSD** image with its layers intact so that you can return at a later time and make different adjustments if you want.

TIP

What truly impresses people, I've discovered, is giving them a greeting card or a message embellished with an attractive piece of artwork. After about 60 seconds, they realize the picture is of a part of their own garden, or their own house, or their own campus. It's the double-take that makes the difference. All of a sudden, it's not just a greeting card with a custom message—it's a piece of the recipient's own life that you're sharing with them, as you demonstrate that (from your perspective) their world is beautiful.

181 Make a Photograph Look Like It Was Drawn

Simulating a pencil sketch using a real digital photo is not so much a process of building a sketch composition based on that photo as it is *undoing* the photo in such a way that it unfolds, like layers of an onion, into a sketch. Photoshop Elements includes several sketching *filters*, but no single filter by itself simulates the composition of a pencil sketch. To pay some homage to the way professional artists sketch, a simulated sketch should be divided into three layers: the foundation, the fuzzy *midtones*, and the hard, dark details.

1 Remove Color from Image

Open the image in the *Editor* in **Standard Edit** mode and save it in Photoshop (**.psd*) format. Using the process outlined in **176** **Change a Color Photograph to Black and White**, convert the image you want to render as a pencil drawing to a black-and-white image. When you're done, the image should have three distinct zones of intensity: heavy darks, middle grays, and lights, grouped unto themselves rather than scattered throughout the image.

2 Create Three Duplicate Layers

If you followed along with **176** **Change a Color Photograph to Black and White**, your image should have two layers, the upper-most of which is called **Red** but isn't red (anymore). In the **Layers** palette, choose the **Red** layer and rename it **Basis**.

Create two more drawing layers by duplicating the **Basis** layer twice. Select **Layer, Duplicate Layer** to do so. In the **Layers** *palette*, from top to bottom, rename the first new layer **Middle values**, and the second one **Dark details**. When you're done, the **Middle values** layer should be on *top*.

Before You Start

✔ **149** Sharpen an Image

✔ **166** Frame a Photograph

✔ **176** Change a Color Photograph to Black and White

See Also

→ **179** Make a Photograph Look Like an Oil Painting

→ **180** Turn a Photograph into a Watercolor

💡 TIP

To ensure that you're dealing with a black pencil on a white page throughout, in the **Toolbox**, click the **Default Colors** box that appears between the fore-ground and background color boxes. Then set the **Foreground** color so that its saturation (**S**) is **0%**, and its brightness (**B**) is **54%**. This is the graphite tone of a #2 pencil.

2 Create Three Duplicate Layers

1 Remove Color from Image

3 Apply Texture to Basis Layer

4 Apply Outlines to Details Layer

5 Compose Smooth Grays for Midtones Layer

6 Apply "Whitewash" Frame

7 View the Result

③ Apply Texture to Basis Layer

For the foundation of the image, we want to apply some fuzzy zones of pigment that appear to be embedding themselves in the grain of the paper. In the **Layers** palette, choose the **Basis** layer. From the menu bar, select **Filter**, **Sketch**, **Water Paper**. In the dialog box, set **Fiber Length** to a medium-high value such as **35**, **Brightness** to a medium value such as **58**, and **Contrast** to a high value such as **80**. The result should look like you used a very soft-lead pencil to zone in the basic areas of the drawing, and then perhaps smudged some of the larger zones with your finger to work them in. Click **OK**. You won't see the results in your main image just yet because they're obscured by two other layers.

④ Apply Outlines to Details Layer

In the **Layers** palette, choose the **Dark details** layer. From the menu bar, select **Filter**, **Brush Strokes**, **Ink Outlines**. In the dialog box, set **Stroke Length** to a low value such as **11**, **Dark Intensity** to a low value such as **14**, and **Light Intensity** to its maximum setting of **50**. With the darks very dark and the lights very light, this filter will generate free, squiggly outlines without any middle grays. The **Sketch** category of filters generally presumes that the pencil moves in one direction throughout the entire image; few real sketches are ever produced that way. This is why we turned to the **Brush Strokes** category of filters, which allows for twists and turns. Click **OK**.

In the **Layers** palette, set the *blend mode* for the **Dark details** layer to **Vivid Light** and the **Opacity** to **66%**. (You can hide the **Middle values** layer for a moment to see what's happening: click its eye icon in the **Layers** palette). These settings let some of the graphite grays from the **Basis** layer bleed through the **Dark details** layer.

⑤ Compose Smooth Grays for Midtones Layer

In the **Layers** palette, choose the **Middle values** layer (make it visible if necessary). The effect we're going for on this layer is to create the intermediate shades an artist achieves when drawing lightly with a soft lead pencil. Unlike pen drawing, which produces strokes with a uniform tone, pencil drawing enables variable tones, which some drawing filters tend to forget exist.

◢ NOTE

Technically, if you were actually drawing the image, you'd apply the dark details last. But in this case, we're only simulating the final effects, so we'll do the dark details next.

To accomplish this effect, we apply three filters on top of one another to the **Middle values** layer. For the first filter, select **Filter, Sharpen, Unsharp Mask**. In the dialog box, an **Amount** setting between **100%** and **150%** isolates the gray areas (surrounding them with overbrightened whites) without losing them entirely. Set **Radius** to **50** pixels to overextend the bright areas quite a bit, and **Threshold** to **0** so that no regions are exempt. By creating bright halos and isolated grays, you're setting up for a common sketch effect, where the artist tends to fill in an outlined area *just close to the border but not quite there*, leaving a little paper showing through. Meanwhile, the dark zones are becoming *very* dark, as well as losing detail. You don't need detail in the very dark areas; artists often apply dark tones broadly and aggressively. To apply the filter, click **OK**.

With the **Middle values** layer still chosen, from the menu bar, select **Filter, Brush Strokes, Accented Edges**. In the dialog box, set **Edge Width** to its minimum of **1**, **Edge Brightness** to its minimum of **0**, and **Smoothness** to a high value between **8** and the maximum of **15**. We want the zones we've created to have a distinct, crisp edge. The only reason we want that is to make it easier for the next filter to decide what areas to sketch within, because it's about to "color" within borders that won't be there once this process is done.

To move directly from here to the **Graphic Pen** filter, in the dialog box, open the **Sketch** list from the center pane, and from the list of samples, choose **Graphic Pen**. Set **Stroke Length** to **12** (or more for higher-resolution images than 150 PPI) and **Light/Dark Balance** to **40**. Click **OK**. This layer should now be entirely graphite gray. In the **Layers** palette, leave the blend mode set at **Normal**, and set **Opacity** to **40%**. Now, the rich darks will show through the grays.

TIP

Because pencil sketching, even among masters, is a simplistic process, it's easier for the viewer's eyes to discern the methodology behind it than it is for a more complex process, such as oil painting. As a result, it's actually a lot harder to effectively pull off a simulation of a sketch than it is an oil painting. Photoshop Elements includes its own drawing tools, with which you could conceivably enhance the simulation effect considerably by doing some drawing yourself. But this method of applying filters on three layers will give you a foundation with which you can work.

⑥ Apply "Whitewash" Frame

In the **Styles and Effects** palette, in the **Effects** category, under **Frames**, you'll find that Photoshop Elements offers several automatic picture frame and matting styles, including variations of a simple, splashy, brushed, white border. I find the one that's most compatible with the effect we've just simulated is **Strokes Frame**. Double-click this frame thumbnail in the **Styles and Effects** palette to flatten all visible layers, and apply a jagged border to the image.

7 View the Result

After you're satisfied with the result, make any other changes you want and save the PSD file. Resave the result in JPEG or TIFF format, leaving your PSD image with its layers intact so that you can return at a later time and make different adjustments if you want.

182 Make a Photograph Look Like Andy Warhol Painted It

When most people think of modern, pop art, they think of Andy Warhol. One of his most famous paintings is of a tomato soup can, elevated to the level of art. Another famous painting is of Marilyn Monroe. Marilyn's face is reduced to simple lines, making her look almost like a statue rather than a warm-blooded human being. The canvas of this painting was divided into nine equal parts, with the same copy of Marilyn's face occupying each square. The painting became a study of light and color, as each of the nine Marilyns was rendered in a limited complementary color scheme.

When Andy Warhol painted people, he didn't want them to necessarily look like people, so he always placed them on plain backgrounds. Removing the background from your image will remove its context, giving your subject a kind of statuesque or robotic look. So, as you look for a suitable portrait to render in the Warhol technique discussed in this task, keep in mind that it's the person you'll be emphasizing and not the background.

1 Crop Image

Open an image in the *Editor* in **Standard Edit** mode and save it in Photoshop (*.psd) format. Click the **Crop** tool on the **Toolbox** and crop the image in a square. I selected the 5" × 5" **Preset** from the **Options** bar and cropped my image using that size. You'll end up with a square anyway, even if it doesn't measure exactly 5" × 5".

2 Remove the Background

To remove the background from your image, click the **Background Eraser** tool on the **Toolbox**. On the **Options** bar,

Before You Begin

✔ **91** About Layers and the Layers Palette

✔ **107** Crop a Portion of an Image

✔ **146** Adjust Hue, Saturation, and Lightness Manually

✔ **164** Replace a Background with Something Else

🎣 TIP

As you crop, keep in mind that you'll be removing the background, so try to fill the cropping border with your subject. You might want to crop to only the face, or to the face and part of the upper body instead of the whole person because focusing in that tightly will help your image look more like art and less like a colored photograph.

TIP

If you don't like the effect of the **Cutout** filter on your image, try the **Posterize** filter instead (**Filter, Adjustments, Posterize**). The **Posterize** filter also reduces the number of tonal levels in an image.

 TIP

Sampling for the **Color Replacement** tool takes place at the crosshairs in the tool's center. You use this tool very similarly to the **Background Eraser** tool. It replaces all color within the area of the brush tip that either matches the sample color or, alternatively, matches the background color. Set **Sampling** to **Continuous** to have the tool absorb a new color to replace at the crosshairs point each time you begin a new brushstroke. Set **Sampling** to **Once** to have the tool sample *only the first brushstroke* and continue to replace the sampled color with each successive stroke. To go a different route altogether, set **Sampling** to **Background Swatch**. Set the background color to the color you want to replace (you can use the **Eyedropper** tool for this purpose). Then you don't have to worry about sampling at all; your tool will simply replace the background color whenever and wherever it finds that color.

adjust the **Diameter, Limits, Tolerance,** and other options as desired. Drag the brush along the edge of your subject, removing elements behind your subject from the background. Clean up areas not removed by using either the Magic Eraser or the Eraser. See **97 Erase Part of a Layer** for details on using these tools.

❸ Blur Image

Blur the image to remove unnecessary detail: choose **Filter, Blur, Smart Blur**. The **Smart Blur** dialog box appears. Set **Radius** to the medium value of **50**. Set the **Threshold** value to **10** (higher for images whose resolution is above 150 *PPI*). Then gradually reduce the **Radius**, keeping it above **1**, until you've eliminated or reduced the texture of skin and clothing, without losing too much detail. (Watch the preview window to see the results of your manipulations.) Click **OK** to accept your changes.

❹ Simplify Image

The next task is to simplify the image by reducing the number of colors. Choose **Filter, Artistic, Cutout** from the menu bar. The **Cutout** dialog box appears. Set **Edge Simplicity** to **0**. Set the **Number of Levels** to between **4** and **6** because Andy generally used no more than six solid colors in a portrait. Slowly increase the **Edge Simplicity** slider until you have removed most of the detail, but have retained color variation so that your subject can still be identified. Try not to lose the darks of your subject's eyes. The effect you're going for approximates the use of cutout construction paper, glued together to make a recognizable, if slightly crude, face. Click **OK** to accept your changes.

❺ Replace Colors

The image is probably looking fairly artsy by now, but it might lack the vibrant colors it needs to achieve that Warhol look. Click the **Color Replacement** tool on the **Toolbox**. In the **Options** bar, select **Color** from the **Mode** drop-down list and **Continuous** from the **Sampling** drop-down list. These settings instruct the tool to replace both hue and saturation values ("color") for the shade directly beneath it, and to keep doing that wherever it finds that color. Adjust the **Diameter, Tolerance,** and **Limits** values as needed.

2 Remove the Background

3 Blur Image

1 Crop Image

4 Simplify Image

6 Fill Background

7 Increase Canvas Size

10 Recolor Each Layer

5 Replace Colors

8 Duplicate Layers

11 View the Result

9 Move Layers into Position

TIPS

You can also replace color using the **Replace Color** dialog box (**Enhance, Adjust Color, Replace Color**). Click on the image to select the color you want to replace, and pixels with that color show up in the preview. Select a color to replace those pixels with, and click **OK**.

Where needed, smooth any jagged edges and reduce the number of colors in an area by painting with the **Paint Brush** tool instead.

Sometimes, the **Background Eraser** tool can leave semi-opaque pixels along the outside edge of what you thought was a perfectly cut-out selection. As a result, filling in the background with the **Paint Bucket** tool might leave a transparent halo around your subject. If this happens, use the **Magnetic Lasso** tool to select all the image that is *supposed* to be completely transparent. Then press **Delete** to remove its contents. See more about the **Magnetic Lasso** tool in **75 Select an Object By Tracing Its Edge**.

Set the *foreground color* to the color you want to paint with. To mimic the Warhol palette, you'll want to choose any hue—literally *any* hue—with saturation of **66%** or above and a brightness of **75%** or above. You don't have to have a lifelike palette—cyan skin is perfectly acceptable. When you've chosen a foreground color, click the color in the image you want to replace. Drag with the brush over the area that contains that color to replace it with the selected foreground color. Depending on the **Tolerance** value you've set, you can replace variations close to the color you clicked with similar variations of the foreground color. Generally, you'll have best results with a *low* **Tolerance** setting, such as **5**. Repeat the color replacement process until you've reduced the image to four or five basic colors in various shades.

6 Fill Background

Now that you've painted the image with the colors you want to use, you're ready to fill in the background. Press **Ctrl** and click the *thumbnail* for the image's only *layer* on the **Layers** *palette*. This action selects your subject. To select the transparent background so that you can fill it with color, choose **Select, Inverse**.

Click the **Paint Bucket** tool on the **Toolbox**. Fill the selected background with an adequately contrasting, highly saturated color. It should probably not be a middle tone; the color you use should be relatively light or relatively dark.

7 Increase Canvas Size

Andy copied Marilyn's face a total of nine times in his famous painting, but we'll do a smaller version that uses only four copies. To accommodate a two-across-by-two-down layout, double the size of the *canvas* (increase the canvas size of the image by another 100%). Choose **Image, Resize, Canvas Size**. The **Canvas Size** dialog box appears. Enable the **Relative** option. Type **100%** for both the **Width** and **Height** values. In the **Anchor** pane, click the arrow in the upper-left corner. Click **OK**. The canvas size is doubled, and your current image appears in the upper-left corner of the canvas.

8 Duplicate Layers

Rename the current layer **Upper Left** and then choose **Layer, Duplicate Layer** to copy the layer. Name the new layer **Upper**

Right. Repeat this process to create two more layers: **Lower Left** and **Lower Right**.

9 Move Layers into Position

On the **Layers** palette, select the **Lower Right** layer. To help you position these layers properly, select **View**, **Snap to Grid** from the menu bar. Click the **Move** tool on the **Toolbox**. Drag the image downwards and to the right, into the lower-right corner of the canvas. Repeat this process to move the image on the **Lower Left** and **Upper Right** layers into position.

10 Recolor Each Layer

On the **Layers** palette, click the **Lower Right** layer. Recolor the image on this layer by choosing **Enhance**, **Adjust Color**, **Adjust Hue/Saturation**. The **Hue/Saturation** dialog box appears. Enable the **Preview** check box. Select **Master** from the **Edit** list. Drag the **Hue** slider until you find a different color combination you like. Adjust the **Saturation** and **Lightness** as well, if it helps to balance the overall distribution of color and light for this layer. Click **OK**.

Repeat this step to recolor the images on the **Lower Left** and **Upper Right** layers.

TIP

You don't have to stop at simply recoloring each layer: You can hand-paint an element into one layer; you can adjust the brightness or saturation of one element rather than the entire layer; or you can vary the backgrounds for each layer.

11 View the Result

After you're satisfied with the result, make any other changes you want and save the PSD file. Resave the result in JPEG or TIFF format, leaving your PSD image with its layers intact so that you can return at a later time and make different adjustments if you want.

Jennifer says: This photograph of my mother-in-law, Maria, was one of her favorites. She was an artist, and I'm sure she would have appreciated this rendition of her portrait. Look for it in the Color Gallery.

Scott says: Mom never particularly understood the appeal of pop artists. During her 47-year teaching career, Mom had some students who insisted she help them create versions of the Campbell's Soup can or the Marilyn portrait. In helping them out, she would convey every indication of a lady stepping out of her element, like a cellist in a rock band. What she wouldn't admit out loud was that she was enjoying herself. She'd always find some way to find herself in her work, whether she was working in her own method or in the method of any master of any genre. Jennifer produced this Warhol-inspired portrait in honor of an artist who found herself in everything she made, and in the making, improved it. I hope you take the time to find a piece of yourself in your work with Photoshop Elements, whether or not a computer is necessarily "your element."

24

Adding and Embellishing Text

IN THIS CHAPTER:

183 Add a Text Caption or Label

184 Bend Text

185 Create a Sales Sign

186 Add a Backscreen Behind Text

187 Create Metallic Text

188 Create Text That Glows

189 Emboss Text

190 Fill Text with an Image

191 Add Copyright Information

You add text to an image using one of the **Type** tools: the **Horizontal Type, Vertical Type, Horizontal Type Mask,** or **Vertical Type Mask** tool. You'll use the **Type** tools to add text; you'll use the **Type Mask** tools to create a selection in the shape of text on the current layer, just as you do with any other selection tool. I often use a text selection to mask a fill or adjustment layer (see (100) **Mask an Adjustment or Fill Layer**) or on a clipping mask (see (163) **Mask an Image Layer**), or as a selection I can use to copy or cut data or fill with another image (see (90) **Copy Data into a Selected Area**).

When you add regular text to an image (as opposed to a text selection), a text layer is automatically created for it. A text layer can contain only *vector* text. Vector data, you might recall, is not displayed on screen as a set of pixels, but rendered instead using a formula. This means that the text content, style, size, and position on the layer can be changed over and over as needed, by simply selecting and retyping the text, making different choices from the **Options** bar, or using the **Move** tool (see (99) **Move, Resize, Skew, or Distort a Layer**).

Although Photoshop Elements provides some effects you can apply to vector text, your choices are limited mostly to *layer styles* and specific text *effects*. To apply pixel-based commands such as a brightness or contrast adjustment, edit with a painting tool such as the **Brush**, or apply filters or non-text effects (such as **Motion Blur**, **Liquify**, or **Bricks**) to text, you must convert the vector text to *raster* (bitmapped) data. See (96) **Simplify a Layer** for more information on converting a text layer to a regular layer.

In this chapter, you will learn how to add text to an image and modify the text later on. You will learn how you can use special effects to make the text look metallic or embossed. You will also learn how to fill the text with an image.

NOTE

You can add text to any image you create or modify in the *Editor*. Even so, the Editor will never be mistaken for a word processor—which means that the kind of text you create with its tools is the short, decorative kind. You might add text to a card or invitation, an image copyright, callout or quote; or you might make it large and apply artistic effects to make the text a feature element.

---

183 Add a Text Caption or Label

You add a text label or caption to your image using the **Type** tool on the **Toolbox**. When you select the **Type** tool, you can customize how the text will look by selecting the appropriate options such as font, size, style (such as bold, italic, or underline), orientation (such as left-aligned or centered), and color on the **Options** bar. You typically select the text settings before typing to create your text label. If you decide to change the text settings after typing the text, you must change to the **Type** tool again (if you've been doing something else), select the text, and then edit it or change the **Options** bar settings.

You add a text label to your image as either vertical (up and down) or horizontal (left to right) text. You specify the direction of the text by clicking either the **Horizontal Type** or **Vertical Type** tool. However, because text is just an object, you can rotate, skew, or distort it after the fact by using the **Move** tool (see **99** **Move, Resize, Skew, or Distort a Layer**). You can also change its direction from horizontal to vertical if needed, and make other adjustments as well. This task shows you how to add text to an image; to learn how to add text as a selection you can fill, modify, and use just like any other selection, see **190** **Fill Text with an Image**.

1 Select Type Tool

Open an image in the Editor in **Standard Edit** mode and save it in Photoshop (*.psd) format. On the **Layers** palette, select the layer *below* which you want the text layer to appear. The text layer will be inserted *above* the layer you choose. Select the **Type** tool on the **Toolbox**.

2 Select Text Orientation

In the **Options** bar, click the **Horizontal Type** tool to have the text display horizontally across the image. Click the **Vertical Type** tool to have the text display vertically down the image.

3 Select Font and Size

Click the arrow next to the **Font** drop-down list box and select the font you want to use for your text label or caption. From the **Size** drop-down list, select a font size or type a size (in points) in the **Size** text box.

See Also

→ **184** Bend Text
→ **185** Create a Sales Sign
→ **187** Create Metallic Text
→ **188** Create Text That Glows
→ **189** Emboss Text
→ **190** Fill Text with an Image
→ **191** Add Copyright Information

NOTE

Normally, when choosing fonts to use in a file that you intend to share with other people, you should select a font you know they also have, or risk having your text re-rendered in an alternative font. However, unless you're going to share your actual PSD working file, you can use any font you like because the vector text will be converted to raster when you flatten the image to save it in a single layer format such as non-layered TIFF, JPEG, or GIF. See **102** **Merge or Flatten Layers into One.**

2 Select Text Orientation

Vertical
Type Tool **3** Select Font and Size

4 Select Text Color and Style

Horizontal
Type Tool

1 Select Type Tool

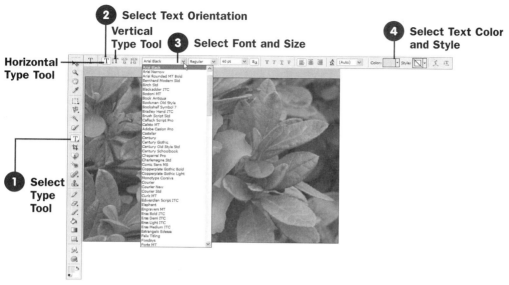

Bold, Italic, Underline, Strikethrough

Anti-aliased

Alignment

Leading

Set Other Options

Change Text Orientation

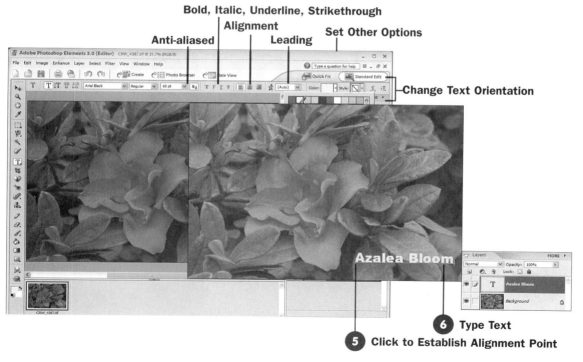

Azalea Bloom

6 Type Text

5 Click to Establish Alignment Point

4 Select Text Color and Style

Text color is set to the current *foreground color* automatically, but you can choose a different color now by opening the **Color** list and selecting a color from the swatch palette. To pick a color using the **Color Picker**, click the **More Colors** button just below the swatch palette. The color you choose will be added to the **Colors** drop-down list box.

You can apply a *layer style* to the text layer by choosing one from the **Style** list.

Click the **Anti-aliased** button located just to the right of the **Size** box to soften curves in your text. Add bold, italics, underline, or strikethrough attributes, choose a text alignment, and set the leading to **Auto** or specify a specific value (if you plan to type multiple lines of text).

5 Click to Establish Alignment Point

Click in the image where you want to align the text.

6 Type Text

Start typing. If you chose **Center text** in step 4, for example, the text you type is centered on the point where you clicked in step 5. Press **Enter** to begin a second line of text. Make changes to the text as needed. You can press **Backspace** to erase characters to the left of the vertical cursor, or press **Delete** to remove characters to the right.

When you are satisfied with your text label or caption, click the **Commit** button on the **Options** bar (the check mark), or click **Cancel** (circle with slash) to not add the text. The text is also added when you click another tool in the **Toolbox**. The text is added to your image on a new text layer, which is named using the text you wrote. The text layer is marked in the **Layers** palette with a large *T* on its layer thumbnail.

Make additional changes to the image. When you're satisfied with the image, save the PSD file. Then merge the layers together and resave the result in JPEG or TIFF format, leaving your PSD image unflattened so that you can return at a later time and make different adjustments if you want.

 NOTE

You can select portions of text by dragging over it and apply formats such as bold to just those characters.

TIPS

To change text after committing it, click the text layer on the **Layers** palette and then choose a **Type** tool or double-click the text layer's thumbnail. Select the text and then make the changes to the settings on the **Options** bar. To change horizontal text to vertical text or vice versa, select the text and click the **Change the Text Orientation** button.

If you do not like the positioning of the text after committing, select the text layer in the **Layers** palette and click the **Move** tool on the **Toolbox**. A *bounding box* appears around the text object. Click within this box and drag the text to the desired location on the layer.

184 Bend Text

Before You Begin

✔ **183** Add a Text Caption or Label

See Also

→ **171** "Melt" an Image

**NOTES**

Using the **Warp Text** option, you can warp vector text. You can also distort or skew vector text using the **Move** tool. See **99** **Move, Resize, Skew, or Distort a Layer.**

If you've converted the text to raster data (simplified the text layer), you can warp it manually using the **Liquify** filter. See **171** **"Melt" an Image.**

You can warp text when you first create it if you prefer. Just type your text and click the **Create Warped Text** button (the arc with a bent *T* over it) at the right end of the **Options** bar to display the **Warp Text** dialog box.

Typically when you add text to an image, it is aligned on a straight line, either vertically or horizontally on the image. However, using the **Warp Text** option, you can bend the text to fit a shape, creating a different effect. In the **Warp Text** dialog box, you select one of several bending shapes, and the text is distorted to fit that shape. Each of these bending shapes can be applied either horizontally or vertically to the text. For example, if you select the **Arc** style and then the **Horizontal** radio button, the text is bent like a rainbow, with a fat arc on top, and a narrow arc below. Choose the **Vertical** option instead, and warp shape is rotated 90 degrees. The text is now bent like a fan, with its fattest arc on the left and its smallest arc on the right.

You can customize the way the text bends even more using the **Bend**, **Horizontal Distortion**, and **Vertical Distortion** options on the **Warp Text** dialog box. The **Bend** option controls the direction and severity of any curves. Adjust the warp shape both horizontally and vertically using the **Horizontal Distortion** and **Vertical Distortion** options.

1 Select Text Layer

Open an image in the Editor in **Standard Edit** mode and save it in Photoshop (***.psd**) format. Select the text layer you want to warp in the **Layers** palette.

2 Open Warp Text Dialog Box

Choose **Layer**, **Type**, **Warp Text** to display the **Warp Text** dialog box.

3 Select Text Bending Options

From the **Style** drop-down list in the **Warp Text** dialog box, select a warp shape. The text on the layer is bent to fill this shape. A preview of how the text will look displays in the *Editor* window.

To rotate the warp shape 90 degrees to the left, click the **Vertical** radio button. To rotate it back, click the **Horizontal** button. Typically, when warping horizontal text, choose the **Horizontal** option; when warping vertical text, choose the **Vertical** option instead. However, "going against the grain" by choosing the opposite option can create some interesting effects.

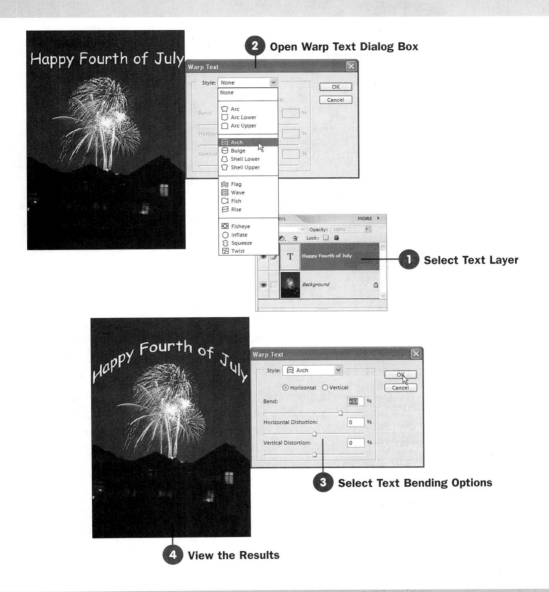

2 Open Warp Text Dialog Box

1 Select Text Layer

3 Select Text Bending Options

4 View the Results

To change the direction and the amount of bend in the text, drag the **Bend** slider. The further away from the center point, the more bend you get. To reverse the direction of the bend (the place where the highest point of the arcs occur), drag the slider in the opposite direction.

To twist the text horizontally, drag the **Horizontal Distortion** slider. Again, the distortion gets more severe the further away from the center point you drag. To reverse the direction of the distortion, drag the slider in the opposite direction.

To twist the text vertically, drag the **Vertical Distortion** slider. To increase the distortion, drag the slider away from the center point. To reverse the direction of the distortion, drag the slider in the opposite direction.

Watch the text in the image window; when you have the desired settings, click **OK** to close the **Warp Text** dialog box and apply the settings to the selected text. The layer thumbnail for the text layer changes to display the **Warp Text** icon (an arc with a twisted *T* over it). This icon helps remind you that warping has been applied to the text layer.

TIPS

You can remove the **Warp Text** settings from the text by opening the **Warp Text** dialog box and selecting **None** from the **Style** drop-down list.

You can change the location of the text on the image while the **Warp Text** dialog box is open. To move the text, click it and drag it to the new location.

4 View the Results

When you're satisfied with the image, save the PSD file. Then merge the layers together and resave the result in JPEG or TIFF format, leaving your PSD image unflattened so that you can return at a later time and make different adjustments if you want.

In this example, I wanted to make my text wrap around the top of the fireworks. To do this, I decided to use the **Arc** style with a **Bend** of about **53%**. I also had to move the text down after I applied the style. To accomplish this, after warping the text, I selected the **Move** tool in the **Toolbox** and dragged the text down to the desired location on my image.

One thing to keep in mind, even though you have altered the look of your text by bending it, the text is still editable. For example, you can select the text and change it to say something else, change the font size, and so on.

185 **Create a Sales Sign**

One common use for *graphics editors* such as Photoshop Elements is to create signs or posters. You might want to create a *For Sale* sign to advertise an item you want to sell. To do that, you'll need to create a new image, add some graphics, enter some text, apply a few finishing touches, and print the result. You could follow these same basic steps to create signs advertising a school or church event, yard sale, or a lost pet—just about any image that combines text and graphics.

When you use the *Editor* to create signs or other documents you want to print, you have to be concerned not only about what it looks like on the screen, but also how it will look when printed. If you plan to print your sign on an 8 1/2 × 11-inch sheet of paper, you should set your image size to match so that the image isn't stretched or distorted during printing. You set the image size in the **New** dialog box that opens when you create the image.

Typically, a sign has multiple lines of text and some type of graphic image. When you add the text, you'll typically want to type each line of text onto a separate layer. For example, to advertise a motorcycle that my husband is selling, I would create one layer with the words *FOR SALE* and a separate layer for the text *Off-Road Motorcycle*. Placing related phrases on separate layers allows me to apply different fonts, sizes, color, and so on to the text on each layer, and also position each line of text separately.

1 **Create a New Blank File**

Choose **File**, **New**, **Blank File** from the menu bar or click the **New** button on the **Shortcuts** bar to display the **New** dialog box. Type **Sales Sign** in the **Name** box. To print the sign in *landscape orientation* on a standard 8 1/2 × 11-inch sheet of paper (allowing for margins), set the **Width** to **10** inches and the **Height** to **8** inches. Reverse these dimensions if you plan to print the sign using *portrait orientation*. Adjust these values if you want to print on a paper size other than 8" × 10".

Before You Begin

✔ **183** Add a Text Caption or Label

See Also

→ **44** Create a New Image

→ **66** Print an Image

🔍 **TIP**

If you want to move two text layers at the same time, link them. Just select one of the layers in the **Layers** palette and click the link icon (the space in front of the image thumbnail) of the other layer. After they've been linked, you can move, copy, resize, and perform other functions on the layers as if they were one. See **101** **Group and Organize Layers.**

📐 **NOTE**

If you want to use a color for the background of your image rather than white or transparency, set the *background color* swatch on the **Toolbox** to that color before choosing the **File, New, Blank File** command.

1 Create a New Blank File

3 Add Text

2 Add Images

Text Layer

Pasted Image on Separate Layer

4 Position Text

5 Print the Sign

Typically a **Resolution** value of 300 DPI works well when printing, although you might choose a higher resolution if you're going to include photos and print on photo paper. Set the **Color Mode** to **RGB Color** if you want to create a color sign. If you want the sign to be black and white, select **Grayscale**. From the **Background Contents** list, select what you want to use for the background color of the image: transparent, white, or current *background color*. See **44** **Create a New Image** for more help.

Click **OK** to create the file. You might want to save the file immediately in Photoshop (***.psd**) format by clicking the **Save** button on the **Shortcuts** bar.

❷ Add Images

Paste and position images that you want to add to the sign. You can paste a copy of another image file by copying it to the Clipboard and then choosing **Edit, Paste** in the new image file. When you paste a copied graphic into your image file, a new layer is added for that graphic. To reposition or resize a pasted graphic, use the **Move** tool as described in **99** **Move, Resize, Skew, or Distort a Layer**.

❸ Add Text

On the **Layers** palette, select the layer *below* which you want the new text layer to appear. The text layer is added above the layer you select.

Select the **Type** tool on the **Toolbox** and select the font, size, color and other options you want to use for the first line of your sign. Click in the image to specify the alignment point for your text, and then type the text you want to add. Edit the text if necessary and click the **Commit** button (the check mark) on the **Options** bar to create the text layer.

Repeat the process for each line of text you want to place on the sign. A new text layer is added for each line of text. If you want several lines of text to use the same font, size and other attributes, you can place all text in the same layer. To start a new line of text, press **Enter** and then continue typing.

 TIP

You can customize the font, style, size, and color of the text you type (even after the fact) using the **Options** bar. See **183** **Add a Text Caption or Label** for more information on setting text font options.

4 **Position Text**

Select the **Move** tool on the **Toolbox** and then select the text layer you want to position in the **Layers** palette. Click and drag the text to the desired position on the sign. See **99** **Move, Resize, Skew, or Distort a Layer** for more information about moving text and image layer contents.

5 **Print the Sign**

After you're satisfied with the image, save the PSD file. Then merge the layers together and resave the result in JPEG or TIFF format, leaving your PSD image unflattened so that you can return at a later time and make different adjustments if you want. Print this JPEG or TIFF version by clicking the **Print** button on the **Shortcuts** bar or choosing **File, Print** from the menu bar. The **Print** dialog box appears.

Because you sized the image to fit your intended paper size, you probably don't have to do anything here except verify that the preview looks correct. If necessary, adjust the settings and click **Print** to display the **Print** dialog box, and then click **Print** again to print the sign. See **66** **Print an Image** for more help.

TIP

If you're not printing on 8.5" × 11" paper, printing in landscape orientatioon (as shown) or if you are using photo paper or a heavy bond paper, you'll need to adjust the print options before printing. See **65** **Set Print Options**.

186 Add a Backscreen Behind Text

Before You Begin

✔ **183** Add a Text Caption or Label

See Also

→ **185** Create a Sales Sign

→ **191** Add Copyright Information

If your text seems to get lost in the detail of your image, you might want to try adding a backscreen to the text. *Backscreening* is a popular technique used by graphic artists to help make text stand out when it is placed on top of a busy background. Typically, a backscreen occupies an area in the original image, but the backscreen has been lightened, blurred, or corrected in some fashion so that text is easier to read against it.

In this example, we are going to select a portion of the image under the text and copy that section to a new layer. Then we will modify that layer by adjusting the brightness so that the text can stand out against it.

PART IV: Sharing, Creating, and Having Fun

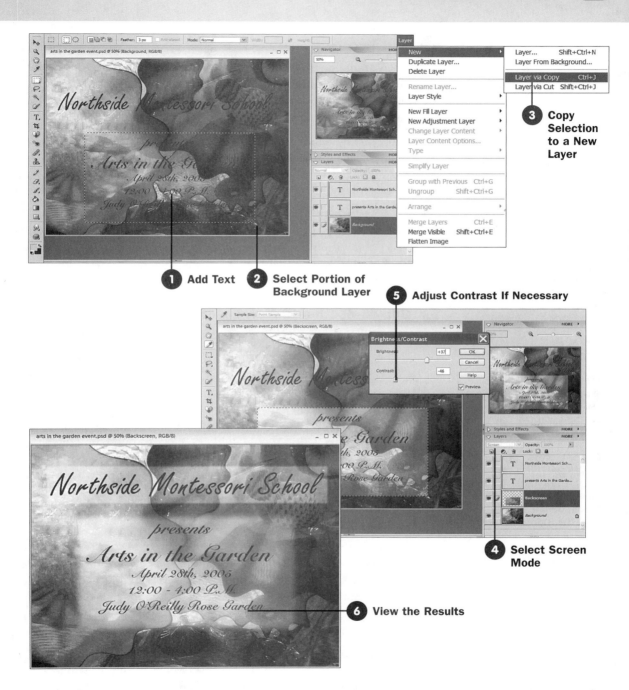

1 Add Text **2** Select Portion of Background Layer

3 Copy Selection to a New Layer

5 Adjust Contrast If Necessary

4 Select Screen Mode

6 View the Results

NOTE

Use the font, size, and color you want for your text. Don't worry if you can't clearly see the text against the image right now. In this example, the black text detailing the time and location of the event is hard to see against the mottled background, but backscreening will fix this problem nicely.

TIP

If you've drawn a rectangular selection behind your text and want to reposition it so that it fits nicely, make sure that you still have the **Rectangular Marquee** tool active, and then click its **New Selection** button on the **Options** bar, position the mouse pointer over the selection marquee or inside its boundaries, and drag to move the marquee.

❶ Add Text

Open an image in the Editor in **Standard Edit** mode and save it in Photoshop (***.psd**) format. On the **Layers** palette, select the layer *below whiIch* you want the text layer to appear. The text layer will be inserted *above* the layer you choose.

Select the **Type** tool from the **Toolbox** and add text to your image. See **183** **Add a Text Caption or Label** for more information on adding text.

❷ Select Portion of Background Layer

In the **Layers** palette, select the **Background** layer. Use one of the selection tools on the **Toolbox** to select a portion of the **Background** layer under the text you typed. The **Rectangular Marquee** tool works well for selecting a rectangular-shaped area.

❸ Copy Selection to New Layer

Choose **Layer, New, Layer Via Copy** from the menu to create a new layer that contains a copy of the portion of the **Background** layer you selected in step 2. Name this new layer **Backscreen**.

❹ Select Screen Mode

On the **Layers** palette, set the blend **Mode** of the **Backscreen** layer to **Screen**. This setting should lighten the background, making it easier to see the text. If you want to darken the backscreen to make light text show up better against it, select the **Hard Light** or **Soft Light** *blend mode* instead.

❺ Adjust Contrast If Necessary

In some cases, you can improve the readability of your text by lowering the contrast and increasing the brightness of the **Backscreen** layer. Press **Ctrl** and click the image thumbnail for the **Backscreen** layer. This action selects all the opaque pixels for you.

Choose **Enhance, Lighting, Brightness/Contrast.** The **Brightness/Contrast** dialog box appears. Drag the **Contrast** slider to the left to lower the contrast. Drag the **Brightness** slider to the right to increase the brightness a little. Watch the image window as you make adjustments; when your text is clearly readable, click **OK** to apply your changes.

6 **View the Results**

When you're satisfied with the image, save the PSD file. Then merge the layers together and resave the result in JPEG or TIFF format, leaving your PSD image unflattened so that you can return at a later time and make different adjustments if you want.

After making the appropriate adjustments to your backscreen layer, the text should be easy to read on your image. Alternative methods you can try include making a selection, creating a new layer, and filling the selection with white, another solid color, or a gradient and then using a blend mode on the **Backscreen** layer such as **Screen** or **Soft Light**. You can try lowering the **Opacity** on this layer as well. Another method to try involves making a selection and creating an adjustment layer (such as **Levels** or **Brightness/Contrast**) which automatically affects just that selection.

Here, I placed a backscreen behind both pieces of text. I set the blend **Mode** to **Screen** and reduced the **Contrast** to improve the text visibility.

 TIPS

You can use any tool to adjust the **Backscreen** layer to improve the readability of the text. For example, you can apply a filter such as **Gaussian Blur** to blur the **Backscreen** layer and further reduce the distraction of a busy background.

Add a **Bevel** or **Drop Shadow** *layer style* to your **Backscreen** layer for a finished look.

187 Create Metallic Text

Sometimes, plain text is just not what you are looking for to set off an image. Photoshop Elements provides several different *effects* for modifying the text on your image, including an effect that makes the text look like chunks of metal.

You can find the available effects on the **Styles and Effects** *palette* on the right side of the *Editor* window. If you do not see the **Styles and Effects** palette, open it by selecting **Window, Styles and Effects** from the menu bar. The palette contains many effects, filters, and layer styles you can apply to text, including many metallic textures. To apply these textures, you may have to select the text first, or simplify it (convert it to *raster data*). See **96** **Simplify a Layer**. Here you'll learn how to apply a simple brushed metal effect.

Before You Begin

✔ **98** Apply a Layer Style
✔ **183** Add a Text Caption or Label

See Also

→ **188** Create Text That Glows
→ **189** Emboss Text

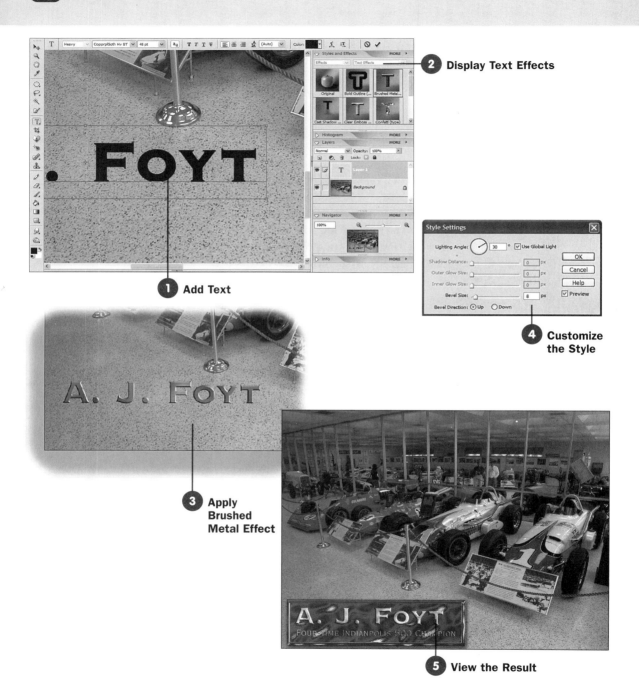

1 **Add Text**

2 **Display Text Effects**

3 **Apply Brushed Metal Effect**

4 **Customize the Style**

5 **View the Result**

1 Add Text

Open an image in the Editor in **Standard Edit** mode and save it in Photoshop (***.psd**) format. On the **Layers** palette, select the layer *below* which you want the text layer to appear. The text layer will be inserted *above* the layer you choose.

Select the **Type** tool from the **Toolbox** and add text to your image. It doesn't matter what *foreground color* you use to create the text; all the **Brushed Metal** effect cares about is the *shape* of the text. See **183 Add a Text Caption or Label** for more information on adding text.

For most tasks, you'll want to use a font with enough size and body to be recognized by the eye as metallic. The exception, as you'll see in this example, is when one passage of text accompanies a larger passage with a bolder, thicker style. In such a case, the smaller text can participate in the effect along with the larger text that substantiates the effect.

2 Display Text Effects

In the **Styles and Effects** palette, select the **Effects** option from the first drop-down list. From the second drop-down list, select **Text Effects**. The palette changes to show thumbnails for the various text effects from which you can choose.

3 Apply Brushed Metal Effect

In the **Layers** palette, select the text layer. Double-click the **Brushed Metal** thumbnail in the **Styles and Effects** palette.

The effect is applied to your text. The **Brushed Metal** effect is actually a combination of several different filters. Photoshop Elements applies each filter to your text to create the effect of metallic text.

You can remove the effect from your text by right-clicking the layer in the **Layers** palette and selecting the **Clear Layer Style** option from the context menu that appears.

4 Customize the Style

To customize the effect for any passage of text in your image, in the **Layers** palette, double-click the **f** icon next to that layer's name. The **Style Settings** dialog box appears.

TIP

Some text effects, including **Brushed Metal**, are made possible by Photoshop Elements's vast array of custom *layer styles*. When you attribute a layer style to a layer (whether or not you intended to in the first place), in the **Layers** palette, a lowercase *f* icon appears to the right of the layer's name. Click this icon to make adjustments to the style. See **98 Apply a Layer Style** for more about finding and using custom layer styles.

Other metallic textures you might try include the Chrome filter; the Gold Sprinkles and Rusted Metal effects; and the Wow Chrome, Brushed Metal, Diamond Plate, Copper, Chrome Fat, Rivet, or Molten Gold layer styles.

You can adjust the **Lighting Angle** for the text by typing a value in the field or twisting the **Lighting Angle** knob. To ensure that the text is given the same lighting angle as all other 3D effects in the image, enable the **Use Global Light** check box. You can adjust the bevel size by dragging the **Bevel** slider or by typing a value. The **Bevel Direction** option designates whether the appearance of the metal bevel is raised (**Up**) or lowered (**Down**). Click **OK**.

5 View the Result

When you're satisfied with the image, save the PSD file. Then merge the layers together (if any) and resave the result in JPEG or TIFF format, leaving your PSD image unflattened so that you can return at a later time and make different adjustments if you want.

For this example, I created two text passages and gave them both the **Brushed Metal** text effect. Behind these text layers is a simple rectangle to which I applied the **Wow-Chrome** layer style. (See **98** **Apply a Layer Style** for details.) Both passages use variants of a font called Copperplate (which is not shipped with Photoshop Elements). To make A.J.'s metal plate stand out from the rectangular metal plate, I increased A.J.'s **Bevel** size to **8**.

To help the text layers incorporate some of the lighting effects from the chrome layer beneath them, I changed their blend modes to **Color Dodge**. This mode uses the color of one layer to lighten the color of the one beneath it. See **111** **About Tool Options** for a discussion of blend modes and how they work.

💡 TIP

To create gold text, apply one the **Wow Chrome** layer styles, then group it with a **Hue/Saturation** adjustment layer that you use to colorize the text with a **Hue** of 59, **Saturation** of 58, and **Lightness** of -26.

---

188 Create Text That Glows

Before You Begin

✔ **84** Save a Selection for Reuse

✔ **183** Add a Text Caption or Label

See Also

→ **187** Create Metallic Text

→ **189** Emboss Text

→ **190** Fill Text with an Image

When I think of the term *glowing*, I infer from it the concept of emitting light. The best way I know to suggest that something gives off light is to show something that the light is reflecting off. Surprisingly, the *Editor*'s **Outer Glows** *layer styles* are not too convincing. It's **Wow Neon** layer styles are better, but what I prefer is an effect that looks like one of those shadow-box neon signs, where light is emitted from the *back* of the letter blocks and bounces off the back plate, illuminating the area *around* the letters. This task shows a homemade version of a far more convincing glowing text style.

Add Text

Build Text Body Selection

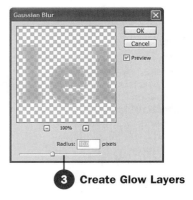

Create Glow Layers

Create Shimmer Layer

View the Result

Create Block Layer

Add Text

Open an image in the Editor in **Standard Edit** mode and save it in
Photoshop (***.psd**) format. On the **Layers** *palette*, select the *layer
below* which you want the text layer to appear. The text layer will
be inserted *above* the layer you choose.

NOTE

Fonts on your computer are managed by Microsoft Windows, not by Adobe Photoshop Elements. If you installed Photoshop Elements with the standard options, you should have more fonts on your computer than you did before. But if you have other fonts on your system, installed with any other application (for instance, Microsoft Office), those fonts are also available to you in the Editor.

TIP

The range of text sizes available with the **Type** tool might not be large enough for many purposes, such as adding a big banner to an image. If **72 pt** isn't large enough, just type the point size you want to use in the **Size** box.

Select the **Type** tool from the **Toolbox** and add text to your image. See **183** **Add a Text Caption or Label** for more information on adding text. For your foreground color, choose either a rich, bright, well-saturated color or a light pastel, but try to keep the total intensity (the **B** component in HSB) at about 150. This method compounds brights on top of brights, so the final product will actually be brighter than the foreground color you choose.

You will want to use a large font size with a wide body to make the glowing text *effects* more apparent. Try adding the **Bold** attribute to give the glow effect enough surface to work on.

When the text passage appears exactly where you want it to and is the size you want it to be, and you've checked its spelling and contents for accuracy, from the Editor's menu bar, select **Layer**, **Simplify Layer**. This command converts the text layer to a *raster* layer, enabling you to apply artistic effects to that layer. Name this new layer **Base**.

❷ Build Text Body Selection

In the **Layers** palette, choose the **Base** layer. From the **Toolbox**, click the **Magic Wand** tool. Click any area of the image that is *not* text. This action selects only the background. Then choose **Select**, **Inverse** from the menu bar. Now the text is selected. To omit the holes in characters (for instance, in an **O**, **p**, and **8**), with the **Alt** key held down, click all the holes in the text passage's characters.

You'll be using this selection pattern more than once in this task, so choose **Select**, **Save Selection** from the menu bar to save the selection. In the **Save Selection** dialog box, enter **Text** as the selection's name and click **OK**. See **84** **Save a Selection for Reuse** for more about saving and reusing selected regions.

❸ Create Glow Layers

Choose **Select**, **Deselect** to remove the selection marquee from the text. With the **Base** layer still chosen, select **Layer**, **Duplicate Layer** from the menu bar. Name the new layer **Glow** and click **OK**.

With the **Glow** layer chosen, select **Filter**, **Blur**, **Gaussian Blur**. For the blur effect to be effective in creating a glow, set **Radius** to **10.0** or higher. Click **OK**.

In the **Layers** palette, set the *blend mode* for the **Glow** layer to **Screen**. To compound the effect, duplicate the **Glow** layer (select **Layer, Duplicate Layer**). The **Glow copy** layer will dramatically brighten the glow effect.

If you like what you see, *you can stop here* and save your results. The next steps make your text look like it's produced by a box sign.

4 Create Shimmer Layer

In the **Layers** palette, turn off visibility (click the eye icon) for the **Glow** and **Glow copy** layers. You'll want to be able to see the new effect you're about to create.

Choose **Select, Load Selection** from the menu bar. In the **Load Selection** dialog box, under **Selection**, choose **Text** and then click **OK**. Now choose **Select, Feather** from the menu bar. For large, bold text above 72 points in size, you'll want to enter a large **Feather Radius** amount, such as **20**; for 72 points and smaller, enter a smaller feather value. Click **OK**. The effect you're going for is to reduce the selection to a series of blobs, as if you'd left the selection out in the hot sun too long and it melted.

In the **Layers** palette, choose the **Base** layer. Then select **Layer, New, Layer via Copy** from the menu bar. Rename the layer **Shimmer**. Change its blend mode to **Pin Light**. To see what you've made, turn off visibility for the **Base** layer for a moment. Each letter should look like it's been lit by individual, soft light bulbs.

5 Create Block Layer

In the **Layers** palette, turn on visibility for the **Base** layer (click its eye icon), and turn off visibility for **Shimmer**. With the **Base** layer chosen, load the **Text** selection again. Then choose **Select, Modify, Contract** from the menu bar. In the **Contract Selection** dialog box, enter a value about one-fourth the amount you entered in step 4 for the **Feather Radius**. Click OK.

Choose **Select, Modify, Smooth**. In the **Sample Radius** dialog box, enter a value about one-half the amount you entered in step 4 for **Feather Radius**. Click OK.

With the **Base** layer still chosen, select **Layer**, **New**, **Layer via Copy**. Name the new layer **Block**. Then set its blend mode to **Difference**. Now your letters have a glowing rim and a second tier of glow on the inside.

6 View the Result

When you're satisfied with the image, save the PSD file. Then merge the layers together and resave the result in JPEG or TIFF format, leaving your PSD image unflattened so that you can return at a later time and make different adjustments if you want.

Although it's nice to have a handful of one-touch layer styles you can apply with ease to get a job done quickly, after you become familiar with the tools and techniques of the Editor, you'll find yourself wanting to experiment with methods that let you apply adaptations, nuances, and your own personal touch. I discovered the technique used here one day after experimenting with the effects of blend modes on blurs, and realizing that you can create blurs that compound or reduce the effect of other blurs. One of my favorite twists on this technique is to pick one letter and eliminate the selection for that letter before creating the **Shimmer** layer, thus making it look like the lights have burned out on one of the letters.

189 Emboss Text

Before You Begin

✔ **183** Add a Text Caption or Label

See Also

→ **184** Bend Text

→ **187** Create Metallic Text

→ **188** Create Text That Glows

→ **190** Fill Text with an Image

A popular *effect* when working with text is to use embossing. Embossing creates a pleasant, almost invisible effect to text. If you watch network television, you're no doubt familiar with the "logo bug" in the lower-right corner, which was an effect introduced by MTV in the early 1990s. It's the most prominent example of embossed text today, and you can produce a similar effect quite easily using the **Emboss** *filter*.

1 Add Text

Open an image in the Editor in **Standard Edit** mode and save it in Photoshop (***.psd**) format. On the **Layers** *palette*, select the layer *below* which you want the text layer to appear. The text layer will be inserted *above* the layer you choose.

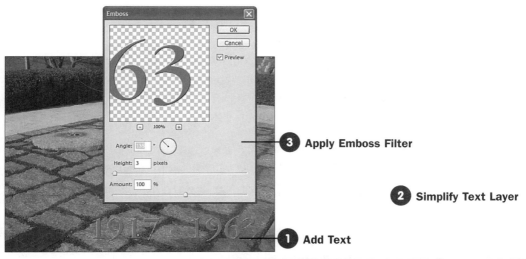

3 Apply Emboss Filter

2 Simplify Text Layer

1 Add Text

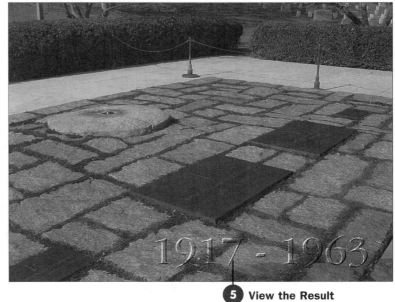

4 Apply Blend Mode

5 View the Result

Select the **Type** tool from the **Toolbox** and add text to your image.
See **183** **Add a Text Caption or Label** for more information on
adding text.

You will want to use a large font size to make the embossing more apparent. A faceted font, such as one with a strong serif, shows off the embossing effect more. Your text's foreground color is only important in that it will be used as the shadow color for your embossed text. The reflected light color will be a light shade of gray, and the flat surface color will be 50% gray. There's a reason for this color scheme, as you'll see momentarily.

2 Simplify Text Layer

In the **Layers** palette, select the text layer. Choose **Layer, Simplify Layer** from the menu bar to convert the text layer to a *raster* layer.

3 Apply Emboss Filter

With the text layer still chosen, select **Filter, Stylize, Emboss** from the menu bar. The **Emboss** dialog box appears. Enable the **Preview** check box.

In the **Angle** field, specify a value between **–180** and **180** degrees to indicate the angle from which simulated light is directed toward the surface. You can use the twister control to point toward the light source. In the **Height** field, indicate the height of the simulated bevel, in pixels.

In the **Amount** field, specify the relative degree of contrast between the light side and the dark side of the embossing. At **100%**, the *filter* applies pure white on the light side and a pure, untainted foreground color on the shadow side. At less than 100%, the light side is colored more softly and the *background color* is applied to the shadow side more diffusely. At greater than 100%, a blur effect is used to extend the area of both light and shadow sides into the gray area.

To finalize your choices, click **OK**.

4 Apply Blend Mode

The reason the **Emboss** filter uses 50% gray for its surface color is not because gray is a particularly fashionable color or this year's beige. It's because the results of the filter are intended to be blended with underlying layers, generally using one of the *blend modes* from the fourth group in the **Mode** drop-down list in the **Layers** palette. For a crisp embossing effect, choose **Overlay**. For a more emphasized effect, choose **Linear Light**. The 50% gray *disappears*, leaving just the embossed region.

NOTE

If needed, increase the brightness and contrast of the text layer to make the embossed text more visible.

5 **View the Result**

When you're satisfied with the image, save the PSD file. Then merge the layers together and resave the result in JPEG or TIFF format, leaving your PSD image unflattened so that you can return at a later time and make different adjustments if you want.

The term *embossing* seems to have overtones of something chunky or bold, when in fact embossed seals on heavy paper are often subtle. For this simply produced example, the **Screen** blend mode lets the embossed text play a reduced role. It reminds the viewer of the context of this image, while helping to keep the composition simple and quiet, like the setting itself.

190 Fill Text with an Image

You can make your text more interesting by filling it with another image rather than a color. When you do this, the image is visible only inside the letters of the text. In effect, your text becomes a frame that holds the image. The process of creating this wizardry is amazingly simple: You choose either the **Horizontal** or **Vertical Type Mask** tool and type your text; a selection is created, in the exact shape and size of the text you typed. You can do anything you want with this text selection, including making modifications to it using any of the selection tools (such as the **Selection Brush**), filling it with a gradient or pattern using the **Paint Bucket** or **Gradient** tool, and even saving it for reuse.

You can fill text with an image using one of two methods: In the first method, you can paste all or part of an image into a selection (a process that resizes the image to fit as much as possible into the selection you've made). You can create a text selection using this method and then paste copied data into that shape. But you have little control over what portion of the image shows up within the text "frame," and manipulating the image so that the exact portion you want to see shows through is difficult because you can't see the image as you make your adjustments (see **90** Copy Data into a Selected Area).

Before You Begin

✔ **183** Add a Text Caption or Label

See Also

→ **184** Bend Text

→ **187** Create Metallic Text

→ **188** Create Text That Glows

→ **189** Emboss Text

① Select Type Mask Tool

② Set Options

③ Type Text Selection

⑤ View the Result

④ Copy and Paste into Final Image

You can also fill text by creating a text selection and using that selection to copy the portion of the image you want to fill your text (as explained in this task). The advantage is that you can maneuver the selection over the image and copy exactly the data you want. If the image doesn't fill the selection adequately no matter where you move it, you can change the selection text's size or font to find a better fit.

1 Select Type Mask Tool

In the *Editor*, in **Standard Edit** mode, open the source image you want to use for the interior of your text. On the **Layers** palette, select the layer *below* which you want the text layer to appear. The text layer will be inserted *above* the layer that contains the data you choose.

Click the **Horizontal Type Mask** tool or the **Vertical Type Mask** tool on the **Toolbox**.

2 Set Options

On the **Options** bar, select a fairly wide **Font** and a large **Size**. Set other options such as **Anti-aliased** (which helps soften any jagged curves in the text selection).

3 Type Text Selection

Click on the image in the area you want to use to fill your text and type the text. A red mask appears over your image, and the text is revealed as you type. This red screen (the mask) helps you see how the image below will fill the text.

Edit the text if needed; because this is a selection and not actual text, you won't be able to go back later and make changes to it after you commit. See **183** **Add a Text Caption or Label** for more information on adding text.

When you have created a text selection that's the size and shape you need, click the **Commit** button (check mark) on the **Options** bar. At this point, you have only created *a selection*.

4 Copy and Paste into Final Image

Select **Edit, Copy** to copy the data within the text selection. Select **Edit, Copy Merged** instead if you want to select all visible pixels within the selection and not just those on the current layer.

Open the image in which you want the text to appear and save it in Photoshop (*.**psd**) format. On the **Layers** palette, select the layer above which you want the filled text to appear. Select **Edit, Paste**. The filled text appears on its own layer within the image, above the layer you selected.

 TIP

For my source image, I typically pick something that's dense with texture or color. You're probably not going to be able to make out a lot of the image detail within the text, so the criteria for selecting a source image is just the overall look and how well you think the image will fill the text.

NOTE

If the text-shaped selection is not positioned to select the exact area of the image you want to use, move the selection after committing it by clicking any selection tool (but not the **Selection Brush**), enabling the **New Selection** option on the **Options** bar, and dragging the selection marquee.

TIPS

You can move the filled text because it's on its own layer. See **99** **Move, Resize, Skew, or Distort a Layer**.

You can also rotate the filled text layer if you like; see **89** **Rotate the Data in a Selection or Layer**.

⑤ View the Result

When you're satisfied with the image, save the PSD file. Then merge the layers together and resave the result in JPEG or TIFF format, leaving your PSD image unflattened so that you can return at a later time and make different adjustments if you want.

In this example, I started with a photograph of my daughter, selected a fat font, and used the **Move** tool to position the selection so that it was centered on her face. I copied the text selection to an image of me leaning against a railing, changed the **Joy** layer's blend mode to **Luminosity**, and found the result I was looking for.

191 Add Copyright Information

Before You Begin

✔ **183** Add a Text Caption or Label

See Also

→ **44** Create a New Image

→ **53** About Image Information

→ **99** Move, Resize, Skew, or Distort a Layer

If you plan to share images that you create and photographs you have taken, you should consider copyrighting them. All the photographs you take are already your property and are protected by law. It is not necessary to fill out any forms or contact the U.S. Copyright Office before copyrighting your images. Still, the government isn't going to compensate you if someone steals your work, and because it's easy to protect your images against unauthorized use, why not do so?

The Editor provides two ways to protect your work. The first method involves typing a copyright notice in the **File Info** dialog box, as discussed in **53** **About Image Information**. The notice becomes a part of the file's *metadata*, and most *graphics editors* such as Photoshop and Photoshop Elements can read this metadata and display the copyright on the image's title bar when the image is opened. There are a lot of programs (including the Editor) that can not only view an image's metadata, but allow the user to change it as well. So, if you add a copyright notice in this manner, keep in mind that it's a simple public notice, and that it can be easily removed or altered.

The best way to protect your work is to add a notice that can't be removed because it's part of the image itself. To copyright your images in this manner, you'll create a copyright file that you can copy into each image you want to protect against misuse. To create the copyright file, you'll type the text you want to use for the copyright and apply the **Emboss** filter to give it a raised appearance. After pasting the copyright into an image you want to mark, you'll use the **Hard Light** *blend mode* to make the copyright see-through, like a watermark, Finally, you'll merge all the layers together, blending the copyright text with the image pixels permanently. This is the image copy you should share online because it can't be altered to look like it was created by someone else. A key here is to make sure that you place the copyright in an integral part of the image so that it cannot be cropped away and the rest of the image used anyway.

❶ Create a New Image

In the *Editor*, choose **File, New, Blank File** from the menu bar or click the **New** button on the **Shortcuts** bar to display the **New** dialog box. Type **Copyright** in the **Name** box. Set the **Width** to **900** and **Height** to **300** pixels. Set **Resolution** to **300** pixels per inch (PPI), or whatever resolution you typically use for images you share or use online. Set the **Color Mode** to **RGB Color.** From the **Background Contents** list, select **white.** Click **OK** to create the new file. See **44** **Create a New Image** for more help.

❷ Add Copyright Text

Select the **Type** tool on the **Toolbox,** choose a font and size and a dark **Color.** Click in the image and type the copyright text: Hold down the **Alt** key and type **0169** on the numeric keypad to enter the copyright symbol (©), and then type the year and your name. See **183** **Add a Text Caption or Label** for more information on adding text.

❸ Create a Border

Click the **Rectangular Marquee** tool on the **Toolbox.** Draw a selection just inside the image border. Choose **Select, Inverse** to invert the selection. You now have a selection along the outer edges of the copyright image.

Select the **Background** layer on the **Layers** palette. Click the **Paint Bucket** tool on the **Toolbox.** Fill the selection with black.

❹ Merge Layers

Merge the layers together by choosing **Layer, Flatten Image.** The two layers are merged into a single layer called **Background.**

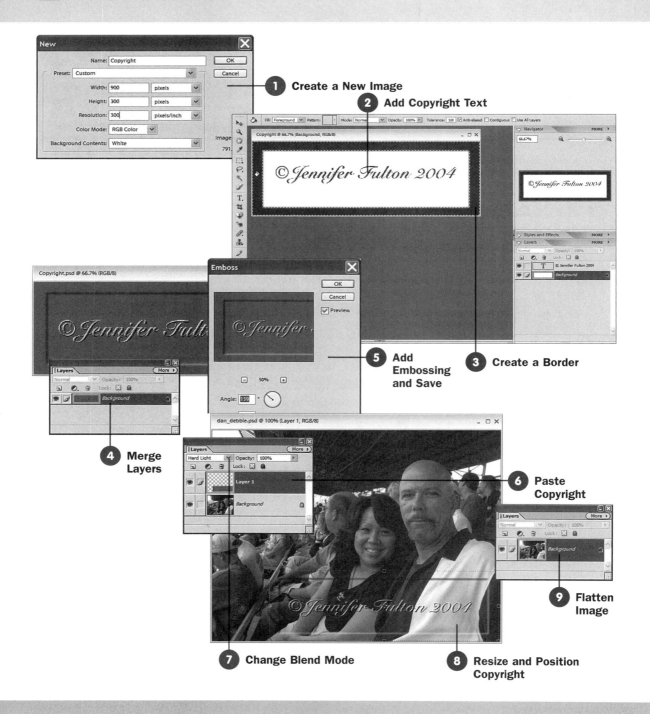

1 Create a New Image

2 Add Copyright Text

3 Create a Border

5 Add Embossing and Save

4 Merge Layers

6 Paste Copyright

7 Change Blend Mode

8 Resize and Position Copyright

9 Flatten Image

5 Add Embossing and Save

To give your copyright a raised appearance, apply the **Emboss** filter. Choose **Filter, Stylize, Emboss**. The **Emboss** dialog box opens. Typically, the default settings work just fine for this purpose, but you can adjust the settings if you don't like the look. See **189** **Emboss Text** for details. Click **OK**.

Click the **Save** button to save the image in PSD format. Use the filename **Copyright.psd**.

6 Paste Copyright

In the **Copyright** image you just created, choose **Select, All** and then **Edit, Copy** from the menu bar to copy the entire image to the Clipboard.

Open an image you want to copyright. Save this image in Photoshop (***.psd**) format. Then select **Edit, Paste** to paste the copyright data onto a new layer in the image.

7 Change Blend Mode

Change the blend **Mode** of the copyright layer to **Hard Light**. The copyright is now transparent.

8 Resize and Position Copyright

Click the **Move** tool on the **Toolbox**. On the **Options** bar, enable the **Show Bounding Box** option. Click and drag the copyright to move it into a good position on the image.

You can resize the copyright as well by dragging a corner handle. Make sure that you enable the **Maintain Aspect Ratio** option on the **Options** bar so that the text does not become distorted. See **99** **Move, Resize, Skew, or Distort a Layer**.

9 Flatten Image

When you're satisfied with the image, save the PSD file. Then merge the layers together by choosing **Layer, Flatten Image** and resave the result in JPEG or TIFF format, leaving your PSD image unflattened so that you can return at a later time and make different adjustments if you want. For example, you might return to the

NOTE

You'll want to position the copyright over some important part of the image that would be impossible to crop out, and yet not obscure the image so much that it's no longer enjoyable to look at. Balance your need to protect with your need to share.

TIP

To apply a quick copyright to an image, type some text and apply the **Clear Emboss** effect. The result is a lot more subtle than what's shown here, and it may be easier to remove as a result, but it's quick and incredibly easy.

PSD file and resize it or change its resolution to fit your current sharing situation.

With the TIFF or JPEG image flattened, your copyright notice cannot be easily removed from the image, and you can share it online without worry. To copyright another image, keep your **Copyright.psd** file open and repeat steps 6–8.

Index

SYMBOLS

[(left bracket), increasing brush sizes, 292

] (right bracket), increasing brush sizes, 292

NUMBERS

180° command, rotating image, 392

3D Transform command (Filter menu), 633

3D Transform dialog box, 633

3D Transform filter, wrapping image around object, 633-636

90° Left command, rotating image, 392

90° Right command, rotating image, 392

A

Acrobat Reader, 64

Action Menu button, 84-86

Actual Pixels button, 85, 217

Adaptive algorithm, 239

Add Anchor Point tool, 635

Add Caption to Selected Items command (Edit menu), 130

Add New Address link, 590

Add Noise dialog box, 636

Add Noise filter, 638

Add Photos dialog box, 259

Add Recipient button, 584

Add to Selection operation, 314-316

additive process, light science, 11

Adjust Color command (Enhance menu), 486

Adjust Color Intensity slider, 539

Adjust Date and Time command (Edit menu), 102

Adjust Date and Time dialog box, 102

Adjust Hue/Saturation command (Enhance menu), 487, 540-542, 646

Adjust Lighting command (Enhance menu), 472, 638

adjustment layers, 21, 336

Adjustment layers
  Brightness/Contrast, 346
  creating, 346-349
  defined, 346
  Gradient Map, 346
  Hue/Saturation, 346
  Invert, 346
  Levels, 346
  masks, 365-366
  Photo Filter, 346
  Posterize, 348
  Threshold, 348

Adjustments command (Filter menu), 275, 466, 507

Adobe button, 29

Adobe Color Picker, 425

Adobe Gamma
  ICC color profile, 378
  installation check, 388

monitor calibration, 381
  adjusting gamma, 385-386
  chromaticity selection, 381-384
  Control Panel mode, 386-392
profile, 379
tool, 388

Adobe Gamma dialog box, 388

Adobe Photo Downloader dialog box, 51

Adobe Photoshop Services, 6

Adobe Photoshop Services dialog box, 263, 588

Adobe Reader, 64

Adobe website, 12, 574

Advanced button, 379

airbrushes, painting photos, 439-440

albums, scrapbook pages, 618

Aligned option, 458, 609

All command (Select menu), 467

Allow Photos to Resize option, 84

Allow Videos to Resize option, 84

alpha channels, 211, 313

alpha transparency, 191, 201, 206

Amount slider, 403

Anchor pad, 234

anchor points, 234

Angle gradient style, 445

Angled Spectrum layer style, 26

animated images, graphics editor, 19

anti-aliased text, 191

anti-aliasing, 7, 301, 549

Anti-aliasing slider, 633

archival quality prints, online services, 247

arranging images, 213-215

artifacts, 26, 190, 203, 241

artistic photographs
  Andy Warhol technique, 677-682
  changing to black and white, 650-653

colorizing, 656-662

drawing effect, 673-676

making look old, 644-650

negative images, 654-655

oil painting effect, 662-668

watercolor effect, 668-672

As a Copy option, Save dialog box, 194

Aspect Ratio list, 395

Attach Selected Items to Email dialog box, 575, 582

Attach to Email dialog box, 582

Attach to Email command (File menu), 582

audio

captions, 84, 88, 133-135

files

photo review exclusion, 84

photo well display, 38

playing, 96-99

thumbnails, 146

Auto button, 401

Auto Contrast tool, 401-402

Auto Fix command, 182

Auto Fix dialog box, 37, 376, 395

Auto Fix feature, 101

Auto Fix Photo command (Edit menu), 186

Auto Fix Selected Photos command (Edit menu), 182

Auto Fix tool, Organizer, 139

Auto Fix Window command (Edit menu), 37, 182, 376, 395

Auto Hide option, 176

Auto Levels command (Enhance menu), 401

Auto Levels tool, Quick Fix tools, 401

Auto Smart Fix command (Edit menu), 376

automatic importing, media files, 66-68

automatic photographs, digital photography, 13

Automatically check for updates option, 586

Automatically Tile Windows button, 169-170, 213, 222, 609

Automation Tools command (File menu), 66

.AVI video format, 99

B

Back button, 36, 142

Back to All Photos button, 37-38, 44, 47, 68, 141, 148, 160

Background Contents drop-down list, 181

Background Eraser tool, 355-357, 560

bland sky, 610

replacing background, 604-607

Background from Layer command (New menu), 350

Background layer, 235, 334-336, 467

blend mode, 334

converting into regular layers, 350-352

creating Image layers, 339

Normal blend mode, 335

transparent areas, 336

Background Music list, 84

backgrounds

bland sky replacement, 607-610

blurring, 13, 558-563

changing with graphics editor, 18

colors, 7, 178, 320, 326, 424-425

fake water, 639

layers, 21, 320, 326

creating new images, 178

increase area around images, 233

replacing, 604-607

selection, 181

sharpening photos, 551

subject on snowy background, 515-519

How can we make this index more useful? Email us at indexes@samspublishing.com

717

Backscreen layer, 696

backscreening text, 694-697

Backup command (File menu), 73

backups

    catalog, 139

    Organizer catalog, 73-76

batteries, care, 12

Bend slider, 689

Best quality, 563

Bicubic resampling, 228

Bicubic Sharper resampling, 228

Bicubic Smoother resampling, 228

Bilinear resampling, 228

Billing screen, 266

bitmaps, 26

    color mode, 181, 237

    converting to, 241

    mode, 241

bits, 237

Black & White forces, 240

black points, 513-514

black-and-white photos, changing from color, 650-653

black-and-white photos, graphics editor, 18

Blank File command (File menu), 179, 691

blemishes, removal, 483-485

blend modes, 323, 334, 339

blended colors, 10

blending images, 615-617

blends, color, 9

blizzard effect, 26, 636

Bloat tool, 630

blue channel, 543

blue speaker icons, 146

Blur Center pane, 563

Blur command (Filter menu), 478, 555

blur filters, 483-485

    remove graininess, 555-558

Blur More filter, removing graininess, 555-558

Blur tool, repairing surface defects, 455

blurring images

    creating depth of field, 558-560

    remove graininess, 555-558

    spin effect, 561-563

    unsharp mask, 550

Border command (Select menu), 614

Border option, 255

bounding boxes, 319, 328, 448, 619

    handles, 328

    straightening images, 400

brightness

    color degree of light, 10

    color models, 9

    faded pictures, 511-515

    flashes

        too close, 525-528

        too far away, 528-531

    histograms, 500-507

    improving, 507-510

    nighttime photos, 523-525

    portion of images, 520-523

    selecting areas of similar brightness, 288-290

    subject on snowy background, 515-519

Brightness and Contrast pane, 389

Brightness slider, 509

Brightness/Contrast command (Enhance menu), 509

Brightness/Contrast dialog box, 507-509, 531

Brightness/Contrast layers, 346

Browse command (File menu), 133

Browse Folders command (File menu), 211

Browse for Folder dialog box, 67

Brush Presets palette, 522, 566

Brush Pressure, 632

Brush Strokes filters, 641

Brush tool, 25-27, 32, 365, 433, 438

   reducing edge sharpening, 553

   repairing surface defects, 455

   small blemishes, 463

brushed metal effect, 699

brushes

   colors, airbrush painting, 439-440

   presets, 423-424

   size increasing/decreasing, 292

Burn command (File menu), 78

Burn tool

   bland sky, 607

   exposure corrections, 520-523

   eyeglasses glare removal, 491-494

   grayscale stains, 466

Burn/Backup Wizard, 74, 78

By Caption or Note command (Find menu), 150-151

By Color Similarity command (Find menu), 162

By Filename command (Find menu), 149

By History command (Find menu), 158

By Media Type command (File menu), 101, 147

Byte Order option, TIFF, 200

C

Calendar (Date View), 152

calendars, 152-156

calibration, monitors, 381

   adjusting gamma, 385-386

   chromaticity selection, 381-384

   Control Panel mode (Adobe Gamma), 386-392

camera-to-subject distance, 14

cameras

   Adobe support, 12

   digital

      file formats, 5

      image information, 378-380

      JPEG format, 191

      noise spottiness, 459-462

      storage capabilities, 4

canvas, 233

Canvas Size command (Image menu), 612

Canvas Size dialog box, 234

captions, 685, 687

   audio, 133-135

   finding items, 150-152

   text, adding, 130-132

catalog

   backup, 73-76, 139

   copying to CD-ROMs and DVDs, 76-79

   finding items, 139-143

   item organization, 106-109

      assign markers to item, 119-122

      audio captions, 133-135

      changing marker, 127-129

      creating group or category, 114-116

      deleting marker, 122-123

      marker creation, 117-119

      marker icon change, 125-127

      markers, 109-113

      Organize Bin display, 113-114

      text captions, 130-132

   locating moved files, 70-73

   Organizer, 15, 34, 51, 139

   removing items, 68-70

   scanned photos, 18

   updating images, 94-96

Catalog command (File menu), 75

Catalog dialog box, 75
categories
    changing, 127-129
    creating, 114-116
    deleting, 122-123
CCD noises, 459-462
CD-ROMs
    copying from catalog, 76-79
    importing media files, 47-50
cell phones, 591. *See also* mobile phones
    camera images, 60
    images
        folders, 61
        importing media files, 60-61
    noise spottiness, 459-462
Center Image option, 253
Change the text orientation button, 687
channels, alpha, 211
Choose border color box, 255
Choose Color button, 116
Choose Location dialog box, 586
chromaticity selection, 381-384
circular areas, selecting, 278-279
clarity
    adding motion, 567-568
    blurring
        creating depth of field, 558-560
        remove graininess, 555-558
        spin effect, 561-563
    improving, 550-554
    sharpness basics, 548-549
    softening selected details, 564-566
Clear Date Range command (Find menu), 158
Clear Undo History command (More menu), 32
clipping mask, 21, 292, 600
Clipping Mask layer, 338, 602-603

Clone Stamp tool, 400, 483, 494
    bland sky, 607-610
    eyeglasses glare removal, 493
    remove unwanted objects, 596-600
    repairing surface defects, 454
Clone tool, 465
cloning
    Aligned option, 458
    source point, 599
Close button, 170
Close Palette Bin button, 222
Close Photo Bin button, 176
CMYK color mixing system, 11
Collapse All Collections command (View menu), 113
Collapse All Tags command (View menu), 113
collection markers, 138, 211
    assigning to items, 119-122
    catalog organization, 109-113
    changing, 127-129
    creating, 117-119
    deleting, 122-123
    finding items, 143-145
        adding criteria, 146
        dragging to Find bar, 145
        searches, 145
    icon change, 125-127
    image organization, 34
    reviewing images, 82
collections, 15, 109
Color Management command (File menu), 390
Color Mode drop-down list, 181
Color Picker, 9-10, 235-236, 424-428
Color Picker dialog box, 239, 344
Color Replacement tool, 544
Color Settings command (Edit menu), 391
Color Settings dialog box, 391

Color Swatches palette, 175

Color Table dialog box, 239

Color Variations command (Enhance menu), 486, 537-540

Color Variations dialog box, 490

colorizing photos, 542, 656-662

colors

backgrounds, 7, 178, 320, 326

blended, 10

cast

balance, 534

correcting manually, 534-537

removing, 472

Quick Fix tool, 401

corrections

Color Variations command, 537-540

manually, 534-537

saturation for specific area, 544-546

value manually, 540-544

depth, 179

fading repair, 470-473

finding items by similarity, 160-162

graphics editor, 18

intensity, 539

layers, 342-345

blend modes, 241

fills, 344

management, 376-377

image information, 378-380

printing images, 245

reasons for, 376-378

mixing system, 11

mode, 179-181, 236-242

models, 8-10

photos, changing from black and white, 650-653

profiles, 11

restoring balance, 402

retouching photos

airbrush painting, 439-440

Eyedropper tool, 430

gradient, 443-446

patterns, 441-442

selection, 424-428

selecting areas of similar colors, 288-290

slider, 10

commands

Edit button, 37

Edit menu

Add Caption to Selected Items, 130

Adjust Date and Time, 102

Auto Fix Photo, 186

Auto Fix Selected Photos, 182

Auto Fix Window, 182, 376, 395

Auto Smart Fix, 376

Color Settings, 391

Contact Book, 579

Copy, 317-318, 330, 467

Copy Merged, 317-318, 330, 709

Cut, 317

Define Brush from Selection, 442

Delete, 321

Delete from Catalog, 70

Delete Selected Items from Catalog, 70

Edit with XXX, 182

File Association, 186

Finish External Edit, 182

Paste, 317, 467

Paste Into Selection, 329-331

Preferences, 30, 56, 61, 112, 176, 183

Preset Manager, 422

Redo, 32

Resize, 227

Select All, 68

How can we make this index more useful? Email us at indexes@samspublishing.com

721

Stack, 93
Undo, 32
Undo Delete Selected Items from
    Catalog, 70
Update Thumbnail, 95
Update Thumbnails, 96
Version Set, 184-185, 189
Enhance menu
    Adjust Color, 486
    Adjust Lighting, 472, 638
    Auto Levels, 401
File menu
    Attach to Email, 582
    Automation Tools, 66
    Backup, 73
    Browse, 133
    Browse Folders, 211
    Burn, 78
    By Media Type, 101
    Catalog, 75
    Duplicate, 196
    File Info, 210
    Get Photos, 43, 46, 51, 61
    Import, 58
    New, 179, 321-323
    Open, 94
    Open Recently Edited File, 186
    Order Prints, 263
    Page Setup, 249
    Place, 319
    Print, 253, 694
    Process Multiple Files, 230
    Reconnect, 72, 231
    Rename, 70, 230
    Restore, 75
    Save, 195
    Save As, 195-197, 230

Save for Web, 203-205
Watch Folders, 66
Filter menu
    Adjustments, 275, 466, 507, 654
    Blur, 478, 555
    Distort, 480, 630-633
    Filter, 23
    Noise, 456, 460
    Pixelate, 636
    Render, 633
    Sharpen, 490, 549-551
    Sketch, 619
    Stylize, 638
Find menu
    By Caption or Note, 150-151
    By Color Similarity, 162
    By Filename, 149
    By History, 158
    By Media Type, 147
    Clear Date Range, 158
    Items with Unknown Date and Time, 156
    Set Date Range, 157
    Untagged Items, 146
Image menu
    Crop, 395
    Divide Scanned Photos, 58
    Mode, 237, 478
    Resize, 223, 247
    Rotate, 328, 392, 639
Layer menu
    Delete Layer, 277, 338, 518
    Duplicate, 467
    Duplicate Layer, 275, 338, 478
    Group with Previous, 603
    Layer from Background, 469
    Merge Down, 371, 603
    Merge Linked, 371

Merge Visible, 371
New, 317
New Adjustment Layer, 348, 523
New Fill Layer, 612
Rename Layer, 338
Simplify Layer, 354, 619, 632
Type, 688
Layer Style menu, Scale Effects, 361
Modify menu
 Expand, 296
 Smooth, 301
More menu, Clear Undo History, 32
New Fill Layer, 344
New menu
 Background from Layer, 350
 Image From Clipboard, 293, 321-323
 Layer via Copy, 325
Select menu
 All, 467
 Feather, 306, 649
 Grow, 298-300
 Inverse, 308-310, 649
 Load Selection, 314, 649
 Modify, 296, 648
 Save Selection, 312, 648
 Similar, 298-300
View menu
 Collapse All Collections, 113
 Collapse All Tags, 113
 Expand All Collections, 113
 Expand All Tags, 113
 Grid, 177, 400
 Media Types, 97, 146
 Menu Types, 38
 New Window for XXX, 221
 Organize Bin, 111

Rulers, 176
Snap to Grid, 177
Timeline, 157
Window menu
 Dock Properties in Organize Bin, 130, 212
 File Browser, 230
 Histogram, 506
 How To, 177
 Images, 170, 213-215, 599, 609
 Info, 176, 470
 Navigator, 218
 Organize, 145
 Organize Bin, 116
 Properties, 130, 211-212
 Reset Palette Locations, 174
 Undo History, 32
 Welcome, 29
composite images, 622-624
composition, graphics editor, 17
compressing images
 GIF format, 200-203
 JPEG format, 203-206
CompuServe GIF option, Format drop-down list, 202
Confirm Deletion from Catalog dialog box, 70
Confirmation screen, 266
Constrain Proportions check box, 227
Contact Book
 groups, 579
 name sorting, 581
 Organizer, 579-581
Contact Book command (Edit menu), 579
Contact Book dialog box, 579
contact sheets, 86, 256-259

contrast

corrections, Color Variations command, 537-540

faded pictures, 511-515

flash

too close, 525-528

too far away, 528-531

histograms, 500-507

improving, 507-510

Median filter, 461

nighttime photos, 523-525

portion of images, 520-523

Quick Fix tool, 402

scanned photo quality restoration, 476

subject on snowy background, 515-519

Contrast command (Select menu), 648

Contrast command (Style menu), 613

Contrast Selection dialog box, 296, 649

Contrast slider, 510

Control Panel, Adobe Gamma tool, 388

Control Panel mode (Adobe Gamma), monitor calibration, 386-392

conversions, Background layer into regular layers, 350-352

Convert Anchor Point tool, 635

Convert Photos to JPEGs option, 585

Cookie Cutter tool, 16, 600-604, 619

Copy command (Edit menu), 317-318, 330, 467

Copy Merged command (Edit menu), 21, 317-318, 330, 709

copying

data into selection areas, 329-331

Organizer catalog, to CD-ROMs and DVDs, 76-79

selections, 317-321

Copyright Notice text box, 211

copyrights, 211, 232, 710-714

corrections, photos, 376

Adobe Gamma, 381-392

color management, 376-380

cropping images, 394-398

Quick Fix tools, 401-403

rotating images, 392- 394

straightening images, 398-400

cosmetics, graphics editor, 17

creases, repairing, 465

Create Adjustment Layer button (Layers palette), 344, 348

Create and Apply New Tag dialog box, 91

Create button, 84, 170

Create Category dialog box, 116

Create Collection dialog box, 118

Create Collection Group dialog box, 116

Create New Layer button (Layers palette), 338

Create Tag dialog box, 118

Create Texture option, 462

Create warped text button, 688

creating

files, photo review exclusion, 84

new images, 178-181

Organizer, 15, 34

searches by filenames, 148

criteria, finding items, 146

Crop button, 395

Crop command (Image menu), 395

Crop to Fit Print Proportions option, 253

Crop tool, 248, 395, 400

cropping

images, 248

quick corrections, 394-398

cross-hairs, 177

Cube tool, 633

current display, 36

current layers, 329

Current Position slider, 99

curves, anti-aliasing, 7

Custom command, rotating image, 393

Custom Shape tool, 602, 613

Custom Size option, 253

Cut command (Edit menu), 317

cutting, selections, 317-321

Cylinder tool, 633

Cylindrical Mapping option, 627

D

Daily Note, 152

damage

    photos, graphics editor, 18

    repairing large areas, 463-470

Darken Amounts, 481

Darken blend mode, 458, 609

Darken Highlights setting, 518

Darken Highlights slider, 402

data

    copying into selection areas, 329-331

    images, alpha channel, 211

    layering, 20

    rasters, 7

    rotating data in, 326-329

    vectors, 7

Date View, 106, 152

Date View button, 154, 170

dates

    files, 138

    finding items, 152-158

    images, changing, 101-104

    sorting, 89, 154

Decrease Red button, 490

Default Colors button, 646

Define Brush from Selection command (Edit menu), 442

Delete Anchor Point tool, 635

Delete command (Edit menu), 321

Delete from Catalog command (Edit menu), 70

Delete key, deleting selection points, 287

Delete Layer button (Layers palette), 338

Delete Layer command (Layer menu), 275-277, 338, 518

Delete Selected Items from Catalog command (Edit menu), 70

deleting. *See also* erasing

    catalog items, 68-70

    layers, 338

    markers, 122-123

    selection points, 287

depth of field, 14

    blurring images, 558-560

    panorama, 625

depths, color, 179

desaturation, photos, 520

Description category, Organizer, 211

Description page, 211

Despeckle commands (Filter menu), 460

Despeckle filter, 455, 460

    removing noise, 459

    scanned photo quality restoration, 474

dialog boxes

    3D Transform, 633

    Add Noise, 636

    Add Photos, 259

    Adjust Date and Time, 102

    Adobe Gamma, 388

    Adobe Photo Downloader, 51

    Adobe Photoshop Services, 263, 588

    Attach Selected Items to E-mail, 575, 582

How can we make this index more useful? Email us at indexes@samspublishing.com

725

Attach to Email, 582
Auto Fix, 37, 376, 395
Brightness/Contrast, 507-509, 531
Browse for Folder, 67
Canvas Size, 234
Catalog, 75
Choose Location, 586
Color Picker, 239, 344
Color Settings, 391
Color Table, 239
Color Variations, 490
Confirm Deletion from Catalog, 70
Contact Book, 579
Contract Selection, 296, 649
Create and Apply New Tag, 91
Create Category, 116
Create Collection, 118
Create Collection Group, 116
Create Tag, 118
Display Properties, 388
Dust & Scratches, 456-458
Edit Collection, 119, 125
Edit Collection Icon, 125
Edit Tag, 119, 125
Edit Tag Icon, 125-127
Emboss, 713
Feather Selection, 306-307, 649
File Info, 210-212, 232, 379
Forced Color, 239-240
Frame From Video, 63
Gaussian Blur, 478, 527, 560
Get Photos by Searching for Folders, 43
Getting Photos, 44, 47-50
GIF Options, 203
Gradient, 345
Gradient Map, 523
Grain, 648

Hue/Saturation, 473, 542
Image Size, 223, 227, 247
Indexed Color, 202
Items Not Imported, 44, 47-50
Items Shown, 97
JPEG Options, 205
Level, 472, 503, 511
Liquefy, 630
Load Selection, 314, 649
Median, 461
Missing Files Check Before Backup, 75
More Options, 257
Motion Blur, 567, 638
Name, 424
New, 179
New Contact, 579
New Group, 581
New Layer, 340-341, 344, 348, 398, 649
Open, 186
Page Setup, 249
Pattern Fill, 345, 649
PDF for Image Import, 64
Photo Filter dialog box, 349
Photo Review, 84
Photomerge, 625
PNG Options, 207
Pointillize, 636
Preferences, 30-31, 61, 183, 319-321, 577
Print, 256, 694
Print Preview, 224, 245, 248, 253
Print Selected Images, 245, 248
Print Selected Photos, 224, 257-260
Process Multiple Files, 230-231
Properties, 251
Radial Blur, 562
Reconnect Missing Files, 72
Reduce Noise, 461

Remove Color Cast, 536

Save As, 46, 58, 188, 197

Save For Web, 202

Save Selection, 312-314, 648, 702

Select Audio File, 133-135

Select Icon, 127

Send to Mobile Phone, 591

Set Date Range, 156-157

Shadows/Highlights, 518

Smart Blur, 556

Smooth Selection, 301, 649

Style Settings, 26, 359

Threshold, 517

Time Zone Adjust, 104

Unsharp Mask, 476, 490, 551, 652

Warp Text, 688-690

Watch Folder, 66

Diamond gradient style, 445

Diffuse Glow command (Filter menu), 480, 646

Diffuse Glow filter, 480, 646

diffusing errors, 241

Diffusion Dither, 242

Diffusion option, 241

Digimarc Corporation, watermarking plug-in, 711

digital cameras

   file formats, 5

   image information, 378-380

   importing media files, 51-54

   JPEG formats, 191

   noise spottiness, 459-462

   PPI (pixels per inch), 247

   storage capabilities, 4

digital photography, 4-6

   color models, 8-10

   objects, 6-8

   optically appealing photographs, 12-15

   printing, 10-12

   processing principles, 4-6

   resolution, 6

   storage media, 5

   text, 6-8

digital retouching artist, 455

digital video files, viewing videos, 99-101

dimensions, images, 227

Direct Selection tool, 635

Discard Layers and Save a Copy option, TIFF, 200

Displace command (Filter menu), 633

Display icon, 379

Display Properties dialog box, 388

Distort command (Filter menu), 480, 630-633

distorting layers, 361-362, 364

distortion filters, 630

dithering, 201

Divide Scanned Photos command (Image menu), 58

Do this step for me hyperlink, 177

Dock Properties in Organize Bin command (Window menu), 130, 212

Dodge tool

   exposure corrections, 520-523

   sharpening eyes, 488-494

   stain repairs, 466

   whitening teeth, 486-487

Dolly slider, 635

dots per inch (DPI), 6, 222, 247

DPI (dots per inch), 6, 222, 247

drawings

   changing photo, 673-676

   selections, freehand, 280-282

   shapes, retouching photos, 448

drivers, printer color management, 378

Duplicate command (File menu), 196

How can we make this index more useful? Email us at indexes@samspublishing.com

727

Duplicate command (Layer menu), 467

Duplicate Layer command (Layer menu), 338

Duplicate Layer menu commands, Duplicate Layer, 275

duplicating image window, 220-222

Dust & Scratches command (Filter menu), 456

Dust & Scratches dialog box, 456-458

Dust & Scratches filter, 455-456

    scratch removal, 456-458

    small spot removal, 461

DVDs

    copying from catalog, 76-79

    importing media files, 47-50

dye sublimation printers, 6

E

Email button, 584

E-mail Client drop-down list, 577

E-mail command (Edit menu), 577

E-mail to Mobile Phone option, 591

earth tones, blended colors, 9

Edge Contrast option, 286

edges

    images, selecting, 273-277

    masks, 551

    selections, softening, 306-307

Edit and Enhance Photos button, 63

Edit and Enhance Photos option, 168, 179

Edit button, 168, 179

    image arrangement in Editor, 213

    stacking images, 92

    updating images in the catalog, 96

Edit button commands, 37

Edit Collection dialog box, 119, 125

Edit Collection Icon dialog box, 125

Edit Contacts button, 584

Edit icon, 337

Edit Icon button, 125

Edit menu commands

    Add Caption to Selected Items, 130

    Adjust Date and Time, 102

    Auto Fix Photo, 186

    Auto Fix Selected Photos, 182

    Auto Fix Window, 182, 376, 395

    Auto Smart Fix, 376

    Color Settings, 391

    Contact Book, 579

    Copy, 317-318, 330, 467

    Copy Merged, 317-318, 330, 709

    Cut, 317

    Define Brush from Selection, 442

    Delete, 321

    Delete from Catalog, 70

    Delete Selected Items from Catalog, 70

    Edit with XXX, 182

    File Association, 186

    Finish External Edit, 182

    Paste, 317, 467

    Paste Into Selection, 329-331

    Preferences, 30, 56, 61, 112, 176, 183

    Preset Manager, 422

    Redo, 32

    Resize, 227

    Select All, 68

    Stack, 93

    Undo, 32

    Undo Delete Selected Items from Catalog, 70

    Update Thumbnail, 95

    Update Thumbnails, 96

    Version Set, 184-185, 189

Edit Tag dialog box, 119, 125

Edit Tag Icon dialog box, 125-127

Edit with XXX command (Edit menu), 182

editing. *See also* modifying

    images, 182-185

        brightening face, 495-498

        creating soft focus effect, 478-480

        eyeglasses glare, 491-494

        opening, 186-189

        red eye removal, 481-483

        sharpening eyes, 488-491

        whitening teeth, 486-487

    photos, 16

        during review, 86

        effects, 24-25

        file formats, 26-27

        filters, 23-24

        graphics editor capabilities, 16-20

        layer styles, 25

        layering, 20-22

        pen tablet, 27-29

        selecting portions, 22-23

Editor, 3, 168-170

    catalog, 18

    color models, 8

    digital retouching artist, 455

    grids, 176-177

    How To palette, 177

    image touch up, 186

    images

        arranging, 213-215

        information display, 210-212

        placing PDF images into, 319

    Options bar, 171-172

    Palette Bin, 172-175

Photo Bin, 175-176

photo corrections, 376

    Adobe Gamma, 381-392

    color management, 376-380

    cropping images, 394-398

    Quick Fix tools, 401-403

    rotating images, 392-394

    straightening images, 398-400

photo editing, 16

    capabilities, 16-20

    effects, 24-25

    file formats, 26-27

    filters, 23-24

    layer styles, 25

    layering, 20-22

    pen tablet, 27-29

    selecting portions, 22-23

printing

    images, online services, 263

    single image, 244

publishing, 19

Quick Fix window, 182

Red Eye Removal tool, 481-483

rulers, 176-177

saving images, 194-195

selections. *See* selections

Shortcuts bar, 170-171

soft focus effect, 478-480

Standard Edit window, 182

Toolbox, 171-172

effects

    creating images, 181

    digital photography, 6-8

    editing photos, 16

graphics editor, 18, 24-25

visual

creating weather, 636-638

melting images, 630-632

water reflection, 639-641

wrapping image around object, 633-636

elements, graphics editor, 17

Ellipse tool, 446

Elliptical Marquee icon, 278

Elliptical Marquee tool, 299, 561

Elliptical Selection tool, 558

email

clients, 574

sharing photos, 582-585

basics, 574-575

Contact Book, 579-581

online service selection, 586-587

online service sharing, 588-591

Organizer set up, 576-578

sending to mobile phone, 591-593

Emboss command (Filter menu), 713

Emboss dialog box, 713

Emboss filter, 704-707

embossing text, 704-707

Enhance menu commands

Adjust Color, 486

Adjust Lighting, 472, 638

Auto Levels, 401

Epson, PIM (Print Image Management), 380

Equalize command (Filter menu), 476

Equalize filter, scanned photo quality restoration, 476

Eraser tool, 29, 469, 480, 485

erasers

Background Eraser, 355-357

pen tablets, 29

tolerance, 357

erasing. See also deleting

layers, 355-358

errors

diffusion, 241

messages, saving to text files, 233

event banners, 152

Exchangeable Image File. See EXIF

Exclusion blend mode, 21

EXIF (Exchangeable Image File), 139, 211

image information, 378-380

scanning images, 140

Exif Print option, 258

Exit button, 86

Expand All Collections command (View menu), 113

Expand All Tags command (View menu), 113

Expand command (Modify menu), 296

Expand command (Style menu), 613

expanding selections, 296-298

Export Clipboard option (Preferences dialog box), 318-321

exposure corrections

faded pictures, 511-515

flashes

too close, 525-528

too far away, 528-531

histograms, 500-507

improving brightness and contrast, 507-510

nighttime photos, 523-525

portion of images, 520-523

subject on snowy background, 515-519

Exposure scale, 521

Eyedropper tool, 206, 240, 430

eyes

glasses glare removal, 491-494

sharpening, 488-491

F

face, brightening with makeup, 495-498

faded pictures, improving, 511-515

fake water, 639

Favorites tag markers, 121

Feather command (Select menu), 306, 649

Feather Selection dialog box, 306-307, 649

feathering, 8, 201, 272, 306-307, 558

    defined, 272, 301

    radial blur effect, 563

    selections, 23

Field of View slider, 635

File Association command (Edit menu), 186

File Browser, Metadata palette, 211

File Browser command (Window menu), 230

File Browser method, 231

File Info command (File menu), 210

File Info dialog box, 210-212, 232, 379

File menu commands

    Attach to Email, 582

    Automation Tools, 66

    Backup, 73

    Browse, 133

    Browse Folders, 211

    Burn, 78

    By Media Type, 101

    Catalog, 75

    Duplicate, 196

    File Info, 210

    Get Photos, 43, 46, 51, 61

    Import, 58

    New, 179, 321-323

    Open, 94

    Open Recently Edited File, 186

    Order Prints, 263

    Page Setup, 249

    Place, 319

    Print, 253, 694

    Process Multiple Files, 230

    Reconnect, 72, 231

    Rename, 70, 230

    Restore, 75

    Save, 195

    Save As, 195-197, 230

    Save for Web, 203-205

    Watch Folders, 66

filenames, finding files, 148-149

files

    dates, 101-102, 138, 211

    formats, 26-27

    formatting, 5

    locating, 138

        by caption or note, 150-152

        catalog, 139-143

        color similarity, 160-162

        dates, 152-156

        filenames, 148-149

        Hidden tags, 162-164

        history, 158-160

        media types, 146-148

        same markers, 143-146

        within date range, 156-158

    organization, 139

    renaming, 230

fills, layers, 21, 336

    colors, 344

    gradients, 342

    masks, 342, 365-366

    patterns, 344

Film Grain filter, 646

Filter command (Filter menu), 23

Filter menu commands
  Adjustments, 275, 466, 507
  Blur, 478, 555
  Despeckle, 460
  Distort, 480, 630-633
  Filter, 23
  Noise, 456
  Pixelate, 636
  Render, 633
  Sharpen, 490, 549-551
  Sketch, 619
  Stylize, 638
filters, 24, 646
  blur, 483-485
  creating images, 181
  digital retouching artist, 455
  Gaussian Blur, 310, 478
  Gradient Map, 276
  graphics editor, 18, 23-24
  Invert, 276
  making photo look old, 644-650
  Posterize, 276
  sharpness basics, 548-549
  Threshold, 276
  Threshold adjustment, 276
Find bar, 140-143
  Back to All Photos button, 148
  dragging markers to, 145
  Organizer, 37
Find button, 127
Find menu commands
  By Caption or Note, 150-151
  By Color Similarity, 162
  By Filename, 149
  By History, 158
  By Media Type, 147
  Clear Date Range, 158

  Items with Unknown Date and Time, 156
  Set Date Range, 157
  Untagged Items, 146
finding items, 138
  by caption or note, 150-152
  catalog, 139-143
  color similarity, 160-162
  dates, 152-156
  filenames, 148-149
  Hidden tags, 162-164
  history, 158-160
  media types, 146-148
  same markers, 143-145
    adding criteria, 146
    dragging to Find bar, 145
    searches, 145
  within date range, 156-158
Finger Painting check box, 564
Finger Painting option, 465
Finish External Edit command (Edit menu), 182
Fit On Screen button, 217
Fixed Aspect Ratio mode, 278
flashes
  correcting
    too close, 525-528
    too far away, 528-531
  graphics editor, 17
Flatten Set command (Edit menu), 185
flattening layers, 370-371
Flip Horizontal command, rotating image, 393
Flip Layer Horizontal command (Image menu), 617
Flip Vertical command, rotating image, 393
flipping images, 392
floating palettes, 173
focus, graphics editor, 17

Fog layer style, 358

Folder Location option, sorting images, 91

folders

  importing media files, 44-47

  watches, importing files, 68

fonts, 702

For Sale signs, 691-694

Forced Color dialog box, 239-240

Foreground Color swatch, 612

foreground

  colors

    gradient patterns, 345

    retouching photos, 425

    Smudge tool, 564

  Finger Painting option, 465

Foreground to Background gradient, 523

foreground-background colors, retouching photos, 424-428

Format drop-down list, 202

formats, saving images, 189-193

formatting

  files, 26-27

  memory cards, 12

  RAW, 5

  TIFF, 5

Forward button, 37, 142

Frame From Video dialog box, 63

Frame layer, 614

frames

  increasing area around image, 233-236

  photos, 610-614

framing, digital photography, 15

freckles, removal, 483-485

Free Rotate Layer command (Image menu), 394, 398

free-floating palettes, 217

freehand drawings, selections, 280-282

Frequency option, 286

From Camera or Card Reader command (File menu), 51

From Mobile Phone command (File menu), 61

Front Image button, 395

Full Color Management option, 391

full-screen photo reviews, reviewing images, 82

G

gammas, 383, 503

  monitor calibration, 385-386

  white and black points, 513

gamuts, 376-377

  EXIF information, 378

  monitor chromaticity, 382

  sRGB, 378

Gaussian Blur command (Filter menu), 478, 560

Gaussian Blur dialog box, 478, 527, 560

Gaussian Blur filter, 310, 478, 555, 558-560

Get Photos button, 37, 46

Get Photos by Searching for Folders dialog box, 43

Get Photos command (File menu), 43, 46, 51, 61

Getting Photos dialog box, 44, 47, 50

GIF format

  compressing images, 200-203

  files, Organizer, 43

  saving images, 189

GIF Options dialog box, 203

glare, removal from eyeglasses, 491-494

Glass filter, 630

Glow Amounts, 480, 647

glowing text, 700-704

How can we make this index more useful? Email us at indexes@samspublishing.com

733

Go to Quick Fix command (Edit button), 37

Go to Standard Edit command (Edit button), 37

Go to Standard Edit option, 179

Grab Frame button, 63

Gradient command (New Fill Layer menu), 344

Gradient dialog box, 345

Gradient Map command (Layer menu), 523

Gradient Map dialog box, 523

gradient maps, 523

   filter, 276

   layers, 346

gradients

   layers, 342-345

   retouching photos, 443-446

   tool, 342, 366, 602

Grain command (Filter menu), 648

Grain dialog box, 648

Graininess values, 480

graphics. *See also* images, photos, pictures

   Editor, 3, 168-170

      grids, 176-177

      How To palette, 177

      Options bar, 171-172

      Palette Bin, 172-175

      Photo Bin, 175-176

      rulers, 176-177

      Shortcuts bar, 170-171

      Toolbox, 171-172

   images, Organizer, 3

graphics editors, 3, 16

   capabilities, 16-20

   effects, 24-25

   file formats, 26-27

   filters, 23-24

gamma adjustments, 385

image information, 379

layer styles, 25

layering, 20-22

pen tablet, 27-29

selecting portions, 22-23

grayscale

   color mode, 181, 237

   converting to, 241

   images, filters, 24

   increasing mode to RGB, 237

   mode, removing surface defects, 455

Grayscale command (Image menu), 650

green channel, 543

greeting cards, scrapbook pages, 618

Grid command (Edit menu), 177

Grid command (View menu), 177, 400

gridlines, straightening images, 400

grids

   changing properties, 177

   Editor, 176-177

Group with Previous command (Layer menu), 603

Group with Previous option (New Layer dialog box), 344, 348

groups

   changing, 127-129

   collection markers, 112

   Contact Book, 579

   creating, 114-116

   deleting, 122-123

   images, processing, 229-233

   layers, 368-370

   palettes, 173

Grow command (Select menu), 298-300

H

Hand tool, 215, 219, 402
    retouching photos, 406
    scrolling images, 219
handles, 328, 448
Hard Mix blend mode, 21
Healing Brush, 16, 222, 597
    repairing surface defects, 455
    scratch removal, 458
height adjusting, 179
Help Contents button, Editor, 168
Hidden tags, 162-164
    category, 111
    markers, 121
hidden tools, Toolbox, 172
hiding layers in images, 337
Histogram command (Window menu), 506
Histogram palette, 16, 174-175, 503, 506
histograms, 500-507
history, finding items, 158-160
History States value, 32
History tab (Properties pane), 102, 212
holes
    repairing, 454-455
    repairing large areas, 467-470
Horizontal Distortion slider, 690
Horizontal tool, 330, 342, 621
Horizontal Type Mask tool, 709
Horizontal Type tool, 685
How To command (Window menu), 177
How To palette, 172, 177
HSB (hue, saturation, and brightness), 8-10, 427
HTML color, 10, 427

hue
    correcting manually, 540-544
    optical color wheel, 10
    saturation levels, 10
Hue slider, 403, 466, 542-543
hue, saturation, and brightness (HSB), 8-10, 427
Hue/Saturation command (Filter menu), 466
Hue/Saturation dialog box, 473, 542
Hue/Saturation layers, 346

I

ICC color profiles, 11, 212, 378, 386
    Adobe Gamma, 378
    loading, 388
    monitor chromaticity, 381
    paper, 245, 378
ICC Profile option, Save dialog box, 194
ICM (Image Color Management), 378
ICM profiles. *See* ICC color profiles
icons
    Elliptical Marquee, 278
    markers, changing, 125-127
    photo well, 39
    Rectangular Marquee, 278
Ignore Palettes option, 217
Image Color Management (ICM), 378
Image command (Window menu), 215
Image Compression option, TIFF, 199
Image Effects style, 361
Image from Clipboard command (New menu), 293, 321-323

Image layers, 336, 469, 603
  creating, 339-341
  opacity, 341
  raster data, 339
Image menu commands
  Crop, 395
  Divide Scanned Photos, 58
  Mode, 237, 478
  Resize, 223, 247
  Rotate, 328, 392, 639
Image Size command (Edit menu), 227
Image Size command (Image menu), 245-247
Image Size dialog box, 223, 227, 247
images. *See also* pictures, photos, graphics
  adding layers to, 337
  arranging in Editor, 213-215
  cell phone cameras, 60
  changing date and time, 101-102
    change options, 104
    entering new date or time, 104
    selection of image, 102-104
    viewing result, 104
  colors
    changing mode, 236-242
    find by similarities, 160-162
  creating
    from selections, 321-323
    new, 178-181
  cropping, 248
  deleting layers, 338
  editing, 16, 182-185
    brightening face, 495-498
    creating soft focus effect, 478-480
    effects, 24-25
    eyeglasses glare, 491-494
    file formats, 26-27
    filters, 23-24

    graphics editor capabilities, 16-20
    layer styles, 25
    layering, 20-22
    pen tablet, 27-29
    red eye removal, 481-483
    selecting portions, 22-23
    sharpening eyes, 488-491
    whitening teeth, 486-487
  Editor, 168-170
    grids, 176-177
    How To palette, 177
    Options bar, 171-172
    Palette Bin, 172-175
    Photo Bin, 175-176
    rulers, 176-177
    Shortcuts bar, 170-171
    Toolbox, 171-172
  filling text, 707-710
  group processing, 229-233
  hiding layers in, 337
  icon, 125
  increasing area around, 233-236
  information display, 210-212
  layers. *See* layers
  magnifying work, 220-222
  opening for editing, 186-189
  Organizer, 3
  PDFs, placing into Editor, 319
  printing, 227, 246-248, 252-256
  resolution, 222-229
  reviewing, 82
    applying controls, 85-86
    displaying photos for review, 84
    editing photos, 86
    Photo Review button, 84
    setting options, 84

viewing mode selection, 85

zoom adjustment, 85

Sample radius value, 303

saving, 5, 189-190

   Editor, 194-195

   formats, 189-193

   GIF format compression, 200-203

   JPEG format compression, 203-206

   PNG format, 206-208

   printing preparation, 247

   PSD format, 195-197

   selections, 312-314

   TIFF format, 198-200

scrolling, 219

selecting areas of, 268, 273

   circular areas, 278-279

   edges, 273-277

   rectangular areas, 278-279

   selection marquee, 268-273

size, 222-229

   changing, 225-229

   printing preparation, 248

stacking, 91-94

thumbnails, 38

updating in the catalog, 94-96

version sets, 92

Zoom tool, 215

zooming

   Navigator palette, 217-219

   Zoom tool, 215-217

Images command (Window menu), 170, 213, 599, 609

Import Addresses button, 264

Import Batch option, sorting images, 91

Import command (File menu), 58

Import Folders button, 43

importing

   dates

      images, 101-102

      sorting items, 91

   media files

      automatically, 66-68

      CD-ROM or DVD, 47-50

      cell phone images, 60-61

      digital camera, 51-54

      from folders, 44-47

      multiple scanned images, 57-60

      scanned images, 54-57

      scanning Organizer for, 40-44, 47-50

      video files, 61-64

   PDF documents, 64-66

Include All Subfolders option, 231

Include in the Organizer option

   Save As dialog box, 46

   Save dialog box, 194

Indexed Color dialog box, 202

Indexed Color mode, 237

Individual Attachments option, 585

Info command (Window menu), 176, 470

Info palette, 174-176, 470

information

   device acceptance, 378-380

   images, 210-212

ink jet printers, resolution, 181

Inmatrix website, 100

Instant Tag button, 91, 106, 121

interlacing, 191-192

interleaving, 192

Intersect with Selection operation, 316

Inverse command (Select menu), 308-310, 649

inverse selections, 308-310

Invert command (Filter menu), 466

How can we make this index more useful? Email us at indexes@samspublishing.com

737

Invert filter, 276

Invert Image option, 256

Invert layers, 346

iris, 481

Items Not Imported dialog box, 44, 47-50

Items Shown dialog box, 97

Items with Unknown Date and Time command (Find menu), 156

J

jagged selections, smoothing edges, 301-303

Joint Photographic Experts Groups. *See* JPEGs

JP2 format, saving images, 191

JPEG Options dialog box, 205

JPEGs (Joint Photographic Experts Groups), 26, 146

    2000 format, 191

        compressing image, 204

        saving images, 191

    compressing images, 203-206

    digital cameras, 191

    image saving, 5

    saving images, 190

JPG format, saving images, 190

K - L

keywords, searches, 141

Keywords category, 211

khaki colors, blended colors, 9

kiosks, printing photos, 5

Kodak Picture Maker, 34

labels, 231, 685-687

Labels option, 231

Labels pane, 231-232

landscapes

    digital photography, 15

    orientation, 249, 349

large damages, repairing, 463-470

Lasso tool, 23, 298

    drawing selections freehand, 280-282

    selecting, 286

Layer 180° command, rotating layers, 394

Layer 90° Left command, rotating layers, 394

Layer 90° Right command, rotating layers, 394

Layer Flip Horizontal command, rotating layers, 394

Layer Flip Horizontal command (Image menu), 394

Layer Flip Vertical command, rotating layers, 394

Layer from Background command (Layer menu), 469, 491, 602

Layer menu commands

    Delete Layer, 277, 338, 518

    Duplicate, 467

    Duplicate Layer, 338, 478

    Group with Previous, 603

    Layer from Background, 469

    Merge Down, 371, 603

    Merge Linked, 371

    New, 317

    New Adjustment Layer, 348, 523

    New Fill Layer, 612

    Rename Layer, 338

    Simplify Layer, 354, 619, 632

    Type, 688

    Visible, 371

Layer Style list box, 25

Layer Style menu commands, Scale Effects, 361

Layer via Copy command (Layer menu), 493, 517

Layer via Copy command (New menu), 325

layers, 27, 300

  adding to images, 337

  adjustment, 336

    Brightness/Contrast, 346

    creating, 346-349

    defined, 346

    Gradient Map, 346

    Hue/Saturation, 346

    Invert, 346

    Levels, 346

    masks, 365-366

    Photo Filter, 346

    Posterize, 348

    Threshold, 348

  background, 21, 320, 326, 334-336

    blend mode, 334

    converting into regular layers, 350-352

    creating Image layers, 339

    creating new images, 178

    increase area around images, 233

    Normal blend mode, 335

  blend mode, 339

  Brightness/Contrast, 346

  colors, 342-345

    blend modes, 241

    fills, 344

  cropping, 395

  current, 329

  deleting, 338

  distorting, 361-364

  Edit icon, 337

  erasing, 355-358

  fills, 21, 336

    colors, 344

    gradients, 342

    masks, 342, 365-366

    patterns, 344

  flattening, 25, 370-371

  free rotating, 398

  Gradient Map, 346

  gradients, 342-345

  graphics editor, 20-22

  groups, 368-370

  hiding in images, 337

  Hue/Saturation, 346

  Image, 336

    creating, 339-341

    opacity, 341

    raster data, 339

    TIFF format, 188

  Invert, 346

  Layers palette, 334-339

  Levels, 346

  linking, 338

  Lock Transparency icon, 337

  locking, 337

  masking images, 600-604

  merging, 248, 370-371

  moving, 361-364

  opaque pixels, selecting, 337

  organization, 368-370

  patterns, 342-345

  Photo Filter, 346

  Posterize, 348

  raster, 7

  repairing stains, 466

  rotating, 392-394

  selections, creating, 323-325

  Shape, 336

How can we make this index more useful? Email us at indexes@samspublishing.com

739

simplifying, 336, 352-354

sizing, 361-364

skewing, 361-364

styles, 25, 334, 446

    applying, 358-361

    creating images, 181

    Fog, 358

    graphics editor, 18, 25

    Image Effects, 361

    Radioactive Outer Glow, 331

    scale, 26

    Toy, 358

Threshold, 348

transforming contents, 362

Type, 336

vector, 7

Visible icon, 337

Layers option, Save dialog box, 194

Layers palette, 21, 26, 172, 334-339

    Create Adjustment Layer button, 344, 348

    Create New Layer button, 338

    Delete Layer button, 338

    Link icon, 338, 369

    Lock All button, 337-338

    Lock button, 338

    Lock Transparency icon, 337

    lowering opacity, 480

    New Layer button, 341

    Opacity setting, 338, 341

    printing images, 248

    rotating layers, 392

    Visible icon, 337

left bracket ([), increasing brush size, 292

Less Saturation button, 539

Levels command (Enhance menu), 472, 505, 511

Levels dialog box, 472, 503, 511

Levels layers, 346

libraries

    loading, 424

    patterns, 442

light points, color fading repair, 472

Lighten button, 490

Lighten Shadows setting, 518

Lighten Shadows slider, 402

lighting

    color fading repair, 470-473

    digital photography, 12

    white balance, 13

lightness

    correcting manually, 540-544

    slider, 543

Limits option, Background Eraser tool, 604

Linear gradient style, 445

Link icon (Layers palette), 338, 369

linking layers, 338

Liquify command (Filter menu), 630

Liquify dialog box, 630

Liquify filter, 630-632

Liquify tools, melting images, 630-632

Lite-Brite toys, 7

Load button, Preset Manager window, 424

Load Selection command (Select menu), 314, 649

Load Selection dialog box, 314, 649

loading, saved selections, 314-316

Local options, 239

locating files, 138

    by caption or note, 150-152

    catalog, 139-143

    color similarity, 160-162

    dates, 152-156

    filenames, 148-149

    Hidden tags, 162-164

history, 158-160

media types, 146-148

same markers, 143-146

within dates range, 156-158

Lock All button (Layers palette), 337-338

Lock button (Layers palette), 338

Lock Transparency icon, 337

locking layers, 337

log files, 233

low-resolution

digital photographs, 12

images, printing, 252

luminance, 507, 540

Luminosity channel, 507

M

Magenta channel, 544

Magic Eraser tool, 355-357, 606

Magic Wand, 23, 308

Magic Wand tool, 300, 312, 354, 461, 517, 702

Magnetic Lasso tool, 284, 286-287, 303, 325, 331

magnification, images, 220-222

Maintain Aspect Ratio button (Options bar), 362

makeup, brightening face, 495-498

management, colors, 376-377

image information, 378-380

reasons for, 376-378

manual color correction, 534-537

markers

assigning to items, 119-122

catalog organization, 109-113

changing, 127-129

collections, 109

creating, 117-119

deleting, 122-123

finding items, 143-145

adding criteria, 146

dragging to Find bar, 145

searches, 145

icon change, 125-127

marquee selections, 296, 303-305

moving, 320

reloading, 314

selecting image portions, 268

Marquee Selection tools, 278

Marquee tools, 23

Mask layer, 553, 614

masks, 27, 211, 554

Adjustment layers, 365-366

clipping, 21, 292, 338

defined, 365

fill layers, 342

image layer, 600-604

layer fills, 365-366

overlays, 268

saved selections, 312

Master options, 239

Mat layer, 614

Match Location command (Window menu), 170, 215

Match Zoom command (Window menu), 170, 215

Matte color, 206

Matte drop-down list, 205, 240

Maximize button, Editor, 168

Maximize Compatibility option, 27

Maximize mode, 16, 169, 175

Maximize Mode button, 170

measuring objects, Info palette, 176

How can we make this index more useful? Email us at indexes@samspublishing.com

741

media files
  CD-ROM or DVD importing, 47-50
  cell phone image importing, 60-61
  digital camera importing, 51-54
  importing from folders, 44-47
  multiple scanned image importing, 57-60
  scanned image importing, 54-57
  scanning Organizer for, 40-44, 47-50
  video, 61-64
Media Player, 135
Media Player window, 99, 135
media types, finding files, 146-148
Media Types command (View menu), 97, 146
Median command (Filter menu), 461
Median dialog box, 461
Median filters, 455, 461
  contrast, 461
  noise removal, 459
  scanned photo quality restoration, 474
melting images, 630-632
memory cards, 12, 51
Menu Types command (View menu), 38
Merge Collections option, 123
Merge Down command (Layer menu), 371, 603
Merge Linked command (Layer menu), 371
merge neighbors, 371
Merge Tags option, 123
merging
  layers, 248, 370-371
  tags and collection markers, 123
metadata
  copyrights, 710
  images, 210-212
Metadata button, 211
Metadata palette, 211
Metadata pane, Properties pane, 379

Metadata tab, 212
metallic text, 697-700
Method area, 242
Midtone Contrast slider, 402
midtones, 385, 503, 518
Minimize button, 168-170
Missing Files Check Before Backup dialog box, 75
mistakes, Undo feature, 32
Mobile Phone command (Edit menu), 61
mobile phones, sending images to, 591-593
Mode command (Image menu), 237, 478
modified dates, 101-102, 211
Modify command (Selection menu), 296, 648
Modify menu commands
  Expand, 296
  Smooth, 301
modifying. See also editing
  selections, 296
    adding areas similar to current selections, 298-300
    adding areas to similar current selections, 298-300
    expanding selections, 296-298
    shrinking selections, 296-298
moiré patterns, 24, 227, 474
  removing, 247
  scanned photos, 474
monitors
  calibration, 381
    adjusting gamma, 385-386
    chromaticity selection, 381-384
    Control Panel mode (Adobe Gamma), 386-392
  chromaticity, 381
  color management, 245, 376-377
    image information, 378-380
    reasons for, 376-378

onscreen images, 7

PPI (pixels per inch), 6

Month button, 154

More button, 32

More menu commands, Clear Undo History, 32

More Options button, Print Selected Photos dialog box, 257

More Options dialog box, 257

More Saturation button, 539

motion, adding to image, 567-568

Motion Blur command (Filter menu), 567

Motion Blur dialog box, 567, 638

Motion Blur filter, 567-568

.MOV video format, 99

Move tool, 312, 320, 361, 467, 621

moving

    layers, 361-364

    selection marquee, 303-305, 320

.MP3 format, 133

.MPG video format, 99

Multi-window mode, 16, 169

Multi-window Mode button, 170

multiple images, printing, 246

N

Name dialog box, 424

Navigator command (Window menu), 218

Navigator palette, 175, 215

    scrolling images, 219

    zooming, 217-219

Nearest Neighbor resampling, 228

negative images, creating, 654-655

neighbors

    merge, 371

    pixels, 395, 428, 551

neutral gray points, 514

New Adjustment Layer command (Layer menu), 348, 523

New command (File menu), 179, 321-323

New command (Layer menu), 317

New Contact button, 579

New Contact dialog box, 579

New dialog box, 179

New Fill Layer command (Layer menu), 612

New Fill Layer menu commands, 344

New Group button, 581

New Group dialog box, 581

New Layer button, 341

New Layer dialog box, 340-341, 344, 348, 398, 649

New menu commands

    Background from Layer, 350

    Image From Clipboard, 293, 321-323

    Layer via Copy, 325

New Selection operation, 316

New Window for XXX command (View menu), 221

Next Day button, 155

Next Item button, 155

Next Month button, 154

Next Photo button, 86

Next Year button, 154

nighttime photos, correcting exposure, 523-525

Noise command (Filter menu), 456, 460

Noise option, 241

noises, 455

    removing graininess, 555-558

    scanned photo quality restoration, 474

    spottiness, 459-462

Nokia Suites 6.2, 61

None option, 241

Normal blend mode, Background layer, 335

How can we make this index more useful? Email us at indexes@samspublishing.com

743

notes
  adding, 130-132
  finding items, 150-152
NTSC standard TV resolution, 223

O

objects
  digital photography, 6-8
  graphics editor, 17
  removing with Clone Stamp tool, 596-600
  selecting, tracing edges, 284-287
observation, digital photography, 15
Ocean Ripple filter, 630
offline storage, 48, 138
Ofoto website, 246, 588
oil paintings, changing photo, 662-668
old photos
  graphics editor, 18
  repairing
    color fading, 470-473
    large damaged areas, 463-470
    scanned photo quality restoration, 474-476
    scratch removal, 456-459
    specks, 459-462
    spots, 459-462
    surface defects, 454-455
online services, 247
  printing images, 263-266
  printing photos, 6
  selection, 586-587
  sharing images, 588-591
onscreen images, size, 7

Opacity
  blurred layers, 480
  pixels, 301
  selecting areas of similar opacity, 288-290
Opacity setting (Layers palette), 338, 341
opaque pixels, layers selection, 337
Open command (File menu), 94
Open dialog box, 186
Open Recently Edited File command (File menu), 186
Opened Files option, 231
opening images for editing, 186-189
optical illusions
  creating weather, 636-638
  melting images, 630-632
  water reflection, 639-641
  wrapping image around object, 633-636
optics, color models, 8-10
Options bar, 297
  Editor, 171-172
  Maintain Aspect Ratio button, 362
  Organizer, 39
  Show Bounding Box option, 362
Orange Glass layer style, 25
Order Online button, 264
Order Prints command (File menu), 263
Order Summary frame, 264
organization
  items, 139
  layers, 368-370
  photos, 15
Organize & Share command (Edit menu), 577, 586
Organize Bin
  changing display, 113-114
  Organizer, 38
  selecting markers, 145

Organize Bin command (View menu), 111

Organize Bin command (Window menu), 116

Organize command (Window menu), 145

Organizer, 3-5, 15

  basics, 34-36

    Options bar, 39

    Organize Bin, 38

    photo well, 38-39

    Timeline, 37

  by caption or note, 150-152

  catalog, 18, 34, 139

    backup, 73-76

    copying to CD-ROMs and DVDs, 76-79

    item organization, 106-135

    locating moved files, 70-73

    removing items, 68-70

  color similarity, 160-162

  cropping images, 262

  Date View button, 170

  dates, 152-158

  editing image, 186

  emailing photos, 575, 582-585

    Contact Book, 579-581

    online service selection, 586-587

    online service sharing, 588-591

    sending to mobile phone, 591-593

    set up, 576-578

  filenames, 148-149

  Find bar, 37, 141-143

  finding items, 138

  fixing images, 182

  GIF or PNG files, 43

  Hidden tags, 162-164

  history, 158-160

  markers, finding items, 143-146

media files

  CD-ROM or DVD importing, 47-50

  cell phone images importing, 60-61

  digital camera importing, 51-54

  importing automatically, 66-68

  importing from folders, 44-47

  multiple scanned image importing, 57-60

  scanned image importing, 54-57

  scanning for, 40-44, 47-50

  video files, 61-64

media types, 146-148

PDF document, importing from, 64-66

picture package printing, 260

printing

  groups of images, 244

  images, online services, 263

Properties pane, 212

rotating images, 392

searches, 140-141

orientation, 249

Orientation option, Page Setup dialog box, 249

Output Levels slider, 514

Overlay Color list, 292

overlays (masks), 268

Oversharp layer, 491

P

packages, 259-262

Page Duration list, 84

Page Setup command (File menu), 249

Page Setup dialog box, 249

Paint Brush tool, 621

How can we make this index more useful? Email us at indexes@samspublishing.com

745

Paint Bucket tool, 342, 354, 365-366, 603, 614, 636

Paint Shop Pro, file format, 47

painting

   retouching photos, airbrush, 439-440

   selections, 290-293

palette

   gamuts, 377

   Layers, New Layer button, 341

Palette Bin, 16, 172-175

Palette option, 238

palettes, 172-175

   colors, 238

   free-floating, 217

   Layer, 334-339

      Create Adjustment Layer button, 344, 348

      Create New Layer button, 338

      Delete Layer button, 338

      Link icon, 338, 369

      Lock All button, 337-338

      Lock button, 338

      Lock Transparency icon, 337

      Opacity setting, 338

      Visible icon, 337

   Image layers, 341

   Styles and Effects, 23-25, 359

Pan Camera tool, 635

panoramas, creating, 624-628

paper

   ICC color profiles, 378

   manufacturer, 245

   photo printers, 252

   photos, 6

   printing images, 245

Paper Size option, Page Setup dialog box, 251

Parent Collection Group list, 116

Paste command (Edit menu), 317, 467

Paste Into Selection command (Edit menu), 329-331

Paste Into Selection option, 319

pasting selections, 317-321

Pattern command (New Fill Layer menu), 344

Pattern Dither option, 242

Pattern Fill dialog box, 345, 649

Pattern option, 241

Pattern Stamp, scrapbook page creation, 619

patterns, 441

   layers, 342-345

   retouching photos, 441-442

   scrapbook page creation, 619

Pause Automatic Sequencing button, 155

.PDD extensions, 27

PDF for Image Import dialog box, 64

PDFs

   documents, importing from, 64-66

   images, placing into Editor, 319

Pen Pressure option, 286

pen tables, graphics editors, 27-29

pen tablets, 546

Pencil tool, 25, 365

Perceptual algorithm, 239

Photo Bin, 16

   Editor, 175-176

   thumbnails, changing to new image, 170

Photo Browser

   button, 156, 170

   sorting media files, 108

   view, Organizer, 82

Photo Browser Arrangement list, 89

Photo Compare button, 85

Photo Compare mode (photo reviews), 85-86

Photo Downloader, 51

Photo Filter dialog box, 349

Photo Filter layers, 346
photo paper
    image sizes, 245
    manufacturer, 245
    printers, 5
Photo Review button, 84-85
Photo Review dialog box, 84
Photo Review mode (photo reviews), 85-86
Photo Review toolbar, 84
photo wells, Organizer, 38-39
photography, digital, 4-6
    color models, 8-10
    objects, 6-8
    optically appealing photographs, 12-15
    printing, 10-12
    resolution, 6
    text, 6-8
Photomerge dialog box, 625
Photomerge Panorama command (File menu), 625
photos. *See also* graphics, images, pictures
    artistic creations
        Andy Warhol technique, 677-682
        changing to black and white, 650-653
        colorizing, 656-662
        drawing effect, 673-676
        making look old, 644-650
        negative images, 654-655
        oil painting effect, 662-668
        watercolor effect, 668-672
    copyrighting, 710-714
    corrections, 376
        Adobe Gamma, 381-392
        color management, 376-380
        cropping images, 394-398
        Quick Fix tools, 401-403

        rotating images, 392-394
        straightening images, 398-400
    digital processing principles, 4-6
    editing, 16
        during review, 86
        effects, 24-25
        file formats, 26-27
        filters, 23-24
        graphics editor capabilities, 16-20
        layer styles, 25
        layering, 20-22
        pen tablet, 27-29
        selecting portions, 22-23
    histograms, 500-507
    organization, 15
    paper, 6, 378
    printers, paper selection, 252
    repairing
        color fading, 470-473
        large damaged areas, 463-470
        scanned photo quality restoration, 474-476
        scratch removal, 456-459
        specks, 459-462
        spots, 459-462
        surface defects, 454-455
    retouching, 406
        airbrush painting, 439-440
        color selection, 424-430
        drawing shapes, 448
        gradient, 443-446
        patterns, 441-442
        preset management, 423-424
    review, 15, 82
    visual impact improvement
        bland sky, 607-610
        blending images, 615-617

composite image, 622-624

framing photo, 610-614

mask image layer, 600-604

panoramas, 624-628

removed unwanted objects, 596-600

replacing background, 604-607

scrapbook pages, 618-621

Pictorico website, 246

pictures. *See also* graphics, images, photos
packages, printing, 259-262

pigment, 11

PIM (Print Image Management), 380

Pixelate command (Filter menu), 636

pixelation, 223

pixels, 6

histograms, 500-507

image size, 222-229

neighboring, 428

opacity, 301

preparing image to print, 246

resampling, 227

saturating, 466

pixels per inch (PPI), 6, 247

Place command (File menu), 319

Place in Palette Bin option, 173

Place Order button, 266

Play Audio Captions option, 84

Play button

playing audio files, 97

viewing video files, 101

playback management, playing audio files, 99

playing audio files, 96-99

PNG files, Organizer, 43

PNG format, saving images, 191, 206-208

PNG Options dialog box, 207

Point Sample option, 428

Pointillize dialog box, 636

Pointillize filter, 636

polarizing filters, 491

Polygonal Lasso tool, 282-284, 287

portrait orientations, rotating images, 392

portraits, 249, 392, 644

positioning objects, Info palette, 176

post cards, scrapbook pages, 618

Posterize filter, 276

Posterize layers, 348

posters, creating, 691-694

PPI (pixels per inch), 6, 247

preferences, changing, 30-31

Preferences command (Edit menu), 30, 56, 61, 112, 176, 183

Preferences dialog box, 30-31, 61, 183, 319-321, 577

preparation, digital photography, 12

Preserve Exact Colors option, 241

Preset drop-down list, 179

Preset Manager, 423-424

Preset Manager command (Edit menu), 422

Presets folder, 424

Previous Day button, 155

Previous Item button, 155

Previous Month button, 154

Previous Photo button, 86

Previous Year button, 154

Primaries forces, 240

primary channels, 543

principles, digital photography, 4-6

Print button, 244, 253

Print command (File menu), 253, 694

Print Crop Marks check box, 255

Print dialog box, 256, 694

Print Image Management (PIM), 258, 380

Print Multiple Images button, Print Preview dialog box, 253

Print photos to a local printer or online service button, 257, 260-263

Print Preview dialog box, 224, 245, 248, 253

Print Selected Area option, 255

Print Selected Images dialog box, 245, 248

Print Selected Photos dialog box, 224, 257-260

Print Size button, 217, 227

Print Size drop-down list, 253

Print Size list, 253

Print This Confirmation button, 266

Printer button, Page Setup dialog box, 249

printers

    color management, 245

    DPI (dots per inch), 6, 247

    drive color management, 378

    image

        information, 378-380

        resolution, 6

    ink jet, resolution, 181

    installing profile, 391

    photo, 6, 252

    quality, 5

    test image, 391

printing

    basics, 244-248

    color management, 376-377

        image information, 378-380

        reasons for, 376-378

    contact sheet, 256-259

    digital photography, 10-12

    Editor versus Organizer, 244

    images, 228, 252-256

    kiosks, 5

    online services, 263-266

    picture package, 259-262

    setting options, 249-252

Process Files From list, 231

Process Multiple Files command (File menu), 230

Process Multiple Files dialog box, 230-231

processing, image groups, 229-233

Product Overview button, 29

professional printing, 246

properties, media files, 73

Properties button, Page Setup dialog box, 251

Properties command (Window menu), 130, 211-212

Properties dialog box, 251

Properties pane, 39, 130-133, 211-212, 259

    History tab, 102

    Metadata tab, 379

    Organizer, 212

Proximity Match option, texture matching, 462

.PSD extensions, 27

PSD format, 188, saving images, 193-197

.pspimage format, Paint Shop Pro, 47

publishing, Editor, 19

Pucker tool, 630

pupils, 481

Puzzle layer style, 26

Q

quality

    digital photography, 12

    printing images, 245

    scanned photos, restoring, 474-476

quick corrections, 376

    Adobe Gamma, monitor calibration, 381-392

    color management, 376-378

    image information, 378-380

How can we make this index more useful? Email us at indexes@samspublishing.com

749

cropping images, 394-398

Quick Fix tools, 401-403

rotating images, 392-394

straightening images, 398-400

Quick Fix

edit tool, 394

mode, 16, 29, 182, 213

tool, 376, 401-403

window, 182

Quick Fix option, 231

Quick Fix pane, 394, 402

Quick Fix Photos button, 63

R

Radial Blur command (Filter menu), 562

Radial Blur dialog box, 562

Radial Blur filter, spin effect, 561-563

Radial gradient style, 445

Radioactive Outer Glow layer style, 331

rain, creating, 636, 638

range markers, file date ranges, 156

rasters, 7

data, 7

conversion from vector data, 8

filters, 24

Image layers, 339

layers, element rendering, 7

RAW format, 5

photo editing, 26

saving images, 193

recompressing stacks, 94

Reconnect command (File menu), 72, 231

Reconnect Missing Files dialog box, 72

Reconstruct tool, 630

Record Audio Caption button, 133-135

rectangular areas, selecting, 278-279

Rectangular Marquee icon, 278

Rectangular Marquee tool, 255, 331, 395

red channel, 543, 652

red eye correction, 481-483

Red Eye Removal tool, 481-483

red, green, and blue. *See* RGB

red-eye graphics editor, 16

Redo button, 32

Redo command (Edit menu), 32

Reduce Noise command (Filter menu), 461

Reduce Noise dialog box, 461

Reduce Noise filters, 455, 459-461, 474

Reflected gradient style, 445

Reflection tool, 630-632

Refresh button, Preferences dialog box, 586

Remember my password option, 264

Remove Color Cast command (Enhance menu), 536

Remove Color Cast dialog box, 536

Remove Color Cast option, 534

Remove from Collection option, 122

Remove Selected Items button, Print Photos dialog box, 259

Remove Tag option, 122

Rename command (File menu), 70, 230

Rename Files check box, 232

Rename Layer command (Layer menu), 338

renaming

files, 232

single files, 230

Render command (Filter menu), 633

Render, Clouds filter, 610

repairs, photos
 color fading, 470-473
 large damaged areas, 463-470
 scanned photo quality restoration, 474-476
 scratch removal, 456-459
 specks, 459-462
 spots, 459-462
 surface defects, 454-455
Repeat Slide Show option, 84-85
Replace menu option, 424
Resample Image option, 228
resampling, 227, 247
 disabling, 229
 images, 225
 Unsharp mask, 229
 when not to, 228
Reset Image button, 540
Reset Palette Locations command (Window menu), 174
Resize command (Edit menu), 227
Resize command (Image menu), 223, 247
Resize Images option, 232
Resize Window to Fit option, 217
resizing images, 232
resolution
 adjusting, 179
 creating new images, 178
 digital cameras, 4
 digital photography, 6, 12
 images, 222-229
 low printing images, 252
 preparing image to print, 246
 printing images, 244-245
 scanners, 6
restorations, graphics editor, 18
Restore command (File menu), 75

retouching
 images, 231
 photos
  airbrush painting, 439-440
  color fading, 470-473
  color selection, 424-430
  drawing shapes, 448
  large damaged areas, 463-470
  gradient, 443-446
  patterns, 441-442
  preset management, 423-424
  scanned photo quality restoration, 474-476
  scratch removal, 456-459
  specks, 459-462
  spots, 459-462
  surface defects, 454-455
Reveal Photos in Version Set command (Edit menu), 184, 189
Revert to Original command (Edit menu), 185
reviewing images, 82
 applying controls, 85-86
 displaying photos for review, 84
 editing photos, 86
 Photo Review button, 84
 setting options, 84
 viewing mode selection, 85
 zoom adjustment, 85
RGB (red, green, and blue), 9, 181, 427
 color mode, 237
 images, filters, 24
 mode, removing surface defects, 8-10, 455
richness, color, 507
right bracket (]), increasing brush size, 292
Rotate command (Image menu), 328, 392, 639
Rotate Image tool, 626
Rotate Left button, 86

Rotate photo 90° clockwise (right) button, 394

Rotate photo 90° counterclockwise (left) button, 394

Rotate Right button, 86

rotations

    data, in selections, 326-329

    images, 392-394

rulers

    changing unit of measure, 176

    Editor, 176-177

Rulers command (View menu), 176

S

sales sign, 691-694

Sample Radius value, high-resolution images, 303

Sample Size option, 428-429

sandy shades, blended colors, 9

saturation

    color models, 9

    corrections

        Color Variations command, 537-540

        manually, 534-537, 540-544

        specific area, 544-546

    levels, 10

    Quick Fix tool, 401

    slider, 403, 542-543

Save As command (File menu), 195-197, 230

Save As dialog box, 46, 58, 188, 197

Save Collections to File option, 117

Save command (File menu), 195

Save for Web command (File menu), 203-205, 212

Save For Web dialog box, 202

Save Image Pyramid option, TIFF, 200

Save in Version Set with Original option, Save dialog box, 194

Save Selection command (Select menu), 648

Save Selection dialog box, 312-314, 648, 702

Save Tags to File option, 117

saving

    images, 5, 189-190

        Editor, 194-195

        formats, 189-193

        GIF format, 200-203

        JPEG format, 203-206

        PNG format, 206-208

        printing preparation, 247

        PSD format, 195-197

        TIFF format, 198-200

    selections

        for reusing, 312-314

        formats, 314

        masks, 312

        reloading previously saved selections, 314-316

    vector data, 8

Saving Files command (Edit menu), 195, 380

Scale Effects command (Layer Style menu), 361

Scale setting, 255

Scale Styles option, 227

Scaled Print Size frame, 255

scanned images

    importing media files, 54-60

    quality restoration, 474-476

scanners

    automatic levels correction, 511

    PPI (pixels per inch), 247

    resolution, 6

scrapbook pages, 618-621

scratches
  removing, 456-459
  repairing, 454-455
  repairing large areas, 463-466
Scroll All Windows option, 215
scroll arrows, date range markers, 156
scrolling images, 219
Search box, Editor, 168
Search button, 43
Search Results frame, 44
Search Results pane, 43
searches
  keywords, 141
  narrowing, 156
  Organizer, 140-141
secondary colors, 543
Select a Frame list, 261
Select All command (Edit menu), 68
Select Audio File dialog box, 133-135
Select Icon dialog box, 127
Select Image tool, 627
Select menu commands
  All, 467
  Feather, 306, 649
  Grow, 298-300
  Inverse, 308-310, 649
  Load Selection, 314, 649
  Modify, 648
  Save Selection, 312, 648
  Similar, 298-300
Select Type of Print drop-down list, 259
selecting
  areas of similar brightness, 288-290
  areas of similar colors, 288-290
  areas of similar opacity, 288-290

image portions, 268, 273
  circular areas, 278-279
  edges, 273-277
  rectangular areas, 278-279
  selection marquee, 268-273
Lasso tool, 286
Magnetic Lasso tool, 286
objects, tracing edges, 284-287
opaque pixels (layers), 337
straight-edged areas, 282-284
Selection Brush tool, 23, 268, 290-293, 303, 527, 603
selection marquee, 23
  moving, 320
  reloading, 314
  selecting image portions, 268
Selection menu commands, Modify, 296
Selection tool, 633
selections
  adding to, 297
  blurring edges, 455
  copying, 317-321, 329-331
  cutting, 317-321
  deleting selection points, 287
  drawing, freehand, 280-282
  expanding, 296-298
  feathered, 23
  images, creating from selections, 321-323
  inverse selecting, 308-310
  jagged, smoothing edges, 301-303
  layers, creating, 323-325
  marquee, 296, 303-305
  modifying, 296-300
  painting, 290-293
  pasting, 317-321
  photo editing, 22

How can we make this index more useful? Email us at indexes@samspublishing.com

753

rotating data in, 326-329

saving

for reusing, 312-314

formats, 314

masks, 312

reloading previously saved selections, 314-316

selecting areas of similar brightness, 288-290

selecting areas of similar colors, **288**-290

selecting areas of similar opacity, **288**-290

selecting objects by tracing edges, 284-287

selecting straight-edged areas, 282-284

shape, 301

shrinking, 296-298

softening edges, 306-307

subtracting from, 297

Send to Mobile Phone dialog box, 591

Sepia layer, 646

Services command (Edit menu), 586

Set as Top Photo command (Edit menu), 185

Set Date Range command (Find menu), 157

Set Date Range dialog box, 156-157

Set Vanishing Point tool, 627

Shadows/Highlights command (Enhance menu), 518

Shadows/Highlights dialog box, 518

shakes, digital photography, 14

Shape layer, 336

Shape tool, 337, 366, 446

shaped borders, cropping images, 395

shapes

retouching photos, 448

selections, 301

vector data, 352

Share button, 582

sharing photos

email, 582-585

basics, 574-575

Contact Book, 579-581

online service selection, 586-587

online service sharing, 588-591

Organizer set up, 576-578

sending to mobile phone, 591-593

file format, 27

Sharpen command (Filter menu), 490, 549-551

Sharpen Edges command (Filter menu), 549

Sharpen Edges filter, 549

Sharpen filter, 549

Sharpen More command (Filter menu), 549

Sharpen More filter, 549

Sharpen tool, 549

sharpening edges, Quick Fix pane, 403

Sharpening layer, improving sharpness, 553

sharpness

adding motion, 567-568

basics, 548-549

blurring

creating depth of field, 558-560

remove graininess, 555-558

spin effect, 561-563

improving, 550-554

softening selected details, 564-566

Shear filter, 630

Shift Pixels tool, 630-632

Shifted layer, 469

Shortcuts bar, 37

Back button, 142

Editor, 170-171

Forward button, 142

Photo Browser button, 156

Print button, 244, 253

Print photos to a local printer or online service button, 257, 260-263

Timeline, 37

tooltips, 37

Show Bounding Box option (Options bar), 253, 362

Show Filenames option, 176

Show More Options check box, 255

Show notifications about Adobe promotions option, 587

Show Only Navigation Controls button, 86

Show or Hide Properties button, 132, 212

Show Printer Preferences button, 257

shrinking selections, 296-298

Similar command (Select menu), 298-300

Simplify Layer command (Layer menu), 354, 619, 632

simplifying, layers, 336, 352-354

Single Photo View button, 88, 133

single-layer images, 27

sizing

    images, 222-225

        changing, 225-229

        printing, 244-248

    layers, 361-364

Sketch command (Filter menu), 619

skewing, layers, 361-364

skies, replacing bland sky, 607-610

slideshows, 84, 584-585

Small Thumbnail Size button, 88

Smart Blur command (Filter menu), 555

Smart Blur dialog box, 556

Smart Blur filter, removing graininess, 555-558

Smart Fix, 402

Smooth command (Modify menu), 301

Smooth command (Select menu), 648

Smooth Selection dialog box, 301, 649

smoothing

    defined, 301

    jagged selection edges, 301-303

Smudge tool, 352, 630

    repair large damages, 463-465

    repairing surface defects, 455

    softening selected details, 564-566

    Strength setting, 465

Snap to Grid command (View menu), 177

Snap to Image option, 625

snow, creating, 636-638

soft focus effects, 478-480

softening

    details, 564-566

    selection edges, 306-307

software, gamma adjustments, 385

Solid Color command (Layer menu), 612

Solid Color command (New Fill Layer menu), 344

sorting, 89

    by Import Batch, 91

    data (Newest First), 89

    date, 89

    items, 89

    location, 91

    Organizer catalog, 106-109

        markers, 109-113

        Organize Bin display, 113-114

Sounds and Audio Devices icon (Windows Control Panel), 99

Source option, Page Setup dialog box, 249

source points, Clone tool, 465

specks, repairing, 459-462

Sphere tool, 633

Spherize command (Filters menu), 635

spin effect, blurring images, 561-563

How can we make this index more useful? Email us at indexes@samspublishing.com

755

Sponge tool, 493
  blending stain edges, 466
  faded color saturation, 473
  saturating pixels, 466
  saturation correction, 544-546
Spot Healing Brush, 16, 483, 597
  blemishes and freckles, 485
  eyeglasses glare removal, 494
  large spot removal, 462
  repairing surface defects, 454
spots
  repairing, 454-455, 459-462
  repairing large areas, 463-466
Sprayed Strokes filter, 641
sRGB gamuts, 378
Stack button, stacking images, 92
Stack command (Edit menu), 93
Stack Selected Photos button, stacking images, 92
stacking images, 91-92
  Edit button, 92
  recompressing stacks, 94
  redisplaying images, 92
  selection of images, 92
  Stack button, 92
  Stack Selected Photos button, 92
  unstacking images, 94
  viewing result, 92
stains, repairing large areas, 463-466
Standard Edit, arranging multiple images, 213
Standard Edit mode, 29, 168, 179, 182, 284, 299
Standard Edit window, 182
Start Automatic Sequencing button, 155
Stationery and Layouts button, 584
Status bar, Close Palette Bin button, 222

storage
  digital photos, 5
  offline, 138
straight-edged areas, selecting, 282-284
Straighten and Crop Image command (Image menu), 398
Straighten Image command (Image menu), 398
straightening images, quick corrections, 398-400
Style Settings dialog box, 26, 359
styles, layers, 25, 334, 446
  applying, 358-361
  creating images, 181
  Fog, 358
  graphics editor, 25
  Image Effects, 361
  Radioactive Outer Glow, 331
  scale, 26
  Toy, 358
Styles and Effects palette, 23-25, 172, 359, 649
  blizzard effect, 636
  brushed metal effect, 699
Stylize command (Filter menu), 638
Stylus Pressure, 632
subject line, email, 585
subjects, snowy background, 515-519
Subtract from Selection operation, 316
subtractions, from selections, 297
subtractive process, purest light, 11
surface defects, repairing photos, 454-455
Sync Pan and Zoom button, 85
System (Mac OS) option, Palette list, 238
System (Windows) option, Palette list, 238

T

tablets, pen, 28

Tagged Image File Format (TIFF), 26

  images

    layers, 188

    saving, 5, 192, 198-200

tags, 109, 138, 211

  assigning to items, 119-122

  catalog organization, 109-113

  changing, 127-129

  creating, 117-119

  deleting, 122-123

  Find bar, 140

  finding items, 143-145

    adding criteria, 146

    dragging to Find bar, 145

    searches, 145

  folder location, 91

  icon change, 125-127

  image organization, 34

  reviewing images, 82

Tags and Collections command (Edit menu), 112

tears

  repairing, 454-455, 465

  repairing large areas, 463-470

teeth whitening, 486-487

temperature, white points, 382

Temperature slider, 403

text

  backscreening, 694-697

  caption, 84, 88, 130-132, 685-687

  copyright information, 710-714

  digital photography, 6-8

  embossing, 704-707

  filling with image, 707-710

  glowing, 700-704

  label, 685-687

  metallic, 697-700

  sales sign, 691-694

  vector data, 352

  warping, 688-690

Text tool, 337, 366, 440

Texture layer, 648

textures, Proximity Match option, 462

Threshold adjustment filter, 276

Threshold command (Filter menu), 507, 517

Threshold dialog box, 517

Threshold filter, 276, 507

Threshold layers, 348

Threshold Level setting, 276

Thumbnail size slider, 88

thumbnails, 5, 38

  audio files, 146

  changing size, 86-88

  changing to new image, 170

  date and time appearance, 88

  Photo Bin, 175

  reducing size, 82

  Small Thumbnail Size button, 88

TIFF (Tagged Image File Format), 26

  images

    layers, 188

    saving, 5, 192, 198-200

Tile command (Window menu), 213, 599, 609

time, changing images, 101-104

Time Zone Adjust dialog box, 104

timeline

  finding items within date range, 156-158

  limiting file dates, 162

  narrowing searches, 156

Organizer, 37

sorting media files, 108

Timeline command (View menu), 157

Timeline in Photo Browser view, 108

Tint slider, 403

tired eyes, sharpening, 488-491

Tolerance option, Background Eraser tool, 604

tolerance settings (erasers), 357

Tool Options pane, 632

toolbars, Photo Review, 84

Toolbox

Brush tool, 463

Burn tool, grayscale stains, 466

Clone tool

repairing large damages, 465

source point, 465

Crop tool, 395, 400

Dodge tool, stain repairs, 466

Editor, 171-172

Eraser tool, 480

Hand tool, 215-219

Move tool, 467

Red Eye Removal tool, 481

retouching photos

airbrush painting, 439-440

color selection, 424-430

drawing shapes, 448

gradient, 443-446

patterns, 441-442

preset management, 423-424

Sharpen tool, 549

Smudge tool

repairing large damages, 463-465

Strength setting, 465

Sponge tool, 493

blending stain edges, 466

faded color saturation, 473

saturating pixels, 466

Zoom tool, 215

tools

Brush, 25

Pencil, 25

retouching

airbrush painting, 439-440

color selection, 424-428

drawing shapes, 448

gradient, 443-446

patterns, 441-442

preset management, 423-424

Toolbox, hidden tools, 172

tooltips, Shortcuts bar, 37

Torn Edges command (Filter menu), 619

Torn Edges filter, 619

Toy layer style, 358

tracing, edges to select objects, 284-287

Trackball tool, 635

transformations, layer contents, 362

Transparency option, 240

transparent areas, Background layer, 336

Transparent option, background color selection, 181

tripods, digital photography, 14

Turbulence Jitter, 632

Turbulence tool, 630-632

Tutorials button, 29

TWAIN, 58

Twirl Clockwise tool, 630

Twirl Counter-Clockwise tool, 630

Type command (Layer menu), 688

Type layer, 336

Type tools, adding text to images, 684

U

Undo command (Edit menu), 32

Undo Delete Selected Items from Catalog command (Edit menu), 70

Undo feature, 32

Undo History command (Window menu), 32

Undo History palette, 32, 175

Uniform option, Palette list, 239

Units & Rulers command (Edit menu), 176

Unsharp mask, resampling, 229

Unsharp Mask command (Filter menu), 476, 490, 549-551

Unsharp Mask dialog box, 476, 490, 551, 652

Unsharp Mask filter, 549-550, 554

unstacking images, 94

Untagged Items command (Find menu), 146

Update Thumbnail button, updating images in the catalog, 96

Update Thumbnails command (Edit menu), 95-96

updating images in the catalog, 94-96

Use All Layers option, 312

Use Lower Case Extension option, Save dialog box, 195

V

vectors, 7
    data, 7-8, 352
    layers, element rendering, 7
    objects, file formats, 193
    text, 684
        file formats, 193
        Warp Text option, 688

Version Set command (Edit menu), 184-185, 189

version sets, 92, 184

vertical axis, flipping images, 392

Vertical Distortion slider, 690

Vertical Text Mask tool, 342

Vertical Type Mask tool, 330, 709

Vertical Type tool, 621, 685

videos, 584
    cards, gamma adjustment, 385
    files
        importing media files, 61-64
        photo review, 84
    viewing, 99-101

View and Organize Photos button, 42, 46, 68

View menu commands
    Collapse All Collections, 113
    Collapse All Tags, 113
    Expand All Collections, 113
    Expand All Tags, 113
    Grid, 177, 400
    Media Types, 97, 146
    Menu Types, 38
    New Window for XXX, 221
    Organize Bin, 111
    Rulers, 176
    Snap to Grid, 177
    Timeline, 157

View Single Gamma Only check box, 390

viewing videos, 99-101

vignette frames, creating, 648

vintage look, 644

virtual drives, 51

viruses, 584

Visible command (Layer menu), 371

Visible icon, 337

How can we make this index more useful? Email us at indexes@samspublishing.com

759

visual effects
  creating weather, 636-638
  melting images, 630-632
  water reflection, 639-641
  wrapping image around object, 633-636
visual impact, improving
  bland sky, 607-610
  blending images, 615-617
  composite image, 622-624
  framing photo, 610-614
  mask image layer, 600-604
  panoramas, 624-628
  remove unwanted objects, 596-600
  replacing background, 604-607
  scrapbook pages, 618-621
Vivid Light blend mode, 21

W-X

Wacom Graphire pen tablet, 28
Warhol, Andy, photo technique, 677-682
Warp Text command (Layer menu), 688
Warp Text dialog box, 688-690
Warp tool, 630
warping text, 688-690
Watch Folder dialog box, 66
Watch Folders command (File menu), 66
watched folders, importing files, 68
water reflections, 639-641
watercolors, changing photo, 668-672
watermarking plug-ins, 711
watermarks, 231-232, 711
.WAV format, 133
Wave filter, 630
Waves layer styles, 394

weather, creating effect, 636-638
Web forces, 240
Web option, Palette list, 238
websites
  Adobe, 12, 574
  Inmatrix, 100
  Ofoto, 246, 588
  Pictorico, 246
Web-safe colors, 427
Welcome window, 29
white balance, 13
White option, background color selection, 181
white points, 382, 513-514
  light chromaticity, 382
  setting manually, 390
white slider, 472
whitening teeth, 486-487
WIA (Windows Image Acquisition), 58
width, adjusting, 179
Window command (Windows menu), 29
Window menu commands
  Dock Properties in Organize Bin, 130
  File Browser, 230
  Histogram, 506
  How To, 177
  Images, 170, 213-215, 599, 609
  Info, 176, 470
  Navigator, 218
  Organize, 145
  Organize Bin, 116
  Properties, 130, 211-212
  Reset Palette Locations, 174
  Undo History, 32
  Window, 29
Windows, Media Player, 99
Windows Control Panel, Sounds and Audio
  Devices icon, 99

Windows Image Acquisition (WIA), 58

Windows menu commands, Dock Properties in
Organize Bin, 212

Wizard mode, Adobe Gamma, 386

WMA format, 133

work area, enlarging, 222

Wow-Chrome layer style, 700

wrinkles, removal, 483-485

Y - Z

Year button, 154

zero origins, 177

zoom, 14

    adjustment, reviewing images, 85

    digital photography, 14

Zoom and Trim option, 264

Zoom In button, 217

Zoom Out button, 217

Zoom tool, 215-217, 402

    melting images, 630

    red eye removal, 481

    window tiling, 215

zooming

    Navigator palette, 217-219

    Zoom tool, 215-217

ZoomPlayer, 100

Key Terms

Don't let unfamiliar terms discourage you from learning all you can about Photoshop Elements 3. If you don't completely understand what one of these words means, flip to the indicated page, read the full definition there, and find techniques related to that term.

Adjustment layer *A special layer that allows you to make a specific color or contrast adjustment to the layers that show through it.* **Page 346**

Alpha channel *Data saved with an image for reuse when needed, such as selections, masks, and creator information.* **211**

Alpha transparency *Variable transparency, or the ability to vary the amount of transparency in an image.* **191**

Anti-aliasing *The addition of semi-transparent pixels along the curved edge of a shape or selection to help curves look smooth.* **7**

Artifacts *Unwanted elements of a digital photo introduced by technology.* **190**

Audio caption *Recorded description of an image, created in the Organizer and associated with the image.* **133**

Background color *The color applied when you erase with the Eraser on the background layer.* **425**

Background layer *The lowest layer in an image; it cannot be moved in the layer stack until it is converted to a regular layer.* **335**

Bounding box *A rectangle that describes the boundaries of a drawn object, cropping border, or selection.* **448**

Canvas *The working area of an image defined by the image's outer dimensions.* **233**

Caption *A text or audio description of a media file.* **34**

Catalog *A collection of organized media files.* **34**

CCD noise *Random distortions introduced into a photo by the CCD chip in a digital camera, cell phone camera, or scanner.* **459**

Clipping mask *Controls what portions of any upper layers grouped with the mask appear in the final image.* **600**

Collection *A marker associated with an ordered group of media files that share the same context or purpose.* **109**

Color cast *The unwanted predominance of a particular color throughout an image.* **534**

Color management *The process of coordinating the color gamut of your monitor with that of your scanner and printer.* **377**

Color mode *Determines the number of colors an image can contain.* **179**

Contact sheet *A printout of a group of images, along with identifying labels, as a collection of miniatures.* **256**

Creations *Greeting cards, calendars, web galleries, slide shows, and other things you can make using the images in the catalog.* **15**

Depth of field *The distance between the closest and farthest in-focus object.* **Page 14**

Distort *To stretch a corner of a layer in any direction.* **361**

Dithering *A technique for simulating a color whose value does not appear in an image's palette by mixing pixels of the two closest available shades.* **201**

DPI (Dots per Inch) *Used to describe printer output. The higher the DPI, the larger the number of pixels used to print an image, and the more detail you get in your printed image. See also PPI.* **6**

Edge mask *A selection that encompasses only the edge pixels in an image, preventing unwanted modification to everything else.* **551**

Editor *The portion of Photoshop Elements you use to make changes to images.* **3**

Effect *Unique combination of filters and other image manipulations to achieve a particular look.* **25**

Email client *A program that sends and receives email on behalf of another application.* **574**

Error diffusion *Any of several mathematical techniques that attempt to compensate for large error values.* **241**

EXIF (Exchangeable Image File) *Data attached to a photo file that contains the key settings the camera used when the photo was shot.* **139**

Feathering *The addition of semi-selected pixels around the edge of a selection to help blend selected data with its new location.* **272**

File date *The date on which an image was taken or scanned into the system.* **102**

Filter *A series of computer instructions that modify the pixels in an image.* **24**

Foreground color *The color applied when you use the Brush, Pencil, or Paint Bucket tool, create text with the Text tool, or create a shape with one of the Shape tools.* **425**

Gamma *The measurement of the contrast of an image or imaging device.* **503**

Gamut *A palette comprised of all the individual colors that can be reproduced by a device. Your monitor and your printer each have separate gamuts, and sometimes, colors between them may match closely but not precisely.* **377**

Gradient *A gradual transition between two colors, sometimes by way of a third (or more) color.* **443**

Graphics editor *An application that allows you to edit your digital images.* **3**